D1165659

Progress
AND ITS
Discontents

═══

Progress

AND ITS

Discontents

═══════

EDITED BY
GABRIEL A. ALMOND,
MARVIN CHODOROW, &
ROY HARVEY PEARCE

*Sponsored by the Western Center of the
American Academy of
Arts and Sciences*

═══════

Berkeley

Los Angeles

London

UNIVERSITY OF CALIFORNIA PRESS

University of California Press
Berkeley and Los Angeles, California
University of California Press, Ltd.
London, England
© 1982 by
The Regents of the University of California
Printed in the United States of America

1 2 3 4 5 6 7 8 9

Library of Congress Cataloging in Publication Data
Main entry under title:
Progress and its discontents.
Papers based on a conference held in Palo Alto,
Calif., Feb., 1979.
Includes bibliographical references and index.
1. Progress—Congresses.   I. Almond, Gabriel
Abraham, 1911-   II. Chodorow, Marvin.
III. Pearce, Roy Harvey.   IV. American Academy of
Arts and Sciences. Western Center.
HM101.P89   303.4   81-11643
ISBN 0-520-04478-9   AACR2

CONTENTS

Foreword JOEL COLTON   ix
Preface   xiii
Introduction GABRIEL A. ALMOND, MARVIN CHODOROW, AND
      ROY HARVEY PEARCE   1

PART I
Historical, Ideological, and Evolutionary Aspects   17

  NANNERL O. KEOHANE
  1. The Enlightenment Idea of Progress Revisited   21

  GEORG G. IGGERS
  2. The Idea of Progress in Historiography and
     Social Thought Since the Enlightenment   41

  ALFRED G. MEYER
  3. The Idea of Progress in Communist Ideology   67

  CRAWFORD YOUNG
  4. Ideas of Progress in the Third World   83

  FRANCISCO J. AYALA
  5. The Evolutionary Concept of Progress   106

PART II
The Progress and Problems of Science   125

  JOHN T. EDSALL
  6. Progress in Our Understanding of Biology   135

  GERALD FEINBERG
  7. Progress in Physics: The Game of Intellectual Leapfrog   161

  BERNARD D. DAVIS
  8. Fear of Progress in Biology   182

  GERALD HOLTON
  9. Toward a Theory of Scientific Progress   202

  MARC J. ROBERTS
  10. Progress in Social Science   226

v

H. STUART HUGHES
11. Contemporary Historiography: Progress, Paradigms,
and the Regression Toward Positivism   240

PART III
The Prospects and Problems of Material Progress   249

MOSES ABRAMOVITZ
12. The Retreat from Economic Advance:
Changing Ideas About Economic Progress   253

HARVEY BROOKS
13. Can Technology Assure Unending Material Progress?   281

NATHAN ROSENBERG
14. Natural Resource Limits and
the Future of Economic Progress   301

HOLLIS B. CHENERY
15. Poverty and Progress   319

PART IV
Political and Social Aspects   333

GIANFRANCO POGGI
16. The Modern State and the Idea of Progress   337

AARON WILDAVSKY
17. Progress and Public Policy   361

G. BINGHAM POWELL, JR.
18. Social Progress and Liberal Democracy   375

SAMUEL H. BARNES
19. Changing Popular Attitudes Toward Progress   403

PART V
Progress and Humanistic Understanding   427

STEVEN MARCUS
20. Conceptions of the Self in an Age of Progress   431

MURRAY KRIEGER
21. The Arts and the Idea of Progress   449

ROBERT C. ELLIOTT
22. The Costs of Utopia   470

MARTIN E. MARTY
23. The Idea of Progress in Twentieth-Century Theology   482

DANIEL BELL
24. The Return of the Sacred:
The Argument About the Future of Religion   501

FREDERICK A. OLAFSON
25. The Idea of Progress: An Ethical Appraisal   524

Contributors   547
Index   551

.

FOREWORD

What has happened in our day to the idea of progress—the belief in the continuing improvement of the human condition? To contemporary ears it has a hollow ring. Yet for two centuries, from the eighteenth to the early twentieth, the belief in progress was an important credo in the West in both intellectual and popular circles, and it accompanied many of the formidable accomplishments of Western civilization. For many it became a surrogate religion, a secular faith: Progress, spelled upper case, replaced Providence. With the continuing accumulation of theoretical and practical knowledge, there seemed to be no barriers to realizing on this earth the deepest human aspirations. Civilization had advanced from the earliest stages of precivilization, was advancing, and would continue to advance in the foreseeable future. Men and women would move forward to ever-increasing material comfort and happiness. A golden future stretched ahead.

Flexibly interpreted, the idea of continuing progress can be traced back to classical and medieval times and can be said to have a 2,500—not a 250—year-old ancestry. But it is more common, and perhaps more convincing, to conceive of it as a modern idea, born with the rise of modern science in the seventeenth century and with the popularization of science, rationalism, secularism, and scientific thinking in the eighteenth-century Enlightenment. Nineteenth-century evolutionary ideas reinforced it. In that same century, a number of deterministic philosophies, Marxism being the most influential and lasting, asked us to interpret progress as inevitable, as the result of impersonal historical forces; human intervention could accelerate or slow the process but not prevent it. Others in the same century, like John Stuart Mill, building on the thought of the Enlightenment philosophers, saw progress as contingent upon human intelligence and human will; denying inevitability, they left a large margin for human rationality and choice. To be sure, there were intellectuals throughout these years who questioned the belief in continuing progress and were less optimistic about human destiny, but no one denied its pervasiveness. No matter what the differences among its proponents, this tenaciously held idea meant, in its simplest form, that each generation could look forward to a richer, happier, fuller, and more peaceful life for itself and its posterity. The very notion reinforced the self-confidence and dynamism of Western civilization as Western influence spread throughout the world.

What then happened to the idea of progress as a popular and intellectual belief so that today it has fallen into disrepute? No contemporary would hold the buoyant view of Tennyson's "Locksley Hall" written in 1842:

For I dipt into the future, far as human eye could see
Saw the vision of the world and all the wonder that would be,
Saw the heavens fill with commerce, argosies of magic sails,
Pilots of the purple twilight, dripping down with costly bales,
Till the war drum throbbed no longer, and the battle flags were furled,
In the Parliament of Man, the Federation of the world.

Today, no contemporary possesses the enthusiasm or optimism of the *New York World* on January 1, 1901, the opening day of the twentieth century: "The *World* is optimistic enough to believe that the twentieth century . . . will meet and overcome all perils and prove to be the best this steadily improving planet has ever seen."

The first powerful shock came in 1914 when the "civilized" nations of Europe—most of them boasting the advances of science and technology, education, and self-government—went to war with one another and quickly brought even non-European nations into the vortex of a global conflict. The world had scarcely recovered from the conflagration when other traumas followed: the Russian Revolution, fought, like the French Revolution, in the name of heroic ideals but demanding from its inception to the present unconscionable human sacrifices; fascism in its Italian and in its generic form; the Great Depression; Nazism, reaching its climax of bestiality in the scientifically organized wartime extermination camps of the Third Reich; the carnage of the Second World War; the war's aftermath of spreading dictatorship and new armed conflicts; and the aborted hopes for democracy and economic advance in the emergent Third World countries. Indeed, the idea of continuing progress received staggering blows in the twentieth century.

To be sure, science and technology continued to move forward with accomplishments exceeding the anticipations of even their boldest prophets. The greatest invention of the nineteenth century, Alfred North Whitehead had once observed, was "the invention of the method of invention" (*Science and the Modern World*, New York, 1925). The harnessing of nuclear energy was one such "invention" in the twentieth century, the Second World War ending with the explosion of the atomic bomb as an awesome portent for the future. In the postwar years the frightening thought spread that for the first time in history

universal planetary destruction was a real possibility. With no adequate international controls and with nuclear proliferation, the atomic
clock ticked on. No one in the heyday of the idea of progress had to
cope with any such lengthening shadow.

Meanwhile people in the mid-twentieth century also took note, as
never before, of the baneful effects of unrestrained technological
growth—the pollution of the atmosphere, the spoliation and exhaustion of natural resources, the depersonalization of the workplace. The
world economy itself did not seem rational or controllable. The essential element in the idea of progress—belief in improved lives for
oneself, one's children, and one's children's children—was incalculably
undermined. Faith in the idea of progress plummeted from the heights.
Future historians will probably record that from the mid-twentieth
century on, it was difficult for anyone to retain faith in the idea of
inevitable and continuing progress. People increasingly now use the
word in quotation marks or with mocking sarcasm or speak not of
progress in civilization but in barbarism. As Western dominance and
self-confidence wane, so too does the idea of progress. Is the idea of
progress, as we once knew it, to be abandoned completely?

No one can deny continuing scientific advances, spectacular discoveries in biochemistry, genetics, and physics, the knowledge explosion, the growth in informational technology, the achievements of
medicine and surgery, space exploration, and increased human longevity. Building on the past, we are still in so many ways moving forward
and can continue to progress. But the critical unresolved question is
whether we can control human and social affairs—prevent a nuclear
holocaust, preserve international peace, provide social and economic
justice, master the economy, protect natural resources, cope with global
overpopulation, assist in overcoming famine and pestilence, and preserve the quality of life as well as prolong life. We are not so sure.

Much has happened to destroy the pristine appeal of the belief in
progress. Yet has it all turned to ashes? Without some faith in the
future—in progress—we lose a precious element of our heritage and
lose self-confidence itself. We know that we cannot turn back nor lock
up atomic or genetic secrets. But we can retain the will to understand
the implications of modern science and technology and remain the
masters and not the servants of our scientific and technological civilization, now no longer Western but worldwide. If we have abandoned
formulas of inevitable and automatic progress or of utopian perfection, we can still, through human will and intelligence, make slow and
steady advances and cope with the dangers of which we are aware.
Chastened by history, we must cut our hopes and dreams down to size,
heeding perhaps the words of John Dewey, who once noted of "progress": "It is not a wholesale matter, but a retail job, to be contracted
for and executed in sections" (*Characters and Events*, New York, 1929).

The older belief in progress need not be abandoned but transformed and circumscribed; too much is at stake for us to drop it completely. Robert Nisbet, a recent historian of the idea of progress and often a critic of the idea itself, pointedly reminds us: "If the idea of progress does die in the West, so will a great deal else that we have long cherished in our civilization" (*History of the Idea of Progress*, New York, 1980).

The distinguished contributors to this volume help us in richly diverse ways to see more clearly the transformation of the idea of progress in our day and its contemporary meaning in the present decade of the twentieth century, both in the Western and the much larger non-Western world, in capitalist and in Marxist-oriented societies, in the many fields of knowledge itself, and in intellectual and general belief. No one who reads these pages can fail to appreciate the importance of the idea of progress in history or the need to reexamine its meaning in our own era thoughtfully and critically through the multifaceted prisms that these thinkers provide.

We lament the deaths, within two months of eath other in 1979, of two men who were deeply involved in the study of the idea of progress. One was John H. Knowles, physician and humanist, who, in his own field of medicine, lamented the advance of technology—"progress"—as interfering with the true mission of the physician-healer to treat the individual whole person. As president of the Rockefeller Foundation, he encouraged this collaborative project.

The second was Charles Frankel, philosopher-humanist and respected scholar, who presided brilliantly over the newly established National Humanities Center in North Carolina. Concerned professionally with the idea of progress ever since writing his doctoral dissertation, *The Faith of Reason: The Idea of Progress in the French Enlightenment* (New York, 1948), he argued eloquently in *The Case for Modern Man* (New York, 1955) and elsewhere that the idea of progress was not necessarily a hubristic challenge to the gods, a belief insensitive to human imperfection and frailty, or a substitute religion; that belief in predetermined, inevitable, and automatic progress obstructed true progress; and that only through human intelligence, will, and action could we salvage something of the older idea of progress and hope to bequeath to future generations the genuine advances of civilized thought and accomplishments—not least, freedom and the toleration of different viewpoints that make continuing advance possible.

JOEL COLTON
Director for Humanities
The Rockefeller Foundation
1974-1981

PREFACE

Plans for this book were first laid in the early 1970s when the utopianism and apocalyptic mood of the counterculture were still running strong. The Western Center of the American Academy of Arts and Sciences had just been established, and its founding committee often discussed the cultural-historical significance of these developments. It held an exploratory conference on what it decided to call the "transformation of the idea of progress" in San Diego, California, in February 1977. The preliminary conference helped us discriminate the various components of the idea, ideologies, and culture of progress, and on this basis we organized a second conference in Palo Alto in February 1979, at which outlines dealing with the various topics in this book were presented and discussed. The essays published in this book are largely those presented in provisional form at that conference.

An interdisciplinary cultural-historical inquiry, as this volume is, must, of necessity, be a collaborative effort. Its editors include a physicist, a social scientist, and a literary historian and critic. Its authors include historians of ideas and of science, philosophers and theologians, biologists, physicists, engineers, economists, political scientists, sociologists, and students of literature and the arts. It has been carried on under the auspices of the American Academy of Arts and Sciences founded just two centuries ago by one of the leading spokesmen of the Enlightenment and one of the principal interpreters of the idea of progress, John Adams. The kinds of questions we raise in this book require this multidimensional exploration, and it is fitting that they be explored under these auspices at the beginning of the Academy's third century.

At various stages of this enterprise the editors have received advice, help, and support from many individuals. John Voss and Alexandra Oleson of the Academy office in Boston took an active and supportive interest in the project from the very beginning and made important substantive and editorial contributions. Joel Colton, former Director for the Humanities at the Rockefeller Foundation, played an active role in planning the conference and the book. Paul Robinson of the Stanford History Department gave us much helpful advice in the early stages of the project. Muriel Bell of the Western Center of the Academy organized the Palo Alto conference and followed up on the preparation and submission of papers. Estelle Jelinek did a thorough and imaginative job of editing the papers and advising on the overall construction of the volume. William McClung, Marilyn Schwartz, and Mary Lamprech of the University of California Press guided the manuscript thoughtfully and helpfully through the deliberative, editorial, and production processes. We want to thank the anonymous readers of the University of California Press for their many helpful suggestions and the many colleagues who took the trouble to read and comment on individual manuscripts. We are grateful to the Rockefeller Foundation for their interest in and support of this project.

GABRIEL A. ALMOND
MARVIN CHODOROW
ROY HARVEY PEARCE

INTRODUCTION

This collection of essays attempts to take our cultural-historical bearings after almost two decades of disquiet, doubt, and disturbance. The questions that have been raised go to the heart of modern culture, the culture of progress. Processes, institutions, and values which have been taken for granted for two centuries have been brought into question. Are science and technology really "progressive" and beneficial in their consequences? Have they led to the enhancement of welfare, greater happiness, and moral improvement? Is the continued growth of material productivity possible? Is it desirable? Are the institutions of progress viable and beneficial: public bureaucracies, business corporations, universities, research centers, political parties, interest groups, and the mass media? The questioning has been comprehensive, penetrating, and corrosive. We can speak of a crisis of modern culture without fear of exaggeration.

THE IDEA OF PROGRESS AS PHILOSOPHY OF HISTORY

Unlike the terms "modernization" and "development," which are used by sociologists and economists to refer to the increase and spread of the institutions, products, and services of modern civilization, "progress" is the name that our historical era of the last two or three centuries has bestowed upon itself. It is the real "name" of a self-conscious historical era, a term full of diffuse connotations and ambiguities. The changes to which it refers are not only changes of a certain sort, but they are changes presumed to be for the better. It represents a cultural self-identification, an assertion of a historical identity. When we speak in this book of the idea of progress, of ideologies of progress, and of the culture of progress, we are referring to different aspects, manifestations, and versions of a historic culture. And when we talk about the discontent with and the transformation of these ideas and ideologies and of this culture, we are probing into the depths of our contemporary experience, in an effort to anticipate how this culture may be changing and what form these changes may be taking.

Though parts and aspects of the idea of progress had been adum-

1

brated earlier, it only began to take on fully elaborated form as a set of interconnected ideas and expectations in the decades after the mid-eighteenth century. At the beginning of this period—between 1751-1772—the thirty-two volumes of Diderot's *Encyclopedia* appeared in Paris, including contributions by a galaxy of eighteenth-century *philosophes*—Buffon, D'Alembert, Holbach, Montesquieu, Quesnai, Voltaire, and many others. Its articles affirmed the belief that through knowledge man could learn to control nature and make it serve his purposes, increase his material welfare, improve his institutions, reform his legislation, perfect his aesthetic tastes and moral standards, and cultivate the satisfactions of industry and peace.

In the succeeding decades Europe and the United States produced a succession of philosophical expositors of the doctrine of progress, including Turgot, Adam Smith, Condorcet, Benjamin Franklin, John Adams, Kant, Hegel, Saint-Simon, Comte, John Stuart Mill, and many others. By the second half of the nineteenth century a number of different versions of the idea of progress had emerged. The most distinctive were those elaborated by Herbert Spencer and Karl Marx, the first theory an individualist and evolutionary interpretation, the second collectivist and revolutionary.

The distinctiveness of the eighteenth- and nineteenth-century idea of progress is suggested when we compare it with earlier philosophical-historical formulations. Philosophies of history tend to take positions on five questions: (1) the *direction* of the historical process, whether progressive, regressive, linear, curvilinear, or cyclical; (2) the *rate* of historical change, whether incremental or characterized by quantum transformations; (3) the *agent* (or agents) of historical change, whether it (or they) is (are) a divine force (or forces) controlling history or a divine plan instituted at the beginning and then working itself out in history, as in the idea of Providence; or whether the agent is human reason and effort; or whether the divine and human together operate in some ratio or combination; (4) the *substance* of historical change, that is, the areas of historical transformation and their interaction, as knowledge, crafts, and arts, material growth and welfare, political institutions and ideas, and moral and spiritual values, and how they are all linked together; and (5) the *identity* of the bearers of history, whether they be Greeks, Jews, Christians, Muslims, or some larger identity as civilized man or all humanity.

Earlier philosophies of history had complex views of historical directionality, positing both regression from a golden age as well as progress, presenting a realm of nonhistorical being as well as one of becoming, as in Plato. In the various Christian versions of history, though historical improvements may be celebrated as in Augustine, there is no getting around original sin and the fall of man, and redemption and salvation as the larger metaphysical frame within which historic time is enclosed. And certainly among Christian theologians the agent of historical change is divine, with humanity fulfilling divine purposes. Knowledge and the material arts, while important, take second place to divine purpose and the world of the spirit.

The idea of progress as it developed in the eighteenth and nineteenth centuries was different from these earlier historical ideologies in all five of the above respects. First, its definition of direction is unequivocally progressive, though in its Hegelian and Marxian version a generally rising curve of progress contained within itself cyclical regressions. Second, historical growth proceeds at an incremental rate, though the liberal view, in some versions, posited a millenary end-state of perfection, and the Marxist view alternated intervals of slow change with periods of rapid revolutionary change, to culminate in a state of perfection. Third, divine agency in the process of historical change is simply not posited or is only loosely and diffusely connected to human reason and will. Fourth, the various components of historical change—the arenas of history—are linked with knowledge as its catalyst, bringing improvement in the mechanic arts and the control of natural forces. These in turn bring about improvements in humanity's material and physical condition, which may make possible political emancipation and pacification. All of these related processes may enhance mankind's moral and aesthetic qualities and sensibilities. Finally, the historical actor in the eighteenth- and nineteenth-century view is unequivocally all of humanity.

It is this combination of properties which differentiates the modern idea of progress from the earlier view of history, particularly in its conception of man, the creator of knowledge, as the agent of progress; of knowledge as the catalytic force that brings about material, political, moral, and aesthetic improvement; and of all mankind as the ultimate actor and beneficiary in this process.

THE EMERGING CULTURE OF PROGRESS

Unlike the earlier ideas of historical progress and improvement, the ideology of progress in the eighteenth and nineteenth centuries followed, accompanied, and produced institutional, technical, and cultural changes of extraordinary scope and increasing momentum. Surely, by the second half of the nineteenth century the ideology of progress had become a historic culture, and self-consciously so. Not long after, or simultaneously with the publication of the works of Auguste Comte, John Stuart Mill, Marx and Engels, and Herbert Spencer—the leading ideologues of progress—the great urban industrial centers of the Western world began one after the other to present enormous displays of the conditions, the dynamics, and the products of progress to millions and tens of millions of people.

The first great international exhibition took place in London in the Crystal Palace in 1851. Half a million persons attended it on opening day alone, and some six million visitors saw its exhibits before it closed. Prince Albert, the Royal Consort, patron of science, presided over the commission charged with organizing the exhibition. He de-

scribed the purpose and meaning of the exhibition in an early instruction to the organizers:

> Science discovers these laws of power, motion, and transformation:
> industry applies them to the raw matter, which the earth yields us
> in abundance, but which becomes valuable only by knowledge: art
> teaches us the immutable laws of beauty and symmetry, and gives to
> our productions forms in accordance with them. Gentlemen, THE
> EXHIBITION of 1851 is to give us a true test and a living picture
> of the point of development at which the whole of mankind has
> arrived in this great task, and a new starting point from which all
> nations will be able to direct their further exertions. I confidently
> hope the first impression which the view of this vast collection will
> produce upon the spectator will be that of deep thankfulness to the
> Almighty for the blessings which He has bestowed upon us already
> here below; and the second, the conviction that they can only be
> realized in proportion to the help which we are prepared to render
> to each other—therefore, only by peace, love, and ready assistance,
> not only between individuals, but between the nations of the earth.[1]

In rapid succession from the mid-century on, these great international expositions took place: Paris in 1855 with four million visitors,
London again in 1862, Paris in 1867, Vienna in 1873, and the Philadelphia Centennial in 1876. The Parisian exhibition of 1878 attracted
thirteen million visitors, and the later one of 1889 drew twenty-seven
million visitors. The largest exhibition of the nineteenth century, the
Columbian Exposition, took place in 1893 on the Midway in Chicago
and celebrated the four hundredth anniversary of the discovery of
America. The nineteenth-century record for attendance was held by
the Parisian Exposition of 1900, with thirty-nine million visitors.

Walt Whitman composed a "Song of the Exposition" for the Philadelphia Centennial of 1876, celebrating the triumph of industry, engineering, and technology and singing of how the wonders of the Old
World paled in comparison:

> Mightier than Egypt's tombs,
> Fairer than Grecia's, Roma's temples,
> Prouder than Milan's statued, spired cathedral,
> More picturesque than Rhenish castle-keeps,
> We plan even now to raise, beyond them all,
> Thy great cathedral sacred industry, no tomb,
> A keep for life for practical invention. . . .

---

1. *Official Descriptive and Illustrated Catalogue of the Great Exposition of the
Works of Industry of All Nations*, Vol. 1: *1851, Part I, Introductory* (London: Spicer
Bros., 1851), p. 4.

Steam-power, the great express lines, gas, petroleum,
These triumphs of our time, the Atlantic's delicate cable,
The Pacific railroad, the Suez canal, the Mont Cenis
    and Gothard and Hoosac tunnels, the Brooklyn bridge,
This earth all spann'd with iron rails, with lines of steamships
    threading every sea,
Our own rondure, the current globe I bring.[2]

The most powerful message conveyed by these enormous and self-conscious displays of the accomplishments of progress was the relation between science and material productivity. Other typical themes developed in exhibits at these great expositions were man's progress in the improvement of welfare, sanitation, and public health, and political development such as the formation of trade unions and the improvement of criminal justice and rehabilitation. The development of the fine arts also had a place in these exhibitions. But there was no doubt in these great cultural displays that science, education, technology, and material productivity held center stage.

THE SYSTEM OF PROGRESS AND ITS PROBLEMATICS

The ideology of progress and the historic culture of progress in its liberal Western European-American version postulated and in part realized a set of interconnected changes of the sort shown in Figure 1.

Fig. 1. The Logic of the Progress System

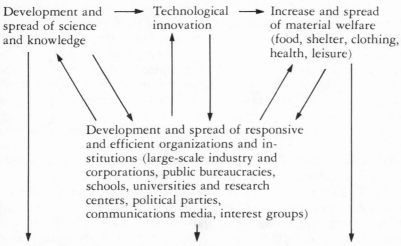

Development and → Technological → Increase and spread
spread of science   innovation   of material welfare
and knowledge   (food, shelter, clothing,
                                      health, leisure)

Development and spread of responsive
and efficient organizations and institutions (large-scale industry and
corporations, public bureaucracies,
schools, universities and research
centers, political parties,
communications media, interest groups)

Intellectual, moral and aesthetic improvement and increasing
human satisfaction

2. Walt Whitman, "Song of the Exposition," in *Complete Poetry and Selected Prose*, ed. James E. Miller, Jr. (Boston: Houghton Mifflin, 1959), pp. 145, 147-48.

The development and spread of knowledge, science, and technology have increased material welfare, and these together have increased political participation and produced modern social, economic, and political organizations (even international ones). Similarly, the development of modern organizations has contributed to the growth and spread of knowledge, the growth of technology, and the increase in welfare. A case could be made for intellectual and moral improvements, and for some significant net increase in the sum and distribution of human satisfaction as well. Unless we argue that there has been no increase in human satisfaction (or a net decline) as a consequence of progress, any positive increment would have to be multiplied by the increase in longevity and human vitality. What we are suggesting is that the problematics of progress cannot be attributed to the failure of the "progress system." In some respects it has been an extraordinary success.

But in recent decades, every relationship suggested in our diagram has come into question—the benignity of science and technology, the possibility and desirability of increased material welfare, the effectiveness of modern institutions and organizations, and the relation of the culture and structure of progress to human satisfaction and improvement. Does this questioning and rejection of progress reflect a genuine cultural-historical change, or is it a repetition of the doubts and alternative views of history that have always accompanied the Enlightenment idea of progress?

Progress as ideology has never fully preempted the field of philosophy of history. A cyclical view of history—of ancient origins—that cultures and societies come into being and pass away has been expressed in modern times by such writers as Nietzsche, Spengler, Sorokin, and Toynbee. Even J.B. Bury, the first major explicator of the origins and content of the idea of progress, a man for whom the notion that progress somehow represented the ultimate stage of man's history on earth had strong attraction, drew back in the epilogue to his book *The Idea of Progress* and asked: "Does not Progress itself suggest that its value as a doctrine is only relative, corresponding to a certain not very advanced stage of civilization; just as Providence, in its day, was an idea of relative value, corresponding to a stage somewhat less advanced?"[3] More than forty years later Frank Manuel, at the conclusion of his study of the philosophy of history, found a consensus among the critics of "Progressism": "They are agreed that the next stage either must or is likely to entail a spiritualization of mankind and a movement away from the present absorption with power and instinctual existence."[4]

3. J.B. Bury, *The Idea of Progress* (New York: Dover, 1955), p. 352.
4. Frank Manuel, *Shapes of Philosophical History* (Stanford, Ca.: Stanford University Press, 1965), p. 159.

More recently, in a book on the history of the idea of progress, Robert Nisbet advances the arresting proposition that "if there is one generalization that can be made confidently about the history of the idea of progress, it is that throughout its history the idea has been closely linked with, has depended upon, religion or upon intellectual constructs derived from religion." Nisbet argues that in recent decades as religious faith has declined and as even secular philosophical coherence has attenuated, faith in progress has declined. In other words, what lies behind the loss of our sense of positive direction is the disappearance of the core sacred beliefs, which, according to Nisbet, have always been at the "heart of any genuine culture." He goes on to argue that behind the fading of our confidence in the basic components of the idea of progress, "the death of the past, the displacement of Western pride of civilization, the waning faith in economic growth and in the works of reason[,] lies the moribundity of religious conviction, of belief in something greater than the life immediately around us. . . ." Nisbet concludes his book on a tentative note of hope for a resurgence of faith in progress, based on what he views as the faint beginnings of a revival in religious belief.[5]

In reviewing this litany of disillusionment with progress, we begin with the direct relationship, suggested in the above schema, among knowledge, science, and technology, and human satisfaction and improvement. There is little doubt that science and technology have been extraordinarily successful in increasing man's understanding and control over nature. But these triumphs have not been unambiguously constructive. They have at least two problematic aspects. First, in many cases a major breakthrough in science and technology produces a sense of uneasiness and threat among both producers and consumers—an urgent need for assessment and the exploration of consequences. Scientific and technological progress has increased man's power to manipulate physical and biological nature by many orders of magnitude, but accompanying it is some sense of helplessness, of powerlessness to keep this manipulative capacity constructive. Thus, from having been the catalysts of benign progress, science and technology have become morally ambiguous. There is a pervasive attitude that something has to be done to keep them from going bad. This attitude may in general be unjustified, but it is certainly true that the amount of intended and unintended evil science and technology are capable of, unless controlled, has increased enormously.

Second, the great progress of science has, in Max Weber's words, dispelled the magic and mystery of the world, replacing it with rational-

5. Robert Nisbet, *The History of the Idea of Progress* (New York: Basic Books, 1980), pp. 352, 354ff. For a penetrating discussion of the Nisbet thesis and an illuminating interpretation of the history of the idea of progress, see Gertrude Himmelfarb, "In Defense of Progress," *Commentary*, June 1980, pp. 53ff.

empirical views and procedures. Even the Newtonian cosmology provided a lawful, diffusely deistic setting consistent with and supportive of rational improvement. But modern cosmology, while it does not threaten a quick contraction and early repetition of the Big Bang, appears to have no connection at all to human culture and aspiration. The implications of the nature of the universe for human striving and aspiration seem ambiguous. The cosmos is seen to be neutral or indifferent; it does not really set the good Apollonian example it used to set in the days when the expectation of progress was green. Science erodes the older bases of moral legitimation and produces none of its own.

Or if we turn to the development and spread of material welfare, it would appear to have become problematic in a number of respects. Though science and technology have proven their capacity to overcome material shortages in the past, they are now under pressure to achieve a much increased rate of innovation, one that would make possible continued growth in the advanced industrial world as well as a spread of the benefits of advanced industrial society to the rapidly growing population of the Third World. And assuming that these technical problems can be solved, there is substantial doubt that mankind's cultural adaptability and political capacity and will are sufficient to meet these grave challenges of growth and distribution on a global scale.[6] That complacency with respect to these problems is inappropriate is also suggested by our growing appreciation of the secondary consequences of technological progress—the threats to ecological balance, the costs, in health and natural beauty, of the various and still not fully understood forms of pollution, and the pressures of technology on the environment.

Thus, progress in the sense of continued, increasingly generalized material welfare is said to be approaching limits, and it no longer seems plausible, as the liberal expectation of progress posited, that improvements in the welfare of poor people and poor countries can be derived from increased growth and productivity and from redistributive measures that stop short of reducing the share of material welfare going to the rich. Sharply redistributive politics is a component of the Marxist expectation of progress, not the liberal expectation.

But the problematics of material welfare go deeper than this if we follow the arguments of some economists. On the one hand, it is asserted that the standardized material products "progress" has produced fail to meet and in some sense preempt human needs for stimulation, variety, and novelty. And, on the other, it is argued that the routinization of activity and confinement of increasing numbers of human beings in large urban agglomerations characteristic of the

6. For a thoughtful projection of the limits in growth in the Third World, see Nathan Keyfitz, "World Resources and the World Middle Class," *Scientific American*, July 1976, pp. 28ff.

modern economy is too high a price to pay for a productivity that seems in part to be of dubious value.

The spread of knowledge, science, and technology and of material welfare has both contributed to and been furthered by the development of modern organizations—political parties, organized interest groups, governmental bureaucracies, corporations, schools and universities, and the mass media of communication. Political parties and organized interest groups have been the instrumentalities that created modern mass representative democracy, made public office generally accessible, democratized and "meritocratized" educational opportunity, and introduced the welfare state. Governmental bureaucracies now preempt between one-third to one-half of the national product of advanced liberal societies for the provision of public goods, such as security, public order, and recreation, and for the redistribution of access to material goods and services.

The modern corporation has been the organized instrument that has made possible the enormous increase in the production and distribution of modern goods and services. The university has served as the major center of scientific discovery, as one of the major centers of technological development, and increasingly as a meritocratic screening device in the recruitment of individuals into desired social positions. The mass media of communication have become major disseminators of knowledge and information and creators of tastes and values.

Each one of these organizations and agencies has become a crucial component of the reality of progress, and each one has developed its own problematics. Political parties are increasingly losing their steady clienteles and, consequently, their capacity for aggregating and organizing popular demand. The representative, pluralist politics of liberalism have to some extent become supplanted by populist and confrontation politics and by media and public relations politics. Modern interest groups have to some extent converted representative democracies into congeries of syndicalist monopolies and single-issue "lobbies," many of which have the capacity to bring vital social and governmental functions to a halt. The older system of interest-group pluralism has been attenuated by the emergence of the shop floor revolt and the flash strike as a principal means of special interest pressure. Thus, the organizations which have previously made for a certain order and reconciliation of demand consistent with responsive and effective public policy and implementation are no longer able to perform these functions effectively.

Governmental bureaucracy, having been the instrument for the provision of security, public order, equality of opportunity, and minimal standards of welfare, is alleged to have become an impersonal and voracious monster, governed by Parkinsonian laws of growth, its various departments and bureaus pursuing technocratic and bureaucratic

values, its parts interminable, the "administrative slice" ever-
increasing at the expense of the service slice.

Thus, there is substantial disillusionment with the political system
of advanced liberal society in both its input and its output aspects. And
yet it is being called upon to cope with and solve problems of an
increasingly urgent and intractable kind. It is not surprising that one
of the major themes of modern political analysis is the "ungovernability" of modern society.

The modern business corporation is viewed as corruptive of politics
and government, inaccessible to governmental control, exploitative of
the economies of poor countries, wasteful of scarce resources, indifferent to environmental values, and a major cause of deterioration of
taste and moral values. The modern university is criticized for producing narrow specialists and technical virtuosi, for failing to transmit
historical culture effectively, and for losing sight of its character-
shaping function. And the mass media of communication are variously
under attack for sensationalizing information, disrupting orderly and
prudent political and policy processes, and brutalizing and vulgarizing
taste and moral standards.

Thus, modern organizations have produced cognitive-technical-
material progress, but they are said to have also brought about a
precarious and threatening state of the world. The notion of progress
in its liberal version has implied a benign, almost automatic process.
Morality was assumed to be an outcome of material improvement and
secular knowledge whereas politics and collective coercion had minimal rule-keeping and security concerns or were called upon for intermittent remedial interventions. Otherwise, an invisible hand converted
self-interest into collective interest or transformed the short-run view
of interest into the long-term view.

THEMES OF THIS BOOK

Progress and Its Discontents is divided into five parts. The first part
deals with progress as a historical, ideological, and evolutionary concept. The second part appraises science and knowledge from the two
perspectives of the prospects for their continued growth and the
problem of the side effects and negative consequences of that growth.
Part Three deals with the prospects and problematics of continued
economic and technical progress. Part Four explores the political and
sociological aspects of progress; and Part Five relates the idea of
progress to the realms of the arts, morality, and religion.

A multiauthored book of this kind cannot aspire to an unambiguous
and definite set of conclusions. There are differences in philosophy
and emphasis among the authors, which become clear in the individual
chapters. Nevertheless, the following themes are advanced in the
course of the book.

1. The Enlightenment polemic about the necessary *linkages* among the various spheres of science and knowledge, material productivity, political, economic, and social institutions, human welfare, morality, and aesthetic creativity is clearly resolved in favor of such skeptics as Voltaire and Diderot. There are undoubtedly strong connections between increasing knowledge and technical innovation and material productivity, but the linkages of these with political and moral improvement are surely not unambiguously positive, as was predicted by Turgot and Condorcet. At the same time, given the dominance of the planet by the ideas, ideologies, and cultures of progress and the enormous and problematic powers which have been let loose, the linkage of political and moral progress with the other components cannot simply be left as an open question. If the notion of an "inevitable" and benign sequence of the components of progress has been set aside, the question may now be raised about whether the culture of progress can survive without making moral and political "progress" of the most fundamental sort.

2. The powerhouse of progress has always been the growth of knowledge, and the pattern which this growth has been held to take has been one of cumulativeness. This model of scientific growth has come under attack and the argument advanced that the notion of cumulativeness be replaced by a more political and dialectical model of scientific progress. This view, by and large, has not been adopted by philosophers and historians of science and, certainly, not by scientists themselves. How science grows is now the subject of a separate historical discipline, and the model which seems to be emerging is one of considerably greater complexity than the classical view, but one in which cumulativeness and progress survive.

3. Although progress, in the sense of cumulativeness, and unification characterize the physical and biological sciences, for the social and historical disciplines progress has an overlapping but differing set of meanings. There have been great achievements in our understanding of economic, social, political, and cultural processes and their interdependences. This increased understanding has been attained in part through the use of scientific procedures of rigorous measurement, experiment, statistical analysis, and mathematical modeling. But in at least two respects progress in the social and historical disciplines differs from the "hard science" model. First, their data—human interactions, behaviors, and aspirations—are not and cannot be standardized. Memory, learning, and invention render them unstable; hence, regularities may decay, and psychological, social, cultural, and economic "laws" may lose their force. Second, efforts to explain culture, social structure, politics, and economics by a reductionist strategy imitative of the successes of the hard sciences in reducing biological processes to chemical and physical ones have turned out to be an

over-sanguine and inappropriate agenda. The serious consequences of the misinterpretation of the nature of the social and historical sciences are most evident in this context of the general treatment of the theme of human progress and its problematics. It is plain that human survival—to say nothing of the continued spread of welfare— will turn on our capacity to resist and overcome "normal," "lawlike" social, cultural, and political propensities and constraints, and to invent and achieve historically unprecedented outcomes.

4. Though the more optimistic Enlightenment philosophers included the arts in their idea of progress, it is evident that the idea of progress is applicable to the arts in limited ways. We cannot argue that modern art objects are more beautiful than ancient ones, that the novels of Tolstoy are more beautiful than the epics of Homer. There is, however, progress in the arts in the sense of the encouragement and fostering of artistic talent, in the display and accessibility of art objects to larger audiences, in the appreciation and interpretation of art objects, and in the enrichment of artistic techniques from the influences of science and technology.

5. The development of mankind has reached a stage at which our problems *and* their solutions are dominated by science and technology. The same science and technology which produce what first seemed to be a beneficial drug also discover the harmful side effects and alternatives which mitigate the side effects. The threat of nuclear destruction and of environmental deterioration brought about by the progress of science and technology has produced an "adversary culture" and a "critical establishment." The adversary culture is a mood of distrust of and resistance to scientific and technological growth among a substantial part of the educated populations of advanced industrial nations; and the critical establishment consists of a collection of interest groups and lobbies which influence public opinion and public policy as they affect scientific activity and technology. This political dialectic has positive consequences, bringing other important values to bear on technological development and economic growth. But the adversary culture and the critical establishment do not fully appreciate the urgency of technological adaptiveness. If the conflict among growth, safety, and aesthetics is always resolved against growth and risk, the creative potential of science and technology, of which we have the most urgent need, may be seriously impaired.

6. The achievement of economic growth in Europe and America in the nineteenth century was accompanied by increasing inequality as modern economic sectors emerged out of primarily agricultural economies. The peoples of contemporary Third World countries seem to be less tolerant of this pattern of economic progress. Material progress in the contemporary world tends to be defined politically as requiring a more equitable balance of growth and distribution. This has begun to reduce confidence in the measures of economic growth. Simple per

capita growth of the national product fails to reflect the distribution of income among various groups in the society.

In the more advanced economies confidence in the present pattern of economic measurement has been impaired by our failure to take into account the externalities of economic growth—the costs in health, amenities, and safety resulting from economic progress. Thus, in general, we can say that a skeptical and more prudent mood has replaced the optimism of the earlier stages of the culture of progress and that the future evaluation of material progress will insist on a reconciliation of these secondary consequences and on an accommodation with considerations of equity.

7. The relation of government to progress is more complex and problematic. From having become the primary instrument of welfare and equity in the last century, government in advanced liberal societies now seems to be encountering intractable problems of economic growth, stability, and equity whereas in the communist world massive government represses liberty and privacy and seems to be encountering its own set of growth and distributive problems. From different starting points, these two sharply contrasting approaches to government are seeking to reconcile growth, stability, equity, and liberty in different ratios and proportions.

It is in the area of international politics that the relation of the state to progress becomes most problematic. The growth of defense expenditures and the concentration of science and technology on the development of increasingly destructive weapons are the very opposite of progress, and it is this development and use of science and technology that have most seriously impaired our faith in a "progressive" future. Surely, in this area progress is to be measured by the establishment of effective controls over armaments and the establishment of limits on the policies of governments that may result in their use.

8. Although democracy continues to perform well by comparison with other alternatives in the advanced industrial societies, it would appear to be less effective in societies seeking to cope with the massive problems of modernization. In the Third World the place of democracy in the overall strategy of progress is still not fully understood. At least at certain points in this process of modernization, technocratic authoritarian regimes seem to produce better results.

9. The growth and diffusion of scientific knowledge have meant the increasing displacement of theocentric and anthropocentric views of the universe and nature. The cosmology of science has replaced these traditional beliefs with the view that the physical universe as now constituted, the emergence of living organisms, and the emergence of man and of his contemporary culture were none of them necessary and inevitable and that their future in the long run is in doubt. Surely, the intellectual impact of the scientific revolution is destructive of traditional culture and of religiously based systems of morality. These

secularizing and demystifying influences have been met in the past and even today by defensive and repressive measures on the part of powerful groups and agencies in society. But this demoralization and alienation may perhaps be only the first generation of reactions to the spread of the culture of science. The view that secularization replaces the sacred is only tenable if one confines the notion of the sacred to traditional definitions. The great discoveries of modern science produce their own humility, awe, and mystery. If anything, the imputation of sacredness to the environment and to the preservation of the species has been enhanced in recent decades. The awareness of the contingent basis of man's emergence and existence may prove to be more supportive of a sober, consequential morality than of nihilism or a mock-heroic existentialism.

10. Although science and the growth of knowledge have eroded traditional morality, they have opened the potentiality of a far-reaching science and technology-based morality. The sense of obligation and responsibility seems to stretch and extend as far and as deep as we can know and understand. Contemporary humankind is asked to assume a responsibility as extensive and as compelling as the sweep and power of modern knowledge. Our obligation to help the poor is not confined to alms but calibrated by criteria of nutrition and indexed for inflation. Our obligation to heal the sick and cure and prevent disease has kept pace with modern medical technology, radically transformed the ratio of births to deaths, increased longevity, and produced secondary and unintended consequences of the gravest and most complex kind.

We cannot argue that there has been a decline in morality as a consequence of modern science and technology. Rather it would appear that we evaluate ourselves and our performance by more and more demanding criteria and hence seem to be falling short of what we require of ourselves. Our charity is less visible since it has become routinized and bureaucratized and rationalized as tax saving. Our regard for human dignity has produced a whole series of affirmative actions relating to race, sex, age, cultures and lifestyles, such that it has now become almost taboo to investigate and assert the existence of differences.

But this science and technology-based sense of moral obligation is specialized and fragmented. Its very success is based upon this specialization. What we have begun to appreciate is that when our humanity is broken up into parts—health, aesthetic sensibility, safety, dignity, privacy—these parts do not add up to a whole identity. The caring for and the cure of souls—once the province of a vital and powerful religious establishment—is now left to psychotherapy and mental health programs. Thus, the fostering of morality by progress is a story of extraordinary accomplishment in detail, at the cost of a fragmentation of the sense of self and of community.

What gives a desperate quality to the modern ethical dilemma is not only that we evaluate ourselves by more exacting criteria but that we seem to have no choice but to stretch and reach them. Thus, the control of nuclear technology can hardly appear as a matter of ethical free choice. The burden of population and technology on environment produces a similar sense of urgency. The growing gap between the developed and developing worlds has similarly threatening overtones. If there is a single phrase that can capture the contemporary version of the idea of progress, it would be progress not as an inevitable sequence of improvements but as aspiration and compelling obligation.

PART I

Historical, Ideological, and Evolutionary Aspects

Part One traces the idea of progress through its intellectual history, its ideological transformations, and its diffusion as idea and ideology throughout the entire world. The concluding essay of Part I is concerned with the biological-evolutionary basis of the idea of progress.

In the opening essay dealing with the origins of the idea of progress, Nannerl Keohane points out that in the eighteenth century, humanity's autonomous creative and adaptive potential is recognized and legitimated for the first time on a substantial scale. To be sure, she points out that not all the philosophers of the eighteenth century share the "simplistic optimism" of the Abbé Saint-Pierre, Turgot, and Condorcet, that knowledge and the progress of reason will solve all humankind's problems. There were skeptics such as Voltaire, Diderot, and Kant, who argued that increasing knowledge and technical development did not necessarily produce political and moral improvement. What did take place in the eighteenth century was a general recognition that new powers were afoot in the world, that through knowledge man was in a position to acquire mastery over nature, but with what political and moral consequences was a matter of debate.

Georg Iggers traces the idea of progress through the social theory and historiography of the nineteenth and twentieth centuries. He describes three approaches to history which carry through from the Enlightenment to modern times. The first of these is the unambiguously progressive approach represented in the eighteenth century by the work of Adam Ferguson, Saint-Pierre, Turgot, and Condorcet. In the nineteenth century Hegel, Saint-Simon, Comte, Marx, and Spencer follow in this same tradition, emphasizing the universality of history and dividing it into progressive stages; however, these nineteenth-century social theorists gave more emphasis to historical and collective tendencies and constraints and to conflict as a progressive dynamic, along with the growth of knowledge and the progress of reason. In the contemporary era this progressive tradition is represented in the "stages" of development studies of Walt Rostow and Cyril Black and in the modernization theories of Talcott Parsons, Neil Smelser, and others.

The second approach emphasizes the ambiguity of progress, the costs, and negative side effects. In the nineteenth century this tradition of skepticism and pessimism about the value of progress is expressed in the work of Alexis de Tocqueville, who stresses the negative consequences of increasing equality; Ferdinand Tönnies, the destruction of community; Emile Durkheim, man's alienation as a consequence of division of labor and specialization; and Max Weber, the secularization and bureaucratization of society.

The contemporary expression of this ambivalent, critical view of progress as historically realized in the twentieth century has a neo-Marxist and a neoconservative version. The neo-Marxist version attacks the exploitativeness of modern civilization and the compulsion to produce and consume without regard to need. The neoconservative version emphasizes the destruction of meaningful cosmology, the bases of morality, and the primary supportive institutions of family, community, and church that result from progress.

In the third approach, the idea of progress was never accepted as an ordering theme for modern history. Its advocates include the historians Leopold von Ranke and Jacob Burckhardt, who emphasized the uniqueness of historical phenomena, each epoch being equal and "immediate to God" and each to be judged according to its own standards. More recently, the popularizers of philosophy of history—Oswald Spengler and Arnold Toynbee—proposed cyclical, organic models for the movement of history. The historical relativism of Ranke and Burckhardt has its contemporary formulation among anthropologists, some of whom tend to stress the uniqueness and equal validity of cultures. This is stated most consequentially in the structuralist school of Claude Lévi-Strauss, who tells us that in a sense magic and science are equally valid ways of knowing.

Iggers concludes that despite the relativism of the historians and the romanticism of the anthropologists

> the modern world is the central historical experience of our existence. This modern world is fundamentally different from all other civilizations and cultures, and this difference rests on its progressive character. Modern society has been one of growth. This growth

in the nineteenth and twentieth centuries has affected the entire world so that one can speak for the first time of world history. . . . The critics of progress. . . . have not invalidated the core of the idea, the moral imperative to create a world in which the conditions for a dignified human existence, which today do not exist for billions of human beings, are achieved.

That the idea of progress and its culture now dominate the world, though with important modifications from the Western version, is the theme of Alfred Meyer's essay on the idea of progress in communist ideology and Crawford Young's on the Third World. Meyer tells us that Marxism and Leninism combine eighteenth-century faith in progress and nineteenth-century critiques of industrialism in a single grand synthesis, with progress becoming a spiral development in which retrogression and alienation are necessary steps toward progress. Unlike the Western, more benign version, Marxism-Leninism as idea and as reality seeks to "push, shove, or drag" backward societies into the progressive tendencies of history by heroic effort. If the Western version of progress accepted the inequalities and inequities of industrial development, preserving areas of freedom, and providing for increasing mass political participation, the communist version of progress accepted the emphasis on science, technology, and material growth but traded off liberty and effective political participation for greater equality and mobilized participation.

Crawford Young traces the diffusion of the idea of progress into the Third World, showing us how it has been adopted with modifications but with enthusiasm for its scientific and technical components. Progress in its historic meaning is not immanent in the beliefs of Islam, Buddhism, Hinduism, or Confucianism. Within each of these major world cosmologies, reform movements sought to reconcile progress with religious doctrine. Other sources of ambivalence regarding the content of progress and modernization have been the reactions against imperialism, postcolonial dependency, and the growing inequality engendered by the introduction of a modern sector. Thus, progress has been embraced in the Third World often in combination with some version of socialism, a strong affirmation of nationalism, and cultural independence.

In the final chapter of Part One, Francisco Ayala approaches the concept of progress from the perspective of the evolutionary biologist. He points to the variety of ways progress has been defined by biologists and criticizes a number of efforts to measure biological progress. In his own view the "ability of organisms to obtain and process information about the environment . . . [is] a criterion of progress that is particularly relevant to the evolution of man." The most fundamental human characteristic, according to Ayala, is this greatly developed (and through culture) constantly increasing "ability to perceive the environment and to react flexibly to it." According to this measure, Ayala argues that man is the most progressive organism on the planet. And it is precisely this ability to perceive, analyze, store, retrieve, and utilize information for purposes of mastery of and adaptation to the environment that is fully recognized in the Enlightenment and implemented in the nineteenth and twentieth centuries.

The import of Part I is that the idea of progress—and the civilization it has produced—is not just another historical phenomenon but that it represents the fulfillment of mankind's potential for the accumulation and interpretation of knowledge and the utilization of this knowledge for technical and organizational innovation in ways and to a degree not equaled by any prior historical experience. Furthermore, this idea of progress and the culture it has produced have come to so dominate the world that the notion that they will give way, short of major catastrophe, to some other, basically different culture would appear to be quite untenable.

1

The Enlightenment Idea of Progress Revisited

NANNERL O. KEOHANE

The idea of progress, conventional wisdom has it, was first preached during the Enlightenment. It became an article of faith in the nineteenth century and remained the dominant doctrine in Western culture until the middle of the twentieth. But somber experiences and multiplying complexities have made the Enlightenment conception of progress obsolescent. The simple faith that things are steadily getting better and, moreover, can be relied on to continue to improve is now vulnerable to powerful opposing evidence and has few professed adherents. We know too much about the human condition to share the naïve optimism that characterized eighteenth-century rationalists or those happy Victorians who flocked to the Crystal Palace in 1851.

This "sadder but wiser" perspective is familiar from numerous contemporary writings. Ironically, one major component of the belief in progress is imbedded in this view. The doomsayers assume that our understanding of the human situation has, with the benefit of a century of experience and research, progressed beyond that available to our ancestors. In thinking about progress, at least, there has been progress. This is but one example of the extent to which the idea of progress, in one guise or another, permeates our perspective on the world.

For some people, this pervasive belief in progress assumes the form of a theory of history, a systematic framework that allows us to account for the entire experience of humankind. Another perspective, represented by Robert Bierstedt, is that the notion of progress "hardly qualifies as an idea at all" but should be construed as "an attitude," an affirmation that some social change gives pleasure or elicits applause, "a phenomenon wholly devoid of objective validity."[1] From yet another vantage point, progress is a durable myth, a rhetorically persuasive ideology that allows people to make sense of past experiences and face the future armed with hope.

Do such contemporary statements about progress describe actual patterns in human activity, or do they merely give one particular perspective on that activity? What difference does it make whether we believe in progress or not? In dealing with such questions, let us first note some of the problems of definition we are likely to encounter and then review the development of the Enlightenment idea.

DEFINING PROGRESS

"The idea of the Progress of humanity," according to its most eminent twentieth-century historian, J.B. Bury, "means that civilization has moved, is moving, and will move in a desirable direction."[2] Although Bury's definition does not approach the compactness of Charles van Doren's "irreversible meliorative change," it compares favorably with Arthur Lovejoy's more cautious "tendency inherent in nature or in man to pass through a regular sequence of stages of development in past, present, and future, the later stages being—with perhaps occasional retardations or minor retrogressions—superior to the earlier."[3] All three definitions share the elements of movement and improvement considered essential to the notion of progress. The idea of movement is fairly easy to grasp in this context. The human experience of alteration over a lifetime combined with accessible records from the past that document such changes make the concept of change itself uncontroversial. The more difficult question is that of melioration or improvement. How do we know that later stages of development are "superior" to earlier ones, that the direction of movement is "desirable"? All three definitions beg this essential question. However, Bury confronts it in his next sentence: "In order to judge that we are moving in a desirable direction, we should have to know precisely what the destination is."[4] The happiness of the species, in this view, is determined only after the fact; statements about progress are then provisional and tentative. Progress, one might say, means movement toward an outcome that would have been chosen had it been foreseen.

Since we can never know the destination in advance, Bury's solution, if rigidly adopted, invalidates the whole concept, but it reminds

1. Robert Bierstedt, "Once More the Idea of Progress," in *The Science of Society and the Unity of Mankind*, memorial volume for Morris Ginsberg, ed. Ronald Fletcher (London: Heinemann, 1974), p. 73.

2. J.B. Bury, *The Idea of Progress: An Inquiry into Its Origin and Growth* (1932; rpt. New York: Dover, 1955), p. 2.

3. Charles van Doren, *The Idea of Progress* (New York: Praeger, 1967), p. 7; Arthur O. Lovejoy and George Boas, *Primitivism and Related Ideas in Antiquity* (Baltimore, Md.: Johns Hopkins University Press, 1935), p. i.

4. Bury, *Idea of Progress*, p. 2.

us that the notion of a goal or destination is closely associated with the idea of progress. We make progress as we advance toward the end of a journey or complete a task such as solving a puzzle or tidying a room. When we speak of making progress in learning Greek or getting to know somebody, we have no expectation of understanding the language perfectly or achieving complete intimacy. But the hypothetical end point establishes the other end of the line along which we are moving. A projected goal allows us to say that our movements have direction; aimless activity gives no basis for assessing progress.

If we turn from everyday activity to the larger philosophical questions with which the idea of progress is concerned, we find that the most ardent Enlightenment proponents of the idea, Saint-Pierre, Turgot, and Condorcet, were staunch utopians, who hypothesized a golden age toward which we were moving. Today, statements about progress are less grandiose, often based simply on a comparison of the present with the past. Lovejoy's definition, which posits a superior later stage, may do the job without requiring Bury's unknown destination. However, this still leaves unanswered the question of desirability or superiority. Unless we are headed in a direction that we all recognize as a desirable one, how can we establish that the direction of our movement is a proper one? What makes succeeding stages superior to earlier ones? The notion of progress is not always associated with desirability. Doctors speak of "the progress of a disease," even though no one desires the deterioration of the sick person. Rakes, as well as pilgrims, have made progress of which others have heatedly disapproved.[5] Nonetheless, we commonly expect the notion to connote acquiring or approaching something worth having. What forms the basis for such judgments? Is it sufficient that *someone* thinks the direction is desirable, or is a consensus required? Can firm benchmarks be established that do not depend on idiosyncratic taste or transient perspectives?

Looking about us, we see increases in diversity and complexity in certain areas of human life; in others, there is growing uniformity and congruence. Both complexity and congruence describe our modern age compared with the traditional past, but are these satisfactory criteria for progress? Is either diversity or uniformity valuable as such? One of the most important changes in the idea of progress in recent decades is that we have ceased to take for granted the desirability of things earlier generations assumed to be beneficial. The notion of progress has become so bound up with those things that we can, paradoxically, agree that "progress" in the conventional sense has taken place, yet deny that the change was for the better.

The idea of progress has often been closely associated with an

5. John Baillie, *The Belief in Progress* (Oxford: Oxford University Press, 1950), Chap. 1. Adam Ferguson's *Essay on the History of Civil Society* (1767) closes with "Of the Progress and Termination of Despotism," an account of the progress of political corruption.

increase in human achievements or transformations. In the eighteenth century, progress was synonymous with refinement, polish, and civility in contrast to crudity, barbarity, and rudeness. Artifice, defined as the highest natural achievement of our species or as counterposed to raw nature, was the core of this conception of progress and the grounds for the association of "cultured" with refined and superior. Benjamin Lincoln, a Revolutionary general and statesman, spoke for most of his contemporaries when he observed in 1792 that "civilization directs us to remove as fast as possible that natural growth from the lands."[6] This attitude is the basis for the present linkage of progress with such things as mechanization, technical innovation, and replacing forests with factories or housing developments. The notion of progress as refinement gave way to the notion as accumulation—of skills, of material comforts, of instruments of sophistication and control. It is not accidental, surely, that today we rarely speak of "progressing" but instead of "making" progress. Yet the very proliferation of techniques and products of technologies excites anxiety and criticism because to some observers the costs of such "refinements" loom larger than the benefits. This attitude was not unknown in the heyday of "the idea of progress." It is far more common today.

Once we accept that progress has its "costs," we can see the value of sorting out different types of progress rather than lumping everything together in the amorphous "civilization" of Bury's definition. Ruth Macklin distinguishes four types and ranks them according to their probability or general acceptability. "It is wholly uncontroversial," she asserts, "to hold that technological progress has taken place; largely uncontroversial to claim that intellectual and theoretical progress has occurred; somewhat controversial to say that aesthetic or artistic progress has taken place; and highly controversial to assert that moral progress has occurred."[7] Each kind of progress requires its own canons to demonstrate improvement and desirability. They all depend, however, on cumulative development. To show that progress has occurred in any of these domains, we must show that sequential advances were not accompanied by equally important losses. In the case of technology this is often easy. In more spiritual domains it is not so obvious that we incorporate the greatest achievements of past generations, avoid their errors, and move beyond them: but advances in techniques and

6. Quoted in Roy Harvey Pearce, *The Savages of America* (Baltimore, Md.: Johns Hopkins University Press, 1953), p. 68; cf. the similar opinion held by Marx and Engels, discussed in Alfred Meyer's essay in this volume, pp. 70–71.

7. Ruth Macklin, "Moral Progress," *Ethics*, 87(4) (July 1977): 370. As Baillie puts it: "Observed progress is mainly technical whereas believed progress is mainly spiritual"; *Belief in Progress*, p. 156. In a working paper for an earlier conference on progress sponsored by the American Academy of Arts and Sciences, H. Stuart Hughes adapted Marx's notion of the "substructure" of technology and productivity versus the "superstructure" of ideas and institutions to locate these two different types of progress.

skills are undeniable. The evidence of length of life, health, and comfort can only with extraordinary perversity be denied the label of improvement.

Such achievements, however, are not necessarily sufficient ground for establishing "net progress" in human welfare (to use Ayala's term; see pp. 110ff.). A *New Yorker* cartoon makes this point neatly; it shows the Four Horsemen of the Apocalypse speeding down a superhighway on motorcycles. Technological progress creates difficulties as well as advantages. It makes possible certain kinds of aesthetic creations that were out of reach before but may also contribute to dullness and ugliness in the environment. It extends the capacities of tyrants and humanitarians alike. The growing complexity of knowledge means that although a few may comprehend more about nature than any human being in the past, most of us understand less about our surroundings, both man-made and natural, than earlier peoples whose lore was simpler but more proportional to their world. As Max Weber pointed out, we ride on streetcars but cannot tell how to build them; "the savage knew incomparably more about his tools."[8] In assessing who is the "we" who have progressed, it is important to recall that collective accomplishments for the species are often lodged in advantages for the few, whether economically privileged or intellectually elite. "We have progressed" does not necessarily imply "I am better off."[9]

A different set of issues is raised by causal questions. What propels change along, and what determines its direction? Since the Enlightenment, there have been three main candidates: the hand of Providence, the unfolding of history, and the activities of human beings.

The idea of progress is sometimes juxtaposed to a belief in Providence. Bury, for instance, asserts that the one supplanted the other as modern thought became more secularized. The distinction rests on the belief in an external cause of change, as opposed to asserting that transformations "proceed from a principle of advancement in the subject itself."[10] However, historically speaking, it is inaccurate to regard the two as mutually exclusive. Early versions of the theory of progress were direct offshoots of the belief in Providence. The "invisible hand" identified by classical economists, which combined individual human activities in a concerted forward movement, was, at the outset, the hand of God. Ernest Tuveson notes how the "dogma of progress, shedding its ecclesiastical trappings, nevertheless retained

8. Max Weber, "Science as a Vocation," in *From Max Weber*, ed. H. H. Gerth and C. Wright Mills (Oxford: Oxford University Press, 1958), p. 139.

9. I am indebted to Ruth Marcus for this insight, offered during a seminar at the Center for Advanced Study in the Behavioral Sciences, Stanford, where a draft of this chapter was presented in March 1979.

10. Adam Ferguson, "Of Man's Progressive Nature," in his *Principles of Moral and Political Science* (Edinburgh, 1792), vol. 1; cf. Bury, *Idea of Progress*, pp. 5-6, 73-74.

a smuggled Providence."[11] This is apparent in numerous "secular" accounts of history as progress, from Adam Ferguson to Hegel and beyond.

The second candidate for the cause of change, the notion that history unfolds according to its own inner tendencies, particularly fascinated eighteenth- and nineteenth-century philosophers of progress. Imposing stages on history, whether four or twenty-four, is a delightful game. However, it is extremely difficult to devise a convincing account of the laws that govern the succession of such stages and to show why we should expect them to be invariant and benign. Almost all such accounts collapse into theories either of providential or of "anthropogenic" progress.[12]

The final candidate for the cause of change is human activity itself. At the heart of most theories of progress is a fascination with human efforts to improve the human condition. One can easily combine all three candidates under this rubric: a divine beneficence created our species to undertake activities that result in unfolding stages of history. Whichever energy or motive force is identified as the root cause, the most striking feature of this dogma of progress is the conviction that knowledge, power, virtue, and happiness buttress one another and will be achieved together. In its most robust and purest form, the belief in progress affirms that increase in human knowledge, the establishment of human control over nature, and the perfecting of the moral excellences of the species will guarantee one another, with a concomitant increase in human happiness. This certainly rests on beliefs drawn from Judeo-Christian and classical sources, combined with seventeenth-century optimism about man's estate.

THE CONSTITUENTS OF THE
IDEA OF PROGRESS

Bury depicts the idea of progress as a monolithic entity waiting to be discovered. He excuses the Greeks for not quite seeing it, despite all their other accomplishments, and makes a good deal of identifying the exact moment when the idea was first formulated. This way of investigating the history of ideas presents some major pitfalls.[13] Several elements have been combined to form what we call a theory or ideology of progress. Each of these elements was familiar from antiquity, and each is still with us. The notion of progress depends on combining them in a particular way.

11. Ernest Tuveson, *Millennium and Utopia* (Berkeley: University of California Press, 1949), p. 201; see also Karl Löwith, *Meaning in History* (Chicago: University of Chicago Press, 1949), p. 60.

12. Van Doren distinguishes "anthropogenic" theories of progress, based on man's "collective or social memory," from "cosmogenic theories," which regard Providence as the source of progress or else ascribe it to some impersonal cosmic principle in the universe itself; *Idea of Progress*, Chap. 2.

13. See Quentin Skinner, "Meaning and Understanding in the History of Ideas," *History and Theory*, 8 (1969): 3-53.

Among the elements prominent in Judaism (and Christianity) is the conviction that man was licensed by his creator to dominate nature for his own use. This conception of the relationship between humankind and other parts of nature, which differs profoundly from that found in other ancient cultures, is central to the notion of progress. It certifies that human conquest of nature is divinely blessed. It teaches us to think of control and power as the proper ends of knowledge. Genesis, however, gives no guarantee that man will progress with such mastery. Although this condition was a feature of paradise, the desire to know and control also led to the expulsion from the garden and the lowering of man's estate.

A second element crucial to the theory of progress in Judeo-Christian doctrine is the belief that history, at least for the chosen or elect, has a happy ending. This divine plan became particularly important to the early Christians, who looked for an early Second Coming and found comfort for their tribulations in a belief in the millennium. The elements of material well-being associated more recently with the doctrine of progress are offshoots of this conviction that the last stage of earthly history will be delightful. Consider the vivid description by Saint Irenaeus (ca. 125-ca. 202):

> The days will come, in which vines shall grow, each having ten thousand branches, and in each branch ten thousand twigs, and in each true twig ten thousand shoots, and in each one of the shoots ten thousand clusters, and on every one of the clusters ten thousand grapes, and every grape when pressed will give five and twenty metretes of wine. And when any one of the saints shall lay hold of a cluster, another shall cry out, "I am a better cluster, take me; bless the Lord through me."[14]

The millennium, however, was expected to follow periods of tribulation and decline. It was a gift of God's grace to the faithful, not an achievement steadily won by human activity.

A third, especially Christian, aspect was the conviction that over time there will be increasing revelation. God's truth was made more and more manifest from the Old Testament to the New, and on through the refinements of the Fathers of the Church. This sense of cumulative truth is closely akin to that professed by the optimistic believers in progress. The image of men sitting on shoulders of giants, able to see further by virtue of their increased stature, is often used as a symbol for progress from the Middle Ages to modern times.[15] It was no doubt connected with the images of the evangelists sitting on the shoulders of the prophets, depicted so memorably in the north transept windows at Chartres Cathedral.

14. *Saint Irenaeus, Against Heresies*, V, 33; quoted in Tuveson, *Millennium and Utopia*, p. 22.
15. Robert Merton, *On the Shoulders of Giants* (New York: Praeger, 1965), offers a delightful account of his researches into the origins of this metaphor.

To these Judeo-Christian contributions must be added those of the Greeks and Romans. Ludwig Edelstein, in his elegant study of early ideas of progress, quotes Xenophanes' succinct expression of the belief in the gradual discovery of truth about the world by human effort, with beneficial results for human life: "The gods did not reveal to men all things from the beginning; but men through their own search find in the course of time that which is better."[16] In *De Rerum Natura*, which offers a detailed description of this process, Lucretius speculates on anthropological history and outlines the stages by which men learned arts and skills for making their lives more comfortable but, therefore, more complex. He presents a set of stages in profane history, rooted in the production of goods and organization of societies, quite different from the stages of sacred history as outlined in the book of Daniel or by Joachim de Floris (ca. 1132-1202).[17] Lucretius uses the term *progredientes*—moving forward step by step—but does not describe the process as an overall increase in happiness. For Lucretius, as for Seneca, the conflicts and corruptions that mark human history are as important as the increase in skills or knowledge and supply evidence of accompanying decadence or decay.

One further aspect of Greek thought is relevant: the Socratic conviction that virtue is knowledge, that men do not willingly perform acts they know will bring pain and unhappiness to themselves. In this view, the increase in human rationality or comprehension of the world constitutes an increase in moral excellence; as individual men discover truth, they learn more about what it means to live life rightly, and they behave more virtuously. But Socrates and his followers (especially Plato) saw no reason to suppose that humankind become more rational over time. To these philosophers, history was cyclical or retrogressive, and, therefore, they cannot be enlisted among the believers in progress. The knowledge they associated with rationality and virtue is far removed from the amassing of what we today call empirical understanding. Nonetheless, they contributed a central moral element to the theory of progress: the association of knowing and acting well.

During the Renaissance, many of these ideas were recovered or expanded. Jurists such as Bodin and Le Roy displayed a new interest in history; artisans developed pride in technical skill and a sense of guild cooperation that helped lay the groundwork for the belief in intellectual and technological advances of succeeding generations;[18] discovery

16. Ludwig Edelstein, *The Idea of Progress in Classical Antiquity* (Baltimore, Md.: Johns Hopkins University Press, 1967), p. 3.

17. For Lucretius, see Ronald Meek, *Social Science and the Ignoble Savage* (Cambridge: Cambridge University Press, 1976), pp. 9-10; for sacred history, see Tuveson, *Millennium and Utopia*, Chap. 1.

18. Edgar Zilsel, "The Genesis of the Concept of Scientific Progress," and A.C. Keller, "Zilsel, the Artisans, and the Idea of Progress in the Renaissance," in *Roots of Scientific Thought*, ed. Philip Wiener and Aaron Noland (New York: Basic Books, 1957), pp. 251-75, 281-86.

and exploration of new worlds offered material for comparison between "civilized" and "primitive" societies and engendered pride in the fruits of sophisticated human artifice.[19] In the seventeenth century these various elements were brought together to give grounds for optimism about future human possibilities, but without a corresponding sense of past achievement. Nonetheless, in the era of Bacon and Descartes, we first recognize a pattern of argument that can sensibly be labeled "the idea of progress."

SEVENTEENTH-CENTURY OPTIMISM

The vigorous optimism of Bacon, Descartes, and their followers about the capacity of the human mind to discover useful truths for the comfort and improvement of the species was a crucial contribution to the notion of progress. Their certainty, however, had nothing to do with past progress. They saw the blind toil of their ancestors as fruitless, men wasting their efforts for want of proper method. "There was but one course left, therefore," announced Bacon in the preface to his *Great Instauration*: "to try the whole thing anew upon a better plan, and to commence a total reconstruction of the sciences, arts, and all human knowledge, raised upon the proper foundations. . . . For of this there is some issue; whereas in what is now done in the matter of science there is only a whirling round about, and perpetual agitation, ending where it began."[20]

Bacon's assurance that the new beginning would issue in unprecedented accomplishment rested on two factors: method and motive. The method was to "establish progressive stages of certainty," beginning with the evidence of the senses and depending upon instruments and machinery rather than unaided logic to establish truth. Technology augments the forces of understanding as it does manual strength. Bacon warned against "anticipations," assumptions not supported by evidence, laced together intricately in systems as insubstantial as a spider's web. This tendency was the main difficulty with intellectual endeavor throughout past history. Bacon asserted:

> Though all the wits of all the ages should meet together and combine and transmit their labours, yet will no great progress ever be made in science by means of anticipations; because radical errors in the first concoction of the mind are not to be cured by the excellence of functions and remedies subsequent. . . . We must begin anew from the very foundations, unless we would revolve for ever in a circle with mean and contemptible progress.[21]

19. See Pearce, *Savages of America*; and Meek, *Social Science*; as well as Margaret Hodgen, *Early Anthropology in the Sixteenth and Seventeenth Centuries* (Philadelphia: University of Pennsylvania Press, 1964).

20. Francis Bacon, Preface to *The Great Instauration*, in *Francis Bacon: A Selection of His Works*, ed. Sidney Warhaft (New York: Odyssey Press, 1965), p. 299.

21. Francis Bacon, *Novum Organum*, Book 1, Chap. 31, in *Francis Bacon*, p. 334.

The second factor—the proper motive—assured rapid progress. If we "consider what are the true ends of knowledge," we will set out to learn "not either for pleasure of the mind, or for contention, or for superiority to others, or for profit, or fame, or power, or any of these inferior things; but for the benefit and use of life," as we "perfect and govern it in charity." According to Bacon, the original sin was not "that pure and uncorrupted knowledge whereby Adam gave names to the creatures," but rather "the ambitious and proud desire of moral knowledge," the revolt from God's legislative power over us. To desire power for oneself, or over one's country, is "vulgar and degenerate," a source of sin; but "if a man endeavor to establish and extend the power and dominion of the human race itself over the universe," his ambition is noble and wholesome, and will be divinely blessed.[22]

Bacon's sense of nature's role in this adventure was complex. We must respect nature to ensure her cooperation—obey her in order to command her—but the goal is human mastery.[23] There is no doubt about God's support for such endeavors. Bacon depicts God as a devotee of hide-and-seek, inviting the "human spirit for his playfellow" at the game of innocent discovery of truth. If we proceed in this spirit, we may hope that the "commerce between the mind of man and the nature of things, which is more precious than anything on earth, may be restored to its perfect and original condition." As we imitate the creative works of God for human good, he will repay the enterprise most handsomely: "Thou wilt make us partakers of thy vision and thy sabbath."[24]

The utilitarian conviction that scientific enterprise must be under-taken "for the benefit and use of life" if it is to bear fruit is balanced in Bacon's work by the pure joy in the discovery of truth. He praises the increase of knowledge itself, "the very beholding of the light," as a "fairer thing than all the uses of it," and "more worthy than all the fruit of inventions." For Bacon, these two aspects of the search for truth are not mutually exclusive but complementary. He asserts that there will never be "much progress in the sciences" until "natural philosophy be carried on and applied to particular sciences, and partic-ular sciences be carried back again to natural philosophy."[25] From this mutual refreshment of pure and applied science we may expect great things; and this is the rule established in Bacon's research utopia, New Atlantis (1627), where the "End of our Foundation is the knowledge

22. Bacon, Preface to The Great Instauration, p. 310; and Novum Organum, Book 1, Chap. 129, p. 375.

23. Bacon, Novum Organum, Book 1, Chap. 3, p. 331; on Bacon's exploitative atti-tude toward nature's bounty, see Carolyn Merchant, The Death of Nature: Women, Ecology, and the Scientific Revolution (San Francisco, Ca.: Harper & Row, 1980).

24. Bacon, Preface to The Great Instauration and concluding paragraph of "The Plan of the Work."

25. Bacon, Novum Organum, Book 1, Chap. 80, p. 253.

of Causes, and secret motions of things; and the enlarging of the bounds of Human Empire, to the effecting of all things possible."[26]

Several of Bacon's successors, including Thomas Burnet and Robert Boyle, were even more optimistic. They carried out their own scientific discoveries in the conviction that they were contributing to the reversal of the Fall from grace and the reestablishment of the human race in its original condition. They assumed that God, like a skillful workman, had built a universe that did not require continual tinkering or supervision but ran of its own accord on regular principles. This means, as Tuveson puts it, that "the plot of nature is written into the structure of the universe itself," and the idea of progress can emerge from that of Providence.[27] As men discover these laws and work in accord with them, they transform the earth for human betterment and also redeem humankind from sin. In this scheme of salvation through "cosmic progressivism," the neo-Platonic vision of the ascent of the soul through the various stages of the good was joined with optimism about the divine plan for history, and thus, the whole story of the Fall was reinterpreted. Burnet described the Fall as a "moral degeneration" extending over many centuries rather than a momentary lapse in a mystical garden.[28] Human failings had swept away the age of gold; God had ordained that human works could bring it back again.

A more secular but equally bold faith marked Descartes' certainty. He was confident that God had not created a fundamentally disordered or malicious universe, so that assiduous and well-intentioned human labors in gathering knowledge by the proper method would yield rich fruits for human life. Descartes' confidence and rationalistic method were just as influential as Bacon's; and the combined legacies of these two thinkers gave their century new enthusiasm about the human capacity to know and control the world. There followed a new optimism about the future. Earlier generations had regarded the pattern of history as ceaseless cyclical movement or overall decline, or they thought that history (apart from sacred history) had no pattern at all. They were humble or skeptical about human reason. Montaigne's dictum was atypical only in its elegance: "Man does not know the natural infirmity of his mind; it does nothing but ferret and quest, and keeps incessantly whirling around, building up and becoming entangled in its own work, like our silkworms, and is suffocated in it."[29] In the seventeenth century, for the first time, many thoughtful persons were convinced that a route had been found out of such sterile whirling, a route that would establish the human race in its proper place in the

26. Francis Bacon, *New Atlantis*, in *Francis Bacon*, p. 447.

27. Tuveson, *Millennium and Utopia*, p. 119.

28. Thomas Burnet, *Theory of the Earth* (1684-1690), discussed in ibid., Chap. 5.

29. Montaigne, "Of Experience," in *The Complete Essays of Montaigne*, ed. Donald Frame (Stanford, Ca.: Stanford University Press, 1958), Book 3, number 13, p. 817.

great chain of being. The future would surely be brighter than the past.

In this climate even Pascal, whose assessment of the corruption and triviality of the human condition unaided by God's grace is as dark as any in literature, was optimistic about human reason and the progress of science. He recalled the Greek belief that the secrets of nature are revealed over time and explained this by the cumulative efforts of generations. Human life is a learning experience; the whole race, like a single individual becoming wiser with age, augments skills and avoids errors. We, maturer and more proficient than our ancestors, are the true "ancients," not the Greeks and Romans who lived in the infancy of the world. For "tous les hommes ensemble y font un continuel progrès à mesure que l'univers vieillit. . . ."[30]

In all this optimism about the human prospect, however, it is rare to find any conviction that men will improve steadily in virtue and brotherhood as knowledge grows. The Christian Platonists' assurance that men work out their own salvation implied progress in virtue; but only faith in God's plan for the species gave grounds for this assurance. Bacon, Descartes, and Pascal all believed that "civil knowledge"—knowledge about morality, society, and politics—is the most difficult to establish firmly. They made no rosy predictions about morals or politics to match their visions in science and technique. In this, they were more akin to our contemporary mood than their successors of the next two centuries.

The awareness that technological sophistication and material comfort can be accompanied by moral and social decadence has been part of the Western consciousness since philosophers first mused on the decay of Greece and the decline of Rome. The fully developed theory of progress required an explanation for such asymmetries between technique and virtue in the past, along with arguments to show why increasing control over our world in the future will assure increasing happiness and moral excellence. Such a theory has been held by only a small number of persons, compared with those in past or present who have endorsed other elements of the idea of progress. Most of those persons lived in the eighteenth, nineteenth, and early twentieth centuries; and the arguments about virtue and happiness that were needed to complete the theory were the contributions of the era of Enlightenment to the idea of progress.

THE FIRST STAGE OF
THE ENLIGHTENMENT

The Abbé de Saint-Pierre, an enthusiastic Cartesian, was first responsible for asserting that progress can be expected not only in physical

30. Pascal, "Preface pour le Traité du Vide" (ca. 1657), in Pascal's *Oeuvres complètes*, ed. Jacques Chevalier (Paris: Gallimard, 1954), pp. 533-34.

science but in social science and morality as well. His age, which spanned the last generation of Louis XIV and the first generation of the Enlightenment, was impressed by the immense gains in knowledge of the natural world and struck by the contrasting stagnation and sterility in the social sciences. The abbé, in his utilitarian treatises and projects, preached the conviction that equally impressive progress in morality and politics would follow the application of the new scientific method to these areas. He assured his readers that the principles of political and moral science are as invariant as those of physics and proposed academies of social science to carry out research and to educate the public.[31] He believed that discoveries in the human sciences solve the most urgent problems of humankind and move it along toward earthly bliss.

Saint-Pierre's arguments depended on the power of human reason, correctly focused and directed, to devise policies for ensuring human happiness. His system involved punishments and rewards to channel behavior toward useful pleasure and away from antisocial vice and depended on the support of strong governments. It appeared obvious to the abbé that civilization was bound to triumph and an earthly paradise was not far away once men put their reason to its proper uses.

Few eighteenth-century philosophers shared such a wide-ranging and simplistic optimism about human reason, and to attribute this mood to the Enlightenment in general is unwarranted.[32] Voltaire, Diderot, and Kant held more complex and guarded views about the human prospect; and Rousseau was the most eloquent of all critics of the idea of progress. However, numerous writers in this era shared a more diffuse optimism about rationality that made progress seem possible, if not inevitable. The instruments of education and legislation upon which Saint-Pierre relied for the success of his science of utility were refined by Helvétius and Condillac. The concept of controlling human behavior, even shaping human nature, to ensure that men would pursue their own secular happiness efficiently became familiar. And a new theory of historical development provided the temporal framework in which such advances could be explained and predicted.

At the Sorbonne in 1750, Turgot delivered a discourse on the stages of civilization in history, a recurrent theme in Saint-Pierre's volumi-

31. See Saint-Pierre's *Ouvrages de Politique*, 16 vols. (Rotterdam, 1733-1741), in which he suggests among other reform projects a more rational orthography. For his ideas on moral and political progress, consult Bury, *Idea of Progress*, Chap. 6; and N. O. Keohane, *Philosophy and the State in France* (Princeton, N.J.: Princeton University Press, 1980), Chap. 12.

32. Carl Becker's provocative *Heavenly City of the Eighteenth-Century Philosophers* (New Haven, Conn.: Yale University Press, 1932) is one source of this attribution. For the opposite opinion, consult Peter Gay, *The Party of Humanity* (Princeton, N.J.: Princeton University Press, 1959); and Arthur O. Lovejoy, *Reflections on Human Nature* (Baltimore, Md.: Johns Hopkins University Press, 1961).

nous writings. Turgot's "Philosophical Review of the Successive Advances of the Human Mind" presented evidence that the human adventure proceeds in a generally positive direction. Using Pascal's analogy, he compares the race to a single individual maturing in wisdom and virtue. "Finally," asserts Turgot, "commercial and political ties unite all parts of the globe, and the whole human race, through alternate periods of rest and unrest, of weal and woe, goes on advancing, although at a slow pace, toward greater perfection."[33]

The evidence Turgot provided was the different condition of human societies, using the "barbarism" of contemporary American savages as the benchmark against which the development of other nations could be measured.[34] This "four stages" theory of economic and social change—from hunting through pastoral life and agriculture to modern commercial economies—became quite popular in the second part of the eighteenth century. Those who embraced it had no doubt that the commercial way of life was superior to and more civilized than the earlier stages. The comparison of Scotland and France with simple hunting tribes in America offered decisive proof of progress in social organization, economic production and commerce, and communication. The "low material and cultural level" of the savage was correlated directly with the absence of sophisticated technology and institutions such as property, hierarchy, and capital.[35]

It was taken for granted in the eighteenth century that the most distinctive human trait was the capacity for social and scientific adaptiveness—the finishing or perfecting of the species, "la perfectibilité."[36] In his *Essay on the History of Civil Society* (entitled *A Treatise on Refinement* at one stage), Adam Ferguson took issue with the venerable distinction between art and nature on the grounds that "art itself is natural to man. He is in some measure the artificer of his own frame, as well as his fortune, and is destined, from the first age of his being, to invent and contrive." It is in our nature to improve ourselves, according to "a principle of progression" implanted in our species. Thus, it is inappropriate to suppose that we have "quitted the state of

33. Turgot's discourse is included in *Turgot on Progress, Sociology, and Economics*, ed. Ronald Meek (Cambridge: Cambridge University Press, 1975), pp. 41-59.

34. Ibid., p. 42; Turgot's explanation for differential rates of progress is the irregularity of nature's bounty; she has bestowed her gifts unequally; therefore, some people advance more rapidly than others.

35. Meek, *Social Science*, pp. 129-55; Pearce, *Savages of America*, p. 85. The indebtedness of Turgot and others to Locke's *Second Treatise of Civil Government* (Chap. 5, on property) is particularly obvious on this point. For a modern statement of the opposite belief, that the movement from hunting and gathering to agriculture was a necessary adaptation to a changing environment that had numerous unpleasant consequences for the species, see Mark N. Cohen, *The Food Crisis in Prehistory* (New Haven, Conn.: Yale University Press, 1977).

36. Even Rousseau's second *Discourse*, on the "Origins of Inequality," a searing indictment of the view that we have "progressed" in virtue and happiness as our technologies and sciences improve, retains the concept of "perfectability" in a neutral form.

nature" since we have begun to proceed; the state of nature is found wherever human beings are.[37]

The seventeenth-century idea that the principle of progress is God's plan for human redemption from the Fall remained prominent in several of these writings.[38] But, in demonstrating that moral progress has occurred and will continue, the Enlightenment authors improved upon their forebears. The proponents of the four stages theory relied on demonstrating that improving communication among members of our species and increasing commerce among societies must necessarily ensure an increase in virtue. According to Lord Monboddo, a prominent figure in the Scottish Enlightenment, "God has so ordered matters, that civil society has furnished a remedy" for the very evils it brings about; for "the love of knowledge has, by means of civil society, and that close intercourse and communication of men which it produces, invented and cultivated arts and science, by which the defect of our intelligence, the cause of all our evils, is ... in some degree remedied."[39] Here is the rationalistic principle that intellectual defects are the source of all other evils, with the concomitant assurance that reparations in intellectual deficiencies will lead to increasing virtue over time. Here we have the last linchpin in the theory of progress: the reliance on civilized society itself to confirm the inevitability of human improvement.

THE ZENITH OF THE
IDEA OF PROGRESS: CONDORCET

This faith that civilized progress perpetuates itself is brought to fullness in the Marquis de Condorcet's *Sketch for a Historical Picture of the Progress of the Human Mind*, composed in a few months in 1793-1794 while Condorcet was in hiding from Robespierre. Notwithstanding its brevity and melodramatic circumstances, this treatise provides the clearest and most uncompromising statement of the Enlightenment theory of progress. Ironically, it affirms Condorcet's implacable faith in a brilliant future on the very eve of his own miserable death at the hands of the forces he identified with progress.

Like Pascal and Turgot, Condorcet also bases his theory on the analogy between the race and the individual, each learning by experience from the simplest sensations to complex ideas. And just as individuals store information, so members of our species create a collective memory and a repertoire of skills and knowledge. Each stage

37. Adam Ferguson, *An Essay on the History of Civil Society* (1767), ed. Duncan Forbes (Edinburgh: Edinburgh University Press, 1966), pp. 6-8.
38. See Tuveson, *Millennium and Utopia*, pp. 195-96; Gladys Bryson, *Man and Society: The Scottish Inquiry of the Eighteenth Century* (Princeton, N.J.: Princeton University Press, 1945), p. 36; Bryson points out that for Ferguson, "progression is the gift of God to all his intelligent creatures."
39. Lord James Monboddo, *Antient Metaphysics* (1779-1799) 6 vols.; quote is from vol. 6, 255, as cited in Tuveson, *Millennium and Utopia*, p. 189. The same idea can be found in Turgot and Ferguson as well.

in history is "the result of what has happened at all previous moments" and influences what happens next. As communication is perfected, progress in all areas of life becomes "a hope that is almost a certainty." Of course there are obstacles: the prejudices that afflict human reason, which are aided by ignorance and supported by powerful interests. But Condorcet has no doubt about the outcome. He sets out to "demonstrate how nature has joined together indissolubly the progress of knowledge and that of liberty, virtue, and respect for the natural rights of man." As soon as enlightenment reaches all parts of the globe and commerce knits them together, "all will be the friends of humanity, all will work together for its perfection and its happiness."[40]

The bulk of Condorcet's treatise describes ten stages of human development, from the simplest hunting societies through the development of agriculture, the division of labor, the origin of government, and thence into the eras of history from the Greeks to the French Revolution. He celebrates especially the invention of the alphabet, advances in education and literacy, and the growing awareness of human rights and dignity. But Condorcet does not end his survey with his own day. He notes that "the forces of enlightenment are still in possession of no more than a very small portion of the globe." His confidence in the future destiny of man rests on his belief that not only European science and technology but also the high moral principles recently discovered in France will be disseminated around the globe by modern communication. When the benefits of human reason are distributed to every member of the race, then we can speak of the true perfection of mankind.[41]

According to Condorcet, progress requires "the abolition of inequality between nations" as well as "the progress of equality within each nation." The equality that he foresees is not a sterile uniformity, but a "condition in which everyone will have the knowledge necessary to conduct himself in the ordinary affairs of life, according to the light of his own reason," to understand and exercise his abilities and rights. The progress of the peoples of Africa and Asia "is likely to be more rapid and certain than our own because they can receive from us everything that we have had to find out for ourselves." His generosity extends also to the female sex. Condorcet identifies the "complete anihilation of the prejudices" on which sexual inequality rests as one of the most important "causes of the progress of the human mind," a central contribution to general happiness. Here he anticipates both Fourier and Marx.[42] Compared with his seventeenth-century precur-

40. Antoine-Nicolas de Condorcet, *Sketch for a Historical Picture of the Progress of the Human Mind*, trans. June Barraclough, introd. Stuart Hampshire (London: Wiennfeld & Nicolson, 1955), pp. 4, 10, 184.

41. Ibid., pp. 169-74.

42. Ibid., pp. 189-90, 193; cf. Karl Marx, "Economic and Philosophic MSS. of 1844," in *The Marx-Engels Reader*, ed. Robert C. Tucker (New York: Norton, 1972), pp. 69-70; and Fourier, *Théorie des quatre mouvements*, quoted in *The Utopian*

sors, who attributed the downfall of Adam (and the race itself) to Eve, Condorcet's ideas are revolutionary. He cuts boldly through the intricate arguments of "the woman question" with his assertion that "this inequality has its origin solely in an abuse of strength, and all the later sophistical attempts that have been made to excuse it are vain."[43]

The central purpose of Condorcet's *Sketch* was to demonstrate beyond any doubt that the several components of progress are inextricably connected and guarantee one another. As human knowledge grows, we also learn more about ordering and classifying what we know so that ideas which at first were grasped only by geniuses become part of the workaday equipment of ordinary human beings. As more and more people are made capable of participating in the advancement of knowledge everywhere, we can expect rapid progress in all parts of science and increasing productivity in industry and agriculture. This in turn ensures a higher standard of living, and thus we can expect population (the standard eighteenth-century measure of human welfare) to increase rapidly. Medical and dietary improvements will extend the span of life till it becomes indefinite, and death itself an exceptional event.[44]

Moral and political sciences will advance as inexorably as all the others, asserts Condorcet, and as they do, the faulty institutions and corrupt laws and habits that are the foundation of human viciousness will surely disappear. We will learn to reconcile, nay, identify, "the interests of each with the interests of all." Men will learn to reflect before they act, and will see the connections between their own good and that of the whole society of which they are a part. Permanent confederations between nations and universal free trade will remove the causes of war, and international organizations will hasten universal brotherhood. In all these ways, ethics are as susceptible to perfectibility as all other areas of human life. For, affirms Condorcet, "nature has linked together in an unbreakable chain truth, happiness and virtue."[45]

The progress of humanity, unlike the maturing of a single individual, has no limit. "The perfection of human faculties," asserts the marquis, will continue until the earth itself is destroyed, or some

---

Vision of Charles Fourier, ed. Jonathan Beecher and Richard Bienvenu (Boston: Beacon Press, 1971), pp. 195-96.

43. Condorcet, *Sketch for a Historical Picture,* p. 193.

44. Ibid., pp. 188-89.

45. Ibid., pp. 189-93; see also p. 168. Condorcet gives no sign of worrying about the complications and problems introduced by the coordination of individual good intentions in activities round the globe. His blindness to this set of problems may have something to do with the initial adoption of the analogy of the race to the individual, which predisposes him to assume that the problems of the former are no more complex than those of individuals set side by side. "The progress of the human mind," he asserts, "is subject to the same general laws that can be observed in the development of the faculties of the individual, and it is indeed no more than the sum of that development realized in a large number of individuals joined together in society" (p. 4).

unexpected change "deprives the human race of its present faculties and its present resources." No "new invasion of the Tartars" need be feared by refined societies since the Tartars themselves will be refined. Condorcet recognizes that a burgeoning population poses a long-term threat. But he reassures his readers that when civilized humanity threatens to exceed the earth's capacity, the rational and virtuous beings who inhabit our perfected orb will curb reproductive growth rather than "encumber the world with useless and wretched beings," recognizing that "if they have a duty towards those who are not yet born, that duty is not to give them existence, but to give them happiness."

Such assurance that the drama of humanity will have a happy ending is a great consolation for the philosopher in his adversity, concludes Condorcet. The vision of human progress is

> for him an asylum, in which the memory of his persecutors cannot pursue him; there he lives in thought with man restored to his natural rights and dignity, forgets man tormented and corrupted by greed, fear or envy; there he lives with his peers in an Elysium created by reason and graced by the purest pleasures known to the love of mankind.[46]

A RETROSPECTIVE VIEW

Condorcet's nineteenth-century successors among philosophers of progress were a heterogeneous group: Saint-Simon, Comte, Hegel, Schelling, Darwin, and Spencer. The technocratic programs of the French social theorists were closely related to the utilitarian projects of Saint-Pierre and the optimistic rationalism of Condorcet. The rich treatises of the German idealists describe history unfolding organically according to its own inner tendencies through the works of humankind. When Darwin referred to the evolution of the species as progressive, theories in history and biology began to reinforce one another.[47]

In all these variations on the theme of progress, an anthropocentric perspective allows the affirmation that progress is occurring. To call the evolution of species, but not changes in the cosmos, "progressive," as Ayala does (see pp. 106ff.), is to be faithful to the history of the concept and its linguistic usage; it reflects the implicit assumption that *human* development is the measure of progress. Few of us would readily attach the label to further developments involving the extinction of our species and the survival of fitter beasts such as cockroaches and snails. Placing our own species at the top of the evolutionary tree corresponds to placing one's own era near the end of history's unfolding, which apostles of progress usually do. Progress turns out to be movement toward wherever the observer is, joined with the certainty

46. Ibid., pp. 201-02.

47. Bury, *Idea of Progress*, p. 336, quotes the conclusion of the *Origin of Species*: "As natural selection works solely by and for the good of each being, all corporeal and mental environments will tend to progress towards perfection."

that things will continue much the same in the future. Adam Smith, said Bagehot, used the idea of progress to show "how from being a savage, man rose to be a Scotchman."[48]

Such an anthropocentric perspective on the theory of progress is closely connected with shifting human valuations of the quality of human life. Moses Abramovitz suggests that progress might be gauged by looking at the kinds of things people are unhappy about (see p. 280). Another way of putting it would be to look at what we take for granted. We depend on innumerable aids and comforts that would have seemed miraculous a century ago; but we have ceased to be able to take for granted things our ancestors regarded as the simplest given things of life—fresh air, clean water, open land.

If we look back at the components of the theory of progress, we can see how each of them is now called into question. We no longer give universal assent to the idea that humanity is the rightful lord of nature, put on the earth to manage and control its bounty in whatever way it thinks best. We can hardly be sanguine about an inevitable happy ending, given all the possibilities for global tragedy brought incessantly to our attention. Even the millennium, it appears, may turn out to be a sterile wasteland from the perspective of human happiness.[49] The sense of cumulative truth fares better, perhaps, but even here there are dissenting voices, as well as a growing awareness of the rich perspectives gone forever in the cultures of the past. And the conviction that virtue is knowledge—that to know the good is to will it—is not one the twentieth century finds generally persuasive.

Isaiah Berlin describes the durable conviction that all good things will fit together perfectly if we can only find the proper formula, as the fallacy on which Western civilization is founded.[50] This same belief that good things come in clusters, that knowledge, power, virtue, and happiness are interconnected and stand surety for one another, is the Enlightenment addition to the theory of progress that is most problematical for us today. Condorcet's visions of technological improvement and material betterment have been overfulfilled. His predictions about morality and politics have a very different sound today. The naïve assurance that our virtue and happiness have steadily progressed seems particularly infused with the wishful thinking to which a philosopher is liable as he consoles himself in his cell.

It is not that we have all reverted to an earlier view of history as a record of moral and social degeneration. Instead, we are becoming aware of a factor of which earlier generations had little notion: increasing social complexity and interdependence, which, far from ensuring advances in intimacy and virtue, multiply the problems of the

48. Quoted in Bryson, *Man and Society*, p. 89.
49. Gunther Stent, *The Coming of the Golden Age: A View of the End of Progress* (New York: Natural History Press, 1969).
50. Isaiah Berlin, "The Question of Machiavelli," *New York Review of Books*, November 4, 1971; and his *Four Essays on Liberty* (Oxford: Oxford University Press, 1962), pp. 154-72.

species at least as fast as our capacity to grasp them—much less solve them satisfactorily and move on. We have discovered that "rationality" splinters our lives as rapidly as it orders them. Human control over human beings, by legislation and by education, was the Enlightenment's final contribution to the theory of progress. It has now become the battleground on which the outcome of all other constituents of progress must depend.

In the eyes of some observers, our only hope for extricating ourselves from the dilemmas of modernity is a "recrudescence of religion," a recapturing of the "aura of the sacred" in our approach to knowledge and to human life. According to Robert Nisbet, theories of progress in the past rested heavily on religious beliefs, and it is the disappearance of this underlying structure that accounts for the evaporation of the belief in progress. His claims on this score are tangled and controversial, but the evidence clearly supports at least one of his central claims: the historical connection between "confidence in the existence of a divine power" and confidence in "design or pattern in the world."[51] Most past theories of progress depended heavily on the conviction that all things work together for good in the long run because a beneficent creator willed it to be so. This gave ground for some certainty that even the messiest human efforts would resolve themselves in rational conclusions.

The belief that an omnipotent, divine agency is ultimately responsible for making sense of our most nonsensical performances carries an element of comfort that cannot easily be matched in any other way. It also carries the potential for greater danger in our current situation. Throughout history, one favored device for describing human progress has been the analogy between the development of the species and the maturation of a single individual, the progressive "education of the human race."[52] Perhaps the mark of maturity in a species, as in an individual, is willingness to take sober responsibility for our own actions and their consequences instead of assuming that a paternalistic Father-God always stands ready to extricate us from our self-imposed dilemmas, a *deus ex machina* eternally prepared to guarantee a happy ending for a species bent on folly. Such a conception of maturity is consonant with either a secular or a religious vision of the world. It is not consonant with a simplistic faith that we can have everything we want without sacrifices or hard thinking. That progress in some areas is quite likely to mean cutbacks somewhere else is an idea to which we have yet to become accustomed. We are not yet "mature," but we may be maturing. We ask questions that would have made no sense to earlier generations. If the answers we give make sense to later ones, that will be time enough to say that progress has occurred.

51. Robert Nisbet, *History of the Idea of Progress* (New York: Basic Books, 1980), pp. 355-56.
52. Ibid., p. 61, shows how this image was broached by Saint Augustine and echoed by numerous subsequent philosophers of progress.

2

The Idea of Progress in Historiography and Social Thought Since the Enlightenment

GEORG G. IGGERS

OVERVIEW

In a quite fundamental way, a sense of history is incompatible with the idea of progress. This at least was the perception of the nineteenth-century historian who has often been considered a founder of history as a modern, professionalized, scholarly discipline, Leopold von Ranke.[1] The idea of progress, he held, was primarily a philosophic notion; but history and philosophy pursued fundamentally different aims, the latter seeking to systematize reality, to reduce it to concepts; the former seeking to grasp the uniqueness of historical phenomena, to restore them in their concrete living reality. From the historical perspective the idea of progress represented a distortion of the past. Instead of comprehending the past in its own terms, the idea of progress viewed the past philosophically as a stepping stone to an end result. It thus reduced history to a scheme which violated the individuality and diversity of the past.

In his critique Ranke had Hegel in mind. But the idea of progress was more than an abstract philosophical notion and proved to be much more compatible with a historical perspective than Ranke admitted. It represented an all-encompassing world view shared by broad segments of eighteenth- and nineteenth-century social thought. Despite their formal rejection of the idea of progress, Ranke and much of

1. See Leopold von Ranke, "On Progress in History (1854)," in his *The Theory and Practice of History*, ed. Georg G. Iggers and Konrad von Moltke (New York: Bobbs-Merrill, 1973), pp. 51-56.

the historical school of the nineteenth century shared the basic assumptions of the idea.[2] It is indeed misleading to seek a concise definition of the idea, for example, as "irreversible meliorative change" and then establish that ideas of progress were a persistent theme in the history of Western thought since the Hebrews and the Greeks.[3] To be certain, there was an awareness in Greek and Roman writings, for example, by Thucydides, Polybius, and Lucretius, as there was for that matter in Chinese historical literature, that the modern age is more complex than the past. Thucydides had already spoken of stages of development: a nomadic culture gave way in Greece to a pastoral, agricultural, and finally a commercial civilization[4]—four stages remarkably similar to those which appear in the writings of the Scottish moral philosophers of the eighteenth century.[5] But this awareness of growing complexity was not accompanied by a confidence in the improvement of man or even in the liberating function of science and education. For Thucydides, this complexity provided the setting for the most awesome war in history. For him as for Lucretius, the very conditions of modern civilization opened a bleak prospect for a future marked by conflict and intellectual decline over which men had little control. But the various attempts by recent theorists to see in the modern idea of progress a secularized form of Judeo-Christian conceptions of Providence are hardly satisfactory.[6] The content of the modern idea of progress is fundamentally different. Even in the Judeo-Christian tradition a clear distinction exists between Hebraic prophetic visions and Christian views from Augustine and Joachim de Floris to Bossuet, in which this worldly strife and misery are overcome in a final, transhistorical redemption in which justice and peace are achieved on earth, albeit through divine intervention. The millenarian conception of the apocalyptic transformation, it has been argued, finds an unintended

2. Cf. Georg G. Iggers, *The German Conception of History: The National Tradition of Historical Thought from Herder to the Present* (Middletown, Conn.: Wesleyan University Press, 1968).

3. Charles van Doren, *The Idea of Progress* (New York: Praeger, 1967), p. 3; see also Robert Nisbet, *History of the Idea of Progress* (New York: Basic Books, 1980). The conception that the idea of progress is a secularization and for some a distortion of a Christian idea is persistent in modern thought. See Warren Wagar, "Modern Views of the Origins of the Idea of Progress," *Journal of the History of Ideas*, 28 (1967): 55-70.

4. Thucydides, *History of the Peloponnesian War*, trans. Rex Warner (New York: Penguin Books, 1978), pp. 35-46; see also Ludwig Edelstein, *The Idea of Progress in Classical Antiquity* (Baltimore, Md.: Johns Hopkins University Press, 1967).

5. Of Scottish philosophers, I have in mind particularly John Millar, Adam Ferguson, but also Adam Smith; see Duncan Forbes, ed., "Introduction" to Adam Ferguson, *An Essay on the History of Civil Society* (1767) (Edinburgh: Edinburgh University Press, 1966); and Ronald S. Meek, *Social Science and the Ignoble Savage* (Cambridge: Cambridge University Press, 1976).

6. See Nisbet, *History of the Idea of Progress*; and Ernest Lee Tuveson, *Millennium and Utopia: A Study on the Background of the Idea of Progress* (Berkeley: University of California Press, 1949).

echo in modern social utopias including Marx's proclamation of the imminent end, of the "prehistory of human society" as the result of the dialectics of history, and the ushering in of "an association, in which the free development of each is the condition for the free development of all,"[7] an age of peace and reconciliation. Yet one can easily make too much of this continuity, for these social conceptions are fundamentally different not only in their this-worldly emphasis but in the central role which they assign to human agency.

It is thus misleading to abstract ideas from their historical context as Mortimer Adler and Charles van Doren proposed when they sought to find a "nonhistorical" definition that would be valid for the entire history of Western thought.[8] Ideas originate within a concrete social, political, and intellectual setting, in part in response to this setting; they are not merely formal concepts but have a specific content that can be understood only with reference to the historical situation. Lucretius' use of the term *progredientes* has a profoundly different meaning from Condorcet's use of the expression "progress of the human mind." The idea of progress has a specific meaning in the context of the eighteenth, nineteenth, and—to an extent still—the twentieth century which differentiates it essentially from ideas of historical progression in the classical Greek or Roman world or in the Hebraic and Christian traditions. The idea of progress belongs to what has sometimes, but not very accurately, been called the age of the bourgeoisie— not accurately since the bourgeoisie as a cohesive class has never existed and the appeal of the idea went beyond the propertied and educated middle and upper classes to broad portions of the working class. Thus, the idea is part of the outlook of a broad segment of opinion, including many who did not formally expound a philosophy of progress. Its appeal was strongest among those sections of the population—particularly of the intelligentsia—that were interested in the transformation of the economy, society and politics from traditional patterns, dominant in the *ancien régime*, to modern conditions of growth. The adherents of progress were committed to science, technology, and to a political society, which, at its minimum, guaranteed civil liberties, equality before the law, and the abolition of traditional privilege—if not popular participation in government.

THE ENLIGHTENMENT IDEA OF PROGRESS

Several ideas have been central to the emerging philosophies of progress in the eighteenth century since Turgot and Condorcet. One is the concept of the unity of man's history. This involves the conception

---

7. Karl Marx, "Preface" to *A Contribution to the Critique of Political Economy* in *The Marx-Engels Reader*, 2nd ed., ed. Robert C. Tucker (New York: Norton, 1978), p. 5; Karl Marx and Friedrich Engels, "Manifesto of the Communist Party," in *Marx-Engels Reader*, p. 491.

8. Mortimer Adler, "Foreword," in Van Doren, *Idea of Progress*.

that civilization is one and universal, that in the place of a variety of separate histories, there emerges one world history. The notion that there is not one history but that the historian tells separate histories was still very much alive in the eighteenth century, even in the monumental *Universal History from the Earliest of Time to the Present*, thirty-eight volumes published in Great Britain in 1736-1765, which consists of a collection of factual accounts of distinct nations. Even Ranke's first work in 1824 still carries the title *Histories of the Latin and Germanic Nations.*[9] Essential to the new conception of a history in the place of histories is the recognition of the role of process and development. There is a central theme to this development, as in Voltaire's *Age of Louis XIV*: the progressive development of intellect, culture, and society. This awareness of a theme fundamentally changes the character of historical writing and introduces a developmental structure to the great narrative historical writings of the eighteenth century (for example, those by Robertson, Hume, and Gibbon) and distinguishes them from the cumulative approach of much of scholarly historiography until this time.

Yet the history of mankind as attempted by Enlightenment historians seldom turns out to be universal history in a true sense, despite the interest of Montesquieu, Voltaire, and Schlözer in intercultural comparison. For it is Europe—and this is the second key component of the idea—specifically France and the English-speaking world, which for Voltaire or Condorcet represents the vanguards of civilization. The history of mankind thus becomes identical with the history of Western civilization. Implicit in the idea of progress, in Condorcet but generally also in nineteenth-century ideas of progress (for example, in Hegel, Marx, Comte, and Spencer) is the notion of the civilizing mission of the European nations.

A third note, which sharply distinguishes the new kind of history inspired by the idea of progress from older conceptions of Providence, is the recognition that history is the work of men. This idea, that man makes history, that human history is filled with conscious purposes and intents, which distinguishes it from both natural and providential history, is given clear expression for the first time in Vico's *New Science* (1725), to be sure in the framework of a very different philosophy of history, which saw limited progress followed by decay as part of a recurrent *ricorso* of slowly upward-moving cycles. The idea that, to quote Marx, "men make their own history" even if "they do not

9. See Anne-Robert-Jacques Turgot, *On The Progress of the Human Mind*, trans. McQuilkin De Grange (Hanover, N.H.: Sociological Press, 1929); and Antoine-Nicolas de Condorcet, *Sketch for a Historical Picture of the Progress of the Human Mind* (New York: Noonday Press, 1955). On the conception of "histories" as against one "history," see Reinhart Koselleck, *Vergangene Zukunft. Zur Semantik geschichtlicher Zeiten* (Frankfurt: Suhrkamp, 1979), pp. 130-43. On Ranke's conception of world history, see Leonard Krieger, *Ranke: The Meaning of History* (Chicago: University of Chicago Press, 1978).

make it just as they please . . . but under circumstances directly found, given and transmitted from the past" so that the consequences they intend do not coincide with the consequences which result, is central to the idea of progress in its eighteenth- and nineteenth-century form. This makes it possible to understand historical behavior because, unlike natural processes, it is purposive. As Droysen suggested, "there is nothing that moves the human spirit or that has found expression through the senses which cannot be understood."[10]

Inextricably linked with the belief in the idea of progress in the eighteenth and nineteenth centuries is an optimistic expectation of the society which human reason can and will construct. This expectation is not necessarily millenarian. It can, as in the case of Condorcet, be based on the attainment of limited, but for the most part achievable, goals. There is, to start with, a firm faith in the emancipatory role of science and technology. From the perspective of the late twentieth century, Condorcet's expectations in the scientific, technological, and medical areas appear by no means utopian. What is problematic are the connections which Condorcet establishes between science and human nature, the possibility through enlightenment, reason, and education of eradicating the manifestations of conflict, particularly war. Indeed, an optimistic conception of man is fundamental to the theories of progress in their classical form. The possibility exists for Turgot, Condorcet, the Saint-Simonians, Comte, Mill, and even Marx of establishing a world society in which the causes of conflict will have been eliminated and the conditions will have been created for a community which through conscious rational planning can get down to the business of achieving advancements in all aspects of life which bear on the fulfillment of the individual.

The history of the idea of progress cannot simply be related as a history of ideas, as Bury and Nisbet have done. If it is narrated as a history of ideas, then the question why these ideas changed must be confronted.[11] Nisbet's explanation of the decline of the idea of progress as the consequence of the dissolution of the Judeo-Christian religious heritage requires an explanation why this heritage lost force. The idea of progress in the eighteenth and nineteenth centuries cannot be understood simply as a secularization of a religious outlook. Even if the idea of progress is viewed as the continuation of the idea of Providence in a secular form, the actual political and social content of

10. Karl Marx, "The Eighteenth Brumaire of Louis Bonaparte," in *Marx-Engels Reader*, p. 595; Johann Gustav Droysen, quoted in Iggers, *German Conception*, p. 110.

11. J.B. Bury, *The Idea of Progress: An Inquiry into Its Origin and Growth* (1920; rpt. New York: Dover, 1955); Nisbet, *History of the Idea of Progress*. For a broadly social perspective, see Sidney Pollard, *The Idea of Progress: History and Society* (London: Watts, 1968). W. Warren Wagar's *Good Tidings: The Belief in Progress from Darwin to Marcuse* (Bloomington: Indiana University Press, 1972) is perhaps the most comprehensive study of the idea in contemporary social thought, including theology.

the idea, which is crucial to an understanding of the idea of progress in its eighteenth- and nineteenth-century contexts, goes far beyond the religious content. It was the rapid changes in the eighteenth and nineteenth centuries—scientific advancement, industrial growth, the expansion of European power, the democratization of society—which provided the background for historical optimism; it was the dissolution of nineteenth-century "bourgeois civilization," the discontent and alienation produced by the social concomitants of industrialization, the trauma of two world wars, the political experiences with modern forms of authoritarianism, the decline of Europe which all-in-all determined the decline of the idea of progress more than specifically intellectual developments, such as the growth of historical and cultural relativism.

The role of the ideal of progress in eighteenth-century European thought should not be overstressed. Neither should the strength of Enlightenment ideas. The eighteenth century was not only the age of Turgot, Lessing, and Adam Smith, it was also the age of Rousseau, John and Charles Wesley, and the Marquis de Sade. Henry Vyverberg and Carlo Antoni have pointed at the deep roots of historical pessimism in eighteenth-century France and the German-speaking world, respectively.[12] Nevertheless, it is in the eighteenth century that for the first time in Western history a pronounced optimism emerges regarding the future of civilization. This optimism does not necessarily entail a schematic philosophy of progress. The future may indeed be open, as for Voltaire, with the possibility and even the likelihood of regression. For him greed and fanaticism are persistent penchants of man, which make unlikely an age of permanent tranquillity devoted to cultural pursuits. Nevertheless, the age of Louis XIV represents for Voltaire a high point in intellectual, artistic, and social achievements. There is a broadly disseminated conviction in the eighteenth century that modern civilization represents not only an advancement over that of the ancients but that it is firmly established, able to resist the challenges from barbarians within and without and open to further development. This note finds expression in Gibbon's firm confidence that modern civilization will not experience a repetition of the fate of ancient Rome; for neither religious obscurantism nor barbarism, the two forces which effected the fall of Rome, continues to hold sway. Nor is Rousseau, as a critic of modern civilization, a historical primitivist. As Vyverberg suggests, the return to nature did not mean for Rousseau a return to an earlier, simpler age—civilization was too firmly established—but rather a recovery of the original nature of man which

12. Henry Vyverberg, *Historical Pessimism in the French Enlightenment* (Cambridge, Mass.: Harvard University Press, 1958); cf. R.V. Sampson, *Progress in the Age of Reason* (Cambridge, Mass.: Harvard University Press, 1956). On historical pessimism in the nineteenth century, see Koenraad W. Swart, *The Sense of Decadence in Nineteenth-Century France* (The Hague: Martinus Nijhoff, 1964). Carlo Antoni, *Der Kampf wider die Vernunft* (Stuttgart: K.F. Koehler, 1951).

had been obscured by the artificialities and inequalities of contemporary society.[13]

The idea of the unity of the history of man, essential for an explicit theory of progress, finds as yet few exponents in the eighteenth century. But the idea, which goes back to Francis Bacon and René Descartes, that existing conceptions must be questioned and replaced by rationally defensible notions has a broad backing. This rational critique is directed primarily at the remnants of feudal institutions and traditional religion and aims at the reconstitution of society along modern lines, modern in the sense of a society in which capitalist economic activity can function with relatively little restriction by traditional practices and will benefit from the wise regulations of an enlightened administrative state. The different political and economic development in Great Britain, France, and the Germanies determines in each of these areas different notions of the form which economic and social policy should take. While English and particularly Scottish theorists of progress consider a laissez faire capitalist order as normative for the future, German thinkers, such as the Göttingen historian August Ludwig Schlözer, stress the contributions which enlightened bureaucracy can make to removing the obstacles in the way of an expanding economy.[14]

In Great Britain explicit theories of progress in the eighteenth century concentrate on the centrality of economics, in France on that of science. In Great Britain, or at least in Scotland, two very different approaches to historical writing coexist—which find parallels in progressivist historical writing on the continent in the nineteenth century —speculative or "conjectural" history on the one hand, narrative developmental history, on the other. John Millar, Adam Ferguson, and in a sense even Adam Smith represent the attempts to write a "conjectural" or "natural" history of mankind, which seeks to establish the laws governing historical development.[15] For them, the pattern of development becomes apparent to the critical philosophic mind. There is a clear gap between this essentially sociologically oriented history, seeking broad generalization and assuming a basic constancy of hu-

13. See Edward Gibbon, *The History of the Decline and Fall of the Roman Empire*, 6 vols. (London: W. Strahan & T. Cadell, 1776-1788); cf. Vyverberg, *Historical Pessimism*, pp. 57-61. Cf. also in Arthur O. Lovejoy, *Essays in the History of Ideas* (New York: Braziller, 1955), pp. 14-37.

14. Cf. Hans Medick, *Naturzustand und Naturgeschichte der bürgerlichen Gesellschaft* (Göttingen: Vandenhoeck & Ruprecht, 1973). On Schlözer's politics, see Ursula A.J. Becher, *Politische Gesellschaft: Studien zur Genese bürgerlicher Öffentlichkeit in Deutschland* (Göttingen: Vandenhoeck & Ruprecht, 1978); Bernd Warlich, "August Ludwig Schlözer 1735-1809 zwischen Reform und Revolution," dissertation, Erlangen-Nürnberg, 1972; Joan Karle, "August Ludwig von Schlözer: An Intellectual Biography," Ph.D. dissertation, Columbia University, 1972.

15. John Millar, *The Origin of the Distinctions of Ranks* (London, 1779); Ferguson, *An Essay*; Adam Smith, *An Inquiry into the Nature and Causes of the Wealth of Nations*, 2 vols. (London, 1776); cf. Forbes, ed., "Introduction," p. xxii.

man nature, and a historiography which builds on the careful examination of sources. Representatives of the latter, such as Hume and Robertson, may be informed by a general optimism about the course of British history, but they cannot embrace a philosophy of progress that sees history as an ascending whole. For the "conjectural" historians, history can be written even if documents are lacking because the pattern of historical development is known. In this vein, the Saint-Simonians wrote half a century later that even if hard information is missing, "it can be affirmed in advance" what the course of, for example, Indian history was. "We do not even hesitate to say that the Europeans alone are able to teach the Indians their own history."[16] For Millar, Ferguson, and Smith, economic factors are decisive. All human societies follow the same pattern—for Smith under the pressure of population growth—from nomadic, to pastoral and agricultural and commercial economies. The establishment of economic laissez faire and liberal representative institutions are the political concomitants of this development. Duncan Forbes, the editor of Adam Ferguson's *Essay on the History of Civil Society* (1767), stressed that the Scots were no unqualified advocates of progress, that Ferguson remained aware that every stage of human history was able to achieve a standard of happiness which was neither superior nor inferior to that of other stages, and that the wealth and luxury of modern societies had not only its beneficient but also its destructive side.[17] Nevertheless, they perceived a persistent development toward a more complex, prosperous, and liberal society.

For the French, the emphasis rested on science rather than on economics. Scientific development, however, did not necessarily spell out social or moral progress. The idea of scientific progress was thus given expression in the seventeenth century by Pascal, who, committed to a theological notion of the limitations of man's nature, regarded the prospects of mankind skeptically. There could be no finality of scientific knowledge for Pascal since scientific knowledge continuously corrected itself. Certain of the *philosophes*, convinced of the potential goodness of man, believed in the applicability of a "moral and political science" to the problems of society. Turgot, in his Second Sorbonne "Discourse on the Successive Progresses of the Human Mind" (1750), established such a relationship but with qualifications. In contrast to nature, which is subject to constant law, the realm of man is marked by diversity and confusion. Nevertheless, out of the chaos progress emerges as the human mind passes from religious superstition to metaphysics and finally to a scientific explanation of reality. Social progress lagged behind intellectual progress. Indeed the passions of men—unreason and injustice—provided a part of the dynamics which

---

16. *The Doctrine of Saint-Simon. An Exposition. First Year 1828-1829*, 2nd ed., trans. and ed. Georg G. Iggers (New York: Schocken Books, 1972), p. 37n.

17. Forbes, ed., "Introduction," p. xiv.

made for upward development toward the final stage when "Commerce and politics will unify at last all parts of the globe."[18]

Progress was certain but precarious. Like Voltaire, Turgot believed that it was constantly threatened by forces of irrationality which sought to interrupt and reverse it. Much more confident, Isaac Iselin from Basel in his *Über die Geschichte der Menschheit* (1764) (On the History of Mankind) undertook to write the history of mankind as the progressive triumph of human reason over ignorance and irrationality, a process in which industry and trade would eliminate poverty, crime, and war.[19] In even more heightened form this confidence marked the Marquis de Condorcet's *Sketch for a Historical Picture of the Progress of the Human Mind*, written in 1794 while Condorcet was in hiding from the Committee of Public Safety. Condorcet was convinced that it was possible to construct a science of society with direct applications to social policy. Condorcet set out to "demonstrate how nature has joined together indissolubly the progress of knowledge and that of liberty, virtue and respect for the natural rights of man." "All errors in politics and morals," he asserted, "are based on philosophical error and these in turn are connected with scientific errors." Thus, social science provided the basis for a rational political order. This order, in turn, would lay the foundation for a society marked by steady growth in technology and subsequent improvements not only in material standards of living and health but also in social relations. Social and economic inequalities would be minimized by equal educational opportunities, equal rights for women, humane treatment of prisoners, and, finally, the end of war after the establishment of a world federation. "The sun [would then] shine only on free men who know no other master but their reason."[20] The progress of civilization would be universal, but the bearer of progress would be Europe, specifically the peoples of France, Great Britain, and the United States. The non-European world would be freed from colonial control and economic exploitation as free trade replaced government monopolies.

"HISTORISM" AND THE NINETEENTH CENTURY

This a priori history which foresaw a pattern for historical development universally was questioned by a broad current of opinion that stressed the uniqueness of historical development. We shall call this current of opinion historism (*Historismus*).[21] A discussion of historism belongs in an essay on the history of the idea of progress because despite surface differences, it shares basic assumptions of the idea of progress and, in turn, introduces conceptions of growth and develop-

18. Turgot, *Progress of the Human Mind*, p. 5.

19. Isaak Iselin, *Über die Geschichte der Menschheit* (Frankfurt: J.H. Harscher, 1764).

20. Condorcet, *Sketch for a Historical Picture*, pp. 163, 179.

21. See Georg G. Iggers, "Historicism," in *Dictionary of the History of Ideas* (New York: Scribner, 1973), II, 456-64.

ment that are fundamental in the transformation of progressivist thought in the nineteenth century. A variety of eighteenth-century historians coming from different theoretical directions share certain of the assumptions of historism—Vico, Montesquieu, Möser, Herder, W. von Humboldt, Edmund Burke, and, in a certain sense, also Hume. These historians and social theorists reject the attempt to apply a theory of stages to history, as Ferguson, Turgot, and Condorcet had attempted; they stress the specific character of each society and link this character to the unique history of the society. They may, as in the case òf Montesquieu,[22] combine an attempt to isolate general factors which affect all societies—geography, climate, etc.—with a specific spirit that has its source in the unique traditions of the society. Historistic conceptions of society often view the societies as organic analogies. A society possesses a spirit which gives it unity and which gives every individual, every idea, and every institution in it its character. Historism often involves a political ethos different from that of progressivist thought. It stresses the diversity of cultures and within each culture the diversity of stations in life. It has a much more positive relation to existing social, political, and cultural institutions and is more likely to affirm the status quo. While Montesquieu stresses a rigorous empirical approach in the study of institutions, the German thinkers, such as Möser, Herder, and Wilhelm von Humboldt, proceeding from a much more idealistic epistemology, wish to understand the culture through empathy (*Einfühlung*). Yet despite these marked differences from the idea of progress, historism functions in an intellectual world that has many common characteristics with the idea of progress. It too believes in growth and transformation. Conservative in certain aspects, it is not necessarily reactionary when turned to the past. It sees history in terms of linear development. In the nineteenth century, historism is often identified with a narrowing of the historical focus on the nation state; in the Enlightenment setting historism is broadly cosmopolitan and culture-oriented. Thus, Herder undertakes a history of the human race. Instead of progressive development to a higher stage, history fulfills itself for him in the inexhaustibility of the cultures which manifest themselves through time. There is indeed a purpose to world history, but it is not found in the progressive perfection of man. The intent of history is rather for all energies to express and develop their unique character. This perception involves an immense optimism regarding the benign function of history. History is the source of knowledge, morality, and culture. The purpose of historical study is the widening of man's humanity. Truth, values, and beauty are not one but many. They are found only in history and manifest themselves in concrete national forms. The fullest development of man's humanity requires his immersion into the diversity of cultures.[23]

22. Montesquieu, *Spirit of the Laws*, 2 vols., trans. Thomas Nugent (New York: Colonial Press, 1900).
23. See Johann Herder, *Ideen zur Philosophie der Geschichte der Menschheit*

There is relatively little space for evil in this view of history. Every age must be understood in its own terms and judged by its own standards. This does not exclude political criticism. The historistic standpoint is particularly well represented in the smaller states of Germany and the Swiss cantons, where traditional corporative institutions still maintain themselves and historical arguments are used against the encroachments of bureaucratic absolutism. But the thinkers who represent a more modern and libertarian orientation such as Herder and, a generation later, Wilhelm von Humboldt, also draw on concrete historical rather than on abstract natural law arguments as they envisage a state closely tied to popular culture.[24]

The French Revolution both strengthened optimistic expectations and undercut the basic assumptions on which these expectations rested. The enthusiasm with which broad segments of middle- and upper-class opinion received the events of 1789 turned into horror once the revolution, in its terroristic and military phase, radically questioned the established order. The French Revolution, which set out to apply rational principles to the transformation of state and society, took on the appearance of an uncontrollable force of nature. In the nineteenth century, basic concepts of historism were integrated into the dominant ideas of progress. Conscious human action was now no longer seen as the decisive agent of historical change. History possessed a logic and dynamic of its own. The course of history was not determined by the conscious actions of men; rather, these actions led to unintended results. From historism, those committed to the ideas of progress also accepted the organic conception of society. Large social groupings, nations or classes, with roots in history, formed the units of history. These units possessed a structure and a spirit. History alone became the key to the understanding of things human. Yet in contrast to the historistic conception that history was fulfilled in every culture and every age, the theories of progress assumed an upward development, generally toward a final society, in which reason would find its fulfillment in concrete social institutions. For Hegel, history was thus the march of reason in history leading to a political organization in which man could find his fullest development. Hegel's conception of the free—that is, rational—society reflected the political and social condi-

---

(1789-1791); English: *Outlines of a Philosophy of the History of Man*, trans. T. Churchill (New York: Bergman, 1966), and *Reflections of the Philosophy of the History of Mankind*, abridged, ed. Frank Manuel (Chicago: University of Chicago Press, 1968). Also Johann Herder, *Auch eine Philosophie der Geschichte zur Bildung der Menschheit* (1774), and *Briefe zur Beförderung der Humanität* (1793-1797), all in *Sämmtliche Werke*, ed. Bernhard Suphan (Berlin: Weidmann, 1877-1913). See also Wilhelm von Humboldt, "On the Historian's Task," *History and Theory*, 6 (1967): 57-71.

24. See Antoni, *Der Kampf*. Wilhelm von Humboldt, "Ideen zu einem Versuch die Grenzen der Wirksamkeit des Staats zu bestimmen," in *Gesammelte Schriften* (Berlin: B. Behr, 1903-1936), I.

tions of early nineteenth century Germany, in particular of the Prussia after the reforms of the Stein and Hardenberg eras, in which a modern capitalistic society, freed from feudal and corporatistic restraints, functioned freely under the protection of a benevolent bureaucratic order.[25] Progress thus found its fulfillment in the peculiar Prussian settlement of a bourgeois society operating under the aegis of an enlightened constitutional monarchy. Reason found its expression, not in scientific planning and the attempts consciously to control and guide society on the basis of scientific insights, but rather in the "recognition of [historical] necessity," of the inevitability with which history, utilizing law but not governed by the actions of men, moved inexorably to its historical fulfillment.

By contrast, in France and Great Britain, and to a lesser extent in Germany, the ideal of a scientifically planned society lived on. Men indeed did not control their past but were the instruments by which society moved to rational foundations. However, the point was, according to Marx, approaching when "the prehistory of human society [is] coming to a close" and, according to Engels, when

> the whole sphere of the conditions which environ man, and which have hitherto ruled man, now comes under the dominion and control of man, who for the first time becomes the real, conscious lord of nature because he has now become master of his own social organization. The laws of his own social action, hitherto standing face to face with man as laws of nature foreign to, and dominating him, will then be used with full understanding, and so mastered by him.

The conception of the political structure of this society controlled by man differed widely. For Comte and to an extent the Saint-Simonians, an elite of scientists would obtain authority over the material and cultural destinies of the population; for Spencer government would increasingly yield to the free play of enlightened economic interests; for Marx and Engels after a transitory period of proletarian dictatorship, "the public power will lose its political character" and the state wither away. The idea that "all traces of government disappear," according to Proudhon, and the "government of men" be replaced by "the administration of things," according to Saint-Simon, in a world without coercion recurs in early and mid-nineteenth century progressivist thought.[26]

25. Georg Hegel, *Philosophy of History*, trans. J. Sibree (New York: Wiley, 1900); Georg Hegel, *Philosophy of Right*, trans. T.M. Knox (Oxford: Clarendon Press, 1965).

26. Marx, "Preface," p. 5; Friedrich Engels, "Socialism: Utopian and Scientific," in *Marx-Engels Reader*, p. 715; Marx and Engels, "Manifesto," p. 490; Pierre-Joseph Proudhon, "The General Idea of the Revolution in the Nineteenth Century," in *The Great Political Theories*, ed. Michael Curtis (New York: Avon, 1962), p. 135; *Doctrine of Saint-Simon*, p. xxi.

Despite the fundamentally different conceptions of the political organization of the future, ranging from autocratic rule by scientifically informed elites to the abolition of traditional political constraints, there is a considerable area of common ground among these doctrines of progress in the affirmation of values to be recognized in history. For Comte, Mill, Buckle, Spencer and also Marx, Condorcet's vision of the future, rooted in the Enlightenment, remains decisive, even if the mechanism by which this vision becomes reality places much greater emphasis on collective forces and historical processes than on intellectual leadership. The entire history of the world points to the achievement of a civilization in which science and industry occupy a central role in the transformation of the conditions of human life. The military repressive patterns of the past will be replaced by the peaceful, productive order of the future. The entire history of mankind finds its culmination in the history of modern Europe. This confidence in the leadership of Europe is shared by Hegel and by German idealist philosophers like Fichte, who, perhaps reflecting the delayed economic and social modernization of Germany, places less emphasis on science and technology. The non-European world will find the completion of its historical development not in the further development of its own heritage but, because its heritage represents an earlier phase in the progress of mankind, in total Europeanization.

For the majority of nineteenth-century theorists of progress, it is conflict which provides the mechanism by which the onward march of mankind proceeds. The Enlightenment idea that intellectual discussion itself provides a major source of the civilizational advancement of modern man is reiterated in the liberalism of John Stuart Mill. But Mill, in his stress on rational dialogue, is somewhat of an exception. For Hegel, Comte, Marx, and Spencer, the rational order of the future is achieved in part unwittingly by the irrational forces of the past. There is no room for fundamental evil in the economy of history; coercion, exploitation, and warfare have thus contributed to their own elimination. The implication is that individuals and whole ages were sacrificed on "the slaughter bank of history" for the redemption of mankind.

Conflict took a variety of forms. For Hegel, as also for Kant, war played a decisive role as the ultimate arbiter in the dialectical confrontation of states, as the concrete manifestation of an ascending succession of philosophic principles. War and the conflict of states remained for Hegel (but not for Kant) a desirable agent of progress also in the future. For the Saint-Simonians and Comte, "organic" epochs, marked by unanimity in basic beliefs and the presence of a centralizing authority providing social cohesion, alternated with "critical" epochs in which individualism and skeptical inquiry dissolved the incomplete unity of the past to provide the possibility of a new, more comprehensive synthesis. For Marx and Engels the agency of human emancipation was the class struggle; for Spencer it was the competition of the marketplace, with its survival of the fittest. The belief in finality and the role of conflict in attaining this finality contained the seed of a political attitude that was willing to sacrifice the individual for an idea. From a libertarian perspective, Proudhon sensed this well when in his *Philosophie du Progrès* he warned against any identification of progress with an absolute end. Progress, Proudhon insisted, is "the affirmation of universal movement, consequently the negation of any static form or formula."[27] Mill questioned the possibility of progress as a "natural law." At most, limited "empirical laws" might be formulated which would describe "certain general tendencies which may be perceived in society," such as the replacement of a military society by an industrial one. Moreover, even if the laws of social change were known, it would not follow that changes were necessarily in a desirable direction. Although Mill shared the belief that "the general tendency is, and will continue to be, saving occasional and temporary exceptions, one of improvement: a tendency toward a better and a happier state," he nevertheless acknowledged, "that progress was not inevitable but the result of conscious human effort based on rational insight." This left the door open to the possibility of real regression.[28]

From the perspective of the new "scientific" historiography which emerged in the nineteenth-century German university, the speculative approach to history, represented by the theorists of progress, was, of course, unacceptable. Ranke rejected the idea of progress on two counts. For one, neglecting a critical examination of the sources, it lacked a scholarly or "scientific" basis. For the other, as we suggested at the beginning of this essay, it violated the historian's sense of the uniqueness of the historical phenomenon. The historian deals with every historical manifestation as something nonreproducible, as an end in itself. For him "every epoch is immediate to God"[29] and must be judged in terms of its own standards. "While the philosopher, viewing history from his vantage point, seeks infinity merely in progression, development, and totality, history recognizes something infinite in every existence, in every condition, in every being, something eternal, coming from God." Yet in this assertion of the ultimate value of every individuality, Ranke in turn occupies a speculative position. Ranke assumed that there is fundamental purpose in history even if this purpose does not express itself in directional movement. Thus, the perfection of history is expressed at every moment in time. This form of historism expresses a historical optimism more radical in a sense than the classical theories of progress. For while the theories of

27. Pierre-Joseph Proudhon, *Philosophie du progrès* (Paris: M. Rivière, 1946), p. 49; the English translation is mine.

28. John Stuart Mill, *A System of Logic*, 7th ed. (London: Longman's, 1868), II, 510, 497.

29. Ranke, "On Progress in History," p. 53.

progress assume that the present represents a point, often marked by dissent and exploitation, to be overcome in a higher stage, the Rankean form of historism suggests that the high point of history has already been attained. Politically, this position implies an acceptance and affirmation of the status quo. In Ranke's words, "it recognizes the beneficient, the existing, and opposes change which negates the existing."[30]

In Ranke's historical writing, this optimism in fact moved close to an affirmation of progress. Notwithstanding his assertion that "all epochs are immediate to God," he distinguished between Western history, which alone he considered to be of world-historical significance, and that of the non-European world. While Hegel still assigned to China and India—in contrast to Africa, which in his opinion had no history—important roles in the early chapters of a world history leading to the modern Germanic world, Ranke denied that these peoples, to whom "we can devote but scant attention," had a history at all. "Their condition," he commented, "is rather a matter for natural history."[31] For Ranke, world history was the history of the making of modern Europe. Indeed, his entire historical work—from his early study of the emergence of the modern state system in 1824 to his *World History* written in his old age—is devoted to the historical foundations of modern Europe. Despite theoretical assertions to the contrary, there is an explicit theory of progress contained in his history. The theme is the rise and success of the Protestant principle of secular government in the German and the English worlds. Reflecting on the peculiar circumstances in Germany, in which effective limitations had been set to liberal forms, Ranke saw a modern conservative principle assert itself successfully against the revolutionary threat of French ideology.

This emphatic endorsement of nineteenth-century Europe recurs in much of historical scholarship in the nineteenth century. The idea of progress is seldom asserted; yet it is implicit in the national traditions of historical writing in Germany, France, Great Britain, and the United States. Generally affirmative of the course of development in their particular nation-states, these writers see in their national histories a progression toward a state of benefit to their own nation and exemplary to the rest of the Western world. With nuances which reflect different political constellations in the respective countries—the Prussian school in Germany, the Macaulay and the Whig interpretation in Great Britain, Bancroft and the democratic orientation, as well as the later Anglo-Saxon school in America; Thierry, Guizot, and Michelet in France—all give expression to a historical optimism which sees in the

30. Leopold von Ranke, "On the Character of Historical Science," in his *Theory and Practice*, p. 38.
31. Ibid., p. 46.

modern European and North American world the highpoint of progress achieved to this point with the prospects favorable to further
advancement.[32]

This optimism was radically questioned by a small minority of historians and social theorists who questioned the assumptions as regards
value upon which historical writing, both progressivist and historistic,
rested. Involved was a rejection or at least a critique of the tendencies
which appeared to dominate in nineteenth-century civilization, the
development of science, technology, production, and the expansion of
democracy identified with bourgeois culture. Only in isolated instances
did this critique come from the Left.[33] For the most part, socialist
thought affirmed the economic and even political values of the "bourgeoisie" and wanted to make the benefits of modern civilization accessible to the working masses. The critique came from an intellectual
elite, which sought to rescue an aristocratic culture from the vulgariza-
tion of a mercantile age.

An early expression of this radical critique was contained in the
writings of Jakob Burckhardt in the 1860s and 1870s. Burckhardt took
to task "the arrogant belief in the moral superiority of the present."
"Morality as a power," he wrote, "stands no higher, nor is there more
of it, than in the so-called barbarous times." "Even progress in intellectual development is open to doubt since, as civilization advanced,
the division of labor may have steadily narrowed the consciousness of
the individual." The notion that there is continuity and growth in
history is to be denied. The chronological approach, which underlies
not only the philosophies of history but almost all historical writing
and which "regards the past as a contrast and a preliminary stage of
our own time" must give way to a study of the "recurrent, constant
and typical." Much more honestly than Ranke, Burckhardt embraces
the historistic position that an epoch be studied for its own worth.
This calls for a history which, unlike the conventional narrative history, does not follow progressions of a selected theme through time
but takes "transverse sections of history," such as the Italian Renaissance, "in as many directions as possible."[34]

Time thus stands still. The Renaissance is regarded not as a link
in a chain but as a unique and one-time expression of the human spirit.
A new criterion emerges for what is historically interesting, and this
criterion is determined by values which move essentially counter to
the popular aspirations of the century. The Enlightenment vision of a
world, which provides security and comfort for all, is abrogated for

32. On nineteenth-century historians, see George P. Gooch, *History and Historians
in the Nineteenth Century* (Boston: Beacon Press, 1959).

33. Georges Sorel, *The Illusions of Progress*, trans. John Stanley and Charlotte
Stanley (Berkeley: University of California Press, 1969).

34. Jakob Burckhardt, "Reflections on History," in his *The Civilization of the
Renaissance in Italy and Other Selections*, ed. Alexander Dru (New York: Washington
Square Press, 1966), pp. 46, 5, 30.

one in which heroic qualities survive. Despite his fear of mass outbursts of the "terribles simplificateurs" and of modern militarism, Burckhardt, like Nietzsche, underestimated the reservoir of violence stored up in the modern world. There is a glorification of struggle. "Evil," he writes, "is assuredly a part of the great economy of world history. It is force, the right of the stronger over the weaker, prefigured in that struggle for life which fills all nature . . . and is carried on in the early stages of humanity by murder and robbery, by the eviction, extermination or enslavement of weaker races, or of weaker peoples within the same race, of weaker states, of weaker classes within the same state and people,"[35] which makes history. Burckhardt emphatically takes morality out of history. On the surface, this stress on struggle, on the survival of the stronger, reminds one of Darwinism. Yet the linear development, the belief that conflict leads to the selection of higher cultures, is radically rejected by a conception which denies the part of direction.

THE TWENTIETH CENTURY

As the nineteenth century passed into the twentieth, there was an increasing sense that there were forces of history at work over which man had no control. The conditions of modern life called forth an ambiguous response from a growing number of social theorists and historians. They agreed that an increasing area of human relations had come under rational control, but rationality was no longer seen as a positive force. If for the thinkers of the Enlightenment reason had been normative in character and had fulfilled a liberating and emancipatory function, reason now was seen as a value-free abstraction, which was applied to control nature and manipulate men for irrational ends. Reason became an instrument of domination. Very early in the nineteenth century, not only conservative Christian thinkers—Novalis, Adam Müller, Louis de Bonald, and Joseph de Maistre—but also socialists such as the Saint-Simonians saw in the dissemination of reason and enlightenment a cause of the fragmentation of society and of the dissolution of common values. For Marx and Engels, but not only for them, the liberation of the economy from a traditional economic order "left remaining no other nexus between man and man than naked self-interest, than callous 'cash payment.'"[36]

But it was less the working class that felt this sense of alienation than a cultural elite, which in a period of rapid industrialization saw its preeminence threatened by what it conceived to be the expansion of a mass culture and a mass society. Ferdinand Tönnies observed the dissolution of *Gemeinschaft* ("community") into a fragmented *Gesellschaft* ("society"); Emile Durkheim described the structure of modern society as one of *anomie*, a condition of relative normlessness, in

35. Ibid., p. 98.
36. Marx and Engels, "Manifesto," p. 475.

which individuals were isolated as common goals vanished. Much of this cultural pessimism was built on a class bias, which failed to take into account the positive aspects of modernization: the increase of education, cultural consciousness, and political responsibility among the broad segments of the working population mobilized by these economic transformations. But the catastrophe of the First World War and the subsequent emergence of efficient authoritarian regimes purportedly based on mass movements intensified the conviction that the development of modern civilization, with its reliance on science and technology and the mobilization of all segments of the population, led inexorably to deterioration of the human condition. In 1872, the *Grand Larousse du XIXe siècle*, only a year after the French national debacle of 1870-1871, could note that virtually all intelligent men now accepted the idea; and Bury could still write in 1920 that "we are so conscious of constantly progressing that we look upon progress as an aim... which it only depends on our effort and good will to achieve".[37] Yet few non-Marxist social theorists or historians in 1980, at a point when many of Condorcet's predictions have been fulfilled, not only in the scientific and technological but also in the social sphere, would still admit the validity of the idea.

Nevertheless, there are marked similarities between modern theories of social development and classical ideas of progress. Three ideas are basic to the classical idea of progress: the incessant growth of scientific knowledge and technological control, the transformation of society from an order of privilege to an order of meritocracy, and the extension of these modern forms of civilization over the universe. All three recur in modern theories of modernization and of industrial society. But what has fundamentally changed is the conception of the basic goodness or malleability of human nature. In its place there enters a recognition of the destructive and aggressive aspects of man. Kant and Hegel were aware of these, but they were convinced that they fitted into the economy of history, into the cunning of reason, which always, like Goethe's Mephistopheles, "wills evil but creates good." Yet this faith in an economy of history collapses. In a world in which the drive to power is ineradicable, science and technology lose their emancipatory function and become instruments of control. Before the ecological and resource crises of the late twentieth century, few social theorists foresaw limits to material growth, but they recognized the ambiguities of progress.

There is a readiness to recognize the direction of development predicted by the theorists of progress and yet to reverse the scale of values they posited. Alexis de Tocqueville saw and hailed the steady

---

37. Ferdinand Tönnies, *Gemeinschaft und Gesellschaft* (Darmstadt: Wissenschaftliche Buchgesellschaft, 1963); Emile Durkheim, *Suicide: A Study in Sociology*, trans. John A. Spaulding and George Simpson (New York: Free Press, 1951); Bury, *Idea of Progress*, pp. 1-2.

advance of equality but, like Mill, discovered danger in its potential power to destroy individuality, foster conformity, favor authoritarian control, and open the doors to new kinds of fanaticized, ideologically directed violence. There is an ambiguity written into Social Darwinist conceptions of progress, which, particularly in their continental forms, for example, Ludwig Gumplowicz, see struggle and violence as necessary elements of progress and thus as ends as well as means. Spencer's optimism turns in the 1880s to a stark pessimism as he witnesses the militarization of the modern states. The vision of the progressivist thinkers of a world marked by prosperity, a sense of security, and peace, is negated and replaced by one in which struggle and heroism are valued. Burckhardt, like Nietzsche, derides the search for "happiness"—"we should try to rid the life of nations entirely of the word 'happiness' and recognize that 'natural history' shows us a fearful struggle for life." "A people actually feels its full strength as a people only in war." The reevaluation of values finds its extreme expression in Spengler's identification of rationality, productivity, humaneness, and humanity as the values of a decadent "civilization" to be replaced by the heroic values of discipline, struggle, and war.[38]

Perhaps one of the best examples of an acute awareness of the ambiguities of the idea of progress is contained in the historical thought of Max Weber. History, or at least the history of the West since Hebrew times, is the scene of the unfolding of reason in time, but in a very different sense from that of Condorcet or Hegel, each of whom envisaged history as the irresistible march of reason. For Weber, the driving force in the Western world in the areas of intellect, social organization, and economics is the accelerating transformation of all aspects of life along rational lines. But reason has lost its normative value and has become a purely abstract instrumentality, free of any inherent value, for the control of the world in the service of irrational ends. For no rational standards can be applied to the selection of values; rationality enters only in examining the inner consistency of these values and in the determination of means by which the desired ends can be attained. Weber projects a grand scheme of modernization, in which he sees all Western societies move forward along similar lines, only partially modified by different historical traditions. For Weber, as for the classical theorists of progress from Condorcet to Marx, the history of the West becomes ultimately the history of the non-West, as the West extends its hegemony over the world. In the realm of intellect, the history of the West since Egyptian times, but with increasing speed in the modern period, is the history of scientifi-

38. See, e.g., Alexis de Tocqueville, *The Old Regime and the French Revolution*, trans. Stuart Gilbert (Garden City, N.Y.: Doubleday, 1955), particularly the passage on the new mad men, p. 157, and Chap. 8, pp. 203-11. Herbert Spencer, *The Man Versus the State* (Caldwell, Idaho: Caxton Printers, 1940); Burckhardt, "Reflections of History," pp. 96, 50; Oswald Spengler, *The Decline of the West*, 2 vols., trans. Charles F. Atkinson (New York: Knopf, 1932).

cation, a process which marks not only growing understanding for purposes of control and manipulation of the forces of nature and to an extent society but also a destruction of old illusions and therewith "the disenchantment of the world"[39] and a recognition of the lack of rational foundation of the traditional values that have informed the society. In the economic realm, the process of "rationalization" and "intellectualization" leads to an exclusion of older moral concerns and the emergence of an ethos, at first religiously motivated, which sees man's calling as maximum production, production for its own sake. In modern society, growth becomes an imperative, an irresistible force "until the last ton of fossilized coal is burnt."[40] The cult of efficiency calls for rational social and political control, the elimination of the personal factor and the increasing establishment of impersonal regulation by means of a bureaucracy. Resistance to the imposition of an iron cage may occur; the nonrational exerts itself momentarily through the charismatic effect of great individuals who go against the stream. But their impact too is ultimately "routinized."

Not all theories of modernization come to these pessimistic conclusions. In the Western as well as in the socialist countries and in the Third World, ideas in many ways akin to the classical idea of progress remain influential in the post-World War II era. In the West these ideas have been linked to the concept of "industrial society," in the socialist countries to that of the "scientific and technological revolution." In a host of writings, in various countries, J. Fourastié in France, Hans Freyer in West Germany, Walt Rostow in the United States, Georg Klaus in the German Democratic Republic, and Radovan Richta and a host of coworkers in an ambitious cooperative project at the Czechoslovak Academy of Sciences offer what the last calls "an entirely new, optimistic view of the future."[41] The basis is laid for a science of the future. The Western formulation of this conception of progress is perhaps most forcefully expressed in Walt Rostow's *The Stages of Economic Growth*. Marx's assertion that there are laws of social development "working with iron necessities toward inevitable results" so that "the country which is more developed industrially only shows to the less developed the image of its own future"[42] is here given a new, capitalist expression. A technological determinism operates here, dif-

39. Max Weber, "Science as a Vocation," in *From Max Weber: Essays in Sociology*, ed. H.H. Gerth and C. Wright Mills (New York: Oxford University Press, 1946), pp. 139, 155.

40. Max Weber, *The Protestant Ethics and the Spirit of Capitalism*, trans. Talcott Parsons (New York: Scribner, 1958), p. 181.

41. Radovan Richta and a research team, *Civilization at the Cross Roads: Social and Human Implications of the Scientific and Technological Revolution* (Prague: International Arts and Sciences Press, 1969), p. 11.

42. W.W. Rostow, *The Stages of Economic Growth: A Non-Communist Manifesto* (Cambridge: Cambridge University Press, 1960); Karl Marx, "Preface to the First German Edition," *Capital: A Critique of Political Economy*, ed. Frederick Engels (New York: International Publishers, 1967), p. 8.

ferent from the more broadly social conception of historical change in the Marxist doctrine of economic determination. The British and the American experience of transformation, through a series of five stages from traditional economies to mature capitalism and mass consumption, stands as the model for other societies including the Soviet Union. Communism appears as a deviation, as "a disease of transition,"[43] which under the pressures of economic development will give way to the social and political concomitants of an affluent consumer society, to a convergence with other highly developed societies. The pressure of development has already led to the "end of ideologies," to the "consensus" of the post-World War II generation of optimistic historians on the American national past.[44] The Marxist formulations of the "scientific technological" revolution, optimistic formulations restricted to Eastern European countries and largely absent from the much more flexible thought of Western Marxists, give greater emphasis to the social effects of industrialization. For them too "the scientific and technological revolution" provides the basis for an unalienated, perfected society. "Only when the productive forces of human life have reached this level," observes the Richta group, "will opportunities exist for new relationships among people and a new concept of human life. We are standing today on the soil of the historically formed industrial civilization, but we are beginning to cross its frontiers and go forward into the unknown civilization of the future."[45]

This stress on the uniformity of economic development is questioned by Alexander Gerschenkron, who stresses the unique historical factors which determine the economic takeoff to industrialization in specific national settings. The unequal economic development of countries at the verge of industrialization prevents a repetition of the British model. In a study of political modernization, Barrington Moore introduces a similar comparative note; differences in social relations related to economic modernization explain the very different roads that the various major national societies took. Raymond Aron accepts the notion of the "industrial society" with its imperative of maximum production, which calls forth uniform forms of control yet which runs into the barriers of societies and individuals whose character has been formed by history.[46] Cultural and national diversity continues to exist under the veneer of technologically conditioned uniformity.

43. Rostow, *Stages of Economic Growth*, pp. 162-64.

44. Daniel Bell, *The End of Ideologies: On the Exhaustion of Political Ideas in the Fifties* (Glencoe, Ill.: Free Press, 1960); cf. Bernard Sternsher, *Consensus, Conflict, and American Historians* (Bloomington: Indiana University Press, 1975); also John Higham, "The Cult of American 'Consensus': Homogenizing Our History," *Commentary*, 27 (February 1959): 93-100.

45. Richta et al., *Civilization at the Crossroads*, p. 278.

46. A. Gerschenkron, *Economic Backwardness in Historical Perspective* (Cambridge, Mass.: Harvard University Press, 1962); Barrington Moore, *Social Origins of*

Yet these varied critiques still proceed from the assumption that industrialization and growth are the destiny of the modern world. A more radical critique takes issue with the fundamental value assumptions of an industrial society. From a fictional perspective, Julian Huxley and George Orwell stress the tendencies to domination inherent in technical rationality. Basic to the Judeo-Christian and the Hellenic-Roman tradition is the faith that the world was given to man to control. From two very different directions, one neo-Marxist, the other structuralist-anthropological, the relationship of man to nature is called into question. In his early philosophical writings as well as in *Capital*, Marx had spoken of the "complete inversion" in the relation between the world of things and the world of man. Max Horkheimer and Theodor Adorno see a similar inversion operating in modern society since the Enlightenment but see it not as a function of private property but as an inherent quality of scientific-technical civilization. Seeking to emancipate man from myth, they argue, the Enlightenment created a new myth. It assumed that thought could best be expressed in mathematical forms and in doing this created a conceptual world in which men were depersonalized. Rationalization and mathematization lent themselves to the manipulation of men in the service of production for its own ends. "Mankind, instead of entering into a truly human condition, is sinking into a new kind of barbarism."[47] Going beyond this, Herbert Marcuse and Norman Brown question the very compulsion to produce.[48] In changing the relationship between man and nature and seeking technical control over the latter, Western civilization laid the bases for the manipulation and control of human beings. The drive to perform, in industry or sexuality, represents a neurosis. The civilization of the West is thus inherently sick. In a Utopian vein, Marcuse sees in the dialectics of industrial society the possibility but improbability that the achievement of an automated industry will free man from the traditional economy of scarcity and the curse of alienated labor and make possible a world in which the pleasure principle will no longer be in conflict with the reality principle.

This attempt to redefine man's relation to nature[49] and thus to question the fundamental value assumptions of Western civilization, and with it the ideology of progress, is expressed in a different form in structural anthropology. Claude Lévi-Strauss questions the unique role of scientific reason as it has been conceived in the Western tradition of

Dictatorship and Democracy: Lord and Peasant in the Making of the Modern World (Boston: Beacon Press, 1966); Raymond Aron, *Progress and Disillusion: The Dialectics of Modern Society* (New York: Praeger, 1968), p. 221.

47. Cf. Marx, *Capital*, I, 310; Max Horkheimer and Theodor Adorno, *Dialectic of Enlightenment*, trans. John Cumming (New York: Seabury Press, 1972), p. xi.

48. Herbert Marcuse, *Eros and Civilization* (Boston: Beacon Press, 1955), and *One-Dimensional Man* (Boston: Beacon Press, 1964); Norman O. Brown, *Life Against Death* (New York: Vintage, n.d.).

49. Cf. William Leiss, *The Domination of Nature* (New York: Braziller, 1972).

philosophy since the Greeks. The mythical and magical thinking of the "savage mind" possesses an equal dignity in its attempt to understand reality. "Mythical" and "scientific" thought do not represent "two stages or phases in the evolution of knowledge. Both approaches are equally valid." Nor is there continuity or process in time. Modern civilization does not represent a higher form of social life; historical knowledge has no claim to superiority over other forms of knowledge. "History is a discontinuous set." It has no objective subject matter. "We need only recognize that history is a method with no distinct object corresponding to it to reject the equivalence between the notion of history and the notion of humanity."[50]

A very similar idea is suggested by Michel Foucault.[51] It is only in one specific period of Western history that men have thought in historical terms. This way of thinking represented an anthropocentric hubris, which gave man a special and illusory status in reality and destroyed the balance between man and nature. But Foucault agrees with Lévi-Strauss that this "golden age of historical consciousness," which marked the world outlook of the eighteenth and nineteenth centuries, "has already passed."[52] In his early work on the history of insanity in the Age of Reason,[53] Foucault had tried to demonstrate the inhumanity of an outlook which seeks to dominate and regulate, in this case the insane, with no understanding of the creative and humane sources of madness.

This attempt at a history, which fundamentally questions the assumptions of historical writing since the eighteenth century of the unity of world history—the notion of development as the framework for historical thought, the special dignity of intellect, and the unique quality of European civilization—is perhaps best represented by the historians and "human scientists" of the *Annales* circle in Paris, although the work of the *Annales* finds its parallel in the historical writing of almost all countries by the 1970s.[54] It is here that a Copernican view of history, for which rational man no longer occupies the center of the stage and Europe appears as one among many cultures, replaces an anthropo- and Europocentric conception. The denial of the unity of world history is not unique. A tradition from Herder

50. Claude Lévi-Strauss, *The Savage Mind* (Chicago: University of Chicago Press, 1966), pp. 259, 263.

51. Cf. Michel Foucault, *The Order of Things: An Archaeology of the Human Sciences* (New York: Pantheon, 1971), and *The Archaeology of Knowledge*, trans. A.M. Sheridan Smith (New York: Pantheon, 1972).

52. Lévi-Strauss, *Savage Mind*, p. 254.

53. Michel Foucault, *Madness and Civilization: A History of Insanity in the Age of Reason*, trans. Richard Howard (New York: Vintage, 1964).

54. Cf. Traian Stoianovich, *French Historical Method: The Annales Paradigm* (Ithaca, N.Y.: Cornell University Press, 1976); J. H. Hexter, "Fernand Braudel and the Monde Braudellien," *Journal of Modern History*, 44 (1972): 480-539; Georg G. Iggers, *New Directions in European Historiography* (Middletown, Conn.: Wesleyan University Press, 1975), pp. 43-79.

through Lasaulx, Danilevski, Brooks Adams, Spengler, and Toynbee[55] has stressed the diversity of cultures and developments. But all of these perceptions still stressed the developmental unity of each culture and saw the culture in an idealistic manner in terms of an underlying spirit. Two ideas are radically questioned by many of the historians of the *Annales* circle. One is the concept of development. Fernand Braudel challenges not only the idea of a continuous development in the unit under investigation—in his treatment of the Mediterranean seen as a geographic historic region or in his survey of the entire world between the fifteenth and the eighteenth centuries—but the idea of the unity of the time. There is not one history of a region, a society, or the world but a variety of histories, a variety of times running parallel to each other but not necessarily integrated.[56] The geographical time of the *longue durée* moves alongside the relatively slow transformations of social and economic structures and cultural patterns and the rapid time of political events. For Braudel, as for Lévi-Strauss, history "is not tied... to any particular object" but "consists wholly in its method."[57] It is important, however, that it is not the realms alone in which consciousness is decisive—culture, politics, or even economics—which are of historical interest, but the broad areas of human existence: the material, biological, and routine everyday activities of human beings. Like the anthropologist, the historian is interested less in the realm of conscious ideas than in "decoding" the pattern of automatic behavior hidden in all phases of life. The link between man and nature is reestablished. This search for history which is synchronic rather than diachronic, which does not move, an *histoire immobile*, finally leads to Emmanuel Le Roy Ladurie's retrospective anthropology in his attempt to grasp the pattern of life in a remote fourteenth-century village in the Pyrenees.[58]

Thus, the idea of progress has run its course in social thought and historiography, but not quite. In two important senses the idea of progress continues to be of relevance to social thought and historiography today: in its contribution to the analysis of the modern industrial age and as a norm for social policy and action. Notwithstanding the

55. Cf. Georg G. Iggers, "The Idea of Progress in Recent Philosophy of History," *Journal of Modern History*, 30 (1958): 215-26.

56. See the following works by Fernand Braudel: *The Mediterranean and the Mediterranean World in the Age of Philip II*, 2 vols., trans. Sian Reynolds (New York: Harper & Row, 1973); *Civilisation matérielle, économie et capitalisme, XVème-XVIIIème siècle*, 3 vols. (Paris: Armand Colin, 1979); *Capitalism and Material Life*, trans. Miriam Kochan (New York: Harper & Row, 1973); and "Time, History, and the Social Sciences," in *The Varieties of History*, ed. Fritz Stern (New York: Vintage, 1972), pp. 403-29.

57. Lévi-Strauss, *Savage Mind*, p. 262.

58. Cf. Emmanuel Le Roy Ladurie, "L'histoire immobile," *Annales: Economies, Sociétés, Civilisations*, 29 (1974): 673-92; Emmanuel Le Roy Ladurie, *Montaillou: The Promised Land of Error*, trans. Barbara Bray (New York: Vintage, 1979).

admonitions of the structuralist anthropologists, who are not entirely free of an element of nostalgic romanticism, the modern world is the central historical experience of our existence. This modern world is fundamentally different from all other civilizations and cultures, and this difference rests on its progressive character. Modern society has been one of growth. This growth in the nineteenth and twentieth centuries has affected the entire world so that one can speak for the first time of a world history. Only in the affluent nations of the West has the desirability of growth been seriously questioned, and even here it remains an integral part of public policy. This growth has never been purely material but has had consequences for all aspects of society.

History as retrospective anthropology has its charm. It also serves the important function of protecting us against a parochialism which takes modern industrial society as its norm. But it does not replace a study of such a society. And such a study must work with concepts of dynamic change. The idea of progress in its Enlightenment form represented the first theory of modernization. Admittedly, the social effects of science and technology have not been uniform. As Raymond Aron has pointed out, the scientific-technological transformation has led universally to both greater uniformity and greater diversity.[59] In the social and cultural realms, institutions and attitudes continue to have a history of their own, which defies the reduction of modern civilization to a common denominator. The study of a modern world thus requires an approach that uses categories indebted to the idea of progress to conceptualize the developments which point to uniformities in modernization yet which at the same time takes into consideration the conditions and traditions that give this development everywhere its unique character.

But neither is the vision of the future contained in the classical idea of progress entirely lost. In its Enlightenment form but also in its nineteenth-century expressions—Marx, Mill, and even Comte—the idea did not resolve into a naïve assumption that scientific and technological advances automatically translated into social improvement. Progress was an affirmation of the belief that men and women were active participants in historical change and that enlightenment should serve as an instrument in the transformation of society along humane lines. There was divergence in the conception of what constituted such a society but also a broad consensus on the values of a world community in which ignorance, disease, want, and, not least important, war would be progressively eliminated, and human beings freed from the yokes of tradition and external control would determine their own lives. The shortcomings of the idea of progress are apparent: the failure to appreciate the resistance to rationality, the very ambiguities of reason, and the powerful needs for domination, which turn science and technology into powerful instruments of control and destruction. Growth

59. Aron, *Progress and Disillusion.*

for the sake of growth has proven to be not only a dubious value from the view of human needs but a threat to human existence; but then growth for its own sake was never what the idea of progress in its classical form was about. Progress was always conceived in broad social terms. A basic assumption of the theorists of progress has been that "man is not merely a natural being: he is a *human* natural being;"[60] that he cannot be submerged fully into the order of nature; that civilization is the setting in which he expresses and develops his humanity. The critics of progress have rightfully pointed out the limits of the idea. They have not invalidated the core of the idea, the moral imperative to create a world in which the conditions for a dignified human existence, which today do not exist for billions of human beings, are achieved.

60. Karl Marx, "Economic and Philosophic Manuscripts," in *Marx-Engels Reader*, p. 116.

3

The Idea of Progress in Communist Ideology

ALFRED G. MEYER

Communism is carrying out the historic
mission of redeeming all people from social
inequality, from all forms of domination and
exploitation, and from the horrors of war,
and it is establishing on earth *peace, labor,
liberty, equality, fraternity*, and *happiness* for
all nations.

From Program of the *CPSU*, 1961

MARX AND ENGELS ON PROGRESS

The ideology of progress might well be called the religion of Western
civilization. It has functioned as a faith or a set of deep convictions, by
which, during the last two centuries, the most trenchant changes have
been justified. Scientific, technological, and economic advances have
demonstrated its reality and have been used to justify disruptions and
destructions of peoples, cultures, and the natural environment. But although progress is, in many senses, a reality, as an ideology it rests on
assumptions, convictions, and beliefs that are fundamentally religious.
In fact, as an ideology it can be traced back to the Western Christian
conception of history as the stages of human salvation. Ultimately,
one cannot understand the Marxian dialectic of progress without ap-
preciating the dialectical interplay of sin and grace and of death and
resurrection in Christian theology. To be sure, Marxism is decidedly
this-worldly. Long before Marx, the faith in salvation had become
secularized, and eighteenth-century theories of progress incorporated

notions about the end of religion and its replacement by science and skeptical philosophy. Nonetheless, the ideas of progress current in the age of Enlightenment cannot be fully appreciated without recognizing many of them as secularizations of notions that go back to Saint Augustine's City of God, Joachim de Floris' dream about the reign of the Holy Spirit, or the medieval mystics' yearning for the unity of all creation with God (see Keohane, pp. 27ff.).

From the philosophers of the Enlightenment, Engels and Marx inherited the well-known commonplace about progress—the conception of history as the development of human powers through science, technology, and rational social organization, which would, once all people became enlightened, culminate in the reign of reason on earth, implying the solution of all hitherto unsolved human problems. By mastering the forces of nature, humanity would secure material comforts; and by mastering passions, superstitions, ignorance, and injustice, humanity would restructure institutions to shape a social world in which freedom, order, and equity would reinforce one another. In the writings of Marx and Engels, these aims are described as the appropriation of nature, the victory over necessity, the leap into the realm of freedom, the realization of all human potential, and the beginning of truly human history. The term they used for this transformation was communism.

In asserting that Engels and Marx were heirs of many ideas associated with the Enlightenment, especially the unshakable faith in progress, one must point out that at every step in their intellectual development the two men voiced sharp criticism of virtually every representative eighteenth-century thinker, including Newton, Locke, Smith, and Kant. At the risk of oversimplification, I shall summarize their objections to these philosophical founding fathers of liberalism by stating that they dismissed the Enlightenment conception of progress as naïve, the entire tradition of thought of which it was a part as shallow, unhistorical, and shamelessly apologetic. And yet the fact remains that the founders of Marxism were thoroughly committed to the basic idea of progress sketched above, and they expressed this commitment in countless ways.

Rejection and acceptance simultaneously—what Freudians call ambivalence—is the attitude that Marxism expresses toward virtually all historic phenomena. With regard to the representative philosophers of the eighteenth century, the ambivalence of Marx and Engels was particularly deep. Contemporary students of Marxism allude to this attitude by arguing that Marxism represents an inversion (*Umstülpung*) of Ricardo's political economy or of liberal ideology in general, including eighteenth-century theories of progress, an inversion of any theory being a system of ideas which *accepts* that theory or some of its basic premises, turns it inside-out and thereby *rejects* it, and in this fashion *enriches* it. Indeed, Marxism sees itself as having precisely that kind of relationship to liberal conceptions of progress.

Guided by this model, we will readily perceive that Marxist theories incorporate and invert such ideas as the Lockean theory of property (Marx's assertion that socialism aims for the "restoration of property" can be understood only in its light); the Smith-Ricardo model of the market; Voltaire's hatred of bureaucratic arbitrariness; the materialistic and atheistic views of Holbach and Helvétius; and the skepticism of Hume. Yet in the writings of Engels and Marx, these ideas reappear in a totally different framework of ideas; and much of this framework is taken from the romantic critics of the Enlightenment tradition, chiefly perhaps from Rousseau.

The work of Jean-Jacques Rousseau offers a passionate indictment of the entire notion of progress, arguing, in effect, that "civilization corrupts." Nowhere does Rousseau spell out this indictment more clearly than in his *Discourse on the Origin and Foundation of Inequality Among Mankind*. How remarkable, therefore, that Engels should single out this work as one of the themes on which the entire Marxist opus is but a set of variations. In his famous popularization of Marxist doctrines, he describes the *Discourse* as a dialectical masterpiece, in which, decades before Hegel's birth, Hegelian philosophy is brilliantly anticipated:

> Thus we have already in Rousseau not only a development of ideas which to a hair resembles that followed in Marx's *Capital*, but also, in detail, an entire series of the very same dialectical turns of language used by Marx: processes which by their nature are antagonistic and contain within themselves a contradiction; the transformation of one extreme into its opposite; finally, as the kernel of the whole thing, the negation of the negation.[1]

What makes such praise by Engels so remarkable is the fact that generally he and Marx were highly critical of Rousseau for several reasons. For one thing, they often argued that the political system suggested in the *Social Contract*, which they regarded as the paradigmatic model of the liberal state, was based on false premises and therefore was naïve and utopian. More important for the purposes of this discussion, Marx and Engels were utterly contemptuous of the ideals Rousseau confessed throughout his life's work and of the romantic ideology which his work helped inspire. One should, perhaps, read the account that Engels wrote about the revolutionary partisan war of 1849, in which he participated, to get the flavor of his disdain for the Rousseauian ideal of the idyllic small community of honest, virtuous, frugal, simple folk not corrupted by greed for power, status, possessions, refined pleasures, or knowledge, nor disturbed by the mighty winds of world history. Some of these remarks, as well as the

---

1. Friedrich Engels, *Anti-Dühring*, in Karl Marx and Friedrich Engels, *Werke*, 39 vols. (Berlin: Dietz-Verlag, 1965-1971), XX, 130-31 (hereafter cited as **MEW**); all English translations in this essay are mine.

numerous scathing observations he and Marx made about the petty bourgeoisie and about democratic ideals, seem similarly to be directed at Rousseau.

But this contempt need not conceal the debt they owed him, a debt which both of them acknowledged. Marx praised him for correctly seeing "political man" as an abstraction and an alienation, and he quoted with approval his description of the capitalist-worker relationship: "I shall permit—says the capitalist—that you will have the honor of serving me on condition that, for my pains in giving you orders, you will give me what little surpluses you have."[2]

Engels, as we have seen, praised Rousseau for his dialectics, particularly for recognizing, first, that the development of inequality was progressive, and, second, that progress was antagonistic, every step toward progress also being retrogressive. "Every new progress of civilization is simultaneously a new progress in inequality. All institutions which the society that has developed with civilization gives itself turn into the opposite of their original purpose," writes Engels, and then illustrates this by a quotation from Rousseau about liberty-destroying institutions of government (princes) which the people have given themselves for the purpose of protecting their liberty.[3]

The two men's intellectual debt to Rousseau and the entire romantic tradition is stated most clearly, perhaps, by arguing that from this tradition they learned to focus their attention on the human cost of progress. The one concept which sums up this cost is, of course, that of alienation; and this Hegelian concept as well as its Marxian elaborations are unthinkable without the inspiration given by Rousseau. To be sure, the preoccupation with the prevalence of evil in a world conceived of as rational, the entire dialectic of good purpose and bad results, of freedom and determination, progressive base and reactionary superstructure—this entire conception in which progress and retrogression intermingle in cunning (*listig*) fashion also goes back to medieval and Reformation Christian ideas, to say nothing of their ultimate source in Aristotle's writings. Still, any reader of Rousseau's *Discourse on the Origin and Foundation of Inequality Among Mankind* will be struck by the number of ideas and phrases that will sound familiar to students of Marxism because they recur, often literally, in the writings of the two founders. Whether he discusses the despoliation of nature, the inauthenticity of civilized humans, the destruction of the natural community, the enslavement of women, or the decline of art, Rousseau offers ideas that we encounter again in *The Holy Family, The German Ideology, Capital*, and in the *Economic-Philosophic Manuscripts of 1844*. He sounds especially Marxian when he

---

2. Karl Marx, *Das Kapital*, I, in *MEW*, XXIII, 774, note 232. The quotation is from Jean-Jacques Rousseau's *Discours sur l'économie politique* (Geneva, 1760), p. 70. See also *Theorien über den Mehrwert*, in *MEW*, XXVI, part 3, 57. The remark concerning Rousseau's view of "political man" is from *Zur Judenfrage, MEW*, I, 370.

3. Engels, *Anti-Dühring*, in *MEW*, XX, 130, 19.

sums up the consequences of the division of labor: "equality vanished, property was introduced, labor became necessary, and boundless forests became smiling fields, which had to be watered by human sweat, and in which slavery and misery were soon to sprout out of, and grow with, the harvests."[4]

In fact, Marxism is not only an inversion of liberalism but is at the same time an inversion of romanticism, accepting not only Rousseau's theory of alienation, but also much of the critique of capitalism offered by romantic conservatives and reactionaries. Indeed Marxism derives its radical-critical impulse from precisely this school. It thus combines both the eighteenth-century faith in progress and nineteenth-century critiques of progress in a grand synthesis, in which history is neither the straight line or ladder from darkness to light that it was for Condorcet nor the equally unilinear path from innocence to corruption that it was for Rousseau; instead, it is a spiral in which retrogression and alienation are themselves necessary steps toward progress.

Ultimately, Marx and Engels were on the side of Condorcet rather than Rousseau. While the latter accepts the alienation of the human being as inevitable and, indeed, in some sense as desirable, seeking to mitigate its consequences in the simple life, they opted for progress, arguing that it would be the *result* of alienation. Thus, their theory turned out to be a humanistic variant of Leibnitz's theodicy, that is, an anthropodicy. They would have agreed with Usbek, of Montesquieu's *Lettres Persanes*, who was convinced that technology, including strange new chemicals and superweapons of mass destruction, would always be controlled and serve human needs;[5] or with Goethe, whose *Faust* begins with the assertion that "in the beginning was the deed" and ends with the assertion that knowledge pursued for the purpose of serving material human needs is knowledge of which even heaven approves, regardless of the sacrifices made en route. The famous remarks Marx made about Greek art, which he greatly and naïvely

4. Jean-Jacques Rousseau, "Second Discourse," in *The Social Contract and Discourse on the Origin of Inequality*, ed. Lester G. Crocker (New York: Pocket Book), p. 220.

5. Cf. a contemporary expression of the same faith:

It's sometimes argued that there's no real progress; that a civilization that kills multitudes in mass warfare, that pollutes the land and oceans with ever larger quantities of debris, that destroys the dignity of individuals by subjecting them to a forced mechanized existence can hardly be called an advance over the simpler hunting and gathering and agricultural existence of prehistoric times. But this argument, though romantically appealing, doesn't hold up. The primitive tribes permitted far less individual freedom than does modern society. Ancient wars were committed with far less moral justification than modern ones. A technology that produces debris can find, and is finding, ways of disposing of it without ecological upset. And the school-book pictures of primitive man sometimes omit some of the detractions of his primitive life—the pain, the disease, famine, the hard labor needed just to stay alive. From that agony of bare existence to modern life can be soberly described only as upward progress, and the sole agent for this progress is quite clearly reason itself. (Robert M. Pirsig, *Zen and the Art of Motorcycle Maintenance* (New York: Morrow, 1974).)

admired, but nonetheless put in its place as the product of the infantile stage of human progress, express the same faith in progress which Engels offered upon his return home from his first two years in Manchester: he raved to Marx about how much the city had developed in such a short time: whole forests have been cut down, he wrote triumphantly.

In countless ways, Engels and Marx expressed their conviction that progress was promoted precisely by the destructive and oppressive trends the romantics denounced. Slavery, the oppression of women, the exploitation of wage labor, the ruination of the peasantry, the despoliation of nature, the mechanization of life, the destruction of religious and cultural traditions, the colonization of formerly independent nations, from Bohemia to India, from China to Mexico—these and other stages in the march of civilization Marx and Engels described in all their horrors and then made sure to add that every one of them was necessary and desirable for assuring the eventual victory of progress. It is as though they were in agreement with Nietzsche's statement that "the magnitude of any 'progress' indeed is *measured* by the mass of everything that had to be sacrificed for its sake."[6] The romantic laments over these costs they always dismissed as sentimental, reactionary, and infantile. They would have scoffed at the contemporary anthropologist Marshall Sahlins for asserting that Western civilization is dangerous "because in the interest of this growth it does not hesitate to destroy any other form of humanity whose difference from us consists in having discovered not merely other codes of existence but ways of achieving an end that still eludes us: the mastery by society of society's mastery over nature."[7] It is noteworthy, in this connection, that Engels and Marx reacted angrily and with incomprehension to suggestions that their own critique of capitalism and its ills might have been inspired or anticipated by romantic reactionaries of previous generations.

The philosophic underpinnings of this faith remain a matter of controversy, and so, to some extent, is the degree of doubt Marx and Engels generated to qualify their faith. Both of them at various times had moments of despair during which they thought history was taking wrong turns toward barbarism rather than toward the communist utopia. Both of them allowed the possibility of such an alternative, though both often reassured each other that, in the final analysis, humanity would fulfill its destiny of creating a world fit for human beings to live in. Moreover, they seem to have made a clear distinction

6. Friedrich Nietzsche, *Zur Genealogie der Moral* (Munich: Goldmann-Verlag, 1877), pp. 65-66. In German, the statement reads as follows: "Die Grösse eines 'Fortschritts' *bemisst* sich sogar nach der Masse dessen, was ihm alles geopfert werden musste."

7. Marshall D. Sahlins, *Culture and Practical Reason* (Chicago: University of Chicago Press, 1976).

between progressive civilizations and those condemned to stagnate unless they were coerced into participation in historic developments by brute force from outside, that is, by colonialism and imperialism. Max Weber's comparison of Chinese and Western civilizations is but a variation on a theme struck more than once by Engels and Marx. At times they dwelled on the human costs of progress so much and waxed so nostalgic about the cozy relationships of feudalism or the idyllic image of primitive society that they sounded like echoes of romanticism. But these were only momentary lapses. By and large, their faith in progress remained unshaken.

This faith is founded either on a neo-Hegelian view of the entire universe as teleological, striving for self-perfection or self-realization, or on a faith in human potential so absolute that the human species is elevated to the role of the creator of the world. Contemporary students of Marxism today tend to attribute the former view to Engels, who, to be sure, spent much effort on an unfinished work on the philosophy of science, which seems to see the entire cosmos as dynamic and, perhaps, imbued with purpose. But Marx probably shared this view. Why else would he have greeted Darwin's discoveries with such enthusiasm that he wanted to dedicate the first volume of *Das Kapital* to him? Marx's enthusiasm was based on the belief that the Darwinist theory of evolution had proven that all of nature participates in the dialectic of progress. There are other statements Marx made which suggest that he at least toyed with such notions of a teleological cosmology in which some creative urge is attributed to all existence. In the final analysis, however, he and Engels were far more interested in human relations and human action; and the ultimate premise for their faith in progress remains their unshakable faith in the unlimited creative potential of the human species. Even in the drafts Engels left for essays on the philosophy of science, what is stressed is not the dynamic nature of "matter" but the progress in knowledge our civilization has made since the Renaissance. The conviction he and Marx shared about the imminent dawn of communism, of course, was based on their belief that they had done for human history what Copernicus and Newton had done for the solar system: they thought they had laid bare its laws of development; and that of which we have scientific knowledge we can begin to control.

Subsequent Marxist schools have stressed one or the other philosophic premise, but all of them have taken for granted the eventual inevitability of progress. The theoretical authorities of the Second International—Kautsky, Mehring, and Plekhanov were the outstanding representatives—subscribed to a deterministic philosophy suggesting a teleological cosmos. Their ideology expressed the smug conviction that communism was the inevitable end product of Western history, and those like themselves who were on its side would soon be in power. This ideology, strangely enough, turned out to be quite compatible with a politics of accommodation to, or gradual reform of, existing regimes.

THIRD WORLD MARXISM AS A THEORY OF PROGRESS

Third World Marxism,[8] from Russian Bolshevism to its Asian, African, and Latin-American variants, sees itself as a civilizing agent promoting progress. Its image of the contemporary world is shaped by the conception of modern imperialism as a regressive, reactionary, and retarding force that promotes and reproduces underdevelopment throughout the Third World; capitalist monopolies similarly retard development, and racism keeps ethnic minorities and nonwhite nations in a dependent and servile position, poorly educated, ill equipped for modern life.

In Third World Marxism, the Marxist theory of inevitable progress has thus transformed itself into a set of programs for modernization, all of them planning economic and technological growth, scientific development, massive resocialization of the population for life in the twentieth century, with the concomitant antagonism to many aspects of traditional culture and incumbent ruling classes, with national liberation from previous dependencies, as well as the mobilization of the masses for participation in this process. Antagonism to incumbent elites and the belief in national independence as an essential precondition for this modernization make Third World Marxism revolutionary; before anything else, it seeks, therefore, to mobilize the masses for revolution.

Third World Marxism thus is a conscious attempt to realize the Marxist goal in precisely those areas of the world which, according to Marx, had not participated in the forward march of Western civilization and thus had not partaken of progress. Hence, although the theorists of the Second International, speaking for growing numbers of workers in highly industrialized societies, could believe that progress was inevitable even if they themselves did little or nothing to promote it, Third World Marxists seek to push, shove, or drag their countries into the progressive tendencies of history by heroic effort. Progress is to be imposed on underdeveloped nations by an elite of professional revolutionaries, who proclaim themselves the enlightened vanguard of the exploited, in the name of which they establish their dictatorship. The primary tasks of this dictatorship are building the economic base for socialism, functioning as substitute capitalist in accumulating the material resources required for a modern economy, training the people to function in it, and inducing work discipline and a "communist" attitude toward work.[9]

8. By "Third World Marxism," I mean those ideologies and movements in underdeveloped countries which "officially" subscribe to the political ideas of Engels, Marx, and Lenin.

9. See V.G. Afans'ev, *Nauchnyi kommunizm* (Moscow: Izdatel'stvo politicheskoi

The leaders of Third World Marxist movements thus see themselves as the pioneers of that universal civilization developed in the West, which, in the name of progress, is to be imposed on all non-Western cultures. Such a program implies either the destruction or the deep transformation of autochthonous cultures; and indeed the Third World Marxist doctrines tend to regard most elements of the old cultures—religion, social structure, mores, and cosmology—as inherently reactionary and thus harmful. At the same time, many Marxist-Leninist theorists have recognized the problem discussed by Crawford Young (see pp. 92ff.), that is, the need to reconcile the universal ideal of amelioration with the deeply ingrained views and attitudes springing out of native cultures. One can see this most clearly, perhaps, in observing how leaders like Mao, Ho, Castro, and Cabral seek to translate the universal currency of Marxist-Leninist terminology into local verbal coinage, linguistic adaptations which at times subtly change not only the vocabulary but also the message and the policies. It is already more difficult to interpret organizational forms and mobilization patterns of various Third World Marxist movements as conscious or unconscious accommodations with native cultures. Altogether, the interplay of universalism and nativism in Third World Marxist movements may be one of the most interesting subjects for study.[10]

Again, for Third World Marxists, the imposition of the universal pattern of amelioration is the primary goal, accommodations to local cultures seen, at their best, as tactical compromises. The Stalinist formula, according to which the Soviet system should be "socialist in content, and national in form," makes this clear; the careful cultivation of selected folk arts, crafts, and customs in the Soviet Union can be compared with the popularity of cowboy rodeos and Bluegrass music in the United States: progress, while destroying the cultures which these activities expressed, has preserved them as pretty or amusing relics and placed them in its museums.

The philosophy of Third World Marxism is an inversion of the ideas of Engels and Marx: consciousness rather than the internal pressure of rapidly growing productive forces is to be the driving force of progress. The superstructure, not the base, is the dynamic element, as the state, established in a backward nation, painfully accumulates the essential means of production for an advanced economy. "The most important distinguishing feature of socialism, as against capitalism," argues a Soviet theoretician, "is that it does not arise spontaneously but is erected consciously by all those who do productive labor under the leadership of the Marxist-Leninist party and on the basis of the theory of scientific communism."[11] The revolution, supposedly, is

---

literary, 1966), p. 196.

10. For a discussion of the general problem, see Alfred G. Meyer, "Communist Revolutions and Cultural Change," *Studies in Comparative Communism* 5(4) (Winter 1972): 345-70.

11. Afanas'ev, *Nauchnyi kommunizm*, p. 194.

promoted not because of highly developed, and decaying, capitalism, but because of its absence. History here is seen not as a teleological process on which humanity might rely but as an obstacle it must overcome. Heroic initiative, swimming against the current, firm leadership against discouraging obstacles—those are the images with which Lenin exhorted his followers to revolutionary action.

PROGRESS AS VIEWED IN SOVIET IDEOLOGY

The immediate goal of the systems which Third World Marxism manages to found is to catch up with the West, economically, militarily, technologically, and scientifically. Western achievements in production and defense are to be replicated, but the free-enterprise society, which in the West promoted these attainments, is to be avoided. To be sure, the ultimate goal envisaged is precisely the combination of democratic self-government and up-to-date technology—at least that is what Lenin's famous definition of communism as "Soviet rule plus electrification of the country" implies. But concerning the relative weight to be given to these two elements, there is sharp disagreement within Third World Marxism; and in practice the temptation to forget about the democratic and egalitarian aims, at least for the time being, has proven overwhelmingly strong so that progress is to be measured much more by the growth of technology and the accumulation of the means of production and destruction than by the rearing of autonomous individuals realizing their full human potentials. An East European reform communist writing under a pseudonym has argued that the resulting socialist systems in Russia and Eastern Europe combine a "socialist" class structure with an essentially capitalist economy and a "feudal" state so that it is progressive and reactionary at one and the same time.[12]

For justification of this failure so far to have reached the communist goal, Soviet theoreticians once more revert to the deterministic interpretation of Marxism that argues that the communist superstructure can develop only after the economic base has been completed. An attempt to have genuine communist relations before the economic preconditions are present is condemned as utopian and infantile. But the same Soviet writer who argues this point, V.G. Afanas'ev, also resorts to the answer given by Malthusians and other nineteenth-century liberals trying to defend the inequalities of capitalism: if equality were granted, if people were to receive goods in accordance with their needs, there would not be enough for all, and too much consumption would slow down the process of capital accumulation.[13] What Afanas'ev omits to point out is that, obviously, vital human needs will meanwhile remain unfilled.

Progress, in Third World Marxism, is thus identified with the

12. Felipe García Casals, *The Syncretic Society* (White Plains, N.Y.: M.E. Sharpe, 1980).

13. Afanas'ev, *Nauchnyi kommunizm*, pp. 206-07.

accumulation of technology. This expresses itself, in its most naïve form, in the conviction that the messier the traffic jam in the capital city, the more advanced is the country. President Eisenhower, when taking Nikita Krushchev to Camp David, was waxing lyrical about the peace and quiet and the lack of bother they would find in that idyllic mountain retreat. "Do you have a place, Mr. Chairman, where you can get away from jangling telephones and other such disturbances?" he asked his guest; and Nikita Sergeevich is reported to have replied, somewhat testily, "Mr. President, we haven't got as many telephones yet as you, but we will."

Within Marxist ideas about progress there has, in short, developed a tension analogous to that between the democratic and the utilitarian traditions in liberalism, the former, perhaps, to be associated with the revolutionary phases of liberalism, the latter with liberalism as an establishment ideology. What can be said about the Victorian or Third Republic idea of "progress" could be said about contemporary Soviet conceptions of progress. Comparable to Saint-Simonians, Comteans, Utilitarians and their twentieth-century successors, communist elites proclaim their intention to travel the road toward progress on the basis of expertise and rational planning within the given system. (In fact, it should be noted, the pattern of development in both systems has been convulsive, with recurrent "great leaps" followed by periods of institutionalization.) Like the establishment liberals of the last one hundred and fifty years, the ideologists of ruling communist parties combine elitist convictions with democratic rhetoric, voice undiminished confidence in the achievements they have made and expect still to make and are reticent or altogether silent about the human costs of progress. In both the establishment-liberal and ruling-communist pronouncements, the ideology of progress supports the increasing bureaucratization of social life. Bureaucratization as an essential element of the vision of progress is linked to the notion of the reign of reason, which is central to both liberal and Marxist ideas of progress. In *revolutionary* liberalism and communism, the reign of reason implied liberty and equality. In both of these schools, once they have begun to justify existing systems, rationality turns into something to be imposed by effective organization and scientific management so that the goal begins to resemble the Weberian model of bureaucracy, based on an organized hierarchy of experts—though usually without the note of regret over the accompanying disenchantment of human life. Both in liberalism and communism the religion of progress becomes morally and aesthetically insensitive and, from the point of view of whoever aims toward the moral improvement of human intercourse, morally objectionable. If this is too strong a statement, at least one can point out that in both schools, once their adherents have come to power, progress is redefined by toning down expectations.

S.G. Strumilin, a noted Soviet economist who has written a great deal about the forthcoming transition to full communism, warned that expectations should not be pinned too high. The transition to communism, he argued, will be a very lengthy process, and one should be realistic, not utopian, in defining it.[14] Meanwhile, Afanas'ev suggests that communism will be achieved by the means of intensifying the societal features of present-day Soviet Russia.[15] Socialist democracy, argues Strumilin, demands a great deal more centralization and coordination than capitalism, hence also continued control by the party as the central planning and commanding agency.[16] Indeed, not only during the transition to communism is it necessary to strengthen both state and party, writes yet another Soviet theorist; even after communism is reached, the state cannot disappear until the entire world has gone communist.[17]

In his critique of the Gotha program of the German socialist party, Marx gave a tantalizingly brief sketch of communism. It would be a system in which people no longer would be enthralled by the division of labor; specifically, the distinction between mental and physical work would disappear. Work would cease to be a means for survival and would, instead, become a vital need for every healthy person. All individuals would be able to develop their many varied gifts and talents, leading to a flowering of creativity. Finally, while each would contribute according to his or her ability, each would receive according to need: abundance would reign. To this description of communism the 1961 program of the Soviet Communist party makes one important addition: communism will be a *highly organized society* in which the party maintains its policy-making functions.[18] Afanas'ev adds that it will be a system in which scientific management reigns not only over the economy but over all social activities so that it will be a society analogous to an efficient machine, in which all spontaneity is eliminated.[19]

One of the implications is the need to mobilize the social sciences and humanities for the double task of managing this society and of educating the citizenry for smooth functioning within it. In discussing these implications, leading Soviet academics have stressed the need for the nationwide coordination of all social science research, the need for more rigorous research methodologies, especially the use of statistics and computer techniques, and the need to bring the social and natural sciences closer together. Finally, they emphasize the growing

14. S.G. Strumilin, *Problemy sotsializma i kommunizma v SSSR* (Moscow: Izdatel'stvo ekonomicheskoi literatury, 1961), pp. 307-08.

15. Afanas'ev, *Nauchnyi kommunizm*, p. 205.

16. Strumilin, *Problemy sotsializma*, p. 15.

17. A.S. Podgalo, *Period razvernutogo stroitel'stva kommunizma* (Moscow: Izdatel'stvo Znanie, 1959), pp. 42-48. See also Afanas'ev, *Nauchnyi kommunizm*, pp. 321ff.

18. *Programma KPSS*, in *Materialy XXII s'ezda KPSS*, p. 366.

19. Afanas'ev, *Nauchnyi kommunizm*, pp. 210ff.

role of the party in deciding scientific issues.[20] And while the social sciences are to be thus mobilized, it is taken for granted, in the manner of the American end-of-ideology school, that no further drastic changes are needed to assure progress. We have reached the threshold of the desirable society, Soviet ideologists argue; all we need now is further peaceful development. For the transition from socialism to communism, no revolution or other drastic change is needed. Between the dictatorship of the proletariat and the communist people's state there is no great difference.[21] In answer to those who might inquire about the promised withering away of the state, we are told that, instead, the stress will be on *discipline* of people who know their place and function in society, will freely contribute their labor for the common good, and will observe the rules of communal life; it will be on *organization*, on a strong order and strict coordination of efforts; and it will be on *leadership* which, in communism, will be like the gentle dictatorship of the orchestra conductor.[22]

As in contemporary liberal rhetoric, these communist ideas about the road to progress are embedded in a great deal of self-congratulation about what has been achieved so far. It would be a mistake to underestimate the meaningfulness of the achievements which Soviet and East European systems have in fact made toward their goal and the potential results that might be expected from them for the flourishing of those qualities in human intercourse and for the comprehensive development of creative potentials in individuals—"give or take some major historical setbacks and a few wars, revolutions, and gruesome barbarities."

> The development and spread of knowledge, science, and technology have increased material welfare, and these together have increased political participation and produced modern social, economic, and political organization. . . . Similarly, the development of modern organizations has contributed to the growth and spread of knowledge, the growth of technology, and the increase in welfare. A case could be made for intellectual and moral improvements as well, and for some significant net increase in the sum and distribution of human satisfaction as well (see p. 6).

CONTEMPORARY WESTERN MARXISM

Such a statement, applied to the U.S.S.R. or the German Democratic Republic, is likely to stick in the throat of anyone preoccupied with the

20. Akademiia Nauk SSSR, *Stroitel'stvo kommunizma i obshchestvennye nauki: Materialy sessii Obshchego sobraniia Akademii Nauk SSSR 19-20 oktiabria 1962 g.* (Moscow: Izdanie Akademii Nauk SSSR, 1962); see esp. the contributions by M. V. Keldysh, L. F. Il'ichev, A. I. Berg, Iu. P. Frantsev, P. N. Fedoseev, V. P. Eliutin, B. P. Konstantinov, A. A. Markov, M. N. Alekseev, A. G. Spirkin, and V. D. Novikov. See also Afanas'ev, *Nauchnyi kommunizm*, p. 214.

21. Afanas'ev, *Nauchnyi kommunizm*, pp. 195, 204.

22. Ibid., p. 324.

heavy price these and other countries have paid and still are paying for their achievements. Western Marxists, in particular, have had difficulty accepting as progress what they might prefer to describe as the "withering away of utopia." This is but one of the many reasons why Western Marxism has tended to stress the romantic elements in Marxism; hence its preoccupation with dialectical contradictions, with the moral and aesthetic perils of radical politics, and with the concept of alienation—a term which for some decades was totally absent from the vocabulary of ruling communist parties. One can trace variations of such attitudes in Jugoslav communism, in Euro-communism, and in the cluster of Marxist intellectuals loosely known as the Frankfurt school. Nonetheless, ultimately they remain Marxists only as long as they refuse to abandon their confidence in the possibility of progress. Contemporary Western Marxism regards itself as an ideology and a movement which seeks to carry out the task which Frederic Jameson identified as that of dialectical criticism: "to pass judgment on the abstract quality of life in the present, and to keep alive the idea of a concrete future."[23] Keeping this idea alive is a confession of faith in progress.

This is defiant, not to say desperate, optimism. From the point of view of Western Marxism, the history of the world since the death of Engels has been a series of disasters likely to shake even the most firmly grounded faith in progress: the general failure of revolutionary socialism in those countries where Marx and Engels thought it would succeed; the victories of Third World Marxism, which to Western critics represents a barbarization of the doctrine; two world wars; the rise of fascism and Stalinism; Gulag and extermination camps; vicious colonial wars in Algeria, Indo-China, and elsewhere; ecological disasters and seeming moral crises. Looking at the world in the twentieth century, even a Marxist must find it difficult to maintain a belief in progress. And in the final analysis, even the most abstruse epistemological and aesthetic issues (to mention only some) with which Western Marxists deal can be understood only as responses to this lingering crisis of confidence.

This same crisis, which in turn is related to so-called postmaterialism, appears to have begun also in the socialist systems of Eastern Europe. The Western press has given much publicity to the great variety of dissenters in all countries east of the Elbe river. We know about national, religious, and cultural revival movements, some of them of considerable strength. Representatives of such currents have fled to the West or been expelled; some of those who are still in the communist world have published their works abroad. The social basis of this dissidence appears to range from peasants, religious believers,

23. Fredric Jameson, *Marxism and Form* (Princeton, N.J.: Princeton University Press, 1971), p. 416.

tribal people, and other groups that never adjusted to twentieth-century civilization, on the one hand, to urban intellectuals, a jaded *jeunesse dorée*, and other beneficiaries of progress on the other, who raise questions quite similar to those asked in the West today (see Barnes, pp. 415ff.).

How deep do such sentiments run in Eastern Europe, in China, or in the Soviet Union? We do not, alas, have reliable ways of ascertaining this. That they are present is clear. Nor are Western observers the only ones to notice them. Communist authorities, too, have paid attention to the emergence of doubts about the blessings of progress. Here is just one typical response. A Romanian weekly recently felt the need to comment on the fact that some people have lost their faith in the future of humanity. The weekly did this, first, by reference to the tremendous strides that have been made in Eastern Europe since the dismal years of World War II, an argument which in that part of the world will ring true to many readers. But, more important, it reaffirmed the Marxist assumption that humanity, having shown itself capable of solving seemingly insuperable problems in the past, is likely also to find solutions to the technological and social problems facing us at the present time. The energy and materials crisis will be solved. The population of the globe will stabilize because ways of increasing the output of foodstuffs are already known. "Do we have good reasons to be optimistic? We do indeed, yet only to the extent to which we understand this optimism not as a passive expectation of what is doomed to happen, but as a firm awareness of the need to work unceasingly, tirelessly and efficiently for making developments take the desired course. . . ."[24]

Ever since the Christian doctrine of salvation turned into a political theory, and through its many secularizations in absolutist, mercantilist, liberal, utilitarian, socialist, and communist ideologies, the religion of progress has assumed two mutually antagonistic forms. It has been an essential element in ideologies of protest, suggesting and justifying change, reform, rebellion, and revolution; and it has served as the underpinning of establishment ideologies, justifying and rationalizing existing economic and political system. Thus, the religion of progress has given confidence to political heroes and martyrs, to charismatic leaders and ovine followers, to rational planners and reckless adventurers, inspiring great benefactors as well as those who committed the most unspeakable crimes against humanity and against the earth. Marxism is the latest denomination in this family of political religions. Its history, like the history of earlier churches in the religion of progress, illustrates this duality of the faith in progress.

What all believers in progress share is the conviction that, ulti-

24. Felicia Antip, "May We Be Optimistic?" *Tribuna României*, 8(151) (February 15, 1979): 10.

mately, human history makes sense and is imbued with a definable goal. Earthly salvation does beckon. This faith implies that, in the final analysis, all the crimes and stupidities committed and tolerated in the name of progress, all the damage inflicted on people and on our environment, will be outweighed by the benefits that will result from it all. Only future historians will be capable of judging whether this ideology itself was a blessing or a curse.

4

Ideas of Progress in the Third World

CRAWFORD YOUNG

> We are citizens of no mean country and we
> are proud of the land of our birth, of our
> people, our culture and traditions. That pride
> should not be for a romanticized past to
> which we want to cling; nor should it
> encourage exclusiveness or a want of appreci-
> ation of ways other than ours. . . . We have a
> long way to go and much leeway to make up
> before we can take our proper station with
> others in the van of human civilization and
> progress. And we have to hurry, for the time
> at our disposal is limited and the pace of the
> world grows ever swifter. . . .
>
> Nehru, *The Discovery of India*

These reflections by one of the most venerated and influential Third
World statesmen, composed in prison shortly before his elevation to
the premiership, serve as fitting prologue. The idea of progress, that
once-sturdy child of the Enlightenment, may appear frail and infirm
in the postindustrial West. Not so in the Third World; as Jamaican
sociologist Orlando Patterson has argued: "To be a leader or a techno-
crat in any Third World society is, whatever one's ideological position,
at the very least, to be wholly committed to the idea of progress."[1]

1. Orlando Patterson, "The Transformation of the Idea of Progress in the Third

Nehru's thoughts reflect those of the communities which shared his time and space: the postcolonial states of Africa, Asia, and Latin America. They embodied a profound faith in material science, which, blended with liberation, would yield transformation. This elixir of change retained the cultural heritage but distilled from the "romanticized past," which might impede "social betterment." Progress was both a possible dream and a categorical moral imperative; the First and Second worlds, after all, had achieved it. The shackles of poverty, whether viewed as millennial curse or imperialist imposition, simply had to be sundered. Yet, as Patterson further notes, a jarring vector of uncertainty enters and has shaken the serene confidence which suffused the Nehru testament: "once the attempt is made to actualize the idea of progress, the reality of the formidable obstacles involved immediately become apparent. For almost all Third World countries, these obstacles have proven to be insurmountable."[2]

Those who discovered the idea of progress and others who elevated it to a commanding precept of the modern world, such as J.B. Bury and Warren Wagar, or those who mourn its decay, such as Judith Sklar and Raymond Aron, locate the concept exclusively in Western thought.[3] Further, their search for the idea lies in the philosophical realm; Bacon, Descartes, Rousseau, Condorcet, and Smith are numbered among its prophets. To extend our quest to the Third World takes us at once into the political realm; Mao Tse-tung, Kwame Nkrumah, and Gamal Abdel Nasser are its spokesmen. It is less a problematic component of moral discourse than a premise which pervades, even saturates, political expression. To them, the Bury mode of analysis, discovering the idea through the philosophers who fashioned it, is a misplaced exercise. Less striking than the existence of the idea is the well-nigh universal assent it commands. Explanation needs to focus upon the social processes which have shaped this intellectual consensus rather than merely cataloguing those who have pledged their fealty to the common creed.

Before plunging into this task, we may pause to concede the apparent impudence of presuming to contain within a single discussion a universe so diverse and amorphous as a "Third World," a figure of speech which originates as a residual geographic category when the Western and communist sets of states are removed. It is indeed breathtaking to lump polities as disparate as Japan and Equatorial Guinea, Argentina and Nepal. Many have come to speak of a "Fourth World,"

World," American Academy of Arts and Sciences (Western Center) Conference on the Transformation of the Idea of Progress, San Diego, February 1977, p. 2.

2. Ibid., p. 3.

3. J.B. Bury, *The Idea of Progress* (1920; rpt. New York: Dover, 1955); W. Warren Wagar, *Good Tidings: The Belief in Progress from Darwin to Marcuse* (Bloomington: Indiana University Press, 1972); Judith Sklar, *After Utopia: The Decline of Political Faith* (Princeton, N.J.: Princeton University Press, 1957); Raymond Aron, *Les désillusions du progrès* (Paris: Colmann-Lévy, 1969).

composed of the most desperately poor group of countries, especially those concentrated in Africa. Yet despite the vast dissimilarities, for our present purposes a quite common pattern of transmission and reception of the idea of progress may be discerned, vehicled through imperial domination by the "First World" and the revolt against it.

ORIGINS OF THE IDEA OF PROGRESS IN THE THIRD WORLD

First, what precisely is the idea of progress in the Third World? Bury, in giving birth to this debate, defines the concept as past, present, and future movement of civilization in a desirable direction. Charles van Doren proposes that we understand the idea as simply "irreversible ameliorative change."[4] Nannerl Keohane offers a useful basis for understanding present uncertainties about the idea in the West by decomposing the concept into four components: increased human knowledge about the world, increased human power over the world, increased human virtue deriving from this knowledge, and increased happiness as consequence of the other three (see pp. 27ff.). The essence of the Third World variant lies in such *passe-partout* metaphors as "development" and "modernity." Poverty, ignorance, and disease are the demons of antiprogress; "irreversible ameliorative change" is achieved through exorcising them. The remedies of knowledge and power are present in the world and need only be seized. Lucian Pye has aptly termed this universally espoused aspiration to "advancement and progress" as a world culture of modernity, "based on advanced technology and the spirit of science, on a rational view of life, a secular approach to social relations, a feeling for justice in public affairs, and, above all else, on the acceptance in the political realm of the belief that the prime unit of the polity should be the nation-state."[5] We may note, at this juncture, that progress thus conceived lies above all in the material realm.

However universal its diffusion, the idea of progress is a recent arrival in the Third World. The concept of ameliorative change was as foreign to the great cosmologies of the non-Western world as it was to the medieval West. Progress is not immanent in the tenets of Islam, Buddhism, Hinduism, or Confucianism. Individuals or human communities may attain greater perfection by a willing submission to divine will or religious prescription, but the underlying materialism of the Western concept of progress is wholly foreign. Periods of moral decay alternated with moments of regeneration through a return to right conduct.

The encounter between this Eastern world view and the Western idea of progress inevitably posed the question as to whether there was

4. Bury, *Idea of Progress*, p. 2; Charles van Doren, *The Idea of Progress* (New York: Praeger, 1967), pp. 3-16.

5. Lucian W. Pye, *Aspects of Political Development* (Boston: Little, Brown, 1966), p. 8.

inherent contradiction between the two. Within each of the major cosmologies, reformers emerged to reconcile the impulse to modernity with religious doctrine. Muhammed Abduh of Egypt, Jamaluddin Afghani of Persia, the Muhammadiya movement in Indonesia for Islam, Swami Dayananda Saraswati and Swami Vivekenanda for Hinduism were among the many who endeavored to demonstrate that acceptance of technological change was not antithetical to the Eastern heritage.[6] But others perceived the Western idea of change as a threat because it was associated with domination (also with the threat of Christian proselytization) and because many of the emissaries of imperialism held non-Western cultures in singularly low esteem; Macauley spoke for an age in his famous dictum that a shelf of good English books was worth all of the wisdom in India. Reformers argued that there was no necessary antithesis between religious heritage and material progress; the real threat was cultural alienation, which could be averted only by mediating progress through heritage. To postulate incompatibility, in their view, was to invite the annihilation of the latter by the former, and with it the extinction of the faith.

These debates touched above all the religious literati of society. At the peasant base of society, the idea of progress was less philosophical anathema than simply beyond the ken of imagination. Observable reality secreted the concept of the "limited good," identified by George Foster and embellished by James Scott.[7] Village life was a zero-sum game, with absolutely finite resources fixed by the narrow limits of hand tools, household animals, family labor, and often by limited access to land. Within this cognitive frame, the expansion of well-being of some could only be achieved by reduction in returns to others. The boundaries of human possibility were not philosophical but empirical; cultural values, embodied in religion, located virtue in willing submission to this bounded existence but did not create the limits. Indeed, Melford Spiro and Manning Nash, in exploring the issue as to whether the Buddhist world view of Burmese peasants inhibited change, offer convincing testimony that the more exacting otherworldy prescriptions of the faith—extinction of desire—rested quite lightly on most villagers. The onerous requirements of transcendence of self through extinction of desire were attainable only by the monks; for ordinary mortals, if the boundaries of the limited good could be slightly expanded by mundane effort, faith offered no barrier.[8] Not

6. Among the numerous works on this theme, see Marshall G. Hodgson, *The Venture of Islam* (Chicago: University of Chicago Press, 1974), vol. 3; Donald S. Smith, *Religion and Political Development* (Boston: Little, Brown, 1970); and Melford E. Spiro, *Buddhism and Society* (New York: Harper & Row, 1970).

7. George Foster, "Peasant Society: The Image of the Limited Good," *American Anthropologist*, 62 (April 1965): 293-315; James C. Scott, *Political Ideology in Malaysia* (New Haven, Conn.: Yale University Press, 1968).

8. Spiro, *Buddhism and Society*; Manning Nash, *The Golden Road to Modernity* (New York: Wiley, 1965).

only the concept of ameliorative change but the sense of the cultural threat of Westernization as ransom of progress were remote to most, though the symbolic resources and political mobilization potential of Islam did, in certain times and places, activate the rural masses against Western intrusion.[9]

The idea of progress, after its birth in the West, was carried to the Third World in the baggage trains of imperial conquest beginning in the fifteenth century. Here we may usefully distinguish three patterns of internalization of the premise of change: (1) the Latin American model (including the Caribbean), based upon radical submergence of indigenous cultures; (2) later colonialism in Africa and Asia, where the superstructure of Western rule effected great changes at the level of material technology and values but eventually retreated before anticolonial nationalism; and (3) a handful of polities in Africa and Asia, such as Japan, China, Thailand, Afghanistan, Iran, and Ethiopia, which staved off conquest by defensive modernization. Each of these merits brief exploration.

European expansion in the Western hemisphere occurred before the emergence of the idea of progress in the West. The major centers of Indian civilization, in Mexico and the Andes, were decapitated by tiny bands of treasure-seeking conquistadors, accompanied by priests whose quest for a harvest of souls was informed by the spirit of the Crusades, and the bitter Iberian struggle to extirpate the influence of Moor and Jew. The result was a demographic and cultural holocaust for indigenous populations. Spanish and Portuguese language and culture were swiftly established at the summit, less by conscious design than by the unexamined assumption that royal and spiritual domain should be extended by the natural law of conquest. The structure of earlier religions was shattered by the razing of the temples and decimation of the priesthood; from their rubble the cathedrals of the new faith militant were erected. The sedentary and fixed populations within reach of centralized state structures were incorporated within the new apparatus of hegemony; the decentralized societies of both Americas had the option of retreat beyond immediate reach of the colonizers.

Epidemics and exploitation took a tremendous toll, entirely depopulating the Caribbean islands, while in Mexico and Guatemala Indian populations fell to one-seventh of the preconquest levels during the first century of Spanish rule.[10] From the early days, a crucial category of racially mixed persons emerged, and these generally identified with Iberian culture. A social continuum thus developed, whose apex was Iberian and Catholic. Mobility was possible, not only through genetic

9. For example, in the various Mahdi movements, or religious reform orders such as Wahabiya, Senusiya, Qadariya, among others.

10. See Eric Wolf, *Sons of the Shaking Earth* (Chicago: University of Chicago Press, 1962), pp. 196-99.

mestization but also by cultural migration through the adoption of European language, dress, lifestyle, and the Catholic religion.

In the plantation economies of the Caribbean and lowland South America (and the American south), economies based on servile labor led to massive importation of African slaves (and, in the nineteenth century, indentured Asians in a few places). Even where the African component was predominant, the cultural dislocation of uprooting and prolonged European hegemony yielded contemporary polities in which immigrant culture was predominant. This was most completely evident in the Hispanic isles (Cuba and the Dominican Republic) but also holds for the English-speaking Caribbean; only Haiti, with its early slave revolution, is a partial exception.[11]

The nation-state system in Latin America arose from the revolt of the socially hegemonic Creole elites against the mercantile-absolutist colonial state at the beginning of the nineteenth century. The new states viewed themselves as culturally European, even though some— such as the Andes republics and Paraguay—were genetically predominantly Indian. There was thus no sense of moral ambivalence in the reception of the idea of progress; the social elites of Latin America were eager to assimilate European currents of thought. The primary nineteenth-century vehicle for progress was the concept of the liberal state, as modified in dialectic with the corpus of Catholic social thought with its corporatist implications. The liberal state, in truth, proved an imperfect instrument of ameliorative change in much of Latin America, as the image of progress was juxtaposed to the reality of social fragmentation, rural paternalism, and coercive authoritarianism. Yet the idea of the liberal state remained the primary incubator of progress until well into the twentieth century.[12]

In much of Asia and Africa, colonialism resulted in the domination but not the submergence of the indigenous culture and society. Its duration was much briefer than it was in Latin America—really less than a century in most areas, with scattered exceptions such as Algeria, South Africa, the Philippines, parts of India, and Indonesia. Here the structures of domination imposed a new state apparatus, ultimately to become the framework for the postcolonial nation-state, which so transformed cultural geography. The new set of power relationships

11. In the Haitian case, European hegemony was quite short-lived, as the French sugar economy of the "pearl of the Antilles" took off only in the eighteenth century, then was swept away by Toussaint L'Ouverture and Henri Christophe at the beginning of the nineteenth century. The predominance of Creole rather than French as the spoken language is evidence of the incomplete assimilation. See Robert I. Rotberg, *Haiti: The Politics of Squalor* (Boston: Houghton Mifflin, 1971).

12. See, especially on these issues, Morris J. Blackman and Ronald G. Hellman, eds., *Terms of Conflict: Ideology in Latin American Politics* (Philadelphia, Pa.: Institute for the Study of Human Issues, 1977); Rex Crawford, *A Century of Latin American Thought* (Cambridge, Mass.: Harvard University Press, 1961); James Malloy, ed., *Authoritarianism and Corporatism in Latin America* (Pittsburgh, Pa.: University of Pittsburgh Press, 1977).

radically altered extant systems of status, which became increasingly contingent on proximity to the colonial structures. The political economy of colonialism closed down earlier pathways to wealth, and the mercantilist order of European rule forced those seeking accumulation into linkage with the extractive mechanisms of the colonial state or, as in many parts of colonial Africa, entirely monopolized wealth within the expatriate community. Social mobility was channeled into the status pathways designated by the colonizer and came to be tightly linked to Western education. An increasingly large and visible portion of roles conferring status and relative prosperity required formal educational qualifications, available through completion of schooling whose higher levels, in the colonial period and beyond, were primarily staffed by Europeans.[13] Among the orientations transmitted by these multiple structures of domination was the idea of progress, rendered ambivalent, however, by its very association with Westernization.

The third pattern of the idea of progress in the Third World, that of defensive modernization, occurred in a small number of Afro-Asian states where, through a combination of diplomacy, strength, and good fortune, Western conquest was averted. The globalizing thrust of Western imperialism became evident by the second half of the nineteenth century. The more perspicacious could identify the sources of this thrust in the knowledge and power attributable to the material engines of progress: science, technology, and industry. Most important of all was power; in the first instance, monarchs such as Menelik of Ethiopia and Mongkut of Thailand needed to gain access to military technology. More broadly, an understanding of Western modes of thought facilitated the diplomatic ingenuity required to deflect the conquerers; Thailand first employed foreigners as drillmasters and advisers to the foreign ministry.[14] Sheer military force also helped; Ethiopian survival was assured by Menelik's defeat of several thousand Italians in 1896, and the martial prowess of Pathan warriors made occupation of Afghanistan simply too costly for Britain.

Success in defensive modernization required opening the gates wide enough to allow the idea of progress in. The first to develop this craft was Peter the Great in seventeenth-century Russia, when a technology gap was beginning to become perceptible. By the nineteenth century, the chasm was wider, and extensive if selective adaptation was indispensable. Students were dispatched to Europe, and some foreign personnel were retained by the state. The artifacts of Western industry were admitted in deference to the insistence by European emissaries

13. For a useful discussion of these themes, see James S. Coleman, ed., *Education and Political Development* (Princeton, N.J.: Princeton University Press, 1965).

14. See David J. Steinberg, ed., *In Search of Southeast Asia* (New York: Praeger, 1971), pp. 114-16. King Mongkut and his chief minister, Suriyaivong, are described as coping with an ominous set of British demands in 1855 by plying the English envoy with cigars and wine while "casually revealing detailed acquaintance with European economic theory and the principles of good government."

on the virtues of trade as the hallmark of civilization. While those directing the defensive modernization process were skeptical about the intrinsic virtues of the West or the happiness that might flow from selective Westernization, they were persuaded that the knowledge and power available in the West constituted not only ameliorative change but was essential for survival.

The most remarkable example of defensive modernization is Japan. Elements of Japanese success are evidently rooted in its history and culture: an unusually homogeneous society amenable to purposive collective action and relatively well endowed with a literate class. These sturdy strands of cultural material, however, were not woven into a conscious creed of modernization until the threat of uncontrollable Western intrusion loomed menacingly by the 1850s. The Japanese response is commonly dated with the Meiji Restoration in 1868, bringing in its train sweeping political and social transformations that released the country's energies for a deliberate modernization program. Japan thus organized itself to deflect Western economic and political expansion from its shores; more than any other defensive modernizer, Japan was able to determine the cultural terms of its model of progress. Western technology was massively assimilated, but the social impact of industrialization was mediated through the unchallenged primacy of the Japanese cultural heritage. Even the disaster of World War II and the American political (though not economic) occupation which followed did not subvert the Japanese synthesis of material progress and cultural heritage. Indeed, shorn of militarism, Japanese capitalism entered a period of unprecedented dynamism in the postwar period, which opened the extraordinary possibility that this Asian nation might in the next century become the world's premier industrial power. Perhaps because the Japanese pathway is so thoroughly grounded in its own cultural heritage, its contribution to the Third World vision of progress has been limited; few southern hemisphere statesmen make pilgrimages to examine the Japanese experience. One may doubt whether the defensive modernization strategy is easily available to those whose political, economic, and cultural strategies are more heavily impacted by the Western imperial era.

The process of transmission of the idea of progress to the Third World was affected by gradually altering perceptions in the Western world. When imperial expansion began in the fifteenth century, there was not a marked disparity in material technology between Europe and the rest of the world. The most important distinction to the first mariners who sailed the uncharted seas was between Christian and "heathen." However, concepts of racial arrogance began to gather force, to come into full flower, in the nineteenth century.[15] As colonial

15. The process is well chronicled by Philip D. Curtin, *The Image of Africa* (Madison: University of Wisconsin Press, 1964).

conquest reached flood tide, the assumption of Western superiority—the nether side of the idea of progress—was scarcely open to question in Europe. Colonial expansion had to be justified primarily to domestic opinion, some of which required persuasion that the "white man's burden" really was profitable to the metropole. In return for the new markets, raw materials, and national aggrandizement presumed to accrue to colonizers, the conquerer offered the blessings of progress in the form of what was usually termed "civilization."

In the political field, this meant a minimalist administrative apparatus, which applied the "principles of good government," translated as enforcement of hegemony of the colonial state, a rudimentary legal apparatus, and fiscal machinery to support this structure. For areas not preempted by a universal religion, Christian evangelization was seen as a necessary condition of uplift. Trade with European mercantile houses was widely believed to have powerful redeeming impact.[16] The higher purposes of mankind were served by the *mise en valeur* of the natural resources of the colonies. These materials otherwise lay idle, as the colonized lacked the capacity to exploit them. As a disinterested service to humanity, *mise en valeur* created the infrastructure of a modern economy for the colonized and made the raw materials available for Western industry. This doctrine was elaborated into a high-minded creed of colonial progress by Lord Lugard in his "dual mandate": tutelage in good government and exploitation in trusteeship of natural resources. Lugard took the gathering protest against imperial rule as validation of its mission: "If there is unrest and a desire for independence, as in India and Egypt, it is because we have taught the people the value of liberty and freedom, which for centuries these peoples had not known. Their very discontent is a measure of their progress."[17] However, the notion of the *mission civilisatrice* as an eleemosynary charter of progress would not long be so comfortably rationalized.

In its waning years, colonialism required a much more elaborated defense. The gathering force of Asian and African anticolonial nationalism and the slowly eroding self-confidence in the West on the legitimacy of domination called for a more active commitment to progress. Gradually, the concept of progress as *mise en valeur* and *mission civilisatrice* was superseded by the goal of "colonial development." This doctrine pledged state-directed economic change accompanied by social policies deemed to assure advancement of the subject population. In Africa, more or less conscious definitions of educational policies were first devised in the 1920s. In 1940, Britain enacted a Colonial

16. Some missionaries, however, viewed traders as a depraved lot from whom their charges should be isolated; see Barbara A. Yates, *The Missions and Educational Development in Belgian Africa 1876-1908*, Ph.D. dissertation, Columbia University, 1967.

17. Frederick Lugard, *The Dual Mandate in British Tropical Africa* (Edinburgh: W. Blockwood & Sons, 1922), p. 618.

Development and Welfare Act; in the authoritative words of Lord Hailey, "a new concept ... had come to be increasingly accepted ... namely, that active State intervention was a necessary lever to the amelioration of social conditions. The aim of good Colonial administration thus came to be defined positively as the promotion of economic and social advance in order to provide the essential basis for political self-rule."[18] In the postwar period, with Asia independent or in armed revolt, other colonizers hastened to follow suit actively to promote socioeconomic uplift in their remaining dependent territories; Belgium launched a well-publicized ten-year plan for public investment in 1950, and France established a Fund for Economic and Social Development (FIDES) in 1946. Until the late 1950s, however, "development" was intended by Belgium and France as an alternative to the nationalist goal of independence. The efficiency of the European colonial mandarinate and the superior resources of the metropole were held to guarantee swifter and safer progress than the adventure of self-rule.

The era of defensive colonialism in Africa coincided with a period of rapidly expanding state revenues fueled by the postwar commodity boom, which ran out of steam only in 1955. The political urgency of these development expenditures and swelling resources available to the colonial state, abetted by relatively modest supplements from the metropolitan treasury, did give real content to the welfare pretensions of terminal colonialism. Formerly skeletal educational and health systems were pushed out into the rural periphery. Roads and water supplies appeared in response to the swelling cry for "amenities." A wide battery of technical services—agricultural, veterinary, sanitation —were added to the older law-and-order infrastructure of regional administration.

The postwar metamorphosis of official dogmas of progress had a powerful impact in extending the sphere of state activity. At the same time, there was a curious paternalism to its legacy. Colonial apologetics always rested on the premise that the powerful were mandated by history to define the future for their subjects. The more comprehensive the colonially defined blueprints for social advancement became, the more pervasive was the paternalism which suffused its inner spirit. The agenda for amelioration was fixed by the state, perhaps abetted by mission partners. The superior wisdom of the state and risks of recourse to immature judgments of its subjects were effortless assumptions of the mandarinate.

PROGRESS AND CULTURAL SELF-AFFIRMATION

The doctrine of progress in the Third World is, in a crucial sense, dialectical. If imperial transmission is thesis, then liberation struggle is antithesis. It is the fusion through struggle of these opposites that is

18. Lord Hailey, *An Africa Survey* (London: Oxford University Press, 1957), p. 203.

the inner core of the creed. Nationalism took form as an ideology of liberation through an increasingly comprehensive critique of colonialism. In its earliest Third World form—the rejection of the absolutist peninisular bureaucracy of the Spanish royal house in early nineteenth-century Latin America—the doctrine was a relatively simple and unadorned demand for local rule and the denunciation of mercantile and bureaucratic abuse. Neither nationalism nor anticolonialism had yet undergone much doctrinal development, and the adversary was only the relatively underdeveloped eighteenth-century colonial state.

Twentieth-century Afro-Asian nationalism took form around the bedrock idea of the right to self-determination and the illegitimacy of foreign rule. The vexed question of what constitutes a "people," who are entitled to exercise this act of sovereign will, was resolved through ultimate acceptance of the imperial partition itself as generative of the human collectivities to claim *their* birthright. By degree, the arbitrary territorial units of partition claimed the sanctity of the modern nation-state. Thus we encounter such curious memorabilia as Ruben Um Nyobe's assertion that "God alone had created the Cameroon" (with Bismarck as silent partner), or the rococo claims of Cabinda separatists that their territory had been bound to Portugal by separate treaty and was thus not properly part of Angola. An estimated one hundred thousand perished in the forlorn struggle to sustain Timor as a territory whose identity derives from Portuguese occupation, and a bitter struggle by a suddenly coalescent Sahroui people was undertaken to avert partition between Morocco and Mauritania.

As nationalism gained momentum, the negative valuation of colonialism and its works became total. Colonialism, conceived in force, born in blood, and matured in oppression, was seen as devoid of redeeming features. Fanon gave voice to these views:

> Colonialism generally manages, at the turning point when history and the nation reject it, to maintain itself as a value. It is not true that it was a good thing for France to have made of Algeria what it is today. . . .
>
> French colonialism will not be legitimized by the Algerian people. No spectacular undertaking will make us forget the legalized racism, the illiteracy, the flunkyism generated and maintained in the very depth of the consciousness of our people. . . .
>
> Instead of integrating colonialism, conceived as the birth of a new world, in Algerian history, we have made it an unhappy, execrable accident, the only meaning of which was to have inexcusably retarded the coherent evolution of the Algerian society and nation.[19]

In its radical form, Afro-Asian nationalism thus refuted all of the claims of colonialism. The *mission civilisatrice* was cultural aggres-

19. Frantz Fanon, *Toward the African Revolution* (New York: Grove Press, 1967), p. 101.

sion; the dual mandate was naked exploitation, and the welfare development program was a cynical fraud. Far from introducing ameliorative change, colonialism had retarded the "coherent evolution" of society. Rather than representing the farthest point of progress, the colonial powers embodied decadence and decay. "Most of the European nations," wrote Nehru, "are full of mutual hatreds and past conflicts and injustices."[20]

True, not all anticolonial nationalism hinged upon the root-and-branch rejection of the imperial legacy. Leaders such as Habib Bourguiba of Tunisia and Leopold Senghor of Senegal made no secret of their admiration for French culture. Kwame Nkrumah, an uncompromising foe of imperialism, nonetheless spoke of the "vast, untapped reservoir of peace and goodwill toward Britain, would she but divest herself of the outmoded, moth-eaten trappings of two centuries ago, and present herself to her colonial peoples in a new and shining vestment of peace and love, and give us a guiding hand in working out our own destinies."[21] Nonetheless, the equation of liberation with progress was unequivocal for all.

A particularly thorny aspect of the dialectic synthesis of the idea of progress was the treatment of the cultural heritage. Nationalist liberation is fundamentally an assertion of self that cannot be denied. At the same time, most nationalist leaders and intellectuals had passed through the portals of the essentially Western educational systems and had been profoundly influenced by Western philosophical discourse, particularly of the Left—liberalism, socialism, and Marxism. Their ideological programs for change were derived from these doctrines, yet a place for affirmation of self through cultural heritage was required. The discovery of India, for Nehru, yielded both "terrifying glimpses of dark corridors which seem to lead back to primeval night" and, at the same time, "a cultural unity amidst diversity . . . a myth and an idea, a dream and a vision . . . the fulness and warmth of the day about her." Change she must, yet her store of wisdom must be treasured.[22]

Various symbolic reconstructions have been proposed, which both reject and incorporate the past. Senghor developed an elaborate cosmology, influenced by Father Teilhard de Chardin.[23] The ultimate triumph of human civilization would result from a cosmic fusion of world cultures at a future "omega point." To prepare the ground, each

20. Jawaharlal Nehru, *Discovery of India* (1946; rpt. London: Meridian Books, 1956), p. 563.

21. Kwame Nkrumah, *Ghana: An Autobiography* (Edinburgh: Thomas Nelson & Sons, 1959), p. 103.

22. Nehru, *Discovery of India*, pp. 578-79.

23. Chardin was himself an architect of philosophic synthesis, much influenced by his prolonged immersion in Chinese culture.

cultural heritage had to vitalize itself—in the African case, through the doctrine of *négritude*.[24]

Nkrumah used an appropriated myth of the past as warrant for the future by christening the reborn Gold Coast as "Ghana" even though this great medieval state did not geographically coincide with its contemporary namesake. "The name of Ghana," Nkrumah explained,

> is rooted deeply in ancient African history.... It kindles in the imagination of modern African youth the grandeur and the achievements of a great medieval civilization which our ancestors developed many centuries before European penetration.... It is reported that Egyptian, European, and Asiatic students attended the great and famous universities and other institutions of higher learning that flourished in Ghana during the medieval period to learn philosophy, mathematics, medicine, and law ... we take pride in the name, not out of romanticism, but as an inspiration for the future.[25]

The cultural heritage invoked by Senghor and Nkrumah was carefully abstracted and detached from any concrete referents which would constrain the blueprints for advance. More specific legacies of the past, such as chiefs, were viewed by Nkrumah as a feudal execrescence blocking the path to change. The creed of "authenticity" put forward by Mobutu Sese Seko of Zaire as national ideology similarly used the past while in effect rejecting its specific characteristics. Recourse to authenticity, Mobutu argued, was not to forsake modernity in favor of ancestral values but was rather a dynamic method of progress without alienation by asserting cultural heritage while pursuing material change.

Mao Tse-tung went further in the specific repudiation of the Confucian heritage as a means to moral regeneration of the peasant mass. Progress, in its Marxist-Leninist vision, required that the age-old ethic of deference to extant social hierarchies be shattered. The organization of the "speak bitterness" campaign in the early 1950s was the catharsis. In being forced to externalize anger at landlord exploitation, the peasant was liberated from the stultifying ethic of submission and internalization of resentment which Confucian socialization had induced.[26]

Another radical synthesis, of growing significance in lands of Islamic heritage, was integralist Islam. This movement, embodied in different ways by Libyan leader Wanis Muammar al-Qadafi, Ayatollah Khomeini in Iran, and the Muslim Brotherhood in Egypt and Sudan,

---

24. Leopold Senghor, "What is Negritude?" reprinted in *The Ideologies of the Developing Nations*, ed. Paul E. Sigmund (New York: Praeger, 1963).

25. Kwame Nkrumah, *I Speak of Freedom* (New York: Praeger, 1961), pp. 67-68.

26. See Richard Solomon, *Mao's Revolution and the Chinese Political Culture* (Berkeley: University of California Press, 1971).

demands a total severance of modernity from Westernization and its evil twin, secularism. Ameliorative change was taken to be possible, indeed necessary, in the delimited sphere of material life; however, such change was a poisoned gift if tied to the decadence and corruption of the West. Material progress was beneficent only if suffused with the just social order inspired by Islam. Muslim Brotherhood ideologist Muhammad Al-Ghazzali argued: "Everybody knows that capitalism is founded on robbery and, what is worse, that it spends all that it steals on the satisfaction of base desires and the spreading of moral, social, and political chaos."[27] Unless guided by Islam, progress in the form of secular materialism leads inexorably to the sort of pervasive corruption symbolized by the Pahlavi state in Iran. An Islamic socialism would permit harnessing new technological possibilities to social justice. Integralist Islam is a combative reassertion of faith and heritage; it ferociously rejects secularism, capitalism, Marxism, and reformist Islam. Yet it goes far beyond mere revivalism and theocracy. Whatever its prospects for survival, the Khomeini Islamic republic in Iran does not repudiate the idea of progress. Rather it seeks to absorb, dominate, and redefine it as handmaiden of a perfected religious order rather than as subverter of the faith.

However, whether the Khomeini synthesis of integralist Islam and material progress is either economically or politically viable is quite another question. The patriarch of Iranian Shi'ism may will the end of prosperity in piety, but he also denies to the officially invested government the means rationally to pursue material goals. Although destruction of the Pahlavi state won applause from a broad spectrum of society, fervor for the new order of the integralist Islamic republic is much narrower. The struggle against social forces, both in the Iranian heartland and the non-Persian (and frequently non-Shi'a) periphery, which do not share the Khomeini vision of the righteous society, is likely to intensify. In this contest, enforcement of piety may well eclipse material progress.

It is interesting to compare the fundamentalism of the Wahabi affiliation of the Saudi ruling house, or of a Qadafi, with the would-be Islamic republic of Khomeini. In the Sunni lands, such as Libya and Saudi Arabia, integral Islam is upheld by political leaders, whose fusion of material and religious goals has a different texture. In both these instances, the vast petroleum revenues are committed to sweeping modernization programs, as well as the promotion of religious causes at home and abroad. In Shi'ite Iran, the relatively structured religious hierarchy has assumed informal but no less direct political power, which gives theological goals more weight. Further, there is little real dissent from the fundamentalist religious philosophy promoted by the state in Libya and Saudi Arabia whereas in Iran the

27. Quoted in Nadav Safran, *Egypt in Search of Political Community* (Cambridge, Mass.: Harvard University Press, 1961), p. 239.

currents of secularism in the center and cultural autonomy on the periphery flow strongly, forcing the religious leaders into bitter struggle to impose their views.

In different ways, a common theme observable in the absorption of the idea of progress in the Third World was rejection of the premise that modernity was defined by Western values. "Progress" was not a seamless web, bound by cultural threads of European provenience. The ideology of the *mission civilisatrice*, central to colonial philosophy, was repudiated. The peculiarly coercive metaphors of Western analysis had imposed the image of the modern-traditional dichotomy. The alchemy of this figure of speech had rendered the non-Western cultural heritage as "traditional" and, therefore, ascriptive, static, and past-centered: the incarnation of antiprogress. To repatriate the idea of progress, some form of valorization of cultural heritage was requisite. Ameliorative change, therefore, was not contingent on self-alienation but was discovered through self-realization.

Above all, the vision of progress that was universally accepted was material. The ethical superiority of Western civilization was dubious; the advance in Western science and technology, essential instruments for environmental mastery, was indisputable. Here we find an intriguing intersection with the transformation of the idea of progress in the West. Confidence in ameliorative change is largely unshaken in the scientific disciplines, where generally agreed standards of measurement exist. Doubt grows stronger as we enter the more incommensurable domains of arts and morals. Murray Krieger points out that technique and critique may have improved, but there is no certain basis for claiming that the intrinsic worth of poetry or painting is greater (see pp. 463ff.). Frederick Olafson is even more skeptical in treating the impact of progress on ethics, suggesting that it tends to function as a justificatory ideology that really dispenses with independent ethical criteria (see pp. 526ff.).

PROGRESS AS DEVELOPMENT

Thus, if we return to the Keohane formulation, we may suggest that the idea of progress as assimilated in Third World thought gives full credence to the knowledge and power components. The enormous investment in educational systems, which consumes a quarter of many Third World budgets, is eloquent demonstration of this point. Even more firmly rooted is the conviction that increasing knowledge— material science—is convertible into greater power over environment; armed with technology, the state can wrest abundance from a reluctant nature. This granite axiom is the foundation for the ubiquitous development plans which articulate the dream of progress. However, the association of accelerating Western material advance with cumulating virtue is as dubious to the Third World as it is to the Western postmaterialists identified by Samuel Barnes (see pp. 415ff.) and

Ronald Inglehart.[28] The most immediate Third World experience of the West was through conquest and exploitation, made possible precisely by the surge of postmedieval knowledge and power. The Western claim to superior "civilization" was daily belied by observed imperial behavior: racism and oppression. Most doubtful of all, in West and non-West, is that higher orders of satisfaction and happiness spill over from Western material progress. Here divergent reasoning leads to a common conclusion. For the affluent, "postmaterialists," the new order of material security made possible by the first two dimensions of progress leads to new dissatisfactions arising from an increasing preoccupation with the aesthetic and moral components of life either untouched by or actually threatened by material advance. In the Third World, the postmaterialist generation has yet to emerge, but there is a general conviction that permitting Western cultural values to migrate with science and technology is a fatal prescription for massive alienation.

Although only the material aspects of the idea of progress were embraced, at the hour of its greatest achievements, in the 1950s and 1960s, Third World nationalism exhibited a mood of exhilarating confidence in their efficacy. The political triumph over imperialism— bitter and bloody in Indochina and Algeria, almost effortless in a number of former African and Asian colonial domains—built a mood of expectation, of exuberance which eroded in the 1970s. The stunning defeats of Western powers once believed invincible in the military domain contributed powerfully to this triumphal mood. Vietnam held at bay first the French, then American expeditionary forces armed with overwhelming firepower. Outmanned and underequipped Algerian guerrillas, at the cost of a million deaths, shattered the centennial myth of *Algérie française*. Egypt bearded imperialism by seizing and efficiently operating the Suez Canal, winning through diplomacy what was lost on the battlefield to Britain, France, and Israel. Fidel Castro and his small band of guerrillas in the Sierra Maestre provoked the collapse of a corrupted citadel of imperialism ninety miles from the Florida shores.

These victories in the political realm at the time seemed easily translatable into economic transformation. "Seek ye first the political kingdom," went the oft-quoted Nkrumah aphorism, "and all else shall be added unto you." Such sentiments are echoed in the ebullient mood revealed in Nasser's *Philosophy of the Revolution*.[29] At the extreme, this might be manifest in declarations of faith in the romanticism of revolutionary transformation expressed by Sukarno, who declared, "I

28. Ronald Inglehart, *The Silent Revolution* (Princeton, N.J.: Princeton University Press, 1977).
29. Gamal Abdel Nasser, *Philosophy of the Revolution* (Cairo: Information Department, 1954).

am inspired by it, I am fascinated by it, I am completely absorbed by it, I am crazed, I am obsessed by the Romanticism of Revolution."[30]

There was much to support this optimistic vision of progress within reach. Western social science was in a positivist mood, with development and modernization theory in the ascendant. Economic growth theory brought the good tidings of the Rostowian "takeoff." The Soviet experience appeared to demonstrate the capacity of the state, through socialist planning, to transform a backward society within the time span of a few five-year plans. Even more inspiring was the example of the Chinese revolution, which—before its post-Mao heirs confessed its technological flaws—seemed to demonstrate an egalitarian escape route from famine and poverty within a generation by the marriage of nationalism and socialist revolution.

Progress, then, as a possible dream, is an inspirational theme in the political testaments of the towering figures of this era—Nehru, Nasser, Nkrumah, Ho Chi Minh, Nyerere, Castro. In more bureaucratic prose, the vision is inscribed in the early five-year plans of the new states. The ideological panoply was broad, but the center of gravity was radical and populist, often socialist. Liberation, cultural resurgence, science, and technology: these are the core dimensions of the idea of progress in the Third World.

Of crucial importance in the universal diffusion of this concept is the existence of a reference point in the First and Second worlds. Here the contrast with the ambiguities of progress in the West is fundamental. Aron points to the paradox of moral disorientation in Western societies in the face of a material success never before imagined. Societies, he argues, do not measure themselves against their past but against their ambitions for the future.[31] We would amend this observation by noting that the future, for advanced industrial societies, is an uncharted sea. For the Third World, the standard of measurement is advanced industrial society itself, with its unparalleled abundance. If we assume that growing segments of First (and presumably Second) World societies have assurance of a satisfactory level of material security, then the future agenda for amelioration lies in the problematic domain of spiritual, psychic, and moral fulfillment. For the Third World, the agenda of progress is starkly clear: to match the material accomplishments of the first two worlds. This elemental fact explains why an idea of progress is both so universal and so material: the extension to the Third World of the concept of "catching up with the United States" cited by Moses Abramovitz (see pp. 260-61). The very existence of the empirical referent serves to override doubts as to whether "progress" is attainable or good.

30. Sukarno, Independence Day speech, August 17, 1960.
31. Aron, *Les désillusions du progrès*, pp. vii-xxiii, 333.

We may detect here an echo of the Condorcet vision cited by Keohane, that human progress in Africa and Asia "is likely to be more rapid and certain than our own because they can receive from us everything that we have had to find out for ourselves." Joined to this was the equally comforting Condorcet assumption that all good things go together; progress could be comprehensive and not a series of anguishing trade-offs. In this perspective, we can also understand why the "limits to growth" debate in the West has so little resonance in the Third World, why a Brazilian delegate to the 1972 Stockholm conference on global environmental problems could invite the developed world to "send us your pollution,"[32] why the extensive clearing of the Amazonian forest for development could provoke concern in the West but not in Brazil.

Another salient divergence between Western and non-Western concepts of progress derives from the differential psychological impact of three calamities that shook the self-confidence of the West. World War I, the Great Depression, and World War II, all within three decades, in their colossal human destruction, ended the serene optimism of 1913. Though the prolonged period of rapid Western growth after World War II partly restored the faith, it jostled with Orwellian images of the ultimate destiny of modern society and postmaterialistic disillusionments. The Third World was affected by these events; huge numbers of colonial soldiers were conscripted to help fight the world wars (ninety-two Senegalese batallions fought on the Western front in World War I), and Third World producers suffered a devastating loss of income through collapse of primary commodity markets in 1930. But the Third World clearly bore no responsibility for the horrors of the holocaust at Hiroshima, for economic crises which threw millions into the breadlines, or for the implausible carnage of the two wars.

PROGRESS AS PROBLEMATIC:
THE RISE OF DISILLUSION

Still, the optimism of an earlier decade relative to the ease of attainment of progress has eroded on a broad front. Models of growth and transformation which once seemed alluring have lost their luster. Many have come to believe that only sternly authoritarian regimes can provide guidance to the promised land of plenty, but the bankruptcy of many of these illuminates their potential costs. Diverse limitations of the nation-state itself have become more apparent, and the possibility of large-scale regression is now clear. Many signs bear witness to the new mood of pessimism for Africa: French radical agronomist René Dumont first gave voice to doubts as to the direction of change in

---

32. Charles W. Anderson, Fred R. von der Mehden, and Crawford Young, *Issues of Political Development*, rev. ed. (Englewood Cliffs, N.J.: Prentice-Hall, 1974), p. viii.

L'Afrique Noire est mal partie, soon followed by the more despairing *L'Afrique peut-elle partir?* of Albert Meister. The sense of progressive nationalist mission in Ousmane Sembene's *God's Bits of Wood* gives way to the biting social criticism of his film *Xala*; James Ngugi of Kenya follows the same trajectory from *Weep Not, Child* to *Petals of Blood.* Ayi Kwei Armah conveys the disillusionments of independence in the feculent imagery of *The Beautyful Ones Are Not Yet Born.* Robert Heilbroner carries the mood of gloom to its farthest point, concluding, "the answer to whether we can conceive of the future other than as a continuation of the darkness, cruelty, and disorder of the past seems to me to be no; and to the question of whether worse impends, yes."[33]

In the 1970s, the models of growth which had once offered inspiration evaporated one by one. The "takeoff" models of growth on Western lines, although they had some successes (Ivory Coast, Malaysia, Taiwan), often yielded massive corruption and gigantic misallocations (Iran) or accentuated inequality (Brazil). The intellectual prestige of socialism remained high, and indeed a new wave of Third World Marxist-Leninist states appeared in the 1970s (Afghanistan, South Yemen, Ethiopia, Angola, Mozambique, Congo-Brazzaville, Benin, among others). As Alfred Meyer notes, these leaders—as often military officers as professional revolutionaries—"proclaim themselves the enlightened vanguard of the exploited, in the name of which they establish their dictatorships." Although they claim to be building the economic base for socialism in societies where fully developed capitalism does not yet exist, yet the very absence today of an authoritative world communist center, as Kenneth Jowitt observes, permits "self-designated 'scientific socialist' African elites to avoid the hard identity choice of bloc alignment internationally and exclusive political choices domestically."[34]

Indeed, the concrete designs for progress through socialist transformation had lost their luster. Long vanished was the kind of admiration once felt for Soviet achievements by Nehru, who spoke of "the tremendous educational and cultural achievements of the masses," the Russians as "almost wholly devoid of racism," while "no other country today presents such a politically solid and economically well-balanced

---

33. René Dumont, *L'Afrique Noire es mal partie* (Paris: Editions du Seuil, 1962); Albert Meister, *L'Afrique peut-elle partir?* (Paris: Editions du Seuil, 1966); Ousmane Sembene, *God's Bits of Wood* (Garden City, N.Y.: Doubleday, 1962); James Ngugi, *Weep Not Child* (London: Heinemann, 1964), and *Petals of Blood* (New York: Dutton, 1978); Ayi Kwei Armah, *The Beautyful Ones Are Not Yet Born* (London: Heinemann, 1968); Robert L. Heilbroner, *An Inquiry into the Human Prospect* (New York: Norton, 1974), p. 22.

34. Kenneth Jowitt, in Carl G. Rosberg and Thomas M. Callaghy, *Socialism in Sub-Saharan Africa* (Berkeley: University of California Institute of International Studies, 1979), p. 144.

picture. [35] The Chinese model, which admittedly attracted more often devotional praise than the truer flattery of imitation, was tarnished by the confessions of material flaws which followed Mao's death, as well as the unseemly alliance in which the People's Republic was discovered in the struggle against the social imperialism of "the new czars." Cuba won widespread respect for its political feat of building a socialist society in the face of unrelenting American hostility, with imposing achievements in the social welfare field. While the prestige yielded by these accomplishments gave Cuba a weight in Third World councils which belied its modest size, the heavy reliance upon Soviet aid and its economic stagnation devalued the model.[36] Vietnam, inspirational in its military struggle against colonialism and imperialism, was tarnished in triumph by the tawdry ransoming of the Sino-Vietnamese populace, its subimperialism in Cambodia and Laos, the blockages of the socialist economy in the South, and the revelation of a Vietnamese Gulag with as many as eight hundred thousand prisoners.[37] Beyond the Marxist family of states, once-prestigious experiments in socialist construction—Velasco's Peru, Nasser's Egypt, Nyerere's Tanzania—encountered serious setbacks. Third World socialism had become an idea without a model.

In Latin America, confidence in the idea of progress was also jolted by the sudden end in the 1960s of what had appeared to be a powerful if not irresistible trend toward democracy in the 1950s, the demise of old dictatorships. It was precisely in the most economically advanced Latin American states where a new form of polity emerged, well labeled by Guillermo O'Donnell as "the bureaucratic-authoritarian state."[38] The social mobilization of the "popular sectors" produced by modernization generates pressures, O'Donnell argues, which can be contained in a capitalist framework only by the erection of a military-bureaucratic leviathan state disposed to silence dissent and demobilize restive lower strata by terror. On the other end of the political spectrum, a small band of Khmer Rouge cadres under Pol Pot tried to compensate for their weakness by a sanguinary reign of terror and brutality which has few historical parallels; it was their apparent logic that only through ruthless destruction of the old society could a new socialist order be securely erected.

The natural course of Third World modernization exhibited certain disconcerting pathologies, which no one seemed able to control. Urban growth in many areas sped forward at 7-10 percent per year, yielding sprawling cities which could supply neither employment nor basic

35. Nehru, *Discovery of India*, pp. 556, 563.

36. The most thorough and balanced recent assessment of the Cuban revolution is Jorge I. Dominguez, *Cuba: Order and Revolution* (Cambridge, Mass.: Belknap Press, 1978).

37. *Le Monde*, October 5, 1978.

38. Guillermo O'Donnell, *Modernization and Bureaucratic-Authoritarianism* (Berkeley: University of California Institute of International Studies, 1973).

services to the new immigrants. Projections suggest that by the turn of the century Mexico City will have thirty million, and Lagos ten million—creating social problems no level of oil revenue can resolve. Education was, in many countries, a quantitative success but a qualitative failure; the mood reflected in a series of conferences in the 1970s on the theme "education and development" was one of disenchantment. The system failed to impart the technological skills presumed central to progress but generated instead a rural exodus—and, to more extreme critics, alienation, Western consumption expectations, and a ruinous financial drain.

Benoit Verhaegen, arguing in the Zaire case that the educational system has been in fact destructive of progress and development, cites the fact that the city of Kisangani houses today 650 university graduates, or ten times as many as during the colonial era. Yet the level of economic activity is much lower, and the forty-five managerial cadres of the only significant productive enterprise in town, a French textile factory, are almost all European. "Far from being the essential condition for autonomous development," Verhaegen concludes, "an increase in national university graduates would seem to be the indicator of stagnation and dependency."[39]

Further, headway has been disappointingly slow, particularly in the poorest set of "Fourth World" countries. Debts, which became a widespread problem in the 1970s, became an intolerable burden for a growing number of countries (Brazil, Turkey, Sudan, Zaire, Zambia, Sierra Leone, among others). Rural development lagged, and many countries with the potential for food surpluses found it necessary to import basic foodstuffs. Not only had material progress fallen short of expectations, but in a number of countries absolute stagnation, or even substantial declines in well-being have occurred. In Burma, by 1961 the per capita gross national product was only 86 percent of that for the late 1930s, and the figure has further declined since.[40] Spiro, in his inquiry in rural and urban Burma in 1961, found that his interlocutors expressed terrible disappointment with their present fate:

> Post-independence Burma has been characterized ... by political and economic disaster, even aside from the military coup and its calamitous aftermath ... the history of post-independence Burmese economy has been one of industrial failure and agricultural stagnation. ...

39. The observation gains in poignancy when one realizes the author has devoted his entire career to university development in Zaire. Benoit Verhaegen, "Universities, Social Classes, and Economic Dependency," conference on the African university and development, Bellagio, Italy, August 1978. See also Benoit Verhaegen, *L'enseignement universitaire au Zaire* (Paris: Edition L'Harmattan, 1978).

40. See Lawrence D. Stifel, "Economics of the Burmese Way of Socialism," *Asian Survey*, 11(8) (August 1971): 803-17; Josef Silverstein, *Burma: Military Rule and the Politics of Stagnation* (Ithaca, N.Y.: Cornell University Press, 1977).

The result has been disillusionment and humiliation. One cannot talk very long with Burmese of any stratum without realizing the depth of their bitterness and frustration. These feelings are especially intense, however, in the upper stratum. As many of them expressed it to me, while the rest of the world—by which, of course, they mean the Western world—has undergone vast economic and technological changes, Burma has stood still. Everything seems hopeless to them; their high dreams have turned into nightmares....[41]

In Uganda, production of all marketed commodities has radically declined under the profoundly destructive "state of blood" created by Amin.[42] In Ghana, the calamitous ravages of hyperinflation and shortages in the face of sustained record prices for the major export, cocoa, are explicable only when one appreciates the enormity of the predatory diversion of resources by the military clique from 1972-1979.[43] The wave of executions of senior military officers in 1979 in a country so little used to political killing finds its logic in the generalized sense of accelerating deprivation. In Zaire, the government trade union issued figures in 1976 demonstrating that urban real wages had dropped to 26 percent of their 1960 level; with 80 percent inflation the following two years, and one 30 percent wage increase, by 1978 the figure was little more than 10 percent.[44] Yet all of these countries have the resources for modest prosperity and reasonable material progress. Nor were these isolated instances; International Labor Organization figures showed in eleven of twenty-one African countries surveyed, the real minimum wage declined between 1963 and 1974.[45] A recent survey in rural Haiti found that there was a widespread conviction among peasants that life was steadily deteriorating and that the only real solution was emigration.[46]

In a number of Third World countries, a crisis of the state itself appeared at hand. While the Iranian revolution of 1978 was an event of far-reaching significance, an alternative formula to the discredited Pahlavi state has yet to emerge. The experiment in Marxist-Leninist rule in Afghanistan is disintegrating. The final demolition of the Amin regime by the Tanzanian army left Ugandan leaders with a

41. Spiro, *Buddhism and Society*, p. 183.

42. So named by one of his former ministers, Henry Kyemba, *A State of Blood* (New York: Ace Books, 1977).

43. For figures, see Crawford Young, "The State and the Small Urban Center," in Aidan Southall, ed., *Small Urban Centers and Rural Development in Africa* (Madison: African Studies Program, University of Wisconsin, 1979), pp. 313-33.

44. Crawford Young, "Zaire: The Unending Crisis," *Foreign Affairs*, 57(1) (October 1978): 169-85.

45. Susumu Watanabe, "Minimum Wages in Developing Countries: Myth and Reality," *International Labour Review*, 113 (May-June 1976): 353.

46. Personal communication, former American Consular officer, Port-au-Prince. For evidence that their perception is correct, see Rotberg, *Haiti*.

shattered state and an economy and a society in disarray. Chad, perennial problem state, finds its political forces so fragmented by thirteen years of civil war that survival has become problematic. The viability of Mauritania has been placed in doubt by the unwise adventure of sharing in the partition of former Spanish Sahara with Morocco, exposing the country to a guerrilla challenge which has dangerously weakened the fabric of the state. Thus, the range of possible outcomes in the pursuit of progress must be extended to include not only results which fall short of the hopes implicit in the idea but absolute regression and even total decomposition.

Yet the idea of progress remains a powerful beacon, at least so far. While the earlier conviction of inevitable success has proven naïve, neither is failure predetermined. Hollis Chenery has entered a convincing brief (see pp. 319ff.) for the possibility of material progress in the best sense, encompassing both growth and redistribution.[47] A fairly broad spectrum of countries, discounting the OPEC set which have experienced windfall gains, have enjoyed at least partial success. However cogent Patterson's critique of "the iniquitous distribution and exploitation of the world's resources" and "a failure of intellect . . . of the social sciences,"[48] progress is a possible dream in the Third World, as elsewhere, at least in the material realm. And the hope embodied in its message is surely an indispensable spur to the political will and wisdom necessary for its realization.

47. See Hollis Chenery et al., *Redistribution with Growth* (London: Oxford University Press, 1974).
48. Patterson, "Transformation of the Idea of Progress," p. 3.

5

The Evolutionary Concept
of Progress

FRANCISCO J. AYALA

Progress presents itself as an obvious attribute of the evolutionary process. The earliest organisms were no more complex than today's bacteria. Three billion years later, their descendants include orchids, bees, dolphins, and human beings, which appear to be, prima facie at least, patently more advanced or progressive than their primitive ancestors. But what do we mean when we say that there has been progress in the evolutionary process? Organisms may be progressive with respect to one or a few attributes, regressive with respect to others. For example, bacteria are able to synthesize all their components and obtain the energy they need for living from inorganic compounds; human beings depend on other organisms. And some evolutionary lineages do not appear to be progressive by any reasonable definition: living bacteria are not very different from their ancestors of two or three billion years earlier. Moreover, many evolutionary lineages have become extinct.

Nevertheless, some form of progress appears to have occurred in biological evolution as the result of a natural process. Hence, it seems worthwhile to investigate the notion of progress as this may have occurred in the biological world. Such investigation might yield a notion of progress applicable to other domains and, perhaps, of general validity.

CHANGE, EVOLUTION, DIRECTION, AND PROGRESS

The notion that living organisms can be classified in a hierarchy going from lower to higher forms goes back to Aristotle and, indeed, even to

106

earlier times: the creation of the world as described in Genesis contains the explicit notion that some organisms are higher than others and implies that living things can be arranged in a sequence from the lowest to the highest, which is man. The Bible's narrative of the creation reflects the common-sense impression that earthworms are lower than fish or birds, the latter lower than man. The idea of a "ladder of life" rising from amoeba to man is present, explicitly or implicitly, in all preevolutionary biology.

The theory of evolution adds the dimension of time, or history, to the hierarchical classification of living things. The transition from bacteria to humans can now be seen as a natural, progressive development through time from simple to gradually more complex organisms. The expansion and diversification of life can also be judged as progress; some form of advance seems obvious in the transition from one or only a few kinds of living things to the more than two million different species living today.

It is not immediately clear, however, what is meant by statements such as, "The evolution of organisms is progressive," or "Progress has occurred in the evolutionary sequence leading from bacteria to humans." Such expressions may simply mean that evolutionary sequences have a time direction or, even more simply, that they are accompanied by change. The term "progress" may be clarified by comparing it with other related terms used in biological discourse. These terms are "change," "evolution," and "direction."

"Change" means alteration whether in the position, the state, or the nature of a thing. Progress implies change but not vice versa; not all changes are progressive. The molecules of oxygen and nitrogen in the air of a room are continuously changing positions; such change would not generally be regarded as progressive. The mutation of a gene from a functional allelic state to a nonfunctional one is a change but definitely not a progressive one.

The terms "evolution" and "progress" can also be distinguished although both imply that *sustained* change has occurred. Evolutionary change is not necessarily progressive. The evolution of a species may lead to its own extinction, a change which is not progressive, at least not for that species. And some living organisms, such as bacteria or horseshoe crabs, do not seem to be significantly different from their ancestors of millions of generations ago.

"Direction" and "progress" are different concepts as well. The concept of "direction" implies that a series of changes have occurred that can be arranged in a linear sequence with respect to some property or feature, such that elements in the later part of the sequence are more different from early elements of the sequence than from intermediate elements. Directional change may be "uniform" or not, depending on whether every member of the sequence is invariably more different from the first than each preceding member, or whether directional change occurs only on the average. (This distinction will also be made later with respect to progress.) If the elements in the sequence are plotted in a two-dimensional graph with time on one axis and some property or feature of the elements of the sequence on the other axis, and all the elements are connected by a line, directional change is uniform when the slope of that line is at every point positive (or at every point negative). The line connecting all the elements in the sequence may be straight or curved but should go up or down monotonically. Nonuniform or "net" (see below) directional change occurs when the line connecting all the elements in the sequence does not change monotonically but only on the average. Some elements in the sequence may represent a change of direction with respect to the immediately previous elements, but, on the average, later elements in the sequence are further displaced than earlier ones.

In discussions of evolution, "directionality" is sometimes equated with "irreversibility": the process of evolution is said to have a direction because it is irreversible. Biological evolution is irreversible (except perhaps in some trivial sense, as when a previously mutated gene mutates back to its former allelic state). Direction, however, implies more than irreversibility. Consider a new pack of cards with each suit arranged from ace to ten, knave, queen, king, and with the suits arranged in the sequence spades, clubs, hearts, diamonds. If we shuffle the cards thoroughly, the order of the cards will change, and the changes cannot be reversed by reshuffling. We may shuffle again and again until the cards are totally worn out, without ever restoring the original sequence. The change of order in the pack of cards is irreversible but not directional.

Irreversible and directional changes both occur in the inorganic as well as in the organic world. The second law of thermodynamics, which applies to all processes in nature, describes sequential changes that are irreversible but are also directional and, indeed, uniformly directional. Within a closed system, entropy always increases; that is, a closed system passes continuously from less to more probable states.

The concept of direction applies to what in paleontology are called "evolutionary trends." A trend occurs in a phylogenetic sequence when a feature persistently changes through time in the members of the sequence. Trends are common occurrences in all fossil sequences sufficiently long to be called "sustained."[1]

The difference between "direction" and "progress" can be explained by the following example. Consider the trend in the evolutionary sequence from fish to man toward a gradual reduction of the number of dermal bones in the skull roof or the trend toward increased molarization of the last premolars which occurred in the phylogeny of the *Equidae* from early Eocene (*Hyracotherium*) to early Oligocene (*Hap-*

1. G.G. Simpson, *The Major Features of Evolution* (New York: Columbia University Press, 1953), pp. 245-65.

lohippus). These trends represent directional change, but it is not obvious that they should be labeled progressive. To label them progressive, we would need to agree that the directional change had been in some sense for the better. That is, in order to consider a directional sequence progressive, we need to add an evaluation, namely, that the condition in the latter members of the sequence represents, according to some standard, a *melioration* or improvement. The directionality of a sequence may be recognized and accepted without any such evaluation being added. Progress implies directional change, but the opposite is not true.

THE CONCEPT OF PROGRESS

Evolution, direction, and progress all imply that there is a historical sequence of events that exhibits a systematic alteration of a property or state of the elements in the sequence. Progress occurs when there is directional change toward a better state or condition. The concept of progress, then, contains two elements: one *descriptive*—that directional change has taken place, the other *axiological*—that the change represents an improvement or melioration.[2] The notion of progress requires that a value judgment be made about what is better and what is worse according to some axiological standard. However, contrary to the belief of some authors,[3] the axiological standard of reference need not be a moral one. Moral progress is possible, but not all forms of progress are moral. The evaluation required for progress is one of better versus worse or of higher versus lower but not necessarily one of right versus wrong or of good versus evil. "Better" may simply mean more efficient, more abundant, or more complex without connotating any reference to moral values or standards.

Progress, then, may be defined as *systematic change in a feature belonging to all the members of a sequence in such a way that posterior members of the sequence exhibit an improvement of that feature.* More simply, progress may be defined as *directional change toward the better.* The antonym of progress is "regress." Regress or retrogression is directional change for the worse. The two elements of the definition, namely, directional change and improvement according to some standard, are jointly necessary and sufficient for the occurrence of progress. Directional change (and progress) may be observed in sequences that are spatially rather than temporally ordered. Biologists use the term "cline" to describe changes associated with geographical displacement, for example, a gradual increase in individual size with increasing latitude. Clines are examples of directional change recog-

2. T. A. Goudge, *The Ascent of Life* (Toronto: University of Toronto Press, 1961).
3. For example, M. Ginsberg, *Moral Progress*, Frazer Lecture at the University of Glasgow (Glasgow: Glasgow University Press, 1944); and R.C. Lewontin, "The Concept of Evolution," in *International Encyclopedia of the Social Sciences*, vol. 5, ed. D.L. Sills (New York: Macmillan, 1968).

nized along a spatial dimension. In evolutionary discourse, however, temporal (historical) sequences are of greatest interest.

The concept of progress just elucidated may be applied to all sorts of sequences and not only to biological ones. The historical development of a human culture (or of mankind as a whole) may be labeled progressive only if sustained (directional) change has occurred and if the change represents an improvement or amelioration. However, progress need not have occurred with respect to all the component elements of that culture (see below the distinction between "general progress" and "particular progress"). The definition proposed above makes it possible to identify in a historical sequence cultural aspects or components according to which progress may have occurred whereas no progress (or retrogression) may have occurred with respect to other aspects or components. Some discussions of human history fail to recognize this possibility. The claim that progress took place in a given historical period is sometimes negated by advancing the counter-claim that with respect to certain feature(s), the historical development was regressive. Appropriate identification of the feature or features according to which progress is predicated from the historical sequence may help to resolve such arguments. Of course, the possibility is not excluded of claiming that progress has taken place, for example, "with respect to a majority of features," or "with respect to those features that are most significant for human welfare," or the like. But claims such as these will require additional value judgments.

The distinction between temporal and spatial sequences, made for the biological world, may be applied to human societies as well. It might be claimed, for example, that one society is more progressive than another contemporary society with respect to certain cultural elements. However, in cultural anthropology and history, as in biological evolution, temporal sequences are often more relevant than spatial ones.

KINDS OF PROGRESS

The concept of progress may be further clarified by distinguishing various kinds of progress that are established by considering one or the other of the two essential elements of the definition. I shall later refer to different types of progress based on different axiological standards of reference. Now, I shall make two distinctions that relate to the descriptive element of the definition, namely, the requirement of directional change. These distinctions also apply, therefore, to the concept of direction.

If we attend to the *continuity* of the direction of change, we can distinguish two kinds of progress: uniform and net. *Uniform progress* takes place whenever every later member of the sequence is better than every earlier member of the sequence according to a certain feature. Let m_i represent the members of a sequence, temporarily ordered from 1 to n, and let p_i measure the state of the feature under evaluation. There is uniform progress if it is the case for every m_i and m_j that $p_j > p_i$ for every $j > i$. *Net progress* does not require that every member of the sequence be better than all previous members of the sequence and worse than all its successors; it requires only that later members of the sequence be better *on the average* than earlier members. Net progress allows for temporary fluctuations of value. Formally, if the members of a sequence, m_i are linearly arranged over time, net progress occurs whenever the regression (in the sense used in mathematical statistics) of p on time is significantly positive.

Some authors have argued that progress has not occurred in evolution (or in human history) because no matter what standard is chosen, fluctuations of value are always found to have occurred. This criticism is valid against the occurrence of uniform but not net evolutionary progress. Also, neither uniform nor net progress requires that progress continue forever or that any specified goal be achieved. The *rate* of progress may decrease with time; progress requires only a gradual improvement in the members of the sequence. It is possible that a progressive sequence may tend asymptotically toward a finite goal, that is, continuously approach but never reach the goal.

The distinction between uniform and net progress is similar but not identical to the distinction proposed between uniform and perpetual progress by C.D. Broad and T.A. Goudge.[4] Perpetual progress, as defined by Broad, requires that the maxima of value increase and that the minima do not decrease with time. Using the symbols given above, Broad's perpetual progress requires that for every m_i there is at least one m_j $(j > i)$ such that $p_j > p_i$, and that there is at least one m_k $(k < i)$ such that $p_k < p_i$. This definition encounters some difficulties in its applications and has the undesirable feature of requiring that the first element in the sequence be the worst one and the last element be the best one. Neither of these two requirements is made in my definition of net progress. Also the term "perpetual" has connotations that are undesirable in the discussion of progress.

The distinction between uniform and net progress is implicit, although never formally established, in Simpson, who applies terms like "universal," "invariable," "constant," and "continuous" to the kind of progress that I have called "uniform" (although he also uses these terms with other meanings).[5]

Other types of progress (and directional change) can be distinguished. With respect to the *scope* of the sequence considered, progress can be either general or particular. *General progress* is that which occurs in all historical sequences of a given domain of reality and from the beginning of the sequences until their end. *Particular*

4. C.D. Broad, *The Mind and Its Place in Nature* (London: Kegan Paul, 1952); Goudge, *The Ascent of Life*.

5. G.G. Simpson, *The Meaning of Evolution* (New Haven, Conn.: Yale University Press, 1949), pp. 239-62; see also Simpson, *The Major Features of Evolution*.

progress is that which occurs in one or several but not all historical sequences, or that which takes place during part but not all the duration of the sequence or sequences.

In biological evolution, general progress would be any kind of progress, if such exists, that can be predicated of the evolution of all life from its origin to the present. If a type of progress is predicated of only one or several, but not all, lines of evolutionary descent, it is a particular kind of progress. Progress that embraces only a limited span of time from the origin of life to the present is also a particular kind of progress. Some writers have denied that evolution is progressive because not all evolutionary lineages exhibit advance. Some evolutionary lineages, like those leading to certain parasitic forms, are retrogressive by certain standards; and many lineages have become extinct without issue. These considerations may be valid criticism against a claim of general progress but not necessarily against that of particular forms of progress.

The distinctions advanced of various kinds of progress may be applicable, beyond evolutionary biology, to all forms of progress. In cultural evolution it is also appropriate to distinguish between uniform and net progress. Progress in a given historical sequence may not have been uniform because periods of regression may have taken place. Nevertheless, this would leave open the possibility that net progress has occurred. Similarly, in order to accept that progress has occurred in human history, it is not necessary that progress be present with respect to each and every element of human life. Even when general progress may not have taken place, it remains possible that there be progress with respect to one or several cultural components.

CAN "PROGRESS" BE DEFINED WITHOUT REFERENCE TO VALUES?

Can one find in biology any criterion by which progress could be defined and measured by an absolute standard without involving judgments of value? Some authors believe that one can. J.M. Thoday has pointed out the obvious fact that survival is essential to life. Therefore, he argues, progress is increase in fitness for survival, "provided only that fitness and survival be defined as generally as possible." According to Thoday, fitness must be defined in reference to groups of organisms that can have common descendants; these groups he calls "units of evolution." A unit of evolution is what population geneticists call a Mendelian population; the most inclusive Mendelian population is the species. The fitness of a unit of evolution is defined by Thoday as "the probability that such a unit of evolution will survive for a long period of time, such as 10^8 years, that is to say will have descendants after the lapse of that time." According to Thoday, evolutionary changes, no matter what other results may have been produced, are progressive only if they increase the probability of leaving descendants after long periods of time. He correctly points out that this definition has the advantage of not assuming that progress has in fact occurred, an assumption which vitiates other attempts to define progress as a purely biological concept.[6]

Thoday's definition of progress has been criticized because it apparently leads to the paradox that progress is impossible, in fact, that regress is necessary since any group of organisms will be more progressive than any of their descendants. Assume that we are concerned with ascertaining whether progress has occurred in the evolutionary transition from a Cretaceous mammal to its descendants of one hundred million (10^8) years later. It is clear that if the present-day mammal population, M_1, has a probability, P, of having descendants 10^8 million years from now, the ancestral mammal populations, M_0, will have a probability no smaller than P of leaving descendants after 10^{16} years from the time of their existence.[7] In fact, the probability that the ancestral population M_0 will leave descendants 10^{16} years after their existence will be greater than P if M_0 has any other living descendants besides M_1. As Thoday himself has pointed out, such criticism is mistaken since it confuses the probability of survival with the fact of survival.[8] The a priori probability that a given population will have descendants after a given lapse of time may be smaller than the a priori probability that any of its descendant populations will leave progeny after the same length of time. There is, however, a legitimate criticism of Thoday's definition of progress, namely, that it is not operationally valid. Suppose that we want to find out whether M_1 is more progressive than M_0. We should have to estimate, first, the probability that M_1 will leave descendants after a given long period of time; then, we should have to estimate the same probability for M_0. Thoday has enumerated a variety of components which contribute to the fitness of a population as defined by him. These components are adaptation, genetic stability, genetic flexibility, phenotypic flexibility, and the stability of the environment. But it is by no means clear how these components could be quantified nor by what sort of function they could be integrated into a single parameter. In any case, there seems to be no conceivable way in which the appropriate observations and measurements could be made for the ancestral population. Thoday's definition of progress is extremely ingenious but lacks operational validity. If we accept his definition, there seems to be no way in which

6. J. M. Thoday, "Components of Fitness," *Symposia of the Society for the Study of Experimental Biology*, 7 (Evolution) (1953): 96-113; see also J. M. Thoday, "Natural Selection and Biological Progress," in *A Century of Darwin*, ed. S. A. Barnet (London: Allen & Unwin, 1958).

7. Francisco J. Ayala, "An Evolutionary Dilemma: Fitness of Genotypes Versus Fitness of Populations," *Canadian Journal of Genetics and Cytology*, 11 (1969): 439-56.

8. J. M. Thoday, "Genotype Versus Population Fitness," *Canadian Journal of Genetics and Cytology*, 12 (1970): 674-75.

we could ascertain whether progress has occurred in any one line of descent or in the evolution of life as a whole.

Another attempt to consider evolutionary progress as a purely biological notion has been made by defining biological progress as an increase in the amount of genetic information stored in the organism. This information is encoded, at least for the most part, in the DNA of the nucleus. The DNA contains the information which, in interaction with the environment, directs the development and behavior of the individual. By making certain assumptions, Motoo Kimura has developed a method to estimate the rate at which genetic information accumulates in evolution. He calculates that in the evolution of "higher" organisms genetic information has accumulated from the Cambrian to the present at an average rate of 0.29 bits per generation.[9]

Kimura's method of measuring progressive evolution by the accumulation of genetic information is vitiated by several fundamental flaws. First, since the average rate of accumulation of information is allegedly constant *per generation*, it follows that organisms with a shorter generation time accumulate more information and, therefore, are more progressive than organisms with longer generation time. In the evolution of mammals, moles and bats would necessarily be more progressive than horses, whales, and men.

A second, more basic flaw is that Kimura is not measuring how much genetic information has been accumulated in any given organism. Rather, he assumes that genetic information gradually accumulates with time and then proceeds to estimate the rate at which genetic information could have accumulated. The assumption that more recent organisms have more genetic information and that, therefore, they are more progressive than their ancestors is unwarranted and completely invalidates Kimura's attempt to measure evolutionary progress. Moreover, there is, at least at present, no way of measuring the amount of genetic information present in any one organism (see below).

Julian Huxley has argued that the biologist should not attempt to define progress a priori but rather he should "proceed inductively to see whether he can or cannot find evidence of a process which can be legitimately called progressive." He believes that evolutionary progress can be defined without any reference to values. Huxley proposes first to investigate the features that mark off the "higher" from the "lower" organisms. Any evolutionary process in which the features that characterize higher organisms are achieved is considered progressive. Like Kimura, Huxley assumes that progress has in fact occurred and that certain living organisms, especially humans, are more progressive than others. The classification of organisms as "higher" or

9. Motoo Kimura, "Natural Selection as the Process of Accumulating Genetic Information in Adaptive Evolution," *Genetical Research*, 2 (1961): 127-40.

"lower" requires an evaluation. Huxley has not succeeded in avoiding reference to an axiological standard. The terms that he uses in his various definitions of progress, like "improvement," "general advance," "level of efficiency," etc., are all, in fact, evaluative.[10]

THE EXPANSION AND
DIVERSIFICATION OF LIFE

I have established above that the concept of "progress" involves an axiological element. Therefore, discussions of evolutionary progress require that a choice be made of the standard by which organisms and evolutionary events are to be evaluated. Two decisions are required. First, we must choose the objective feature according to which the events or objects are to be ordered. Second, a decision must be made as to what direction of change represents improvement. These decisions are in part subjective, but they should not be arbitrary; biological knowledge (or the appropriate kind of knowledge if one is considering progress in a nonbiological process) should guide them. There is a criterion by which the validity of the standards of reference can be judged. A standard is valid if it enables one to say illuminating things about the evolution of life. The choice of appropriate standards also depends on how much relevant information is available and whether the evaluation can be made more or less exactly.

What is known about the evolution of life enables one to decide immediately that there is no standard by which *uniform* progress can be said to have taken place in the evolution of life. Changes of direction, slackening, and reversals have occurred in all evolutionary lineages, no matter what feature is considered.[11] The question, then, is whether *net* progress has occurred in the evolution of life, and in which sense.

The next question is whether there is any criterion of progress by which net progress can be said to be a *general* feature of evolution, or whether identifiable progress applies only to particular lineages or during particular periods. One conceivable standard of progress is the increase in the amount of genetic information stored in organisms. Net general progress would have occurred if organisms living at a later time would have, on the average, greater content of genetic information than their ancestors. One difficulty, insuperable at least for the present, is that there is no way in which the genetic information contained in the whole DNA of an organism can be measured. We do not even know how information is stored in organisms. We could choose the Shannon-Wiener solution, as Kimura has done, by regarding all of the DNA of an organism as a linear sequence of messages made up of groups of three-letter words (the codons) with a

10. Julian S. Huxley, *Evolution in Action* (New York: Harper, 1953); see also Julian S. Huxley, *Evolution, the Modern Synthesis* (New York: Harper, 1942).
11. Simpson, *The Major Features of Evolution*; see also Simpson, *The Meaning of Evolution*.

four-letter alphabet (the four DNA bases).[12] But many DNA sequences are repeated from a few to many thousands of times in any given organism. There are ways to estimate, at least approximately, the "complexity" of the DNA of an organism, that is, the total length of different DNA sequences.[13] However, a large fraction of the nuclear DNA does not encode information in the form of codon triplets, and much DNA may have nonsense messages.

Accumulation of genetic information as a standard of progress can be understood in a different way. Progress can be measured by an increase in the *kinds* of ways in which the information is stored or as an increase in the *number* of different messages encoded. Different species represent different kinds of messages; individuals are messages or units of information. Thus understood, whether an increase in the amount of information has occurred reduces to the question whether life has diversified and expanded. This has been recognized by Simpson as the standard by which what I call general progress has in fact occurred in the evolution of life. According to Simpson, we can find in evolution as a whole "a tendency for life to expand, to fill in all the available spaces in the livable environments, including those created by the process of that expansion itself."[14]

The expansion of life can be measured by at least four different though related criteria: (1) the number of *kinds* of organisms, that is, the number of species; (2) the number of individuals; (3) the total bulk of living matter (biomass); and (4) the total rate of energy flow. Increases in the number of individuals or their bulk may not be an unmixed blessing, as is now the case for mankind, but they can be a measure of biological success. Net progress appears to be a general feature of the evolution of life by any one of these four standards of progress.

Living organisms have a tendency to multiply exponentially ad infinitum without intrinsically imposed bounds. This is simply a consequence of the process of biological reproduction: each organism is capable of producing, on the average, more than one progeny throughout its lifetime. However, the tendency of life to expand encounters constraints of various sorts. Once a certain species has come to exist, its expansion is limited by the environment in at least two ways: first, because the supply of resources accessible to the organisms is limited; second, because favorable conditions for multiplication, even when resources are available, do not always occur; at times, the rate of growth of the population becomes negative because deaths exceed births. Predators, parasites, and competitors, together with the various parameters of the environment encompassed by the term "weather,"

12. Kimura, "Natural Selection."

13. R.J. Britten and E.H. Davidson, "Repetitive and Non-Repetitive DNA Sequences and a Speculation on the Origin of Evolutionary Novelty," *Quarterly Review of Biology*, 46 (1971): 111-38.

14. Simpson, *The Meaning of Evolution*, p. 242.

are the main factors interfering with the multiplication of organisms when resources are available. Drastic and secular changes in the weather, as well as geological events, lead at times to vast decreases in the size of some populations and even of the whole of life. Because of these constraints, the tendency of life to expand has not always succeeded. Nevertheless, it appears certain that life has, on the average, expanded throughout most of the evolutionary process.

Estimates of the number of living species vary from author to author. Probably there are more than two million but not many more than six million species. Although it is difficult to estimate the number of plants that existed in the past (since well-preserved plant fossils are rare), the number of animal species can be roughly estimated. Approximately one hundred and fifty thousand species live in the seas today, probably a larger number than the total number of animal species that existed in the Cambrian (six hundred million years ago) when no animal or plant species lived on the land. Life on the land began in the Devonian (four hundred million years ago). The number of animal land species is probably at a maximum now even if we exclude insects. Insects make up about three-quarters of all animal species and about half of all species including plants. Insects did not appear until the early Carboniferous, some three hundred and fifty million years ago. More species of insects exist now than at most, probably all, times in the past. On the whole, it appears that the number of living species is probably greater in recent times than it ever was before and that at least on the average a gradual increase in the number of species has characterized the evolution of life.

The expansion of the number of species operates as a positive feedback process. The greater the number of species, the greater the number of environments that are created for new species to exploit. Once there were plants, animals could come into existence; and the animals themselves sustain large numbers of species of other animals that prey on them, as well as of parasites and symbionts. Thomas Huxley likened the expansion of life to the filling of a barrel. First, the barrel is filled with apples until they overflow; then pebbles are added up to the brim; the space between the apples and the pebbles can be packed with sand; water is finally poured until it overflows. With diverse kinds of organisms the environment can be filled in more effectively than with only one kind.[15] Huxley's analogy neglects one important aspect of life. A more appropriate analogy would have been that of a balloon or an expanding barrel. The space available for occupancy by other species is increased rather than decreased by some additions.

The number of individuals living on the earth today cannot be estimated with any reasonable approximation even if we exclude microorganisms. It is a staggering number. The mean number of indi-

15. Thomas H. Huxley and Julian S. Huxley, *Touchstone for Ethics* (New York: Harper, 1947).

viduals for insect species is estimated to be around 2×10^8, but some species may consist of more than 10^{16} individuals—and there are more than one million insect species! The number of individuals of *Euphausia superba*, the small krill eaten by some whales, may be greater than 10^{20}. There can be little doubt that the number of individual animals and plants and their biomass are greater now than they were in the Cambrian. Very likely, they are also greater than they have been at most times since the beginning of life. This is more so if we consider the large number and enormous bulk of the human population and of all the plants and animals cultivated by man for his own use. Even if we include microorganisms, it is probable that the number of living individuals has increased, on the average, throughout the evolution of life. An increase in the total bulk of living matter is even more likely than an increase in numbers because larger organisms have generally appeared later in time.

The rate of energy flow has probably increased in the living world faster than the total biomass. One effect of living things on the world is to retard the dissipation of energy. Green plants do, indeed, store radial energy from the sun that would otherwise be converted into heat. The influence of animals goes, however, in the opposite direction. The living activities of animals dissipate energy since their catabolism exceeds their anabolism.[16] The net result of these opposing processes is, however, an increase in the rate at which energy flows through the whole of life. Animals provide a new path through which energy can flow, but, moreover, their interactions with plants increase the total rate of flow through the system. An analogy can be used to illustrate this outcome. Suppose that a modern highway with three lanes in each direction connects two large cities. A need for an increase in the rate of traffic flow can be accomplished either by adding more lanes to the highway or by increasing the speed at which the traffic moves in the highway. These two approaches may appear, at first sight, to work in opposite directions, but together they increase the total flow of traffic on the highway.

INFORMATION ABOUT THE ENVIRONMENT

There are many criteria by which net progress has occurred in some evolutionary sequences but not in others. One of the most meaningful of such criteria is the ability of the organism to obtain and process information about the environment. This criterion is of considerable biological interest because such ability notably contributes to the biological success of the organisms that possess it. The criterion is particularly interesting in reference to humans since among the differences which mark off humans from all other animals, their greatly

16. A.J. Lotka, "The Law of Evolution as a Maximal Principle," *Human Biology*, 17 (1945): 167-94.

developed ability to perceive the environment and to react flexibly to it is perhaps the most fundamental one. All organisms become genetically adapted to their environments, but humans moreover artificially create environments to fit their genes.

Increased ability to gather and process information about the environment is sometimes expressed as evolution toward "independence from the environment." This latter expression is misleading. No organism can be truly independent of the environment. The evolutionary sequence fish → amphibian → reptile allegedly provides an example of evolution toward independence from an aqueous environment. Reptiles, birds, and mammals are indeed free of the need for water as an external living medium, but their lives depend on the conditions of the land. They have not become independent of the environment but rather have exchanged dependence on one environment for dependence on another.

"Control over the environment" has been linked to the ability to gather and use information about the state of the environment. However, true control over the environment occurs to any large extent only in the human species. All organisms interact with the environment, but they do not control it. Burrowing a hole in the ground or building a nest in a tree, like the construction of a beehive or of a beaver dam, does not represent control over the environment except in a trivial sense. The ability to control the environment started with the australopithecines, the first group of organisms that can be called human. They are considered to be humans precisely because they were able to produce devices to manipulate the environment in the form of rudimentary pebble and bone tools. The ability to obtain and process information about the conditions of the environment does not necessarily provide control over the environment, but rather it enables the organisms to avoid unsuitable environments and to seek suitable ones. It has developed in many organisms because it is a useful adaptation.

All organisms interact selectively with the environment. The cell membrane of a bacterium permits certain molecules but not others to enter the cell. Selective molecular exchange occurs also in the inorganic world; but this can hardly be called a form of information processing. Certain bacteria when placed on an agar plate move about in a zigzag pattern, which is almost certainly random. The most rudimentary ability to gather and process information about the environment can be found in certain single-celled eukaryotes.[17] A *Paramecium* follows a sinuous path as it swims, ingesting the bacteria that it encounters. Whenever it meets unfavorable conditions, such as unsuitable acidity or salinity in the water, the *Paramecium* checks its advance, turns, and

17. In eukaryotes the DNA is organized in chromosomes, which exist in a nucleus surrounded by a nuclear membrane. Prokaryotes have genetic information encoded in DNA, but there is no nucleus set off from the rest of the cell.

starts in a new direction. Its reaction is purely negative. The *Paramecium* apparently does not seek its food or a favorable environment but simply avoids unsuitable conditions.

A somewhat greater ability to process information about the environment occurs in the single-celled *Euglena*. This organism has a light-sensitive spot by means of which it can orient itself toward the direction in which the light originates. *Euglena*'s motions are directional; it not only avoids unsuitable environments, but it also actively seeks suitable ones. An amoeba represents further progress in the same direction; it reacts to light by moving away from it and also actively pursues food particles.

Progress as increase in the ability to gather and process information about the environment is not a general characteristic of the evolution of life. Progress occurred in certain evolutionary lines of descent but not in others. Today's bacteria are not more progressive by this criterion than their ancestors of one billion years ago. In many evolutionary sequences some very limited progress took place in the early stages, without further progress through the rest of their history. In general, animals are more advanced than plants; vertebrates are more advanced than invertebrates; mammals more advanced than reptiles, which are more advanced than fish. The most advanced organism by this criterion is doubtless the human species.

The ability to obtain and to process information about the environment has progressed little in the plant kingdom. Plants generally react to light and to gravity. The geotropism is positive in the root but negative in the stem. Plants also grow toward the light; some plants, like the sunflower, have parts which follow the course of the sun through its daily cycle. Another tropism in plants is the tendency of roots to grow toward water. The response to gravity, to water, and to light is basically due to differential growth rates; a greater elongation of cells takes place on one side of the stem or of the root than on the other side. Gradients of light, gravity, or moisture are the clues that guide these tropisms. Some plants react also to tactile stimuli. Tendrils twine around what they touch; *Mimosa* and carnivorous plants like the Venus flytrap (*Dionaea*) have leaves which close rapidly when touched.

In multicellular animals, the ability to obtain and process information about the environment is mediated by the nervous system. All major groups of animals, except sponges, have nervous systems. The simplest nervous system among living animals occurs in coelenterates like hydra, corals, and jellyfishes. Each tentacle of a jellyfish reacts only if it is individually and directly stimulated. There is no coordination of the information gathered by different parts of the animal. Besides, jellyfishes are unable to learn from experience. A limited form of coordinated behavior occurs in the echinoderms, which comprise the starfishes and sea urchins. The coelenterates possess an undifferentiated nerve net; the echinoderms possess, besides a nerve net, a nerve ring and radial nerve cords. When the appropriate stimulus is encountered, a starfish reacts with direct and unified actions of the whole body. The most primitive form of a brain occurs in certain organisms like planarian flatworms, which also have numerous sensory cells and eyes without lenses. The information gathered by these sensory cells and organs is processed and coordinated by the central nervous system and the rudimentary brain; a planarian worm is capable of some variability of responses and of some simple learning. That is, the same stimuli will not necessarily always produce the same response.

Planarian flatworms have progressed farther than starfishes in the ability to gather and process information about the environment, and the starfishes have progressed farther than sea anemones and other coelenterates. But none of these organisms has gone very far by this criterion of progress. The most progressive group of organisms among the invertebrates is the arthropods, but the vertebrates have progressed much farther than any invertebrates.

It seems certain that among the ancestors of both the arthropods and the vertebrates, there were organisms that like sponges lacked a nervous system, and that their evolution went through a stage with only a simple network, with later stages developing a central nervous system and even later a rudimentary brain. With further development of the central nervous system and of the brain, the ability to obtain and process information from the outside progressed much farther. The arthropods, which include the insects, have complex forms of behavior. Precise visual, chemical, and acoustic signals are obtained and processed by many arthropods, particularly in their search for food and in their selection of mates.

The vertebrates are generally able to obtain and process much more complicated signals and to produce a much greater variety of responses than the arthropods. The vertebrate brain has an enormous number of associative neurons with an extremely complex arrangement. Among the vertebrates, progress in the ability to deal with environmental information is correlated with an increase in the size of the cerebral hemispheres and with the appearance and development of the "neopallium." The neopallium is involved in association and coordination of all kinds of impulses from all receptors and brain centers. The neopallium appeared first in the reptiles. In the mammals it has expanded to become the cerebral cortex, which covers most of the cerebral hemispheres. The larger brain of vertebrates compared with invertebrates permits them also to have a large amount of neurons involved in information storage or memory.

The ability to perceive the environment and to integrate, coordinate, and react flexibly to what is perceived has attained its highest degree of development in humans. Humans are by this measure of biological progress the most progressive organisms on the planet. That such ability is a sound criterion of biological progress was indicated earlier by pointing out that it is useful as an adaptation to the environment. Extreme advance in the ability to perceive and react to the environment is perhaps the most fundamental characteristic which marks off *Homo sapiens* from all other animals. Symbolic language, complex social organization, control over the environment, the ability to envisage future states and to work toward them, and values and ethics are developments made possible by the human's greatly developed capacity to obtain and organize information about the state of the environment.

CONCLUDING REMARKS

As stated above, the concept of progress involves an evaluation of better versus worse relative to some standard of reference. Particular forms of evolutionary progress, which obtain only in certain evolutionary sequences and usually for only a limited span of time, may be identified using a variety of criteria. Simpson has examined several criteria according to which evolutionary progress can be recognized in particular sequences. These criteria include dominance, invasion of new environments, replacement, improvement in adaptation, adaptability and possibility of further progress, increased specialization, control over the environment, increased structural complexity, increase in general energy or level of vital processes, and increase in the range and variety of adjustments to the environment. For each of these criteria, Simpson has shown in what evolutionary sequences, and for how long, progress has taken place.[18] Bernhard Rensch and Julian Huxley have examined other lists of characteristics which can be used as standards of particular forms of progress.[19] Ledyard Stebbins has written a provocative essay proposing a law of "conservation of organization" that accounts for evolutionary progress as a small bias toward increased complexity of organization.[20] I have elsewhere examined in some detail the increase in the ability of organisms to obtain and process information about the environment, as a criterion of progress that is particularly relevant to the evolution of man: among the differences that mark off humans from all other animals, perhaps the most fundamental is the human's greatly developed ability to perceive the environment and to react flexibly to it.[21] George Wil-

18. Simpson, *The Meaning of Evolution*; and Simpson, *The Major Features of Evolution*.

19. Bernhard Rensch, *Evolution Above the Species Level* (New York: Columbia University Press, 1947); Huxley, *Evolution in Action*; Huxley, *Evolution, the Modern Synthesis*.

20. G. Ledyard Stebbins, *The Basis of Progressive Evolution* (Chapel Hill: University of North Carolina Press, 1969).

21. Francisco J. Ayala, "The Concept of Biological Progress," in *Studies in the Philosophy of Biology*, ed. F.J. Ayala and Th. Dobzhansky (Berkeley: University of

liams has examined, mostly critically, several criteria of progress.[22] Two brief but incisive discussions of the concept of progress can be found in G.J. Herrick and Theodosius Dobzhansky. A philosophical study of the concept of progress has been made by Goudge.[23]

There is no need to examine here all the standards of progress that have been formulated by the authors just mentioned nor to explore additional criteria. This chapter has been written primarily to clarify the notion of progress as it is used in biology. Writings about biological progress have involved much disputation concerning (1) whether or not the notion of progress belongs in the realm of scientific discourse, (2) what criterion of progress is "best," and (3) whether progress has indeed taken place in the evolution of life. These controversies can be solved once the notion of progress is clearly established. First, the concept of progress is axiological, that is, it involves an evaluation of good versus bad or of better versus worse. The choice of a criterion by which to evaluate organisms or their features is to a certain extent subjective. However, once a criterion of progress has been chosen, decisions concerning whether or not progress has occurred in the living world and what organisms are more progressive can be made following the usual standards and methods of scientific discourse. Second, there is no criterion of progress which is "best" in the abstract or for all purposes. The validity of any one criterion of progress depends on whether the use of that criterion leads to meaningful statements concerning the evolution of life. Which criteria are preferable depends on the particular context in which they are discussed. Third, the distinction between uniform and net progress makes it possible to recognize the occurrence of biological progress even though every member of a sequence may not always be more progressive than every previous member of the sequence. Fourth, the distinction between general and particular progress allows one to recognize progress in particular groups of organisms or during limited periods in the evolution of life.

I believe that the concept of progress as I have defined it and the distinctions I have made may also be useful in the fields of cultural anthropology and, more generally, human history. It may be the case that knowledge in these fields is largely value-free, but we can predicate progress of human historical events only by introducing value judgments. However, once this is recognized, it becomes possible to seek criteria of progress that will yield valuable insights in the study of human history.

California Press, 1974), pp. 337-55; Th. Dobzhansky, F.J. Ayala, G.L. Stebbins, and J.W. Valentine, *Evolution* (San Francisco, Ca.: W.H. Freeman, 1977).

22. C. George Williams, *Adaptation by Natural Selection* (Princeton, N.J.: Princeton University Press, 1966).

23. G.J. Herrick, *The Evolution of Human Nature* (Austin: University of Texas Press, 1956); Th. Dobzhansky, *Genetics of the Evolutionary Process* (New York: Columbia University Press, 1970); Goudge, *The Ascent of Life*.

Claims that progress has occurred in human history need not imply that progress is universal, inevitable, or unlimited. Like biological progress, cultural progress may have occurred in some societies but not others, during certain periods rather than forever, and may be subject to certain limits rather than able to proceed without bounds. Where and how progress has taken place are matters for investigation, which, once a criterion of progress has been selected, can proceed according to the normal standards of scholarly inquiry.

PART II

The Progress and Problems
of Science

Though the various contributors to the idea of progress have differed in their philosophical and ideological perspectives, there has been common agreement about the central role of science and technology. These were certainly to lead to the improvement of material conditions but, also, possibly to more rational forms of government, social organization, and the like.

What has happened to this hope? We find ourselves near the end of a century which has seen the greatest advances in scientific knowledge and technological innovation in the history of mankind. We have gained profound insights into the nature of the physical world, the theoretical structure of physics, chemistry, and biology, and all the hierarchical connections among these fields. As an intellectual achievement, it has been a creation of the greatest beauty, profundity, and depth. In technology, we have developed electric power, the internal combustion engine, the airplane, tremendously productive and varied chemical and pharmaceutical industries, and advances in medicine and medical understanding which have had profound effects on our health and physical well-being. Among these technical achievements, possibly the most flamboyant, a tour de force, has been the landing of a man on the moon, but they also include such far-reaching developments as nuclear energy, the whole field of electronics, communication and computers, the synthesis of drugs and, most recently, the development of recombinant DNA, the consequences of which are still somewhat unclear.

All this technology of the last century has changed the life of humankind in drastic ways, in its effects on comfort, food production, standards of living, medical care, and longevity in the advanced countries and, to some extent, in the developing countries. But now in the last several decades we find that in spite of all of this scientific and technological achievement, there is great concern, some warranted, some expressing only a generalized anxiety, about the effect of technology in terms of, for example, pollution of our biosphere and the adverse side effects of drugs. There have been great difficulties in decision making regarding the use or nonuse of much of our technology. Obviously, a major source of this unease has been the impact of nuclear fission, which, on the one hand, greatly benefits us by providing an abundant source of clean, nonpolluting power (and through the use of breeder reactors, power for hundreds of years) but has also led to the single most dangerous and deadly outcome of technology, nuclear weapons, which, in principle, could wipe out humankind. Certainly, this one morally ambiguous technology has had a major impact on public attitudes not only toward nuclear power but also toward almost all other advanced technologies.

It has been said that Einstein once referred to a colleague, who was particularly noted for his scientific astuteness, originality, and versatility (and it was not intended as a whole-hearted compliment), as an *intelligenz Tier* ("intelligence beast") as compared with a *nage Tier* ("gnawing beast") or a *grasendes Tier* ("grazing beast"). Einstein's epithet could be applied to all of humankind. In the past, various species are alleged to have become extinct because of overspecialization of some particular characteristic not suited to their environment. It is at least thinkable that man, as an "intelligence beast," may disappear for similar reasons.

In reviewing the present status of science and technology as a key element of progress, we have to consider seriously this ambivalence in the attitudes of various elements of society and the unsolved social and political problems resulting from these attitudes. First, as to progress in science, we now have a comprehensive understanding of the whole nature and structure of the physical world as we *experience* it. This excludes much of the subnuclear world, which does not contribute to ordinary physical experience and which we do not yet comprehend with the same completeness as the extranuclear world. The word "comprehensive" is not meant to imply that we can predict or even explain everything in the physical world in *detail*. As we investigate more and more intricate forms of matter, the complexity becomes too great to be able to apply the accepted principles of the physical world in detail. But starting from our precise knowledge of single atoms, we can understand and formulate useful principles about the nature of more complex combinations of atoms so that we can encompass the various branches of chemistry and all its technical products, drugs, synthetics, etc. We can extend all this knowledge about the nature of atomic binding and molecular configurations to the understanding of very complex structures and to the understanding of the chemical nature of living matter embodied in that magnificent scientific complex known as molecular biology, where we can talk with confidence of the detailed atomic constituents, geometric arrangements, and *functions* of the chemical components that constitute living matter and guide its behavior. When the philosopher Arthur Lovejoy spoke of "the great chain of being," he could not possibly have appreciated the aptness of his metaphor to the functioning of DNA.

All of this optimistic description is not to claim an unbroken web of scientific knowledge and understanding but to indicate that all of the partially disjointed portions of the web have obvious common intellectual and conceptual ties. The famous statement by Dirac about quantum mechanics, that "it includes most of low energy physics and chemistry" (and, presumably, biochemistry, etc.), is certainly true in principle, but, in practice, chemistry and biochemistry and molecular biology did not evolve in an elegant, organized way from the principles of quantum mechanics. At critical points in the development of these disciplines, certain organizing principles discovered and used very fruitfully by the scientists in these fields were given much more quantitative justification by developments in atomic physics. For example, the whole concept of valence and the geometrical configurations discovered or postulated by chemists was given greater quantitative substance by the development of quantum mechanics. Also, in many cases, empirical knowledge about such structures was obtained largely by instrumental means developed by physicists, such as various forms of optical spectroscopy, nuclear magnetic resonance, mass spectrometry, and X-ray crystallography, all of which were almost entirely unknown at the beginning of this century. This sweep of physical science, including physics, chemistry, and molecular biology, forms a continuum with no obvious separations. The development of this whole intellectual structure in the last century represents possibly the greatest concentrated intellectual achievement of humankind.

We could not possibly review all of this within the scope of one volume. We have been forced to choose and, therefore, to omit magnificent pieces of the entire tapestry. We have chosen what, one might say, are the two boundaries of this continuous panorama of scientific development. One boundary is the development of physics, the experimental discoveries, and the drastic changes in our understanding of the theoretical and conceptual foundations of the atomic and cosmic world. This is described and evaluated in the paper by Gerald Feinberg. At the other boundary of the physical sciences—the most recent and most startling outcome of the long chain of development of chemistry—is the unfolding of the molecular basis of life, the subject of the paper by John Edsall, on progress in molecular biology and evolutionary biology.

It is relevant to refer here to some views among philosophers and historians of science about such claims of progress. One school of thought asserts that the perception by scientists of the nature of their activity is such that the outcome *must* be progress by definition so that the notion that science progresses is a self-fulfilling judgment. A related judgment then is that to get a true evaluation of scientific progress, one must go outside the scientific community and apply tests or criteria formulated through logical procedures by philosophers of science. Most physical scientists are unaware of such philosophical critiques and modes of analysis, and of those who are aware of these philosophical positions, most would disagree. Several of the authors here point to this conflict in attitudes between the philosophers of science and the scientists. It is worth mentioning also that some of these judgments on progress and methodology in science have had a much greater influence on the social sciences than on the physical sciences. Gerald Holton addresses this matter of the definition of scientific progress, using the developments of physics during the last several centuries and particularly in the last century as a basis for his formulation of the nature of progress in science. To some extent, his essay complements that of Feinberg. The latter describes some of the great theoretical advances of the last century and their impact on the understanding of the physical world, and Holton shows how these advances can help to formulate a general theory of scientific progress. We return to this theme below.

It is interesting to compare the tone and thrust of the Feinberg and Edsall essays. Both have philosophical and, perhaps, religious implications. Physics has given us an image of the nature of the universe and biology of the nature of life, images very different and remote from traditional beliefs. The consequence of this erosion of traditional beliefs may have as great an impact on the human condition as the detailed, scientific impact of these developments on human life. Each essay in Part Two is in an important sense characteristic of the nature of its particular field of science. They span not only the total spectrum of fundamental science but exemplify how the characteristics, problems, and methodologies change as one covers this range.

Feinberg emphasizes the great theoretical and conceptual changes that have occurred in the descriptions of the atom and of the nature of space and time. These did not represent intricate, complex problems; for example, single atoms can be simply described, but it did require the proper conceptual formulation for the understanding of these problems to be achieved. These theoretical constructions clarified the concepts of the atom and of space and time, and we then understood the behavior of more complex physical systems. However, there is little or no consideration in Feinberg's essay of some complex systems which the physicists deal with and in which tremendous progress has been made, for example, the whole field of condensed matter, liquids, and solids. These do represent applications of the fundamental theoretical structure, and they are important, but they certainly do not have the major philosophical impact that the changes in concepts have.

Edsall, on the other hand, focuses on a particular problem, the nature of life and its propagation. Obviously, this is of great importance and as more than just the solution of a scientific problem. He gives us a detailed and fascinating history of the development of molecular biology and evolutionary biology and discusses some of the philosophical and ethical implications of this work.

Feinberg describes the evolution of physics during what was undoubtedly the most revolutionary period in the history of science, which spanned about a century, dating from the death of Maxwell (1879) to the present, covering the era of Einstein, Bohr, Heisenberg, and Dirac. During this period, the content and scope of physics were completely altered in the kind of phenomena that were discovered and the theoretical models used, all leading to a scientific structure that was probably the most successful theory in the history of science. The atom itself, from having been a vague, semiphilosophical concept, acquired real physical meaning and precisely defined physical properties. The entities with which the theory deals, the mathematical organization, the abstractness of the concepts, all differ from anything that had gone before. In many cases, the concepts are remote from direct human experience, and they have been created and used by scientists because they are found to represent successful organizing principles which describe the nature of physical reality very well. Between them, the two major theories created during this period, quantum mechanics and relativity, can explain the nature of the atom, the origins of the universe, and the characteristics of strange and remote astrophysical systems, which exemplify Einstein's general theory of relativity.

The development of this conceptual structure of physical theory is the exemplary model and a central theme in Holton's essay. There he deals with what he considers a limited (and perhaps simplistic) view of science, one consisting of empirical data, plus "propositions concerning logic and mathematics" ("phenomenic propositions" and "analytic propositions"). This view is characteristic of most current philosophies of science, which originated in empiricism or positivism. The deficiency of this description is that it restricts science to data, plus logic, and does not provide for any means of producing axioms and, thereby, a theoretical *structure*. Such a limited, two-dimensional view, in principle, should lead everyone to the same scientific conclusions. Holton asks: "Why is science not one great totalitarian engine?" The missing ingredient, the formulation of axioms which then lead to a theory, is considered in great detail by Holton, using, particularly, the work of Einstein on the nature of theoretical physics.

Einstein's conclusions are best expressed in a quotation: "In the logical sense the fundamental concepts and postulates of physics are the free inventions of the human mind." In his further description of

Einstein's criteria for choosing a particular set of concepts, for making a particular "invention"—simplicity, symmetry, the efficacy of formal mathematical structures, parsimony, unification—Holton might seem to be opening a Pandora's box of personal and possibly idiosyncratic choices representing an act of faith by the inventing scientist, or perhaps an aesthetic choice. In large part, however, these criteria do represent the beliefs of the community of theorists and as guidelines have been remarkably successful not only in Einstein's "inventions" but in all later "inventions"—modern nuclear theory, cosmology, etc. Holton makes a very strong case for the Einstein prescription, which challenges the more conventional philosophic views stemming from positivism or empiricism. The Einstein view has created all the important features of modern physical theory, which do not emerge easily from these alternative approaches.

Edsall deals with progress in the understanding of life at the most fundamental scientific level, in the fields of biochemistry and molecular biology, on the one hand, and evolutionary biology, on the other. In a period of sixty years, from what may be considered as the origins of biochemistry to the present, there has emerged, particularly during the last quarter century, a revolutionary change in our understanding of the chemical basis of life. The developments in the logical organization of chemical concepts and knowledge of chemical structures now provide us with an understanding of metabolism and chemical processes which occur throughout the biological domain, animal, bacterial, and, to a large extent, in the higher plants. What has occurred is a scientific revolution, not in the Kuhnian sense, which Edsall specifically disavows. "No great intellectual construction was overthrown," but a whole host of new concepts were developed, such as the genetic code, which have led to a coherent structure uniting chemistry and biology in a way which has never been achieved previously. "A gene ceased to be a black box and became a known chemical system full of information," all entirely understandable in terms of known physics and chemistry. One outstanding aspect of this development is the unification of two fields that had been quite separate, namely, biochemistry and genetics. This is not to say that all is now known, but now at least we know where to look.

Concurrently, there has been an equally great increase in the understanding of the nature and mechanism of evolution. The combination of a more precise formulation of mathematical genetics, plus a great deal of biological research, has unified the conceptual structure of evolutionary genetics so that the whole process of evolutionary development and the conditions and circumstances for the creation of species are now understood. A major result is the realization of the random nature of the evolutionary process. One cannot predict an evolutionary step, but one can know that it is "compatible with the theory." This is satisfactory for the scientist, but the notion of *contingency* in the evolution of biological beings and, particularly, of man has tremendous impact on all traditional religious beliefs.

Because the subject of molecular biology and evolution is so closely tied to the human condition and human beliefs, there are other ideological and possible social consequences of work in this field, for example, the present status of eugenics, the political implications of research in human genetics, and the field of sociobiology. Edsall feels that there should be no political constraints on such research and that the dangers are probably illusory.

Finally, Edsall comments on the general question of progress and the hope of progress. As a biologist, he is concerned with ecological threats to the future of life, the extinction of some species, the deterioration of certain land areas, for example, tropical rain forests and the like. Though he takes these problems quite seriously, these anxieties are only small perturbations in this generally optimistic view of the future of biological research and the benefits of such research for mankind. He cites a comment by Peter Medawar: "To deride the hope of progress is the ultimate fatuity, the last word in poverty of spirit and meanness of mind."

In contrast to the celebration of scientific progress, of science as an intellectual achievement, are the problems of public attitudes and public concerns about science, the difficulties of public decision making about technology, its benefits and its risks. The essay by Bernard Davis is concerned with this problem. Two others touching on the theme of popular attitudes toward technology—one by Harvey Brooks and one by Nathan Rosenberg—appear in Part Three. (An essay concerned with the same problem was also presented by Arthur Kantrowitz at a symposium prior to the completion of this volume. There is no printed version of Kantrowitz's paper because it overlapped to a great extent the content of the Messenger Lectures, given by Kantrowitz at Cornell.) All of these writers are concerned in one way or another with the conflict in attitudes and judgments of two separate groups: on the one hand, probably the majority of the technical and scientific community, and, on the other, a minority of scientists and many concerned laymen. In general, the consensus of the scientific community is that science and its effects can be *managed* for the benefit of society.

On the other side, in opposition to scientific and technological judgments by people with some expertise is a group of organizations and individuals, which Kantrowitz had referred to as the "critical establishment." Although these groups may have some understanding of technical problems and their concern may sometimes be justified, there is also a tendency to stress the negative consequences of technology, even when such concern is not warranted. This critical establishment transmits to the larger society a generalized distrust of technological innovation, appealing to fears of the unknown, with the common difficulties of assessing risk among laymen.

Kantrowitz has presented a number of cases in which real scientific or technological issues were almost ignored and final decisions made largely on the basis of the political effectiveness of the contenders rather than by any rational method based on estimates of the costs and benefits to society. Kantrowitz has for some time urged the establishment of some due process procedure similar to that of our legal system to deal with disputes about the consequences of technological innovation. Although a proposal of this kind presents many problems, it does reflect a need for some orderly procedure to cope with scientific and technological issues of great consequence for society.

Granted the enormous progress of science and technology, one of its implications is the growing importance of scientific and technological decisions for society and the consequent "politicization" of these decisions. If there is any single problem that is repeatedly pointed up by the essays in this volume, it is the discrepancy between our scientific and technological power and our political capacity for utilizing this technology optimally.

Bernard Davis treats the political repercussions and unreasonable fears which have arisen from the work on recombinant DNA. The problems which can arise in the interaction of scientists and the public include anxieties about improbable consequences of science, naïve expectations of absolute security, a general mistrust of institutions and experts, diffuse blame attaching to science because of some applications of its technology, the guilt of scientists over possible elitism, the increasing complexity and, therefore, decreased accessibility to the public, and, finally, the general undermining of traditional supernatural beliefs by scientific knowledge.

Davis classifies public fears under three headings: dangerous products, dangerous powers, dangerous knowledge, and illustrates these problems by recent experience in biology. Dangerous products are exemplified in the history of recombinant DNA, where events show that the fear of escape from the laboratory of new and threatening organisms was vastly exaggerated. The result has been a substantial bureaucracy to control this activity and the setting of needlessly high and costly standards. The fear of dangerous powers is exemplified by the threat of gene manipulation, gene replacement, and cloning. Scientific opinion now would indicate that all of these powers are not likely to come into being for clear scientific reasons. However, the impact on society will continue and the concern will remain even though any real basis for such concern probably does not exist.

Finally, there is the fear of dangerous knowledge: whether certain fields of science should be studied at all because one might learn something which might be politically dangerous, for example, the study of human behavioral genetics. The fear is that the recognition of genetic differences among human groupings might have political repercussions. Whether political ideology should be a criterion in a matter of this kind is a very delicate matter. Davis's closely reasoned discussion of this problem establishes an agenda on the interaction between science and political goals, which society will ultimately have to consider. In a nonauthoritarian society, such controversies cannot be settled by fiat but, presumably, by some method of informed decision making.

Though the recent successes of the natural sciences have encouraged emulation among the social and historical sciences, from the eighteenth century on there have been sanguine philosophers and social scientists who have argued that human affairs are susceptible to scientific treatment in no way different from physics and the other hard sciences. This was a position taken by the Abbé Saint-Pierre and Condorcet in the eighteenth century, Comte, Marx, and others in the nineteenth century, and advanced again in recent decades by neopositivist philosophers of science such as Richard Braithwaite and Carl Hempel. This hard science approach was led by economists and psychologists who set mathematics, statistics, and experimentation as the methodological criteria of social scientific progress, and the discovery of general laws of social process and change as their goal. Marc Roberts, in his essay on the social sciences, and H. Stuart Hughes, in his paper on historiography, demur from this point of view, arguing that the spillover of expectations and methodologies from the hard sciences into the softer ones has been in part counterproductive, has introduced misleading and unrealizable criteria of progress, and has resulted in a partial misdirection of energy and a misallocation of resources.

Both Roberts and Hughes acknowledge the uses of scientific methods, the value of mathematical formulation and statistical analysis in the development of the human sciences, and the discovery of important regularities and relations in the social and historical process. Roberts argues that the rage for rigor and for order, the overemphasis on quantification and formal theorizing, has diverted the attention of social scientists from the search for solutions to practical problems to which their sciences are more suited. And Hughes claims that the diffusion of positivism into historiography has produced a kind of hyperprofessionalism and loss of contact by historians with larger interpretive themes, such that the meaning of the past is inadequately illuminated by their work.

Thus, the progress of the social sciences and historiography in contrast with the exact sciences is a story, on the one hand, of great constructive accomplishments and somewhat confused identity, on the other. The essays by Edsall and Davis and the ones in Part Three by Abramovitz, Brooks, Rosenberg, and Chenery demonstrate the point that continued scientific progress, the solution of contemporary problems of technology and the protection of the environment, as well as the continuation and spread of material welfare, are dependent on political and cultural adaptations of a substantial sort. Only a minority among social scientists approach the study of human affairs from the perspective of the contemporary biological image of man in the evolutionary process as a creative innovator and problem solver. Their criteria of progress have been drawn from the simplistic reconstructions of the positivist philosophers of science, views generally rejected by the natural scientists themselves.

6

Progress in Our Understanding of Biology

JOHN T. EDSALL

Earlier in this volume, Francisco Ayala dealt with the concept of progress in the development of living organisms and their evolution since life on earth began (see pp. 106ff.). He defined progress as directional change, combined with improvement according to some objective standard. My aim here is different; my concern is not to inquire whether living organisms, and the biosphere in general, have improved over time but whether and how our understanding of life has become deeper and more adequate. There can be no doubt that progress in this sense has occurred; it has indeed accelerated over at least the last four centuries. The transformation of understanding in the present century, and especially in the last forty years, has changed our outlook on the nature of life more fundamentally than ever before. I shall concentrate, therefore, primarily on the twentieth century with emphasis on biochemistry and molecular biology, on the one hand, and evolutionary biology, on the other. Indeed, these two broad areas, once inhabited by quite different groups of scientists who communicated little with each other, have moved far closer together; they overlap, and in some places they merge.

This essay, however, will not be simply a celebration of progress. It is gravely doubtful that the accelerated pace of discovery in the last few centuries can be maintained. A few distinguished scientists have even questioned how much of great significance will still be left to

I thank Ernst Mayr, Francisco J. Ayala, and Bernard D. Davis for their comments on an earlier draft of this paper. I am indebted to the National Science Foundation (Grant SOC 7912543) for continuing support.

discover in another generation or so. Although I believe that the territory still to be explored is immense, one cannot dismiss such thoughts casually. There are also serious threats to the future of biology and to the future of life itself: the simultaneous growth of deserts and of vast urban areas; the destruction of great forest regions, especially of much of the world's tropical rain forests; the exploitation of marginal land to grow food for an increasing human population—all these developments diminish the range of habitats where living creatures can survive and flourish. The present evidence points to the coming extinction of a vast number of plant and animal species over the next generation at a rate unparalleled in past human history. The implications are grave for the future of biology, and they are of course immense for the future of humanity and of life in general. I close with a few reflections inspired by these larger issues.

DANGERS OF THE IDEA OF PROGRESS
FOR THE STUDY OF HISTORY

Before considering our major themes, however, a warning is in order. The idea of progress, involving directional change through time, is in its very essence historical. Such an idea, however, may corrupt and distort the writing of history, including perhaps especially the history of science. Surely it is the proper aim of the historian to understand the people and the period under study in their own terms, to grasp as nearly as possible how the world looked to them and why they thought and acted as they did. The task is formidable, perhaps nearly impossible, especially for times and places remote from our own. Interpretations are uncertain, and historians will continue their disputes. Nevertheless, the aim remains: to see people—their thoughts and actions—as truly as possible and without parochial prejudice.

Herbert Butterfield has characterized the opposite tendency as "the Whig interpretation of history," which he describes as "the tendency in many historians to write on the side of Protestants and Whigs, to praise revolutions provided they have been successful, to emphasize certain principles of progress in the past and to produce a story which is the ratification if not the glorification of the present."[1] All of us, I think, have been exposed to this form of history in one way or another; it gets into school textbooks and stays there in spite of the detailed researches of scholarly historians, whose work undermines the simplicity of such concepts.

The close relation between the Whig conception of history and the idea of progress is obvious. What concerns me here is its effect on the writing of the history of science. The existence of progress in the natural sciences is inescapable; but historians often write to celebrate that progress rather than to understand the course of history. The

1. Herbert Butterfield, *The Whig Interpretation of History* (London: G. Bell & Sons, 1931; reprinted 1951); the quoted passage is from the preface.

danger is particularly great when a practicing scientist like myself turns to the study of the history of science; but even professional historians can easily fall into the trap. It is tempting to extrapolate from the present back to the past and to rate the value of past events and trends in terms of developments that have come to fruition in our own time. Joseph Fruton has warned of this tendency in his important studies on the development of biochemistry.[2] In what follows, I may sometimes fail to heed my own warning, but the reader should remember it.

BIOLOGY SINCE THE SIXTEENTH CENTURY: THE ACCELERATION OF DISCOVERY

The course of discovery in the natural sciences for the last four centuries is probably the most striking example of the conception of the acceleration of history as advanced by Henry Adams. Derek de Solla Price has documented the exponential increase of the scientific literature and of scientific activity in general over this time. Bentley Glass has described the phenomenon recently in considerable detail for the science of biology.[3] He tabulates a list of great discoveries or milestones in biology, as a function of time. For the first half of the seventeenth century he records only two such milestones—Harvey's demonstration of the circulation of the blood (1628) and Van Helmont's analysis of the growth of a willow plant in terms of its uptake of water (1648). For the second half of the century, Glass lists seven discoveries of comparable significance to these. For the eighteenth century he records twenty-two and for the nineteenth the number rises to 136, of which ninety-four fall in the second half of the century. According to this analysis the doubling time for the number of major discoveries is of the order of fifty years in the seventeenth and eighteenth centuries, but the acceleration in the nineteenth is substantially greater. By the twentieth century the pace has so increased that Glass restricts himself to discoveries in his own field of genetics—a field which is essentially a twentieth-century creation beginning with the rediscovery of Mendel's work in 1900. Here he lists 185 major discoveries between 1900 and 1972. The phenomenal acceleration in rates of discovery is still being maintained although one must note that genetics is one of the most active areas in all of biology, and some fields that were active in the nineteenth century—comparative anatomy, for example—have been relatively quiescent in our time. The choice of just what discoveries to include in the list is, of course, to some extent arbitrary, but

2. Joseph S. Fruton, *Molecules and Life: Historical Essays on the Interplay of Chemistry and Biology* (New York: Wiley, 1972).

3. Henry Adams, *The Education of Henry Adams*, ed. with introduction and notes by Ernest Samuels (Boston: Houghton Mifflin, 1974), Chaps. 23, 24; Derek J. de Solla Price, *Little Science, Big Science* (New York: Columbia University Press, 1963); Bentley Glass, "Milestones and Rates of Growth in the Development of Biology," *Quarterly Review of Biology*, 54 (1979): 31-53.

other historians of biology would almost surely acknowledge the validity of the general trend that Glass portrays.

Glass emphasizes a significant fact: the frequency of notable discoveries has indeed been increasing exponentially with time, but at a considerably smaller rate than the exponential growth in the number of papers published, the number of scientific workers, or the funds invested in the support of science. Thus, to maintain the accelerated pace of major discoveries, the demands for the support of science are steadily increasing. By Glass's analysis the fraction of all scientific papers published in biology that represent important advances has been, and is still, declining. This latter statement, indeed, is something that many of us have recognized in a general way, though without the documentation that Glass has now provided.

Nicholas Rescher has stressed both the acceleration in the rates of scientific discovery with time and the increasing effort and expense required to make further progress at a comparable rate. His discussion focuses on the physical sciences, but in large measure it is equally applicable to biology.[4] In the real world exponential processes cannot continue indefinitely. As time goes on, the growth curve must bend over and begin to level off; otherwise, it must end in something analogous to an explosion. I return later to some of the implications of these findings for the future of biology.

However, as Glass would certainly emphasize, an appreciation of the development of biology does not come primarily through a catalogue of discoveries but through perspective on the growth of ideas and concepts. For a study of the major themes of biological inquiry over the preceding centuries, we are indebted to François Jacob, who is probably unique in his historical perspective among the great creators of modern molecular biology.[5] He denotes his study as a history of heredity, but this subject involves practically all the major problems and ideas of general biology. Jacob traces with great insight the major developments, from the early confusion over spontaneous generation and the belief in strange, supposedly possible matings between different species to the fundamental concepts of modern biochemical genetics. In his introduction he sets forth the concept of the genetic program as understood today, a concept which largely reconciles mechanistic and teleological (or teleonomic) views that previously were thought to be in conflict. To this I return later.

My concern, in the rest of this essay, is with the twentieth century and progress in our time, together with the outlook for the future.

PROGRESS IN BIOCHEMISTRY AND MOLECULAR BIOLOGY

Although there was significant progress in biochemistry from the time of Lavoisier on, the subject is largely a creation of the last sixty

4. Nicholas Rescher, *Scientific Progress* (Pittsburgh, Pa.: University of Pittsburgh Press, 1978).

5. François Jacob, *La logique du vivant: Une histoire de l'hérédité* (Paris: Editions

years. The most spectacular developments have occurred in the last quarter century, but the earlier developments were fundamental for all that happened later.[6] From the immense mass of detail I will try to point out a few general conclusions that emerged from the earlier "classical" biochemistry. Its practical achievements were in any case great, notably in revolutionizing the science of nutrition through the discovery of vitamins and the identification of the essential amino acids for synthesis of body proteins, and in the discovery and purification of numerous hormones.

1. It was an arduous and essential undertaking to establish the nature of the substances involved in metabolic processes and the transformations they would undergo. In spite of the fact that the organic chemists had synthesized scores of thousands of compounds, the substances important in biochemistry were, in many cases, still unknown; their transformations in the living cell, or in suitable extracts derived from it, were for the most part unparalleled by anything known in the chemical laboratory. For instance, adenosine triphosphate (ATP), first isolated and characterized in 1929, had not previously been suspected of existing; yet it proved to play an absolutely central role in biochemical energy transformation. The same thing was true repeatedly; the vital substances had to be found by hard work, with little guidance from general principles.

2. Biochemical evidence greatly strengthened the conception of the general unity of life. The major patterns of metabolism proved to be much the same throughout the bacterial and animal kingdoms and, to a large extent, in the higher plants as well. There were of course variations, and special chemical processes were found in certain classes of organisms. For example, a substance as important in the animal world as cholesterol is not found in bacteria or in any but a very few of the higher plants. On the whole, however, the biochemical similarities that prevail throughout the living world are far more striking than the differences.

3. Practically every biochemical process proved to be catalyzed by a

---

Gallimard, 1970); English trans. Betty E. Spillmann, *The Logic of Life: A History of Heredity* (New York: Vintage, 1976).

6. The best single source on the development of biochemistry from 1800 to about 1950 is probably Fruton's *Molecules and Life*. It illustrates in detail the points briefly sketched here. See also the more extensive "History of Biochemistry" by Marcel Florkin in *Comprehensive Biochemistry*, ed. M. Florkin and E.H. Stotz, vols. 30-33 (Amsterdam and New York: Elsevier, 1972-1979). For the developments in molecular genetics, which are discussed below, the most useful reference is probably Gunther Stent and Richard Calendar, *Molecular Genetics*, 2nd ed. (San Francisco, Ca.: W.H. Freeman, 1978; first ed. by Stent alone, W.H. Freeman, 1972). Stent has been deeply involved in research in the field; he writes lucidly and with historical and philosophical perspective. James D. Watson, *Molecular Biology of the Gene*, 3rd ed. (Menlo Park, Ca.: W.A. Benjamin, 1976), is a brilliant portrayal of the current status of the field but is not concerned with the historical background. For the reader from outside the natural sciences who wants to learn about molecular biology, Stent's book is probably the more useful of the two.

specific enzyme. Enzyme-catalyzed processes ran smoothly, at ordinary temperatures, and without the side reactions that troubled the organic chemists when they could not use specific catalysts. J.B. Sumner at Cornell, in 1926, and J.H. Northrop at the Rockefeller Institute, from 1930 on, were the first to demonstrate that pure enzymes are proteins, a conclusion confirmed a thousandfold later on. Proteins were already known to be important and complex and to be composed of more than twenty kinds of amino acids in widely varying proportions. Evidence steadily mounted that they were large and specific molecules of defined structure, with molecular weights of many thousands and sometimes millions, but the details of that structure were still obscure until about 1950.[7]

4. Much was learned about the pathways of energy transformation in living organisms and particularly of the enzyme and coenzyme systems that serve to break down organic compounds in stages, providing an energy yield that can be turned into useful work at each stage; and of the details of the cyclic processes that serve to convert these compounds into carbon dioxide and water as end products.

These points are simply bare indicators of some aspects of biochemical progress. Before 1940 there was relatively little interest in the nucleic acids, though P.A. Levene had made important advances in determining their organic chemical structure. They were supposed to be built on simple repeating patterns, for which no function was apparent. Just after 1940, however, two major developments pointed to the coming union of biochemistry and genetics. One was the work of G.W. Beadle and E.L. Tatum on the metabolism of the bread mold *Neurospora* and the numerous mutants they obtained from it with specific biochemical deficiencies. Each deficiency could be traced, at least by inference, to the loss of function of a specific enzyme by mutation; this led to the formulation: one gene, one enzyme. Essentially, this slogan was correct; the later advances in molecular biology led to the modified version: one gene, one polypeptide chain.[8]

Meanwhile, Oswald T. Avery and his collaborators at the Rockefeller Institute proved in ten years of intensive work that the transforming substance that changed pneumococci from the rough (nonvirulent) to the smooth (virulent) form was DNA. This was in fact a

7. A recent symposium, "The Origins of Modern Biochemistry: A Retrospect on Proteins," *Annals of the New York Academy of Sciences*, 325 (1979): 1-373, is an important source of material on the history of protein biochemistry. Concerning proteins in nutrition, see the papers therein by W.C. Rose and H.E. Carter.

8. Some of the ideas of Beadle and Tatum were anticipated by the English clinician Sir Archibald Garrod in his *Inborn Errors of Metabolism* (Oxford: Oxford University Press, 1909; 2nd ed. 1923). He correctly inferred that certain enzymes, catalyzing intermediate steps in metabolism in normal people, were missing in conditions such as albinism and alcaptonuria. His work was almost forgotten for a time among geneticists, and Beadle and Tatum learned of it only after their researches were largely completed.

genetic transformation, and the inference could be drawn that DNA was the genetic material. Avery did not state this inference explicitly in his published work although he was well aware of it. The immense importance of the work was recognized in some quarters almost immediately, though it required several more years before biologists generally accepted the view that DNA, rather than protein, was actually the material that carried genetic information.

The crucial event occurred in 1953 when J.D. Watson and Francis Crick formulated the double helical structure of DNA. This not only explained the data relating to the chemical structure, but it offered a rational basis for the replication of DNA, with each of the two complementary strands, on separating and unwinding, serving as a template for the synthesis of the complementary strand.

The developments that followed this work have produced what may fairly be called a revolution in biology. However, in agreement with a recent remarkable study of the molecular biologists by Horace Judson,[9] I would stress the importance of two biochemical studies that preceded Watson and Crick. One was the determination by Frederick Sanger of the exact sequence of amino acid residues in the two chains of the insulin molecule. The patterns were specific and unique; insulin behaved as a pure chemical compound, and the molecules were all alike. However, to the surprise of many, there was no sign of any repeating pattern in the specific sequences; they were like messages written in an unknown language. As Jacques Monod remarked in a conversation with Judson, the existence of such a definite, yet nonrepeating pattern implies the existence of a code that prescribes the sequence of the elements in the message.[10]

Likewise, Erwin Chargaff, at about the same time, showed by careful analytical techniques, with DNA from many species, that nucleic acids were not the uninteresting molecules people had supposed, with a simple repeating pattern that could not convey significant information. Chargaff's data liberated biochemists from such restrictions and showed the possibility of an almost infinite variety of sequence patterns among the bases in DNA. Also, he cautiously noted one restriction on this immense range of possibilities: within the limits of analytical error, the amount of adenine (A) was always equal to that of thymine (T), and the amount of guanine (G) was always equal to that of cytosine (C). Nobody knew at that time what the equivalence meant, but it emerged later as a necessary result of the complementary relations between A and T, and between G and C, in the double helix structure. Chargaff has since become deeply disillusioned with what he feels to be the stridency, and the frantic pace, of modern research

9. Horace Freeland Judson, *The Eighth Day of Creation: The Makers of the Revolution in Biology* (New York: Simon & Shuster, 1979). I have reviewed the book and others related to it, *Journal of the History of Biology*, 13 (1980): 141-58.

10. Judson, *Eighth Day of Creation*, p. 213.

workers in molecular biology—"a frantic and noisy search for stunts and 'breakthroughs'" in his opinion, but this should not obscure his fundamental contribution to the subject.[11]

The existence of specific sequence patterns in DNA and proteins, together with much evidence that the nucleic acid somehow directed the synthesis of the protein, led naturally to the search for a code to define the relation between the two. Judson has told in detail of that search and its ultimate complete resolution by experiment,[12] including the evidence that the code is universal: the same for all living things. The details do not concern us here. Essentially, what has emerged is the concept of a genetic program, imprinted in the DNA, executed and controlled by enzymes and regulatory proteins, the structures of which are specified by the program in the DNA.[13] The message from the DNA is transmitted from the cell nucleus to the cytoplasm by messenger RNA, which directs the synthesis of the protein during its attachment to the subcellular structures known as ribosomes, with a specific shape and surface that permit the process to run smoothly and rapidly.

Once the specified sequence of the protein is laid down and it is released from the ribosome, it must fold up into a rather complex three-dimensional structure before it can function as an enzyme or in some other specific way. The DNA and messenger RNA cannot specify the three-dimensional structure but only the sequence. However, it turns out that, given the correct sequence, the folding follows spontaneously; a fact that was boldly predicted by Crick, and has been experimentally verified by C. B. Anfinsen and others. Thus, the specificity of enzymes, antibodies, and other highly specific proteins is all implicitly embodied in the sequence of their amino acid residues. The central feature of the process is the transmission of genetic information through an exactly specified order in DNA to RNA and then to the protein. This pattern of order is faithfully reproduced; a complicated set of chemical controls insures that the exact message is transmitted from DNA to protein; the probability of error in transmission is extremely small.

Thus, the DNA directs the program, and the enzymes operate it— subject, of course, to the provision of food, water, sources of energy, and essential chemical elements in a suitable environment. The program does not remain invariant from generation to generation, of course. Occasional mutations introduce alterations; and, in sexually reproducing organisms, the recombinations that occur among the genes derived from the parents produce endless variations in the genetic make-up of the offspring. Each resulting organism is unique,

11. See Erwin Chargaff's autobiography, *Heraclitean Fire: Sketches from a Life Before Nature* (New York: Rockefeller University Press, 1978). I have reviewed the book in *ISIS*, 70 (1979): 276-77.

12. See Judson, *Eighth Day of Creation*, Chaps. 5, 6, 8.

13. The concept of the program is most explicitly set forth by Jacob in the introduction to his *La logique du vivant*.

and natural selection is in perpetual operation, altering the average distribution of genes in the total gene pool of any species as time goes on. To this matter I return in the next section.

One of the great advances of modern biology is in our understanding, still in an early stage, of the controls that regulate the action of genes and turn them off and on so as to harmonize and coordinate the activity and development of the organism. For bacteria, much is known primarily through the great work of Jacob and Monod.[14] The structural genes determine the sequence of specific proteins. Regulator and operator genes control the rates of synthesis of the proteins through intermediate substances (repressors) synthesized under the influence of the regulator genes and released into the cytoplasm. The specific repressors bind to the operator genes to which they are complementary. An inducing substance, such as lactose in the particular gene system studied by Monod in *Escherichia coli*, causes the repressor to relax its grip on the operator. The message from the operator then gets through to start the synthesis of specific enzymes that are needed to metabolize the inducer or a substance closely related to it. Other repressors can be activated by certain metabolites; they then bind to their complementary operators and shut down the synthesis of the enzymes that catalyze that particular metabolic pathway. In higher organisms our knowledge of the regulatory systems that control development and gene expression is still in a very primitive state; it remains one of the great fields for future discovery in biology.

There is another system of biochemical controls; instead of regulating the *synthesis* of enzymes, it regulates their *activity*. Commonly it functions by feedback inhibition; if there is overproduction of the end product of a metabolic sequence beyond the needs of the organism, some of the end product molecule binds to the first enzyme in that sequence, converting it reversibly to an inactive form. Thus, the whole sequence of reactions is shut down, and wasteful production of the end product is stopped. Enzymes that are subject to feedback inhibition have been termed allosteric enzymes by Monod[15] since the inhibitor binds at a different region of the enzyme molecule from the active site where the substrate binds, and in general it is quite a different kind of molecule from the substrate. The action of many hormones appears to involve a similar conformation change in a specific protein when the hormone binds to it. The existence of molecules with such remarkable built-in controls would, of course, have been seen by our ancestors as evidence of purposeful design by the Creator. These molecules are, in fact, products of mutation and natural selection. Once they are formed,

14. François Jacob and Jacques Monod, "Genetic Regulatory Mechanisms in the Synthesis of Proteins," *Journal of Molecular Biology*, 3 (1961): 318-56.

15. Jacques Monod, Jean-Pierre Changeux, and François Jacob, "Allosteric Proteins and Cellular Control Systems," *Journal of Molecular Biology*, 6 (1963): 306-29. See also Judson, *Eighth Day of Creation*, Chaps. 9, 10.

the organisms that possess them have obviously an immense selective advantage over those that do not. Knowledge of such control mechanisms has begun to establish at the biochemical level evidence for the nature of the harmonious integration of the activities of living organisms, which has been recognized since the time of Aristotle.

One aspect of progress in science is certainly the unification of fields that had been separate. This has occurred with biochemistry and genetics. Early in the century a gene was essentially a "black box," of which we could only say (for eukaryotic organisms) that it was located on one of the chromosomes. Most workers doubted whether the principles of Mendelian genetics applied to bacteria at all. There were guesses that genes might be composed of protein, or nucleoprotein— plain nucleic acid, in those days, seemed too uninformative in structure (to use current terminology) to be of any use in itself. Until the work of Avery there was really no relevant information regarding the chemistry of the gene.[16] Now we know not only that genes are made up of sequences of DNA, but we also know the language of the genetic code. H.G. Khorana and his associates have synthesized a gene in the chemical laboratory, inserted it into a strain of bacteria that lacked it, and shown that it is functional *in vivo*.[17]

Much is still obscure; we know that there are long stretches of DNA in cell nuclei that do not code for any protein and have no known regulatory function. In eucaryotic organisms and some viruses, though apparently not in bacteria, many genes that do code for proteins contain internal regions of DNA that are not translated into the protein sequence. Instead, the corresponding regions of messenger RNA are excised and the cut ends are spliced together to form the sequence that codes for the protein.[18] Discovery of new and unexpected phenomena is still proceeding rapidly, and the great triumphs of molecular biology should not blind us to the vastness of what is still unknown.

PROGRESS IN EVOLUTIONARY BIOLOGY

Progress in the understanding of the nature and mechanisms of evolution in the twentieth century has been immense. At the beginning of this century, the fact of evolution was almost universally accepted among biologists, but Darwin's conception of natural selection, acting on small inheritable variations as the basis of evolution, was widely disbelieved. The rediscovery of Mendelian genetics in 1900 by Hugo

16. Robert Olby, *The Path to the Double Helix* (Seattle: University of Washington Press, 1974). Olby traces in detail the ideas concerning the nature of the gene from 1900 to the work of Watson and Crick and the great variety of experimental approaches that helped to shed light on the problem.

17. M.J. Ryan, E.L. Brown, T. Sekiya, H. Küpper, and H.G. Khorana, "Total Synthesis of a Tyrosine Suppressor tRNA Gene. XVIII. Biological Activity and Transcription, *in vitro*, of the Cloned Gene," *Journal of Biological Chemistry*, 254 (1979): 5817-26.

18. See Francis Crick, "Split Genes and RNA Splicing," *Science*, 204 (1979): 264-71.

De Vries and Carl Correns, essential as it was for the resolution of the problem, led temporarily to an increase in confusion. De Vries proposed that new species evolved by sudden leaps because of drastic mutations that changed the whole character of the organism, and for a time he had many followers. The statisticians, led by Karl Pearson, challenged the whole Mendelian conception of discrete genetic factors since the inheritance of many characters—height, for example—appeared to follow a pattern of continuous distribution within a population rather than being confined to a few discrete categories. Only around 1920 was this objection disposed of as it became clear that such characteristics depended on the mutual action of many genes during development. This could give rise to essentially continuous distributions in the quantitative aspects of such characters in the resulting organisms. Moreover, the expression of genes in the course of development could be modified or selectively inhibited by a variety of control mechanisms, such as the action of hormones.

A far-reaching resolution of the conflicts between the various schools, with a general synthesis of evolutionary concepts, developed in the 1930s. It owed much to the mathematical analysis of mutation and selection in Mendelian populations developed by R. A. Fisher, Sewall Wright, and J. B. S. Haldane in the previous decade, but the new conceptions probably came most clearly to a focus in the work of Theodosius Dobzhansky, whose book *Genetics and the Origin of Species* appeared in 1937. A few landmarks in the field out of a vast literature are books by Julian Huxley, George Gaylord Simpson, and Ernst Mayr.[19] I will try to indicate briefly some of the key conceptions. In at least one area—see item 9 below—there is currently an active debate on important issues.

1. A species, as Mayr states, is a reproductive community, an ecological unit.[20] It interacts with other species with which it shares its environment but does not mate with them. A species is a genetic unit consisting of a large intercommunicating gene pool.

2. The members of a species share a common general pattern of

19. Theodosius Dobzhansky, *Genetics and the Origin of Species*, 3rd ed. (New York: Columbia University Press, 1951). Julian Huxley, *Evolution: The Modern Synthesis* (London: Allen & Unwin, 1942). George Gaylord Simpson, *The Major Features of Evolution* (New York: Columbia University Press, 1953); and his *The Meaning of Evolution*, rev. ed. (New Haven, Conn.: Yale University Press, 1967). Ernst Mayr, *Animal Species and Evolution* (Cambridge, Mass.: Harvard University Press, 1963); and his *Population, Species, and Evolution* (Cambridge, Mass.: Harvard University Press, 1970). This is an updated abridgement of the previous reference; a shorter volume, it is likely to be more useful for the general reader, and it also incorporates more recent developments. For an important perspective on the development of these concepts, see *The Evolutionary Synthesis: Perspectives on the Unification of Biology*, ed. Ernst Mayr and William B. Provine (Cambridge, Mass.: Harvard University Press, 1980). Among the authors are most of the surviving creators of this evolutionary synthesis.

20. Mayr, *Population, Species, and Evolution*, p. 12.

genetic make-up (the total genome), which makes them capable of mating successfully and leaving viable and fertile offspring; but each individual differs genetically from every other in the set of particular genes that he or she carries (such special cases as identical twins are rare enough to be disregarded in this respect).

3. Numerous small mutations are constantly occurring in the DNA of the members of any species, and the distribution of combinations in the gene pool of the species is constantly being reshuffled by recombination processes that give new patterns of DNA. Large drastic mutations, of the sort that interested De Vries, practically never result in offspring of superior fitness and play no part in evolution. However the production of new species is not necessarily, or even perhaps predominantly, the result of slowly accumulated small mutations (see item 9 below).

4. Natural selection operates on organisms in their total environment, not on genes as such. It is misleading to consider a gene as being fit or unfit in itself. Each gene is one component of a total interacting regulatory system that operates as the organism develops. Even though each structural gene specifies the constitution of a specific protein, the regulatory controls that turn genes "off" and "on," including the actions of hormones, can profoundly alter the effects of the presence of a gene as the organism develops. For the higher organisms, the nature of these controls is still largely unknown, but there is no doubt as to their fundamental importance.

5. The adaptations that arise from selection of favored variations are relative to a particular environment; a variation favored in one environment may be deleterious in another. There is, of course, nothing new about this conception; Darwin clearly recognized and emphasized it. This means of course that adaptive variation does not necessarily mean progress if we think of progress in terms of what human beings consider desirable.

6. Evolutionary success depends on leaving surviving offspring that can in turn survive and reproduce. Differential reproduction and survival is the basis of natural selection. The survivors may not, in terms of human values, be the most progressive and desirable. The fittest creatures, in terms of evolutionary population genetics, are the ones that leave most progeny.

7. New species may arise in various ways. An important mechanism is geographical isolation that separates two populations of an originally single species; this might occur, for instance, if some members of the species, during a favorable climatic period, migrate across a mountain barrier, which later becomes essentially impassable with change of climate. The course of subsequent gene mutations among the members of the separated populations may eventually make them so different genetically that they can no longer mate successfully (or desire to mate) if brought together again.

8. Chromosomes and the genes within them (apart from the X and Y chromosomes in male animals and similar sex-differentiating factors in other organisms) come in pairs, one from each parent. Thus, at any particular gene locus the corresponding pair of genes may be either alike (homozygous) or different (heterozygous). Until recently, most geneticists believed that in a well-adapted "fit" organism, the great majority of gene pairs would be homozygous, with identical pairs of presumably "superior" genes. Recent evidence shows the contrary; the proportion of heterozygous loci is large, often of the order of 50 percent in well-adapted healthy animals. A substantial amount of heterozygosity appears to increase fitness; it probably provides for a more flexible adaptation to a varying environment.

Species are populations composed of individuals, no two of which are identical. The distribution of various characters among the members of the species can be described in statistical terms. There is no ideal type to which the members of the species conform, and the statistical distribution of characters varies with time because of natural selection. This description of species in statistical terms was strange to most biologists when Darwin and Wallace proposed the concept of natural selection. The inability to understand it was responsible for a considerable part of the early opposition to the theory.

9. An important debate is currently under way concerning what G.G. Simpson has called the tempo and mode of evolution. Darwin believed that the formation of new species was always slow and gradual, resulting from the operation of natural selection on numerous small inheritable variations over long periods of geological time. This was also the view of the creators of the "Modern Synthesis"—Dobzhansky, Huxley, Simpson, Mayr, and others to whom I have referred above—and it appeared until quite recently to be rather generally accepted. The recent challenge has come primarily from some of the paleontologists; its essence is to be found in an article by Stephen Jay Gould and Niles Eldredge.[21] They argue that the evidence of the fossil record does not suggest a picture of slow gradual evolutionary change. Rather it shows great numbers of organisms persisting, with little or no evidence of visible change, over long periods of geological time; but

21. Stephen Jay Gould and Niles Eldredge, "Punctuated Equilibria: The Tempo and Mode of Evolution Reconsidered," *Paleobiology*, 3 (1977): 115-51. A recent book on the subject is by Steven M. Stanley, *Macroevolution: Pattern and Process* (San Francisco, Ca.: W.H. Freeman, 1979), reviewed by D.J. Futuyama, *American Scientist*, 68 (1980): 694. I have not yet had the opportunity to examine this book, but both Professor Gould, in personal discussion, and Futuyama in his review rate it as a major contribution. See also Roger Lewin, "Evolutionary Theory Under Fire," *Science*, 210 (1980): 883-87; this is a report of a conference in Chicago, where the tempo and mode of evolutionary change were earnestly and sometimes hotly debated for several days. For some important critical comments by several biologists on Lewin's interpretation of the conference and the issues involved, see the letters in *Science*, 211 (1981): 770-74.

these long stretches of stasis are punctuated, from time to time, by the comparatively abrupt appearance of new forms, clearly related to, but obviously different from, those that have gone before. The frequent absence of intermediate forms was explained by Darwin and most of his followers as being due to gaps in the fossil record. Unquestionably the gaps are numerous and serious; nevertheless, Gould and Eldredge argue that the fossil record should be taken as meaning, on the whole, just what it appears to say. If so the formation of new species is likely to occur only at long intervals, but at a rather rapid pace when it does occur, rather than being due to slow accumulation of small variations. The term "rapid" here must be understood in terms of geological time. A rapid process may require tens of thousands of years rather than (perhaps) scores of millions, as in the classical Darwinian view. One should not draw the contrast too sharply; the proponents of these views do not deny the existence of slow gradual change, but they believe that it plays a secondary role in formation of new species.

There is related evidence from the work of the molecular biologists. Consider for instance the contrast between frogs and mammals with respect to evolutionary change. The numerous species of frogs have remained morphologically and (presumably) functionally stable over scores of millions of years, with little evolutionary change. Mammals, in contrast, over the same period have evolved into immensely diverse forms, with new adaptations to a wide range of environments. Yet the rate of appearance of simple point mutations in the DNA, as shown by amino acid substitutions in their proteins, has been much the same in frogs and mammals.[22] This suggests that the major features of genetic change, with formation of new species, are associated with the larger alterations and rearrangements of the genes, rather than with the slow accumulation of point mutations. The whole field of knowledge in this area is now in a state of flux and further discoveries are likely to alter our perspective.

THE STATUS OF EVOLUTIONARY THEORY:
MECHANISM AND TELEOLOGY (OR TELEONOMY)

The theory of evolution differs in status from the theories of the physical sciences or from the concepts of modern molecular biology. In the words of Mayr: "The theory of natural selection can describe and explain phenomena with considerable precision, but it cannot give reliable predictions except through such trivial and meaningless circular statements as for instance, 'The fitter individuals will on the average leave more offspring.'"[23] This represents an important difference between evolutionary biology and the physical sciences. Prac-

22. Allan C. Wilson, Steven S. Carlson, and Thomas J. White, "Biochemical Evolution," *Annual Review of Biochemistry*, 46 (1977): 573-639. See especially the discussion of organismal rates versus molecular rates of evolution, pp. 616-20.

23. Ernst Mayr, "Cause and Effect in Biology," in his collected essays, *Evolution and the Diversity of Life* (Cambridge, Mass.: Harvard University Press, 1976).

tically all concepts in physics are predictive as well as explanatory; they are susceptible to test by experiment or by observations as in the prediction of an eclipse. Likewise, modern molecular biology has led to specific predictions that have been experimentally tested, as in the beautiful experiments of Matthew Meselson and Franklin Stahl, who showed by labeling bacterial DNA with heavy nitrogen and following its density over several generations grown without heavy nitrogen that the results corresponded to the semiconservative process of replication predicted by Watson and Crick from the double helix model.[24] In contrast Mayr says: "Probably nothing in biology is less predictable than the future course of evolution. Looking at the Permian reptiles, who would have predicted that most of the more flourishing groups would become extinct (many rather rapidly) and that one of the most undistinguished branches would give rise to the mammals?"[25]

Monod has made much the same point even more forcefully:

> The biosphere does not contain a predictable class of objects or of events but constitutes a particular occurrence, compatible indeed with first principles, but not *deducible* from those principles and therefore essentially unpredictable ... in my view the biosphere is unpredictable for the very same reason—neither more or less— that the particular configuration of atoms constituting this pebble I have in my hand is unpredictable ... it is enough for us that this actual object, unique and real, be *compatible* with the theory. ... That is enough for us as concerns the pebble, but not as concerns ourselves. We would like to think ourselves necessary, inevitable, ordained from all eternity. All religions, nearly all philosophies, and even a part of science testify to the unwearying, heroic effort of mankind desperately denying its own contingency.

Later he remarks: "The universe was not pregnant with life nor the biosphere with man. Our number came up in the Monte Carlo Game. Is it any wonder if, like the person who has just made a million at the casino, we feel strange and a little unreal?"[26]

Most biologists might not put the matter quite so forcefully as Monod, but I think that nearly all evolutionary biologists would essentially agree. However, we should not ignore, or try to evade, the fact that living organisms do constantly display goal-directed behavior. For a long time, mechanistically oriented biologists frowned on such statements as: "A female sea turtle came on shore to lay her eggs in the sand." The mechanists demanded a simple statement of temporal

24. Matthew Meselson and Franklin Stahl, "The Replication of DNA in *Escherichia Coli*," *Proceedings of the National Academy of Sciences*, 44 (1958): 671-83. Judson gives a good account of this work and how it developed; *Eighth Day of Creation*, pp. 188-92.

25. Mayr, "Cause and Effect," p. 368.

26. Jacques Monod, *Chance and Necessity*, trans. Austryn Wainhouse (New York: Knopf, 1971), pp. 43-44, 145-46.

sequence: "She came on shore and laid her eggs in the sand." The other statement was teleological, they said, and introduced the notion of final causes, which we are trying to banish from biology. Yet it would seem clear to most of us that the first statement expresses something valid and important that is missing in the second. The turtle's behavior was directed to a goal because it was built into the genetic program with which she was endowed, and the program had evolved as a result of natural selection with no necessity to assume any conscious guiding agency to create it.

Given the reality of goal-directed behavior and its universal presence in living organisms, many biologists today do not hesitate to speak of such phenomena as teleological. Ayala distinguishes three classes of teleological phenomena:[27] (1) purposeful activity consciously directed to a goal, as in man and the higher mammals; (2) self-regulating systems, such as those that maintain the composition of the blood nearly constant; homeostatic mechanisms, in the terminology of Walter B. Cannon; human devices, such as thermostats, are also examples of such systems; (3) structures designed to perform a certain function, as the hand is designed for grasping. Here the term "design" simply denotes the fact that the hand is a highly adapted product of mutation and natural selection; it does not imply that these remarkable adaptations resulted from any conscious design on the part of a Creator or from an inner *élan vital* supposed to act like a force propelling evolution in one direction or another. Such hypothetical forces are useless for scientific understanding or explanation. The use of the term "teleology" in the above sense is perfectly compatible with a mechanistic conception of life.

Colin Pittendrigh, wishing to avoid the past association of teleology with the notion of final causes, introduced the term "teleonomic" to denote essentially the same category of phenomena that Ayala terms "teleological." Mayr has adopted Pittendrigh's term, with the following definition: "A teleonomic process or behavior is one that owes its goal directedness to the operation of a program." He tentatively defines the term "program" as "coded or prearranged information that controls a process (or behavior) leading it toward a given end." Such programs may be closed or open. The activities of the sea turtle, cited above, or of a spider spinning a web, or a mammalian infant suckling its mother, provide examples of essentially closed programs, unmodifiable by experience. Hunting behavior in the higher mammals exemplifies an open program: the hunter modifies strategy in the light of circumstances and experience. The varied activities of men and women exemplify open programs in the highest degree; but even so, many of our responses are closer than we realize (or perhaps would like to

27. Francisco Ayala, "Teleological Explanations in Evolutionary Biology," *Philosophy of Science*, 37 (1970): 1-15; see also his "Biology as an Autonomous Science," *American Scientist*, 56 (1968): 207-21.

acknowledge) to the automatic behavior patterns of the spider or the sea turtle. We note that machines also display teleonomic (or in Ayala's usage, teleological) behavior, for human beings have built them so that they will do so.[28]

SOME ILLUSIONS OF PROGRESS: THE RISE AND DECLINE OF THE EUGENIC MOVEMENT

Biological ideas based on inadequate knowledge have on occasion been hailed as representing great progress, with initial enthusiasm followed later by disillusionment. The eugenics movement is a case in point. Initiated in England by such eminent men as Francis Galton and Karl Pearson, eugenics won widespread and often enthusiastic support in the United States in the early twentieth century. Eugenic programs, envisaging great improvement of the human stock by selective breeding of the "best" people and elimination of the "unfit," became intimately entwined with the early applications of Mendelian genetics to human heredity. Prominent American biologists such as David Starr Jordan, William E. Castle, and Edward M. East were supporters of the movement, but its most ardent apostle in the United States was Charles Benedict Davenport, who was for thirty years (1904-1934) director of the Carnegie Laboratory for Experimental Evolution at Cold Spring Harbor, New York. Davenport was well trained in the Mendelian genetics of his day, and he made important scientific contributions, especially in his earlier years. However many of his notions of genetic factors as determinants of human behavior were naïve in the extreme. In a report during the First World War on criteria for selection of naval officers, for instance, he concluded that an inborn thalassophilia (love of the sea) was important and was probably due to a sex-linked recessive factor (sex-linked, presumably, since women did not run away to sea). Likewise, from a study of 350 "wayward girls" he concluded that a dominant gene for "innate eroticism" was a powerful causative factor in prostitution. In the depths of the Depression, during the terrible winter of 1932-1933, he wrote to Frederick Osborn

28. For the first use of "teleonomic," see C.S. Pittendrigh, "Adaptation, Natural Selection and Behavior," in *Behavior and Evolution*, ed. A. Roe and G.G. Simpson (New Haven, Conn.: Yale University Press, 1958), pp. 390-416. For the quotations from Mayr, see "Teleological and Teleonomic: a New Analysis," in *Evolution and the Diversity of Life*, pp. 383-404; the quoted passages are on pp. 389, 393-94. We may note that P.B. Medawar and J.S. Medawar, in their brilliant brief survey *The Life Science: Current Ideas of Biology* (New York: Harper, 1977), consider the term "teleonomy" a "genteelism"; see pp. 11, 171. Indeed, the fear of invoking "teleology" because it suggests the "final causes" of Aristotle may well be due to a misunderstanding of what Aristotle really meant. Ayala remarks: "His error was not that he used teleological explanations in biology, but that he extended the concept of teleology to the nonliving world"; "Teleological Explanations," p. 15. Mayr likewise emphasizes that Aristotle's biological concepts have been seriously misunderstood and that they are in many ways remarkably close to modern views; "Teleological and Teleonomic," pp. 400-01.

that welfare agencies were "a force crushing out civilization" by helping to preserve the unfit. In his personal relations, however, he was unusually kind and helpful to young scientists and others; and he did not share in the racial prejudice that was so marked in many of the advocates of eugenics.

The eugenic movement won widespread popular support; under its influence California and several other states, after 1920, passed laws requiring the sterilization of the feeble-minded. Writers such as Madison Grant and Lothrop Stoddard, who were not biologists but wrote influential propaganda for their view of eugenics, held the Nordic peoples to be the Great Race; those of other origins were inferior, though some were more inferior than others. The immense influence of these views was made manifest in the Immigration Restriction Act passed by Congress in 1924, which favored the admission of immigrants from the nations of northern Europe that had supplied the earlier American settlers, while imposing drastic restrictions on immigration from southern and eastern Europe and on Oriental and African peoples.

Increasingly, from about 1920 on, American geneticists grew disillusioned with the simplistic notions of human heredity promulgated by the eugenic enthusiasts. Biologists such as Castle, Raymond Pearl, and a number of others, who had earlier been sympathetic to a more moderate eugenic program, disassociated themselves sharply from the movement. They realized that the still infant science of human genetics was quite inadequate to serve as a basis for ambitious eugenic programs.

Nevertheless, other countries followed the American example by enacting sterilization laws; in Canada this happened in Alberta and British Columbia, and in Europe, Denmark, Finland, Sweden and Norway followed suit (1928-1933). Germany under the Nazis sterilized more than 200,000 of the allegedly unfit under its "eugenic" law. The fanatical excesses of the Nazis and the later hideous extermination policy directed against the Jews had a powerful influence in giving the whole idea of eugenics a bad name.

Within the last quarter century, our knowledge of human genetics has grown rapidly. Well over one hundred diseases are known to be associated with specific enzyme defects; the total number of gene loci at which known mutations have been identified is over a thousand, and some genes have been located in specific chromosomes. Some specific chromosomal abnormalities have been identified, as in Down's syndrome (mongolism). Genetic counseling is a new but accepted profession. Thus, negative eugenics—the endeavor to prevent or minimize the conception or birth of seriously abnormal children—has obtained a foothold in society again; but its claims are relatively modest, and its practitioners know that our ignorance is still profound. The ambitious programs of the eugenicists of sixty years ago appeared to many at the time to represent great progress; but the scientific foundation on which they were based was weak. The foundation crumbled and the illusion of progress faded. Today a more modest edifice is being built on a much firmer foundation.[29]

PROGRESS AND PARADIGM IN SCIENCE: FASHION AND PRESTIGE IN RESEARCH

Thomas Kuhn has discussed certain deep changes in fundamental conceptual framework in the physical sciences (which he denotes as changes in paradigm) in terms of the overthrow of an old by a new paradigm.[30] The Copernican revolution, the change from the phlogiston theory to the chemical system of Lavoisier, and the change from Newtonian to quantum mechanics are examples. The immense transformation of biological concepts in our time, especially in biochemical genetics and related aspects of biology, has been widely termed a scientific revolution, and I think the term is appropriate. However, I would not consider this revolution to involve a change of paradigm in the sense of Kuhn. No great intellectual construction was overthrown in the process of bringing the new genetics into being. New and fundamental concepts developed such as that of the genetic code. We might well call this set of concepts a new paradigm; but they replaced ignorance, not a rival set of concepts. The gene ceased to be a black box and became a known chemical system full of information. The behavior of genetic systems and of the products whose synthesis they directed turned out to be entirely understandable in terms of known physics and chemistry.

The idea prevalent in the 1930s that the gene was probably composed of protein never became a working basis for experimental programs. I must therefore disagree on this particular point with Olby's major historical study.[31] He considers the change from the conception

29. One useful reference for the history of the American eugenics movement is Mark H. Haller, *Eugenics: Hereditarian Attitudes in American Thought* (New Brunswick, N.J.: Rutgers University Press, 1963); on the rise and spread of eugenic sterilization laws, see especially Chap. 4: "Legislative Battle"; the estimate of more than 200,000 sterilizations performed in Nazi Germany is on p. 180. See also Kenneth M. Ludmerer, *Genetics and American Society: An Historical Appraisal* (Baltimore, Md.: Johns Hopkins University Press 1972). A book of broader scope, as its title indicates, is Charles E. Rosenberg, *No Other Gods: On Science and American Social Thought* (Baltimore, Md.: Johns Hopkins University Press, 1976); in the present connection, see especially Chap. 4: "Charles Benedict Davenport and the Irony of American Eugenics." The expressions of Davenport's views quoted here are on pp. 92, 93, 95. Concerning his personal kindness and lack of racial bias, see Ludmerer, *Genetics and American Society*, p. 150. For the current status of human genetics, see, for instance, Harry Harris, *The Principles of Human Biochemical Genetics*, 2nd ed. (Amsterdam and New York: Elsevier/North Holland, 1975; 3rd ed. 1980). The reader should also consult the essay by Bernard Davis, pp. 182-201, in this volume.

30. Thomas S. Kuhn, *The Structure of Scientific Revolutions*, 2nd ed. (Chicago: University of Chicago Press, 1970).

31. Olby, *Path to the Double Helix*, p. 434.

of the gene as protein to the conception of the gene as DNA as representing a change of paradigm. One should not quarrel over words, but I believe that the situation in molecular biology involves no such radical conceptual shift as those that Kuhn has discussed in the physical sciences.

Kuhn has also made the point that "in the transition from an earlier to a later theory, there is very often a loss as well as a gain in explanatory power." He mentions, as one example, that

> the phlogistonists, who looked upon ores as elementary bodies from which the metals were compounded by addition of phlogiston, could explain why the metals were so much more like each other than were the ores from which they were compounded. All metals had a principle, phlogiston, in common. No such explanation was possible with Lavoisier's theory.[32]

Does any analogous statement hold regarding modern biology? I am inclined to doubt it. In all the cases of which I am aware, the later conceptual framework takes care of all the known relevant facts at least as well as the earlier, while also achieving a great net gain in explanatory power.

It is of course true that the focus of interest in science changes. Some fields of research flourish perhaps for several generations, and then their major interest is more or less exhausted. Workers in a current field of central interest may look rather scornfully on others who follow the older patterns. Experimental biologists of the generation of Jacques Loeb, for instance, often had such an attitude toward the field naturalists. Biochemists and molecular biologists, a generation ago, commonly looked down on the ecologists. This attitude changed as public perception of the significance of ecology changed dramatically in the last twenty years; many who had rather despised ecology jumped on the ecological bandwagon when ecology became a household word.[33]

Progress in biology, as in other subjects, sometimes becomes temporarily lost, and the lost ground has to be recovered later. Sir Andrew Huxley, in studying the history of research in muscle, has shown how some major investigators of the late nineteenth century discovered essential features of the fine structure of muscle, which later came to be disbelieved and largely forgotten. Much later, from about 1950 on, the early work was confirmed and greatly extended by researchers using new and more powerful techniques, notably the electron micro-

32. Thomas S. Kuhn, "The Function of Measurement in Modern Physical Science," in his collection of essays *The Essential Tension: Selected Studies in Scientific Tradition and Change* (Chicago: University of Chicago Press, 1977), p. 211; p. 212, note 50. Kuhn makes the same point again in another essay in the same volume, p. 323.

33. One should perhaps note that the public perception of ecology scarcely recognizes the kind of work that the professional ecologists are actually doing. Nevertheless, the general awareness of the subject is a matter of profound importance.

scope. Nearly all the later workers were ignorant of the work of their nineteenth-century predecessors and discovered the phenomena anew. In this case, there was not progress but retrogression for a period of about forty years in this particular field.[34]

Important fields of research that have practical applications may decline if some new and easier way of attaining the practical goal is discovered. This happened, for instance, with the work of Oswald T. Avery, Michael Heidelberger, and others at the Rockefeller Institute on the specific complex carbohydrates that formed loose, protective capsules on various types of pneumococci. The work proceeded actively from the 1920s to about 1935. It involved biochemical studies of great importance, and was clinically significant for the treatment of penumonia patients with protective antibodies specific for the type of pneumococcus that was infecting the patient. The discovery of sulfonamide antibiotics and later of penicillin and other drugs largely ended this field of research for many years in spite of its great scientific interest. The antibiotics attacked the pneumococci regardless of type, so typing of specific carbohydrates was no longer of clinical importance. Given the increasing number of pneumococcal strains that have developed resistance to antibiotics in recent years, it is likely that interest in this field of research will revive.[35]

One should note, of course, that Avery went on to do his greatest work on the role of DNA in the transformation of pneumococcal types; and Heidelberger went on to his great achievements in placing immunochemistry on a quantitative basis. The result for the progress of science was clearly a net gain. In any case, none of the examples that I have mentioned here seems at all comparable with what Kuhn has suggested concerning the loss of explanatory power in a later theory as compared with an earlier one.

WILL PROGRESS IN BIOLOGY DECLINE AND EVENTUALLY STOP?

Great discoveries in biology have occurred at an accelerated rate over the last four centuries, and the acceleration has even increased in our time. I have already discussed the evidence on this point, presented by Bentley Glass and Nicholas Rescher. Both have emphasized the fact that the costs of achieving such discoveries are steadily rising. The number of workers involved, the total number of papers published, the amount of money spent—all these have been increasing much

34. A. F. Huxley, "Looking Back on Muscle," in *The Pursuit of Nature: Informal Essays on the History of Physiology*, ed. A. L. Hodgkin et al. (Cambridge: Cambridge University Press, 1977), pp. 23-64.

35. Concerning Avery, see especially René Dubos, *The Professor, the Institute, and DNA* (New York: Rockefeller University Press, 1976). See also Michael Heidelberger, "A Pure Organic Chemist's Downward Path," *Annual Review of Microbiology*, 31 (1977): 1-12; and Part 2 of the narrative, *Annual Review of Biochemistry*, 48 (1979): 1-21.

more rapidly than the number of really outstanding discoveries. At the same time, the support of research in the United States has actually declined for the last twelve years; yet the number of papers published —in my own field of biochemistry, for example—continues to rise. Just what is really happening?

Certainly *accelerated* progress cannot continue indefinitely; no exponential curve, describing actual phenomena, can keep rising forever. We may well be close to the end of the period of *exponential growth in science*. Even apart from the limits of financial support that taxpayers are willing to provide, there is a limit to the number of qualified researchers who can be recruited from the total population, especially when research is in competition with other essential social needs. When the scientific community was much smaller, as it was in 1900, the fraction of really gifted and dedicated scientists was undoubtedly larger than it is today. As the community of science expands, the average level of talent must almost inevitably decline. This fact may partially explain Glass's and Rescher's findings of the increased cost of making really significant discoveries; but it is also true that the instruments and techniques needed to make discoveries at the frontier of science are rapidly growing more expensive.

Apart from expense, however, there is among many people a genuine fear of what further advances in science may bring. The development of the technology of nuclear weapons rightly inspires us with deep anxiety; and we know that this technology arose rapidly—in a few years—from discoveries in "pure" nuclear physics. We are now alert, and properly so, to the potential threats in any new developments in basic biology. The potential hazards of recombinant DNA research have been greatly exaggerated in some quarters; but the furor now seems to be dying down. Since Bernard Davis discusses these issues elsewhere in this volume (see pp. 182-201), I merely mention them here, as possible obstacles to progress in biology.

Some people—even some notable scientists—have opposed investigation into the possible genetic factors that may influence intelligence and behavior, on the ground that such research may be unduly disturbing to certain minority groups. I would reject any such view. I believe that the advancement of scientific knowledge, though it might cause temporary distress in certain quarters, will actually serve to dissipate false views on such matters as racial differences and can lead to increased wisdom in dealing with social problems. Likewise, I am totally unsympathetic to the attacks that have been made, on somewhat similar grounds, on E. O. Wilson's *Sociobiology*.[36] Wilson's views concerning the penetration of biological concepts into sociology and on the possible limitations that genetic factors may impose on the range of human behavior certainly call for criticism and debate; but I

36. Edward O. Wilson, *Sociobiology: The New Synthesis* (Cambridge, Mass.: Harvard University Press, 1975).

believe that this can be carried on according to the usual canons of scientific controversy and does not call for the emotional attacks that some critics have made upon Wilson. Such attitudes do represent some of the factors that may threaten progress in biology.

Gunther Stent has raised a more fundamental question.[37] He believes that in molecular genetics the great fundamental discoveries were already made by 1965 or earlier; the immense outpouring of research in the field since then has produced many advances in detail, but there is no longer the excitement of pioneering in a new, major field. Indeed, Stent believes that we may be approaching the end of really significant discoveries in the sciences and of creation in the arts, with a relatively static "golden age" awaiting us.

Stent does indeed consider three areas of biology as still offering great potentialities for future discovery: the origin of life, the processes of development and differentiation in living organisms, and the nature of the workings of the brain. These should be enough to keep eager inquirers active for a long time. Personally, I doubt whether the fundamental problems of molecular genetics are as nearly completely solved as Stent believes. For instance, there are recent discoveries of internal regions of DNA in genes that do not serve to code for any protein but are excised during the formation of messenger RNA, the cut ends then being stitched together by specific enzymes. This represents a major new discovery and a totally unexpected one.[38] Glass has suggested that within another two or three centuries we may have found out everything that is really interesting and fundamental in biology.[39] There would still be many details to map out, but the expense of doing so might be excessive and the motives insufficient. In that case, progress would come to a stop. I will not try to look ahead so far; in the foreseeable future I think that great and challenging problems will remain. Whether the urge to investigate them will still be as strong as it is today, I venture no prediction.

ECOLOGICAL THREATS TO THE
FUTURE OF BIOLOGY

There are far-reaching and ominous changes in the patterns of life on earth today. The spread of deserts continues at a formidable rate. It was estimated at the United Nations Conference on Desertification held in Nairobi in 1977 that the world's annual loss of good land that turns to desert is of the order of 60,000 square kilometers per year: some 32,000 of rangeland, 25,000 of rain-fed cropland, and a signifi-

37. Gunther Stent, *The Coming of the Golden Age* (Garden City, N.Y.: Natural History Press, 1969); and his *Paradoxes of Progress* (San Francisco, Ca.: W.H. Freeman, 1978). The latter book includes the key parts of the former, together with a series of thoughtful and illuminating essays on some of the philosophical and ethical problems raised by modern science.

38. See the account by Crick, "Split Genes" (note 18).

39. See Glass, "Milestones and Rates of Growth" (note 3).

cant amount of farmland. About one hundred countries are directly affected.[40] The conference proposed a broad program to reverse these trends, but it would appear that in spite of high hopes expressed there, little progress has been made thus far.

Likewise, there are formidable losses of agricultural cropland and pasture land. Overgrazing, overplowing, and erosion produce major losses in many countries of the world. Even in the United States where soil conservation practices are better than in most countries, the Soil Conservation Service reported that "in 1975, soil losses on cropland amounted to almost three billion tons or an average of about twenty-two tons per hectare (one hectare equals 2.5 acres, approximately). Although this was excessive, it was less than the estimated four billion tons that would have been lost in 1975 if farmers had followed no conservation practices at all." To maintain crop levels, the report concluded that the loss would have to be reduced to about 1.5 billion tons, about half the present level.[41] In addition, the growth of great modern cities and highways is devouring large areas of good land, with loss not only of farmland but of potential habitat for animals and plants. Many of the world's great forests, especially the tropical rain forests, are also disappearing at a rate unprecedented in past history.[42]

These changes and the pressures from human population growth with which they are associated have created threats to the future of plant and animal life that lead to accelerated extinction. The wildlife specialist Norman Myers estimates that at present we are probably losing one species per day in the rain forests alone and that by the end of the century the rate may be one such species lost per hour. Perhaps a million species may be gone by that time, and the conditions of life will be vastly impoverished for great numbers of others.[43]

The impending loss of many genetic strains of important plants is one serious danger from all these changes. The whole pattern of change obviously represents far more than a threat to the future of the science of biology; it is a threat to the future of mankind, to that of the whole biosphere, and to the value and quality of life in general. For future biologists, however, it clearly represents impoverishment. The natural world that the young Charles Darwin explored during the voyage of the *Beagle* was a far richer world for a biologist than one of

40. See Margaret R. Biswas, "U.N. Conference on Desertification in Retrospect" *Environmental Conservation*, 5 (1978): 247-62; see also Erik Eckholm and Lester R. Brown, "Spreading Deserts—the Hand of Man," *Worldwatch Paper 13* (Washington, D.C.: Worldwatch Institute, 1977).

41. Soil Conservation Service, "Cropland Erosion," U.S. Department of Agriculture, Washington, D.C., June 1977. I take this quotation from Lester R. Brown "The Worldwide Loss of Cropland," *Worldwatch Paper 24* (1978).

42. See also another paper from the Worldwatch Institute, No. 26, by Erik Eckholm: "Planting for the Future: Forestry for Human Needs," 1979.

43. The literature on loss of species is enormous. A good summary is given in another *Worldwatch Paper*, No. 22, by Erik Eckholm: "Disappearing Species: the Social Challenge," 1978; the reference to Norman Myers is on p. 7.

Darwin's successors could find in the same regions today. To some, primarily molecular biologists, this may not seem a tragedy. They could perhaps be happy with *E. coli* and a few higher species, including man. Nevertheless, the loss of large numbers of species in such a short time would be a biological tragedy of major proportions and probably an unprecedented event in the earth's history. There have indeed been widespread extinctions of species in past epochs—rapid indeed in terms of geological time but surely very slow by comparison with the situation that confronts us now.[44]

THE HOPE OF PROGRESS

This discussion has brought us over the boundary of the topic of progress in biology and into the broader area of general human concerns— matters indeed of life and death for hundreds of millions of human beings and perhaps decisive for the total future of our planet. Let me close by quoting and briefly commenting on a statement by a great contemporary biologist, Sir Peter Medawar. Contemplating the fears and anxieties that afflict our times and comparing them with a somewhat similar period in the early seventeenth century, he has written:

> We cannot point to a single definitive solution of any one of the problems that confront us—political, economic, social, or moral, i.e., having to do with the conduct of life. We are still beginners, and for that reason may hope to improve. To deride the hope of progress is the ultimate fatuity, the last word in poverty of spirit and meanness of mind.[45]

Considering the grave and ominous trends that I have just described

44. In one respect, this statement requires modification. Some of the great extinctions of many forms of life in the past may have been very rapid, according to the proposal of L. W. Alvarez, W. Alvarez, F. Asaro and H. V. Michel "Extraterrestrial Cause for the Cretaceous-Tertiary Extinction" *Science*, 208 (1980): 1095-1108. According to their hypothesis, the impact of a large asteroid colliding with the earth could have injected vast quantities of dust into the atmosphere, requiring several years to settle out. The resulting attenuation of sunlight would have largely suppressed photosynthesis, and could have led in a few years to the extinction of the dinosaurs and many other forms of animal and plant life that occurred at the end of the Cretaceous. The hypothesis is far from proven, but the authors have marshaled impressive evidence in its favor. For some expert commentary and criticism see the letters in *Science*, 211 (1981): 649-56.

In any case, regardless of the processes underlying past extinctions, the disappearance of great numbers of species in our time—a process virtually certain to continue on a much larger scale in the next twenty years—represents a loss unparalleled in human history.

45. Peter B. Medawar, "On the Effecting of All Things Possible," in his *The Hope of Progress* (London: Methuen, 1972), p. 127. This article was Medawar's presidential address to the British Association for the Advancement of Science, September 1969. After writing an earlier draft of this essay, I discovered, on reading Nicholas Rescher's "Scientific Progress" that he concludes his book with the last sentence of the same passage from Medawar that I have quoted here. I am happy to acknowledge Rescher's priority in this, but I offer my own response, somewhat different in tone, to Medawar's challenging statement.

—and there are plenty of other causes for anxiety as well—I would still agree with Medawar. It is the *hope* of progress that we must cherish and vigorously maintain in action. Certainty of success, even tentative assurance, we cannot have. Many of our nineteenth-century predecessors, even those with no firm religious belief, still trusted in some vaguely defined external force to propel mankind onward and upward. Today we know that we are on our own; no *deus ex machina* will come to our aid. Thanks largely to science, in the broadest sense of the term, we understand the nature of the problems we face better than we could ever have done in the past. The political and psycholog-cal obstacles to the effective application of that knowledge are immense, and human wisdom is in short supply. What the outcome will be, we cannot tell; but we can face the future with hope, determination, and a willingness to learn.

7

Progress in Physics:
The Game of Intellectual
Leapfrog

GERALD FEINBERG

═══════════

INTRODUCTION

In this essay, I describe and analyze some aspects of the changes that
have taken place as physics has developed, especially over the past
century. I concentrate on what has happened in physics as a study of
natural phenomena rather than as it is applied in human affairs. The
latter question is worth examining in its own right, but it involves
very different considerations and seems, therefore, inappropriate to
treat here along with the former topic.

There is broad agreement among physicists that their science has
shown continual progress since its "founding" by Galileo, Gilbert, and
others in the sixteenth century. There can be differences among us on
whether specific developments represent steps in the right direction,
defined as an ever more thorough understanding of an ever wider
array of natural phenomena. However, these differences tend to be
transitory, and the passage of time usually enforces a consensus on
what is wheat and what is chaff. Even when there are disagreements
about the worth of something, these are usually about a set of ideas—
the content of theoretical physics—rather than about some observations or experiments. To a physicist participating in the daily struggle

I wish to thank Professor Sidney Morgenbesser for many discussions which helped
me greatly in the formulation and expression of these ideas. I wish also to thank
Professor Ernest Nagel for a helpful discussion. This work was supported in part by the
U.S. Department of Energy.

to coax some new fact out of reticent data or to provide a satisfactory interpretation of his colleagues' new fact, it is impossible to escape the sense that whatever may be happening in other human activities, here progress is really taking place.

This impression is strongly reinforced by the fact that the problems of understanding that arise in physics tend to be solved rather quickly, typically in a very few years. Although physics does have its perennial problems, some of which I will mention later, most things that a typical physicist works on have only recently emerged and been recognized as problems at all. The typical reference in a physics article is to work done within the last two or three years. Often it is to work not yet published. This happens not because physicists are intellectually more fickle than workers in other fields but rather because we have been more successful at finding answers to our questions that satisfy us, at least temporarily. That those answers usually lead to yet other questions to be studied in turn is one aspect of the game of intellectual leapfrog referred to in the title of this essay.

We cannot rest content with this sense of day-to-day progress that physicists have since it doubtless occurs in other fields also. An analysis of progress in physics must also deal with long-term trends and examine whether there are general characteristics of the development of physics over generations rather than over years that can be described as progress. Here again, the attitude of most physicists would be that, indeed, physics progresses in the long run also, if not quite in a straight line, at least with a significant component in one direction. This intuition has been questioned by some, including Thomas Kuhn, who have suggested that the discontinuities in explanation that occur in "scientific revolutions" are really akin to a change from one philosophical system to another, with little of the cumulative element that we want to associate with progress.

I find this analysis unconvincing and have argued elsewhere that at least some of the questions that physicists try to answer have a long history, during which there has been a gradual convergence to a complete answer and in which continuity can be traced in the approaches taken by successive generations of physicists.[1] It is, I think, tendentious to attempt to deny physicists the very aspect of their procedure that separates them from workers in many other fields, that is, their sense of the existence of a solid basis of accepted results that they can use as a foundation for their own investigations. Although it is more striking to concentrate on the ways in which a subject changes over time than on its continuities, we should recognize that to some extent this represents an analytical bias. Sometimes, the remarkable thing about an area of a discipline is that it needs no change because of its

---

1. Gerald Feinberg, "Physics and Thales Problem," *Journal of Philosophy*, 63 (1966): 5-17.

success in solving the problems tha: it faced. Progress may be a good, but it is not the only good, even when it has occurred.

I shall not pursue this question any further here as it is not my aim to examine physics from outside itself. Instead, what I intend is to use some parts of the development of physics, especially over the last century, to infer certain generalities about what constitutes progress in physics. My thesis is that physics undergoes changes of different kinds simultaneously and that these changes have varying components of progress in them, some easy to recognize, some more questionable. Some aspects of progress in physics, such as the increase in empirical knowledge, are also characteristic of other branches of science. But other aspects, including the ability to convert axiomatic principles into subjects of theoretical and experimental investigation, seem to me peculiar to physics, perhaps, because it is the most mature of the natural sciences.

In outline, this essay proceeds as follows. I begin with a brief survey of developments in the last century of physics, concentrating on some of the major changes that have occurred by giving three snapshots of physics. The first is taken in 1879, the year in which Einstein was born and James Clerk Maxwell died. The second snapshot is taken in 1929, approximately midway through the century, and the final one is taken in the present. I describe three aspects of the physics of each period: the kinds of phenomena that were known, the theoretical models that were used to understand these phenomena, and the types of explanation that were accepted as legitimate by the physicists of the time. Using this survey as data, I next describe several levels of change over this period and indicate to what extent each of them can be taken as progress. Finally, in my closing section, I discuss briefly some aspects of the future of physics and of its relation to some other areas of science.

THE DEVELOPMENT OF PHYSICS:
1879 TO THE PRESENT

1879: The Age of Maxwell

One way to get some idea of the state of physics in an earlier time is to read some of the discursive rather than technical writings of the leading physicists of the time. A useful source of information about physics a century ago is a series of articles written for the *Encyclopedia Britannica* by James Clerk Maxwell, arguably the most important physicist who lived between the time of Newton and that of Einstein. I will refer only to Maxwell's article "Atom,"[2] written around 1875, but several other articles that he wrote at about the same time present an

2. James Clerk Maxwell, "Atom," in *The Scientific Papers of J. C. Maxwell,* ed. W. D. Niven (New York: Dover, 1952), II, 445-84.

equally fascinating picture of how a man of genius viewed various parts of his subject.

As a result of work by Maxwell, Ludwig Boltzmann, Rudolf Clausius, and others, atoms had become fairly well accepted by physicists by 1879 although a rearguard action against them was still being fought by Ernst Mach and Wilhelm Ostwald. In his *Encyclopedia* article, Maxwell presents some of the evidence for atoms from chemistry and from the kinetic theory of gases. He goes on to give the then recent estimates of the size of atoms, 10^{-8} centimeter, indicating why direct observation of atoms was not feasible. In a prescient aside, he points out that this definite size of atoms implies that germ cells contain only billions of molecules. This raises the problem of how all of the characteristics of a developed organism can be included in so few (!) molecules. Maxwell appears skeptical that this is possible, and it required the advent of molecular biology and of information theory to prove his skepticism unwarranted.

Maxwell and his contemporaries realized that such phenomena as the emission of light must eventually be explained in terms of the properties of atoms. Maxwell raised the question of how it is that a hydrogen atom on earth will emit the same wavelengths of light as one on Arcturus, but the physics of his time was unable to furnish the answer. Maxwell himself seemed to favor some Leibnitzian notion of preestablished harmony of creation as the answer. In reality, this answer was furnished some forty years later through the quantum hypothesis of Niels Bohr.

Finally, Maxwell speculates on the ultimate nature of atoms themselves and presents as the most appealing model of them an idea attributable to Hermann Helmholtz and Lord Kelvin, according to which atoms are rotating vortices in an unobserved fluid pervading space. In this model, the competition between discreteness and continuity would have a paradoxical resolution, in which the atoms, considered to be paradigms of discreteness, are found to be expressions of an underlying continuity. The vortex model of atoms has not survived its contact with physical phenomena, but the competition is not over and reappears in the age of Einstein as the conflict between particle and field.

The other important development of the age of Maxwell was the recognition of the electromagnetic field as an independent part of the world, not reducible to matter, although influenced by it. In Maxwell's hands, this realization led to the explanation of light as electromagnetic waves. In the hands of his successors, it eventually led to the discovery of other types of radiation, such as X-rays, distinguished from light only by wavelength. Heinrich Hertz's radio waves and Wilhelm Roentgen's X-rays both found direct interpretations within Maxwell's synthesis. Later, in the twentieth century, some of these types of radiation were found to have particlelike properties that went beyond Maxwell's theory and required a new theoretical synthesis.

In other areas of physics, fairly complete descriptions of many types of macroscopic phenomena had been achieved by the time Maxwell died. The properties of heat were well summarized in the laws of thermodynamics. Maxwell himself was beginning to search for a deeper understanding of these laws through the ideas of statistical mechanics, in which a combination of Newton's deterministic laws of motion and considerations of probability that are essential for dealing with the immense number of atoms in any macroscopic object were combined. But this had not been really accomplished by 1879. Newton's laws of motion continued to describe accurately the motion of large bodies. As yet, there was no sign of the great extension in the range of phenomena that was to characterize the next fifty years of physics.

1929: The Age of Einstein[3]

Fifty years later, at a time representing the middle of Einstein's career, the face of physics had changed so radically that Maxwell might have found it difficult to recognize. Newtonian dynamics had been replaced in its most hallowed ground—the description of gravity—by Einstein's general theory of relativity. An even more fundamental change had taken place in microphysics, where it had been found that Newtonian determinism itself had to be replaced by probabilistic quantum mechanics, scornfully described by Einstein as involving "God playing dice with the world."

Not only the theories of physics changed radically between 1879 and 1929. Discoveries of new and unexpected phenomena, such as radioactivity, were the driving force behind much of the new theoretical construction. The triumph of atomism, described in Maxwell's *Encyclopedia* article, was soon followed by the recognition that although atoms existed, they were by no means indivisible as their name implied. The discovery that atoms had parts that themselves could be studied was an early indication of two characteristic themes of twentieth-century physics, that the everyday world is only a small part of all there is and that the ideas that guide our understanding of everyday phenomena may not be appropriate for other unfamiliar ones.

Within physics, the most obvious advance between 1879 and 1929 was a thorough exploration and understanding of the inner structure of atoms. The understanding, which followed intense experimental work on spectroscopy and on electrical discharges through matter, required the invention of a new description of physical phenomena—quantum mechanics. The essence of this change is the renunciation of the Newtonian program of following precisely the motion of objects as they move through space. Instead, quantum mechanics deals with objects whose properties remain constant for a while but then change

3. For details about many of the discoveries described here and in the next section, see Gerald Feinberg, *What Is the World Made Of?* (New York: Anchor Press, 1977); and Paul Davies, *Space and Time in the Modern Universe* (Cambridge: Cambridge University Press, 1977).

abruptly at a time that usually cannot be predicted in advance. Only the probability of change is predictable by quantum theory. This circumstance, though in perfect accord with the phenomena of radioactive decay and other subatomic observations, is what critics of quantum mechanics such as Einstein found ultimately objectionable. However, no plausible substitute for quantum theory has been suggested that could avoid this feature.

Meanwhile, physicists, using the new theoretical description, were able to give a fairly complete account of the properties of ordinary matter. This included much of chemistry, the thermal and electrical behavior of solids, and the interaction between light and matter. It was also possible, using quantum mechanics, to predict a number of then unobserved phenomena, such as the stimulated emission of light by atoms, which were eventually observed, for example, through the invention of lasers. It is apparently necessary, although it should not be at this late date, to reemphasize that physicists generally accept and use quantum mechanics because of the immense success they have had in understanding old and new phenomena with it, not because of some demonic urge to overturn the dictates of "common sense."

The other important theoretical advance in the period from 1879 through 1929 was the novel conception of space and time contained in Einstein's special and general theories of relativity. The gist of these developments was that the properties of space and time, rather than being invariant and eternal, were found to depend on the state of motion of observers, as well as upon the matter content of the region involved and of nearby regions. One by-product of this discovery was a new theory of gravity, now described as distortions of space and time. This theory, although it has passed every observational test put to it, was sufficiently close in most predictions to Newton's theory, for objects known by 1929, that it made little practical difference for most phenomena then studied. A more significant result of Einstein's work for the physics of the period being discussed was an increased emphasis on symmetry and mathematical invariance as important aspects of physical theory. This emphasis, in turn, led physicists to use a greater diversity of mathematical methods, especially group theory, in constructing their own theories, a tendency that has continued up to the present.

By 1929, the major theoretical advances of the twentieth century (up until now) had already been made. Physicists were now ready to extend the domain of application of these theories to an immense variety of new phenomena that would be discovered in the next fifty years.

The Present

In the period since 1929, physicists have discovered and explored a wide range of phenomena, which have been successfully described by a combination of quantum and relativity theory. These include the properties of atomic nuclei and of the subatomic particles, both those found in ordinary matter and the large majority that are not. An important and unexpected catalyst of this work was the discovery that the constituents of ordinary matter are just a few of many similar objects, which, under suitable conditions of energy, transform into one another readily in ways governed by the nondeterministic principles of quantum mechanics. The study of these phenomena has progressed to the point where we appear to be in sight of a complete theory of matter, in which all the properties of every type of matter can be explained on the basis of a few principles and a few constants of nature. An important step toward such a theory of matter has been taken in the quark model of the subatomic particles called hadrons. Einstein's dream of a unified field theory has also come close to being realized through ideas relating all of the different interactions of the subatomic particles, although not in the mathematical form that Einstein himself pursued. The themes of invariance and symmetry have played an ever increasing role in the development of these theories while, at the same time, definite patterns of deviation from symmetry have also been discovered and have been integrated into the overall description of subatomic particles.

The ideas of particle physics and of relativity have also been applied to the study of the origin and evolution of the universe, again with substantial success. It has been possible to understand how the present types and distribution of matter in the universe have developed from an earlier state consisting of a hot gas of subatomic particles. Evidence for the accuracy of these speculations has shown up in the form of the so-called microwave background radiation that is thought to pervade the universe as a much cooled-down reminder of earlier times. There have even been suggestions on how to account for the hitherto puzzling datum that our universe contains a surplus of what we call matter over what we call antimatter.

Another important development in this last half-century has been the identification, first in theory and then by observation, of physical systems in which the novel properties of space and time that distinguish Einstein's theory of gravity from Newton's play a major role instead of being a minor correction. These discoveries, including neutron stars and black holes, have revitalized the somewhat dormant interest in general relativity and have helped to bring it closer to other branches of physics, a tendency that is very likely to continue into the future.

Finally, an important aspect of the past fifty years of physics is that quantum theory and relativity have proved capable of meeting all the challenges that the description of new phenomena have put to them. There have been important advances in our understanding of what needs description and of the precise types of model that can be formulated within the framework of relativistic quantum mechanics. But there has been no change in our fundamental way of describing physical systems comparable with those that occurred in the previous period. The passage of time and further discoveries will show how long that situation can continue.

SEVERAL FORMS OF PROGRESS IN PHYSICS

The physics of the past hundred years exemplifies a number of ways in which the science can be said to have progressed. Here I will attempt to disentangle four different modes of progress. These modes can be briefly characterized as follows:

1. The discovery of new phenomena through the development of new experimental techniques or through the application of previously known techniques in different areas.

2. Progress in theoretical understanding of previously known phenomena, either by eliciting new consequences of existing theories or from the invention of new theories.

3. The acceptance of new kinds of explanation for phenomena, especially of types of theory that involve different restrictions than previous theories about what can be known or predicted.

4. Shifts in the view of what aspects of the world need to be understood at all, as opposed to being taken as axioms, in terms of which other things are to be understood.

The first two of these types of progress occur within the subject matter of physics itself; the last two involve the way physics is done, what the Greeks would have called metaphysics. While these four aspects of progress are not completely separable, there are enough differences among them that the distinctions seem worth making.

The Discovery of New Phenomena

For physicists, one of the most exciting things that can happen within the science is the discovery of some new phenomenon, especially one that was previously unexpected. This has happened many times in the last century, and several times the discovery has eventually led to a profound revision of the prevailing views in some area of physics. One example was the discovery in 1896, by Antoine Becquerel, of radioactivity and its subsequent elucidation by Pierre and Marie Curie, and by Ernest Rutherford. Originally thought of as a sidelight of Roentgen's discovery of X-rays, radioactivity instead turned out to be immensely more important in its significance for physics. Among the changes in our view of the world that were required to understand radioactivity were the abandonment of the idea that elements were immutable and the renunciation of the belief that all physical transformations were exactly predictable. The subatomic particles of high energy that certain radioactive substances emit also provided an important research tool in the early twentieth century, which led, among other things, to the theory of the nuclear atom.

Radioactivity was apparently a completely unexpected discovery. Certainly it was not a prediction of any of the then current views of the structure of matter. It is probably that very feature of unexpectedness that impelled physicists to make a thorough study of the phenomena relatively quickly so that within ten years the phenomena themselves had been described almost completely. The fact that radioactivity did not fit at all into the preexisting ideas is what made it such a good catalyst for the introduction of new ideas about the structure of matter. Furthermore, the phenomena of radioactivity are interesting in themselves, for example, involving magnitudes of energy never before encountered by physicists. This circumstance would in any case have made the discovery of radioactivity important even if its explanation had been more prosaic than is the case. All of these factors combine to make radioactivity a paradigm example of how physics progresses through the discovery of new phenomena.[4]

Another example of more recent vintage is the discovery, over a period of four decades, of a large number of distinct species of subatomic particles. Before this process began, with the discovery of the muon in 1937, physicists knew of a small number of types of subatomic particles, all of which played important roles in the phenomena of *ordinary* matter. Thus, it seemed that the study of these particles was a direct extension of the two-millennia-long investigation of the nature of matter begun by the Ionians.

The discovery of the muon, and of many other particles since then, showed that this was not the case. The particles that occur in ordinary matter are but a few examples of hundreds of others, similar to the familiar ones except that they are unstable. Consequently, the task of physics was not only to explain ordinary matter in terms of a few known fundamental objects but also to account for the plethora of subatomic particles themselves, perhaps in terms of unknown, yet more fundamental, things.

As mentioned, there has been substantial progress toward understanding the properties of these subatomic particles. Unlike the case of radioactivity, the discovery of newer particles has not required the invention of any fundamentally new ways of describing nature, at least not yet. Perhaps its greatest effect on the thinking of physicists was that for a period of twenty years or so, it shook the belief that we were close to having a complete theory of matter. This view is now reemerging, thanks to the success of the recent theoretical advances mentioned previously. It remains to be seen how justified this view is now.

4. For a description of some of the early responses to radioactivity, see Abraham Pais, "Radioactivity's Two Early Puzzles," *Reviews of Modern Physics*, 49 (1977): 925-38.

This development in subatomic particle physics raises an interesting general question concerning progress defined as the discovery of new phenomena—that is, what fraction does what we know at any given time represent of "all" there is to know? The answer to this question will help decide whether science has boundaries or is an endless activity. Various thinkers have proposed different answers to the question. Lenin, in his essay *Materialism and Empirio-Criticism*, writes of the "inexhaustibility of the atom,"[5] meaning that there is no end to new phenomena to be discovered and implicitly implying that a science such as physics will never run out of work. Alternatively, it has been argued that even if nature itself is inexhaustible, human beings are not, and there is a limit to human enterprise that will eventually bring the discovery of new phenomena to a close. Still others have claimed that the laws of nature themselves are a finite set and that it was within human ability to understand these laws sufficiently well so that no new phenomena whose explanation is not—at least in principle—contained in these laws could be discovered. Indeed, there have even been suggestions that specific physical theories already put us within sight of that goal. An example of this is the notorious comment of a physicist at the end of the nineteenth century that the only remaining task for physicists was to measure the next decimal place.

It seems premature to decide about what physicists can discover throughout eternity in view of the mere four centuries over which physics has been practiced. However, there is a pattern that can be discerned in what has been happening, especially over the last fifty years, that is, that unanticipated discoveries tend to come in areas that become available for study as the result of new observational techniques. There are few major new discoveries about phenomena that have been studied for a long time, and these are usually the result of attempts to verify predictions of theories that encompass these fields and so are not unanticipated. As examples of what I have in mind, there is, on the one hand, radio astronomy, in which the invention of a new type of instrument revealed phenomena such as quasars that were surely not anticipated and have not even yet been fully understood. On the other hand, there is the transistor, a device of utmost technological importance, whose invention was made possible by theoretical understanding in solid state physics over a period beginning twenty years earlier.

It has been remarked by Enrico Fermi, I believe correctly, that we should not expect any real surprises in future investigations of physical phenomena on the ordinary human scale akin to the discoveries of radioactivity or X-rays. The reason for this is not that we have systematically examined all such phenomena. On the contrary, it is very likely

5. V.I. Lenin, *Materialism and Empirio-Criticism* (Moscow: Foreign Language Publishing House, 1947), p. 271.

that there are many very interesting things to be discovered on this scale. Rather, Fermi was expressing some confidence that our present understanding of phenomena on this scale is accurate enough that any new discoveries will also fit easily into the picture we have and so will not really be so surprising. The statement is, therefore, as much one about the relation between theory and observation as about new discovery, and it is time that I turned to that aspect of progress in physics.

Progress in Theoretical Understanding

The relation between progress in observing new phenomena and progress in theoretical understanding of physical phenomena can be illustrated by simple diagrams. At any time, physicists know of a certain restricted set of phenomena, indicated by the areas with horizontal lines in Figure 1. At the same time, the available physical theories are able to explain some part of these phenomena, but not all of them. These theories are indicated by areas with vertical lines in Figure 1.

Fig. 1. Observation and Theory in Physics at Some Time

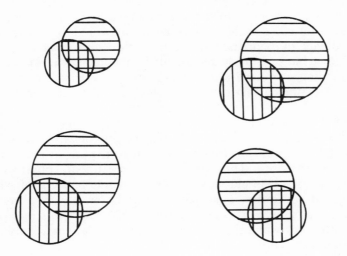

The "explained" phenomena are those represented by the intersection of the two circles. These theories also can account for yet undiscovered phenomena, indicated by the regions that have only vertical lines within the circles. In this snapshot of physics, I am ignoring possible inconsistencies between theories that are used to explain disparate phenomena. Such situations have occurred for some intervals, as in the particle and wave pictures of light in the early twentieth century, but they tend not to last very long.

The undiscovered phenomena predicted by theories at any time provide a direction for further progress in physics that is complementary to the unexpected new phenomena discussed above. As a result of both of these types of discovery, if we take another snapshot of the state of physics at a later time, we would see something like that in Figure 2. Here some of the previously undiscovered but predicted

Fig. 2. Changes in Theory and Observation Over Time

phenomena have been found so that there is more overlap between theory and experiment. On the other hand, new phenomena not encompassed by older theories have been discovered, which furnish a new challenge to theorists. Finally, theoretical advances have brought some known but previously unexplained phenomena within bounds of understanding and have also led to predictions of still more undiscovered phenomena that can be searched for by experimental physicists.

All of this is a kind of intellectual leapfrog, in which theorists and experimenters are constantly meeting one another's challenges and also setting new problems for one another. At the same time, developments within theoretical physics or within experimental physics induce progress in each subfield that is somewhat independent of what is going on in the other. Examples of this latter situation were the development of experimental spectroscopy in the latter half of the nineteenth century and the creation of general relativity theory in the early twentieth century.

One measure of progress in physics is the extent to which the things that have been observed up to some given time are understood through the theories available at that time. By that criterion, physics progresses when theoretical breakthroughs, such as quantum mechanics, are made, and that certainly agrees with the physicist's intuition. However, the use of this criterion alone might also suggest that physics retrogresses when new phenomena, such as radioactivity, are discovered which do not fit into existing theories. That conclusion would certainly be counterintuitive. Therefore, there must be other criteria by which progress can be said to occur in these circumstances.

Another such criterion for progress involves the logical union of those phenomena that have been observed and those that are implied by a set of theories that are both logically consistent and consistent with all observations that have been made up to the time in question. This union represents the maximum set of phenomena that physicists have reason to believe in at any given time. To the extent that there is an increase in either of the two components, progress has occurred. According to this criterion, theory and experiment operate somewhat independently. Experiments that confirm existing theories do not represent progress by this criterion, nor do theories that simply reproduce known observations. Only an extension of one aspect beyond the bounds of the other would be regarded as progressive. For example, the fact that Maxwell's theory of electromagnetism could interpret light as an electromagnetic wave was not progress in this sense. However, this theory did predict similar waves of different frequency, which were eventually observed by Hertz. The theory, therefore, was progressive in that sense whereas Hertz's confirmation of the theory was not.

Of course, there can also be experimental discoveries that are inconsistent with existing bodies of theory. These discoveries show that something believed to be true was not true, and thus they can diminish the range of believable phenomena since all of the implications of the now discredited theories are discarded. Such discoveries do not represent progress by either of the criteria I have mentioned. Perhaps a further criterion involving the removal of erroneous views could cover this type of development, but I am not sure how to formulate that criterion.

The intuition that the second criterion of progress attempts to capture is that it is easier to make theories that account for known phenomena than it is to predict new phenomena correctly. Perhaps a similar intuition is behind Karl Popper's view that falsifiability is the essence of a proper physical theory. However, I think that Popper's view, and the second criterion I have described, underestimate the difficulty in making any theory that accounts for an existing body of observation. Especially in a mature branch of science, in which there is a substantial "backlog" of knowledge, it is usually an intellectual feat to find any set of ideas from which this knowledge can be deduced. That is why I think that at least two separate criteria, rather than a single notion, must be used to judge progress.

New Modes of Explanation

One of the striking features of physics during its history has been the extent to which changes have been required in the type of theory that is acceptable as an explanation for phenomena. An early example was the shift from explanation in terms of innate properties of individual objects, as in the Aristotelian theory of motion, to an explanation in terms of interactions between bodies, as in the Newtonian theory of gravity. A more recent example was the development of statistical thermodynamics in the late nineteenth century, in which notions of chance entered into physics for the first time.

This type of shift is always difficult for physicists to accept and is perhaps the leading cause for "generation gaps" when they occur in physics, with a resisting older generation gradually giving way to an accepting younger generation. I do not think that such changes are due mainly to the desire of each new generation to separate itself intellectually from its predecessors, although that fact may play some role. Rather, I think that in most cases, physicists have been driven to such changes by the need to account for new phenomena. I do not know whether the same is true in other fields in which such changes occur.

I have mentioned two examples of this type of change, that is, the shift from deterministic to statistical explanations that took place with the invention of quantum mechanics, and the expanded use of "preformed" mathematical structures to describe subatomic particles in the last half of this century. Actually, quantum mechanics exemplifies the second shift also, as its earliest formulation relied on the preexisting mathematical structure of matrix algebra, and its ultimate expression in the work of Paul Dirac also utilized earlier work in pure mathematics.

However, the shift in mode of explanation between quantum mechanics and previous theories is in some ways even deeper than the distinctions I have indicated. The very notion of what a physical theory should accomplish changed also. One way to see this is to compare a statement of Lord Kelvin about the preferred types of explanation with one by Dirac.

Kelvin, in his *Lectures on Molecular Dynamics*, says: "I never satisfy myself until I can make a mechanical model of a thing. If I can make a mechanical model, I understand it."[6] This comment was meant as a criticism of Maxwell's electromagnetic theory of light, but it can be taken as a statement of a characteristic nineteenth-century attitude about what kind of physical explanation was acceptable.

Dirac, in his influential text *Quantum Mechanics*, writes: "it may be remarked that the main object of physical science is not the provision of pictures, but is the formulation of laws governing phenomena, and the application of these laws to the discovery of new phenomena. If such a picture exists, so much the better, but whether a picture exists or not is a matter of only secondary importance."[7] In these words, Dirac is trying to provide a philosophical justification for the impossi-

6. William Thomson (Lord Kelvin), *Lectures on Molecular Dynamics* (Baltimore, Md.: Johns Hopkins University Press, 1884), pp. 131-32.

7. P. A. M. Dirac, *Quantum Mechanics*, 3rd ed. (Oxford: Oxford University Press, 1947), p. 10.

bility, according to quantum mechanics, of following the detailed motion of subatomic particles through space and time. The statement can be taken as characteristic of an attitude toward physical explanation held by many twentieth-century physicists.

The change from Kelvin's view to Dirac's goes in the direction of loosening the requirement that physical phenomena be explained in terms of concepts taken from everyday life. Kelvin's mechanical model is abstracted from how familiar things behave, and his criterion for understanding is essentially that everything should be explicable in terms of these concepts. The "pictures" that Dirac mentions are visualizations of phenomena in terms of behavior that we have seem among everyday things. His rejection of their necessity for atomic phenomena is a recognition that concepts cannot necessarily be extended indefinitely far beyond the phenomena from which they are abstracted. This recognition is not new, of course. It is at least as old as Galileo and Newton, who rejected the idea that planets needed a continual push to keep them in uniform motion, as terrestrial bodies often do.

This tendency toward accepting unfamiliar concepts in physical explanations has been strengthened by the expanded use of mathematics in modern physics. To some extent, physicists have substituted coherent mathematical structures for the pictures that Dirac tells us to abandon. Dirac's own work is a prime example of this approach, as is much of the present work on the theory of subatomic particles. In case after case, physicists have found that mathematical structures, either previously studied by mathematicians or invented for the purpose at hand, can be used to describe varieties of physical phenomena. The reasons for this kind of "preestablished harmony" between mathematical creations and the physical world are unclear and have been the subject of speculation both by physicists, such as Eugene Wigner, and mathematicians, such as Jacob Schwartz.[8] Whatever the reasons, the development of theoretical physics has involved an ever widening range of mathematical concepts, and this process shows no sign of abating.

There is some variation in the opinion of physicists as to the significance of mathematical "explanations " in physics. Some physicists are content when a mathematical structure clarifies a set of phenomena whereas other physicists seek an underlying explanation of the fit. As one example of this, it was discovered by Murray Gell-Mann around 1960 that a certain mathematical structure, the group

8. Eugene Wigner, "The Unreasonable Effectiveness of Mathematics in the Natural Sciences," in his *Symmetries and Reflections* (Bloomington: Indiana University Press, 1967), pp. 222-37; Jacob Schwartz, "The Pernicious Influence of Mathematics on Science," in *Logic, Methodology, and Philosophy of Science: Proceedings of the 1960 International Congress*, ed. E. Nagel, P. Suppes, and A. Tarski (Stanford, Ca.: Stanford University Press, 1962), pp. 356-60.

SU(3), could be used to give a surprisingly accurate classification of many properties of the known subatomic particles. Many physicists were content with this, but others, notably Gell-Mann himself, went further and several years later realized that the applicability of this group could be understood if these known subatomic particles were actually composite objects made up of three types of undiscovered but simpler objects, which Gell-Mann called quarks. Since then, overwhelming evidence for this conclusion has been obtained, and the original mathematical description has become a minor aspect of the quark theory.

After a mathematical structure has been used successfully for a time in physics, its content becomes sufficiently intuitive that physicists can use it about as easily as they can use models taken from everyday life. This has happened with the continuous functions of calculus, with the expansions in periodic functions of Fourier analysis, and is now happening with group theory. So one should not regard the trend toward a wider use of mathematical concepts as a renunciation of intuition by physicists. Rather, I think that one can regard this trend as itself a kind of progress in the arsenal of weapons that can be wielded by physicists in their efforts to cut through the tangle of phenomena to a systematic account of the physical world. Physics teachers can see this in their own experience, as they find their students at home with mathematical techniques that they themselves have mastered with difficulty, if at all. Here again is an indication of the ultimate source of progress in science: the human ability to pass on the insights of one person to those who follow, making it unnecessary for the latter to start from scratch. It is this type of transtemporal collaboration, not the greater intelligence of its practitioners, that has made science more successful than other human activities at dealing with its chosen problems.

What Needs to Be Understood?

Modern science, unlike its Greek counterpart, does not attempt to understand everything in terms of necessary truths. It is content with the more modest aim of explaining some phenomena, taken as secondary, in terms of others, taken as primary. So Newton explained the motion of the planets in terms of the laws of motion and the force of gravity but gave no explanation of gravity itself. For this, he was strongly criticized by some of his contemporaries, but time showed this renunciation to be a fertile approach to eventual progress in physics.

But such renunciation is never permanent. Some minds react adversely to the notion that any idea is to be accepted as given, not to be analyzed any further. Accordingly, there has been a change over time as to which principles of physics were to be taken as axioms. The change has generally been in the direction of explaining some axiom in terms of other principles, now recognized as yet more fundamental. The outstanding example of this is doubtlessly the geometry of space. Euclidean geometry was considered by Kant to be a logical necessity. In the early nineteenth century Karl Gauss and Nikolai Lobachevski showed that alternative geometries were at least logically possible. In the late nineteenth century, Georg Riemann and William Clifford raised the question of whether such alternative geometries might apply to our actual space. Finally, in the twentieth century, Einstein extended this question to the newly discovered space-time and showed that actual geometry depended in a fundamental way on the content of matter in space-time. Thus, what for earlier generations was an unquestionable basis for thought about the world has become a contingent fact, explicable in terms of other properties of the universe.

There are other examples of this type of progress. In some cases, things previously taken as given have been explained whereas in other cases, the question of how to explain them has been raised, although no convincing explanation is yet forthcoming. One example of the latter is the value of certain physical constants, such as the ratio of masses of different subatomic particles, or the so-called fine structure constant, which measures the probability of emission of light by charged particles. In existing physical theories, these numbers must be provided as input from experiment, after which other physical quantities can be calculated in terms of them. But physicists as far back as Arthur Eddington in the 1930s have raised the question of whether deeper theories exist, in which these constants themselves could be calculated in terms of pure numbers. Something like this has happened in other cases in the past. The ratios of weights of atoms of different elements were originally quantities that had to be furnished empirically and could be used to describe mass relations in chemical reactions. The nuclear theory developed in the 1930s made it possible to calculate these atomic weight ratios fairly precisely and so removed them from fundamental to derived quantities. In this case, it is not a principle that changed its status but a set of facts.

Of course, such changes occur in step with the other types of progress that I have discussed. Discovery of new phenomena as well as new theories make possible the explanation of what were previously axiomatic principles or empirical facts. But it is an important thing about physics that it builds downward as well as upward, reassessing its own foundations from time to time. A confirmed Platonist might argue that in spite of its renunciation, physics is seeking for an ultimate theory, in which everything is explained in terms of nothing, that is, in which no purely empirical elements enter at all, apart perhaps from the existence of the universe. This view, insofar as anyone holds it, does not seem appropriate to me. Although any given empirical proposition may eventually be explained, there is no indication that the purely empirical content of physics is decreasing with time. What has happened is that the empirical and axiomatic presuppositions have become more and more removed from everyday experience, referring now to properties of the subatomic particles and to the microstructure and large-scale structure of space and time. A wide variety of phenomena can be explained in terms of these assumptions, but they do not seem any closer to laws of pure thought than those of previous stages of physics. As yet, physics has found no way to learn about the actual world by logic alone in spite of occasional claims to the contrary by scientists such as Eddington.

I do not think that other sciences have followed the same process as physics in regard to systematically deepening their own foundations. One reason for this is that science tends to be reductive, not only within a science but between sciences. When biology looks for the explanation of genetics, it finds it not in some deeper biological truth but instead in the chemistry of nucleic acids. This appears similar to what happens in some subfields of physics, whose axioms are explained in terms of other subfields, as, for example, when Maxwell explained lightwaves in terms of electromagnetism. Physics, having no underlying science to reduce itself to, can explain its foundations only by appealing to yet other aspects of physics. Perhaps a similar process occurs in mathematics, where there has also been a gradual shift in the notion of what is to be taken as axiomatic, but there the matter appears to involve more controversy among mathematicians than does the corresponding question in physics.

In sum, physics can be said to have progressed in several ways over the past century and over its entire history. Some of these forms of progress, such as the increase in knowledge of phenomena, are shared with other disciplines. Other forms, such as the conversion of axioms into things to be explained, are more specific to physics. The conviction among physicists themselves that their science has undergone great progress is based on a combination of these different forms, with the emphasis depending very much on the individual. Experimenters, such as I.I. Rabi, tend to emphasize the discovery of unexpected phenomena as the essential ingredient of progress. Theorists such as Einstein point to the creation of theoretical structures that encompass a wide variety of phenomena while possessing a high degree of inner coherence. Philosophically minded physicists, like Bohr, are especially struck by the change in the form of explanation, both in regard to the continuities and discontinuities involved in the change. But all of these commentators would agree that physicists today understand more about nature than those of the past, and this is the ultimate criterion of progress in physics.

FUTURE PROGRESS IN PHYSICS

After reviewing the history of progress in physics, I cannot resist some speculation on what progress the future may bring. Of the four types of progress that I have mentioned, the two that lend themselves to such speculation are progress in theoretical understanding and progress in the conversion of axioms into contingencies. The discovery of unexpected phenomena is almost by definition impossible to anticipate, except in the general sense that we can expect it to happen. Shifts in the accepted mode of explanation can usually be recognized only after the fact and are difficult to anticipate for that reason.

The aspects that seem ripest for future advances in understanding are the properties of "empty" space and time, which physicists refer to as the vacuum. I have indicated that we appear to be near a fairly complete theory of matter, that which fills space-time. However, the behavior of matter has, especially recently, been found to depend profoundly on the characteristics of the space-time that it inhabits. For example, it appears that many of the differences among subatomic particles are not intrinsic to the particles but instead arise from the surrounding in which the particles are found. Such discoveries suggest a need for a deeper understanding of these surroundings. If we are interested in A, and we find that B influences A significantly, it is usually good practice to learn all that we can about B.

Some efforts along this line have already been made. The present description of subatomic particles through a mathematical system called quantum field theory implies that even empty space-time should have a structure as a result of innumerable processes of creation and destruction of particles, each lasting for very short times but recurring again and again. This structure of the vacuum is one of the influences on particles imbedded in space-time. Other influences arise from variations in the value of quantum fields from one region of space-time to another, variations which at present can only be detected through their effect on subatomic particles. We are still far from understanding all of the things that can influence the structure of the vacuum, and it seems very likely that the physics of the near future will concern itself increasingly with this question.

A somewhat related problem for future physics is the further analysis of space-time itself. Of course, this problem has already been attacked earlier in this century through the two theories of relativity, but many questions remain unanswered. Some of the properties of space-time have the character of axioms in present physics, and these may be converted into contingencies. For example, there is the matter of why space has three dimensions and time one dimension, a question sometimes raised but never satisfactorily answered. There is the question of why time flows in a unique direction, whose answer is now thought by many physicists to be related to the expansion of the universe but which is not completely resolved. Finally, there is the question implicitly raised by Ernst Mach in the nineteenth century about the extent to which all the properties of space-time are determined by the matter in it or near it. All of these questions seem to be well posed even now, an indication that their solution may not be far off.

It is not clear whether progress on either of these subjects can be made within the context of the existing theories in physics or whether new theories will be needed for them. This is a part of the more general question as to what changes in accepted ideas the future of physics may bring. Although new theories are often introduced in physics as the result of some "crisis"—a contradiction between theory and observation or between two theories—this pattern is not invariable. General relativity did not arise in this way, for example. The present state of physics does not seem to involve any such crises, but appearances may deceive us. Sometimes physicists think that the successful application of an existing theory to some unexplained phenomenon is just a matter of sufficient calculational ingenuity whereas actually entirely new ideas are necessary for the explanation. This may be the situation in regard to the description of very compact objects, such as the legendary black holes. The existing descriptions of such objects lead to a number of paradoxical results. It is believed by many physicists that these paradoxes result from the omission of quantum effects from the description and that inclusion of these quantum effects would eliminate the paradoxes. Perhaps this is so, but perhaps also something really new is needed to deal with black holes. Regrettably, there is as yet little observational evidence about them, so the question is entirely one of theory. But it does seem likely that if surprises are to occur in the near future in physics, this is one of the more promising areas in which to look for them.

Finally, there is the question of the relation between physics and other sciences. There is little doubt that physics has been successful in extending the scope of its explanations to areas that have traditionally been the domain of other sciences. This has happened to astronomy, to chemistry, and, in the past few decades, to biology. I think that this process will certainly continue and that some of these subjects will disappear as independent sciences. Chemistry and molecular biology may become as much a part of physics as are thermodynamics and electromagnetism. It is not so obvious whether there will be a reciprocal influence of these other subjects on physics. This did happen in the past, for example, when atoms were reintroduced into physics in the nineteenth century through the influence of chemistry. If other sciences are to influence physics in the future, a plausible way for this to occur is through the need to deal with the complex systems that sciences such as biology involve. If physics is to bring even molecular biology under its sway, physicists will have to develop better intellectual tools for handling complex systems.[9]

9. See Gerald Feinberg, "Post-Modern Science," in his *Consequences of Growth* (New York: Seabury Press, 1977), pp. 94-106.

There is one further aspect of the relation between physics and other sciences that is worth mentioning. On the most fundamental level, physicists have been able to identify sufficiently simple elements of the world, such as some of the subatomic particles, so that the methods of physics have led to a substantial understanding of these elements. This has given physicists confidence to apply the laws that successfully describe these elementary phenomena to more complex phenomena, such as atoms and molecules. Here the success is more limited although still significant. Often to describe these more complex phenomena, new models must be introduced, which cannot be rigorously justified in terms of the fundamental ideas but are presumably still consistent with them.

This process of going from more fundamental entities to more composite entities, and at the same time from more simple to more complex phenomena, is repeated over and again in the process of going from particle physics, to atomic physics, to molecular physics, to chemistry, and to biochemistry. Each step from one level to the next in the indicated series can be done only approximately, and after two or three such steps, very little of the basic ideas of the lower level is apparent. Thus, the red, white, and black balls that biochemists use to symbolize the atoms in biomolecules show little of the quantum mechanical behavior that electrons and nuclei display to the particle physicist. Nevertheless, as time goes on, we can expect to see each link in the chain between simple and complex phenomena grow gradually stronger. This will reinforce the view held by most physicists and many other scientists that we are dealing with a single subject matter and that a single set of fundamental laws ultimately governs all natural phenomena.

8

Fear of Progress in Biology

BERNARD D. DAVIS

THE CHANGING CONTRACT BETWEEN
SCIENCE AND SOCIETY

For centuries the scientific community enjoyed virtually complete autonomy in choosing the directions of its research and also in regulating any attendant hazards; and the record seemed to be one of almost pure benefit and achievement. In recent years, however, we have seen increasing concern about where science is taking us and increasing demands that the public determine what scientists may or may not do.

This new attitude arose in response to belated recognition that the technological applications of the physical sciences generate large social costs as well as benefits—costs that range from the threat of nuclear annihilation to despoliation of the environment. The biological sciences at first seemed immune, since their major applications—increased control over disease and increased food production—are so obviously humanitarian. To be sure, these successes have also created problems: the resulting population explosion may turn out to be the greatest underlying cause of social unrest, and the development of very expensive medical procedures raises problems of distributive justice. But these issues, though present, do not yet seem to loom large in current public apprehension over biomedical research. Instead, attention has been focused largely on possible or hypothetical future dangers, and control is therefore demanded over the basic research itself rather than over its applications.

Before discussing these presumed dangers from biology, I would like to note briefly some of the more general reasons for the recent growth of disaffection with science. (1) The rapid advances in many areas of science have caused even the most improbable future projections to be taken seriously. Accordingly, scenarios belonging in science fiction become sources of anxiety—especially in biology. (2) Many short-term benefits of technology have turned out to have long-term costs, and the scale is growing. Technological advance in general has therefore become suspect. (3) Because of the success of science and technology in reducing many of mankind's traditional ills and hazards, expectations of absolute security have replaced a mature recognition that costs generally accompany benefits. (4) The important distinction between science and technology is often blurred. For example, even pure biology is tainted by the use of defoliants in Vietnam. (5) Since science is inherently elitist (in a sense depending on ability and achievement rather than on social origin), the egalitarian thrust of our era has created guilt among many scientists and has weakened their confidence in the moral status of their enterprise. This development and the increasing dependence of research on public funds have encouraged acceptance of the neo-Marxist view that science is primarily an instrument of the prevailing political system rather than a methodology for seeking universal, objective truths about nature. (6) Major failures of our political institutions, often linked to advice from academic experts, have led to a general mistrust of institutions and experts. (7) As science and technology become more complex, they influence the life of the ordinary citizen more, while at the same time he understands them less. The disparity, as well as the speed of the resulting changes in our way of life, generates uneasiness. (8) When scientists hold conflicting views, the mass media find it hard to assess their judgment and credentials, and those with more sensational claims of hazard are likely to be featured.[1] (9) The cohort of activist students of the 1960s has now reached influential positions in the media, and also in science. In particular, such groups as Science for the People have chosen genetics, rather than our political and economic structure, as their focus, and they have acquired attention far beyond their numbers. (10) The program of the Enlightenment has failed: the relative freedom from want created by technology and the spread of rationality encouraged by science have not resulted in general moral progress. In fact, science has undoubtedly contributed to a weakening of the moral order by undermining the traditional supernatural foundation for a moral consensus without providing an alternative.[2] Moreover, while the uncompromising emphasis of science on objectivity has provided great

1. The temptations of even the most respectable media, and their difficulty in judging credentials in science, are vividly illustrated by an extraordinarily scary picture of recombinant DNA research in the *New York Times Sunday Magazine* of August 22, 1976. The author, a molecular biologist, was famous for his remarkable insistence that DNA is a quadruple helix. This article included the even more remarkable statement that "this research may produce yet another Andromeda strain"—as though the fantasy of the first strain were a reality.

2. I have discussed this problem further in "The Importance of Human Individuality for Sociobiology," *Zygon*, 15 (1980): 275-93.

intellectual strength, the price has been a shift of much of our intellectual focus away from subjective values. (11) The Judeo-Christian assumption of man's right to unlimited multiplication and to unlimited dominion over nature arose at a time when the spread of agriculture encouraged an increase in population. The present need to reevaluate this assumption, in the light of diminishing resources, adds another dimension to our sense of moral crisis.

On all these grounds, changing public attitudes could lead to a real contraction in the support and the prestige of science. Such a development would seem sad to those of us who still see science as a source of major benefits to society: power to improve our physical conditions and our security, deeper understanding of ourselves, and delight in the expression of man's intelligence and creativity.

We might note that Gunther Stent has also predicted a contraction in science, but on quite different grounds: the exhaustion, quite soon, of the possibilities for further interesting scientific progress. He suggests that we will then replace the Faustian striving for personal accomplishments and for increased control over nature by the Taoist goal of a static, harmonious adjustment to nature.[3] Elsewhere in this volume (pp. 155-157) John Edsall has considered this possible limitation to future progress in biology. I would simply like to add my doubts that the end of an exciting age of fruitful exploration could lead smoothly to a comfortable golden age of enjoying the fruits. Instead, a dense world population, competing increasingly for dwindling and unevenly distributed resources, seems more likely to drift desperately into a flight from science and rationality, and hence into a new Dark Age.

Against this rather discouraging background, I shall try to assess the reality of the assumptions underlying three widespread fears about advancing knowledge in genetics: fear that these advances will create dangerous products, dangerous powers, and dangerous insights into human nature. I shall close by discussing the role of objective knowledge in our intellectual life, emphasizing not only its value but also its limits.

POSSIBLE DANGERS FROM GENETICS

Dangerous Products

Though microbiologists have been cultivating pathogenic organisms for a century, public concern about possibly dangerous biological materials did not become widespread until the recent development of the recombinant DNA methodology. In this technique a segment of DNA from any source can be spliced into a DNA molecule in the test tube and then replicated (cloned) in bacteria. It has thus become possible to

3. Gunther S. Stent, *The Coming of the Golden Age* (New York: Doubleday, 1969).

isolate any gene in quantity, to study its function in a simplified environment, and to manufacture many desired products. A decade ago such a discovery would have been greeted solely as a remarkable breakthrough. In the current atmosphere, however, public discussion focused much more on the risk of inadvertently creating and releasing dangerous new organisms.

This contingency was initially raised by a group of molecular biologists. Their concern was very much in the tradition of responsible science. But they departed from tradition in one respect: perhaps in order to disprove the recent charge that scientists have been elitist in making decisions for the public, they expressed their concern publicly before they had time to explore the matter extensively. Their candor was acclaimed initially, but it soon gave rise to widespread public anxiety, particularly after a handful of other scientists raised an alarm.

By now much of the apprehension has subsided. It may be of interest to summarize briefly the main scientific reasons, which I have reviewed elsewhere in greater detail.[4] (1) After several years of work, in hundreds of laboratories, with such chimeric bacteria, the hazards have remained entirely conjectural: no illness or environmental damage has been traced to this source. (2) Mutant bacterial strains have been developed with a remarkable, novel safety feature: they require special nutrients that are lacking outside the laboratory, and without these compounds the cells rapidly self-destruct. (3) It has recently become clear that bacteria transfer DNA from one species to another promiscuously (employing, in fact, the same enzymes that investigators extract and use for in vitro recombination). This finding makes it extremely likely that the recombinants with human DNA now being made in the laboratory would not be a novel class of organisms after all, since *E. coli* in the mammalian gut would occasionally take up DNA released from dying host cells (as well as DNA from other bacterial cells). (4) In nature novel mutants are continually being generated, and only an infinitesimal fraction of these innovations pass through the sieve of natural selection and survive. Moreover, this survival depends not on the properties of a single gene but on the adaptive value of a balanced set of genes; and insertion of DNA from a distant source, in the new technique, is almost certain to impair that balance. (5) Since this insertion adds only about 0.1 percent to the DNA of the host *E. coli*, a recombinant will retain the mode of spread of *E. coli* and will be restricted to the habitat of that organism (the vertebrate gut). Hence, epidemiological experience with pathogens closely related to *E. coli* is pertinent—and it is reassuring. Indeed, from the inception of the debate no expert in epidemiology or infectious disease supported the view that *E. coli* might inadvertently yield

4. Bernard D. Davis, "The Recombinant DNA Scenarios: Andromeda Strain, Chimera, and Golem," *American Scientist*, 65 (1977): 547-55.

recombinants as hazardous as the already known major bacterial pathogens—organisms that have already been selected in evolution for the ability to spread, and that may turn up in any diagnostic laboratory at any time. Moreover, though the history of microbiology includes several thousand laboratory infections, and a few microepidemics, no large epidemic of any pathogen has ever arisen from a laboratory. (6) Ironically, views on the possible spread of tumor virus genes by bacteria, which started the discussion, have rotated 180 degrees. Viral DNA cloned in bacteria, from which it can be released only as naked DNA, is over a million times *less* infectious to an animal than the same DNA released from its natural animal cell host, as a complete viral particle with a protective coat.[5] Hence, an investigator can now prepare such DNA more safely in bacteria than by the conventional (and unregulated) methods in animal cells. (7) Since mild pathogens are much more common than severe ones (for example, the common cold versus the influenza virus), it seems exceedingly unlikely that a serious pathogen could be inadvertently produced without any warning.

With these developments, and after an enormous amount of discussion, public anxiety abated. The very real threat of restrictive and even punitive legislation has been dropped, and the National Institutes of Health guidelines regulating this research have gone through two successive stages of relaxation. But reason prevailed only after a great deal of time and money had been spent fighting exaggerated or nonexistent dangers. Moreover, a large regulatory bureaucracy was set up. Starting on this slippery slope may be the greatest price of all, unless the experience helps us to develop better mechanisms for evaluating risks in highly technical areas. For such bureaucracies not only are costly in time and money, and occasionally obstructive: their rigidity also inhibits the sense of playfulness and of artistic creativity that has characterized much of the best scientific research.

THE NEED FOR IMPROVED ASSESSMENT
OF POSSIBLY DANGEROUS ACTIONS

Concern over actions that might create dangerous materials is clearly legitimate in principle. Moreover, in practice scientists have had little trouble in agreeing with public agencies on regulations over demonstrably dangerous materials—inflammable, explosive, toxic, or radioactive. Problems arise, however, when the hazards are matters of judgment more than of demonstrable fact. In both circumstances the assessment of the hazards is a technical job, best handled by those with the requisite special knowledge, while the subsequent process of making policy should involve a wider group.

5. M. A. Israel, H. W. Chan, M. A. Martin, and W. P. Rowe, "Molecular Cloning of Polyoma Virus DNA in *Escherichia coli*: Oncogenicity Testing in Hamsters," *Science*, 205 (1979): 1140-42.

A move in this direction would require an adjustment of attitudes in both the general community and the scientific community. On the one side, having recognized that science and technology present hazards as well as benefits, we cannot go back to an earlier era in which scientists were trusted to make all decisions that involved science. But I believe the record justifies a restoration of public trust in the sense of responsibility of the scientific community when it is asked to provide objective and informed judgments on the technical matters in which its members have special knowledge. At the same time, scientists must recognize that risks and benefits are generally noncommensurable and are unevenly distributed in society, and that balancing them involves not simply technical questions but also value judgments; hence the general community must be involved in the later stages of decision making.

In asking for trust, scientists must also recognize a new responsibility toward the public. With the growing impact of technology on society and with large economic stakes biasing many sources of information, we need greater watchfulness and initiative on the part of those scientists closest to a new development—willingness not only to provide answers when asked but also to expose abuses as soon as they become identifiable. In addition, the scientific community must not pretend to more expertise or more objective knowledge than it has, especially in those fields where the knowledge is diluted by a great deal of uncertainty.

It is not obvious how confidence in the scientific community can be restored. In a broad sense education is perhaps the only way. But I would suggest that for this purpose an informed public is not simply one that is exposed to news about recent discoveries. Much more important, and more difficult, is education on the nature of scientific activity. Legislators, in particular, need to know that discovery is inherently unpredictable, and not purchasable quite like a commodity. Another point, particularly important in asking for trust, is that scientists are intensely trained to be honest in handling their data—not because they are more virtuous than other people but because their findings are valueless unless verifiable, and they know that nature has the last word. Finally, though scientists are not infallible, and though at the growing points of science interpretations rise and fall, the scientific community has evolved extraordinarily effective communal mechanisms for discriminating between true and false conclusions. And that community sometimes needs quite a bit of time to digest and exchange information before a conclusion is firm enough to warrant public attention.

Perhaps we can learn a lesson from the reaction to recombinant DNA, which retrospectively seems to have been close to hysteria. The record of the scientific community was certainly a highly responsible one. Indeed, the problem arose because the molecular biologists who created the novel techniques were carried away excessively by concern over the theoretical possibility of creating novel epidemics, and it took time for the highly reassuring information from epidemiologists and evolutionists to have an impact. If the matter could have remained within the scientific community in the first state of a two-stage process, we would have avoided a futile and expensive exercise—expensive in terms of time, money, public anxiety, and the morale of the scientific community.

Dangerous Powers from Genetics

Let us now shift from research that may yield dangerous products to research whose results may give us dangerous powers—a problem that raises quite different issues of social policy. In the biomedical sciences the powers most feared are those of genetic engineering, that is, directing changes in the genome of an organism.

In medicine the phrase genetic engineering, with its cold overtones, does not seem very apt, for the goal is simply gene therapy: replacement of the single defective genes that cause various hereditary diseases. By itself such a replacement would surely be as legitimate as the daily replacement of a gene product, such as insulin. Nevertheless, the idea has generated alarm. Some critics see such manipulation as something akin to sacrilege—the invasion of sacred territory. But most of the concern no doubt has a more pragmatic basis: fear that if we develop such techniques for medical purposes, those in power may employ them for political purposes—not to cure or to prevent diseases but to manipulate personalities. This belief, as an undercurrent, clearly added to public anxiety in the recombinant DNA debate.

If I believed such political applications of genetics were at all likely, I would share this apprehension. But just as with the dangers from recombinant DNA, I find the technical facts highly reassuring, on several grounds. First, even therapy of single-gene defects still seems far off (except for the precursors of circulating blood cells, which are so loosely organized in the bone marrow that they could conceivably be replaced by other cells). In addition, even if gene therapy for monogenic diseases should be achieved, the complexity of the genetic contribution to individual differences in behavior presents a huge technical obstacle to its manipulation. For though we know virtually nothing about these genes, we can be sure that their number must be very large. Intelligence, or altruism, or any other behavioral trait is polygenic, that is, it is not determined by a single gene but instead is influenced by many genes, interacting with each other and with the environment. The problem of identifying such a large, coordinated set of genes, and replacing them in a predictable way, is very much greater than that of single-gene therapy.

Still another obstacle to genetic manipulation of personalities arises from the fact that the function of the brain depends on an intricate network of specific cell-to-cell contacts, and most behavioral genes act by guiding the development of that circuitry. Since these genes will have done their work before birth, gene transfer could not conceivably rewire an already developed brain. In principle, one could circumvent this difficulty by replacing genes in germ cells. But this procedure not only would be technically even more difficult: it would also be useless, for one would be investing great effort to change some genes in a germ cell whose other genes were still an unknown, chance combination.

Social factors further limit the possibility of genetic control of behavior. Though it has been suggested that genes might be manipulated secretly (for example, by dissemination in a virus), such fantasies cannot be taken seriously, if only because of the complexity of the complement of behavioral genes. We must therefore assume that genetic manipulation would require cooperation of the subjects; and any population willing to cooperate in this way would already have lost its freedom. Moreover, genetic manipulation of personalities, if ever feasible, would have to compete with other, less elaborate, and less costly means that are already at hand or in process. These include the familiar psychological methods (amplified by modern methods of mass communication) and the methods of pharmacology, neuro-surgery, and even eugenics (that is, selective breeding for the desired traits).

For these many reasons discussions of ethical aspects of gene replacement—recently a major topic in the field of biomedical ethics—may be seen as theoretical exercises in moral philosophy rather than as analyses of present or imminent social problems. Indeed, that so many scholars have taken the issue seriously testifies to the penetration of science fiction into the contemporary image of science. The alarm may abate as the issue is clarified and the anticipated powers remain remote. On the other hand, because of their emotional appeal the attacks on genetic engineering may threaten the highly desirable medical goal of gene therapy, just as similar attacks have effectively discouraged research on chromosomal aberrations in infants.[6]

Unlike gene replacement, another type of genetic manipulation of humans has seemed quite close at hand: the creation of genetic copies of an individual. Such cloning has been successfully accomplished with frogs, by implanting nuclei from somatic cells of an embryo into egg cells. Ten years ago it seemed self-evident that improvements in technique would sooner or later extend the procedure to mammals, and

6. See E. B. Hook, "Geneticophobia and the Implications of Screening for the XYY Genotype in Newborn Infants," in *Genetics and the Law*, ed. A. Milunsky and G.J. Annas (New York: Plenum, 1976) pp. 73-86; and Bernard D. Davis, "XYY: The Dangers of Regulating Research by Adverse Publicity," *Harvard Magazine*, 79 (October 1976): 26-30.

this scientific advance, of obvious value in agriculture, would create serious moral problems if it should be extended to man.[7] However, the prospect has now changed, with recent indications—though not yet decisive evidence—that various fully differentiated cells do not have quite the same genetic information as the embryonic cells. Hence cloning of mammalian adults may well be unachievable, for fundamental reasons rather than for reasons that might be overcome by advances in technique. If so, human cloning by nuclear transplant, aimed at copying individuals with already demonstrated traits, loses its potential interest—and its threat.

Should We Ever Restrict Knowledge That Might Yield Dangerous Powers?

I suggested earlier that in principle restrictions on research procedures involving potentially dangerous materials are clearly legitimate: the problem is how best to go about the job of assessing hazards when they are uncertain. However, when we consider research that might give us dangerous powers we face a more fundamental question: not how to improve procedures for setting limits, but where the limits should be set. Should we limit the search for certain kinds of knowledge, or only limit its applications? Waving the flag of Galileo may no longer be an adequate answer. For even though open societies have a long tradition of defending free inquiry as a mode of free expression, we find serious people today suggesting that science has now reached a stage where it might yield powers too hot to handle.

We cannot logically exclude this possibility. The problem is that we cannot identify such undesirable knowledge in advance. Being able to foresee a conceivable dreadful application is not enough. All knowledge is double-edged; and to justify proscribing any knowledge, we should be able to provide convincing evidence that the probable peril outweighs the probable gain.[8] No basic scientific knowledge has yet met this test.[9] Indeed, it is difficult to see how any knowledge could meet the test, for we simply cannot foresee all the applications of any knowledge; even less can we foresee all the social consequences of these applications. It would follow that we can still best serve society not by blocking any particular knowledge but by better controlling its

7. Bernard D. Davis, "Prospects for Genetic Intervention in Man," *Science*, 170 (1970): 1279-83.

8. See T.I. Emerson, "The Constitution and Regulation of Research," in *Regulation of Scientific Inquiry*, ed. K.M. Wulff, AAAS Selected Symposium 37 (Boulder, Colo.: Westview Press, 1979).

9. Nuclear energy might be considered to fall into the class where the peril outweighs the promise. Yet even here, as our civilization is threatened by dwindling energy supplies, only the future will be able to balance the benefits against the risks. And in any case, how could we have arranged for the advance of physics to stop short of this discovery?

applications. We should therefore seek to improve our methods for recognizing early the costs and dangers, as well as the benefits, of various applications, and we should resist economic and other pressures for automatically proceeding with all possible applications (the technological imperative).

Knowledge Believed to Endanger Social Justice

Let us now consider the third concern over advances in genetics: the production of knowledge that would undermine the foundations of public morality. This is the oldest source of fear of scientific progress, having arisen with the heliocentric theory, and reappearing in the reaction to Darwin. After the Scopes trial it seems unlikely that this form of antiscience would remain a matter of concern. But today we see not only increasing interference by creationists with the teaching of biology in public schools. A much more serious problem is an ideological attack, spearheaded within scientific circles, on the study of the biological roots of our behavior, and particularly on the study of human genetic diversity. This subject cuts even closer to the bone than did the earlier question of man's origin, for the results may conflict directly with assumptions about human nature that underlie strong political convictions. And a restriction on presumably dangerous insights is not simply a problem for biologists: it raises the question of intellectual freedom for the whole scholarly community.

It is ironic that human implications of evolution and genetics are now opposed primarily from the left. Darwin, in contrast, was seen as a threat not by liberals but primarily by religious traditionalists. Moreover, in the 1930s the distinguished British geneticist and Marxist J.B.S. Haldane could strenuously oppose Hitler's pseudogenetics and at the same time emphasize that real study of human behavioral genetics offers great promise for education.[10] More recently, the sad fate of genetics in the Soviet Union under Lysenko has offered a vivid warning against subordinating the search for objective knowledge to ideology. Nevertheless, the current attack has evoked wide sympathy, and it has created an atmosphere of intimidation: few graduate students today are likely to enter the field of human behavioral genetics.

The reasons for fear of this field are evident. One is the widespread conviction today that genetic differences between people, however real, should not be discussed in public lest they discourage or limit egalitarian aims. An older reason is the past history of political misuses of genetics. Dr. Edsall (pp. 151-153) has reviewed the enthusiasm of some early geneticists for a naïve eugenics program. Even more serious were the simplistic extrapolation from early evolutionary concepts to Social Darwinism and the use of pseudogenetics to support the racism of Nazis and white supremacists. Given this tragic history, we must

10. J.B.S. Haldane, *Heredity and Politics* (New York: Norton, 1938).

recognize that genetics could indeed again be misused to rationalize discriminatory practices; and we should be especially concerned about this possibility today, when we have finally begun to rectify our legacy of race discrimination.

But though this history has led to the assumption that studies of evolutionary and genetic aspects of human behavior are bound to have a reactionary social impact, this conclusion does not follow. For if we look closely at the past abuses of this area of science, we will find that in each case the politics has distorted the science, rather than being derived from it. This recognition leads to a paradoxical conclusion: the ideologically oriented critics of behavioral genetics today are the true spiritual heirs of the tradition that they appear to be opposing. For the proponents of genetic inquiry are defending the universality and objectivity of science against political undermining, from either the right or the left, while their critics would again subordinate scientific knowledge, though in a different direction, to social preconceptions.

One might counter that some kinds of knowledge could threaten the goals and values of a just and decent society, and so it is callous for the scientist to seek knowledge, in the tradition of disinterested inquiry, without regard to its political consequences. But however humanitarian the intent of this criticism, it misconstrues the relation between knowledge and justice. Justice is a social construct, and it is constantly evolving as we adapt to changing circumstances. Moreover, scientific findings cannot specify a particular construct as the correct one. They can only test some of the assumptions about human nature that underlie our efforts to develop adaptive social institutions; and the degree of correspondence between these assumptions and reality strongly influences the success or failure of our social experiments. Since science may thus reveal, but does not create, the reality that plays this role, it is difficult to see how scientific knowledge itself can be a threat to justice. To be sure, in its social applications knowledge can also be distorted, or misunderstood, or prematurely extrapolated. But as with knowledge that creates double-edged powers, discussed above, our problem is to avoid the abuses, not the possession of knowledge that creates insights.

This point can be illustrated more concretely by a deeper look at the history of the problem of racial justice. While genetics has been subject to very well-known past abuses in this area, as we have just noted, it has also made a positive (but unrecognized) contribution to our modern conception of racial justice. Specifically, the nature of race was viewed for centuries in *typological*[11] terms, that is, on the basis of the Platonic view that any class of entities is best understood in terms of an ideal type, the concrete variations between individuals being of trivial im-

11. Ernst Mayr, *Animal Species and Evolution* (Cambridge, Mass.: Harvard University Press, 1963), p. 5.

portance compared with the essential characteristics of the type. This prescientific view led to the belief that a person's race defines his potentials, thus providing a rationalization for racism (that is, for discriminatory treatment of individuals on the basis of identification with a given race). However, this assumption has been demolished as modern evolutionary theory and population genetics have replaced the earlier, vague social notion of race by a precise biological concept. Biologists now define races not in typological terms but in statistical, *populational* terms, that is, as subpopulations, within any species, that have been separated for enough generations so that their total gene pools have evolved significant differences in gene (allele) frequencies. Moreover, human races are highly heterogeneous (that is, they consist of individuals with widely varying potentials), and they all overlap in their distributions.

I would suggest that this biological insight has made a major, hidden contribution to the modern revolution in our social attitude toward race. The fundamental arguments for eliminating racism are, of course, moral and political; but these arguments are built on a tacit understanding that the earlier, typological view of race is false. If that view still prevailed, it is doubtful that the moral arguments would be convincing. Again, our problem is not to avoid scientific knowledge in socially sensitive areas but to avoid unsound or misinterpreted knowledge.

SCIENTISM AND OBJECTIVITY

The Dangers of Scientism and the Value of Objectivity

Having discussed public concern over both real and conjectural dangers generated by science and technology, I shall now discuss another source of public disaffection with science: inflated claims for its power. One kind of reaction is illustrated by genetic engineering. In the early, heady days of molecular genetics it was tempting to boast about future possibilities for reshaping man; but as the possibilities have seemed to be coming close, these boasts have now stirred up fears.

A much broader source of exaggerated claims has been the view called "scientism": the expectation that the advance of science will ultimately provide definitive solutions for the problems of society.[12] Our failure to find these solutions leads to criticism of scientists for wasting their talents on the wrong problems.

It is quite understandable that scientistic predictions should have been widely accepted at an earlier time, for science seemed to be a universal problem-solving machine, with no inherent limits in its

12. F.A. Hayek (*The Counter-Revolution of Science* [Glencoe, Ill.: Free Press, 1952], p. 15) uses the term "scientism" to denote the error of trying to build the social sciences in "slavish imitation of the method and language of science," rather than simply in its general spirit of disinterested inquiry. But this focus on method leaves out the question of goals and limits.

application to increasingly complex problems. Today, however, we recognize limits to its scope. One reason is that human social problems are more complex than those in the related natural science disciplines (neurobiology, ethology, and evolutionary biology). Another is that in social processes small causes can have large effects. But the most fundamental reason is epistemological: social actions involve value judgments, and in principle problems of values have no objectively demonstrable correct solution. Hence solving a problem in physics or in biology does not have the same meaning as solving a social problem. Indeed, in the absence of objective criteria, some would say that we can only try to manage, and should not speak of solving, social problems.

These limits, however, do not imply that science is irrelevant to social problems. On the contrary, it can help in several ways. First, through the tools provided by technology it can broaden our control over nature and hence our range of options. (Of course, increased options also create new problems.) More fundamentally, science is very good at predicting consequences of alternative actions—and such predictions enter, tacitly if not explicitly, in our selection of a value system, and in making concrete decisions within that system. And most directly, the development called sociobiology reflects a recognition that human social behavior has biological as well as cultural roots, and a hope that a deeper understanding of both will be helpful. As E. O. Wilson has pointed out, "the genes hold culture on a leash": our values are neither entirely arbitrary cultural constructs, on the one hand, nor rigidly determined products of our genes, on the other.[13]

Nevertheless, the leash is long, and it encompasses a very broad range of possible social patterns. Sociobiology therefore cannot be expected to prescribe any particular pattern as correct for a given set of circumstances, nor can it tell us how we ought to balance conflicting values. But it should be able to have an adjuvant role, helping us to incorporate a deeper knowledge of the realities of human nature— including its diversity as well as its universals—in deciding between alternative courses of action. It would be presumptuous to try to estimate how large this role will become, but meanwhile it seems important to avoid scientistic predictions, which can lead both to fear of their fulfillment and disappointment at their failure.[14]

The social sciences are the largest area where scientism has created disillusion. For despite the emphasis of these disciplines on objective,

13. E. O. Wilson, *Sociobiology* (Cambridge, Mass.: Harvard University Press, 1975).

14. For example, as I have spelled out at greater length elsewhere (note 2), Wilson's striking accomplishment, in launching sociobiology as a major discipline and in forcing a reexamination of the prevalent extreme environmentalism, may be diluted by such concepts as "a biology of ethics" and "a genetically accurate and hence completely fair code of ethics"; E. O. Wilson, *On Human Nature* (Cambridge, Mass.: Harvard University Press, 1978).

rigorous, and quantitative studies, in most areas their conclusions and predictions are far less certain than those in the natural sciences. Nevertheless, governmental and other social agencies have sometimes relied on these predictions as a basis for action, as though they were virtually infallible products of an all-powerful scientific method. The resulting disappointment has no doubt contributed to the antiscience movement, because the public (and even the National Academy of Sciences) closely identifies the social sciences with the natural sciences. Public education on the nature and the limits of science should therefore include a clear distinction between these two uses of the word "science."[15]

Soft-core Scientism: The Role of
Objective Knowledge

Gunther Stent, long a stimulating commentator on the idea of progress, has recently put forth a more extended conception of scientism. He agrees with the view that science cannot provide authoritative, correct solutions to moral problems—an expectation that he calls "hard-core" scientism. However, he disagrees with the view, which I have defended above, that solutions to moral problems will be more effective if they are not contradicted by reality, and that we should therefore always welcome the "adjuvant" function of objective knowledge. He calls this view "soft-core" scientism: "the dubious empirical proposition that the realization of moral aims is necessarily impeded by acts which are motivated by objectively false beliefs."[16]

Stent cites two examples. In the first he concedes that the false belief of the Hopi Indians in the effectiveness of the rain dance may have harmed their agriculture, but he suggests that it may nevertheless have provided a greater benefit by promoting communal cohesion. His second example comes closer to home: the problem, already discussed above, of research on the hereditary basis of intelligence. Stent criticizes equally those who consider such research essential and those who consider it pernicious, because both accept the assumption that if there is genetic diversity, it ought to be taken into account in the organization of society. He proposes, instead, that we should ignore such diversity because the communal cohesion fostered by the false belief in innate human equality could outweigh the losses due to the resulting falsely based educational system.

15. In the English language the confusion between natural and social sciences is increased by the sharp separation of both from the humanities. In German *"Wissenschaft"* refers to scholarly knowledge, which is divided into the exact, the social, and the humanistic categories.

16. Gunther S. Stent, "The Decadence of Scientism," in his *Paradoxes of Progress* (San Francisco, Ca.: W.H. Freeman, 1978), p. 207. Also in *Foundations of Ethics and Its Relationship to Science*, vol. 2, ed. H.T. Engelhardt and D. Callahan (Hastings, N.Y.: Hastings Institute of Society, Ethics, and the Life Sciences, 1977); and in *The Hastings Center Report*, 6(6) (1976): 32-40.

But a myth can promote communal cohesion only if it is widely enough accepted by the community. The Hopis could all believe in the power of the rain dance because their world view would not lead them to test it. In a modern, science-based society, in contrast, any testable assumption or claim will inevitably be tested, and if it proves to be objectively false, it will be disputed. The expected communal cohesion then becomes dissension between rationalists and believers. (We need only note how Western religions have increasingly narrowed their jurisdiction, abandoning their earlier role of providing supernatural explanations in areas now taken over by science.) Accordingly, however convenient it would be if everyone would ignore any questions of fact in the troubled area of heredity and intelligence, for the sake of peace and harmony, this simply cannot happen. Our society is too committed to the reality principle, at least in areas that bear on our bread-and-butter activities. And the question of the distribution of intellectual potentials arouses intense reactions precisely because it bears on central issues in many aspects of social policy. Stent's prescription would only prolong the dispute.[17]

The struggle to reconcile inspiring myths with harsh realities will always be with us. But the political costs of deliberately suppressing objective knowledge, in order to protect a myth, can go far beyond merely prolonging specific disputes. Though such suppression is always based on dedication to what the advocates consider a noble cause, Plato's noble lie all too easily becomes Hitler's big lie—and noble deception all too easily slides over into self-deception.

Is Objective Knowledge Possible?

Having emphasized the value of building on an objective recognition of reality, I shall close by considering briefly recent criticisms of the assumption that we can ever acquire such objective knowledge. One major source of this skepticism is the frustration of social scientists over the difficulty of separating the analytic content of their studies from the frequent policy implications. Another source is the search of philosophers for a rigorous epistemological foundation for science. The first topic has been discussed with great good sense by Charles Frankel,[18] and I shall consider only selected aspects.

Many social scientists have thrown up their hands at the problem

17. Another essay in Stent's book (*Paradoxes of Progress*, p. 1) illustrates the contradictions created by an effort to defend rationally the deliberate disregard of objective knowledge for the sake of social coherence. In criticizing Peter Medawar's call for continued confidence in progress through science, and advancing his own pessimistic predictions—which are surely less likely to promote present social coherence—his defense is his "accurate assessment of the actual situation."

18. Charles Frankel, "The Autonomy of the Social Sciences," in *Controversies and Decisions: The Social Sciences and Public Policy*, ed. C. Frankel (New York: Russell Sage Foundation, 1976).

of eliminating bias, holding that the honest investigator can do no better than to warn the reader by declaring his bias at the outset. Indeed, some even argue that in the social sciences the choice between alternative conclusions should take into account not only evidence and logic but also the anticipated social costs. This view is tempting when we are dealing with conclusions that impinge on our moral convictions. Nevertheless, its acceptance would remove such studies altogether from the realm of science. For the cardinal characteristic of science, and the key to its success, has been the requirement that we abandon any preconception, however treasured, in the face of compelling evidence to the contrary. To a natural scientist this problem of separating research findings in social science from their application to public policy resembles closely a problem in the natural sciences that we have discussed above: the separation between basic knowledge and control of its applications. In both areas the findings and the logical inferences derived from them can in principle be objective, but policy decisions are then made by a process that also introduces values.

We can sharpen this discussion by considering further the question of the heritability of intelligence, which has become the present test case in the periodic struggle to defend the objectivity of science against political attacks. This question is often treated as one in social science, but it really lies squarely in biology. To be sure, it has important social implications—but so does man's origin, or the distribution of the sickle cell gene. In addition, unlike various monogenic hereditary diseases, any behavioral trait depends very much on the interaction of genes with the environment, and it also depends on so many genes that we cannot locate them individually or identify their molecular product. Accordingly, the available methods can provide only statistical information, rather than identification of individual genotypes. But neither this limitation nor the relevance of the findings for human affairs justifies the assumption that the investigator in behavioral genetics is bound to be influenced by bias, any more than one who studies the distribution of blood group genes: the scientist does not create the reality that he discloses. And the problem of accepting the relevance of this field will increase when the advance of neurogenetics eventually permits us to identify individual behavioral genetic differences directly: Haldane's dream for optimizing education (see note 10 above).

We should also consider a more far-reaching denial of the objectivity of science, which has been advanced in recent years by certain philosophers and historians of science. This trend seems to have several sources. (1) The possibility of acquiring any objective knowledge has been attacked by neo-Marxists—perhaps to protect ideological dogmas from the danger of contradiction by reality. In an era of disillusion with our social institutions, and of disappointment at the failure of technological progress to solve our social problems, this view seems to have spread widely in academic circles. (2) Our knowledge of reality is acquired by nervous systems that have evolved to deal with a particular range of dimensions; and as Heisenberg has shown in the uncertainty principle, and Einstein in the theory of relativity, phenomena at dimensions outside that range do not fit into the perceptions of time, space, and matter natural for us. By a rather large and unwarranted leap these insights have been thought to weaken confidence that any scientific observations and inferences, even at the level of visible dimensions, correspond reliably to reality. (3) Science as an *activity* involves large subjective elements (and hence value judgments). These elements include the individual's choice of a problem, his choice of what experiments to perform, and society's choice of what work to support. Even more fundamental is the crucial role of hypothesis, for sophisticated students of the philosophy of science (especially Whewell, Peirce, Popper, and Medawar) have recognized that Baconian induction—the spontaneous emergence of a general principle from a collection of observations—fits only the early, descriptive stages of a science. It certainly does not reflect experimental sciences, whose logic involves a continual exchange and feedback between observation, imaginative creation of explanatory hypotheses, logical deduction of additional consequences, and tests of these predictions.

Since science thus has subjective as well as objective elements, it clearly is not value-free in *all* of its aspects. Recognition of this fact, together with preoccupation with the ambiguous term "value-free," has led some to the spurious inference that if values enter anywhere into the activities of a scientist, they also must influence his conclusions: the vaunted objectivity of science is therefore considered a myth. However, this view fails to recognize the dialectic between creation and criticism in science: a methodology that selects, in a sort of Darwinian process of testing and elimination (falsification), the objectively supportable from the false among the many conceptual products of its subjective, creative, value-laden activities. This selection occurs continually in the activities of the individual scientist, and it is further refined through finely honed communal activities.

In addition, we should recognize that scientific conclusions are based ultimately on probabilities, rather than on an absolute causal determinism. Objectivity thus does not imply absolute truth: in principle every conclusion is subject to future refutation or refinement. But in the intellectual edifice constructed by science every addition confirms the reliability (that is, the probability of correspondence with reality) of the foundations on which it builds. I conclude, then, that the biological sciences can indeed reach objective, reliable scientific conclusions about their subject matter. Obviously, at the growing points much that is stated in the name of science does not prove to be verifiable: what science produces might be described in terms of a gradient of reliability.

I am not here opposing the epistemological analysis of the meaning of objectivity, at the level of technical philosophy: what is disturbing is the denial of objectivity at the level of the interaction of science and society. Such extreme cognitive relativism, like extreme moral relativism, is a dangerous doctrine, easily used to persuade troubled people to replace common sense by nonsensical arguments couched in philosophical terms. The politicization of science thus becomes an avenue to political manipulation in a broader sphere.

SUMMARY AND CONCLUSIONS

While concern over the possible production of dangerous organisms by recombinant DNA research was in principle legitimate, a reassessment of the controversy suggests that in practice an excessive early involvement of the public and a lack of confidence in the sense of responsibility of the scientists involved slowed a reasonable resolution. As an alternative approach I have advocated a two-stage process of evaluating and regulating such potential hazards, with complementary roles for the scientific and general communities.

With respect to concern over knowledge that may give us dangerous powers, I have emphasized that we are not able to foresee the full range of positive and negative consequences of any basic knowledge. We should therefore try to control not the knowledge but those applications whose effects are demonstrably harmful or too costly. In the basic biomedical sciences, in particular, ethical challenges have been seen in applications that are far too distant for profitable discussion, and in some cases perhaps even impossible: for example, genetic blueprinting of personalities and human cloning.

A third concern, over increased insights into genetic aspects of human nature, is more complex. On the one hand, evidence from this field may conflict painfully with cherished preconceptions. On the other hand, civilization today has a growing sense of crisis—and though this feeling may derive largely from the consequences of the rapid growth of science and technology, we are not likely to improve our responses by refusing to use the power of science. On the contrary, in the long run increased insight into the biological roots of our behavior should aid us in meeting the crisis. If we should cut off the flow of such insights, in order to sidestep immediate problems, we may pay dearly in the long run—not only through deprival of valuable knowledge but also through damage to the ideals of an open society.

All three of the concerns that I have considered involve uncertain conjectures over future possible catastrophes. They therefore lend themselves to demagogic appeal. To truly protect society's interests, and not simply to create the illusion of protection, we must develop better social mechanisms, both for assessing and controlling those activities that may be dangerous and for protecting those that offer promise. But however much we would like to identify incipient dangers early, we cannot expect to see very far ahead. Hence we must continue to rely largely, like the evolutionary process, on trial and error. The real problem is whether we can develop sufficiently rapid corrective mechanisms, in an age when our errors may be so much more costly than in the past.

In a broader perspective, concern over progress in biology is symptomatic of a more general concern about the goals of our society. Even the scientific community has become shaken in its confidence in several former articles of faith: that truth is a supreme end, that progress in science is good for society, and that the scientific community can be trusted with a high degree of autonomy.[19]

The problem is pressing. As Philip Handler recently stated to the National Academy of Sciences: "For better or worse, the terms of a new social contract between the scientific community and the larger society are being forged. It behooves us to help optimize the terms."[20] But this is not easy, when dealing with critics who focus entirely on the dangers or costs of science and technology while taking the benefits for granted.

Perhaps this overreaction will only be part of a historical cycle between romantic interest in good intentions and classic interest in objective truth.[21] The antiscience movement could then prove to be a transitory stage, and even a useful prod, in our struggle to define more clearly what we seek when we speak of progress. For in contrast to our nearly exponential progress in science and technology, progress in a moral sense, or in the sense of overall human welfare, is difficult to demonstrate. Indeed, it is even difficult to define, because it involves

19. The changed attitude is reflected in recent actions of several central institutions. (1) In earlier years the U.S. National Academy of Sciences, if faced with the recombinant DNA problem, would doubtless have set up a committee that would have sifted the evidence and produced a presumably authoritative report. In the recent climate, however, the academy felt obligated to set up a forum open to the public. A group of activists, invading the first session, provided more dramatic news for the media than the scheduled speakers. (2) Similarly, in *Science* the news columns on recombinant DNA over a period of two years paid much more attention to the arguments against this research than to the counterarguments, though the latter would seem closer to the parent organization's goal of "the advancement of science." (3) Finally, an editorial in *Nature* [271 (1978): 391] suggested that we should refrain from acquiring knowledge in certain areas, such as the genetics of intelligence, because it would threaten a just and decent society. However, this journal later did publish a balancing guest editorial [272 (1978): 390].

20. Philip Handler, Presidential Address, U.S. National Academy of Sciences, April 24, 1979.

21. See Stephen Toulmin, "From Form to Function: Philosophy and History of Science in the 1950s and Now," *Daedalus*, Summer 1977, pp. 143-62.

normative concepts. We can no longer share the confidence of Condorcet or Spencer or Marx in the perfectibility of man and of society. Though man has increasing control over his fate, the contradictions in his nature, as well as the role of chance, create limits to this control. Tragedy is therefore still inevitable. Perhaps a particularly valuable kind of progress today would be a more realistic recognition of the limits of what we can control, and of the underlying biological reasons for these limits.

The antiscience movement also reflects discouragement over the huge challenges that have been amplified by technology: to develop sufficient harmony, between and within nations, to save us from our capacity to destroy civilization overnight; to learn how to use finite resources with foresight; and to broaden the opportunity for fulfillment of individual potentials. Evolutionary and neurobiological insights will not solve these problems, but they may help us to manage them better, and to decrease the amount of tragedy in our lives.

9

Toward a Theory of Scientific Progress

GERALD HOLTON

INTRODUCTION

My objective in this essay is to sketch the rationale for and the outlines of a theory of scientific progress. My hope is to do justice both to the ongoing work pursued by scientists today and also to the long-range view of the development of science as it appears in the findings of historians of science.

The notion of scientific progress is undergoing a transformation at the present time. Though a matter of great consequence, the discussion of this issue seems to be limited, however, by the very conceptual tools that are being applied to it. There is little consensus on whether it is possible even in principle to determine the direction and magnitude of a change of scientific understanding or to what degree the activities of scientists are on the whole cumulative. On the contrary, much of the recent philosophical literature claims that we are only staggering from one fashion, conversion, revolution, or incommensurable exemplar to the next in a kind of perpetual, senseless Brownian motion, without discernible direction or *telos*.

Change as such, it would seem, should be relatively easy to determine. But it has turned out that superficially appealing measures, such as quantitative science indicators, are quite problematical. Also, for the purpose of evaluating scientific progress, changes in a specific field of endeavor lose their significance when considered in isolation, just as the concept of the absolute motion of a planet has no meaning since motion must be referred to an interlocking system of reference frames—the solar system, the galaxy, and the cluster of galaxies.

"Progressive" change or development is a doubly sophisticated notion. It must be true to the aims and methods of advance on the part both of the individual scientist and of the larger community in which he works. Some recent attempts to ascertain "progressiveness" by means of "rational reconstruction" have been unsuccessful primarily because they have not dealt with the actual scientific development. We shall see, rather, that "progressiveness" is an indicator of the direction and magnitude of scientific change with respect to specifiable reference systems—for example, the new acquisition of some analytic or phenomenic result in the service of an implicit or explicit goal, or of a centuries-long effort to achieve some conceptual synthesis. Moreover, we shall see that the reference systems themselves are in large part determined by their thematic content.

THE INTUITIVE MODEL

Efforts to formulate a theory of scientific progress are a fairly recent development. Most scientists at the bench are doing very well without such a self-conscious analysis of their efforts and results. Until recently, even in the historiography of science, the conception of science as inexorably "progressing" has been a relatively unexamined assumption. George Sarton, the first of the modern historians of science, asserted:

Definition: Science is systematized positive knowledge or what has been taken as such at different ages and in different places.

Theorem: The acquisition and systematization of positive knowledge are the only human activities which are truly cumulative and progressive.

Corollary: The history of science is the only history which can illustrate the progress of mankind. In fact, progress has no definite and unquestionable meaning in fields other than the field of science.[1]

Most scientists, when they leave their laboratories to make public announcements or to justify research funding, tend to adopt this euphoric, Sartonian imagery of unending horizons. Privately, many are sensitive to the fragility of "advances," to the difficulty of proving that the physics of Max Planck was better than that of Aristotle, to the need to forego some interesting questions as the cost of an advance (as Lavoisier's oxygen-based chemistry put an end to the fascination with flame and color in chemical reactions, questions which could not be taken up again until after Bohr's atomic theory). But, on the whole, there is a tacit attitude that advances of understanding patently do occur and are in some sense advances in improving our ever-incomplete understanding of "external reality," even though this last notion has been so battered that it is being held as an unconfessed belief,

1. George Sarton, *The Study of History of Science* (1906; rpt. New York: Dover, 1957), p. 5.

fringed by awareness that it may only be a nostalgic remnant of the prepositivistic (therefore "unscientific") period.

Scientific activity may be divided roughly into two kinds: that which is directed toward *analysis* and *accretion*, and that which is concerned with *synthesis*. For work of the former kind—by far the larger fraction—Pierre Duhem's description applies:

> This task of continual modification by which the laws of physics avoid more and more adequately their refutations provided by experiment play ... an essential role in the development of the science.... Physics makes progress through this unceasing struggle and the work of continually supplementing laws in order to include the exceptions.... Physics makes progress because experiment constantly causes new disagreements to break out between laws and facts, and because physicists constantly touch up and modify laws in order that they may more faithfully represent facts.... The laws of physics cannot be maintained except by continual retouching and modification.[2]

The second type, synthesis-oriented work—rarer but more transforming—envisions progress as equivalent to an increase in the inclusiveness of separate subject matter and in the parsimony or restrictiveness in the separate fundamental terms and assumptions. An exemplar is the heliocentric system of Copernicus. By virtue of its combination of inclusiveness and parsimony, Copernicus' system of planets had, as he explained, the great merit that "not only [do the] phenomena follow therefrom, but also the order and size of all the planets and spheres and heaven itself are so linked together that in no portion of it can anything be shifted without disrupting the remaining parts and the universe as a whole." In his system, nothing is arbitrary; there is no room for the ad hoc rearrangement of any orbit, as had been possible before his work, and hence there is revealed a sparse rationale, a necessity that binds each detail to the whole design. Hence it carries the conviction that we understand why the planets are disposed as they are and not otherwise.

The Galilean synthesis of celestial and terrestrial physics is another example, as is Newton's *Principia*, particularly in its theory of lunar motions. Newton's gravitational analysis allowed the prediction, from fundamentals, of the periods and magnitudes of known "inequalities." His success put forward a vision that the concepts of force and mass, and the efficacy of mathematical and observational techniques, sufficed to discover an overwhelming unity of physical science (one which Newton privately thought would eventually encompass also the sphere of moral philosophy).

2. Pierre Duhem, *The Aim and Structure of Physical Theory* (New York: Atheneum, 1962), pp. 176-278.

In our century, the incorporation of Newtonian mechanics into the general relativity theory was a further example of scientific progress by synthesis. At the end of his *Principles of Quantum Mechanics*, P. A. M. Dirac confidently declared that since "quantum mechanics may be defined as the application of equations of motion to atomic particles," the domain of applicability of the theory "includes most of low-energy physics and chemistry." These, it was implied, are essentially solved problems, the past rather than the future of science. However, the latter beckoned:

> Now there are other kinds of interactions, which are revealed in high-energy physics and are important for the description of atomic nuclei. These interactions are not at present sufficiently well understood to be incorporated into a system of equations of motion. . . . It is to be hoped that with increasing knowledge a way will be found for adapting the high-energy theories into a scheme based on equations of motion, and so unifying them with those of low-energy physics.[3]

In almost every scientific research journal, this model of scientific progress by means of greater inclusiveness and parsimony can be found. For example, Victor Weisskopf[4] takes six of the known physical constants—the mass of the proton, the mass of the electron and its electric charge, the light velocity, Newton's gravitational constant, and the quantum of action of Planck—and a few of the known fundamental laws (for example, de Broglie's relations concerning connecting particle momentum and particle energy with their wavelength and frequency, and the Pauli principle). Putting these data and laws together, he *derives* from them a host of predictions that in fact correspond to facts of observation: the size and energy of nuclei, the mass and hardness of solids such as rocks, the height of mountains, and the size of our sun and similar stars. All these seemed at first unconnected and are spread over an enormous range of magnitudes. Now they are seen to be different consequences of a few fundamental posits.

This is indeed Newton's program, triumphant. And if any one of the six physical constants on Weisskopf's list, now considered to be separate, could be derived from the other five—for example, if the charge of the electron were found to be deducible from some of the other fundamental constants—then you would know you are progressing, indeed an immense distance.

A by-product of scientific progress achieved through the continual

3. P. A. M. Dirac, *Principles of Quantum Mechanics* (Oxford: Clarendon Press, 1958), p. 312.

4. Victor Weisskopf, "Of Atoms, Mountains, and Stars: A Study in Qualitative Physics," *Science*, 187(4177) (1975): 605-12.

decrease in the number of fundamental axioms and, simultaneously, through the increase in the range of phenomena covered, is an emerging synergism with respect to techniques and methods. Results in one field become useful in another, far distant one, and often in a surprising way. The theoretical tools of condensed-matter physics that handle macroscopic phenomena such as ferromagnetism, superconductivity, and superfluidity are now understood in terms of concepts and theories applicable at the submicroscopic level, where they connect with problems of the structure of stellar bodies, nuclear physics, particle physics, and field theories. Robert Sachs wrote recently:

> Symmetry principles, and the concepts of gauge theories and spontaneously broken symmetries, turn out to play a common role so that theorists working in one such field may borrow methods from another. Just as all fields have shared in common methods of solution of linear equations, it now appears that new approaches to the solution of nonlinear equations, discovered first in connection with hydrodynamic problems, may be of great importance for the understanding of both condensed matter and elementary particles.[5]

From a historical point of view, one must add at least in passing that all such ideas of scientific progress lack a component that, until the mid- or late nineteenth century, would have been taken for granted quite generally. These modern views are characteristically *demythified*; that is, all traces of a coupling between scientific progress and moral philosophy or theology are gone. Even Duhem dared only to hint at the fundamentally religious underpinnings of his theory of scientific progress, and only at the very end of his treatise: "In a word, the physicist is compelled to recognize that it would be unreasonable to work for the progress of physical theory if this theory were not the increasingly better defined and more precise reflection of a metaphysics; the belief in an ordered, transcending physics is the sole justification of physical theory."[6] Practically all such moral speculations have now gone underground or disappeared. Typically, scientists assume that the criteria of successful work are internal to science, the corollary of that view being that the effects upon society, both technological and cultural changes, are relatively slow, therefore digestible, and beneficial even though unforeseeable.

So much for the largely intuitive, "working-model" notion of scientific progress current among scientists, and evidently adequate in the present surge of excellent work. Nonetheless, these and more explicit conceptions of scientific progress have come under severe attack recently from some philosophers of science. They hold that the outcome of scientific activity is *by definition* inevitably progress, hence that the

5. Robert G. Sachs, "Structure of Matter: A Five-Year Outlook," *Physics Today*, 32(12) (December 1979): 27.
6. Duhem, *Aim and Structure*, p. 335.

perception of progress is self-fulfilling and, therefore, illusory. Other philosophers of science claim that scientific work must be measured against universal criteria, drawn up as "statute law" so that "degenerating" programs can be identified by these philosophers and thus denied research support and publication. By these criteria, however, Boltzmann's kinetic-atomic research program would have been considered in a state of "degeneration" between 1880 and 1905. As one commentator correctly observed,

> Fortunately, the scientific community at that time was more tolerant of dissent. . . . Boltzmann, Lorentz, Smoluchowski, Gibbs, Jeans, and other followers of the kinetic program, including Planck and Einstein after 1900, did not have too much difficulty in getting their work published. But [today], with intense competition for research funds and journal space, application of the methodology of scientific research programs might well be disastrous. . . . Beware of the philosopher kings and philosopher research administrators![7]

During the last decade, these externally imposed criteria have attracted a good deal of attention, at least in circles outside science itself. But the inherent futility of all such attempts to set normative standards, and their distance from science as it is really done, have begun to be more and more obvious. Therefore, I shall not go over that ground here. Instead of attempting to amend all such ad hoc, largely intuitive models, the more important task is to obtain a more disciplined model from the actual practice of scientists in the modern period.

THE TWO-DIMENSIONAL MODEL

We start by differentiating among the main components of scientific thought, each of which has its own potential and mode of progressive development. For this analysis there seems to be no better way than to select as a point of departure the credo of a scientist whose work to a large degree has determined the predominant direction of scientific advance in his field from the early part of this century to our day and whose approach has been absorbed, consciously or not, by most current practitioners. I mean of course Albert Einstein. He wrote extensively on the methods and direction of scientific development, and an appropriate entry for formulating a theory of scientific advance is his essay of 1933, "Zur Methodik der theoretischen Physik,"[8] which Philipp

7. S.G. Brush, "Review," *American Journal of Physics*, 45 (1977): 687-88.
8. Usually translated as "On the Method of Theoretical Physics," this was Einstein's Herbert Spencer lecture, given at Oxford on June 10, 1933. The original manuscript of Einstein's essay was in German and has been published in his collection *Mein Weltbild* (Frankfurt am Main: Ullstein, 1977), pp. 113-19. An English translation appeared as a small booklet by Oxford University Press in 1933; but it left a good deal to be desired, and a different English translation was prepared (by Sonja Berg-

Frank, Einstein's biographer and colleague, called the "finest formulation of his views on the nature of a physical theory."[9]

Einstein begins with an important warning, but one which, by itself, would make it mysterious how scientific progress can be achieved on any model: he notes first of all to pay "special attention to the relation between the content of a theory," on the one hand, and "the totality of empirical facts," on the other. These constitute the two "components of our knowledge," the "rational" and the "empirical"; these two components are "inseparable"; but they stand also, Einstein warns, in "eternal antithesis." To support this conception, Einstein refers to a dichotomy built into Western science. The Greek philosopher-scientists provided the necessary confidence for achievement of the human intellect by the introduction into Western thought of the "miracle of the logical system," which, as in Euclid's geometry, "proceeds from step to step with such precision that every single one of its propositions was absolutely indubitable." But "propositions arrived at by purely logical means are completely empty as regards reality"; "through purely logical thinking we can attain no knowledge whatsoever of the empirical world." Einstein tells us that it required the seventeenth-century scientists to show that scientific knowledge "starts from experience and ends with it."

Up to this point, we are left, therefore, with a thoroughly dualistic method for doing science. On the one hand, Einstein says, "the structure of the system is the work of reason"; on the other hand, "the empirical contents and their mutual relations must find their representation in the conclusions of the theory." Indeed, virtually all of Einstein's commentators have followed him in stressing this dualism— and have left it at that. It is a view of science of which there are many variants. I consider it a two-dimensional view. It can be defended up to a point and may be summarized as follows. Science deals with two types of meaningful statements, namely, propositions concerning empirical matters that ultimately boil down to meter readings and other public phenomena, and propositions concerning logic and mathematics that ultimately boil down to tautologies. The first of these, the propositions concerning empirical matters of fact, can in principle be rendered in protocol sentences in ordinary language that command the general assent of the scientific community. I call these the phenomenic

---

mann) when Einstein later published a collection of his essays in the book *Ideas and Opinions* (New York: Crown, 1954). The translation appears on pp. 270-76. In quoting from Einstein's essay and from his other writings, I refer to the pages of the English translations in *Ideas and Opinions*, but I have gone back to the corresponding original German essays and corrected the published English versions as necessary. In this connection, I wish to acknowledge with thanks the help of Helen Dukas and the kindness of the Estate of Albert Einstein for its permission to quote from Einstein's writings.

9. Philipp Frank, *Einstein: His Life and Times* (New York: Knopf, 1947), p. 217.

propositions. The second type of propositions, meaningful insofar as they are consistent within the system of accepted axioms, I call analytic propositions. As a mnemonic device, and also to do justice to Einstein's warning about the "eternally antithetical" nature of these propositions, one may imagine them as the projections lying on a set of orthogonal axes representing the two dimensions of a plane within which scientific discourse usually takes place. A scientific statement, in this view, is therefore analogous to an element of area in the plane, and the projections of it onto the axes are the aspects of the statement that can be rendered, respectively, as protocol of observation (for example, "the needle swings to the left") and as protocol of calculation (for example, "use vector calculus, not scalars").

Now it is the claim of most modern philosophies of science that trace their roots to empiricism or positivism that any scientific statement has "meaning" only insofar as it can be shown to have phenomenic and/or analytic components in this plane. And, indeed, in the past, this Procrustean criterion has amputated from science its innate properties, occult principles, and all kinds of tantalizing questions, for which the consensual mechanism could not provide sufficiently satisfying answers. A good argument can be made that the silent but general agreement to keep the discourse consciously in the phenomic-analytic plane, where statements and routines can be shared, is the main reason why science has been able to grow so rapidly in modern times. While the degree of consensus at the developing edge of science is usually far less than most model makers of science realize, consensus about an area rises rapidly as the edge moves on. Hence, the two-dimensional model is widely used to characterize science when it is rewritten for pedagogic purposes or "rationalized" for epistemological discussion.

LIMITATIONS OF THE
TWO-DIMENSIONAL MODEL

Nevertheless, this two-dimensional view has its costs. It overlooks or denies the existence of active mechanisms at work in the day-to-day experience of those who are actually engaged in the pursuit of science; and it is of little help in handling questions every historian of science has to face consciously, even if the working scientist, happily, does not. To illustrate, let me mention two such problems. Both have to do with the direction of scientific advance, and both will seem more amenable to solution once the dualistic view is modified.

First, sound scientific discourse is directed entirely by the dictates of logic and of empirical findings. Why is science not one great totalitarian engine, taking everyone relentlessly to the same inevitable goal? The laws of reason, phenomena, and human skills to deal with both are presumably distributed equally over the globe; and yet the story of, say, the reception of Einstein's theories is strikingly different in Germany and England, in France and the United States. On the level of *personal* choice of a research topic, why were some of Einstein's contemporaries so fatally attracted to ether-drift experiments whereas he himself, as he put it to his friend de Haas, thought it as silly and doomed to failure as trying to study dreams in order to prove the existence of ghosts? As to skills for navigating in the two-dimensional plane, Einstein and Bohr were rather well matched, as were Schrödinger and Heisenberg. And yet there were fundamental antagonisms in terms of programs, tastes, and beliefs, with occasional passionate outbursts among scientific opponents.

Or, again, how to understand the great variety of different personal styles of scientists, all engaged in what they agree to be the "same" problem? If science *were* two-dimensional, the work of scientists in a given field might sooner or later be governed by a rigid, uniformly accepted exemplar. The documented existence of pluralism at all times points to a fatal flaw in the two-dimensional model—and also to its cure.

A second question that escapes the simple model, and to which I have devoted a number of case studies in recent years, is this: why are many scientists, particularly in the nascent phase of their work, willing to hold firmly, and sometimes at great risk, to what can only be called a suspension of disbelief about the possibility of falsification? Moreover, why do they do so sometimes without having any empirical evidence on their side or even in the face of disconfirming evidence?

Among countless examples of this sort, Max Planck, responsible for the idea of the quantum but one of the most outspoken opponents to its corpuscular implications, cried out as late as 1927: "Must we really ascribe to the light quanta a physical reality?"—this four years after the publication and verification of Arthur H. Compton's findings. On the other hand, when it came to explaining the electron in terms of what Planck called "vibrations of a standing wave in a continuous medium," along the lines proposed by de Broglie and Schrödinger, Planck gladly accepted the idea and added that "these principles have already [been] established on a solid foundation"—all that before Planck had heard of any experimental evidence along the lines provided by Davisson and Germer.[10]

Einstein was even more daring. To select just one among many illustrations, in 1916, when he wrote his book *Über die spezielle und die allgemeine Relativitätstheorie*, he had to acknowledge that his general relativity theory so far had only one observable consequence, the precession of the orbit of Mercury, whereas the predicted bending of light and the red shift of spectral lines owing to the gravitational

10. Quoted in Richard K. Gehrenbeck, *C. J. Davisson, L. H. Germer, and the Discovery of Electron Diffraction*, Ph.D. dissertation, University of Minnesota, 1973, pp. 343-44.

potential were too small to be then observed. Nevertheless, Einstein drew this conclusion, in a daring sentence in which he ended his book in its first fifteen printings, from 1917 through 1919: "I do not doubt at all that these consequences of the theory will also find their confirmation." It is an example of the suspension of disbelief, an important mechanism in the practice of experimental and theoretical scientists.[11]

THE ROLE OF PRESUPPOSITIONS

What, then, must one conclude from Planck's predisposition for the continuum and against discreteness, from Einstein's predisposition for a theory that encompasses a wide rather than a narrow range of phenomena and so allows him to risk his reputation on a daring prediction, from many examples of suspension of disbelief in the face of missing tests and even contrary data? Such cases serve to indicate that some *third mechanism* is present in determining the choices scientists make in the nascent phase of their work, in addition to the phenomenic and analytical mechanisms. Indeed, we can find it in Einstein's lecture on the method of theoretical physics: the two-dimensional model initially prominent in it gives way, on closer examination, to a more sophisticated and appropriate one. In addition to the two inseparable but antithetical components, there is indeed a third one, located above the plane bounded by the empirical and logical dimensions of the theory.

Einstein launches his argument by reminding his audience, as he often did, that the previously mentioned phenomenic-analytic dichotomy prevents the principles of a theory from being "deduced from experience" by "abstraction"—that is to say, by logical means. "In the logical sense [the fundamental concepts and postulates of physics are] free inventions of the human mind" and in that sense different from the unalterable Kantian categories. He repeats more than once that the "fundamentals of scientific theory" are of "purely fictitious character."[12] Or as he put it soon afterwards: the relationship between sense experience and concept "is analogous not to that of soup to beef, but rather to that of check number to overcoat."[13]

The essential arbitrariness of reference, Einstein explains, "is per-

---

11. After the observation of the bending of light, published in November 1919, Einstein amended this sentence for the edition printed in 1920: now there remained only one consequence drawn from the theory which had not been observed (the red shift of spectral lines); but, he added, "I do not doubt at all that this consequence of the theory will also find its confirmation soon." Albert Einstein, *Über die spezielle und die allgemeine Relativitätstheorie*, 7th ed. (Braunschweig: Vieweg, 1920), p. 70.

12. E.g., Einstein, *Ideas and Opinions*, p. 272. The quotations in the next six paragraphs are from the same source, pp. 273-76.

13. In the essay "Physik und Realität," 1936, translated as "Physics and Reality," in Einstein, *Ideas and Opinions*, p. 294.

fectly evident from the fact that one can point to two essentially different foundations"—the general theory of relativity and Newtonian physics—"both of which correspond with experience to a large extent"—namely, with much of mechanics. The elementary experiences do not provide a logical bridge to the basic concepts and postulates of mechanics. Rather, "the axiomatic basis of theoretical physics ... must be freely invented."

With this declaration, Einstein has, of course, exposed the emptiness of all attempts to impose external standards of "scientific rationality" on the practice of scientists or on the historical study of scientific achievements and hence to condemn as "irrational" scientific work that fails to meet such criteria. Thus, he shows that good scientific reasoning follows the precepts of neither the Dionysians nor the Apollonians. Einstein is, however, quite aware that his insight leads immediately to a basic problem, and he spells it out: How "can we ever hope to find the right way? Nay, more, has this right way an existence outside our illusions? Can we hope to be guided safely by experience at all when there exist theories such as classical mechanics, which do justice to experience to a large extent, but without grasping the matter in a fundamental way?"

We have now left the earlier, confident portion of Einstein's lecture far behind. But at this very point, Einstein issues a clarion call: "I answer with full confidence that there is, in my opinion, a right way, and that we are capable of finding it." Here, Einstein goes suddenly beyond his earlier categories of empirical and logical efficacy and offers us a whole set of selection rules with which, as with a good map and compass, that "right way" to an implicit *telos* may be found. Here, there, everywhere, guiding concepts emerge and beckon from above the previously defined plane to point us on the right path.

The first directing principle Einstein mentions is his belief in the efficacy of formal structures. The "creative principle resides in mathematics"—not, for example, in mechanical models. Then there unfolds a veritable hymn to the guiding concept of simplicity. Einstein calls it "the Principle of searching for the mathematically simplest concepts and their connections," and he cheers us on our way with many examples of how effective it has already proven to be:

> If I assume a Riemannian metric [in the four-dimensional continuum] and ask what are the *simplest* laws which such a metric can satisfy, I arrive at the relativistic theory of gravitation in empty space. If in that space I assume a vector field or antisymmetrical tensor field which can be derived from it, and ask what are the simplest laws which such a field can satisfy, I arrive at Maxwell's equations for empty space.

And so on, collecting victories everywhere under the banner of simplicity.

Later in the lecture, we find two other guiding concepts in tight embrace: the concept of parsimony or economy and that of unification. As science progresses, Einstein tells us, "the logical edifice" is more and more "unified," the "smaller the number [is] of logically independent conceptual elements which are necessary to support the whole structure." Higher up on that same page, we encounter nothing less than what he calls "the noblest aim of all theory," which is "to make these irreducible elements as simple and as few in number as is possible, without having to renounce the adequate representation of any empirical content."

Yet another guiding concept to which Einstein gladly confesses is the *continuum*, the field. From 1905 on, when the introduction of discontinuity in the form of light quantum forced itself on Einstein as a "heuristic" and therefore not fundamental point of view, he clung to the hope and program to keep the continuum as a fundamental conception, and he defended it with enthusiasm in his correspondence. It was part of what he called his "Maxwellian program" to fashion a unified field theory. Atomistic discreteness and all it entails was not the solution but rather the problem. So here he again considers the conception of "the atomic structure of matter and energy" to be "the great stumbling block for a unified field theory."

One cannot, he thought, settle for a basic duality in nature, giving equal status both to the field and to its antithesis. To be sure, neither logic nor experience forbade it. Yet it was almost unthinkable. As he wrote to his old friend, Michele Besso: "I consider it quite possible that physics might not, finally, be founded on the concept of field— that is to say, on continuous elements. But then out of my whole castle in the air—including the theory of gravitation, but also most of current physics—there would remain *nothing*."[14]

We have by no means come to the end of the list of presuppositions that guided Einstein. But it is worth pausing to note how plainly he seemed to have been aware of their operation in his scientific work. In this too he was rare. Sir Isaiah Berlin, in his book *Concepts and Categories*, remarked: "The first step to the understanding of men is the bringing to consciousness of the model or models that dominate and penetrate their thought and action. Like all attempts to make men aware of the categories in which they think, it is a difficult and sometimes painful activity, likely to produce deeply disquieting results."[15] This is generally true; but it was not for Einstein, for at least two reasons. It was he, after all, who first realized the "arbitrary character" of what had for so long been accepted as "the axiom of the absolute character of time, viz., of simultaneity [which] unrecognizedly was anchored in the unconscious," as he put it in his "Autobiographical

14. In Pierre Speziali, ed., *Albert Einstein, Michele Besso, Correspondence 1903-1955* (Paris: Hermann, 1972), p. 527.
15. Isaiah Berlin, *Concepts and Categories* (New York: Viking Press, 1979), p. 159.

Notes." "Clearly to recognize this axiom and its arbitrary character really implies already the solution of the problem."[16] Giving up an explicitly or implicitly held presupposition has indeed often had the characteristic of the great sacrificial act of modern science; we find in the writings of Kepler, Planck, Bohr, and Heisenberg that such an act climaxes a period that in retrospect is characterized by the word "despair."

Having recognized and overcome the negative, or enslaving, role of presuppositions, Einstein also saw their positive, emancipating potential. In one of his earliest essays on epistemology he wrote:

> A quick look at the actual development teaches us that the great steps forward in scientific knowledge originated only to a small degree in this [inductive] manner. For if the researcher went about his work without any preconceived opinion, how should he be able at all to select out those facts from the immense abundance of the most complex experience, and just those which are simple enough to permit lawful connections to become evident?[17]

Much later, in his "Reply to Criticisms," he reverted to the "eternal antithesis" by way of acknowledging that the distinction between "sense impressions," on the one hand, and "mere ideas," on the other, is a basic conceptual tool for which he can adduce no convincing evidence. Yet he needs this distinction. His solution is simply to announce: "We regard the distinction as a category which we use in order that we might the better find our way in the world of immediate sensation." As with other conceptual distinctions for which "there is also no logical-philosophical justification," one has to accept it as "the presupposition of every kind of physical thinking," mindful that "the only justification lies in its usefulness. We are here concerned with 'categories' or schemes of thought, the selection of which is, in principle, entirely open to us and whose qualification can only be judged by the degree to which its use contributes to making the totality of the contents of consciousness 'intelligible.'" Finally, he curtly dismisses an implied attack on these "categories" or "free conventions" with the remark: "Thinking without the positing of categories and concepts in general would be as impossible as is breathing in a vacuum."[18]

ON THEMATA

Einstein's remarkable self-consciousness concerning his fundamental presuppositions throughout his scientific and epistemological writ-

16. Albert Einstein, in *Albert Einstein: Philosopher-Scientist*, ed. Paul A. Schilpp (Evanston, Ill.: Library of Living Philosophers, 1949), p. 53.

17. Albert Einstein, "Induktion und Deduktion in der Physik," *Berliner Tageblatt* (Supplement), December 25, 1919.

18. Einstein, in *Albert Einstein*, pp. 673-74. See also p. 678: "categories are necessary as indispensable elements of thinking."

ings allows one to assemble a list of about ten chief presuppositions underlying his theory of construction throughout his long scientific career: primacy of formal (rather than materialistic or mechanistic) explanation, unity or unification, cosmological scale in the applicability of laws; logical parsimony and necessity, symmetry (as long as possible), simplicity, causality (in essentially the Newtonian sense), completeness and exhaustiveness, continuum, and, of course, constancy and invariance.

These ideals, to which Einstein was obstinately devoted, explain why he would continue his work in a given direction even when tests against experience were difficult or unavailable, or, conversely, why he refused to accept theories well supported by the phenomena but, as in the case of Bohr's quantum mechanics, based on presuppositions opposite to his own. Much of the same can be said of most of the major scientists whom I have studied, from Johannes Kepler to our contemporaries. Each has his own, sometimes idiosyncratic "map" of fundamental guiding notions that may be considered in principle separate, like the band structure of chromosomes, seen microscopically during mitosis of a cell nucleus.

With this finding, we must now reexamine the mnemonic device of the two-dimensional plane. I remove its insufficiency by defining a third axis, rising perpendicularly out of it. This is the dimension orthogonal to and not resolvable unto the phenomenic or analytic axes. Along it are located those fundamental presuppositions often stable, many widely shared, that show up in the motivation of the scientist's actual work, as well as in the end product for which he strives. Decisions between them, insofar as they are consciously made, are judgmental (rather than, as in the phenomenic-analytic plane, capable in principle of algorithmic decidability). Since these fundamental presuppositions are not directly derivable either from observation or from analytic ratiocination, they require a term of their own. I call them *themata* (singular *thema*, from the Greek θέμα; that which is laid down, proposition, primary word).

On this view—and again purely as a mnemonic device—a scientific statement is no longer, as it were, an element of area on the two-dimensional plane but a volume-element, an entity in three-dimensional space, with components along each of the three orthogonal (phenomenic, analytic, and thematic) axes. The projection of the entity down upon the two-dimensional place continues to have the useful roles I stressed earlier; but for our analysis it is also necessary to consider the line element projected onto the third axis, the dimension on which one may imagine the range of themata to be entered. The statements of differing scientists are therefore like two volume-elements that do not completely overlap but have some differences in their projections.

The scientist is generally not, and need not be, conscious of the themata he uses (even if he is sometimes vaguely aware of them, as when he notices that the concepts he works with are "theory-laden"). But the historian of science can chart the growth of a given thema in the work of an individual scientist over time and show its power upon his scientific imagination. Thematic analysis, then, is in the first instance the identification of the particular map of various themata which, like fingerprints, can characterize a scientist, or a part of the scientific community, at a given time.

It can be shown that most of the themata are ancient and long-lived. Many come in opposing dyads or triads that show up most strikingly during a conflict between individuals or groups that base their work on opposing themata. I have been impressed by the small number of thematic couples, or triads; perhaps fewer than fifty have sufficed us throughout the history of the physical sciences. And of course I have been interested to see that, cautiously, thematic analysis of the same sort has begun to be brought to bear on significant cases in other fields.[19]

With this conceptual tool we can return to some of the puzzles we mentioned earlier. Where does the conceptual and even emotional support come from which, for better or worse, stabilizes the individual scientist's risky speculation and confident suspensions of disbelief during the nascent phase? The result of case studies is that choices and decisions of this sort are often made on the basis of loyal dedication to thematic presuppositions. Or again, if, as Einstein claimed, the principles are indeed free inventions of the human mind, should those not be an infinite set of possible axiom systems to which one could leap or cleave? Virtually every one of these would ordinarily be useless for constructing theories. How then could there be any hope of success, except by chance? The answer must be that the license implied in the leap to an axiom system of theoretical physics by the freely inventing mind is the freedom to make such a leap but not the freedom to make *any leap whatever.* The freedom is narrowly circumscribed by a scientist's particular set of themata that provides constraints shaping the style, direction, and rate of advance of the engagement on novel ground.

And insofar as the individual sets of themata overlap, the so-called progress of the scientific community as a group is similarly constrained or directed. Otherwise, the inherently anarchic connotations of "freedom" could indeed disperse the total effort. As Mendeleev wrote: "Since the scientific world view changes drastically not only from one period to another but also from one person to another, it is an expression of creativity. . . . Each scientist endeavors to translate the world view of the school he belongs to into an indisputable principle of

19. A brief survey of thematic analysis is provided in the Introduction and Chapter 1 of Gerald Holton, *The Scientific Imagination: Case Studies* (New York: Cambridge University Press, 1978).

science." However, in practice there is far more coherence than this implies, and we shall presently look more closely at the mechanism responsible for it.

THE "NEED TO GENERALIZE"

Of all the problems that invite attention with these tools, the most fruitful will be a return visit to that mysterious place, early in Einstein's 1933 essay, where he speaks of the need to pay "special attention to the relations between the content of the theory and the totality of empirical fact." The *totality* of empirical fact! It is a phrase that recurs in his writings and indicates the sweep of his conscious ambition. But it does even more: it lays bare the most daring of all the themata of science and points to the holistic drive behind "scientific progress."

Einstein explicitly and frankly hoped for a theory that would ultimately be utterly comprehensive and completely unified. This vision drove him on from the special to the general theory and then to the unified field theory. The search for one grand, architectonic structure itself was of course not Einstein's invention. On the contrary, it is an ancient dream. At its worst, it has sometimes produced authoritarian visions that are as empty in science as their equivalent is dangerous in politics. At its best, it has propelled the drive to the various grand syntheses that rise above the more monotonous landscape of analytic science. This has certainly been the case in the last decades in the physical sciences. Today's triumphant purveyors of the promise as applied to particle physics, who in the titles of their publications casually use the term "The Grand Unification," are in a real sense the successful children of those earliest synthesis-seekers of physical phenomena, the Ionian philosophers.

To be sure, as Sir Isaiah warned in *Concepts and Categories*, there is the danger of a trap. He has christened it the "Ionian Fallacy," defined as the search, from Aristotle to Bertrand Russell and our day, for the ultimate constituents of the world in some nonempirical sense. Superficially, the synthesis seekers of physics, particularly in their monistic exhortations, appear to have fallen into that trap—from Copernicus, who confessed that the chief point of his work was to perceive nothing less than "the form of the world and the certain commensurability of its parts," to Einstein's contemporaries such as Planck, who exclaimed in 1915 that "physical research cannot rest so long as mechanics and electrodynamics have not been welded together with thermodynamics and heat radiation,"[20] to today's theorists who, in their more popular presentations, seem to imitate the founding father of science among the ancient Greeks, Thales himself, and announce that all is ineffable quark.

20. Max Planck, "Verhältnis der Theorien zueinander," in *Die Kultur der Gegenwart*, ed. Paul Hinneberg, Part III, vol. 1 (Leipzig: B.G. Teubner, 1915), p. 737.

A chief point in my view of science is that scientists, insofar as they are successful, are in practice rescued from the fallacy by the variety of their themata, a multiplicity which gives them the flexibility that an authoritarian research program built on a single thema lacks. I shall develop this below, but I can also agree quickly that something like an Ionian Enchantment, the commitment to the theme of grand unification, was upon Einstein. Once alerted, we can find it in his work from the very beginning. In his first published paper (1901), he tries to understand the contrary-appearing forces of capillarity and gravitation and exclaims in a letter to his friend Marcel Grossmann, "It is a magnificent feeling to recognize the unity [*Einheitlichkeit*] of a complex of phenomena that to direct observation appear to be quite separate things"—such as capillarity and gravitation, the physics of micro- and macro-regions. In each of his next papers we find something of the same drive, which he later called "my need to generalize." He examines whether the laws of mechanics provide a sufficient foundation for the general theory of heat and whether the fluctuation phenomena that turn up in statistical mechanics also explain the basic behavior of light beams and their interference, the Brownian motion of microscopic particles in fluids, and even the fluctuation of electric charges in conductors. And in his deepest work of those early years, in special relativity theory, the most powerful propellant is Einstein's drive toward unification. His clear motivation is to find a more general point of view which would subsume the seemingly limited and contrary problems and methods of mechanics and of electrodynamics. In the process he showed that electric and magnetic fields are aspects of one commonality viewed from different reference frames; that space and time are not separate; that energy and mass are fused in one conservation law; and, soon after, that reference systems with gravitation and with acceleration are equivalent. Again and again, previously separate notions were shown to be connected.

Following the same program obstinately to the end of his life, he tried to bring together, as he had put it once, "the gravitational field and the electromagnetic field into a unified edifice," leaving "the whole physics" as a "closed system of thought." In his longing for a unified world picture—a structure that would yield deductively, and thus master, the "totality" of empirical facts—one cannot help hearing an echo of Goethe's Faust who exclaimed that he longed "to detect the inmost force that binds the world and guides its course"—or, for that matter, Newton himself, who wanted to build a unifying structure so tight that the most minute details would not escape it.

THE UNIFIED *WELTBILD*
AS "SUPREME TASK"

In its modern form, the Ionian Enchantment, expressing itself in the search for a unifying world picture, is usually traced to Von Humboldt and Schleiermacher, Fichte and Schelling. The influence of the nature philosophers on physicists such as Hans Christian Oersted—who in this way was led directly to the first experimental unification of electricity and magnetism—has been amply chronicled. At the end of the nineteenth century, in the Germany of Einstein's youth, the pursuit of a unified world picture as the scientist's highest task had become almost a cult activity. Looking on from his side of the channel, J. T. Merz exclaimed in 1904 that the lives of the continental thinkers are

> devoted to the realization of some great ideal. . . . The English man of science would reply that it is unsafe to trust exclusively to the guidance of a pure idea, that the ideality of German research has frequently been identical with unreality, that in no country has so much time and power been frittered away in following phantoms, and in systematizing empty notions, as in the Land of the Idea.[21]

Einstein himself could not easily have escaped being aware of these drives toward unification even as a young person. For example, we know that as a boy he was given Ludwig Büchner's widely popular book *Kraft und Stoff* (*Energy and Matter*), a work Einstein often recollected having read with great interest. The little volume does talk about energy and matter; but chiefly it is a late-Enlightenment polemic. Büchner comes out explicitly and enthusiastically in favor of an empirical, almost Lucretian scientific materialism, which its author calls a "materialistic world view." Through this world view, the author declares, one can attain "the unity of energy and matter, and thereby banish forever the old dualism."[22]

But the books which Einstein himself credited as having been the most influential on him in his youth were Ernst Mach's *Theory of Heat* and *Science of Mechanics*. That author was motivated by the same Enlightenment animus and employed the same language. In the *Science of Mechanics*, Mach exclaims: "Science cannot settle for a ready-made world view. It must work toward a future one . . . that will not come to us as a gift. We must earn it! [At the end there beckons] the idea of a unified world view, the only one consistent with the economy of a healthy spirit."[23]

Indeed, in the early years of this century, German scientists were thrashing about in a veritable flood of publications that called for the unification or reformation of the "world picture" in the very title of their books or essays. Planck and Mach carried on a bitter battle, publishing essays directly in the *Physikalische Zeitschrift*, with titles

21. J. T. Merz, *A History of European Thought in the Nineteenth Century* (London: William Blackwood & Sons, 1904), I, 251-52.

22. Ludwig Büchner, *Kraft und Stoff: Empirisch-naturphilosophische Studien*, 9th ed. (Leipzig: Theodor Thomas, 1867), p. 89.

23. Ernst Mach, *Die Mechanik in ihrer Entwicklung, historischkritisch dargestellt*, 2nd ed. (Leipzig: F. A. Brockhaus, 1889), pp. 437-38.

such as "The Unity of the Physical World Picture." Friedrich Adler, one of Einstein's close friends, wrote a book with the same title, attacking Planck. Max von Laue countered with an essay he called "The Physical World Picture." The applied scientist Aurel Stodola, Einstein's admired older colleague in Zurich, corresponded at length with Einstein on a book which finally appeared under the title *The World View of an Engineer*. Similarly titled works were published by other collaborators and friends of Einstein, such as Ludwig Hopf and Philipp Frank.

Perhaps the most revealing document of this sort was the manifesto published in 1912 in the *Physikalische Zeitschrift* on behalf of the new *Gesellschaft für positivistische Philosophie*, composed in 1911 at the height of the *Weltbild* battle between Mach and Planck. Its declared aim was nothing less than "to develop a comprehensive *Weltanschauung*," and thereby "to advance toward a noncontradictory, total conception [*Gesamtauffassung*]." The document was signed by, among others, Ernst Mach, Josef Petzold, David Hilbert, Felix Klein, Georg Helm, Albert Einstein (only just becoming more widely known at the time), and that embattled builder of another world view, Sigmund Freud.[24]

It was perhaps the first time that Einstein signed a manifesto of any sort. That it was not a casual act is clear from his subsequent, persistent return to the same theme. His most telling essay was delivered in late 1918, possibly triggered in part by the publication of Oswald Spengler's *Decline of the West*, that polemic against what Spengler called "the scientific world picture of the West." Einstein took the occasion of a presentation he made in honor of Planck (in *Motiv des Forschens*) to lay out in detail the method of constructing a valid world picture. He insisted that it was not only possible to form for oneself "a simplified world picture that permits an overview [*übersichtliches Bild der Welt*]," but that it was the scientist's "supreme task." Specifically, the world view of the theoretical physicist "deserves its proud name *Weltbild* because the general laws upon which the conceptual structure of theoretical physics is based can assert the claim that they are valid for any natural event whatsoever.... The supreme task of the physicist is therefore to seek those most universal elementary laws from which, by pure deduction, the *Weltbild* may be achieved."[25]

There is of course no doubt that Einstein's work during those years constituted great progress toward this self-appointed task. In the developing relativistic *Weltbild*, a huge portion of the world of events

24. Cf. "Aufruf," *Physikalische Zeitschrift*, 13 (1912): 735-36; and Friedrich Herneck, "Albert Einstein und der philosophische Materialismus," *Forschungen und Fortschritte*, 32 (1958): 206. I thank Dr. Herneck for kindly making available to me a copy of the original typescript of the Manifesto.

25. Albert Einstein, "Motiv des Forschens"; a somewhat loose English translation was published in Einstein, *Ideas and Opinions*, pp. 224-27.

and processes was being subsumed in a four-dimensional structure which Hermann Minkowski in 1908 named simply *"die Welt"*—the world conceived as a Parmenidean crystal in which changes, for example, motions, are largely suspended and, instead, the main themata are those of constancy and invariance, determinism, necessity, and completeness.

LEAVING OUT NOT A SINGLE EVENT

Typically, it was Einstein himself who knew best and recorded frequently the limitations of his work. Even as special relativity began to make converts, he announced that the solution was quite incomplete because it applied only to inertial systems and left out entirely the great puzzle of gravitation. Later he worked on removing the obstinate dualities, explaining for example that "measuring rods and clocks would have to be represented as solutions of the basic equation . . . not, as it were, as theoretical self-sufficient entities." This he called a "sin" which "one must not legalize." The removal of the sin was part of the hoped-for perfection of the total program, the achievement of a unified field theory in which "the particles themselves would *everywhere* be describable as singularity-free solutions of the complete field-equations. Only then would the general theory of relativity be a *complete* theory."[26] Therefore the work of finding those most general elementary laws from which by pure deduction a single, consistent, and complete *Weltbild* can be won, had to continue.

There has always been a notable polarity in Einstein's thought with respect to the completeness of the world picture he was seeking. On the one hand, he insisted from beginning to end that no single event, individually considered, must be allowed to escape from the final grand net. We noted that in the Oxford lecture of 1933 he is concerned with encompassing the "totality of experience," and he declared the supreme goal of theory to be "the adequate representation of any

---

26. In *Albert Einstein*, pp. 59-61, 81; emphases in original. In the Spencer lecture, Einstein raises this whole problem only gently, and at the end, by saying: "Meanwhile the great stumbling block for a field theory of this kind lies in the conception of the atomic structure of matter and energy. For the theory is fundamentally nonatomic insofar as it operates exclusively with continuous functions of space" (p. 275), unlike classical mechanics, which by introducing as its most important element the material point, does justice to an atomic structure of matter. He does see a way out:

> For instance to account for the atomic character of electricity the field equations need only lead to the following conclusion: The region of three-dimensional space at whose boundary electrical density vanishes everywhere always contains a total electrical charge whose size is represented by a whole number. In the continuum theory, atomic characteristics would be satisfactorily expressed by integral laws without localization of the entities which constitute the atomic structure. (p. 276)

In referring to the total electric charge whose size is represented by a whole number, he points of course to the result of R.A. Millikan's work.

content of experience."[27] He even goes beyond that; toward the end of his lecture he reiterates his old opposition to the Bohr-Born-Heisenberg view of quantum physics, and declares, "I still believe in the possibility of a model of reality, that is to say a theory, which shall represent the events themselves [*die Dinge selbst*] and not merely the probability of their occurrence." Writing three years later he insists even more bluntly:

> But now, I ask, does any physicist whosoever really believe that we shall never be able to attain insight into these significant changes of single systems, their structure, and the causal connections, despite the fact that these individual events have been brought into such close proximity of experience, thanks to the marvelous inventions of the Wilson-Chamber and the Geiger counter? To believe this is, to be sure, logically possible without contradiction; but it is in such lively opposition to my scientific instinct that I cannot forego the search for a more complete mode of conception.[28]

Yet even while Einstein seemed anxious not to let a single event escape from the final *Weltbild*, he seems to have been strangely uninterested in nuclear phenomena, that lively branch of physics which began to command great attention precisely in the years Einstein started his own researches. He seems to have thought that these phenomena, in a relatively new and untried field, would not lead to the deeper truths. And one can well argue that he was right; not until the 1930s was there a reasonable theory of nuclear structure, and not until after the big accelerators were built were there adequate conceptions and equipment for the hard tests of the theories of nuclear forces.

Einstein's persistent pursuit of a fundamental theory, one so powerful that it would not leave out a single datum of experience, and yet excluded nuclear phenomena, can be understood as a consequence of his suspension of disbelief of an extraordinary sort. It is ironic that, as it turned out, even while Einstein was trying to unify the two long-range forces (electromagnetism and gravitation), the nucleus was harboring two additional fundamental forces and, moreover, that after a period of neglect, the modern unification program, two decades after Einstein's death, began to succeed in joining one of the nuclear (relatively short-range) forces with one of the relatively long-range forces (electromagnetism). In this respect, the labyrinth through which the physicists have been moving appears now to be less symmetrical than Einstein had thought it to be.

For this and similar reasons, few of today's working researchers

27. Einstein, *Ideas and Opinion*, p. 272. The phrase was translated in the first English version of the 1933 lecture delivered by Einstein as "the adequate representation of a single datum of experience."
28. Einstein, "Physik und Realität," p. 318.

identify their drive toward the "grand unification" consciously with Einstein's. Their attention is attracted by the thematic differences, expressed for example by their willingness to accept a fundamentally probabilistic world. And yet the historian can see the profound continuity. Today, as in Einstein's time, and indeed that of his predecessors, the deepest aim of fundamental research is still to achieve one logically unified and parsimoniously constructed system of thought that will provide the conceptual comprehension, as complete as humanly possible, of the scientifically accessible sense experiences in their full diversity. This ambition embodies a *telos* of scientific work itself, and it has done so since the rise of science in the Western world. Most scientists, working on small fragments of the total structure, are as unselfconscious about their participation in that grand monistic task as they are about, say, their fundamental monotheistic assumption, carried centrally without requiring constant avowal. Indeed, Joseph Needham may well be right that the development of the concept of a unified natural science depended on the preparation of the ground through monotheism so that one can understand more easily the reason that modern science rose in seventeenth-century Europe rather than, say, in China.

THEMATIC PLURALISM AND THE DIRECTION OF PROGRESS

Diversity in the spectrum of themata which individual scientists carry, and yet overlap among these sets of themata: this formula in brief seems to me to answer the question why the preoccupation with the eventual achievement of one unified world picture did not lead physics to a totalitarian disaster, as an Ionian Fallacy by itself could well have done. At every step, each of the various world pictures in use is seen as a preliminary version, a premonition of the holy grail. Moreover, each of these various, hopeful, but incomplete world pictures of the movement is not a seamless, unresolvable entity (unlike a "paradigm"). Nor is each completely shared even within a given subgroup. Each member of the group operates with a whole spectrum of separable themata, with some of the same themata present in portions of the spectrum in rival world pictures. Indeed, Einstein and Bohr agreed far more than they differed. Moreover, most of the themata current at any one time are not new—they very rarely are—but are adopted from predecessor versions of the *Weltbild*, just as many of them would later be incorporated in subsequent versions of it. Einstein freely called his project a "Maxwellian program" in this sense.[29]

29. The case is quite general. Thus, Kepler's world was constructed of three overlapping thematic structures, two ancient and one new: the universe as theological order, the universe as mathematical harmony, and the universe as physical machine. Newton's scientific world picture clearly retained animistic and theological elements.

It is also for this reason that Einstein saw himself with characteristic clarity not at all as a revolutionary, as his friends and his
enemies so readily did. He took every opportunity to stress his role as
a member in an evolutionary chain. Even while he was working on
relativity theory in 1905, he called it "a modification" of the theory of
space and time. Later, in the face of being acclaimed the revolutionary
hero of the new science, he insisted, as in his King's College lecture:
"We have here no revolutionary act but the natural development of a
line that can be traced through centuries." Relativity theory, he held,
"provided a sort of completion of the mighty intellectual edifice of
Maxwell and Lorentz."[30] Indeed he shared quite explicitly with Maxwell and Lorentz some fundamental presuppositions such as the need
to describe reality in terms of continua (fields) even though he differed completely with respect to others, such as the role of a plenum.

On this model, we can understand why scientists need not hold
substantially the same set of beliefs either to communicate meaningfully with one another in agreement or disagreement or in order to
contribute to cumulative improvement of the state of science. Their
beliefs have considerable fine structure; and within that structure
there is, on the one hand, generally sufficiently stabilizing thematic
overlap and agreement and, on the other hand, sufficient warrant for
intellectual freedom that can express itself in thematic disagreements.
Innovations emerging from such a balance, even as "far-reaching
changes" as Einstein called the contributions of Maxwell, Faraday, and
Hertz, require neither from the individual scientist nor from the
scientific community the kind of radical and sudden reorientation
implied in such currently fashionable language as revolution, Gestalt
switch, discontinuity, incommensurability, conversion, etc. On the
contrary, the innovations are coherent with the model of evolutionary
scientific progress to which Einstein himself explicitly adhered and
which emerges also from the actual historical study of his scientific
work.

Thus, I believe that, generally, major scientific advance can be understood in terms of an evolutionary process that involves battles over
only a few but by no means all of the recurrent themata. The work of
scientists acting individually or as a group, seen synchronically or

---

Lorentz's predominantly electromagnetic world view was really a mixture of Newtonian mechanics as applied to point masses, determining the motion of electrons, and
Maxwell's continuous-field physics. Ernest Rutherford, writing to his new protégé,
Niels Bohr, on March 20, 1913, gently scolds him: "Your ideas as to the mode of origin
of spectra in hydrogen are very ingenious and seem to work well; but the mixture of
Planck's ideas [quantization] with the old mechanics make it very difficult to form a
physical idea of what is the basis of it." In fact, of course, Bohr's progress toward the
new quantum mechanics via the correspondence principle was a conscious attempt to
find his way stepwise from the classical basis.

30. Einstein, "On the Theory of Relativity," in *Ideas and Opinions*, p. 246.

diachronically, is not constrained to the phenomenic-analytic plane alone and hence is an enterprise whose saving pluralism resides in its many internal degrees of freedom. Therefore we can understand why scientific progress is often disorderly, but not catastrophic; why there are many errors and delusions, but not one great fallacy; and how mere human beings, confronting the seemingly endless, interlocking puzzles of the universe, can advance at all—even if not inevitably, or in our time, to the Elysium of the single world conception that grasps the totality of phenomena.

10

Progress in Social Science

MARC J. ROBERTS

But of course economics cannot be compared
with the exact physical sciences: for it deals
with the ever changing and subtle forces of
human nature.—ALFRED MARSHALL

Any discussion of progress in science eventually comes around to the
apparently embarrassing question of the social sciences. Next to the
triumphs of the "hard" sciences, from nuclear weapons to genetic
manipulation, what do the "soft" sciences have to offer? True, we have
not had a replay of the Great Depression, but our economics has not
allowed us to avoid the joys of 8 percent unemployment coupled with 12
percent inflation. We may well have more knowledge of how individuals, organizations, and political systems behave, but that knowledge
has not been sufficient to enable us to achieve such basic objectives as an
honest and efficient government or reconciliation among racial and
ethnic groups.

Have the social sciences really made less progress than the natural
sciences? If so, why should that be the case, and how might the
situation be changed? Indeed, how can the relative "progress" of various disciplines be measured and compared? In this brief essay I will
offer some necessarily elliptical arguments on all of these points.

I begin by trying to disentangle the meaning of the term "progress." Having offered an analysis of that question, I suggest a series of
reasons as to why the social sciences can in fact expect to progress
more slowly than some other areas of study. I then argue that these
general expectations are borne out by what we have and have not

learned about various political and economic processes. I close with a series of injunctions to my fellow social scientists about what we all must try to do in order to progress more quickly.

Although my title refers to "social science," my own background is in economics, with some spillover into political science, history, organization theory, and management. Thus, my discussion will be heavily influenced by what I know of these areas. I am noticeably less informed about areas like anthropology and personality theory; thus, these play a lesser role in the argument that follows.

THE MEANING OF PROGRESS

How can a self-respecting academic discuss progress in science without first being tempted to analyze the meaning of that term? It is a temptation I too am unable to resist. This does not simply reflect a weakness for pedantry, for much of my later argument will depend upon the explication of this key concept.

What can we hope to accomplish when we set out to clarify the meaning of a term? Except for the Platonists among us,[1] most contemporary scholars accept the notion that there is no metaphysical reference point that can be used to resolve arguments about the "correct" meaning of a word. Words and concepts are human creations. They can be, and are, nothing more or less than what we make them. This means we can ask two questions about the definition of a word. First, how *is it used* by various speakers in various situations? Second, if we want to make an argument about how a word *should be used*, we can only make a pragmatic one, that is, we can try to show that one or another usage would be advantageous for various reasons. It would take too long here to make the argument that might allow one to derive the characteristics of a "good" definition from more basic objectives like expanding our ability to understand and control experience. Suffice it to say that I believe that such characteristics include clarity, internal consistency, consistency with other concepts, consistency with common current usage, and embodying distinctions that are predictively and normatively relevant.

From that perspective, what do we mean by "progress"? Popular usage, I suggest, involves some fuzzy notions of achieving a goal, or making something better or easier, or expanding knowledge, etc. At one time in Western thought, there may have been relative agreement about goals and objectives and how movement forward was to be measured. In our day, however, such consensus is less evident. Various individuals ask, with more seriousness than clarity, whether or not certain discoveries *really* constitute progress. Those who do not

1. In Plato's *Republic* there is a well-known discussion of how "forms" or "ideal types" exist as supernatural objects to resolve definitional ambiguities. See, for example, Book 7 for the allegory of the cave, where the idea is presented.

like the consequences of a particular change often try to seize a rhetorical advantage by contending that the change in question does not really involve progress after all.

In order to decide whether the social sciences have progressed relatively slowly we have to clarify this issue. Let me therefore suggest a simple resolution. All we have to do is use "progress" to mean the increased achievement of some specified objective. This implies immediately that it is not possible to ask whether some event does or does not constitute progress without first specifying the goal or objective. Furthermore, this usage makes it clear that "progress" for one can be "regress" for another—provided that their objectives are sufficiently divergent.

In this view, the relative progress of various disciplines simply involves their achievement of various objectives. Disagreements over evaluating their relative progress can thus arise both from differences as to the objectives accepted as relevant and from differences in belief about what the world is like. Would a faith healer and a psychiatrist agree about what changes in behavior and belief constitute progress in an individual suffering from paralysis without apparent physiological origins? Furthermore, as long as progress is multidimensional, some sort of weights, some index or aggregation function, has to be used to compare progress in various areas of study. As a consequence, any metric of progress involves values not only in defining the objectives but also in determining the relative size of the gains along those dimensions. Thus, in order to decide whether social science has made more or less progress, we are going to have to decide what objectives we wish to use and develop some way to calibrate the relative meaning and significance of what has been achieved.

Before proceeding, I should note that this whole analysis implies a need to modify some well-known arguments of Thomas Kuhn,[2] who has contended that major developments in science involve "revolutions," shifts in concepts, methods and generalizations, so profound that individuals on one side of the change cannot make compelling arguments to those on the other side of the disagreement. Instead, a switch from one perspective to another is more like a religious conversion than a matter of being persuaded by logic and evidence. How, then, can one call revolutionary changes progress since the definition proposed above involves some continuity of objective and measures of achievement that apply on both sides of the revolutionary divide?

Part of the answer lies in an argument I have made elsewhere, namely, that the conceptual structures in science typically have a hierarchical structure.[3] Epistemological assumptions and some speci-

2. Thomas S. Kuhn, *The Structure of Scientific Revolutions*, 2nd ed. (Chicago: University of Chicago Press, 1970).

3. Marc J. Roberts, "On the Nature and Condition of Social Science," *Daedalus*,

fication of objectives lie at the base of these structures. More specific methodological rules and assertions about the world are derived from these, and still more derivative are specific numerical estimates of parameters defined by the conceptual system. From this viewpoint, Kuhn's dichotomous distinction between "revolutionary" and "normal" science becomes replaced with a continuous notion of the relative fundamentality of a given scientific change. When confronting a new theory, we have to ask how basic or fundamental is the conceptual change we have to make in order to accept the new idea.

This analysis suggests that even in an apparently profound "revolution," some of the most fundamental aspects of the conceptual structure of a science may well remain intact. When that is the case, some consensual definition of progress may be possible, once passions have cooled and implications clarified. Otherwise, there may not in fact be agreement as to whether or not a new model or theory constitutes progress. Nor will there be any neutral place to stand, outside the system, to resolve this question. Insofar as science now appears to have made steady progress on its own terms, this reflects both the less-than-total nature of many conceptual revolutions and the tendency of even radical changes to seem "progressive" in terms of the criteria they lead us to accept.

To return to our main argument, what goals or objectives and what metrics should we use to measure the relative progress of social and natural science? Elsewhere I have argued that science has in fact pursued three distinct objectives.[4] First is the goal of understanding and explaining—telling stories that make it plausible that observable phenomena should behave as they do. It is in this role that science is at its most religious—making man feel at home in the universe. Many scientists adopt some explicitly aesthetic criteria for judging scientific explanations from this viewpoint, for example, simplicity, economy, elegance, and generality. The second objective, control, is science in its pragmatic role. Good science from this vantage point depends on achieving those changes in human experience we desire. The third objective, prediction, serves both ends—diminishing uncertainty and allowing humans to prepare for it.

How important should these distinct objectives be in assessing relative progress in various realms of study? I offer as a partial answer a normative principle that I realize some readers may find objectionable. The explanatory/aesthetic motive, I believe, should be most compelling where in fact phenomena are most well ordered! That is, we should care most about elegance and generality when by striving

103(3) (summer 1974): 47-62. A further amplification is to be found in Marc J. Roberts and Jeremy Bluhm, *The Choices of Power* (Cambridge, Mass.: Harvard University Press, 1981), Chap. 2.
    4. Roberts, "On the Nature and Condition of Social Science."

for these ends we also can account for a great deal of data. By contrast, when dealing with disorderly and transitory phenomena, I urge instead the primacy of the pragmatic test. For here the "rage to order" can lead to empirical inaccuracy. In a sense, we should accept the inevitable. Why pursue simplicity and elegance in those cases where they are not in fact likely to be found?

HOW MUCH PROGRESS SHOULD WE EXPECT FROM SOCIAL SCIENCE?

In raising this question, I hope to persuade the reader of an admittedly apologetic answer, that is, on the whole, we should have only modest expectations for progress in social science because the subject matter is so difficult![5] Thus, the apparent failure of political science to generalize as broadly and successfully as chemistry arises in part from the more difficult tasks the former confronts. Yet, as I argue below, social scientists have not made as much progress as they might have if they had made a more perceptive methodological response to the problems they confront. Exactly because economics is harder than physics—or at least different—it cannot be most fruitfully pursued with exactly the same methods.

As a crude first approximation, we might compare the ex post facto adequacy of the models offered by two sciences in terms of generality and accuracy—that is, over what range of space-time they apply and what percentage of the observed variation they account for. There are deep issues, indeed, in actually choosing a specific statistical criterion of "goodness of fit," but we will ignore these in this inexact and intuitive discussion.[6]

What is it about phenomena that implies that they will lend themselves to exact and widely applicable formal representation? Surely their inherent regularity is critical. One cannot generalize accurately about that which in fact is not well ordered. This leads to a deeper question—what is it about phenomena that leads them to be well ordered?

Let me suggest that such order arises when the objects of study are both homogeneous and regular in their structural variation so that they respond in similar and ordered ways to similar stimuli, or at least their responses vary predictably as a function of their characteristics.[7] If

5. There is a well-known, and perhaps apocryphal, story that Max Planck once told John Maynard Keynes that he had started out in economics, only to later give it up for physics, because economics was too hard.

6. It matters a great deal, for example, whether one uses the sum of the absolute value of the errors or the sum of the squares of the errors, and so on. In part, choice of a criterion will reflect one's belief about the nature of the random events in the system, and in part it should reflect one's view about the "losses" involved in making errors of various magnitudes.

7. For an interesting discussion of the problems of imposing "arithmomorphic"

they are homogeneous, then even if the number of objects involved in a system is large, their average behavior may still be predictable despite individual randomness. Alternatively, if the objects of study are unique and varied, then we should hope that they are linked together in relatively simple systems with only a few objects. Otherwise, the complexity and variation of system behavior will undermine generalizability.

What kinds of objects then are homogeneous and ordered in their structure and behavior? In many cases sheer physical simplicity and disaggregation are critical. Complex aggregated objects—like trees, people, sailboats, and hurricanes—do vary greatly in their internal structure and hence in their behavior. These categories, to use John Stuart Mill's terminology, do not reflect "real kinds."[8] They do not denote genuinely distinct and homogeneous classes of objects. Indeed, we may not be able to create the necessary categories except by looking at very disaggregate objects and systems. For these reasons it is more plausible to attempt to generalize about electrons, oxygen atoms, and DNA molecules than it is to do the same about families, business firms, and political parties.

Social science, however, deals with such variable, varied, and complex objects of study. Thus, it is more like yacht design, or weather forecasting, or vulcanology than it is like Newtonian mechanics or molecular biology. The objects of study are often unique, highly varied in structure and behavior, and embedded in extremely complex systems. Is it any wonder that our generalizations are so limited in time and space and that the more specific we make them (numerically), the more limited in scope they are?

Social science confronts still other difficulties. For one, history typically performs poor experiments. For example, many things vary together as the economy goes up or down. This makes inference difficult.[9] Furthermore, politics and morality make better experiments difficult or impossible to perform. Yacht design is difficult, but at least yacht designers can build models and run careful sea trials.

Difficulties of experimentation are especially serious because social systems are so complex. Typically, numerous variables are all relevant to some extent. Their effects also tend to be both nonlinear and interdependent. This makes it extremely difficult to disentangle their role on the basis of the experience history offers. It also makes it very

concepts as a complex reality, see Nicholas Georgescu-Roegen, *Analytical Economics* (Cambridge, Mass.: Harvard University Press, 1966), Chap. 2.

8. John Stuart Mill, *System of Logic* (New York: Harper Brothers, 1843), Chaps. 7, 18.

9. This is even true when we evaluate public policies. We seldom are able to discover appropriate "control groups" that would allow us to know what would have happened if the policy had not been put into place.

dangerous to extrapolate beyond the range of known experience because there may be large changes of behavior just beyond the range of recent observation.

I say "recent observation" because another problem of social science is novelty. People learn and change and behave in new ways. Social science results can themselves become part of the system. Once businessmen believe that the government can prevent depressions by deficits, they will curtail their own spending less in a downturn—thereby helping to prevent the downturn they believe the government can avoid. Admittedly, some natural sciences face novelty as well—as virologists working on flu vaccine will tell you. But the problem seems especially widespread and serious in social science. Where is the particle physics analogy to the civil rights movement, women's liberation, and OPEC?

THE RESPONSE OF SOCIAL SCIENTISTS
TO THE DIFFICULTY OF SOCIAL SCIENCE

For various reasons, social scientists have not responded as effectively as they might to the inherent difficulties of their chosen area of inquiry. Instead, seeing certain modes of thought lead to progress in the natural sciences, they have tended to conclude that progress in social science would come by adopting a similar approach. Nor were any and all natural sciences the model. Instead, ironically, perhaps the least relevant analogy became the ideal—namely, physics. Geology, meteorology, ecology—all might have been a closer match in terms of the nature of the subject matter. But from the 1870s onward, economists in particular explicitly looked for the analogy to "Newtonian laws" of economic motion.[10] After all, it was in physics where "real progress" was being made! The possibility that much of that success came from the nature of the phenomena being studied—particularly their simplicity and inherent order—was not widely considered.

It is worth focusing especially on economics for the moment because that discipline itself has become so intellectually imperialistic—sending out columns of conceptual and methodological converts, who have in turn captured significant shares of the traditional territory of political science and sociology. Based perhaps on a false image of natural science, economics has adopted two main methodological precepts. The first is that a conceptual or theoretical argument is not really respectable unless it can be put into mathematical terms. The second is the notion that only numerical data, statistically analyzed, are really legitimate. Almost all of the work published today in professional journals follows these ground rules.

I don't want to appear as rejecting these commitments. On the

---

10. This analogy was quite explicit in the work of some of the earlier pioneers of mathematical economics such as Jeuons in England or Cournot in France.

contrary, they clearly facilitate certain kinds of scientific progress. Contemporary science depends in part on logical reasoning to spin out the implications of assumptions and on subjecting proposed generalizations to verification by methods that are replicable by others, not only by the initial experimenter. Mathematical models facilitate the first task and statistical methods the second, but not all important phenomena are easily reduced to the highly simplified format required for formal representation and numerical data gathering. As Percy Bridgeman argued, thought is simpler than reality, language simpler than thought, and mathematics simpler than language.[11] Furthermore, apart from testing existing concepts, science also involves creating new ideas and offering new assumptions. In the latter process, it may be especially important not to be limited to those formulations that can be easily explored with arithmetical methods, especially where the phenomena to be studied are complex and subtle.

In order to do statistical analysis, we must make the assumption that we are observing various instances of a homogeneous process—exactly the sort of assumption which will often be unwarranted. Furthermore, given data limitations (some data may be unavailable and some concepts hard to capture in numerical indices), we have a tendency to focus on ideas that are testable in this form. This can lead us to ignore potentially important arguments.[12] Equally, unless we are prepared to use very sophisticated mathematical techniques—techniques beyond the competence of most economists, myself included—there are real limits as to the subtlety of the causal interactions we can build into our models. Instead, the sorts of simple mathematical systems usually constructed by economists allow only for an impoverished account of the phenomena in question. We often rush into hypothesis testing by using some existing database and devote insufficient time to understanding the phenomena or to generating more relevant—if difficult to test—hypotheses.

On the other hand, the methodological expansionism of economics has come about, to an extent, because there were few articulated countervailing notions to stand against it. Much of political science, sociology, and history has involved individual detailed case studies, but although these may convey the uniqueness and complexity of a particular situation, they often failed to engage what occurred with enough precision to lead to any potential generalizations that might be applied to other cases. Too often, cases were described and classi-

11. Percy Bridgeman, *The Nature of Physical Theory* (Princeton, N.J.: Princeton University Press, 1936).

12. For example, all of classic consumer theory is predicated on the notion that choice problems can be effectively represented as being merely quantitative—as deciding "how much" of a list of various commodities the buyer wishes to purchase. All qualitative variation within such decisions is suppressed as a second-order, unimportant problem.

fied without clear reference to what the phenomenon was that was to be explained. In the midst of a taxonomic enthusiasm, the dependent variables were often not clearly specified. Thus, one study was piled on another, and yet it was hard to know what they all added up to. Unless clear and generally accepted questions are posed to successive investigators, the cumulative work on which "progress" depends is not likely to occur.

There is yet another force in the methodological evolution of the social sciences. Case studies have the disadvantage that their virtue is difficult for an outsider to judge. How do I know if your account is accurate if I do not know the situation myself? In contrast, numerical theorizing and statistical testing carry with them self-contained evidence of excellence in the form of the technical skill exhibited in the analysis. This makes it easier for practitioners to judge and authenticate one another's competence. This is no small concern when journal editors or promotion committees have to make decisions they can defend to themselves and others. In a kind of reverse Gresham's law (Gresham argued that people tend to hoard hard currency and spend soft), hard methods tend to drive out softer ones in the contemporary academy.

The sociology of social science affects its practice in other ways as well. Individuals who become academics are often those in whom the "rage to order" is especially strong.[13] The aesthetic attractiveness of simple models and monocausal theories to such individuals surely helps explain their repetitive appearance despite their obvious empirical limitations. Similarly, in the contemporary academy there is some value to clear arguments, to novelty, and to disagreement. Advance a sufficiently bold idea and even if you are later proved wrong, your name will remain in the literature while your critics and detractors, however better informed, will linger in obscurity, unknown to all except a very few aficionados. Thus, the cumulative exploration of a given question is not often pursued. The rewards that come from building on someone else's ideas are too small compared with those that come from innovation—especially when all the existing theories look too simplified to be worth exploring anyway.

WHAT PROGRESS HAS SOCIAL SCIENCE MADE?

Despite these difficulties, social scientists have made some real gains in recent years, albeit to an extent of a negative nature. The combination of detailed case study and statistical observation has taught us that many earlier and optimistic views of social phenomena are not really accurate. For example, we have less faith now in the ability of either education or public participation (of the sort embodied in the poverty program) to alter individual behavior. We now know that we know less than we thought we knew about the combined effects of fiscal and

13. I am indebted to Donald Brown for making this point to me fifteen years ago.

monetary policy on inflation and unemployment. We have a more accurate and realistic view of the legislative process and the problems of government policy implementation.

The technology of large-scale samples and systematic data gathering does sometimes pay off with surprising results. One recent study concluded that most Americans do not lack adequate access to medical care—indeed that even among the poor, overutilization was not uncommon.[14] Public opinion and voting data are routinely gathered and occasionally illuminatingly analyzed. Similarly, the process of constructing large-scale mathematical simulation models is now at the core of quite a number of policy-making areas. How else is the President to tell the Congress what effect his proposed tax will have on oil imports or whether a proposed change in the Clean Air Act will put the Midwestern coal industry out of business?

What I find interesting is that this "success," this "progress," has typically been *either* qualitative *or* specific. We have found either insight or a quantity highly limited in its applicability in time or space. By the pragmatic criteria of control and prediction, we may not be doing so badly. But if our aesthetic demands widespread, simple, elegant formulas and numerical generalizations, then social science has made precious little progress. Yet, what should we expect? Social science *is* like meteorology or engineering. One can gain some insight from general principles and the study of simple cases, but to be really helpful in a specific case, a great deal of work is needed to produce a result of admittedly limited applicability. Each storm, each bridge, each business cycle, is in some sense a new problem.

Even within economics, numerical methodologies have not necessarily led to cumulative progress. This is in part because such progress depends on some continuity with regard to the specific questions being explored and the methods being employed. In some cases, better data and more sophisticated methods have been combined with small, if steady, conceptual advances to develop a cumulatively improved-upon analysis. In some areas of social science—studies of voting behavior, perhaps, and studies of the causes of industry profitability (to name two examples), this appears to have occurred,[15] but there are not that many examples that could be cited.

WHY HAVE WE NOT HAD MORE PROGRESS IN SOCIAL SCIENCE?

Some of the reasons for this only modest progress can be found in our previous discussion of the nature of the phenomena social science

14. *Special Report*, No. 1 (Princeton, N.J.: Robert Wood Johnson Foundation, 1978).

15. For a summary of the latter studies, see Leonard Weiss, "Quantitative Studies of Industrial Organization," in *Frontiers of Quantitative Economics*, ed. Michael D. Intriligator (Amsterdam: North Holland, 1971), pp. 362-402.

deals with: novelty, the complexity and irregularity of the system, and so on. A second cause involves the inappropriate methodologic biases noted above. The conceptual systems that can be formulated mathematically and analyzed with algebra and calculus may be far too simple to explain the behavior we are interested in. Economists now have literally dozens of models of the business firm to choose from and yet no well-documented evidence as to which ones work best and where.[16] All tend to be so unrealistically oversimplified that it is hard to even translate their predictions into observations about a modern multiproduct firm operating under conditions of costly information and great uncertainty. This makes it difficult to disprove as well as to demonstrate their applicability. Until we recognize that most of the entities social science studies (like business firms) are not all alike and try to ask what internal features their behavior depends upon, we will not be in a position to initiate a cumulative process of coherent empirical work.

The multiplicity of models and the lack of cumulative refinement of results stem from yet another difficulty as well. That is the large and unavoidable role social values play in the conduct of social science. Modern decision theory has clarified the fact that when the evidence on a point is uncertain, there is no way totally to avoid the risk of making one or another kind of error.[17] In order to decide which risks to take, we have somehow to compare both the likelihood and the unattractiveness of the various consequences. We might prefer to accept the higher probability of making a minor error rather than risk even a low probability of an error that would lead to a major disaster.

This simple argument leads to a radical conclusion. In an important sense, facts depend on values. Since evidence is often ambiguous, what we choose to accept as "fact" may and should depend on how serious we expect the consequences to be when we are wrong by acting on that premise, as compared with the risks we incur by acting on alternative assumptions. Furthermore, the relative "seriousness" of consequences is not just an empirical, but also a normative, matter. It depends upon what we care about, that is, on our values.

In much of natural science, there are no action-forcing choices waiting in the wings. Agnosticism is often defensible in the presence of uncertainty. Also various scholars often do not have highly different evaluations of the costs of making different sorts of errors. In social science the opposite is often true on all these counts. There are decisions to be made, and individuals have strong and highly different views on whether, for example, inflation or unemployment is the more serious risk to be avoided.

16. Joseph W. McGuire, *Theories of Business Behavior* (Englewood Cliffs, N.J.: Prentice-Hall, 1964).

17. The classic work on these issues is R. Duncan Luce and Howard Raiffa, *Games and Decisions* (New York: Wiley, 1957).

Since experts do not like to confront the limits of their own expertise, there is some tendency to suppress or avoid making explicit these value differences. This in turn leads to some tendency, conscious and unconscious, for social scientists to exaggerate their disagreements about "facts" (that is, about the probabilities that alternative accounts are accurate) in order to argue for the decisions they prefer. Economists who dislike unemployment tend to overestimate its likelihood in order to make the case that antirecession measures are called for. Indeed when action-forcing decisions are at hand, the same dynamic invades natural science. Those who believe that the consequences of a nuclear power plant accident will be especially severe also tend to argue that such accidents are relatively likely.[18]

Value differences among social scientists also show up in the very questions they ask and the models they employ. This is made possible in part by the variation in causality in social systems between the short and the long run. In the short run, the characteristics of various social organizations and arrangements and the ideas of various citizens are given. They are independent variables in the system. In the longer run, these same phenomena may be dependent variables—the results of longer-run evolutionary and historic systemwide forces. Thus, operationally oriented ameliorators define short-run questions and focus on manipulable magnitudes as independent variables. In contrast, would-be revolutionary skeptics focus on the role of long-run, unmanipulable, system magnitudes.

POSSIBLE AIDS TO PROGRESS

Given all this, what can social scientists do to increase progress? My first recommendation has to do with expectations. We should place greater weight on the pragmatic and less on the aesthetic. This means that social science should try to be policy-relevant because in a sense that is what we can do best—or perhaps even all we can do. We should spend less time teaching our students admittedly elegant arguments and theories that are obviously oversimplified and more time inculcating in them the desire to explain actual phenomena. If people are going to do the hard work needed to find out about the real world, we have to convey to them that that is what we want and expect, and professional status and reward systems will have to be altered accordingly.

I am contending that as social scientists, we should accept the fact that we are engineers—or, as John Maynard Keynes urged, dentists— and stop trying to imitate the physicists. It means taking seriously the

18. For an analysis of one case where the relationship between the scientists and policy analysts has been documented, see Alan S. Manne and Richard G. Richels, "Probability Assessments and Decision Analysis of Alternative Nuclear Fuel Cycles," in *National Energy Issues—How Do We Decide?*, ed. Robert G. Sachs (Cambridge, Mass.: Ballinger, 1980), pp. 241-64.

argument of the eminent economist Kenneth Boulding, who suggested that the reason economists have not found any simple sweeping regularities, parallel to the laws of planetary motion, may be that they are not out there to discover.[19]

As part of such methodological self-criticism, we also should rethink the value of mathematical theorizing and quantitative, large-sample data. Although they are helpful techniques, it is foolish to rely solely on these intellectual approaches. Qualitative case study data do have their role, as does verbal theorizing. The problem we face is in using such data coherently as a basis for suggesting, testing, and refining proposed generalizations. In this connection, we have to develop an increased appreciation of the role of hypothesis generation as well as hypothesis testing. And we have to learn to distinguish between the nonnumerical and the nonsystematic. We can at least loosely "test" hypotheses against the evidence offered by a given case study without running formal statistical procedures, indeed without even reducing the argument to arithmetic terms.

Cumulative work also requires continuity with respect to the questions we explore and the conceptual systems we employ. Part of our problem in achieving such continuity has arisen because we have not confronted the realization that the definition of a question is a moral and aesthetic as well as a technical issue. We need, in a sense, more input from normative political and social philosophy in order to better distinguish among phenomena in ethically compelling ways. Today, one of the few, perhaps the only, well-articulated reference points is the notion of "efficiency" embodied within the utilitarian framework of contemporary welfare economics. That in turn provides a definition of "market failure" and gives rise to a whole host of questions about market performance. I suggest that one reason political scientists and sociologists find it so hard to agree on what dependent variables they should try to explain is that it is not clear which variables, and outcomes, are ethically interesting. Until we get a clear statement of what questions are really important, it will be hard to persuade various investigators to participate in their coherent, cumulative, and collective exploration.

Finally, social scientists need to confront more clearly the decision-theoretic structure of their activities and the irreducible role of values in their work. Once these are confronted, individuals can then work together—despite their differences in values—to clarify the "facts" in mutually acceptable ways. Here again, however, limited ambitions and pragmatic objectives have a role to play. Such clarification will be relatively easier in the context of a well-defined policy decision that allows all concerned at least to state the issue in question precisely.

19. Kenneth E. Boulding, "The Verifiability of Economic Images," in *The Structure of Economic Science*, ed. Sherman R. Krupp (Englewood Cliffs, N.J.: Prentice-Hall, 1966).

In all, social scientists will progress faster if they focus clearly and realistically on what they can do and on how that might be accomplished. Are we in fact ready, however, to embrace relevance at the price of elegance? Especially in economics, are we ready to spend less time on empty model building and hypothetical theorizing about cases and situations that seldom, if ever, occur? Are we willing to go back to the harsh test of "what actual and important phenomena does it explain" in determining professional status and rewards? As a social scientist looking at social science, I believe that issue is, at best, still very much in doubt.

11

Contemporary Historiography: Progress, Paradigms, and the Regression Toward Positivism

H. STUART HUGHES

If one so desired, one could establish a schematic sequence labeled "'progress' in historical thought and writing." In such a succession, the first stage would be associated with the location and verification of manuscript sources, beginning in the seventeenth century and frequently deriving its motive power from the polemics of Protestant and Catholic divines. A second stage—overlapping with the first—would be characterized by the scholarly accumulation of data, with nineteenth-century Germany as its focal point. Following this and building on its elaboration of exacting standards, one might trace an early twentieth-century stage of adapting criteria of interpretation derived from other disciplines—a stage to which I shall return very shortly. Finally, one might discern in the post-Second World War period a phase of technological improvement in research methods through quantification, the use of computers, and the like. In this four-stage perspective, in which each is seen as reinforcing its predecessor, our own time—or, more precisely, the 1950s and the 1960s—could well appear as a culmination or flowering.

To present matters in such a fashion, however, would be to leave out or abstract from the analysis the aesthetic and philosophical dimension that is central to historical discourse. It would suggest that one was operating at a level of sophistication only slightly higher than the old notion of historiography as a single imposing structure to which each historian lovingly contributes his or her particular brick of knowledge. To do anything of the kind is far from my purpose.

Nor, when I refer to a philosophical dimension, do I mean to discuss either of the two main guises under which the term "philosophy of history" travels. One of these ranks as respectable, the other as disreputable. The respectable kind functions as a branch of contemporary analytic philosophy and tries to provide historians with a theory of knowledge and a definition of the nature of their craft. The disreputable kind—what one may call the cosmological or metahistorical mode—seeks to impose an overarching order on the chaos of events, to find pattern, meaning, and direction in a succession of epochs.

Both of these I find valid subjects of inquiry—even the second, provided one reads it not as gospel but as a kind of poetry whose resonances and promptings may stir the mind from lethargy. Yet neither furnishes a point of departure. My concern, rather, is with a third or intermediate level—the level at which the historian likewise tries to discern a pattern, but a pattern within manageable boundaries of time and space. If he works primarily in temporal sequence, we say that he is tracing a process; if he runs a more static cross-section, we refer to his findings as typology or structure. In either case, the historian who deals in middle-level generalizations never argues—or never should argue—that he is directly at grips with his "facts." Nor does he lay claim to having discovered some ultimate truth. He simply asserts with becoming modesty that he is looking for an organizing principle—or possibly a heuristic device—that will enable him to establish a preliminary ordering for his data. These data, he recognizes, are always at least one remove from the schema he imposes upon them. He is similarly ready to grant that there is an inescapable element of the arbitrary in the order he has established.

Nor is he even sure how to name what he has done. Historical generalizations at the intermediate level go under a variety of titles, most of them inappropriate. "Theory" is too grand a term—"thesis" too combative. "Hypothesis" will do, but it may suggest an excess of caution. "Model" implies a solid and "closed" quality that is foreign to the historian's mind. Perhaps Thomas S. Kuhn's expression "paradigm" comes closest to conveying the notion of a mode of interpretation which has proved helpful in one context and is worth applying to others. In any case, whatever name the reflective historian gives his labors, he admits to two crucial limitations upon them: first, the paradigm in question is a radical simplification; second, competing paradigms deserve respectful attention.

BASIC PARADIGMS

The progenitors of these modes of interpretation were bolder in their claims. Whether German, Austrian, or French, they usually viewed their results as constituting in some sense "the truth." It may be useful at this point to review the paradigms that stimulated European historians most often during the first two generations of the twentieth century and that eventually found their way to the United States. Such a review will suggest the eclecticism with which historians have borrowed from the great theorists in other fields and the simultaneous acceptance of rival paradigms, which to my profession is almost second nature.

The first and most obvious mode of interpretation was the Marxian. Very few first-rate historians ever subscribed fully to the canon of dialectical materialism, and the more sophisticated of those who call themselves Marxists today employ concepts recognized as illuminating even by conservative scholars. As it passed into the mainstream of European historical thinking just after the turn of the century, Marxism reduced itself to two basic propositions, which won adherents far beyond its own ranks: the primacy of the economic substructure as the conditioning environment for occurrences or artifacts in what was conventionally viewed as the "higher" spheres, and the struggle of classes as the major propellant in social change.

A similar stripping down to the essentials was apparent in the vicissitudes of another great paradigm—the Freudian—whose acceptance began only with the twentieth century's second generation, that is, approximately thirty years after Marxism became common property. In this second case, the adoption of a single principle proved sufficient to push an individual historian across the ill-defined line separating the defenders of psychoanalysis from its opponents. The principle, of course, was the primacy of the unconscious. (We may note in passing that with Freud's legacy, as with that of Marx, the residue of dogma to which historians felt able to subscribe amounted to giving first rank to a particular aspect of human existence.) The other basic psychoanalytic concepts—infantile sexuality and the Oedipus complex—encountered greater resistance or suspicion.

For the most part, in Europe and, subsequently, in the United States, the Marxian and the Freudian paradigms went their separate ways and enlisted contrasting types of individuals among historians who had in common only their readiness to entertain unfamiliar explanations. Marxist history and psychoanalytically oriented history have in general been mutually exclusive. Yet from time to time historians, like philosophers and social scientists, have tried to find a meeting point or "fit" between these two modes of interpretation. The most sustained and far-reaching of such efforts was that of the so-called Frankfurt school—the circle gathered about Theodor W. Adorno, Max Horkheimer, and, more fleetingly, Herbert Marcuse.[1] Neither the Frankfurt philosophers nor anyone else, to my mind, really suc-

---

1. On the Frankfurt school, see my *The Sea Change* (New York: Harper & Row, 1975), Chap. 4; and Martin Jay, *The Dialectical Imagination* (Boston: Little, Brown, 1973).

ceeded in closing the gap in question. For a long time this failure puzzled me. It is only recently that I have concluded that the reason can be found in a basic conceptual dissimilarity between the Marxian and the Freudian paradigms.

The incongruity of the two was not a matter of substance—not the fact that they gave primacy to different substructures, in the one case, economics, in the other, the unconscious: the true incompatibility lay in the level of the paradigms themselves. The Marxian worked on a plane of large-scale generalization: in its charting of successive epochs or time sequences, human actors took second rank or even disappeared. The Freudian was anchored in clinical discoveries about recognizable individuals. Both paradigms offered a mixture of temporal and typological explanation. But although at the Marxian level, major shifts from old to new structures have been readily apparent, in the psychoanalytic mode it has proved difficult to extend the developmental thrust beyond a restricted number of cases. Yet this very limitation suggests the abiding relevance of the Freudian approach as a corrective to excessive abstraction. The power of the psychoanalytic paradigm has lain precisely in its return of the individual to center stage by giving a coherent account of human motivation.

At this point it may clarify matters to observe that a third mode of interpretation, Max Weber's, was almost exclusively typological. Moreover, unlike Marx and Freud—or his contemporary Emile Durkheim —Weber never founded a school. He lacked the temperament for it, and he died too young. Yet in a diffused and haphazard way, his work, particularly after the Second World War, won greater respect among historians than that of any other European master. The reasons are not far to seek. For one thing, Weber was a meticulous scholar, whose documentation, except perhaps in an early work such as *The Protestant Ethic*, could seldom be faulted. Perhaps more important, his ideal-type method sanctioned the notion of plural (or even competing) explanations dear to the historian. To put it in the simplest terms, following in Weber's footsteps did not entail subscribing to any substantive principle, as in the case of Marx or Freud. His method was open-ended by definition, and his roster of ideal types could presumably be multiplied ad infinitum—although the relationships among them frequently remained obscure. It is characteristic of Weber's influence that those of us who regard ourselves as most in his debt find it difficult to specify exactly what it is that we owe.

An even greater imprecision surrounds a fourth and final legacy from Europe—this time from France. What is usually referred to as the school of the *Annales* (after the *Annals* that were its professional organ) derived in a roundabout fashion from Durkheim. But its founders were historians, and in this respect it was unique among the modes of interpretation I have been tracing. Moreover, it could scarcely be said to have proposed a paradigm comparable with those I have surveyed up to now. What Marc Bloch and Lucien Febvre first argued in the 1930s—and what reached America a generation later—was rather a series of precepts for conducting a search.[2] As with Durkheim, the search was for the bases of social solidarity or group identity. The precepts called for looking beyond the conventional evidence contained in documents, exploiting such oral or tangible sources as folklore, architectural monuments, and methods of tilling the soil. For the school of the *Annales*, field work became a primary concern. Quite literally they let fresh air into the musty, claustrophobic business of historical research. Not only did they share in Durkheim a common ancestor with the anthropologists: they enjoined similar procedures and pursued similar goals. At their hands history became something resembling a retrospective cultural anthropology.

By the 1950s and 1960s, then, as the last of the four great waves of interpretation washed up on our shores, historians like myself felt braced and invigorated. Although we might differ as to the relative weight to assign each of the influences in question, we agreed that our discipline had received exactly the tonic it needed—and that a great future lay before it and us. In so doing, we subscribed to at least a qualified notion of progress in historical studies—a notion close to the one advanced by Kuhn himself in answer to the charge of "relativism."[3] We tacitly maintained that the paradigms in question were "better" than their predecessors: we found that they both cut deeper and covered a wider range of observed cases. With their guidance, we believed, we could reach new heights of intellectual rigor and interpretive grasp.

THE CURRENT OUTLOOK

Today I feel rather differently. Instead of heralding intellectual victories, I must point to a substantial regression. The symptoms of retreat may be subsumed under the notion of a return to a primitive variety of positivism. To trace these danger signals requires a shift from intellectual history to the sociology of knowledge.

Initially, in the obvious organizational sense, few can have failed

2. On the school of the *Annales*, see my *The Obstructed Path* (New York: Harper & Row, 1968), Chap. 2; Traian Stoianovich, *French Historical Method: The Annales Paradigm* (Ithaca, N.Y.: Cornell University Press, 1976); R. Colbert Rhodes, "Emile Durkheim and the Historical Thought of Marc Bloch," *Theory and Society*, 5 (January 1978), 45-73; the special double issue on "The Impact of the *Annales* School on the Social Sciences," *Review: A Journal of the Fernand Braudel Center for the Study of Economies, Historical Systems, and Civilizations*, 1 (winter/spring 1978), 2 (summer 1978); Samuel Kinser, "*Annaliste* Paradigm? The Geohistorical Structuralism of Fein and Braudel," *The American Historical Review* 86 (February 1981): 63-105; and the annual volume of *Selections from the Annales*, ed. Robert Forster and Orest Ranum (Baltimore, Md.: Johns Hopkins University Press, 1975-).

3. Thomas S. Kuhn, "Reflections on My Critics," *Criticism and the Growth of Knowledge*, ed. Imre Lakatos and Alan Musgrave (Cambridge: Cambridge University Press, 1970), pp. 244-45, 264.

to notice a hyper-professionalization of the historical guild. In our country, each subspecialty now has its own society, its own roster of accredited members, and usually its own journal. Both national and topical groupings—British history and economic history, for example—are professionally equipped in this fashion. The result has been a vast proliferation of the boxes into which historians are sorted out. In the case of someone whose work ranges over a wide number of specialties, it has become impossible to belong to all the organizations relevant to his or her concerns, let alone to follow their activities.

Now there is nothing intrinsically wrong about those with common interests getting to know one another; perhaps some such professionalization is the only way to deal with the pressure of numbers in a discipline whose ranks swelled enormously in the quarter century following the Second World War. The problem, rather, is the mentality that this organizational fever engenders. By defining too narrowly a historian's peers, it encourages that individual to keep digging away in the ground already plowed by the Ph.D. thesis rather than broadening the vista to new pastures. Stuck in a professional rut at the age of thirty, the American historian today has little incentive to climb out and above it. Those who set the standards within each subdiscipline have a vested interest in maintaining its boundaries intact, and their juniors learn with pathetic rapidity to subscribe to the same self-definitions.

One might object that such is true of virtually every other field of knowledge, that history is not peculiar in this regard. But what *is* special about history is the fact that subdisciplinary demarcations do not coincide with the major modes of interpretation I have outlined. All of these paradigms are relevant to *every* subdiscipline. All require a flexibility of mind that can shift with dexterity and ease from one to another specialty and back. Within the subdisciplines, on the contrary, the emphasis falls on the mastery of a particular foreign language or of a particular technical set of tools. The not unpredictable result has been a return to the earlier obsession with archival research.

No conscientious historian could possibly object to the exploitation of unpublished documents: it has always and quite appropriately figured as the nitty-gritty on which apprentice scholars cut their teeth. But it is only the beginning, not the end of knowledge. In the late 1940s and the 1950s esteem in the historical profession was conferred primarily on those who wrote works of synthesis, works based for the most part on published sources alone. Today the reverse is the case. Historians in this country seem to have forgotten—if they ever properly learned—the simple truth that what one may call progress in their endeavors comes not merely through the discovery of new materials but at least as much through a *new reading* of materials already available.

The situation of two research approaches currently much discussed

—quantification and psychohistory—may illustrate what I have in mind. The first is riding high; the second finds itself relegated to a kind of academic ghetto. The quantifiers—and once more I have no intrinsic quarrel with them—fit perfectly today's positivist mood. They deal in "hard" data; their findings have none of the messiness usually associated with the historian's results. Their successes—for example, in demography—are so apparent as scarcely to require special celebration. I can only applaud the fact that a computer may now provide a rapid and tidy solution to a technical problem which in former days, with pencil and arithmetic, would have consumed the better part of a scholar's lifetime. But I cannot accept the hubris into which these successes have led historians trained to the computer, nor the condescension with which so many of them regard the efforts of colleagues still wallowing in old-fashioned imprecision. The spectacular results achieved with new research tools do not automatically confer a similar exalted station on the subject matter to which those tools are applied. The computer specialists neglect to notice that not all historical problems lend themselves to quantification—indeed, that the largest issues seldom do so. They too need to be reminded of a simple truth, that their special knowledge amounts to no more than a technique and that it can add little or nothing to the major paradigms of historical interpretation.

If the pretensions of quantification are imperial and extend across the board, psychohistory, in contrast, seems to have settled for a grudging professional recognition. By now psychohistorians have won a place as members of a topical subdiscipline. Yet the majority of the profession regard their efforts as eccentric or at best marginal. They inhabit one of the tolerated enclaves assigned to holdouts left over from the academic revolution of the late 1960s—black history, women's history, and the like. Denied the support of researchers in social history or demography, the psychohistorians are thrown back on their own limited resources; they receive little encouragement from their colleagues in their efforts to extend the Freudian paradigm from private sentiment to the realm of public action.

This was not the original intention of the founders of psychohistory in the United States. The handful of scholars who in informal meetings a decade and a half ago charted the goals of psychoanalytic interpretation wanted to illuminate the entire range of historical studies. They aimed at superseding the conventional notions of human motivation; they argued that the psychoanalytic view should be directed at all varieties of human behavior—even economic—and that a deepened understanding would result therefrom. They also hoped that by the same process the historical profession as a whole could be led to reflect in a more sustained fashion on its research tasks.

Such might also have been the effect of a systematic reassessment of history's Marxian heritage. Not surprisingly the late 1960s brought a clamorous revival of Marxist-oriented studies. But only in rare cases did it yield rewarding results, notably in the writings of Eugene Genovese. For the most part, the young Marxist scholars produced crude and polemical work. With their energies absorbed in documenting the evils of their own country's society and foreign policy, they took their time about making contact with like-minded scholars in Europe whose understanding of Marxism was more subtle and better-informed than theirs. Not until the end of the 1970s did a still younger generation of American Marxists begin to reach the intellectual level of their counterparts in Britain or Germany, France or Italy.[4] In Europe, Marxist historical scholarship has held and enlarged its place in the mainstream; in the United States it lingers in a precarious status.

So we are back to the situation of the four major paradigms. With the Freudian tucked off in a corner, the Marxian still at a fledgling stage, the Weberian honored by a respectful nod, we are left with the legacy of the *Annales*. This paradigm too, despite the esteem it enjoys, has fallen short of the aspirations of its founders. Here once again the chopping up of the profession into subdisciplines has limited the range of historical speculation. Not unexpectedly, the teachings of Marc Bloch and Lucien Febvre and their heirs have been appropriated by the economic and social historians. And in *this* subdiscipline the quantifiers rule supreme. In contrast, studies directed toward what the French call "mentalities" remain amorphous and without theoretical underpinnings. Thus, the concern for psychology, which the first generation of the *Annales* reckoned as of equal or even superior importance to economics, has been reduced to second rank—just at the moment when psychoanalytically oriented history might have come to its aid.

In the broadest terms, the American historical profession is threatened by a situation in which *Sitzfleisch* alone will be prized, and thought will be at a discount. I scarcely need add that such tendencies are reinforced by the current desperation in the job market; the young scholar today, alert to the realities of professional employment, is well advised to establish as early as possible a reputation as a solid and reliable toiler in one of the subdisciplines. He or she finds little incentive to pose major problems, whether of epistemology or of interpretation. The rewards attendant on developing an existing paradigm or possibly finding a new one will be too long deferred or may never materialize. In the meantime, academic tenure will doubtless have passed the imaginative historian by. And what will have been lost for the profession as a whole will be the courage to risk making a grand but illuminating mistake.

4. See, for example, the biographical study by Andrew Arato and Paul Breines, *The Young Lukács and the Origins of Western Marxism* (New York: Seabury Press, 1979).

CONCLUSION

So much for the dismal aspects of the historical discipline's current sociology. To reach a conclusion, we need to return to the level of ideas themselves—to define the content of the regression toward positivism. I have referred to it as "primitive" in order to distinguish it from the neopositivism of twentieth-century analytic philosophy, which, although of little help to historians, is at least intellectually fastidious. The sort of positivism I am speaking of harks back, rather, to the nineteenth century in its epistemological naïveté.

Early in this essay I referred to the attitude with which sophisticated historians approached their middle-level generalizations or paradigms. I suggested that they recognized what was arbitrary in their constructions and that they made no claim to possessing "the truth." I further specified that they took account of the gap between themselves and their data, of the fact that the data almost never conveyed an unambiguous message and that even the simplest narrative carried along with it a freight of interpretation. All these postulates the positivist-minded historians of today implicitly deny.

I say "implicitly" because most of the time the epistemology of positivism is not spelled out. It is simply taken for granted. But what it amounts to is the conviction, first, that the data are "out there" somewhere and need only be located; second, that a particular historian has no right to go beyond the obvious meanings that other historians will readily recognize as valid—to transcend the conventionally apparent lies in the dangerous realm of guesswork or inference, or possibly of the imagination.

In such a universe of discourse, what becomes of the great paradigms? They all have in common a powerful imaginative component; they all by implication stand condemned. Claude Lévi-Strauss once characterized both Marxism and psychoanalysis as "geologies";[5] both, he maintained, dug down to find the subterranean strata that surface appearances concealed. I should extend his remark to the whole range of major historical interpretation. Everything in it is geology in Lévi-Strauss's sense: the mark of a masterwork in history as opposed to a journeyman's product is precisely the quality of exposing what had lain unrecognized, the revelation that things were not as they had been supposed to be.

To make such a contribution to historical understanding requires a leap of the intelligence. It requires a quality of mind that can discern connections where others have seen only a random succession of events. Such minds are rare; there are no more than a handful in every generation of historians. To discourage this tiny minority—this "saving remnant"—is devil's work. If the new positivists have their way, the historical mind will leap no more.

5. Claude Lévi-Strauss, *Tristes Tropiques*, trans. John and Doreen Weightman (New York: Atheneum, 1974), pp. 57-78.

PART III

The Prospects and Problems
of Material Progress

In the opening essay, Moses Abramovitz analyzes contemporary disillusionment about the prospects and desirability of continued economic progress. He writes of four distinct components in this "retreat" from earlier sanguine expectations regarding economic growth and its relation to welfare and happiness. The first is the widespread belief that growth is impossible to sustain because of scarcities and dangerous to pursue because of the destructive burden on the environment. The second is a growing distrust of the measures of growth. Reports of economic growth are said to be illusory since they fail to include substantial but difficult-to-measure costs of growth. A rising gross national product is no longer viewed as an unmixed good. The third component is the declining satisfaction yielded by more material goods going to people who already have much. And, finally, growth is associated in the minds of some with a dehumanizing and threatening technology. These four themes have become elements of an "adversary culture" which is propagated and implemented in politics and the policy process by a critical "establishment" of pressure groups, lobbyists, and politicians. The arguments advanced in Part Three suggest that our problems with technology and economic growth are not inherent in these processes but rather lie in the realm of cultural and political values and power balances.

The essay by Harvey Brooks deals in detail with the first theme suggested by Abramovitz, the limits-to-growth view of the future. The general set of constraints predicted by this "Malthusian" school includes the depletion of resources, increased environmental pollution, inadequacy in food production, and overcrowding. Brooks's analysis of various of these predictions would indicate that many of the concerns of the Malthusians about this problem are overly pessimistic and based, in some cases, on somewhat simplistic models of the future developments in technology. Brooks's analyses show that from the point of view of the previous history of technology, the pessimism of the Malthusians is unwarranted. We can anticipate improvements in, for example, recovery of minerals from ores, recycling, and appropriate uses of energy, presumably from nuclear sources and/or solar ones.

The question of environmental pollution is really three separate problems: (1) general chemical and radiation contamination because of industrial and agricultural practices, (2) deterioration of natural ecosystems because of the preemption of more land for human use, and (3) changes in global climate because of the buildup of CO_2 and/or other general atmospheric contamination. These consequences are all different in their causes, the intensity of their threats, and the degree to which technology, careful social planning, and regulation can control their adverse effects.

Brooks suggests that a great deal of concern arises from a generalized increase in public sensitivity to some of these problems rather than from precise indications of real and immediate dangers. He arrives at the same conclusion which pervades many of these essays concerning, on the one hand, the discrepancy between our technology and intellectual achievements and the possibilities these offer for coping with our problems, and, on the other hand, the inadequacy of our political and social skills to implement and utilize these achievements for the common good. He points up, perhaps more than any other author, the political and cultural dilemma of modern society in which decisions regarding the application of technologies have to be made by a leadership and a public insufficiently informed on technological and scientific questions.

Pursuing one of the themes developed by Brooks, Nathan Rosenberg argues that pessimistic projections of future growth have assumed a fixed technology whereas in actual fact technological innovation has in the past continually redefined and expanded the resource base. There is no reason to believe that this relation between technology and resources cannot continue for a considerable time into the future. However, a second trend has seriously begun to affect this relation between technology and economic growth. This is the value transformation taking place in affluent societies, stressing the negative environmental consequences of economic growth and thereby slowing down technological adaptation and making it more costly. Rosenberg concludes by asking the sobering question "whether we will have the collective wisdom to modify our institutions in ways which will incorporate these relatively neglected concerns without at the same time destroying that complex balance of incentives upon which efficiency and growth depend."

None of these problems of growth and technology seriously troubles most of the Third World. Their demand for material progress, as Crawford Young argued in an earlier essay, tends to be sustained, though there are intermittent traditionalist reactions. It is also true that the Third World has experienced significant economic growth on the average, with both striking successes and failures to show as a result of the last decades of effort. Hollis Chenery makes the point that many, perhaps most, of the countries of the Third World reject the experience of the West, in which growth in the first part of the nineteenth century was accompanied by increasing inequality. Their demand is for growth with equitable distribution. That this is possible is demonstrated by the experience of such countries as Taiwan, South Korea, and Singapore. Growth successes such as those of Brazil and Mexico essentially benefit the upper-income groups. This leads Chenery to the conclusion that a simple per capita measure of national income is misleading, that we require a new method of computing economic growth weighted by the distribution of the growth in income among the various income groups.

To estimate the prospects for a significant alleviation of poverty in Third World countries in the next decades, Chenery and his colleagues prepared a simulation of growth and distribution over the next twenty years. It shows that the absolute number of poor defined by current criteria in the year 2000, assuming the continuation of current trends, would be at about the same level as in 1960, though the proportion of poor might drop from 50 percent to 20 percent of the population in developing countries. A policy mix that would reduce poverty in the Third World is well understood; the problems are essentially of a political, social, and cultural order.

12

The Retreat from Economic Advance: Changing Ideas About Economic Progress

MOSES ABRAMOVITZ

A vision of the possibility of economic growth lies close to the center of the idea of progress in general. Francis Bacon, the great precursor of the idea, proposed that progress could be founded upon a steady increase in knowledge gained by the application of experimental methods. But Bacon also held that the real and legitimate goal of the sciences is "the endowment of human life with new inventions and riches" and, in J.B. Bury's words, "the amelioration of human life, to increase men's happiness and mitigate their sufferings."[1]

Bacon's outlook immediately suggests how closely intertwined are the notions of progress and economic progress. They are not the same since progress broadly conceived includes intellectual, moral, and spiritual advance, as well as other satisfactions, which are not closely constrained by the supply of scarce goods. The starting point of their connection, however, seems to be the possibility of increasing our command over nature and the output of goods. At the same time, there is a strongly held and plausible idea that if we are to cultivate our nonmaterial, intellectual and spiritual, potentialities, we can do so only to the degree that we are relieved from elementary poverty and repetitive toil.

Considering how crucial economic progress is to the idea of progress generally, it is perhaps ironic that classical economics emerged as a source of skepticism and disbelief in the possibilities of progress rather than as a source of support. Malthusian population theory and

1. J.B. Bury, *The Idea of Progress* (New York: Dover, 1955), p. 52.

Ricardian diminishing returns on the land made the outlook for an indefinite rise of the common man's living standards doubtful even though the "industrial arts" themselves might continue to improve. This skeptical outlook was orthodox academic doctrine during the entire half-century between Malthus' *Essay* of 1798 and Mill's *Principles* of 1848. In Mill's words:

> Hitherto . . . it is questionable if all the mechanical inventions yet made have lightened the day's toil of any human being. They have enabled a greater population to live the same life of drudgery and imprisonment, and an increased number of manufacturers and others to make fortunes. They have increased the comforts of the middle classes. But they have not yet begun to effect those great changes in human destiny which it is in their nature and in their futurity to accomplish. Only when, in addition to just institutions, the increase of mankind shall be under the deliberate guidance of judicious foresight, can the conquests made from the powers of nature by the intellect and energy of scientific discoverers become the common property of the species and the means of improving and elevating the human lot.[2]

This somber vision was originated and fostered by the political economists. But it was far from being merely academic. It largely dominated the views of educated and influential people in Britain and only to a lesser degree in the United States. Because it made the fate of common people depend largely on their own procreative tendencies, it was powerful support for conservative politics.

All this changed in the next twenty-five years under the experience of rising English and American incomes and falling birth rates. When Alfred Marshall, the still young but immensely sober ascendant head of Anglo-Saxon economics, wrote his essay "The Future of the Working Classes" in 1873, he was able to envisage an England very different from Mill's:

2. It is easy to oversimplify and misrepresent the positions of Ricardo, McCullogh, Mill, and the others of the time. They were not, of course, enemies of progress, and they believed that the common man was best off in a "progressive state" of society, that is, in a state in which the "industrial arts" are flourishing and advancing and in which returns to capital are still sufficiently high to induce net accumulation. They did not think that these processes would soon come to a halt. On the other hand, they did not believe that technical advance and capital accumulation would continue at a rapid pace indefinitely or that even the pace of their own era, speedy as they thought it, was sufficient to outrun that of population growth and to permit a cumulative rise of general living conditions. Insofar as the idea of progress comprehends that of indefinite advance in material standards for ordinary people, they did not accept it. See John Stuart Mill, *Principles of Political Economy*, ed. W.J. Ashley (London: Longman's Green, 1909), p. 751. Kenneth Boulding's quip, "One has to be either a lunatic or an economist to believe in the possibility of indefinite economic growth," does not apply to the classical economists.

It is to have a fair share of wealth, and not an abnormally large population. Everyone is to have in youth an education which is thorough while it lasts, and which lasts long. No one is to do in the day so much manual work as will leave him little time or little aptitude for intellectual and artistic enjoyment in the evening. Since there will be nothing tending to render the individual coarse and unrefined, there will be nothing tending to render society coarse and unrefined.... every man will be surrounded from birth upwards by almost all the influences which we have seen to be at present characteristic of the occupations of gentlemen....[3]

If achieved, could such a utopian state of affairs be maintained? It could be and it would be.

the only labour excluded from our new society is that which is so conducted as to stunt the mental growth.... Now it is to such stunting almost alone that indolence is due.... The total work done per head of the population would be greater than now, less of it would be devoted directly to the increase of material wealth, but far more would be indirectly efficient for this end. Knowledge is power; and man would have knowledge. Inventions would increase and they would be readily applied.[4]

Could such a condition then be achieved? It could be and, in fact, already was.

if we look around us, do we not find that we are steadily, if slowly, moving towards that attainment? All ranks of society are rising; on the whole they are better and more cultivated than their forefathers were; they are no less eager to do, and they are much more powerful to bear, and greatly to forebear.... In the broad backbone of moral strength our people have never been wanting; but now by the aid of education, their moral strength is gaining new life.[5]

Marshall's optimism represented a wave of opinion which spread and gained strength for decades. The spread was based on a growing faith in the possibilities of technological advance accompanied by falling, not rising, rates of natural increase of populations and by land rents which declined as a share of national income. So far as concerned the beneficence of such developments, one could observe in all the industrializing countries rising levels of nutrition, health, housing, and education and longer life expectancies. Successive technological marvels were seen as enlarging the scope and variety of people's lives, opening up new worlds of travel, communication, information, entertainment, and convenience. The belief became common that release

3. In *Memorials of Alfred Marshall*, ed. A. C. Pigou (London: Macmillan, 1925), pp. 110, 111.

4. Ibid., pp. 111, 112.   5. Ibid., p. 115.

from deep poverty, greater command over material goods, and lightening of labor would conduce to a more cultivated life for the common man. Charles Beard, writing at the depth of the Great Depression, catches the mood of a time that already seems somewhat distant:

> in dealing with the effect of technology upon social evolution, we are not confronted by accomplished work alone, but also by a swiftly advancing method for subduing material things. . . . there is something intrinsic in technology which seems to promise it indefinite operation. . . . The solution of one problem . . . nearly always opens up new problems for exploration . . . the passionate quest of mankind for physical comfort, security, health and well-being generally is behind the exploratory organs of technology. . . .
>
> Through the press, the radio, the railway, the post office and enormous educational plants, [technology] extends literacy, distributes information, widens the social consciousness. . . .
>
> If no Saint-Pierres, Comtes, and Spencers appeared in the United States to give theoretical formulation to what was taking place, there was no doubt about the course of events. Immense energies, physical, intellectual, and moral were being applied to the conquest of the earth, with a view to raising the standard of life, decreasing the death rate, overcoming illiteracy, eliminating physical suffering and providing the comforts of a rational being.[6]

Needless to say, academic economists did not remain outside this mainstream of opinion. They gave it expression in the "older welfare economics." This connected economic growth with human welfare according to an argument which rested on Benthamite utilitarian conceptions.[7] The argument starts from the notion of "total or social welfare," a vaguely defined entity identified with people's states of consciousness, a matter of how people feel, their levels of satisfaction. Welfare depends on people's command over goods and services but also on other things: friendship, family affections, love, and the like. It has a place for moral and aesthetic values and satisfactions. "Economic welfare" is "that part of total welfare that can be brought directly or indirectly into relation with the measuring rod of money."[8] It reflects the satisfaction of human needs and desires for goods whose production requires scarce resources. The greater the supply of such goods per head, the greater, other things being equal, the level of satisfaction or welfare. The national product or national income, finally, was proposed as the objective measurable counterpart of economic welfare.

National product estimates were never regarded as ideal measures

6. Charles A. Beard, Introduction to Bury, *Idea of Progress*, pp. xxii-vi, xxxv.

7. My statement about the place of economic growth in the older welfare economics follows A.C. Pigou, *The Economics of Welfare* (London: Macmillan, 1932), Chap. 1.

8. Ibid., p. 11.

of output relevant to economic welfare. With some qualifications, they measure only those outputs which move through markets; they count as costs only those which must be paid for by private producers; and they value goods according to the prices which individual purchasers are willing to pay. Thus, conventional national product figures make no allowance for productive work that takes place at home or for the satisfactions that people obtain from their leisure time activities. The estimates take no account of the depreciation imposed by production on those parts of the national wealth which are not privately owned; so they do not subtract the costs of air and water pollution or of damage to other elements of the environment, which producers are permitted to use without charge. Similarly, the estimates neglect the losses which one person's consumption activity may cause to the satisfaction of others when he adds to the congestion in streets and roads or in the use of other facilities provided without a proper service fee. As a practical matter, though not in principle, national product estimates understate the growth of many services because, in effect, they neglect such increase as may occur over time in the productivity of the labor employed in some parts of the service sector. Finally, the estimates grossly understate the rise in effective output that takes the form of qualitative improvement in goods and services. The difference between treating pneumonia with poultices instead of penicillin nowhere appears in the national product figures.[9]

When economists deal with national product data carefully, they are inclined to say that they are adequate indexes of short-term—year to year or quarter to quarter—changes in the flow of goods and services but very uncertain guides to longer-term growth relevant to welfare. That is because the division of time between market work and home work or between work and leisure changes only slowly and continuously and may be neglected when considering the fluctuations in output which are prominent in the short run. And similarly with environmental damage and other "external" costs and with advance in quality. Such developments cumulate over longer periods, however, and may become important compared with measured output change over the decades and quarter-centuries which are of concern for long-term growth.

Economists, however, have not always been careful. Lacking better

9. These issues and a number of others are defined and discussed in detail in *The Measurement of Economic and Social Performance*, ed. Milton Moss (New York: Columbia University Press, 1973). This volume also republishes the well-known experiment by Nordhaus and Tobin in providing a set of national product estimates which allow for many of the deficiencies of conventional national product when viewed as an index of output relevant to welfare. Their "Measure of Economic Welfare," except on extreme assumptions, appears to confirm the common impression that conventional national product can serve as a rough index of long-term growth useful for welfare judgments.

figures, they make the practical judgment that the conventional national product can be used as a rough-and-ready substitute for the long-term index they want. Comparisons of long-term growth between countries and over time were, and still are, often made as if conventionally measured national products per capita were fully satisfactory indications of comparative growth in economic welfare. When, therefore, the national product, usually in its gross version—the GNP —became a household word, the public also came to think of national product figures as satisfactory indexes of output relevant to welfare. Economic growth in popular parlance came to mean growth of GNP. It then emerged, as we shall see, that what are no more than criticisms of the conventional GNP figures as *measures* of growth serve as arguments to discredit economic growth itself.

The deficiencies of national product as a measure of long-term growth relevant to welfare inject an element of ambiguity into the debate over growth. Because national product growth, as conventionally measured, is the conception of economic growth that most people concerned with the issue have in mind, it is convenient to adhere to that meaning. We should not forget, however, that the underlying meaning of economic growth for economists is, as it should be for everyone, increase in a fully comprehensive measure of *net* output per head—net after allowing for the costs of all scarce resources (including the air, the water, the landscape, etc.) which may be used up in production, inclusive of the values produced in the home as well as in the market and adjusted for the improvement or deterioration of quality that accompanies quantitative growth.

Just as increase of conventional national product is an uncertain guide to the growth of economic welfare, so a rise of economic welfare may be obtained at the expense of noneconomic aspects of human satisfaction. Manifestly, the way income is earned and the way it is spent affect the very nature of people and the relations among them. The older welfare economists, however, argued that in the absence of special information, we are entitled to rely on a practical, if rebuttable, presumption that changes in economic welfare also change total welfare in the same direction, if not in the same degree. Economists' favorable appraisal of growth in per capita national product, therefore, rested on a series of practical judgments about the relations between national product and economic welfare and between economic and total welfare. Their appraisal was bolstered by considering the miserable levels of average income from which poor people were rising in each successive generation as well as by the broad indexes of advances in well-being, health, and education already mentioned as concomitants of growth.

A commonsensical Benthamite psychology of fixed wants, the satisfaction of which conduced to happiness, formed the sometimes explicit, always implicit, basis for this outlook. As theoretical welfare economics developed, however, it became more austere. When writing for one another, economists became anxious to empty their subject of entities like happiness, which they could neither define nor measure. They recoiled before the realization that a welfare interpretation of growth demanded interpersonal comparisons of satisfaction among gainers and losers and between populations of different membership at different times. Lacking a clear basis for such comparisons, welfare judgments in any rigorous sense entailing comparisons of experienced satisfaction were held to be impossible. Economic growth in the technical literature came to mean only a greater capacity to produce and, therefore, a wider range of choice among goods, between goods and leisure, and in the distribution of goods among people. What might then be chosen and what that might mean for people were other matters about which objective judgment was impossible.[10] In principle, one might say, if one wished, that enlarging the range of choice is itself a good thing; but one cannot say more than that. Economists' practical judgments, however, did not change. As with people generally, economists as a group continued to support the view that economic growth conduces to welfare. By and large, they still do, and the basis of their position is the series of practical judgments on which the older welfare economics rested. It is those judgments which are now increasingly in question.

POSTWAR EMPHASIS AND ACHIEVEMENT

The opening of the postwar period may be taken to be the bicentennial anniversary of the idea of progress at large—if we think of the mid-eighteenth century as the time when optimism about the possibilities of meliorative change first became widespread. And it can be taken to mark the centennial, counting from about 1850, of the idea that technological progress and capital accumulation could be the basis for sustained progress in human welfare based upon growth in output per head. The quarter-century following World War II was remarkable in three respects.

In the first place, there was, for the first two decades of the period, a still more pronounced interest in economic growth.[11] Growth became

10. Readers will find a thorough review of the subtle and sophisticated literature concerning the possibility of welfare judgments based on output comparisons in Amartya Sen, "The Welfare Basis of Real Income Comparisons: A Survey," *Journal of Economic Literature*, 17(1) (March 1979): 1-45.

11. A more elaborate explanation of the heightened postwar interest in growth along the general lines of the text may be found in H. W. Arndt, *The Rise and Fall of Economic Growth: A Study in Contemporary Thought* (Melbourne: Longman Cheshire Pty., Ltd., 1978). See also Moses Abramovitz, "Economic Growth and Its Discontents," in *Economics and Human Welfare*, ed. Michael J. Boskin (New York: Academic Press, 1979).

the premier goal of social policy throughout the world. This heightened emphasis rested, at bottom, on all the considerations already advanced; but these obtained added support from a variety of special circumstances and influences. In many European countries, there had been a serious check to growth since the outbreak of the First World War, that is, for some thirty-five years. In those years, the United States had forged ahead in industrial power and wealth and established a new standard of affluent living for common people. Since it was widely realized that the gap between European and American incomes was much wider than could be justified by any differences in technological capacity or in experience with commercial, industrial, or governmental organization, there was a natural determination to reduce the income gap rapidly. In the Soviet Union, the same determination was spurred not only by great poverty but also by the reigning political doctrine, which held that the advance to a true communist order was dependent on the achievement of material plenty. In the new countries of the Third World, nationalist governments properly regarded commercial and industrial development as necessary conditions for establishing their fledgling states on stable foundations. In the Cold War between the Soviet Union and the United States, military and political power were, for a time, largely equated with GNP. Since the market economies of the West still lived in the aftermath of the Great Depression, the minimization of unemployment rivaled growth itself as an economic goal. Jobs for an expanding labor force then meant growth, at least in the aggregate, if not per capita. Given technological progress, it meant both. Finally, in both Europe and America, the working classes had become a much stronger political force. Their demands for higher incomes could be more easily met from the fruits of average growth than by redistribution. Their demands for higher levels of mass education, health care, and economic security—for the Welfare State—could be more easily accommodated if incomes were rising than if they were stagnant. In the United States there was also the special problem of the blacks. It seemed far easier to reduce discrimination and to open a better place for blacks in schools, jobs, and professions in an atmosphere of rapid growth and full employment than in a stationary or slowly growing economy.

The second, perhaps still more impressive, feature of the postwar decades was that the heightened interest in economic growth was matched by the achievement. During the twenty-five years from 1948 to 1973, American growth in labor productivity was faster than it had been in any earlier quarter-century in even this country's notable record. Increase of per capita output just failed to establish a new speed record but only because the share of working age people in the total population was declining. More to the point, however, the period passed without a serious depression, and output per head rose by 2.4

percent per year and real disposable income per head by 2.3 percent.[12] Average real incomes, therefore, rose by nearly 80 percent during the quarter-century. And in Western Europe and Japan, growth proceeded even more rapidly and steadily. The per capita rate in those countries averaged some 4 percent per year for the decades of the fifties and sixties.[13] With hardly a pause, their average level of per capita output, which had been under one-half the U.S. level in 1950, rose to almost 70 percent of the now much higher American level in 1973.[14] In that year average incomes in the other industrialized market economies were well above the unprecedentedly affluent American levels of the early fifties. The growth that was so ardently desired was therefore obtained. The American level of consumption became much higher, and large numbers of people in Europe and Japan began to live at the level and in the manner of American consumers. The rise of living standards in those countries reached all classes of people, and the welfare state became established.

The third feature of the postwar period was, therefore, all the more notable. As the experience with rapid growth proceeded, doubts emerged. In the United States and Western Europe, though not in the collectivist societies or in the impoverished Third World, a mood of disappointment in the achievement spread. A critical movement of opposition to future growth appeared and became more powerful. The mood and the movement are not yet dominant. Public policy is still, in principle, pro growth. But the opposition is widespread in intellectual and professional circles and in popular writing. Individual communities seek to bar population expansion, and they make industry and commerce unwelcome. Moreover, both the ordinary person's attitude and public policy itself have become ambivalent. They welcome growth but they resist its concomitants—environmental damage and congestion and the risks posed by new products, materials, and industrial processes. The transformation of opinion is as marked in

12. *Economic Report of the President,* transmitted to the Congress, February 1979 (Washington, D.C.: Superintendent of Documents, USGPO), Tables B-2, B-22.

13. These are unweighted average rates for countries based on the national product estimates of the Organization for Economic Cooperation and Development. Averages weighted by population would be still more impressive since they would give relatively great weight to the larger countries, Germany, France, Italy, and Japan, which were also the faster growing.

14. The 1950 figures are estimates by the present writer. They are extrapolated from data for 1965 worked out by Angus Maddison, "Comparative Productivity Levels in the Developed Countries," *Banca Nazionale del Luvoro Quarterly Review,* no. 83, December 1967, pp. 3-23. The Maddison figures translate European and Japanese incomes in 1965 into 1965 U.S. dollars by weighing outputs in different classes by U.S. relative prices. The 1965 figures were then carried back to 1950 using national growth rates. The 1973 comparisons are from Irving Kravis, Alan W. Heston, and Robert Summers, "Real GDP *Per Capita* for More Than 100 Countries," *Economic Journal,* 88(350) (June 1978): 215-42, Table 4, Col. 9.

Europe and Japan as in the United States. The recoil from growth is as curious as it is unexpected. The next section deals with its rationale.

THE REAPPRAISAL OF ECONOMIC GROWTH

The new attack on growth may be viewed as proceeding on four broad fronts. On the first—which this essay only mentions but does not develop—continued growth is said to be both impossible to sustain and dangerous to pursue. It is unsustainable because growing scarcities of food, basic raw materials, and means of disposing of waste products must eventually halt the growth of aggregate world output and then force a decline. Further advance of per capita output could then proceed only in the measure that population decline might outrun that of production. But pushing output to such limits is also dangerous because we may at any stage overshoot the mark by establishing levels of populations and output, which later prove unsustainable. Rapid and catastrophic reductions of per capita income, accompanied by severe population pressure, would then ensue, leaving the world to face a truly Malthusian adjustment by war, famine, disease, and misery. This essay says no more about this ultimate, gloomy, but possibly very remote, prospect.

On the other three fronts, critics attack growth from several directions. They argue, first, that growth entails costs which national product does not measure; so real growth of net output relevant to welfare is slower than the national product accounts suggest. Next, growth affords but limited consumer satisfactions and benefits to already affluent people; the enhanced satisfaction we seek is a will-o'-the-wisp which vanishes as it is approached. Finally, growth is gained by dependence on a technology and mode of organization which rob work of interest and stimulus. It entails a system of rewards the justification of which is efficiency but whose outcome is injustice. It implies a society which poisons people's characters and the relations among them.

Unmeasured and Badly Measured Costs—and Benefits

If one starts from net national product as the conventional measure of economic growth, the first general criticism holds that the measure is a misleading guide to the growth of economic welfare. Its best known, but not necessarily most important, failing is that it neglects the external costs of production and consumption.[15] These costs are the losses of valuable and scarce resources, which, because they can be used as free goods by producers and consumers, fail to be subtracted from the aggregate net product. If such costs are rising, the true net growth rate is smaller than that of the conventional measure. Familiar examples of such uncounted external costs are the pollution of water and air

15. A standard contemporary discussion is E.J. Mishan, *The Cost of Economic Growth* (New York: Praeger, 1967).

by industrial activity, by automobiles, and by household heating and sewage. Congestion on the highways and streets is another.[16] Damage to wilderness areas and the depopulation or extinction of certain species of wildlife are still others.

No one knows how large these costs may be because no one is asked to pay for the right to do the damage he does. And no one is asked to pay—or, at any rate, asked to pay a rationally determined fee—because no one knows how to value the damage any individual or firm may do. To the dedicated environmentalist, the value of the damage seems beyond all price, and it would be worth the blockage of any incremental output to prevent the occurrence of the smallest increment of environmental harm. To the ordinary urban worker, the problem is the obsession of overly affluent, overly idle sentimentalists. So long as their own drinking water remains potable, many people's tolerance for smoky air and congested national parks is very great. They would sacrifice very little in the way of a pay raise to save the bald-headed eagle. And, in between, the generality of people have their own particular interests and unexamined valuations. We shall learn something more about the valuations as the cost of environmental protection comes to be more systematically studied and better known.

As things stand, few would say that the negative external by-products of production are growing at a rate which would offset as much as one-half percentage point of a per capita growth, which until recently was approximately 2 percent a year in the United States.[17] Any figure of that order of magnitude, however, is important. It is accepted principle that we ought to spend "what it is worth" to us to offset environmental damage. And the expenditure—except for capital equipment and for making good past, rather than current, damage—should be counted as a cost of production, not as part of current net output. In the nature of the case, the value of environmental damage cannot be objectively fixed, and the sum to be expended in

16. Ibid., Chap. 8.

17. Edward F. Denison, *Accounting for Slower Economic Growth* (Washington, D.C.: Brookings Institution, 1979), has estimated that total expenditure on reducing damage from air and water pollution has been offsetting about 0.25 percentage points in the growth rate since 1973. This figure, however, includes expenditures for capital formation to help reduce future pollution and to correct past damage. So it exaggerates the growth of resources to offset current costs. Since there is now a general belief that the levels of air and water pollution are no longer rising, Denison's figure may be a useful upper bound to growth costs of that nature. This, of course, would still take no account of other externalities, congestion, noise, damage to wilderness and wildlife, flood control, etc. To get a sense of orders of magnitude, one should consider that net national product in the mid-seventies was running at about $1,500 billion a year. To offset one-half percentage point in the growth rate, the annual *increment* to currently caused environmental damage would have had to be $7.5 billion. This could be the case if we valued total annual environmental loss at, say, 10 percent of current net output, that is, at $150 billion, and considered that the loss level was rising at 5 percent a year. These are both very large figures, which few would accept.

environmental protection will remain as an issue to be settled politically, in the confused way that political issues are ever settled.

The measurement of net national product relevant to welfare is beset by still other troubles. Some, as critics emphasize, tend to overstate the conventional, measured growth rate, but others work the other way. Much of the cost of government is arguably devoted to supporting the private production and consumption activity, which turns out the goods we want and obtain from the private sector. It therefore represents "intermediate" production, like cotton yarn in the ladder of activity which yields us clothing. To include it is double-counting; and since government expenditure has been rising faster than the total, its inclusion exaggerates the measured growth rate. We should not forget, however, that much government, like some private, expenditure has positive, as well as negative, external effects. Education, for example, benefits not only the recipient but society at large in ways which go beyond the acquisition of productive skills. Its value is understated by its cost; and the educational effort has been rising fast.

National product neglects production that does not pass through the market. This includes housewives' services and other home production, which have been rising slowly because women have gone to "work" in increasing numbers and because standard hours of work-for-pay have been falling slowly. Including production at home would slow down the growth rate. So would including the value of leisure time activity since that has been rising only slowly. If we included the productive value of the time spent by working age students in school, however (because they are creating "human capital" by raising their skill levels), this would have operated to raise the growth rate during recent decades. So would an allowance for rising labor productivity in parts of the service sector, where productivity growth is neglected in the conventional measures. And, most important, so would an adequate allowance for improvement in the quality of goods and services, which is now almost entirely overlooked by the standard measures, or at least so most people would say.

For what is quality? The national product account yields a dollar total into which the myriad goods and services produced enter with dollar weights, which are their market prices. The prices reflect the relative values placed on products by consumers who are viewed as good judges of the capabilities of different things to satisfy each person's own needs and tastes. Similarly, workers' wages, which help to determine relative prices, are supposed to reflect their knowledge about the relative toilsomeness, unpleasantness, and dangers of their jobs. For most consumer goods and for most jobs, especially long-familiar goods and jobs, these are plausible assumptions. Until a few decades ago, all goods were made of homely materials—grains, cotton, wood, iron. Power for tools came from boiling water transmitted by leather belts. When horses gave way to gasoline engines, a farm boy could still understand and fix a motor. But many modern products and processes have become mysterious entities. What we eat and what we use are now often in the realms of an incomprehensible chemistry, biology, and physics.

In our imaginations, and to some extent in reality, our goods and our jobs assault us with unseen emanations. They deposit unknown substances that cumulate within us and years afterwards visit us with life-threatening diseases. In one instant, we are carried aloft on a silent wind; in the next, we may be smashed and incinerated. People sense that their bargains for goods and jobs have become deceitful. New products and processes proclaim their benefits openly: larger harvests of less perishable foods, warmer houses, faster, more comfortable transport, better wages based on higher productivity in pleasanter circumstances. Innovations contract with us according to their visible promise, but they do not at the outset reveal the full terms of the arrangement. They permit us to discover when and as we can, perhaps years later, that they may exact an uncertain additional price. Just as the national product does not measure the improvements in automobiles or in medical diagnosis and remedy, so it does not measure the concealed costs of innovation. A vague terror of novel technology, therefore, has spread. Critics of growth work to foster distrust of consumer products and working conditions and to slow down the pace of innovation in order to uncover and reduce its risks.

When all is said and done, there may still be some presumption that growth of national product per head is an indicator of growth of output relevant to welfare. That, at any rate, is the suggestion of such efforts as have so far been made to construct more adequate measures than conventional product itself.[18] These efforts, however, still fall short of our needs, and no one can say with confidence what the growth rate of a fully comprehensive and accurate measure of output growth relevant to welfare would be. Better measures are possible, but some problems are, in principle, beyond solution. We shall never be able to assign values, comparable with ordinary goods, to the externalities of production and consumption, neither to the negative effects, like environmental damage, nor to the positive effects, like education. Nor shall we be able to take full account of the values of the qualitative improvements and of the hidden costs embodied in new goods and

18. William Nordhaus and James Tobin, "Is Growth Obsolete?" in *The Measurement of Economic and Social Performance*, ed. Milton Moss (New York: Columbia University Press for National Bureau of Economic Research, 1973), pp. 509-32. See also the discussion of the national product treatment of expenditures to control environmental damage and the like in Thomas Juster, "A Framework for the Measurement of Economic and Social Performance," in *Measurement of Economic and Social Performance*, pp. 25-84.

jobs. Critics of growth understandably focus on the hidden costs; proponents, on the unvalued benefits. We have to learn to use the dubious national product numbers we have, or the better ones we may contrive, without assuming that the story they tell is decisive.

The Limited Satisfaction from Growth in Consumption

There can be little doubt of the human values of growth where the common pattern is at or near subsistence and where the largest part of increased production is devoted to a gain in elementary physical well-being—reduction of moribidity and mortality. In that case growth is life-giving and life-saving, restorative if not redemptive, permissive if not creative. To question growth there is to question the value of life itself.[19]

But what about the uses of higher income when people are already well off? In the commonsensical approach to growth, as well as in the outlook of the older welfare economics, people have fixed needs, wants, and desires. Goods help to satisfy these wants. In that somewhat ingenuous view, neither the intensity of their needs and desires nor the capacity of goods to satisfy them is affected by other people's incomes. A larger command over goods for the average person, therefore, means a higher level of satisfaction, happiness, or "welfare." As people become richer, increments of goods may, it is true, serve to satisfy less urgent needs and, therefore, yield proportionately smaller increments of satisfaction: this is the well-known "law of diminishing marginal utility." But the direction of the effect is unchanged. More continues to be better.

This simple doctrine, however, is now widely disputed. For one thing, there appears to be some evidence that in a rich country like the United States, growth of average income is not accompanied by an increase in people's happiness as they themselves perceive it. The evidence comes from repeated surveys carried out in the United States by the Gallup Poll and the National Opinion Research Center. In these surveys, intermingled with other questions, some of which established the income level of the respondents, people were asked to say whether they were "very happy," "pretty happy" (or "fairly happy"), or "not so happy." The results of those surveys were brought together and analyzed by Richard Easterlin.[20] They suggest a striking and puzzling conclusion. Easterlin found a contradiction in the association

19. Robert J. Lampman, "Recent U.S. Economic Growth and the Gain in Human Welfare," in *Perspectives on Economic Growth*, ed. Walter W. Heller (New York: Random House, 1968), p. 158.

20. R. A. Easterlin, "Does Economic Growth Improve the Human Lot?" in *Nations and Households in Economic Growth*, ed. P. A. David and M. W. Reder (New York: Academic Press, 1974), pp. 89-125.

between income and reported happiness. If one considers people in a given country at a given time—say, as they reveal themselves in any single survey in the United States—one finds, as expected, a strong, consistent, positive association between income and happiness. A much larger fraction of people in the upper income groups report themselves "very happy" than in the lower. This positive association across income groups runs through all the individual surveys. On the other hand, if one compares the reports over time during which average U.S. incomes have risen markedly, there is no associated rise in reported happiness. The percentages reporting themselves "very happy" remain about the same.[21] How can these paradoxical results be reconciled? There are several mutually supporting explanations.

THE INCOME RELATIVITY OF ASPIRATIONS. Easterlin's own explanation of his paradox is that the satisfaction a person gets from his income depends not on its absolute level but on its relation to those of others in the same community. If a person stands high on the income ladder, he is the happier for it. But if there is an increase in the level of income with no change in people's relative positions, nobody feels better off. The idea is commonplace and plausible; and it is consistent with age-old observations of social critics about the vanities of wealth and its self-defeating dissipation in competitive display and status seeking.[22]

The relative income hypothesis, moreover, also helps explain why it has proven so difficult to eliminate poverty as incomes rise. By any absolute standard, we have made great progress. The proportions which contemporaries regard as in poverty, however, tell a different story. As incomes rose, the level which the community regarded as tolerable, and which, indeed, was presumably needed for people to function as full-fledged community members, also rose. The rising poverty standard was embodied in the income tests used by state and private agencies to fix eligibility for welfare aid. The result is that welfare rolls in the United States did not decline as a proportion of the population for many years. And several studies, both

21. Easterlin also analyzed the results of a considerable number of cross-country surveys made both by the Gallup Poll and by Hadley Cantril, *The Patterns of Human Concerns* (New Brunswick, N.J.: Rutgers University Press, 1965), and found the same contradictory results—a strong positive association between income and reported happiness across income groups within given national surveys, but no significant association across countries among which average income levels varied a great deal. This result, of course, bolsters the intertemporal findings for the United States. One may well ask, however, whether the standard according to which an Italian would feel justified in reporting himself very happy is the same as that of a Swede. The same question may, in principle, also be addressed to historical comparisons within a single country, but it is surely a less disturbing problem.

22. I have presented a somewhat extended version of these views in "Economic Growth and Its Discontents."

in the United States over time and across countries, suggest that countries tend to set the poverty threshold at about one-half the median income in the country, whatever that happens to be.[23]

HABITUATION.

In prewar days well-to-do people had elaborate meals and had a number of servants to work for them. Now they have simpler meals and do their own work. After they have become accustomed to the new conditions, are they less happy than before? It is doubtful whether a moderately well-to-do man is appreciably happier now than he would be if transplanted back to the pre-railway age and attuned to the conditions of that age. . . .[24]

This quotation suggests a second hypothesis. Suppose that people's feelings of satisfaction depend not on the level of their incomes but on the novelty and stimulation of experiencing a higher income than they are used to—and the reverse with feelings of dissatisfaction. This helps explain the Easterlin paradox because higher-income groups are likely to contain a relatively large proportion of people whose incomes have recently risen whereas low-income groups will contain a relatively large proportion of those whose incomes have recently fallen. That difference would tend to produce the observed positive association between income level and reported happiness in comparisons across income classes at any given time and place. But if the proportions of recent arrivals in the various income groups remained fairly constant, there would be no change in the proportions who declared themselves happy in comparisons over time.

Tibor Scitovsky has shown how this limitation on the power of rising income to yield an increase in the average person's satisfaction can be deduced from contemporary psychological theory.[25] In the older psychology, needs and desires, if unfulfilled, cause tension, anxiety, and alertness, what psychologists would now call a raised level of *arousal*, which is uncomfortable. People try to reduce arousal by satisfying the desire which gave rise to it. The lower the level to which arousal can be brought, the greater the feeling of comfort or satisfaction. The older welfare economics incorporated the same idea.

Backed by much experiment, modern psychological theory proposes a different view. Arousal can fall too low. The comfort of fulfillment, initially satisfying, becomes boring. Animals and humans then find pleasure in action or experience that raises the arousal level, which is

23. Cf. V.R. Fuchs, "Redefining Poverty and Redistributing Income," *The Public Interest*, 8 (1967): 88-95.

24. A.C. Pigou, "Some Aspects of Welfare Economics," *American Economic Review*, 41 (June 1951): 294.

25. Tibor Scitovsky, "The Place of Economic Welfare in Human Welfare," *Quarterly Review of Economics and Business*, 13(3) (autumn 1973): 7-19; and his *The Joyless Economy* (New York: Oxford University Press, 1976).

stimulating. The keys to stimulation are novelty, challenge, and risk, which provide new desires, experiences, or goals and which renew or heighten the interest in meeting them. Such stimulus is found in hard and challenging work, artistic creation or connoisseurship, in exploration of all kinds, and in sports when seriously pursued. People also find stimulus—and this is the immediately relevant point—in the *process* of satisfying a previously unfulfilled desire. There is pleasure, therefore, in exploring the novel possibilities of a higher level of income but not in its routine use. It is a theory that has a disturbing implication. It says that the level of satisfaction depends not—or at least not only—on the level of income but on its growth rate. Other things being equal, we should have to grow *faster* in order to be happier, and we should have to keep on growing in order to stay in the same place. Is it any wonder that some people find the pursuit of satisfaction from higher income self-defeating?

THE RISING PRICES OF SPACE AND TIME. The built-in frustrations arising from the income relativity of aspirations and from habituation, it will be noted, rest on the structures of individual and social psychology. There are, however, frustrations which are more truly economic in origin. When people think about the concrete things they lack, the possession of which might make them happier, it is natural to envisage them in terms of the particular goods and services that form the lifestyle of people who already enjoy a larger income. Two lifestyle differences between relatively poor and relatively rich bear particularly on our problem. One is that the rich live more spaciously. They enjoy larger living quarters with larger grounds about their houses, their locations commonly afford easier access to the countryside, they can pay for comfortable transportation, and both at home and on holiday, they can, if they wish, have quiet, privacy, and seclusion. The other difference is that the rich can, or could, afford servants and, more generally, a large command over "services." If a family can raise its level of income relative to that of other families, it can, of course, adopt the style of life of the richer families to which it aspires. On the other hand, if a family's income rises together with everyone else's, that will not be the case. A general rise of incomes brings with it an increase in the prices of space and personal service. The average family with rising income cannot afford much more of these goods than they had before, certainly not as much as they had imagined they would; and many who used to command a great deal cannot afford as much. This is a third explanation of Easterlin's paradox.

It is, indeed, true that so far as space and related matters are concerned, there are countervailing considerations. Higher income has brought better housing to the average family. Automobiles have given ordinary people a wider choice of location, great freedom of movement, and easier access to mountains and seashore. On the other hand, as Fred Hirsch has emphasized, a large part of the rise of incomes with which people try to buy spaciousness, seclusion, quiet, a pleasing landscape, or an occasional taste of unspoilt wilderness is dissipated because the competition of more people for the same limited space has, in effect, raised the price of what they seek.[26]

There are also complications as regards servants and services. It is not true that the prices of all services rise with average income. There has been rapid technological progress in the production of some services. More knowledge, better diagnostic equipment, antibiotics, and so forth have made medical care more effective. On the other hand, servants have been virtually priced out of employment, productivity in the production of most services has lagged behind that in goods production, and their relative prices have risen steeply. Indeed, on the extreme assumption that the productivity of an hour's service remains constant, there is a neat paradox, which makes the issue clear.[27] The average person, no matter how rich he or she becomes, can never command the service of more than one other average person—even if he spends his entire income to buy it. In this respect the "poor" cannot ever hope to live like the "rich," no matter how rich they become.

The rise in the price of services is the form which the rising price of time takes in the marketplace. There is also the rising price of time at home, the price of time for productive activities around the house or for leisure time activities. This is the development which Stefan Linder has dramatized in *The Harried Leisure Class*.[28] Linder builds his case on the basis of an old proposition, which holds a central place in the relatively new economic theory about the allocation of time. This asserts that consumption consists, not in the purchase of consumer goods and services but rather in combining such purchased materials with a person's own time and effort to produce final utilities or satisfaction. As with ordinary production, consumers may combine purchased materials with labor (that is, leisure) time in varying proportions to produce the largest output of utility with the resources available. In the production of final satisfaction, consumers have a finite amount of time at their disposal, and this they must divide to best

26. Fred Hirsch, *The Social Limits to Growth* (Cambridge, Mass.: Harvard University Press, 1978).

27. I owe this point to Sir Roy Harrod, "The Possibility of Economic Satiety: Use of Economic Growth for Improving the Quality of Education and Leisure," in *Problems of United States Economic Development* (New York: Committee for Economic Development, 1958), I, 207-14. Of course, if productivity were constant in the production of everything, per capita incomes would not rise at all. What gives the apparent paradox its point is that productivity in producing services rises very slowly, even as productivity in other sectors rises fast.

28. Stefan B. Linder, *The Harried Leisure Class* (New York: Columbia University Press, 1970).

advantage between work, which provides purchased raw materials, and leisure or, better, leisure time activity, which is the source of value added in consumption.

What happens to this division? Year by year, in the course of economic growth, people have access to more goods. This has two counteracting effects. On the one hand, the value of extra leisure rises because there are more goods to use and to use up per leisure hour. On the other hand, the price of such time also rises because with the rise of labor productivity, more purchasable goods must be foregone if working hours are cut. There is, therefore, no clear presumption that working time will be reduced to afford more leisure to consume more goods. And there *is* a clear presumption that, even as work hours are reduced, the division of time will be made such that we consume more goods per leisure hour. It is true that over the whole course of industrialization, working hours have declined, but this was conspicuously not the case in the United States and in some other affluent countries in the postwar period. On a family basis, with regard to the larger participation of women in the labor market, the opposite was true. So we end up with Linder's vivid picture of a typical Scandinavian evening at home, the prosperous householder desperately reading the *New York Times*, listening to Italian opera, sipping Brazilian coffee and French cognac, and smoking an Havana cigar while still entertaining his beautiful Swedish wife as well as he can.

All this, of course, means that increments of ordinary net national product yield diminishing increments of satisfaction since the leisure time-goods ratio has declined—always provided that there has been no rise in our own consumption skills, that is, in our ability to convert goods into satisfaction per unit of time. And this source of diminishing marginal utility is over and above the source we usually have in mind, namely, that incremental goods serve to satisfy less and less urgent needs and desires.

The rising price of time may act to reduce the value of growth to affluent people in still another way toward which Scitovsky's ideas point. As goods become cheap compared with time, the pattern of consumption should shift away from activities which require much time for their pursuit and toward those in which lots of goods are used. Goods-intensive consumption is, by and large, directed to desires, which, when met, lower people's levels of arousal. Their routine satisfaction leaves us bored, dissatisfied, and in need of stimulus. But experience and activities that are sources of stimulation—the arts, literature, active sports, travel, companionship, and so forth—generally demand considerable preparation, training, and active involvement. They are time-intensive, but the rising price of time and the cheapness of goods seduce us to other more immediately comforting but ultimately unsatisfying habits.

TECHNOLOGY, ORGANIZATION, AND "LIFE"

The title of this section is pretentious. It has to be. The contemporary debate about economic growth reaches into realms usually inhabited only by English poets, German philosophers, and American sociologists. This is uncomfortable for an economist. The point of departure is the character of the technology, which is the basis of productivity growth, and the character of the organization needed to exploit the technology.

The technology which enables us to apply science to utilitarian ends demands both massive and specialized equipment and highly trained and specialized workers. The organization needed to make economical use of very large units of specialized physical and human capital consists of either great integrated companies (large factories served by large sales, purchasing, warehousing, financing, research and administrative divisions, themselves divided into still more specialized subdivisions) or functionally specialized companies, often very large (professional, service, finance, insurance, transport, etc.). In either case, the finely divided activities of individuals, groups, divisions, departments, and companies are brought into cooperation either by command and higher authority within firms or by the impersonal operation of trade and markets among firms. In the economy of industrialized society (this is the critical view), individuals are trained to perform narrow and repetitive tasks and, endowed with appropriate personal attitudes and goals, they are led by a self-interested commercial drive to cooperate toward the grand unperceived end of producing a large GNP. To the critics of growth, the analogy between industrialized society and the subhuman life of the anthill is inescapable. In the human anthill, however (this is again the view of the critics) the nicely articulated but unconsciously directed efforts of individuals do not conduce to the preservation and improvement of either the individual or the species. Rather they block the full development of the one and promote the destruction of the other.

Work

The older conception of industrialization, still shared by many, sees it as the basis of an immense improvement in the character of work. Viewed across the decades, work has become lighter, safer, cleaner, and conducted in more pleasant surroundings. Jobs are more secure and workers are better protected against the arbitrary authority of supervisors. With the most physically demanding work taken over by machines, the mental and, in a sense, the moral capabilities of people are more important and more actively employed. The great expansion in the ancillary functions of production (professions, trade, finance, services, government) supports this tendency. It opens the world of work more widely to women and provides a material incentive for the spread of education.

The critics have a different vision. Their ideal is preindustrial. They see a craftsman, owner of his own tools and master of his trade. He sets his own hours and his own pace. He works with or near his family to design and then himself to build a well-constructed, finely proportioned utilitarian object. It will function well, it will last, and it pleases the eye. Or they see the village peasant. He works hard, but his work is part of both a seasonal and communal round. He lives close to nature, consumes the produce of his own work, and is free of market pressures. He and his neighbors are friends and cooperators, not competitors or objects of each other's sales efforts.

Industrialization, the critics complain, destroys these humanly satisfying work patterns. The economic organization demanded by advancing technology cuts off work from the rest of life, removes its connection with home and family, deprives it of its communal character, and leaves it shorn of ceremonial, religious, or other mystic elements. Workers, from being masters of their own time and their own tools, become tenders of a company's machinery. Specialized in content, organized on a large scale, knowing neither its beginning nor end, work, for many people, is left simply a burden, increasingly calculated to render them isolated, insecure, and unfulfilled.

It is not hard to recognize this picture of preindustrial work and life as largely mythic and fallacious. Few preindustrial workers were masters of their own time and tools. Labor, both rural and urban, was brutally hard and long. It was shared by children and women. As Marshall tells us, it precluded schooling for the young and left adults without time or energy for "intellectual and artistic enjoyment in the evening." It rendered the individual and, therefore, society "coarse and unrefined."[29] The myth of preindustrial fulfillment in work, however, is hardy. Presumably it projects to the past a human need or desire still unsatisfied for many by contemporary working life.

Country and City

The great cities which grew up in the course of industrialization were the creatures of the more intense trade, professional services, abundant skilled labor, finance, and transport facilities, which were, in turn, needed to support specialized, large-scale production. After basic problems of concentrated populations were overcome—pure water, sewage disposal, police and fire protection—modern cities came into their own as centers of education, art, music, libraries, newspapers, restaurants and cafes, and of social life generally. They were seen to provide a stimulating background for living, a far better combination of facilities for both work and "life" than the dull and torpid village.

Matters, however, did not remain in balance. Ever-growing densities of population and their superconcentration in skyscrapers and in com-

29. Marshall, *Memorials of Alfred Marshall*, pp. 110, 111.

mercial and industrial lofts made business and homelife geographically incompatible. The interesting intermixture of living quarters, shops and cafes, which fills the memories of older Europeans, broke down. First, whole sections of cities became specialized to work, alive by day but dead at night. The computer railway and the automobile carried the process further by making dispersal to suburbs possible. The city then changed its character. Its population tended to become polarized toward the few rich and the many poor. In the United States, the removal of the middle classes to the suburbs created a chronic financial problem for the cities, which made for physical deterioration. The life of the streets was cramped by growing crime. And the suburban dispersal of so many important elements of the urban community restricted its intellectual activity. In the eyes of its critics, economic growth had produced conditions in which people, seeking to better their individual lives, were destroying a great social asset.[30]

The Compulsions of Growth

Defenders of growth regard material advance as an enlargement of people's range of choice and, therefore, of their freedom. Critics regard it as an instrument of compulsion. Defenders of growth tend to take people's tastes and attitudes as fixed by human nature. Technological progress presents a set of opportunities for satisfying those tastes more fully. Markets, private enterprise, and the free search for profits and for remunerative occupations are the instruments that release people's energies to exploit the opportunities presented by technical advance. The speed of exploitation is determined by the rate of technical advance itself and by people's choices regarding the pace of capital accumulation, by how much present income they are willing to divert to the building of physical capital, to the training of youth, and to research. The outcome is a rising level of labor productivity that offers people the chance to have both more goods and more leisure in the combination that best pleases them, as well as a wider choice among an increased variety of goods and services.

Critics see the same facts as restricting rather than enlarging the realm of choice. The nature of technological progress, built on economies of scale, increasingly confines the goods that are supplied to the standardized products of mass production. It restricts the jobs that are available to specialized, subdivided, robotlike occupations. In these, people are reduced to analogues of mechanical parts, and for their effective nonabrasive meshing, they are subject to the psychological and social lubrication of corporate administration. At the same time, a portion of the potentialities of the human spirit are stunted. To the great loss of instinctive social sympathy, feelings of solidarity, and tendencies to cooperate, people are encouraged to think and to behave

30. Mishan, *Costs of Economic Growth*, Chap. 8.

as if their only extrafamily relations were those of contract and trade, competition or authority. Deliberate manipulation, by advertising or otherwise, is not central to the process. The compulsions are implicit in the existence of an industrialized civilization. The social pressures of a society adapted by education, demonstration, and emulation to accepting the kinds of goods and jobs that mass methods imply are pervasive, thorough, and largely unnoticed by the people on whom they act. Behavior in conformity with these pressures is not only foreordained; it is even perceived as freedom by the generality of people. And it is only consistent with this state of affairs that those who may try to adopt an alternative pattern of work, consumption, and communal relations are regarded by the rest of society as "dropouts."[31]

WHERE ARE WE?

Since this essay's main purpose is to present the rationale for the contemporary attack on the growth of per capita national product, it cannot also attempt an appraisal of the grounds for the attack. It is perhaps possible to say something about the present state and implications of a debate which now goes on not only explicitly but also implicitly in the political and bureaucratic processes concerned with environmental regulation, occupational and consumer safety, sources of power, income redistribution, and the like.

It helps one understand the place of the contemporary attack on growth to realize that little in it is new. An analysis of the "external effects" of growth, its unmeasured costs in terms of environmental damage and the like, was a central feature of the earliest writings on the economics of welfare.[32] It has always been understood that true growth had to be measured net of such costs. The preacher in Ecclesiastes knew all about the vanities of wealth. Adam Smith and J. S. Mill, to say nothing of Thorstein Veblen, said most of what needs saying about the income relativity of aspirations, and Pigou[33] was equally clear about the effects of habituation in eroding satisfaction from higher income. Contemporary complaints about the effects of specialization, subdivision of labor, or the workers' loss of control over tools and product stem from Marx. The separation of work from family and communal life was mourned by Oliver Goldsmith in *The Deserted Village*. John Ruskin, William Morris, and many others deplored the passing of the artisan and his craft. Thomas Carlyle aimed his strongest diatribes against the rise of industry and commerce because they

31. Views of this sort fill the New Left literature. Representative references are Herbert Marcuse, *One-Dimensional Man* (Boston: Beacon Press, 1964); William H. Whyte, Jr., *The Organization Man* (New York: Simon & Schuster, 1956); and J. K. Galbraith, *The Affluent Society* (Boston: Houghton Mifflin, 1958).

32. A. C. Pigou, *Work and Welfare* (London: Macmillan, 1904).

33. Pigou, "Some Aspects of Welfare Economics."

involved people in trade and reduced personal relations to an exchange of monetary values, a cash nexus. Rousseau was the precursor of Marcuse and of all those who decry industrial civilization because, like any civilization, it shapes and constrains man's natural, supposedly benevolent, impulses.

These old arguments did not sway opinion seriously during the two centuries culminating in the 1960s when industrialization was spreading and becoming more intense. The belief that economic growth conduces to human welfare rested firmly on the widely accepted assumption that critical considerations might qualify but could not offset the solid benefits of a greater capacity to turn out goods. Somewhat elaborated, the old critical arguments are now the basis of a powerful attack in the richer, industrialized market economies. In those countries, a considerable shift of opinion has taken place and public policy has moved in many ways that limit the pace of growth. What happened to make the old arguments more persuasive to many, if not most, people? The answers are to be found partly in some elements of contemporary technology itself, partly in the widespread affluence and large populations it has brought into being, and partly in our cumulating experience with the unmeasured costs of measured growth and its social by-products. These have combined to change the balance of advantage and disadvantage that people achieve.

The level of affluence achieved is itself a main reason for the change. When the proportion of people living in poverty—as measured by past standards—has been drastically reduced, when large numbers have incomes which are not only comfortable but provide margins for education, recreation, and travel, the most obvious and obtrusive benefits of growth tend to fade from view. Growth then appears less, to use Lampman's words, as a "life-giving and life-saving" force.[34] It is no longer needed to free life for something besides toil. Questions about the possible contributions of higher incomes to happiness then seem more pertinent, and the frustrations which underlie Easterlin's paradox loom larger.

When per capita output has become high and populations large and increasingly concentrated, the external, unmeasured costs of growth become much more important. Rivers, lakes, and the atmosphere itself can carry off great masses of waste before there is a significant loss of purity. The wastes of still larger output and its necessary concentration in and around cities, however, reach and increasingly surpass these threshold capabilities. The external costs of production then rise disproportionately. A power technology based on burning fossil fuels aggravates the problem, and the affluent comfort achieved in other directions makes people more sensitive to atmospheric and other environmental discomfort.

34. Lampman, "Recent U.S. Economic Growth," p. 158.

There is a similar story in other spheres. Streets and parks can absorb a considerable rise of population and usage without the appearance of intense congestion and disturbing noise, but these limits are increasingly surpassed. And given the need for population concentration, it is hard to expand thoroughfares, parks, and other such facilities adequately. The spread of private motor vehicles compounds the difficulty within the cities and helps carry it to the countryside.

From another angle, as the technology on which growth is based becomes more powerful, it also becomes more mysterious to ordinary people. The science that gives rise to new materials and processes also reveals its concealed by-products, dangers, and risks. In their strangeness and apparent power to strike invisibly, at a distance and after long intervals, hidden dangers surround the new technology with a sense of pervasive threat. Again, as the urgency of need for still more goods declines, people's willingness to tolerate risks they have come to feel, but which they are unable to understand and appraise, also declines.

The attack on growth also reflects interests and feelings that transcend any appraisal of the direct benefits and costs of rising productivity. That is because its ability to generate the growth that people want is one of the main supports of capitalistic economy and bourgeois society. To an increasing number of people, that society lacks a moral basis, and others find its taste and style of life unattractive. People who hold these views and who, in one degree or another, have become members of an adversary culture, may then oppose growth for reasons whose real thrust is different from the considerations they advance. Their ostensible and sincerely held aim may be environmental protection or consumer safety. Their underlying, perhaps not quite explicitly formulated, purpose is to render less effective an economy and society which they find distasteful.[35]

An economy is a mode of social cooperation based on a system of rewards and incentives. The system may be regarded as just and legitimate or as unjust and immoral. The capitalistic economy, which relies on trade and markets to offer incentives and to determine rewards, found its traditional legitimacy in the Protestant Ethic and its view of work, thrift, and prudence, and both together as good in the eyes of God. The development of a highly complicated commercial economy and the emergence of large, bureaucratic corporations made the connection between work, thrift, and their rewards more remote and hard to discern. At the same time, the decline of the religious temper weakened the claim of work to be a mark of merit, to say nothing of

35. Irving Kristol and Daniel Bell have published compact elaborations of the argument in this and succeeding paragraphs. See their essays in Bell and Kristol, eds., *Capitalism Today* (New York: Basic Books, 1970); and also Bell's *The Cultural Contradictions of Capitalism* (New York: Basic Books, 1976), Chaps. 1, 2.

the claim of wealth itself to be a sign of grace. Indeed, the most sophisticated defenders of capitalism, such as Friedrich Hayek, have abandoned any contention that capitalistic rewards are proportioned to merit, as the following bears witness:

> Most people will object not to the bare fact of inequality but to the fact that differences in reward do not correspond to any recognizable differences in the merit of those who receive them. The answer commonly given to this is that a free society on the whole achieves this kind of justice. This, however, is an indefensible contention if by justice is meant proportionality of reward to moral merit. . . . The proper answer is that in a free society it is neither desirable nor practicable that material rewards should be made generally to correspond to what men recognize as merit. . . .[36]

Hayek's argument, one will notice, opposes a free society and a just society, and, as Irving Kristol has said: "men cannot accept the historical accidents of the marketplace—seen merely as accidents—as the basis of an enduring and legitimate entitlement to power, privilege, and property."[37] That the market's distribution of rewards and property may, in a generalized way, still be the basis for a wonderfully effective system of production and growth is, indeed, a powerful alternative justification. It is, however, only a pragmatic defense. It will not persuade those who are impatient with the merely pragmatic or those to whom distributive justice seems an attainable ideal or those who are, on other grounds, antipathetic to the bourgeois society which capitalism implies.

It is in this last regard that the attack on growth gains strength from tendencies in the contemporary culture. The culture in question is "high culture," that is, the feelings, sensibility, and style characteristic of leading circles in literature, the arts, and social criticism. This culture has for long been out of sympathy with capitalism and the bourgeois mode, as earlier references to Rousseau, Carlyle, Morris, and Ruskin have suggested. The bourgeois style is sensible, measured, steady, rational, functional, and optimistic. The high culture is expressive, romantic, tragic, heroic, idiosyncratic, and, more recently, anti-intellectual and instinctual.

The disjunction, to use Bell's term, between economy and culture gains in importance from the altered role of the adversary culture in contemporary society. In the nineteenth century, the adversary culture provided a refuge and living space for a tiny minority of eccentric spirits who had little connection with society at large. But the rise in

---

36. Frederick Hayek, from his *Constitution of Liberty* (1960), as quoted by Irving Kristol, "'When Virtue Loses All Her Loveliness'—Some Reflections on Capitalism and 'The Free Society,'" in *Capitalism Today*, p. 6.

37. Ibid., p. 9.

levels of income and education has permitted and encouraged a much wider segment of the population to consume and enjoy the products of high culture, to identify with it, and to adapt it to the tastes and intellectual capabilities of still wider circles. In consequence, the high culture has tended to meld into a "mid-culture." The exponents of the former have become contributors to journals of large circulation. Journalists, movie makers, television writers and producers, fashion designers, and the like have adopted the outlook of the adversary culture and become its translators to a broader public. The result is a conflict in the minds of a large and influential wing of opinion, which seeks its occupation and rewards within the capitalistic economy but is, at the same time, predisposed to attack and hamper its operation and to thwart its effectiveness.

The shift of opinion regarding the benefits of economic growth has been matched by a transformation in the process by which social decisions regarding growth are taken. Until very few years ago, such decisions were made without apparent conflict. They were largely the unconscious outcome of private choices about work and saving and about the technological innovations profitable to introduce and develop. Markets determined the value which the consuming public gave to these decisions and, by fixing the rewards they would carry, either ratified or vetoed them. Decisions, it is true, were not wholly private and market-controlled. Government in the United States was involved especially through its support of education and by its role in the development of transportation. In continental Europe and Japan, governments took a still more active part. Yet even in public decisions, debate did not turn on the desirability of growth but rather on the effectiveness of alternative policies and their cost.

The largely unconscious process which, especially in the United States, governed the pace and nature of growth has now been transformed into a political struggle. This is inevitable. The government is now so large that its taxing and spending activities, regardless of their direct and immediate objectives, have a significant indirect bearing on private choices regarding work, saving, and enterprise. It is inevitable also because the attack on growth is largely concerned with the diffused physical and social by-products of production and consumption. People seek protection against environmental damage and against health risks whose dangers they cannot appraise. They seek to guard their communities against the intrusion of more people or against commercial and industrial activity. In many spheres, the market cannot give people the protection they want, and in others they do not trust it to do so. The debate ranges very widely and connects matters as seemingly trivial to our environment as the fate of the notorious snail darter with matters as patently vital to economic growth as the provision of electric power.

It is an awkward fact that the political struggle over growth is necessarily carried on with little, if any, knowledge concerning the trade-offs that are involved. By way of example, we lack any way of measuring the values which people derive from and attach to various degrees of air or water purity. Nor can we say how much the achievement of such purity costs us in terms of future income. We are, indeed, beginning to measure the costs of compliance with government standards for waste disposal and the like. But no one knows how much future growth is lost because of the delays, expenses, and risks which the regulatory process imposes on investment and innovation. Nor can we know what importance people would place on the extra income which they are, in effect, losing.

This last issue is of special importance because even in countries as rich as America, there are still families who live on the edge of poverty and who would be lifted above it by the growth of average income. For many more, the skeptical views flowing from the "happiness surveys" can hardly be decisive. Progress, as Frank Knight, the great economic philosopher of the twenties, was fond of saying, is less a question of happiness than of what it is that people are unhappy about. Many, therefore, would strongly prefer the disappointments and frustrations of living at a higher rather than at a lower level of income, even if they could be persuaded that they would be no happier in doing so.

Beyond these continuing private interests in higher income, growth enlarges our capacity to deal with social problems. Engaged in fierce international rivalries for mortal stakes, growth is the basis for an adequate national defense. Committed, as in general we are, to a more nearly equal chance in life for the relatively poor and their children, it is politically more practicable to try to provide it from the fruits of growth than by redistributing a stagnant total income. Anxious, as we have now become, to guard ourselves better against the risks of work, product failures, and environmental damage, we look to the growth margin to pay the costs of protection.

The fact that the very size of government, the physical and social by-products of growth, and the social questions dependent on its pace and direction have thrust economic growth squarely into the political arena is perhaps the most important aspect of the present conjuncture. We must rely on a highly imperfect political process, with its confusing struggle of special and general interests, acting with inadequate knowledge, to adjudicate immensely complex conflicts of values. For the foreseeable future, therefore, our limited political capabilities may well be the most binding constraint on our ability to achieve a pace and direction of growth compatible with true human progress.

13

Can Technology Assure Unending Material Progress?

HARVEY BROOKS

INTRODUCTION

That the last three hundred years have seen a dramatic improvement in the material conditions of life for almost everybody on earth is open to little dispute. By measures such as gross national product per capita, average life expectancy, infant mortality, levels of education, or the quantity and quality of housing per capita, life has been getting better. If it is disputed whether or not these material measures represent progress, it is not the facts themselves that are in question but their interpretation. The critics of material progress question whether, in the forms in which it has occurred, it represents a net improvement in the human condition or an increase in the sum of human happiness. They point to the fact that material gains have been unevenly distributed, that economic growth has produced luxuries for a minority while generating barely perceptible improvements for as much as a third of the human population. At the same time, progress in agriculture and public health has helped to produce a population explosion. Communications and transportation have created a revolution of rising, and unrealizable, expectations. Sophisticated technology has resulted in the proliferation of weapons of mass destruction. This last promises to make even the material progress that has been achieved quite ephemeral and to render ultimate collapse of world civilization highly likely.

Nonetheless, the purpose of this essay is to assess the prospects for continuing material progress, taking for granted that, other things being equal, "material" progress constitutes "true" progress. Other essays in this volume deal with the relation of material progress to moral and cultural progress and to the sum of human happiness. I will deal with such issues only to the extent that deterioration of the moral and cultural milieu may threaten the conditions for continued material progress itself.

There is little doubt that progress in science and technology goes hand in hand with material progress. The overwhelming evidence from economic studies of the last twenty years establishes that between 25 and 75 percent of the economic growth in the industrialized world is accounted for by factors other than labor, material, and capital inputs to the production process, and these factors are generally identified with the increase in knowledge and its embodiment in improved quality of the factors of production, including the "human capital" represented by management and labor.[1] Again the precise interpretation of this "residual factor" and its relationship to conventional research and development are frequently disputed, but that technological and managerial innovation are together the main sources of growth is not in doubt. Thus, I assume that technical progress is the main engine of economic growth and that its continuation, however defined, is a prerequisite for the continuation of this growth and for the overcoming of any constraints to growth that may otherwise be posed by the natural world. This means that science and technology are *necessary* conditions for material progress, though they are not necessarily *sufficient*. In fact, the major issue for the future is whether the social conditions and attitudes produced by material progress are incompatible with the conditions for creating technical progress and hence with continued growth.[2]

From the beginning of the postwar European recovery in 1948 to the Arab oil embargo in 1973, the world enjoyed an unprecedented period of economic growth—unprecedented both in the compound rate of growth and in its continuity and lack of major interruptions. There were three driving forces for this growth: (1) the expansion of the world trading system and the trend toward free trade and a more efficient international division of labor, (2) the availability of abundant cheap energy largely from Middle East oil reserves with remarkably low production costs and from natural gas in North America and later in Europe, and (3) the rapid growth of scientific and technological knowledge and of the size of the technical community accompanied by rapid diffusion of their knowledge and skills through cheap transportation and communications. World trade and production by multinational enterprises grew at nearly twice the rate of world production as

1. U.S. National Science Foundation, *Research and Development and Economic Growth/Productivity*, NSF 72-303 Papers and Proceedings of a Colloquium (Washington, D.C., USGPO, 1971); see esp., Leonard L. Lederman, "Summary of the Papers," pp. 3-7.

2. See for example, Andrew Hacker, *The End of the American Era* (New York: Atheneum, 1970).

a whole. Expenditures on research and development grew at a comparable rate and were embodied in new goods and services. To be sure, much of this was for military or quasi-military purposes whose "spin-off" to the civilian economy is a matter of some dispute. Nevertheless, one indisputable spin-off from the military R&D (plus procurement) was the worldwide transportation and information network which greatly facilitated the diffusion of technology and the transnational organization of production and marketing. Inexpensive energy in easily usable forms, such as fluid fuels and electricity, stimulated the growth in productivity of both labor and capital, and it was these unprecedented rates of productivity growth, especially in Western Europe and Japan, which resulted in high economic growth rates worldwide and at an annual rate of 5 percent.

During the postwar period, there was rapid inflation and scattered commodity shortages. This led to a high level of concern about resources as a constraint on growth, expressed in such actions as President Truman's appointment of the Paley Commission in 1951.[3] This commission warned that the long-term demand for materials and energy might eventually outrun supply; but during the subsequent twenty-one years of high economic growth with declining materials and energy prices, the warning was quickly forgotten. The expansive mood of the period is well expressed in the report of the Interagency Energy Study commissioned by President Kennedy, which was published in 1966 under the title "Energy R&D and National Progress."[4] Its most striking sentence is the following: "Thus, rather than fearing a future day when fossil-fuel resources will be largely exhausted and the nation will want for energy, we are concerned for the day when the value of untapped fossil fuel resources might have tumbled because of technological advances and the nation will regret it did not make greater use of these stocks while they were still precious."[5]

Nevertheless, by the end of the 1960s warnings again began to be raised about the exhaustion of resources and the growing dependence of the United States on foreign sources of raw materials, especially oil. Could the momentum of growth be sustained, and if so for how long? World rates of population growth were still rising, with little prospect of tapering off, especially in the populous developing world, and it was clear, even to the greatest optimists, that this could not go on indefinitely. The question was whether the world was beginning to bump against the ceiling of resource and environmental constraints, or whether it still had time to make the gradual transition toward a

3. *Resources for Freedom*, Report to the President by the President's Materials Policy Commission (Washington, D.C.: USGPO, 1952).

4. In Ali B. Cambel, ed., *Energy R&D and National Progress: Findings and Conclusions* (Washington, D.C.: USGPO, 1966).

5. In Ali B. Cambel, ed., *Energy R&D and National Progress* (Washington, D.C.: USGPO, 1964), p. 55.

steady state, in which population and resources were in balance. Equally important was the question of what the material level of living corresponding to a steady state might be. The Malthusians were those who thought the time of reckoning was at hand and that the living level of the affluent quarter of the world's population was already well beyond what the globe could sustain on a long-term basis. The cornucopians were those who believed that technology would be able to surmount apparent resource and environmental constraints and bring about the necessary transition, ending in a material level for all mankind comparable with, or perhaps exceeding, that enjoyed in the most affluent countries.

THE LIMITS TO GROWTH DEBATE

The Malthusians got a shot in the arm from several events which followed each other in short order during the early 1970s. The Club of Rome, with unprecedented skill in disseminating its views, supported two studies, which resulted in *World Dynamics* by Jay Forrester, one of the fathers of the modern computer, and *Limits to Growth* by his disciples.[6] Their computer models of the world predicted a catastrophic increase in death rates throughout the world during the first decades of the twenty-first century largely as a result of resource shortages. And if resource shortages did not get us, global pollution would a few years later in an even greater catastrophe. The basic thesis was that the longer this catastrophe was postponed by "technological fixes," the more drastic would be the final collapse. These seemingly scientific predictions exercised a wide fascination among intellectuals, despite screams of protest from the economics profession, and a deluge of literature appeared on both sides.[7]

The impact might have died away had it not been for a series of events which occurred within two years of the appearance of the books. First came the Arab oil embargo in October 1973, followed by OPEC's success in raising the price of oil by 300 percent with the stroke of a pen. Coming in the midst of an overheated world economy, this rise precipitated an explosion of commodity prices, with spot shortages and panic buying. At the same time, there was a worldwide failure of the grain harvest in 1974 and a rapid draw-down of grain reserves to historic low levels. Finally came a recession and unemploy-

---

6. Jay W. Forrester, *World Dynamics* (Cambridge, Mass.: Wright-Allen Press, 1971); Denis H. Meadows, Donella L. Meadows, Jørgen Randers, and William W. Behrens III, *Limits to Growth: A Report for the Club of Rome's Project on the Predicament of Mankind* (New York: Universe Books, 1972).

7. See H. S. D. Cole, Christopher Freeman, Marie Jahoda, and Keith L. R. Pavitt, *Models of Doom* (New York: Universe Press, 1973). For a full discussion of reactions to *Limits to Growth*, see Martin Greenberger, Matthew A. Crenson, and Brian L. Crissey, *Models in the Policy Process: Public Decision Making in the Computer Era* (New York: Russel Sage Foundation, 1976, pp. 141-46.

ment, the steepest decline in economic activity since World War II but accompanied, in contrast with earlier recessions, by rampant inflation, dubbed "stagflation" by the economists. All this seemed to confirm the dire predictions of Forrester and Meadows et al. about thirty years ahead of time.[8] At the same time, the environmental movement, which had been gathering force in the late 1960s, acquired sufficient influence to put a series of stiff new environmental laws on the books and to make "ecology" a household word among the U.S. public. Perusal of the preambles of some of these laws reveals the extent to which the new perspective of "limits" had penetrated into the political psyche. Conflict in the Middle East, environmental battles in the U.S. courts, the debate over the Alaska pipeline and over off-shore oil exploration on the Atlantic seaboard, the natural gas crisis in the winter of 1977, the coal strike in the winter of 1978, and finally the Iranian revolution of 1979 followed by further price jumps in crude oil kept resource issues constantly before the public. That this debate was largely confined to elites, however, is suggested by the fact that in 1976 nearly half the general public was unaware that the United States imported oil.[9]

The world models suggested four constraints on both population and economic growth. They were, in order of the times at which they were first expected to appear: (1) resources, (2) environmental pollution, (3) food, and (4) overcrowding. The models purported to show that as each of these constraints was partially removed by technology, the next one would result in an even larger catastrophe.

Resources

In this model, finite nonrenewable resources collide with exponential demand. The consumption of these resources must thus be regarded as only a transient episode in human history, a sort of binge that can last at most a century, starting from about 1900. After exhaustion of these finite resources must come either worldwide famine and deprivation or a transition to an indefinitely sustainable regime, stabilized at a level far below the material standard now enjoyed by the affluent populations of the world.

The critics of this picture point out the fallacy of the "spaceship earth" image that it evokes. In a spaceship, the stock of resources really is finite, and wastes are ejected into space. But on earth nothing is really lost; it merely become less accessible and can be recovered at a

---

8. For a lucid account of these events, see Edward R. Fried, "International Trade in Raw Materials: Myths and Realities," in *Materials: Renewable and Nonrenewable Resources*, ed. Philip H. Abelson and Allen L. Hammond (Washington, D.C.: American Association for the Advancement of Science, 1976), pp. 5-10.

9. Opinion Research Corporation, Highlight Report, 24(NTIS PB-261 165/5BA) (1976).

certain cost, provided sufficient energy is available, either through recycling of discarded materials or through extraction of lower concentration ores. The necessary energy, the critics argue, is available in several different forms, ranging from nuclear fission breeders to various forms of solar power.[10] Even more important, nonrenewable resources come in various degrees of accessibility and can be considered finite only if one specifies an upper limit to the cost one is prepared to pay to find, extract, and convert them to usable forms. Oil, for example, is available in the form of heavy oils, tar sands, and oil-bearing shales. It is much more expensive to extract from these sources than from conventional fields, but the total resource base is much larger. Similarly, large amounts of natural gas are believed to exist in Devonian shales and geopressured brines along the Gulf Coast as well as possibly in deeper geological formations than have so far been drilled. As prices rise with the depletion of conventional resources or as technology advances, these sources will gradually come into production. Similarly, iron and aluminum, two of the most commonly used metals, constitute more than one-quarter of the earth's crust and could be extracted, given the proper price and technology. With increased recycling, they could last essentially forever. Generally speaking, the extension of resources results both from new geological knowledge and improved exploration techniques and from advances in technology, which make hitherto uneconomic ores accessible to processing in an economically competitive manner. This last effect is usually more important than the first two in terms of the total new resources made available.[11]

Indeed, for most resources we now use, improvements in the technology of exploration, extraction, and processing have more than offset increased costs associated with lower-grade or inaccessible areas such as off-shore areas or the Arctic. Petersen and Maxwell have examined trends in real prices for a variety of minerals in the twentieth century.[12] They point out that these prices exhibit three phases: (1) a period of falling prices in the early stages of commercial exploitation, with rapidly increasing consumption stimulated by the discovery of new uses; during this stage technological advances in production and economies of scale resulting from increased production dominate the countervailing effects of declining grade or geological accessibility. (2) A period of stable prices with reduced consumption growth, a relatively stable end-use market, and with technological advances about offsetting declining grade and accessibility. And (3) a period of gradual but

10. See Douglas B. Brooks and Peter W. Andrews, "Mineral Resources, Economic Growth, and World Population," in *Materials*, pp. 41-46; and H. E. Goeller and Alvin Weinberg, "The Age of Substitutability," in ibid., pp. 68-73.

11. Brooks and Andrews, "Mineral Resources."

12. Ulrich Petersen and R. Steven Maxwell, "Historical Mineral Production and Price Trends," *Mining Engineering*, January 1979, pp. 25-34.

slowly accelerating price rise as declining grade or accessibility begins to outweigh technological improvements; in this stage the search for substitute resources based on more abundant raw materials tends to be intensified in response to price competition.

Petersen and Maxwell point out that most resources have barely entered the beginning of the third phase as yet. Because of the tendency of resources to be more abundant and more widely distributed as ore grade or geological accessibility declines, the rising price phase tends to be prolonged. Thus, for example, Häfele and his colleagues have suggested the oil production will tend to reach a plateau extending for as long as fifty years, with production from unconventional sources gradually replacing the declining production from conventional sources as production costs and prices gradually rise.[13] Substitute energy sources are also necessary, of course, to meet rising consumption demands so that oil gradually will have to be replaced, but the necessary replacement rate may be much slower than would be suggested by the conventional picture of a bell-shaped production curve for a finite resource which reaches a maximum as the resource is half depleted.[14]

In addition to the effect described above on the production side, as an economy becomes more mature, its resource intensity, defined as the ratio of resource consumption to real gross domestic product (GDP), tends to go through a maximum and then decline. Thus, steel consumption per unit of GDP is about half in the United States what it is in countries in an earlier phase of economic development. In Britain the energy consumption to GDP ratio reached its maximum in 1880 and is now about half of what it was then—about the same as in 1800. For the United States the drop has been about 40 percent. Since these declines are due to advancing technology, the peak of energy and resource intensity in presently developing countries will tend to be reached earlier in their development and be lower than it was historically in the countries which industrialized earlier; this is because the newly industrializing countries can take advantage of more recent technology and are not condemned to retrace the steps of the developed countries. This latter point is well illustrated in the case of Japan, many of whose industrial processes are 25 to 40 percent more energy-efficient than comparable older installations in the United States.[15]

The resource picture outlined above is supported by the history of many mineral reserves between 1950 and 1970. Reserves are defined

13. Wolf Häfele, A. M. Khan, and H. H. Rogner, "Geographic Diversity in Energy Supply and Demand," invited paper, First Arab Energy Conference, Abu Dhabi, March 4-8, 1979.

14. See M. King Hubbert, "Energy Resources," in *Resources and Man*, ed. Preston Cloud (San Francisco, Ca.: W. H. Freeman, 1969).

15. Umberto Colombo and O. Bernardini, *A Low Energy Growth 2030 Scenario and the Perspectives for Western Europe*, report prepared for the Commission of the European Communities, Panel on Low Energy Growth, July 1979.

as the total proven resource which can be produced with existing technology at existing prices. The known resource is already much larger than reserves, and there is also a large, undiscovered resource which can be inferred from general geological considerations. As technology improves or prices rise, uneconomic known resources are converted into reserves while the resulting stimulation to exploration locates undiscovered resources which are ultimately converted into reserves. There is little economic incentive to generate reserves that represent more than ten to twenty years of supply at current rates of consumption. For oil and gas in the United States, the reserve-to-production ratio is about ten years whereas in the world as a whole it is around thirty years, largely because of the size of the Middle East oilfields. On the other hand, because of the extent of coal deposits, the reserve-to-production ratio for coal is nearly four hundred years. During the 1950-1970 period, reserves of most minerals increased many times; in many cases the increase in reserves was more than the cumulative production during the intervening period. The reserve increase has been a factor of forty-five in the case of phosphates, a factor of six in the case of oil, a factor of thirteen in the case of iron, and a factor of four in the case of aluminum.[16]

When we compare the price of minerals to the earnings of labor during the twentieth century, we find an even more dramatic result. A day's wages buys eight times as much copper in 1970 as it did in 1900, six times as much iron, nearly thirty-two times as much aluminum, and ten times as much crude petroleum—still more than twice as much of the latter even after the latest round of price rises. In the early 1970s a day's wages could buy six times as much residential electricity as in 1945 and ten times as much gasoline.[17]

Geologists have criticized this optimistic picture by pointing out that many resources do not exist in a continuous gradation of ore quality or geological accessibility. The simplistic idea of a smoothly and monotonically rising curve of abundance versus price is an economic abstraction that is not well supported by geological evidence, especially in the case of the less abundant minerals such as uranium, chromium, manganese, or mercury, for which we are dependent on ore bodies having more than one hundred times the average concentration of the element in the earth's crust. The favorite example of the economists is copper, which indeed does appear to show a continuous distribution of ore grade versus abundance, but this seems to be not the most common case.[18] Where there are gaps in ore grade distribu-

16. Donald B. Rice et al., *Government and the Nation's Resources, Report of the National Commission on Supplies and Shortages* (Washington, D.C.: USGPO, 1976), esp. Chap. 2.

17. Ibid., p. 19.

18. There is still significant disagreement on this point. See Thomas S. Lovering, "Mineral Resources from the Land," in *Resources and Man*, pp. 109-34; and Brooks and Andrews, "Mineral Resources."

tion, there is much less certainty that market prices will provide sufficiently strong signals to induce timely investment in the finding and development of the less available resources. This is especially so because the lead times required for the development of the more exotic sources are much longer than for conventional sources, and thus the pay-back periods for both development and investment are greatly extended. The only alternative appears to be government planning and development of the more remote technologies. To some extent, this has taken place in such areas as breeders, fusion, solar energy, and synthetics, but the relative roles of government and private investment are poorly defined, and the criteria for setting priorities among government actions tend to be set more by political fashions than by careful analysis.[19]

A second criticism of the economists' model has to do with the effects of rising prices in a world characterized by very unequal income distributions. From a macroscopic viewpoint it is true that market prices should provide adequate signals to curtail consumption and find new or substitute resources or technologies and thus bring supply and demand back into equilibrium. But changing prices also have differential effects on different income levels and geographical regions and can even preclude access of the least advantaged groups to the minimum necessities of life. As the world population increases, the marginal product of labor may become insufficient to purchase enough of a resource to sustain life. For a whole country or geographical region changing relative prices of resources may preclude its earning sufficient foreign exchange to purchase the inputs necessary to keep its economy going in the long run. The late Emile Benoit has remarked rather wryly that "a famine that kills half the population would not be regarded as a food shortage, provided that there were no rationing or price controls and those who could afford it paid the free market price for food."[20] As an example, rising affluence in Europe, Japan, and the U.S.S.R. has resulted in increased per capita consumption of grain in the form of animal protein. The same has happened within developing countries in the growing middle class. This demand for what is an inefficient form of consumption (from a caloric standpoint) has raised the price of grain to the poor, frequently exacerbating malnutrition. In a somewhat similar manner the use of oil and gas in Europe, Japan, and the United States to generate electricity has helped to "tighten" the world oil market. The use of petroleum products in recreation vehicles or for chemical fertilizer on golf courses can also be cited as examples of demand for a scarce resource in affluent countries, which may decrease its availability to the poor. In each case a basic resource needed to sustain life has been converted to a more convenient form

19. Goeller and Weinberg, "The Age of Substitutability," pp. 68-73.
20. Emile Benoit, "The Coming Age of Shortages," *Bulletin of the Atomic Scientists*, 32 (January 1976): 7-16.

through the superior relative purchasing power of the affluent and thereby reduced its availability to the poor. In some countries, such as China and Sri Lanka, this dilemma has been met by rationing, that is, by ensuring the availability of certain basic minima at an affordable price.[21] Similar proposals have been made for energy in developed countries but have nowhere been implemented as yet. The difficulty with the rationing approach is that it does not increase total supply and may even discourage producers, at least in the absence of government subsidies to production. Thus, in a world with highly unequal income levels the price system can result in the absolute denial of certain necessary resources to a segment of the world population even when there is "enough to go around" in a basic physical sense. Yet unless other steps are taken to enhance total supplies, the rationing approach will eventually result in deprivation for all as population continues to increase.

Marchetti has attempted to show how, from a purely technical standpoint, the world could support a population of 10^{12} people.[22] Of course, it would be a far different world than we have today. Two-thirds of this population would live on artificial islands at sea, the other one-third on land at a density about five times the present density of the Netherlands. Structural materials would be based on aluminum, iron, and magnesium for metals since all of these are for practical purposes infinitely abundant in the earth's crust and can be increasingly recycled. Nonmetals would be combinations of the elements carbon, silicon, calcium, oxygen, and hydrogen, all of which are infinitely available, given sufficient energy. Ashby has predicted that in the twenty-first century, as the supply of alloying elements declines, alloys will be replaced by composites based on nonmetallic compounds made from abundant raw materials.[23] Energy use per capita is about the same as that in North America today, with the earth's heat balance maintained by regional albedo control, with not more than 0.1 change over any area. The energy source is some combination of nuclear (breeders or fusion) and solar. None of this requires implausible technical extrapolations from present technological knowledge, given sufficient time and the social discipline necessary to effect the transition. The latter is, of course, a very large condition. In fact, time may be the most serious constraint because to put in place the necessary infra-

21. For a comprehensive discussion of food policy in China, see A. Doak Barnett, *China and the World Food System*, Monograph 12, Overseas Development Council, April 1979.

22. C. Marchetti, *On 10¹²: A Check on Earth Carrying Capacity for Man*, Research Report RR-78-7, International Institute for Applied Systems Analysis (Laxenburg, Austria, May 1978).

23. See Michael Ashby, "The Science of Engineering Materials," in *Science and Future Choice*, ed. Philip W. Hemily and M. N. Özdas (Oxford: Oxford University Press, 1979), I, 19-48.

structure requires an enormous investment. Unless population growth slows down, savings from current consumption may be insufficient to generate the resources necessary for this investment (money or raw materials). What this suggests is that the resource dilemma is created more by the *rate* of population growth and economic growth than by the absolute size of the world population or the world economy at any one point in time. It is this rate of growth, both in gross world product (GWP) and in population, that is without precedent in human history and that thus makes the present human dilemma unique.

Environmental Pollution

The second Malthusian argument is that material progress will so pollute the environment as to threaten human health and the life-supporting properties of the biosphere on which human existence depends. There are really three separate issues involved here: (1) General chemical or radioactive contamination of the environment spreading outward from industrial and agricultural activities or other human activities such as transportation; this contamination creates a direct threat to health from chronic low level exposure, especially to novel chemicals or other sources of stress to which evolution has not adapted the human organism. (2) General deterioration of natural ecosystems due to the preemption of more and more land to human use, with resulting indirect effects on human health and well-being through loss of the genetic diversity on which we rely to maintain our monocultures for human support. (3) Changes in the global climate due to build up of CO_2 and other trace gases or aerosols in the atmosphere.

With respect to the first of these, it is hard to estimate the prospects because of probable progress in pollution abatement technology and because of the difficulty in separating real increases in environmental contamination from heightened public sensitivity to environmental quality. Indicators of public health such as cancer incidence do not presently support the general public perception of an epidemic of environmentally related diseases.[24] On the other hand, pessimists can argue with some plausibility that many environmental contaminants arising from human activity have built up rapidly quite recently, and because of the long induction periods associated with low-level chronic exposure, they have not had time to show up in gross health statistics. Local episodes of occupational exposure to asbestos and vinyl chloride monomer are cited as examples to indicate how large cumulative exposures can be built up before evidence of serious health effects becomes sufficiently widely accepted to generate defensive ac-

24. Robert W. Kates, "Assessing the Assessors: The Art and Ideology of Risk Assessment," *Ambio*, 6(5) (1977): 247-52.

tion.[25] Measurement of ground-water contamination from hazardous chemical waste dumps and some evidence of localized health effects attributable to human exposures from these dumps are taken as further warning signs.[26]

At the same time, more sensitive analytical techniques, combined with an enlarged effort in environmentally oriented research, have stimulated both expert and lay awareness of numerous potential hazards to health resulting from the release of novel chemicals to the environment. It is impossible to establish that the hazard is really serious to large populations in a gross sense, but it is equally impossible to prove that such a dire hazard does not exist, and even local effects can be serious for individuals though insufficient to affect gross statistics.

Thus, both the public and the scientific debates get stalemated on the value-laden question of where the burden of proof should lie with respect to the continuation or expansion of industrial activities ranging from nuclear or coal-burning utilities to the manufacture and sale of specific chemicals or pharmaceuticals. The problem is further compounded by the sheer multiplicity of substances, their chemical transformations within the environment, and their synergistic interactions in the human body.

By and large, I feel that this chemical hazard, serious as it may occasionally become in local episodes, is not likely to be a major constraint on future material progress or to be a source of abrupt deterioration of the human condition such as is pictured in the world models of Forrester and his followers. It is true that some forms of contamination, such as heavy metals and artificially radioactive elements, may be irreversible or reversible only at prohibitive cost. We are highly conscious of such a threat today because of our sudden realization of the large backlog of pollution resulting from older habits. Certainly we cannot hope to continue on the basis of past practices without courting eventual disaster. But from a broader standpoint, the environment differs little from other nonrenewable resources. As it gets used, its assimilative capacity is reduced, and it becomes more expensive to use cleanly, just as low concentration ores are more expensive to mine and process. The cost of mitigating environmental contamination may, in fact, temporarily slow economic growth as conventionally measured by diverting both research and investment to

25. "New Ethical Problems Raised by Data Suppression," FAS Professional Bulletin, 2(8) (November 1974): 1, 2, 3, 4, 6; A.K. Ahmed, D.F. McLeod, and J. Carmody, "Control for Asbestos," Environment, 14(10) (December 1972); "An Ounce of Prevention," FAS Professional Bulletin, 2(7) (October 1974): 1, 2, 5, 8.

26. Subcommittee on Oversight and Investigations of the Committee on Interstate and Foreign Commerce, U.S. House of Representatives, Ninety-Sixth Congress, First Session, "Hazardous Waste Disposal, Together with Additional and Separate Views" (Washington, D.C.: USGPO, 1979).

the defense of the environment instead of to increased production of privately marketed goods and services. However, in terms of more revealing measures of gross welfare, which we presently lack, the apparent slowing down of economic growth due to environmental efforts might be less evident. Environmental quality is just as much a social good as better housing or improved medical care, though it is not properly measured in GNP.

The more subtle phenomenon of indirect effects on welfare (as opposed to direct threats to human health), resulting from the deterioration of natural ecosystems, is more difficult to deal with. The ecosystems which comprise the biosphere are incredibly complex interacting systems, and we have little present capacity to predict the effect of disturbances of these systems engendered by human activity. The fear is that we may do irreversible damage inadvertently through the fact that our capacity to alter nature to our purpose progresses much more rapidly than our understanding of nature's complexities and hence of the ultimate effects of our alterations. There is no agreement, for example, on how robust the system as a whole is with respect to the size of the perturbations we are capable of making in the natural biogeochemical cycles. Are we dealing with a highly resilient system, with many internal compensating mechanisms, or are we dealing with a system that is in very delicate balance, where a relatively small change might trigger a shift to an entirely new and less benign stable state? We do not know for sure, but there are several historical instances, such as the deforestation of the Southern Mediterranean littoral, which suggest that human activities can produce major shifts. What we do not know is the extent to which simultaneous natural changes were also involved in these events.

One of the biggest fears for the future is the possible disappearance of the diversified gene pool from wild nature that we have used in the past as a source of breeding stock for new varieties of plants and animals that are more productive or more resistant to constantly evolving pests and pathogens. Thus wild nature may be thought of as constituting a huge genetic information bank, on which we may have to draw in the future to preserve the key monocultures on which the long-term sustenance of humanity may depend.[27] The other side of this argument, of course, is that with the advent of the possibility of genetic engineering, man may free himself from such heavy dependence on the varieties provided by nature.

There is also the question of the degree to which man is psychologically dependent on nature. Will the gradual separation of man from the "rejuvenating" effect of contact with nature eventually sap his

27. Harvey Brooks, "Environmental Decision-Making: Analysis and Values," in *When Values Conflict*, ed. Laurence H. Tribe, Corinne Schelling, and John Voss (Cambridge, Mass.: Ballinger, 1976), pp. 115-35.

creative energies, or is this fear a mere romantic nostalgia associated with the present phase of our cultural development?

The third issue, that of global environmental changes brought about by man, is more serious. Here the most obvious problem is the build-up of carbon dioxide in the atmosphere due to the burning of fossil fuels and its effect on global climate.[28] We are also beginning to identify other trace constituents of the atmosphere that are affected by man and may also change climate or change the stratosphere, or both.[29] These effects also have a long latency period; we could have irrevocably committed ourselves to a future effect before any contemporary change was measurable. For example, recent work suggests that the ultimate climatic consequences of a given level of CO_2 in the atmosphere may be delayed twenty years because of the thermal inertia of the oceans.[30] Similarly, the effects of fluorocarbons on the stratosphere are delayed by decades because of the long diffusion time from the troposphere to the upper stratosphere where photochemical decomposition and the production of the free chlorine that catalyzes the destruction of ozone occur.[31] Though most experts believe that radioactive wastes can be isolated from the biosphere until they have decayed to harmless levels, there is a fear that nothing can be done if the experts are wrong.

There is also a good deal of disagreement about the actual magnitude of the human consequences following from global climate changes or from worldwide radioactive contamination. Climatic change is not instantaneous. Its main effect will be on the productivity of agriculture in different regions, and some have argued that by the time it is serious, forms of food production not dependent on land or climate will have been developed.[32] Even the melting of the continental ice sheets would probably occur slowly enough so that human settlements could be moved. The predicted climatic effects of CO_2 will occur when man's technological capabilities are much greater than they are now. Progress in the efficiency of use of fossil fuels and the penetration of alternate energy sources such as nuclear or solar power may slow the CO_2 build-up enough so as to increase the opportunity for the development of new technical capabilities for adjustment. Again we see that, as in the case of resource depletion and other

28. Jules Charney et al., "Carbon Dioxide and Climate: A Scientific Assessment," report of an ad hoc study group on CO_2 and climate, based on workshop held at Woods Hole, Mass., July 23-27, 1979, Climate Research Board, NAS-NUR, 1979.

29. Stephen P. Budiansky and Michael B. McElroy, "Interactions of the Atmosphere and Biosphere," unpublished manuscript, 1979.

30. Charney et al., "Carbon Dioxide and Climate."

31. John W. Tukey et al., *Halocarbons:Environmental Effects of Chlorofluoromethane Release*, NAS-NRC, September 10, 1976.

32. C. Marchetti, "On Energy and Agriculture," *Options*, a IIASA News Report, no. 2, 1979.

forms of environmental degradation, the rate of material growth may be a more important factor than the particular level of material consumption.

Food

On balance, food seems likely to be the most serious technical problem for the world in facing the twenty-first century. Although world production of cereal grains has continued to grow faster than population, the economic demand for grains has tended to outrun production in many regions because of the increasing conversion of grain to animal protein. The world food system has become increasingly precarious and vulnerable to both natural and social disruptions, as is illustrated by the Sahel drought, the unprecedented depletion of world grain reserves in 1974, and also by the tragedies in Biafra and Cambodia.

The largest potential for increased grain production lies in populous developing areas such as Southeast Asia. This potential comes from increased inputs of chemical fertilizers, pest controls, and irrigation, combined with new seed varieties. Some estimates indicate that world food production might be quadrupled through a combination of agricultural development of new land and intensified cultivation of existing land.[33] However, it is unlikely that contemporary modes of agriculture can support a world population of much more than eight billion, taking into account increases in economic demand as incomes rise with industrialization.

There is also some doubt as to whether such increases in production are ecologically sustainable. They imply extensive monocultures in tropical climates, and we have little precedent for predicting the vulnerability of such systems to sudden infestations of pathogens or pests. The quantities of chemical fertilizers and pesticides involved are enormous although capital requirements are not unreasonable. Again, we have little precedent for evaluating the ecological effects of such massive chemical inputs.

As in the case of nonrenewable resources, food production is critically dependent on the availability of energy for cultivation, irrigation, and all the other necessary inputs for intensive agriculture.[34] It is possible that eventually present forms of cultivation could be replaced by entirely new methods that are independent of land, such as fermentation of fossil fuels, but in order for this method to make a major contribution to world food supply, an extraordinarily extensive development would be required. Closed-cycle agriculture, in which water and nutrients are recycled in closed systems powered by solar energy

33. See Sterling B. Hendricks, "Food from the Land," in *Resources and Man*, pp. 65-85.
34. See Marchetti, "On Energy and Agriculture."

inputs, is also a possibility but, again, long in the future.[35] Agriculture, as the oldest and most locally adapted of all technologies, may be the slowest to change. The adoption of more productive processes involves tens of millions of decisions by individual producers and the detailed adaptation of new technologies in millions of local situations. Agriculture is an area where the gap between technology demonstrated in experimental situations and that adopted by the average producer is likely to remain large.

The dramatic growth of cereals production in the last two decades has depended on the exploitation of basic knowledge that has been available since the 1940s. The "green revolution" was successful primarily because it was a "catch-up" phenomenon, possible in the context of the backwardness of indigenous agricultural research in most developing countries.[36] During the last few years a consensus has grown up that further major advances in agricultural productivity will depend increasingly on new basic knowledge. Many agricultural economists believe that there is currently a gross underinvestment in agricultural research worldwide, especially in more fundamental and advanced types of biological research relating directly to agriculture. One basis for this belief is the estimate that marginal economic returns to present agricultural research, especially in the international institutes, are much larger than returns to conventional investment.[37]

Overcrowding

The fourth limiting factor suggested by the world models is social. In the simplest version of this model, population density reduces birth rates and raises death rates in such a way as to reverse population growth.[38] In my discussion I would prefer to consider the "crowding" limitation as a surrogate for general social disintegration or for the growing human incapacity to manage the complexity by an increasingly technological and interdependent civilization. Complexity is a consequence of both population and affluence since both increase the number of interactions between individual decision-making units, which are not necessarily compelled to behave in a mutually consistent manner. In a simpler period, disaster could be localized; the world consisted of a large number of essentially self-contained systems so that, for example, social disintegration did not spread from one to the

35. Roger Revelle, "Let the Waters Bring Forth Abundantly," in *Arid Zone Development: Potentialities and Problems*, ed. Yair Mundlak and S. Fred Singer (Cambridge, Mass.: Ballinger, 1977), pp. 191-200.

36. Robert E. Evenson, "Comparative Evidence on Returns to Investment in National and International Research Institutions," in *Resource Allocation and Productivity in National and International Agricultural Research*, ed. Thomas M. Arndt, Dana G. Dalrymple, and Vernon W. Ruttan (Minneapolis: University of Minnesota Press, 1977), pp. 237-58.

37. Ibid., pp. 245, 253.   38. See Forrester, *World Dynamics*, pp. 44-45.

other. Economic development was based on local resources; when they ran out, the center of civilization shifted somewhere else. If the inhabitants of the Mediterranean shores destroyed their forests or if the Spanish aristocracy destroyed the basis of their wealth through over-grazing of sheep, there were other societies that could take over the continuation of material progress. Today a revolution in Iran can affect the whole world, serving as a focus for social unrest among a billion people and profoundly perturbing the world economy. The question is whether this vulnerability is balanced by other capabilities to quarantine the source of trouble or to design around it.

There seems little question that the problem created by resource depletion, environmental degradation, and the food/population balance can only be resolved through the deployment of new science and technology on a scale not hitherto achieved or envisioned. The growth of the world technical community in the last three decades ensures that the capacity to create the necessary science and technology exists. What does not exist is the capacity to mobilize this capability or to deploy the sociotechnical systems which it might create if mobilized. For almost any one of the physical problems created by population and affluence, we can envision a model of a solution and test it in principle on a small scale. What we cannot seem to do is to reproduce it in numerous copies on a large scale—a large enough scale to make a real dent on the problem to which it is a solution in principle.

A good illustration is provided by the current energy problem in the United States. The technical capacity exists in principle for drastic reduction in the rate of growth of energy consumption without adverse effects on economic growth or welfare. This can be brought about mainly through the replacement of present capital equipment and consumer durables by much more efficient models. In the case of buildings, for example, major energy savings can be realized on a relatively short time-scale by various simple retrofits.[39] It is true that this cannot be achieved overnight, and in total it will require a huge investment spread over decades. The problem is how this investment can be brought about when it involves literally millions of individual decisions by consumers, businesses, and institutions. Even if fuel prices and government subsidies or tax credits are such as to make these investments economically rational, it is uncertain whether they will actually be made or how much political compulsion would be necessary or acceptable to accelerate the adjustment. The temptation has been to depend more on the alternative of substituting new large-scale energy supply technologies, such as synthetic fuels or an expedited nuclear or solar energy program. This has the political advantage of being easier to manage because it consists of a relatively small number of discrete

---

39. Robert Socolow, "Twin Rivers Project on Energy Conservation and Housing: Highlights and Conclusions," *Energy and Building*, 1(3) (April 1978): 207-43.

large investments and hence does not appear to require the concerted actions of millions of individual decision makers. Although it is fairly clear that the solution of our energy problems in the United States and in the world will require both conservation and new supply technologies, it also appears that under present conditions the investment cost per unit energy saved through improved efficiency is lower than the investment cost for an equivalent unit of new energy supply which is secure against interruption.[40]

The supply route is also technically feasible, though more expensive, and it does appear to entail lower political cost under current conditions. The subsidy of supplies with tax money while limiting price increases through controls has been a popular policy in the United States until recently. It requires fewer changes on the part of consumers, and at the same time it can be paid for (or appears to be paid for) by higher-bracket taxpayers and hence has fewer redistributional effects than higher energy prices. But this policy has not succeeded, in part because our institutions have been unable to operate in a sufficiently concerted manner to plan for the supply increments required to compensate for lower prices. Problems of environmental regulations, of regional social disruptions, and of conflicting values regarding safety and risk seem likely to paralyze decision making on domestic supplies until events overtake us. The result has been rapidly rising oil imports, declining domestic energy production, especially of oil and natural gas, and improvements in energy efficiency which have been insufficient to offset the effects of an increasingly turbulent world petroleum market. Yet none of these effects is physically or technically inevitable. The energy supplies and the new energy conversion technologies exist, but politically we have been unable to take advantage of them.

One of the characteristics of affluent societies is the great increase in the number of individuals who wish to have a say in the social and technological decisions which they see affecting their lives. Fewer people regard government decisions or the workings of the economic system as external events to which they must adjust as best they can. Affluence also means that they can enjoy the luxury of divergent values and interests. At the very time that society is becoming more intertwined and interdependent and hence dependent on internally consistent collective actions, it is becoming even harder to secure the consensus necessary for such action. Too many interests have to be consulted. We have built in de facto veto mechanisms through expansion of the notion of individual rights and of the applicability of due process. Yet to give up these procedural safeguards for the sake of the consensus necessary for collective action in a technological society

40. FAS Council, "Conservation: Try it, You'll Like It," *FAS Public Interest Report*, 32(8) (October 1979).

may involve sacrificing the very values and principles which seem to constitute the justification and purpose of our type of society—the very ends to which our increasingly sophisticated technological means have supposedly been directed.

Moreover, what applies within the national societies of the democratic welfare states also applies increasingly to world society as well. Small countries that were once passive recipients of the impersonal decisions of the world market now claim sovereignty over the disposition of resources that are vital to the very existence and functioning of other countries. In the last three decades the world system of energy supply and consumption has become truly global, with 60 percent of petroleum and more than one-third of all energy resources moving in international trade. This is beginning to happen with other key resources, but there is no exact parallel to energy because the huge bulk of oil means that the cost of storing it is a large part of its economic value. Today the world depends on a global trading system which assumes the free mobility of key economic resources across national boundaries; roughly speaking, the richer the country, the greater this dependence. Yet politically we are living in a world of national sovereignties, with more than one-third of these key resources under the sovereignty of "have-nots." Furthermore, unlike the situation that tends to exist domestically, the "have-nots" are not content to calculate only their own economic self-interest; on the contrary, they are apparently willing to sacrifice economic self-interest to other goals, which the rest of the world often cannot understand.

CONCLUDING REMARKS

In summary, given continued scientific and technological progress and the capacity to embody such progress in new capital investments and new institutions, and given the continuation of a relatively free world trading system in which both materials and knowledge can move freely across national boundaries from where they are produced to where they can be used, there do not appear to be any fundamental physical or technical obstacles to continued material progress in the world. The question is whether these two "givens" can be assumed to continue into the indefinite future and whether the worldwide social cohesion necessary for them is compatible with the diversity of individual and group aspirations or, indeed, even with an equitable distribution of power and influence in the world.[41] In other words, the obstacles to continued material progress in the world are social, political, and institutional; they are determined not by the relations between humans and nature but by the relations of humans to one another. This is more than just the perversity of human nature; it may well be that what we regard in most of the world as desirable goals for the

41. Brooks and Andrews, "Mineral Resources," p. 46.

relations among humans cannot be reconciled with the necessities of interdependence and technological progress. We just do not know. One thing is clear: the rate of change may be the most important negative factor in trying to reconcile material and social goals, and this rate of change is paced more by the rate of population increase than by the absolute level of population.

14

Natural Resource Limits and the Future of Economic Progress

NATHAN ROSENBERG

The 1970s witnessed a drastic thinning of the ranks of those who professed a belief in the possibility of a continuation of rapid economic progress. The idea of progress, in the economic arena at least, has clearly fallen upon hard times. This is scarcely surprising in a decade dominated by commodity shortages, increasing concern over environmental pollution, an unprecedented escalation in energy costs, stagflation, and sharply falling rates of productivity growth. Surely under these circumstances only the most determined Panglossian would fail to make a drastic downward revision in earlier optimistic expectations concerning future rate of material improvement.

To discuss systematically all of the elements that played a significant role in this transformation of expectations concerning the economic future would be to undertake a major treatise rather than an essay. Consequently, I propose to confine my attention primarily to one dimension: the view that there is an inexorable constraint imposed upon future growth by the scarcity of natural resources. The concern over the adequacy of natural resources (including, especially, sources of energy) to sustain economic growth on "spaceship earth" was certainly one of the dominating reasons for revision of earlier more optimistic views during the past decade.

A CHANGE IN PERSPECTIVE

Not too many years ago a view seemed to be emerging in the economic profession—it was never sufficiently widely held to be called a consensus—that the Ricardian-Malthusian demons were finally being exorcised, at least as far as the future of the industrialized West was concerned. With respect to natural resources in particular, numerous studies suggested that they had been playing a role of declining importance within the favored circle of industrialized countries. There was of course the compelling evidence of the agricultural sector, which, as Simon Kuznets had authoritatively demonstrated, had declined in relative importance in all economies that have experienced long-term economic growth.[1] Within agriculture itself, the implicit Ricardian assumption that there were no good substitutes for land in food production had been belied by a broad range of innovations, which sharply raised the productivity of agricultural resources and at the same time made possible the widespread substitution of industrial inputs for the more traditional agricultural labor and land—machinery, commercial fertilizer, new seed varieties, insecticides, irrigation water, etc. As early as 1951 Ted Schultz called attention to the fact that Harrod, in his notable book, *Toward a Dynamic Economics*, published in 1948, entirely omitted land as an input in the productive process.[2] Although it is doubtful that many economists concerned with economic growth would presently wish to go that far,[3] a growing sense of agreement did emerge with respect to some weaker propositions. This became strikingly apparent in 1961 with the publication of a collection of conference papers in a volume titled *Natural Resources and Economic Growth*.[4] Although the contributors approached the subject from a wide variety of different perspectives, there were two propositions which recurred with striking frequency: (1) the pervasive influence of classical economics in its Ricardian-Malthusian variant had resulted in a vast exaggeration of the importance of natural resources and an overstatement of the constraints which they imposed upon an economy's development possibilities, and (2) the relative importance of natural resources is a declining function of development itself. Charles Kindleberger, for example, made what seemed like only a grudging concession to the economic significance of natural resources in the growth process: "It may be taken for granted that some minimum of

1. Simon Kuznets, *Modern Economic Growth* (New Haven, Conn.: Yale University Press, 1966), Chap. 3.

2. Schultz's article bore the significant title "The Declining Economic Importance of Land," *Economic Journal*, 61(244) (December 1951): 725-40. Schultz cites the following statement from page 20 of Harrod's book: "I propose to discard the law of diminishing returns from the land as a primary determinant in a progressive economy.... I discard it only because in our particular context it appears that its influence may be quantitatively unimportant."

3. Most of the growth literature of the 1950s in fact followed Harrod's practice in ignoring land and resources. Indeed, even the early measures of factor productivity simply lumped land together with capital.

4. J.J. Spengler, ed., *Natural Resources and Economic Growth* (Washington, D.C.: Resources for the Future, 1961).

resources is necessary for economic growth, that, other things being equal, more resources are better than fewer, and that the more a country grows the less it needs resources, since it gains capacity to substitute labor and especially capital for them."[5]

In a similar spirit, Harold Barnett and Chandler Morse drew the following conclusions:

> The Conservationsts' premise that the economic heritage will shrink in value unless natural resources are "conserved," is wrong for a progressive world. The opposite is true. In the United States, for example, the economic magnitude of the estate each generation passes on—the income per capita the next generation enjoys—has been approximately double that which it received, over the period for which data exist. Resource reservation to protect the interest of future generations is therefore unnecessary. There is no need for a future-oriented ethical principle to replace or supplement the economic calculations that lead modern man to accumulate primarily for the benefit of those now living. The reason, of course, is that the legacy of economically valuable assets which each generation passes on consists only in part of the natural environment. The more important components of the inheritance are knowledge, technology, capital instruments, economic institutions. These, far more than natural resources, are the determinants of real income per capita.[6]

Empirical data to support this mood of buoyant optimism, at least for the United States, were not hard to come by. According to one study, the long-term trend of the output of resources as a proportion of gross national product (GNP) declined drastically from 1870 on—from 36 percent of GNP in 1870 to 27 percent in 1900 to 12 percent in 1954.[7] The authoritative Potter and Christy study, *Trends in Natural Resource Commodities*, failed to show evidence of an upward trend in (appropriately deflated) natural resource commodity prices. The evidence between 1870 and 1957 certainly does not show any long-term upward trend, and the recent updating of the price data by Manthy does not suggest any drastic alteration in the long-term trend—at least not up to 1973.[8] Rather, the overall picture is one of a high degree of stability in

5. Charles Kindleberger, "International Trade and Investment and Resource Use in Economic Growth," in ibid., p. 172.

6. Harold Barnett and Chandler Morse, *Scarcity and Growth* (Baltimore, Md.: Johns Hopkins University Press, 1963), pp. 247-48.

7. Joseph Fisher and Edward Boorstein, *The Adequacy of Resources for Economic Growth in the United States*, Study Paper no. 13, materials prepared in connection with the Study of Employment, Growth, and Price Levels (Washington, D.C.: USGPO, 1959), p. 43.

8. N. Potter and F.T. Christy, Jr., *Trends in Natural Resources Commodities: Prices, Output, Consumption, Foreign Trade, and Employment in the U.S., 1870-1957* (Baltimore, Md.: Johns Hopkins University Press, 1962); Robert S. Manthy, *Natural*

the long-term trend of resource prices. There are numerous episodes of short-term price increases, but these are followed by subsequent declines. In the post-World War II period there was a sharp decline in natural resource prices until the late 1950s, then a period of considerable stability until 1971, after which there was a sharp upturn. Up until 1973, therefore, there was no clear evidence of a permanent departure from the picture of long-term stability. Finally, a study by William Nordhaus shows a pervasive downward trend in the twentieth century in the prices of the eleven most important minerals when these prices are compared with the price of labor (see Table 1).

TABLE 1
Relative Price of Important Minerals to Labor, 1970 = 100[a]

	1900	1920	1940	1950	1960	1970
Coal	459	451	189	208	111	100
Copper	785	226	121	99	82	100
Iron	620	287	144	112	120	100
Phosphorus	——	——	——	130	120	100
Molybdenum	——	——	——	142	108	100
Lead	788	388	204	228	114	100
Zinc	794	400	272	256	126	100
Sulphur	——	——	——	215	145	100
Aluminum	3,150	859	287	166	134	100
Gold	——	——	595	258	143	100
Crude Petroleum	1,034	726	198	213	135	100

[a]Values are the price per ton of the mineral divided by the hourly wage rate in manufacturing. Data are from *Historical Statistics, Long-Term Economic Growth, Statistical Abstract*.

SOURCE: William Nordhaus, "Resources as a Constraint on Growth," *American Economic Review Papers and Proceedings*, 64 (May 1974): 24.

Why should the future be totally unlike this past? Is there incontrovertible evidence that during the 1970s we suddenly and discontinuously entered a new epoch in the history of industrial societies? Such a view—that there are immanent limits to growth, which have been imposed upon us by nature—is now widely held. It is not one of the purposes of this essay to discuss whether there are, in fact, limits to growth. That is, in a sense, a trivial question. Of course there are

_____

Resource Commodities—A Century of Statistics (Baltimore, Md.: Johns Hopkins University Press, 1978).

limits to growth. The serious questions revolve both around the time specification attached to such assertions as well as the analysis of the process by which the system moves to its "end of growth" stage.[9] Just how far down the road are these limits? Is it, as some contend, within the life span of a new-born infant? Does the experience of the last decade really support the view that we have already entered the era of sharply defined, inexorable constraints? Just how binding are the limits?

Ever since the Arab oil embargo, of course, the energy problem in particular has become a central preoccupation. There are good reasons, both of a short-term and of a long-term nature, why we should be especially concerned over this particular resource constraint. Aside from the obvious fundamental importance of energy in general to an industrial society, energy is also the key to the solution of many other materials problems. This is so because a large number of basic raw materials exist in abundance in nature in low concentration ores, and their extraction as well as subsequent refining is heavily dependent upon energy-intensive techniques.[10] For this reason I will focus primarily upon the energy problem and some of its ramifications.

THE EFFECT OF TECHNOLOGICAL CHANGE

Our concern with the adequacy of the natural resource base to support continued economic growth requires that technological change be introduced into the discussion as a central variable. Technological change is a multidimensional phenomenon. There are many aspects of it which we might want to emphasize depending upon the problem at hand. What, after all, determines the startling differences in the apparent technological *capacities* of different societies or of the same society at different points in its own history? Even the most cursory survey of the economies of the world would reveal truly astonishing differences in the capacity to *generate* or to adopt technological innovations. The rate of innovative activity, as we know, varies greatly from one country to another.

The aspect of technological change that I wish to emphasize, however, is not simply its rate but rather the manner in which technological change serves as a mechanism of *adaptation* to a world in flux. This aspect of technological change is peculiarly important in considering the relationship between the availability of natural resources and the prospects for future economic growth. The fact is that techno-

9. The same thing might be said about the Law of Entropy in terms of its implications for the growth process. Doubtless it imposes some ultimate limit to growth, but the urgency of this limit is far from clear.

10. To some degree the energy-intensive nature of low-quality resource exploitation must reflect earlier price regimes which dictated the substitution of fuel for labor. The extent to which this is so, and therefore the extent to which it may be possible to substitute capital and labor for energy in the future, is less clear.

logically dynamic societies use their technological skills to adapt to changing patterns of resource availability over time.

In an environment of rich natural resources, the adaptiveness of early American technology often consisted of searching out methods which were natural resource intensive—which substituted natural resources, wherever possible, for scarcer labor or capital. The characterization of nineteenth-century American technology as labor saving is common enough. It is less commonly noted that this same technology frequently had a resource-intensive bias. In fact, this was very often the case. In a country where natural resources were very abundant and labor scarce, it made a great deal of economic sense to search out technologies which substituted such resources for scarcer labor. Thus, Americans used far more wood, land, energy and other mineral inputs per person than their European counterparts in the first half of the nineteenth century. As economic growth and an expanding population eventually reduced the extent of this advantage, the technology also changed in a way that involved less intensive use of natural resources or shifted to a dependence upon more abundant resources.[11]

If we consider the past century or so, we find that countries with strong technological capabilities like the United States and Japan have been highly successful in shaping new technologies to suit their changing needs over time. Indeed, the ability to make these adaptations at a sophisticated level is primarily what distinguishes the highly industrialized countries from the rest of the world. Moreover, it has not mattered very much whether the technologies originated domestically or whether they originated abroad and were imported and subsequently modified. What has mattered historically is the capacity to use technological means to make the desired adaptations. In fact, in the case of two of the most spectacularly successful industrial economies, the United States and Japan, their earliest successes were achieved with technologies that had originated elsewhere. Both these economies have been exceedingly skillful at modifying and exploiting technologies regardless of their place of origin. In addition, they each made highly successful adaptations to very different kinds of factor endowments, the United States to one of resource abundance and labor scarcity and Japan to one of labor abundance and resource scarcity. Perhaps with respect to both countries we may say that the common underlying force was a powerful and pervasive social commitment to the desirability of economic growth. Given that commitment, each country eventually found a path appropriate to its own resource endowment.[12]

11. See Nathan Rosenberg, *Perspectives on Technology* (New York: Cambridge University Press, 1976), Chaps. 2, 14.

12. For a valuable and skillful comparison of the different historical paths of Japan and the United States in the agricultural sector, see Uujiro Hayami and Vernon Ruttan, *Agricultural Development* (Baltimore, Md.: Johns Hopkins University Press, 1971).

ENLARGING RESOURCE BASES

Our discussion up to this point has emphasized the adaptive aspect of technological change in dealing with natural resource scarcities. Such an emphasis captures an essential element of the historical impact of technological change in industrial societies. However, it is still excessively static in nature. It ignores the deeper point that a dynamic technology does not merely *adapt* to the resource base; in a fundamental sense, it redefines and enlarges that base.

Consider the case of energy. Industrial growth created voracious new energy needs. This involved not only an aggregate growth in the demand for energy but, perhaps equally important, it required energy with specific characteristics, or energy which could be delivered in certain forms. Thus, our discussion so far has been excessively static because it has not taken into account the fact that the expansion in energy use was not simply a *precondition* for industrialization. Rather, in a fundamental sense, these expanded energy sources were *creatures*, or *creations*, of advancing industrial societies. They did not exist in the status of "resources" in any meaningful sense *prior* to industrialization. Industrial growth created not only the incentive but also the capacity to expand the available energy base. It would be more appropriate to say that what was unique about industrializing societies was that they had developed a sophisticated capacity to respond in a creative way to their own emerging resource needs. Among their central characteristics were (1) a growing body of scientific knowledge concerning the physical environment and (2) an expanding technological sophistication which enabled them to devise new ways of manipulating the physical environment in order to achieve an expanded production of material goods. It cannot be too strongly emphasized that what constitutes a valuable resource at any time is, itself, a human artifact and not something which is intrinsic in separate components of the natural environment. Moreover, the definition of what constitutes an economic resource—as opposed to a mute fact of geology—is continually changing as a result of the interaction between the changing needs of an industrial establishment and improvements in human knowledge and technical skills. Ores containing a high uranium content were in no sense a part of the inventory of energy resources forty years ago. Again, as recently as the 1930s, natural gas was still regarded as an unavoidable and dangerous nuisance, which needed to be safely disposed of. Unless fortuitously there happened to be some markets nearby, it was typically treated as a waste material and flared —as it still is in some parts of the world. It required the perfection of the technique of producing high-pressure pipelines to transform natural gas from a waste product to our most attractive household fuel, a fuel which currently also plays a major role in many industrial markets and now constitutes a large fraction of our energy resources.

It is only in recent years that oil deposits on the continental shelf have become valuable resources as our capacity to deal with the formidable problems of off-shore exploration, drilling, and extraction have been drastically improved. But what it is easy to forget is that as recently as a century ago, when the oil industry had already been brought into existence, there was no awareness that oil represented a great new power source! The rapidly expanding search for oil which followed upon Drake's successful drilling through seventy feet of rock in Titusville, Pennsylvania, in 1859 was, in fact, a search for a new illuminant. Standard Oil Company was founded (in 1879) and developed its refining and shipping capacities in order to satisfy the compelling need for a more abundant fuel to be used in oil lamps. The early refineries were mainly producers of kerosene for lighting purposes. At that time it was the most volatile fraction of the oil—gasoline—which was treated as an awkward waste product that somehow had to be disposed of. It was only after the development of the internal combustion engine that gasoline was transformed from a waste material to a highly sought-after fuel. The ability to use petroleum as a fuel in turn gave rise to some highly complex problems in the refining process and in turn led to the development of an entirely new technology, beginning with thermal cracking in 1913, which made it possible to increase the yield of the most valuable fuels obtained from a given amount of the raw material. (The ability to alter the products by manipulating the molecules of the hydrocarbon raw materials in order to accommodate the particular needs of the market also marks the beginning of an entirely new industry, the petrochemical industry.)

Thus, even a casual glance at history forcefully emphasizes that the relations between energy and economic growth must be conceived of as dynamic and interactive. Technological breakthroughs are capable of putting natural resources to new and wholly unanticipated uses. Any long-term assessment of energy sources which is based upon a static view of that relationship is likely to be irrelevant in a technologically dynamic society.

The historical cheapness of energy in the United States has pushed the American economy in a highly energy-intensive direction. This energy-intensive thrust has been further intensified in a variety of ways, many of them the result of government policies.[13] The widely shared perception that the availability of power was closely linked with opportunities for more rapid economic and social progress has led to government subsidy of electric power to specific constituencies, as in the creation of the Rural Electrification Administration and the

13. Between 1960 and the Arab oil embargo in 1973 the growth in energy consumption accelerated to 4.1 percent—a rate substantially higher than the preceding post-World War II years. See Richard E. Balzhiser, "Energy Options to the Year 2000," *Chemical Engineering*, 84(1) (January 3, 1977): 73-90, 88.

Tennessee Valley Authority. Price controls and other regulations with the ostensible purpose of protecting the consumer have kept certain prices artificially low, as was most conspicuous in the case of natural gas. The imposition of acreage controls in agriculture served to reinforce the tendency, already strong, toward energy-intensive methods of cultivation—which would raise output per acre—especially with respect to fertilizer use. In the public utility sector, the electric power companies for many years attempted to influence the demand for their output by becoming aggressive salesmen of electricity-using appliances. Thus, the intensity of energy use in the United States reflects a trajectory which was developed in an energy-abundant environment as well as a combination of government and business policies which have had the effect—often deliberate—of intensifying that bias.

ENERGY SAVING IN THE PAST

What does our past history tell us about the possibilities for redirecting the economy in a more energy-saving direction, one which will shift us to a lower trajectory between energy use and economic growth? Perhaps the first and most important thing is that the question itself may be a dangerous one to ask if we repose too much confidence in answers based upon the present state of our knowledge. This is because our past experience with energy has been full of surprises, not only of unexpected difficulties but also of totally unanticipated opportunities, and that therefore any mechanical extrapolation of past trends or tendencies will almost certainly be misleading in some serious respects. It is terribly important to develop policies and programs which allow for the possibility—indeed the likelihood—of surprises and to maintain sufficient flexibility in our system to allow for the creative response to surprises.

In addition, the historical record in America tells the story of a pattern of adaptation in an environment where the economic pressures all militated in the direction of energy-intensive technologies, not energy-saving ones. How successful are we likely to be in moving in a new direction? One easy, initial response is that such a redirection is not likely to be successful without a restructuring of economic incentives which will make it worthwhile for individuals and organizations to move in this new direction. Although the market mechanism, if left entirely to itself, is not likely to provide a satisfactory solution to energy problems, such solutions are far *less* likely if they require people to behave contrary to the incentives of the marketplace. The historical record *does* consistently demonstrate a remarkable degree of technological dynamism. The problem is to develop new institutions and incentives that will harness this dynamism and direct it toward different goals.

Actually, the historical record does already provide much evidence of energy saving, especially in those industries where energy has constituted a large share of total costs. This includes, most obviously, the public utilities themselves. The cost, in terms of fuel, of a kilowatt-hour of electricity is far less than it was fifty or sixty years ago.[14] In the highly energy-intensive cement industry, although American fuel consumption per ton of cement is, as one might expect, considerably higher than in West Germany or Sweden, it was reduced by about 25 percent over the period 1950-1974.[15] In iron and steel, much of the industry's history has been taken up with the exploitation of innovations of a specifically energy-saving nature. In some cases these have been organizational as well as purely technological, as in the case of the integrated steelmill, which reduced fuel costs by locating the separate stages in steel production in close proximity to one another, thereby reducing the amount of fuel previously devoted to reheating. More recently, even the widely held view that mineral production will inevitably become more fuel-intensive as we move down the gradient toward the use of leaner ores seems to have been successfully challenged. Experience over the last twenty-five years with the pelletization of low-grade taconite ores (about 25 percent iron content) has made possible substantial energy (and labor) savings per ton of molten iron at the blast furnace compared with the older, more conventional techniques exploiting the naturally concentrated hematite and geothite ores (50 percent or more iron content).[16] The increased energy required for pelletization has been more than offset by reduced transportation costs and, more particularly, by the increased chemical efficiency of the blast furnaces. It is important to note that the recently acquired capacity to exploit taconite ores has resulted in a vast increase in this country's usable iron ore resources, which, as a result, are now far greater than they were twenty-five years ago.

THE NEW PESSIMISM

In view of such past experience, how are we to account for the pervasive pessimism which has come to dominate the discussion of economic

14. In 1920 it required slightly over three pounds of coal to produce a kilowatt-hour of electricity. By the mid-1950s this fell to less than a pound. During the 1960s there was a slight upward drift from a low of 0.86 pounds per kilowatt-hour in the early 1960s. In 1970 the number was 0.91 as compared with 3.05 in 1920. For additional data, including other fuels, see U.S. Department of Commerce, *Historical Statistics of the United States: Colonial Times to 1970* (Washington, D.C.: USGPO, 1975), Part 2, p. 826.

15. See Bo Carlsson, "Choice of Technology in the Cement Industry: A Comparison of the United States and Sweden," in Bo Carlsson, Gunnar Eliasson, and Ishaq Nadiri, *The Importance of Technology and the Permanence of Structure in Industrial Growth* (Stockholm: Almqvist & Wiksell International, 1978), Figure 4, p. 110.

16. Peter Kakela, "Iron Ore: Energy, Labor, and Capital Changes with Technology," *Science*, 202(4373) (December 15, 1978): 1151-57. Between 1954 and 1975, Kakela found, "The shift in ore technology toward pelletization produced net energy savings of 17 percent" (p. 1151). By 1975, pelletization or some other form of agglomeration was involved in over 80 percent of blast furnace activity.

growth prospects in the past several years? The ease and speed with which perceptions may shift is worth noting. In the post-World War II period up to the early 1960s, it was almost universally believed that the United States enjoyed some sort of decisive and unassailable technological superiority over the other highly industrialized nations of the world. Although the notion of a "technological gap" was never precisely defined, it was widely accepted that the United States possessed an unquestioned technological advantage and that this advantage was fraught with the most dangerous economic and political consequences for other countries, particularly those of Western Europe. At the very least, the view was widely held in Western Europe that only a drastic overhauling of political machinery would make it possible to face up to the "American Challenge," as J.-J. Servan-Schreiber characterized it in his widely discussed book, bearing that title, which was published in 1968. Failing some decisive action, Western Europe was destined to slip into the status of an American colony, totally dependent upon the United States for both economic and technological leadership.

The speed with which these dominating views were displaced by something approaching their polar opposite was breathtaking. Within a couple of years the view of American technological hegemony gave way to the view that the United States was being overtaken throughout a wide range of high technology exports by the burgeoning economies of Western Europe and Japan. By 1974 a distinguished American economist published an article bearing the somewhat ominous title "An American Economic Climacteric?" and proceeded to suggest an affirmative answer to his question.[17]

Are we just going through yet another of those recurrent cycles of pessimism that seem to have afflicted us at intervals in the past, or is there something genuinely new and different about our present state? There are many possible levels at which an answer to this question might be attempted. A mere economic historian cannot offer an explanation for the persistent tendency in our society to predict dismal futures quite different from a more illustrious past. He can, however, point to certain distinct ways of modeling reality, certain intellectual artifacts with which we attempt to probe the future. But I do not propose even to attempt to account for the popularity of such models or artifacts in the face of the abundant historical evidence which should cast them into instant disrepute. (It must be readily admitted that the last decade has not been the most spectacularly successful in our history. But neither, I hasten to add for the benefit of those under forty years of age, is it the first bad decade we have ever had.)

One dimension seems to loom very large in the differing assessments of the prospects for future economic growth. Optimistic assessments of future growth prospects are usually founded upon the con-

17. Charles Kindleberger, "An American Economic Climacteric?" *Challenge*, 16(6) (January-February 1974): 35-55.

ception of the economy as a social system with at least a substantial capacity for adaptation to changing conditions whereas pessimistic assessments are based upon models in which the capacity for such adaptation is either understated or ignored. Alternatively, the issue may be expressed in terms of substitution possibilities. The pessimists see no significant substitution possibilities for natural resources whereas for the optimists the elasticity of substitution of capital and labor for natural resources is very high. The Club of Rome model is simply one extreme end of this spectrum. It is, indeed, a model whose essential feature is precisely the *lack* of a capacity to adjust. Not only is there no technical change in the model, there is no process generating the discovery of new resources or new substitution possibilities, nor even the most rudimentary elements of a price mechanism to induce the substitution of abundant for scarce resources. That such a system soon encounters inexorable limits to growth should be neither surprising nor alarming.

Although the Club of Rome model simply excludes new technologies and other mechanisms that can generate adjustments, others recognize the existence of those forces but deny that they can serve as effective adjustment mechanisms. Many of those who view the future with deep alarm seem to treat both science and technology as totally autonomous forces, unlinked and unresponsive to social or economic considerations. Thus, Ezra Mishan has stated:

> Notwithstanding occasional declarations about the unlimited potentialities for social betterment science is not guided by any social purpose. As with technology, the effects on humanity are simply the by-products of its own self-seeking. As a collective enterprise science has no more social conscience than the problem-solving computers it employs. . . .[18]

In some important respects Mishan's view is not unrepresentative of the one which dominated almost the entire economics profession until very recently. With a few distinguished exceptions such as Marx and Schumpeter, economists neglected technological change shamelessly for generations. The subject has received extensive consideration only since Abramovitz and Solow awakened economists from their dogmatic slumber twenty-five years ago by calling attention to the great apparent quantitative importance of that phenomenon in the American growth process.

The more optimistic outlook of the economics profession seems to

18. Ezra Mishan, *Technology and Growth* (New York: Praeger, 1969), p. 129. Mishan's writings over the past ten or fifteen years constitute perhaps the most forceful statement of an antigrowth view, which has originated within the economics profession. It seems fair to say, however, that Mishan's writings are much more an assertion of his distaste for the consequences of economic growth than an assertion of the impossibility of the continuation of economic growth.

be due to two interrelated facts: (1) the greatly heightened awareness on the part of present-day economists of the historical impact of technological innovation, precisely the phenomenon which was so underrated by Malthus and Ricardo; and (2) the necessarily intense preoccupation on the part of economists with substitution possibilities. An awareness that any goal may be pursued through a multiplicity of means and that goals themselves may be redefined, modified, or catered to in functionally very different ways all militate in the direction of emphasizing the flexibility that may be latent in a dynamic economic system.

As a result, a curious reversal of roles has taken place with respect to the discussion of the possibility for future economic progress. Back in Malthus' time and after, it was the economics profession which was most prominent in expressing the view that there were sharp limits to the possibility for future economic growth. Indeed, it was precisely because economics had become so closely identified with a pessimistic outlook on man's future that the discipline earned the derisive description of "the dismal science." Malthus, it will be recalled, consciously wrote his famous essay as a refutation of those rosy predictions of future improvement which were given such wide circulation during the French Revolution. This is apparent even in the full title of the essay when it first appeared in 1798: *Essay on the Principle of Population as It Affects the Future Improvement of Society, with Remarks on the Speculations of Mr. Godwin, M. Condorcet, and Others.* Today, by contrast, the most prominent "Malthusians" are no longer economists. They are biologists, ecologists, systems analysts, etc. Economists are, by and large, much less alarmist and include the most forceful spokesmen for the view that continued economic growth is both possible and desirable.

ENVIRONMENTAL CONCERNS

Let us return now to the earlier question: How are we to account for the emergence of a widespread pessimism concerning the prospects for future economic progress? I will argue that several trends have been at work in the past ten or fifteen years, which, however they may differ in other respects, have had the effect of limiting the effectiveness of the mechanisms which have been largely responsible for the flexibility and adaptability of the economy in the past. Perhaps the most inclusive way of expressing the point is to say that we have been experiencing a broadening of goals and concerns, as a result of which the "alternative ends" which we seek have an ever-expanding non-material component. I am inclined to see this, at least in large part, as a product of growing American affluence. A sufficiently large proportion of American society has been attaining to income levels at which they are revealing a high-income elasticity of demand for "products" which were not previously on their shopping lists, for example, a nonpolluted environment.[19] However intrinsically desirable these other things may be, I merely want to insist that their attainment is costly in a variety of ways and that, as a result, the process of making adaptations to changing economic conditions has been subjected to additional and often very expensive constraints.

Consider the growth of the large constituency that is now intensely concerned with problems of pollution and the improvement of environmental quality, a concern which is now institutionalized not only in the private Sierra Club but in the public Environmental Protection Agency. Perhaps what is most astonishing about this movement from a historical perspective is that it took so unconscionably long in coming, and I cannot repress the speculation that the abusive manner in which Americans have treated their natural environment has been yet another inheritance of our historical experience in an environment of abundant resources. Everyone has his own favorite litany of the ways in which industrial man has managed to foul his own nest, and I will not inflict my own upon you. The present point is simply that a major concern over environmental impact seriously affects the speed and the cost with which we can respond to a sudden rise in fuel prices by strip-mining western coal, drilling for off-shore oil, or constructing a nuclear power plant. The requirement that utilities introduce stack gas scrubbers as a means of protecting the environment from sulfur dioxide emissions involves not only considerable cost but an array of additional complexities.[20] Further, government regulations, however well intentioned and even (perhaps especially) when they are effective in some important respects, are likely to have the result of increasing still further the uncertainties concerning the future, which can act as a serious deterrent to decisive action. The uncertainties over future regulatory directions are likely themselves to become an independent force discouraging innovation. Thus, much of the uncertainty in the development of nonpetroleum energy sources derives from a present

19. See Gerald Gunderson, *A New Economic History of America* (New York: McGraw-Hill, 1976): "In 1900, Americans said that the large cities were dirty, noisy, crowded, and unpleasant to live in, but that was the way they had always been. In the 1960s Americans said that the large cities were dirty, noisy, crowded, and unpleasant to live in, and the situation was intolerable and something should be done about it" (p. 451).

20. See Allen L. Hammond, "Coal Research (IV): Direct Research Lags Its Potential," *Science*, 194(4261) (October 8, 1976): 172-73: "It is no secret that the power industry has, to varying degrees, been reluctant to adopt scrubbers. The equipment is expensive—$75 to $125 per kilowatt, a substantial fraction of the cost of the power station itself. . . . Scrubbers also consume as much as 5 percent of the power output of a generating plant and introduce a whole new order of complexity, that of chemical processing, into the operation." Hammond also pointed out: "Despite the unresolved problems, stack gas scrubbing has much to recommend it—not least that it now appears to be a far cheaper way of cleaning up coal for power generation than conversion of the coal to a synthetic fuel" (p. 173).

lack of coherence in environmental protection regulations. Just how strict are safety regulations going to be for nuclear-power-generating plants? How restrictive will government regulations with respect to air pollution in urban areas be for the utilization of coal in electric power generation? When federal legislation is eventually enacted, how will it affect the costs of strip-mining operations? Will automobile emission standards be strengthened or relaxed in the future?

Thus, I am suggesting that the attainment of relative affluence in the industrial economies has led to an increased demand (through the addition of new arguments to individual utility functions or the greater subjective weights assigned to such arguments) for goods of a sort not previously demanded with much intensity, such as clean air and water, relative quiet, and other collective goods. As it happens, many of these new "goods" are inherently not amenable to provision through the market mechanism. Their public good nature entails governmental intervention and regulation. Now, the *fact* of this growing governmental regulation of certain private activities has, itself, generated substantial uncertainties for private business. The uncertainty is really a central aspect of what is in fact an adaptation process, which is being mediated through the political rather than the market mechanism. Such a process of the political achievement of certain goals through the detailed regulation of private market activity inevitably introduces its own peculiar lags, frictions, and distortions into the adaptation process, a condition that is further aggravated by the fact that the technologies for the achievement of these goals are not well specified.

OTHER DEBILITATING CONCERNS

Although environmental concerns have become very conspicuous since the 1960s, other concerns have also served to weaken our earlier, more single-minded pursuit of (a very narrowly defined) economic efficiency. Some of these overlap substantially with purely environmental considerations but nonetheless warrant separate recognition. I include here the emergence of a consumerist movement committed to the improvement of product safety. I include also the increasing assumption, especially on the part of government regulatory agencies, of responsibility for matters concerning public health and occupational safety. I would also include the multitude of ways in which questions of worker morale and job satisfaction are leading to a reorganization of the productive process in ways which may have important implications for economic efficiency. However laudable these goals are individually and collectively, their presence necessarily means that we have lost some degree of freedom in adapting to changing economic circumstances.

Another aspect of the new regulatory thrust into such matters as pollution abatement and occupational health and safety is that they have a very different incidence upon different industrial sectors. For example, a relatively small number of manufacturing industries, such as steel, industrial chemicals, petroleum refining, and paper, are likely to bear the brunt of pollution abatement expenditures. It will therefore be difficult to determine the eventual economic impact of such regulatory activities until this industry-by-industry impact is better sorted out and understood than it is at present.[21]

In attributing these recent "quality of life" concerns to a kind of inexorable working out of Engel's Law, I do not mean to suggest that this is the whole story but merely a very important part of it. I would not want to deny, for example, that the scale, power, and intensity of many new technologies have often resulted in objectively measurable, more disruptive ecological effects. On the other hand, it is also true that some highly pollution-intensive technologies have been displaced or have vastly declined in significance—horses and coal fires—and unfortunately we have no single, unambiguous index with which we can trace the overall rise or decline of pollution.[22] There is, however, a related and more subtle point. Improvements in scientific knowledge expand our awareness of interrelationships and therefore enhance our ability to perceive and to anticipate *possible* costs which *may* be associated with specific new technologies. Often these relationships cannot be firmly established because many of the putative consequences appear to be slow-acting but cumulative in nature. Thus, an improved but still highly imperfect understanding tends to be consistently biased in terms of raising our assessment of some of the possible costs involved in the exploitation of new technologies. At best, in many cases, we can make only probabilistic statements about the likelihood of an unfortunate event. Often we are confronted with situations concerning, for example, accidents, where the *likelihood* of the event is extremely small but the *consequences*, should the low likelihood event occur, are extremely serious: damage to the earth's ozone layer from the fluorocarbons in aerosol sprays, accidents at nuclear power plants, the unintentional development of new and highly pathogenic substances as a result of DNA recombinant research. Perhaps it is right to err on the side of caution, especially in those cases, such as aerosol sprays, where substitute methods are readily available; but it needs to be remembered that caution too may inflict substantial costs in terms of opportunities foregone or flexibility sacrificed.

As this discussion implies, problems are generated or intensified by the fact that some of our newly emerging goals are in conflict with

21. See John G. Myers et al., "The Impact of OPEC, FEA, EPA, and OSHA on Productivity and Growth," *The Conference Board RECORD*, April 1976.

22. There have been some highly successful instances of dealing with urban pollution, e.g., in Pittsburgh and London, but for some reason improvements do not seem to be regarded as newsworthy.

other goals. An increasing concern over safety or environmental pollution may lead to a slowing down of the rate of technological innovation, thus raising costs and slowing down the speed of response to changing economic conditions. Concern over limiting one set of hazards may lead, however inadvertently, to increasing exposure to another sort of hazard. In a broader sense, expanding the number of items on the public agenda leads to unavoidable conflict as the pursuit of one desideratum leads to measures that reduce the attainment of others. The legislation adopted in the early 1960s tightening FDA regulation of new-product introduction in the pharmaceuticals industry was clearly aimed at consumer protection. However, this legislation may also have had the effect of increasing concentration in the industry (because of the high fixed costs of the more demanding testing procedure), as well as reducing technological innovation, thus exacerbating two other market inefficiencies as a side effect of regulations ostensibly directed toward consumer protection. On the other hand, antitrust action against IBM and AT&T, in attempting to make the economy more competitive, *may* reduce the rate of innovative activity. More generally, our growing concern with equity has meant that an increasing number of social options are effectively proscribed because of possible unfavorable effects upon the distribution of income. Thus, the mere pursuit of an increasing number of goals, each one individually desirable, may be self-defeating or may, at the very least, involve far more serious trade-offs than we are presently aware of.

Consequently, whereas there is good reason to believe that the technological capacities at our disposal are sufficient to render the natural resource constraints to economic growth relatively tractable, it is more difficult to deliver a confident judgment about other dimensions of the problem. There is a distinct possibility that the addition of more and more items to the public agenda by an increasing number of interest groups will have the effect of blunting the efficiency of our economic institutions. Indeed, there is already a considerable body of evidence that this is now happening.[23] In one sense, what is at issue is

23. See, for example Edward Denison, "Effects of Selected Changes in the Institutional and Human Environment upon Output Per Unit of Input," *Survey of Current Business,* 58(1) (January 1978): 21-44. Denison has attempted to determine the effect upon the measured output of the economy of three categories of changes in the environment in which American business operates: (1) new requirements to provide greater protection against pollution; (2) new regulations dealing with the safety and health of workers; and (3) the rise in dishonesty and crime.

By 1975, the last year for which this article provides estimates, output per unit of input in the nonresidential business sector of the economy was 1.8 percent smaller than it would have been if business had operated under 1967 conditions. Of this amount, 1.0 percent is ascribable to pollution abatement and 0.4 percent each to employee safety and health programs and to the increase in dishonesty and crime. The reductions had been small in 1968-1970 but were rising rapidly in the 1970s. The increase in their size cut the annual change in output per unit of input from

a weakening of our commitment to economic growth and a growing unwillingness to suppress other goals and values in the pursuit of material improvement.

Almost 150 years ago, de Tocqueville made the following observation concerning American society:

> As they are always dissatisfied with the position which they occupy, and are always free to leave it, they think of nothing but the means of changing their fortune, or of increasing it. To minds thus predisposed, every new method which leads by a shorter road to wealth, every machine which spares labour, every instrument which diminishes the cost of production, every discovery which facilitates pleasures or augments them, seems to be the grandest effort of the human intellect.[24]

To a society as preoccupied as ours is with environmental impact studies, risk reduction, product and occupational safety, and distributional equity, de Tocqueville's observations have a quaint, anachronistic ring. And indeed there is much to applaud in the passing of a society to which such a characterization was appropriate. Most of us surely think it appropriate that a society which has attained a very high standard of material well-being should show an increasing concern with other aspects of human welfare than the narrowly material one and that we should deal in a more systematic way with some of the genuine costs of economic growth. The more difficult question is whether we will have the collective wisdom to modify our institutions in ways which will incorporate these relatively neglected concerns without at the same time destroying that complex balance of incentives upon which efficiency and growth depend. The evidence so far is not totally reassuring.

1972 to 1973 by 0.2 percentage points, the change from 1973 to 1974 by 0.4 percentage points, and the change from 1974 to 1975 by 0.5 percentage points. (p. 21)

How large are these magnitudes? Denison further observes:

> A reduction of 0.5 percentage points in the annual growth rate, the reduction reached by 1975, is equal to a large fraction of the growth rates that have been achieved in the past. For example it is equal to nearly one-fourth of the annual growth rate of output per unit of input from 1948 to 1969 (2.1 percent) and nearly one-fifth of the growth rate of output per person employed during that timespan (2.6 percent). The fractions are even larger if comparisons are made with more recent growth rates, which are lower for other reasons besides the impact of pollution abatement, employee safety programs, and crime. (p. 22)

24. Alexis de Tocqueville, *Democracy in America*, trans. Henry Reeve (New Rochelle, N.Y.: Arlington House, n.d.), I, 45.

15
Poverty and Progress

HOLLIS B. CHENERY

Dissatisfaction with the goal of material progress seems to be directly related to the level of income that a country or group has already attained. Thus, achieving the objectives of rich countries depends at least as much on other aspects of social change as on further economic growth. In poor countries, on the other hand, economic advance is viewed as the primary condition for achieving other basic goals and informs the ideology of virtually all types of governments.

Concepts of progress in the Third World are also heavily conditioned by its colonial past (see Young, p. 83). Many developing countries express their objectives in terms of "catching up" to the advanced industrial societies and pattern their economies on this model. This tendency is reinforced by political objectives in countries that wish to acquire military power and influence. The main alternative view of progress focuses more on achieving an equitable society and reducing poverty, with growth regarded as a necessary, but by no means sufficient, condition.

From a scientific point of view, the postwar experience of rapid growth in developing countries provides a rich body of data that is only now being studied. Since there is relatively little established theory to guide this analysis, the collection of data and the formulation of hypotheses have gone hand in hand. Although substantial progress has been made in understanding the economic forces at work, the results to date are largely speculative and fall considerably short of the needs of policy makers.

This essay explores some of the implications of the prevalent views of progress in developing countries in the light of the available infor-

I am indebted to Moses Abramovitz, Clive Bell, and Paul Streeten for helpful comments.

mation. I will consider in turn the dimensions of material progress, the main patterns of growth and distribution, and the possibilities for reducing world poverty.

THE DIMENSIONS OF MATERIAL PROGRESS

"Catching Up"

The concept of "catching up" to the industrial leaders is a product of the Industrial Revolution and its outward spread from Britain and Western Europe. This concept both provides a goal for social action and suggests a means by which this goal can be achieved. The technology and forms of economic organization created by the advanced Western countries have provided the means for accelerated growth to countries in all parts of the world. Nations following this model have differed primarily in their choice of the economic and social elements to be incorporated in their societies and of those that they have tried to avoid.

The phenomena associated with catching up were first noted in the history of countries of southern and eastern Europe. Alexander Gerschenkron has described "the spurtlike character of the past century's industrialization on the European continent" and the "pressures for high-speed industrialization" in terms that could apply equally to the recent history of Brazil, Turkey, China, or Korea.[1]

The prototype of a successful process of catching up is Japan, whose economic structure and income level in 1910 were not significantly different from those of the poor countries of today.[2] Econometric estimates of the sources of Japanese growth suggest that the process of borrowing technology from more advanced countries is now virtually completed and that Japan is likely to attain the income level of the United States by 1990.[3]

The Japanese example has had a powerful effect on Taiwan, Singapore, Korea, Thailand, and other countries of East Asia. All of these economies are growing considerably faster than those of the advanced countries, and some may be able to complete the transformation from a state of underdevelopment to one of maturity in less than the sixty years taken by Japan.

Several of these Far Eastern countries provide modern approximations to the earlier idea of progress as a process in which "good things come in clusters" (see Keohane, p. 39). Unlike most developing

1. Alexander Gerschenkron, *Economic Backwardness in Historical Perspective* (Cambridge, Mass.: Harvard University Press, 1962), p. 26.
2. See Hollis Chenery, Shuntaro Shishido, and Tsunehiko Watanabe, "The Pattern of Japanese Growth, 1914-1954," *Econometrica*, 30(1) (January 1962): 98-139.
3. Dale Jorgenson and Mieko Nishimizu, "U.S. and Japanese Economic Growth, 1952-1974: An International Comparison," *Economic Journal*, 88(352) (December 1978): 707-26.

countries, in Japan, Taiwan, Singapore, and Korea, the benefits of growth have been sidely distributed and the incomes of the poor have grown almost as fast as those of the rich. Many postwar governments have been growth-minded, though somewhat authoritarian, and these countries have ranked high on most indicators of social progress. In more typical cases—for reasons explained below—growth has been achieved at the expense of increasing concentration of wealth and income, and the poor have benefited much less.

In summary, the material success of the industrialized West has been a powerful incentive to the rest of the world to adopt elements of Western experience that are conducive to accelerated growth. The success of countries with different historical backgrounds and varying economic and political systems has served to reinforce this objective. The main differences in the ways developing countries view the idea of progress arise from the value that they place on other objectives, such as social equity, independence, and democracy.

Equity

Although the more equitable sharing of income features prominently among the political objectives of virtually all governments, it is taken much less seriously in practice than is the objective of rapid economic growth. Even though government intervention in production and income distribution is justified largely on the grounds of improving equity, most studies of the effects of government revenue collection and expenditure in developing countries show that on balance they favor the upper-income groups rather than the poor.

A few developing countries have gone beyond the endorsement of equitable growth and adopted policies designed to achieve it. Notable examples include China, Israel, Yugoslavia, Sri Lanka, India, Tanzania, and Cuba. Although their social goals vary with the form and extent of government control of the economy, there is a common emphasis on providing a minimum level of income to the poorest groups. In the more extreme socialist formulations, greater equity is considered a goal in itself even if it is achieved by lowering the incomes of the rich without substantially raising those of the poor.

A pioneering attempt to reconcile the objectives of growth and poverty alleviation in an operational framework was made in 1962 by the Perspective Planning Division of the Indian Planning Commission under the direction of Pitumbar Pant.[4] In this formulation the rate at which poverty can be reduced in India is determined by the growth of the national income and the extent of redistribution considered feasible

---

4. Indian Planning Commission, "Perspective of Development (1961-1976): Implications of Planning for a Minimum Level of Living," reprinted in T.N. Srinivasan and P.K. Bardhan, *Poverty and Income Distribution in India* (Calcutta: Statistical Publishing Society, 1974).

in the light of experiences in other countries. This approach has been refined in recent studies and forms the basis of the comparative analysis in the following section. If the idea of a feasible limit to the redistribution that can be achieved with a given set of institutions is accepted, the conflict between growth and distribution is reduced.

A further refinement in the concept of poverty alleviation has been achieved by shifting from an income measure of poverty to physical estimates of the inputs required to achieve minimum standards of nutrition, health, shelter, education, and other essentials. This "basic needs" approach provides a way of evaluating the effectiveness of any set of policies designed to reduce poverty.[5] It focuses particularly on the distribution of education, health, and other public services as a necessary aspect of poverty alleviation, an area in which some of the more effective socialist societies such as China now show marked improvement.

Reformulating Social Objectives

The social goals of developing countries—and of international bodies representing them—tend to be stated in political terms that confuse ends and means and ignore the different dimensions of progress. For example, the goal of catching up to more advanced countries is a poor proxy for improving welfare because it often leads to emphasis on heavy industry and other policies that concentrate growth in the modern sectors of the economy. Similarly, most of the goals announced by international agencies, such as attainment of given levels of nutrition, education, shelter, or industry, are misleading because they ignore the need to achieve a balance among the several dimensions of social progress.

The economist's answer to this problem is to replace a set of separate objectives by a social welfare function which defines the goal of a society in utilitarian terms as the increase in a weighted average of income or consumption of its members over time. Although the national income is one such average, the typical income distribution gives a weight of over 50 percent to the rich (the top 20 percent) and less than 5 percent to the poor (the bottom 20 percent). Maximizing national income, therefore, implies giving ten to twenty times as much weight to a 1 percent increase in the incomes of the rich as to a 1 percent increase in those of the poor.[6]

In principle, any set of weights could be applied to the income or consumption of different groups to remedy this defect. One possibility is to give equal weight to a given percentage increase in the income of

5. See Paul Streeten, "Basic Needs: Premises and Promises," *Journal of Policy Modeling*, 1 (1979): 136-46.

6. The implications of this approach are discussed in Montek Ahluwalia and Hollis Chenery, "The Economic Framework," in *Redistribution with Growth*, ed. Hollis Chenery (New York: Oxford University Press, 1974).

each member of society, which is the equivalent of weighting by the population in each group. A more extreme welfare function, which corresponds to the announced goals of a few socialist societies, concentrates entirely on raising the incomes of the poor and gives social value to increasing other incomes only to the extent that they contribute to this objective.

Although there is no scientific way to determine the appropriate welfare function for any given society, the concept is useful in bringing out potential conflicts in the idea of progress and in deriving alternative measures of performance. It will be used for this purpose in the following section.

LESSONS OF EXPERIENCE

Perceptions of the nature of progress have evolved considerably as a result of the varied experience of the postwar period. Many of the early postcolonial governments set forth optimistic objectives that now seem highly oversimplified. However, there has also been a notable willingness to learn from experience in countries with varying ideologies. Equity-oriented countries such as China, Cuba, Sri Lanka, and Tanzania have found it necessary to give greater attention to economic efficiency and growth, and some of the leading exponents of rapid growth—Brazil, Thailand, Turkey, Mexico—are now taking poverty alleviation more seriously

Although scholarly interest in these relations has expanded rapidly in recent years, the statistical measures needed to test and refine hypotheses are only now becoming available. Some of the recent results are outlined below in order to provide a better empirical basis for discussing the dimensions of economic progress. I will take up first the general tendency for early phases of growth to be unequalizing and then illustrate the effects of different strategies of development.

The Concentration of Growth

Twenty-five years ago Simon Kuznets addressed the question "Does inequality in the distribution of income increase or decrease in the course of a country's economic growth?" Although his answer was based on evidence for only a handful of countries and was labeled "perhaps 5 percent empirical information and 95 percent speculation," it has provided the starting point for empirical work in this field.[7] Kuznets hypothesized that the distribution of income tends to worsen in the early phases of development and to improve thereafter. This "U-shaped curve" hypothesis is amply verified in several recent cross-country studies based on samples of fifty or sixty countries.[8]

7. Simon Kuznets, "Economic Growth and Income Inequality," *American Economic Review*, 45(1) (March 1955): 1-28.

8. Montek Ahluwalia, "Inequality, Poverty, and Development," *Journal of Development Economics*, 3 (September 1976): 307-42.

There are several reasons for the incomes of middle- and upper-income groups to rise more rapidly than those of the poor. Development involves a shift of population from the slow-growing agricultural sector to the higher-income, more rapidly growing modern sector. In this process inequality is accentuated by more rapid population growth in rural areas and ultimately reduced by rising wages produced by more rapid absorption of labor in the modern sector.[9] The more capital-intensive type of development strategy followed by Mexico or Brazil absorbs less labor and produces greater concentration of income whereas the more labor-intensive forms of Taiwan and Korea distribute the benefits of modernization more widely. A number of other factors, such as the greater demand for skilled than for unskilled labor and the concentration of public expenditure in urban areas, also contribute to growing inequality in many countries.

My present concern is with the broader aspects of the relations between growth and distribution. How universal is the tendency of distribution to worsen in developing countries? Does it lead to an absolute decline in welfare for some groups? What kinds of policies have served to offset these tendencies? Is social conflict an inevitable concomitant of economic advance? Although none of these questions can be answered with great confidence, the average relationships and the variety of individual experience can be brought out by combining the available cross-country and time series evidence for the postwar period.

The average relationship between rising income and its distribution is best shown by Montek Ahluwalia's estimates of the Kuznets curve from data for all countries having comparable measures in some recent period.[10] Although Ahluwalia computed the variation in income shares separately for each quintile, the general phenomenon is adequately depicted by considering only two groups: the rich (upper 40 percent) and the poor (lower 60 percent). As national income rises from the lowest observed level to that of the middle income countries, the share received by the poor declines on average from 32 to 23 percent of the total. In a hypothetical country following this average relationship, 80 percent of the increase in income would go to the top 40 percent of recipients.

The relations between the income growth of different groups and that of the whole society can be brought out more clearly by expressing this relationship in terms of per capita income of each group. This is done in Figure 1, which plots the per capita income of the poor against that of the rich. Since the income level of the society (Y) is a weighted average of the two groups ($Y = 0.4Y_a + 0.6Y_b$), the downward

9. These relationships are discussed in *Income Distribution and Growth in the Less-Developed Countries*, ed. Charles R. Frank and Richard C. Webb (Washington, D.C.: Brookings Institution, 1977), Chap. 2.

10. Ahluwalia, "Inequality, Poverty, and Development," p. 311.

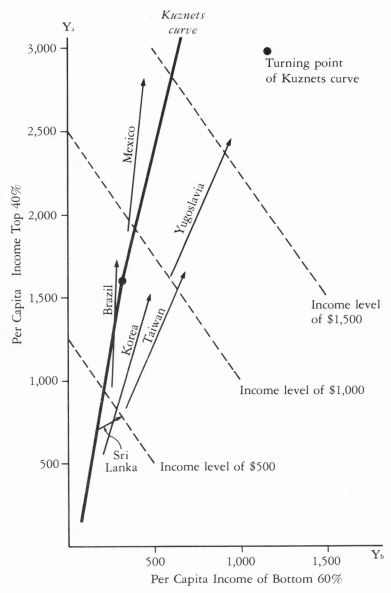

Fig. 1. The Kuznets Curve with Country Observations[a]

[a]The units are 1970 U.S. dollars of constant purchasing power, which in the poorest countries are between 2.5 and 3 times the per capita income converted at official exchange rates.
SOURCE: Montek Ahluwalia, Nicholas Carter, and Hollis Chenery, "Growth and Poverty in Developing Countries," in *Structural Change and Development Policy*, ed. Hollis Chenery (New York: Oxford University Press, 1979).

sloping straight lines define given levels of per capita income. Points on these lines indicate different distributions, making it possible to compare countries at the same level of per capita income. For example, the graph shows that Yugoslavia's per capita income of $1,000 is a weighted average of about $1,600 per capita received by the rich and $600 received by the poor. In Mexico, by contrast, the lower 60 percent had a per capita income of only $360 at the same national level and will only reach the Yugoslav or Taiwan levels when the whole society becomes much richer.

A growth process with a constant distribution is represented by a straight line through the origin, as in Yugoslavia. A vector deviating toward the vertical axis indicates growing inequality, as in the case of Mexico or Brazil. Conversely, Sri Lanka and Taiwan illustrate growing equality.

The Kuznets curve shown in this figure represents the average experience of all countries. It consists of two segments: a phase of worsening distribution up to an income level of about $800 and a phase of improving distribution thereafter.[11] In the first phase the per capita income of the rich grows from about $300 to $1,600 whereas that of the poor increases from about $100 to $300. For the poorest 20 percent, the rate of growth is considerably less. Since an increase in national income of this magnitude may take forty or fifty years even with the relatively rapid growth rates recently experienced in developing countries, in the typical country the very poor cannot look forward to an annual increase of much more than 1 percent—even though the economy is growing at two or three times that rate. Furthermore, there is nothing automatic about the improvement in distribution above $800, as shown by Mexico and Brazil.

The Varieties of Experience

Although acceptable time series data are available for only a dozen or so countries, they indicate a considerable variation around this average relation. Table 1 gives selected measures of overall growth and of the share going to the lower 60 percent for countries having observations for a decade or more. They are divided into three groups according to the share of the increment in income going to the poor. The five good performers show over 30 percent of the increment to the bottom 60 percent whereas the three poor performers show less than 20 percent. Whether distribution is getting better or worse is indicated by comparing these increments to the initial distribution and

11. This analysis is adapted from Montek Ahluwalia, Nicholas Carter, and Hollis Chenery, "Growth and Poverty in Developing Countries," in *Structural Change and Development Policy*, ed. Hollis Chenery (New York: Oxford University Press, 1979). The units are 1970 U.S. dollars of constant purchasing power, which in the poorest countries are between 2.5 and 3 times the per capita income converted at official exchange rates.

by the ratio of the growth of the per capita income of the poor to the national average.

This information, together with less complete data on other countries, provides a basis for describing the following patterns of growth and distribution:

1. *Growth-oriented pattern*, illustrated by Brazil and Mexico.
2. *Equity-oriented, low growth*, illustrated by Sri Lanka.
3. *Rapid growth with equity*, illustrated by Taiwan, Yugoslavia, and Korea.

These cases illustrate the main types of deviation from the average pattern that can be observed in the twelve countries of Table 1.[12]

These examples suggest the following observations on the relations between income growth and social welfare in developing countries. First, a small group of countries has achieved rapid growth with considerable equity. In addition to Taiwan, Korea, and Yugoslavia, it includes Israel, Singapore, and probably China. The policies underlying this successful performance vary from primary reliance on market forces in Taiwan, Korea, and Singapore to substantial income transfers and other forms of intervention in Yugoslavia and Israel.

Second, substantial trade-offs between growth and equity are illustrated by the other cases. Although Sri Lanka has grown much less rapidly than Mexico or Brazil, the poor have done considerably better in the former. Cuba presents an even more extreme trade-off since the welfare of the poor has risen despite a continuous fall in aggregate per capita income since 1960.[13]

In sum, it is only in the few cases where economic growth has been both rapid and fairly equitably distributed that it is possible to make unambiguous comparisons among countries—or among different development strategies for a single country. In other cases it is necessary to define some properties of a social welfare function to make such comparisons. To take two extreme cases from Table 1, the incomes of the poor have grown four times as fast over a decade in Sri Lanka as in Brazil whereas the opposite is true of the incomes of the rich. Since the latter receive greater weight in GNP, per capita income has grown 50 percent faster in Brazil; conversely, a population-weighted index of welfare increases 50 percent faster for Sri Lanka. Even this limited sample demonstrates that judgments about economic progress cannot be separated from social and ethical postulates. In general, it is not true that "all good things go together" although there is, perhaps, less conflict in the developed countries at the upper end of the spectrum.

12. Countries whose experiences closely follow the Kuznets curve are India, the Philippines, Turkey, and Colombia.
13. See Dudley Seers, "Cuba," in *Redistribution with Growth*, pp. 262-67.

TABLE 1
Changes in Income and Its Distribution

Country	Period of Observation	Initial Year	Total	Top 40%	Bottom 60%
			Income Level[a]		
				Increments	
Good Performance					
Taiwan	1964-1974	562	508	758	341
Yugoslavia	1963-1973	1,003	518	822	316
Sri Lanka	1963-1973	388	84	58	101
Korea	1965-1976	362	540	938	275
Costa Rica	1961-1971	825	311	459	212
Intermediate Performance					
India	1954-1964	226	58	113	21
Philippines	1961-1971	336	83	155	35
Turkey	1963-1973	566	243	417	128
Colombia	1964-1974	648	232	422	106
Poor Performance					
Brazil	1960-1970	615	214	490	31
Mexico	1963-1975	974	446	944	114
Peru	1961-1971	834	212	435	63

[a]The income level is measured by per capita income expressed in 1970 U.S. dollars of constant purchasing power.

REDUCING WORLD POVERTY

Attempts to extend the concept of material progress to a global scale run up against more acute problems of equity than the national issues described above. Although most governments recognize their national income as one dimension of national welfare, no one has suggested that global income has much relevance to an assessment of global welfare. Instead, political and economic efforts of international institutions are increasingly focused on the reduction of poverty and other aspects of equity as objectives that command the support of people of widely varying political views.

In recent years considerable efforts have been made to establish

Distribution			Growth Rates		
Share of Bottom 60%					
Initial	Final	Incremental	Total	Bottom 60%	Bottom ÷ Total
0.369	0.385	0.395	6.6	7.1	1.1
0.357	0.360	0.365	4.2	4.3	1.0
0.274	0.354	0.513	2.0	4.6	2.3
0.349	0.323	0.311	8.7	7.9	0.9
0.237	0.284	0.336	3.2	5.1	1.6
0.310	0.292	0.258	2.3	1.6	0.7
0.247	0.248	0.250	2.2	2.3	1.0
0.208	0.240	0.279	3.6	5.1	1.4
0.190	0.212	0.240	3.1	4.3	1.4
0.248	0.206	0.155	3.1	1.2	0.4
0.217	0.197	0.180	3.2	2.4	0.8
0.179	0.179	0.179	2.3	2.3	1.0

SOURCE: Montek Ahluwalia, Nicholas Carter, and Hollis Chenery, "Growth and Poverty in Developing Countries," in *Structural Change and Development Policy,* ed. Hollis Chenery (New York: Oxford University Press, 1979), Chap. 11.

measures of poverty based on standards of nutrition, health, shelter, education, and other basic needs. Conservative estimates of the proportion of the world's population that falls below a poverty line appropriate to conditions in poor countries are between 20 and 25 percent. Although this proportion has declined somewhat in the past thirty years, the absolute number of people below this poverty line has continued to grow and is currently on the order of 900 million.[14]

In technical terms, the reduction or even elimination of world poverty seems deceptively easy. If resources could be shifted to satisfying

14. World Bank, *World Development Report* (Washington, D.C.: World Bank, 1978).

the needs of poverty groups efficiently, it would require only a reallocation of 2 to 3 percent of world GDP per year to meet the identifiable costs of eliminating poverty by the year 2000.[15] Since three-quarters of the world's poor live in very poor countries, however, the annual cost of eliminating poverty in these countries is more meaningfully stated as equal to about 15 percent of their gross national product (GNP) even if expenditures could be designed to serve only the target groups. In the light of the distributional experience outlined in the previous section, the problem is seen to be vastly more difficult.

In order to think somewhat realistically about this problem, it is necessary to identify some of the principal constraints involved. These include: (1) the multiple objectives of nation states, among which the alleviation of poverty is usually subordinated to a variety of nationalistic goals; (2) the limited scope for resource transfers in the existing international economic order. Official development assistance from the Western industrial countries has declined from 0.5 percent of their GNP in 1960 to 0.35 percent or less since 1970. Transfers from the oil exporting countries, while substantial, do not offset the negative effects of higher oil prices on the growth of the oil importing developing countries; and (3) rapid growth of population, which will double in the next thirty-five years even though the rate has started to decline.

To determine the possibilities of progress in the face of these and other constraints, Ahluwalia, Carter, and Chenery have simulated income growth and numbers in poverty over the next twenty years for a large sample of developing countries.[16] A continuation of the trends of the past twenty years—a period of relatively rapid growth of income— would leave the number of absolute poor in 2000 at about the same level as in 1960. This represents rapid progress in one sense since the proportion of the poor would fall from 50 to 20 percent of the population of developing countries. However, since this result would be achieved only by a reduction in absolute poverty in middle-income countries that offsets the rising numbers in the very poor countries, it does not point to a long-term solution.

Improvements in this prospect will have to come from one of three sources: improved distribution, accelerated growth, or a more rapid decline in population. Improved distribution is particularly important in many middle-income countries, such as in Latin America, where income is quite unequally distributed, but some acceleration of growth is essential in the poor countries of Africa and South Asia. Although there are some short-term trade-offs between growth and distribu-

15. See Paul Streeten and Javid Burki, "Basic Needs: Some Issues," *World Development*, 6(3) (1978): 411-21. The authors estimate annual investment costs of $18 billion and operating costs of $30-40 billion for all developing countries. I have doubled these figures in relating the total to world income.

16. Ahluwalia, Carter, and Chenery, "Growth and Poverty in Developing Countries," Tables 3, 5.

tion, in the longer term it is more likely that all three types of policy will be mutually reinforcing. Even within restrictive limits to capital transfers, the OECD countries can considerably improve the outcome by giving greater priority to poverty alleviation in allocating aid among countries.[17]

These projections show that although the elimination of poverty is much more difficult than is sometimes suggested, it remains a plausible goal for international policy. One of the principal means to this end would be accomplished if the tendency of the poor to lag behind the higher-income groups in the process of development could be eliminated. Enough examples of how this can be accomplished have been cited in economic systems ranging from socialist to free enterprise to suggest that this is a feasible objective.

OVERVIEW

However disenchanted some in the advanced societies may be with the goal of material progress, it is being eagerly pursued by the less developed countries. The Western model of industrial development based on the transfer of technology and skills has provided a basis for accelerated growth in many countries. Its main drawback has been that the benefits of growth have usually been concentrated in the modern sectors of the economy, and increasing inequality has often led to social tensions.

Various development strategies have been tried to achieve a more equitable pattern of growth. The results to date suggest that success can be achieved under a wide variety of policies and that there is no single ideal model. However, the necessity for growth has been reaffirmed for the poor countries, even though it is only one of the conditions for material progress. Countries that have started out to improve equity have had to give greater emphasis to growth, just as growth-oriented policies have been modified to alleviate poverty more rapidly.

At the international level, there is an even greater difference between growth of world income and any plausible measure of material welfare. The tendency of the poorest countries to grow more slowly than others compounds the problem of lagging incomes of poor people within countries. As a result, there is increasing acceptance of the idea that international efforts should be more directly focused on reducing poverty in order to offset this tendency of the international system.

This conclusion leaves several fundamental issues unresolved. To what extent should poverty alleviation replace the principle of self-help as a guide to international action? To achieve this objective, will

17. The scope for reallocation is examined in John Edelman and Hollis Chenery, "Aid and Income Distribution," in *The New International Economic Order: The North-South Debate*, ed. J.N. Bhagwati (Cambridge, Mass.: MIT Press, 1977).

it not be necessary to establish enforceable standards of performance to assure that the benefits actually reach the poverty groups? The new emphasis on poverty alleviation does not resolve these old dilemmas in the field of international economic cooperation and may even accentuate them.

PART IV

Political and
Social Aspects

Although the linkage among science, technology, and material growth is clear and unambiguous in both the idea and reality of progress, only the more sanguine Enlightenment theorists viewed the linkage between progress and politics as positive and strong. Three essays in Part Four interpret the evidence on the historical relations of politics and progress, the first by Gianfranco Poggi on the state, the second by Aaron Wildavsky on public policy, and the third by G. Bingham Powell on democracy. A fourth essay, by Samuel Barnes, presents evidence on changing popular attitudes toward progress.

Gianfranco Poggi points out that the "modernization of the state" preceded the Enlightenment. The consolidation of rule and the imposition of a larger-scale legal-political order on smaller principalities was well underway in Western Europe several centuries before the Enlightenment. In its first phases, the modernization of political rule meant the enhancement of the capacity of rulers to extract resources from their societies for their own purposes and glory. The development of public policies intended to foster economic growth, as in mercantilism and in the introduction of the *Rechtsstaat* or the "rule of law," were in the first instance means to enhance the glory of kings, their successful conduct of wars, and the maintenance of an elaborate court life. Enlightenment philosophers viewed the state with considerable ambivalence, as war maker, as waster of resources, and as source and perpetuator of injustice. Progress has its locus and promise in society among the industrious bourgeoisie, the educated and the learned, and the inventors and technicians.

There was some accommodation between the state and the Enlightenment in the eighteenth century as "progressive" despots drew on intellectuals for advice in rationalizing their bureaucracies and public policies. An even greater accommodation occurred in the nineteenth century with the development of popular nationalism, which turned the state into an instrument for the accomplishment of social purposes—the provision of education, social welfare, and the like. In the twentieth century the state and progress became tightly entwined with the emergence of the welfare state in the advanced industrial societies; in the late-developing societies of Eastern Europe, Asia, Latin America, and Africa the state became the main provider of progress in the sense of creating and administering educational and research institutions and investing in and otherwise controlling the economy. Poggi concludes on this paradoxical note of the shift in role and character of the state from enemy or indifferent observer of progress to primary agent. Even more grimly paradoxical is the fact that this same nation-state which provides education and underwrites welfare is also the maker of war and now controls a military technology that can destroy the world.

Aaron Wildavsky's essay on public policy carries us into some of the problematics of the contemporary relationship between government and the public welfare in the larger sense. The growth of the state in scope and penetration—as the main supporter of science and education, the guardian of economic development, and the guarantor of welfare, equity, and justice—now tends to be viewed with disillusionment. Wildavksy attributes this disappointment with modern government to the "overcrowding of policy space." In the earlier phases of the development of the welfare state, income maintenance programs, health programs, educational programs, and the like had positive and measurable consequences. But as public sector expenditures have risen to higher and higher proportions of the gross national product, the effectiveness of these programs has been rapidly diminishing, taxes have been rising to ever-higher levels, inflationary tendencies have been building themselves into the economy, and investment in economic growth has been attenuating.

These unintended consequences and frustrations of public policy have tended to overshadow the substantial progress in public welfare through governmental intervention in recent decades. What seems to be the clear implication of this historical experience is that, close though the linkage between government and welfare may be, there are serious limits to the possibilities of governmental action in the elimination of social evils.

If the Enlightenment philosophers were skeptical about the relation between the state and progress, some of them were even more doubtful about the linkage of progress to liberal, democratic government. Historical experience confirms a strong relationship between progress in the sense of socioeconomic modernization and the political mobilization of those affected by it. The typical components of modernization—industrialization, urbanization, the spread of education, and increased exposure to the media of communication—unquestionably produce political mobilization, but this mobilization does not necessarily take the form of democratic participation. It may take the form of mobilized participation as in communist societies. Bingham Powell explores the relationship between socioeconomic progress and liberal democracy in logic and in reality, presenting the arguments for the mutually supporting effects of both socioeconomic progress and liberal democracy and then examining the empirical evidence. On the evidence of performance of democratic and nondemocratic regimes in the last few decades, he concludes that social progress seems to contribute to sustaining democracy and that democracy contributes to sustaining liberty and personal security.

But Powell also points out that in recent years doubt has grown regarding the mutually supportive relations of liberal democracy and social progress. On the one hand, the argument has gained resonance that as we move into an age of resource scarcity, political conflict will increase in intensity and threaten democratic stability. At the same time liberal democratic regimes are said to lack the kind of concentrated authority and will necessary to control conflict and to contain threats to productivity and growth. Although he sees grounds for concern about the continued connection between progress and democracy, he argues that neither logic nor evidence sustains a vision of the future of declining social progress and collapsing democracies. The essential discovery of the Enlightenment—the power of science and the promise of knowledge—holds out the possibility of a strong and positive connection.

Samuel Barnes, in his essay on changing popular attitudes toward progress, summarizes the evidence on changing values and attitudes in modern Western societies. In what respects do there seem to be changes in popular values and expectations of the future? The evidence of recent attitude surveys in Western countries shows a decline of optimistic expectations of the future and a shift away from material and security values and toward libertarian and "life quality" values, particularly among the educated and younger strata of the population. These value changes seem to be associated, on the one hand, with the attainment of a measure of material welfare for most members of Western societies and, on the other hand, appear to be accompanying the declining pace of economic growth. There is then some evidence that materialist values have been moderating and that an ethic of conservation has been spreading in Western societies, trends that are consistent with a declining rate of growth and the increasing burden of an industrial economy on the natural environment.

Thus, the political and social scientists represented in this book respond to the challenge of the scientists, engineers, and economists in earlier chapters, by arguing that the outcome is by no means foreclosed, that the potential for effective and humane politics and timely public policy is there, but that the progressive political adaptations and decisions of the past have been the easy ones. Those confronting us now and in the future are the really fateful and difficult problems of choice and adaptation.

16

The Modern State and the Idea of Progress

GIANFRANCO POGGI

In the long Western history of sustained, scholarly reflection on social affairs, the modern phase differs from the premodern chiefly in its rejection of the assumption that the course of historical events unfolds according to a divine, eternal design, which it is the task of the student to decipher. Rather, those events are assumed to be in principle contingent and as such to carry their own meaning (if any) within themselves; they establish that meaning as they take place rather than revealing a preexistent one. To adopt the incisive Marxian rephrasing of the old theatrical metaphor for sociohistorical experience, man is both actor *and* playwright. The world of society and man is produced by the (more or less) open-ended doings of men. History is as history does.[1]

This vision of a contingent, man-made historical reality, on the one hand, affirms man's dignity as a free, creative being. On the other, it evokes disturbing doubts over the meaningfulness of human events, anxiety over the destination of their course. As a consequence, various theoretical attempts are made to reconcile the contingency of man's doings with some assurance of the intrinsic significance of their outcomes, to balance that contingency with the steadying vision of some regularity and necessity hidden behind it.

Both the idea of progress and the dialectical conception of history can be seen as such attempts, and to that extent they constitute two more

This essay is dedicated to the memory of Paolo Farneti.

1. For this characterization of the broader assumptions of modern social thinking, see Charles Taylor, *Hegel* (Cambridge: Cambridge University Press, 1975), Chap. 1.

or less secularized, modern versions of the Christian notion of Providence.[2] Leaving aside the dialectic (with which it is in any case related), the idea of progress both attributes to men's doings a contingent leverage upon the contexts of their existence *and* contends that, over sufficiently lengthy periods of time, such leverages make a cumulative, positive difference to those contexts; they impart to history an identifiable and favorable direction; they perfect man.

In this essay I explore the bearing of this vision upon the construction and the evolving activities of the central institutional reality of modern, Western politics—the nation-state. I do not claim that the idea of progress made a strong, causal impact upon the story of the state. A cynic might suggest, in fact, that what is involved in the relation between the latter and the idea of progress is merely a matter of some thoughtful, sometimes self-important bystanders applauding what rulers had been doing on their own account, without much guidance from the idea of progress or any other vision, and at best advocating more of same. Though this view strikes me as excessively simpleminded, I shall sidestep the question it poses, of what difference if any the idea of progress made, and simply detail some apparent correlations (whether causally significant or not) between the evolving political implications of the idea of progress, on the one hand, and the main trends in the state's structures and activities over the last two centuries, on the other.

POLITICS AND PROGRESS:
EARLY TENSIONS AND THEIR RESOLUTIONS

It should be noted that the existence itself of any such correlations, the very possibility of a specifically political impact of the idea of progress, constitutes something of a paradox in view of the original ideological matrix of that idea. The latter originated as one aspect of the forceful vindication by the Western bourgeoisie, in the latter phase of the *ancien régime*, of the autonomy of the civil society vis-à-vis the state and was focused primarily on the realities of the former sphere.[3] Progress was seen to reveal itself, both as a past trend and as a promise of the future, first and foremost in the accumulation of scientific knowledge, then in the improvements of technique and in increasing wealth, then in the refinement of mores and manners and in the growing sophistication of artistic and literary taste, and only last, and least conspicuously and assuredly, in the advances made by legal institutions and by political arrangements.[4]

2. See Karl Löwith, *Meaning in History: The Theological Implications of the Philosophy of History* (Chicago: University of Chicago Press, 1949).

3. See Gianfranco Poggi, *The Development of the Modern State: A Sociological Introduction* (Stanford, Ca.: Stanford University Press, 1978), pp. 77-86.

4. Reinhart Koselleck, "Fortschritt," in Otto Brunner, Wilhelm Conze, and Reinhart Koselleck, *Geschichtliche Grundbegriffe* (Stuttgart: Klett-Cotta, 1977), II, 390ff. I have made much use of this excellent, compact presentation of the evolution of the modern concept of progress.

One might even say that the more visible political phenomena entered the vision of progress only negatively, by way of a contrast. Court intrigue, the vicissitudes and brutalities of war, predatory fiscal exactions, the cruel spectacle of public executions, the machinations of glory-seeking dynasts, "the law's delay, the insolence of office"—all those phenomena of the political sphere appeared as a backdrop against which better to descry the advances of science, the economy, and the arts of civilization. The tempo of progress, continuous and steady (or, in some views, steadily accelerating), was not that of political events with their discontinuities and their apparent repetitiveness. The subject and beneficiary of progress, increasingly seen as constituted by mankind as a whole, cut across state boundaries. The confidently proclaimed necessity and predictability of progress contrasted with the inherent arbitrariness of the central political experiences—war and law making—seen to depend on the brute clash of opposing forces and on the rulers' whim.

For all these reasons, in many of its early (and some later) proponents, belief in progress was associated with an antipolitical animus, an implicit or explicit unwillingness to concern themselves with the phenomenon of rule, or a preference for restricting its leverage upon social affairs at large. Yet for two reasons this original diffidence of progressive thinking toward the political sphere was bound to prove temporary and to yield to that series of meaningful correlations this essay explores.

First, it can be argued that over the few centuries preceding the emergence of the idea of progress, the beginnings and early phases of state building in most European lands had in fact constituted a massive, visible embodiment of the central experience later thematized as progress—the steady, quasi-necessary, ultimately constructive and beneficent cumulation of individually contingent and apparently unconnected acts of choice and sequences of events. Behind the revenges which *fortuna* randomly took upon the *virtù* of individual rulers, behind the vagaries of dynastic policies, the oscillations in the balance of power, the wearily repetitive spectacle of usurpation, depredation, cruelty and folly, enacted within and between polities—behind all this one could detect the steady pull of long-term policies imposed upon states by their own *raison*: the tendency to construct larger and larger political units, their increasing sovereignty; the secularization of political interests and discourses; the increasing cost of military conflict, hence the increasing size of the fiscal take and of military and administrative establishments.

Thus, the first reason for the later encounter between the idea of progress and the modern state lay in the fact that the early stages in the construction of the state(s) had constituted an embodiment of progress *avant lettre*. A second set of reasons has to do with some implications of the idea of progress itself, which over time confronted it with the phenomenon of rule as one to be reckoned with positively.

The first of these implications concerned the collective units concretely involved in the advance of progress, and the necessity that such units be somehow politically constituted and bounded. On the face of it, in the classical formulation of the idea of progress, progress was a universal phenomenon, having mankind as its subject and beneficiary; and mankind was a metapolitical entity. By the same token, however, it was also a kind of transcendental subject, whose unity was only morally postulated or was to be realized, if ever, only *in statu termini*, at the end of the historical process. More concretely speaking, mankind could claim the authorship (and the benefits) of progress only through the mediation of discrete, bounded sections of humanity: through a plurality of historically given collectivities, each endowed with distinctive resources and each burdened with distinctive responsibilities for fostering the progress of mankind at large by means of its own accomplishments.

In fact the proponents of the idea of progress widely assumed that such individual sections of humanity would differ not only in the nature but also in the timing of their contributions, that they would reach (or had reached) the peak of their accomplishments at different points in history. This assumption, in particular, inspired the adoption of the comparative method on the part of nineteenth-century theorists of progress. It was feasible to determine the trajectory of progress from *contemporary* materials only insofar as they referred to units located at different points on that trajectory.[5]

Now, if one sought to locate concretely those changing collective protagonists of the venture of progress and to identify the mechanisms which had made it (and were making it) possible for them to operate as distinctive units, one was brought up against the primary, or at any rate the very considerable, significance of political boundaries and of arrangements for rule. Even students whose cosmopolitan self-identification with wider, morally based communities (such as Freemasonry[6] or "the republic of scholars") made politically constituted and militarily guarded boundaries distasteful to them, could not deny that such boundaries marked off the various sections of humanity from one another with particular visibility, effectiveness, and finality; that over time such boundaries and the related political communities generated in separate populations an intense, cogent, often invidiously proud sense of their collective destiny.

To be sure, that sense could best emerge and could best sustain and inspire each population's unique contribution to the progress of mankind when it encompassed and mobilized other commonalities—of language, religion, ethnic origin, or folkways and mores. Yet, significant as such commonalities could be (particularly when they over-

5. See Robert A. Nisbet, *Social Change and History* (New York: Oxford University Press, 1969), Chap. 6.
6. See Reinhart Koselleck, *Kritik und Krise* (Freiburg: Alber, 1959).

lapped closely), one could not in their name gainsay the significance of a shared political existence, of the dependency on and the loyalty to a single center of rule. (The awareness of this lay behind the attempts made, especially in the nineteenth century, to bring about, in the name of nationality, a close correspondence between state frontiers and the boundaries of those commonalities.)

From this perspective, the idea itself of mankind as a universal subject could be seen as not so much negated and impeded by the political separateness of its parts as rather constituted by and resting upon their however tension-filled coexistence in the concert of nations, each capable of standing next to the others precisely to the extent that they were all politically bounded, protected, and unified. In any case, people entertaining the idea of progress or bringing it to bear upon practical public concerns were led to assume that the social processes they were dealing with, however prepolitical or nonpolitical in nature, took place within one or the other of a set of relatively extensive, unified, and internally fairly homogeneous political frameworks; that they presupposed a state operating, as it were, as the "container" of those social processes.[7]

Second, as I have previously suggested, most early formulations of the idea of progress saw in science the *locus electionis* of progress, where the idea of it seemed most plausibly and triumphantly applicable, where a constructive rationality, generated and controlled by public discourse, reigned supreme. By contrast, the sphere of politics, where questions were settled by the whim of the powerful or by the clash of arms and where as consequence critical events seem to take place randomly and unconstructively, appeared as the realm of human endeavor least amenable to progress.

This very contrast, could (and in effect did) suggest to imaginative and self-confident minds a way of bringing political phenomena within the scope of progress. If science was the progressive human experience par excellence and politics the least progressive, then the remedy might lie in bringing sustained, informed, rational thinking to bear upon politics, to enter and reorder the processes of rule. Instead of repeating Count Oxenstierna's bitter comment, "Knowest thou not, my son, by how little wisdom is the world ruled?" and abandoning politics to its erratic course, one could attempt to make the exercise of rule depend upon or even consist in the informed application of properly established and acquired knowledge.

Thus, a connection between "progress thinking" and the political sphere is mediated through the project of a scienticization of politics, on the threefold assumption that a science of politics is indeed possible; that once developed it would be acted upon, make a difference to

7. François Quesnay's *Tableau économique* (1758), for instance, explicitly and unproblematically treats the (French) state as the necessary framework of all processes of production of wealth.

political *pragma*; and, finally, that such difference would represent a positive advance from the vantage point of progress.

This is not the place to discuss the tenability of those assumptions. One may point out, instead, that the project in question did not appeal exclusively to well-meaning and/or ambitious literati seeking political effectiveness, such as for instance the Abbé de Saint-Pierre.[8] The project was put over sometimes from the *demand* side, on the part of tough-minded practitioners of rule, in order to make the exercise of it less wasteful, more enlightened, more predictable, and more responsive to the opportunities and challenges of the state system; less burdensome to the sovereign's subjects and more formidable to his enemies. Some among the founders of the Prussian *Kameralwissenschaft*, for example, were not self-important academics enamored with the idea of progress. They were in charge of the most sophisticated fiscal arrangements of their time, and in *that* capacity they were keen to pursue systematically and scientifically their felt concern to improve those arrangements further.

A final consideration helps explain why, in spite of their initial conceptual distance from one another, the idea of progress came to be brought to bear upon the realm of politics. So far, I have been referring to "the idea of progress" in rather undifferentiated fashion; but here one should note that it presented itself in two main versions, the Enlightenment and the romantic-historist version.[9] The latter—to draw on Hegel's overworked simile—is like Minerva's bird that spreads its wings at dusk and detects in the course of past events a direction toward progress which it does not impute to the intentionality of past actors and does not seek to impart to present and future ones. The Enlightenment version, however, was originally conceived as not just an interpretation *of* but a directive, a program, *for* history. It possessed an interventionist edge, a passion for purposeful realization, and an urge to validate itself through the positive services rendered to a wider reality to which it was finalized.

Those who forged or shared the Enlightenment view of progress were almost unavoidably led to look for a demiurge through whose agency those aspirations could be realized—and to find it in the state. Some of them merely sought to influence the established powers, others to seek power for themselves through constitutional or revolutionary means. In either case, they reflected the position formulated by Kant when he argued that in the German situation, "the advance toward improvement" could not be expected "through the course of things from below, but rather from the top down."[10] That is, they

8. The abbé saw as a central plank in his effort a "project pour faire faire à la Science du Gouvernement un beaucoup plus grand progrès en peu de temps qu'elle n'ait fait jusqu'ici"; quoted in Koselleck, "Fortschritt," p. 396.

9. Saffo Testoni, "Progresso," in *Dizionario di politica*, ed. Norberto Bobbio and Nicola Matteucci (Turin: UTET, 1976), p. 794.

10. Quoted from Immanuel Kant, *Streit der Fakultäten* (1798), in Koselleck, "Fortschritt," p. 399.

sought positively to harness rule to social tasks of intrinsic progressive significance.

We can at this point both summarize the argument so far and preview what follows. Although in its early formulations the idea of progress possessed an antipolitical animus or perhaps a studied indifference toward political phenomena, it contained implications which would sooner or later, more or less widely and openly, bring it to bear upon the phenomenon of rule and place the state within its focus of attention. The first implication is the awareness that mankind exists (as it were) in bundles, each tied together largely though not exclusively by political commonalities; hence, a tendency for progressive thinking to conceive of the state as a "container" of the social processes wherein progress is realized. Below, I characterize the resultant progressive impulse as the "consolidation of rule."

A second impulse is that of making the exercise of rule depend upon (or consist in) the application of an appropriate body of knowledge. I label this the "rationalization of rule." Finally, I characterize as the "functionalization of rule" the progressive tendency to employ the state as an instrumentality for the attainment of wider social purposes. In our century, this tendency culminates in the view of the state as the engine itself of progress, empowered to activate and direct the potentialities for progress inherent in nonpolitical forces, and where necessary to counteract those forces when they tend to impede, distort, or arrest progress.

Of course, these correspondences between, on the one hand, the implications of the idea of progress leading it to become focused upon the phenomenon of rule and, on the other, the processes of rule consolidation, rationalization, and functionalization, are intended purely as devices for organizing the argument that follows. Its arrangement suggests that those three processes succeeded one another; but also this suggestion is to be taken with caution, in view of the overlaps, conceptual and chronological, which obtain between those processes. Finally, I barely need mention that my discussion will be highly selective and is in no way intended as a properly grounded account.

CONSOLIDATION OF RULE

There are two main, overlapping aspects to the process I call the "consolidation of rule": the political units become larger, extend their radius of action over wider territories; also, they gather into one set of central institutions all facilities and faculties of rule previously dispersed among a plurality of semiautonomous political bodies. Most particularly, they vest into the political center the monopoly of the legitimate exercise of coercion. Associated aspects of the process are constituted by the fiscal, monetary, legal, and linguistic unification of the territory placed under the jurisdiction of each center of rule.

The consolidation of rule had long been under way in most European countries by the time the idea of progress developed, and political progressive thinking both applauded it in retrospect and, by and large, favored its further advance. Why, we may ask, did this trend deserve approval from the standpoint of progress?

It is easy to see the progressive significance of a given center of political rule enlarging its radius of action, whether by curbing the autonomy of a subordinate center of rule within its own territory or by adding new lands to the latter (two not always distinguishable processes, in the nature of the case). One immediate result is to diminish the number of interfaces, of points of contact and friction between competing power centers, along and around which armed conflict and disorder are likely to occur. Phrased otherwise, the consolidation of rule promises, in principle, to reduce the "turbulence potential" of the political environment.

Furthermore, whatever resources the "reduced" or "annexed" territory (and its population, of course) possesses that can be put to political use are likely to be more efficiently utilized when added to those already available to the strengthened center, if only because a smaller proportion of such resources need go toward the system's overheads. In other terms, there are potential economies of scale in running governments. Also, the variety (as distinct from the entity) of the resources now available to the center may be increased, with positive effects for the center's adaptive capacity.

On these and other accounts, insofar as there already are larger units within the political environment, there is a premium on each of the others increasing its own size in order to increase its ability to withstand the pressure and the challenge of the others. Of course, given the highly unelastic nature of the basic resources of land and population, a greater competition for these resources will also result; and this may more than offset, over the environment as a whole, the decrease in turbulence effected by the units' enlargement. However, in the eighteenth and nineteenth centuries, progressive political thinking seems to have assumed that once the disturbances arising from the realization of the principle of nationality were over, the resulting political environment would be less turbulent than one characterized by a great number of smaller units and where many territorial subunits maintained and managed autonomously some resources for coercion.

But from the progressive standpoint, diminished turbulence and improved resource utilization were not the sole advantages of the increased size and greater unity of states. The latter lay as great store by other, less direct (and less immediately political) implications of the same trend. For instance, the reduction of the autonomy of peripheral subunits generally deprived the corresponding local bodies of juridical norms and customs of their political support and, thus, of their effective chances of enforcement. This development was generally favored by progressive thinking on two counts. First, simply by being there, such bodies of rules hindered the application to the whole territory of uniform sets of legal norms; second, their narrow local base generally imparted to them a strongly traditionalistic make-up, a preference for vernacular, poorly elaborated and systematized legal principles. On the other hand, the norms issuing from the center of a wider juridical system are likely to be more systematically connected, formulated at a higher degree of abstraction, and to that extent more general, more responsive to change, and capable of standardizing the legal requirements and consequences of a greater number and variety of open-ended operations and transactions.[11]

In turn, these legal implications of the power center's increasing radius of action, together with other, related effects (such as that of clearing away the restrictions placed on the circulation of goods and people by the fiscal arrangements of the peripheral jurisdictions now eliminated) favor the formation of wider markets and the advance of the division of labor among the productive units operating in the territory. In other terms, they facilitate those processes of commercialization and industrialization of the economy, which in the eighteenth and nineteenth centuries found unhesitating (though not unqualified) acclaim on the part of progressive opinion.

One might point at many further positive consequences (some rather remote) of the increased territorial reach and unification of the systems of rule. It has been suggested, for instance, that the resultant "pacification" of European societies made illegitimate at least some manifestations of the previously quite unrestrained right of male heads of households to employ force against *their* womenfolk; and that in the long run this advanced the cause of female equality or at any rate "gentled" the relations between the sexes.[12] It can also be suggested that the very notions of public order and of citizenship (around which a great many further progressive advances were to be made) require that all private individuals be deprived in principle of legitimate access to means of coercion. (This at any rate is the European, and particularly the British, view, which I personally find more creditable than that embodied in the U.S. Constitution, affirming the right to bear arms.)

RATIONALIZATION OF RULE

During and after the process of consolidation of rule most European states undertook that of its "rationalization": that is, they developed constitutional and administrative arrangements which would make the exercise of rule more purposeful, dependable, and enlightened. Above, I have connected with the project of the scienticization of politics this undertaking because at its heart lay, as we shall see, the

11. See Giovanni Tarello, *Storia della cultura giuridica moderna, I: Assolutismo e codificazione del diritto* (Bologna: Mulino, 1976), Chap. 9.

12. See Randall Collins, *Conflict Sociology: Toward an Explanatory Science* (New York: Academic Press, 1975), Chap. 5.

intent of making *knowledge* (though not exactly "science" in the common English meaning of the term) inspire, direct, and control most activities of rule. This complex undertaking deserves attention because of its significance from the progressive standpoint. To point up that significance, let us characterize briefly the standard arrangements for the exercise of rule in the premodern Western polities of the feudal-patrimonial type.

In this kind of political order, facilities and faculties of rule were typically held and exercised by individuals and bodies as a matter of right, in the course and as an aspect of and as a means to the pursuit of their own interests. Those carrying out tasks of rule were expected to do so *if, to the extent that, and in the manner that* it suited them, at their own discretion, as an expression of their vested powers of disposition.

This did not mean, of course, that rule was exercised utterly at anybody's whim: it devolved, again, only upon those claiming a *right* to exercise it; and every such right had to be grounded in tradition, was limited by other concurrent rights, and had to be backed by a corresponding capacity for coercion. In any case, I repeat, the structural components of the system of rule were (differentiated, overlapping, often contentious, mutually limiting) *rights to exercise rule*. This applied at all levels of the system—excluding, of course, the populace, who possessed no such rights and were exclusively the addressees of rule.

Seen against this background, one basic aspect of the building of the modern state (and a key strategy in the rationalization of rule) consisted in shifting the exercise of rule from a right (or a privilege) to a *duty* base. This produced a system where at all levels (up to but generally excluding the very top) individuals and bodies holding and exercising facilities and faculties of rule do so as a matter of dutiful compliance with binding obligations, not as a matter of making use of their entitlements. Their activities do not in principle express and realize their own will in the pursuit of their particular interests but obey a will other then their own, serve interests higher than their own. The ultimate structural component of the system of rule has ceased to be a protected (because rightful) sphere of freedom, a quantum of private power of disposition; it has become a bundle of constraints and of directives. In principle, whoever exercises faculties of rule must suspend consideration of his own particular interests while doing so.

The significance from the progressive viewpoint of this "right/duty shift," as it can be labeled, is apparent. Right-based acts of rule are liable to be discontinuous, narrowly self-serving, and poorly standardized in their modalities and little predictable in their consequences for those affected by them. The relations between sets of such rights of rule held by different individuals or bodies are frequently a matter of contention to be settled through the appeal to obscure traditions and ultimately through the forceful confrontation of the parties. It is difficult to coordinate from above a plurality of such acts of rule into a coherent, comprehensive undertaking aimed at interests transcending those of the individuals immediately concerned. It is difficult to treat them as elements within a reasonably unified and homogeneous system of rule and to orient them swiftly and uniformly to emergent needs and opportunities.

Contrast with these liabilities of "right" the advantages of "duty" as the institutional basis on which to place authority relations. Duty-based acts of rule perforce depend upon directives, and these can make rule continuous and prompt in its operation, reliable in its consequences. Each act of rule can be controlled and corrected by comparing the directive authorizing or mandating it with the course actually taken by the act (or the omission of the latter). And as the directives themselves can be issued according to higher directives, the repetition at various levels of this form of control-and-correction can maximize the "top-to-bottom coherence" of the system of rule, which operates as a hierarchically ordered set of agencies.

Note that these advantages of placing the operation of the system on a basis of duty are increased when the directives orienting the individual acts of rule are not themselves ad hoc commands but are of a general nature (increasingly so as they relate to successively higher levels in the hierarchy) and when they are clearly stated, officially promulgated, and systematically related. They can then become the object of discursive, teachable, testable knowledge and, as such, be brought to bear upon activities of rule objectively and impartially. If, furthermore, the directives in question are changeable in content, they can activate in a consistent and predictable fashion huge numbers of duty-based acts of rule at the bottom of the system, making them, if necessary, observe new modalities, take into account the requirements of changing circumstances.[13]

These considerations lie behind the progressive preference for the organization of the system of rule and the regulation of its operations by means of laws and by-laws, the formation of which comes to be seen as the supreme expression of sovereignty. The elaboration and implementation of general, binding rules is intended to eliminate those features of unrationalized rule which progressive opinion castigates as the chief sins of the *ancien régime*: the covert nature of its decisional processes (the *arcana imperii*), the overreliance on tradition, on the one hand; arbitrium on the other.

Insofar as it expresses itself through laws, seen in turn as (in Montesquieu's phrase) "les rapports nécessaires qui dérivent de la nature des choses"[14] and in their dutiful application to individual

13. See Niklas Luhmann, *Legitimation durch Verfahren*, 2nd ed. (Neuwied: Luchterhand, 1975), pp. 141-50.

14. Quoted from Charles-Louis de Secondat baron de Montesquieu, *L'esprit de lois*

circumstances, rule opens itself to the controlling influence of knowledge. At any rate in their everyday aspects, activities of rule, motivated by the agent's devotion to duty, are oriented chiefly by the knowledge of norms and by the dispassionate ascertainment of factual circumstances. Rule is to operate primarily on the basis of *Einsicht und Gründe*, as Hegel says, that is, through informed and reasoned judgment. Thus, a phenomenon once seen by progressive opinion as characterized by arbitrariness, wilfullness, brutality, and partiality is seen to acquire the features of objectivity, impersonality, and rationality.

FUNCTIONALIZATION OF RULE

The consolidation and rationalization of rule produced, in the modern Western state, a political organism unprecedented in the amount and quality of human effort it could activate, in its ability to monitor and control a multitude of aspects of social existence of vast populations, in the regularity, continuity, and efficiency of its operations. But this very success of the state's century-long development, the enormity itself of the power potential now accumulated within it, made problematical the previous justifications of its existence and of its increasingly massive impact upon other aspects of social life.

In its earlier, patrimonial phase, the state's existence could still be justified as the expression of the ruling dynasty's greatness and as an instrument for the increase of its majesty and possessions. Later, the increasing saliency of the institutional, impersonal aspects of the state's structure and mode of operation discredited that justification and made credible another, according to which the state constituted an end in itself, and the aggrandizement of its power was the sole reason for its existence.

In the nineteenth century, progressive opinion began to find untenable this form of legitimation of the state. It was too abstract and potentially irrational; it generated too wide a chasm between, on the one hand, the realm of politics, which saw a few titanic protagonists—the states themselves—locked in a perpetual, demoniac struggle, and, on the other, the lived social experiences of the population, the concrete public and private concerns of individuals. The alternative, progressive mode of legitimation of the state's existence and of its growing effects upon the people's existence I term the "functionalization of rule." That is, political life is seen as but one aspect, no matter how distinctive and significant, of social life at large, one aspect which presupposes, *and is meant to serve*, a plurality of others. Thus, the state itself appears as but a set of differentiated structures among the many sets making up an increasingly complex society; its vocation has become purely secular, not just in the sense of making no

---

(1748), in Jürgen Habermas, *Strukturwandel der Öffentlichkeit*, 5th ed. (Neuwied: Luchterhand, 1971), p. 71.

reference to religious beliefs and rejecting any subordination to ecclesiastical authority but in the sense of relating rule ultimately to the matter-of-fact concerns and needs of concretely existent populations rather than to the abstract pursuit of power for its own sake.

By and large, this is still the dominant progressive justification of the state's existence (not valid, of course, for those sectors of progressive opinion which perceive the state as purely a partisan force or exclusively a de facto, unjustified, though inescapable presence on the social horizon). However, the progressive understanding of the entity to whose services rule is to be finalized has changed over time. In the nineteenth century significant advances toward the functionalization of rule were made in the name of the idea of the "nation." In view of the fact that today this idea has a bad name from a progressive viewpoint, I shall review the connotations it had from that same viewpoint over a century ago.

First, if we compare the concept of nation with that of the state itself as the potential beneficiaries (as it were) of the state's own activity, the former concept suggests a more comprehensive entity, richer in its determinations, the locus of a plurality of spontaneous, differentiated social processes. Second, a nation is conceived as an inclusive entity, embracing vast numbers of people and where in principle some measure of intrinsic significance attaches to every individual; membership in the nation (if one can so express oneself) vests in each individual a claim to some recognition of his/her dignity, an entitlement to some expression of solidarity and trust from others. Furthermore, a nation is perceived as a dynamic entity, which lives an open-ended, historical existence and whose destiny reveals and fulfills itself through ever-new shared experiences: a nation is always in a state of becoming. Finally, a nation is seen as possessing shared, irreducible interests of its own, transcending those utterly particular to each of its members in their private capacities. In this sense, by being conceived as a nation, a state's population ceases to be purely the object or addressee or, for that matter, purely the beneficiary of rule; it comes to be seen as possessing a political identity of its own, as being the constituent of the system of rule and its ultimate base.

In the nineteenth century, those progressive connotations of the idea of nation became institutionally embodied in the political structures characterizing liberalism, constitutionalism, and (increasingly) democracy. In their several ways, such structures established significant connections between a state's population and its government; they allowed the population to define those distinctive interests postulated by the idea itself of nation as a collective entity, and to bring those interests to bear upon the government's activities. This was the intended (and, to a considerable extent, the achieved) import of such diverse institutional innovations as military conscription, the expansion of the suffrage, the rise of public education, the adoption of "civil service rules" for the manning of state agencies, the publicity of trials and the involvement in them of juries, the constitutional consecration of civil liberties, and the emergence of party systems.

It can be fairly claimed that progressive thinking played a significant role in promoting those constitutional advances, though of course only in association with other causal influences, in particular those flowing from the growing commercialization and industrialization of the economy. But it is in the very nature of progressive thinking that it should treat past advances as signposts to further ones. Thus, by the end of the nineteenth century progressive opinion to a great extent had come to see the functionalization of rule to the interests of the "nation" as a partial and dangerous attainment. *Partial* because the entity in question was not secular enough; the idea of nation asserts the existence of a collective entity with interests irreducible to the concrete cares and pursuits (particularly economic ones) of living and breathing individuals; and in the process of identifying and celebrating such transcendent interests, it tends to generate mystical and volatile passions which ill agree with the increasingly sober and matter-of-fact progressive mentality. *Dangerous* because (often through the inebriating effects of such passions) the national idea tends to degenerate into nationalism and, thus, to heighten and sharpen the tensions inherent in interstate relations.

In our century, the basic progressive answer to that problem has been, in one word, "society." But since this term first acquired a political significance in the eighteenth century, one must point out the changes that significance has since undergone. The main elements of continuity between the early and the contemporary acceptations of "society" (though in the eighteenth century the preferred term was "civil society") are the following. Both assume the priority of *economic* interests and thus project a social reality whose main dynamic revolves around questions of exchange, property, technique, production, wealth, and security. Both, accordingly, treat conflict, or at any rate competition, as the primary mode of relation among a society's components, each conceived as primarily concerned to increase its own material well-being at the expense of the others.

Against these elements of continuity stand the following elements of *dis*continuity. In its eighteenth-century meaning, the notion of "(civil) society" conveyed a relatively restricted set of actors, those enabled by the possession of property and/or education to act autonomously and responsibly; whereas in the twentieth century "society" means the most comprehensive social reality possible, embracing all individuals, much as they differ in various significant capacities. Also, in the earlier imagery, society was envisaged as a plurality of individuals, at most connected with one another by impermanent, contractual ties; whereas today we conceive of society primarily as a manifold of groups, given visibility and permanence by large-scale, formal organizations. Furthermore, although, as I indicated, economic concerns (and conflicts) are perceived as central to society in both acceptations, today's society is seen to possess a much more differentiated structure, to be much more complex. Finally, whereas in the eighteenth century the "(civil) society" was conceived as a reality contrasting with or complementary to "the state," in the twentieth century the relationship between these two realities is one of increasing mutual interpenetration. Society is no longer viewed as a field of interests and activities intrinsically distinct from those of the political sphere, attended to and pursued by individuals purely in their private capacities. On the contrary, all manner of social interests are conceived, *as such*, as suitable for the state to regulate, direct, and foster.

This last point is central to the twentieth-century version of the functionalization of rule. The state is envisaged primarily as a facility through which the society can exercise leverage upon itself and promote social welfare. It is charged with the responsibility to serve the (national) society not just by regulating it as if from outside but by actively managing it, by positively directing its development.

Clearly, in order to perform these various tasks, the state must take on an active, interventionist posture since some inherent dynamic tendencies of the society are to be encouraged and supported whereas others need to be actively resisted. For instance, the increasing sophistication of productive technology, on the one hand, makes available increasing resources to be put (also) to political uses; on the other, it tends to exclude from active social participation large sectors of the population no longer or not yet capable of contributing needed skills to the economy—and this tendency must be countered or moderated by public policies reaffirming the comprehensiveness of the societal framework, validating the notion of citizenship in its generality. Forms of discrimination (for example, racial and sexual) rooted in prejudice and socially sanctioned must be challenged politically. The conflict of groups must be legally regulated and institutionalized; positions of pronounced social, economic, and cultural disadvantage must be corrected. Authoritative decisions and inputs of public resources must compensate for the market's inability to regulate the economic processes autonomously. The tendency for privileged social interests to acquire irresponsible social power must be monitored and kept from being abused.

In spite of its abstractness, this statement of the expectations placed upon the state by progressive opinion in our century suggests that the state, to become and remain functional to the society, has had to undergo vast and momentous structural changes. In seeking to build up its capacity to form and to carry to execution relevant and effective policies, the state has chiefly undergone the following closely associated developments: (1) an increase in the absolute and relative entity of the economic resources absorbed and allocated by state agencies; (2)

an increase in the total size of the state's administrative apparatus; (3) an increase in the internal differentiation and structural ramification of that apparatus. The state's internal layout, so to speak, has had to match the society's growing complexity; and (4) an increase in the amount and sophistication of the information on the most diverse societal developments made available to and acted upon by the state; hence, the necessity for it to employ an increasing number and variety of professionally trained workers.

It should be noted at this point that the well-known developments I have (selectively) summarized are largely common to both Western, liberal-democratic regimes and to those of Eastern European countries. It is equally the case in both regimes that, as an obvious consequence of those developments, the fortunes and standing of individuals and groups have come to depend to a large extent on their relations to the state, on the direction of relevant public policies; accordingly, they all acquire an equal interest in (but not an equal capacity for) influencing the state's operations in their own regard.

From this standpoint, the chief difference is that only the Western system allows the legitimate formation and the more or less unimpeded and autonomous operation of organizations whereby a group's resources and claims can be brought to bear upon public policy. The existence in the Western regimes of bi- or multiparty systems is probably more significant today as a manifestation of this more general phenomenon, the freedom for groups to organize and operate—a *relative* freedom, of course, considering the costs of organization and entry—than for its specific impact on the dynamics of interest representation and on policy formation, which should not be rated very high.

Seen from the progressive perspective, the point of the twentieth-century developments we have reviewed is that they make the state into the societal organ specifically charged with the promotion of social progress. In the early formulations of the idea, the political realm stood furthest from the sphere of science, seen as best embodying the experience and the promise of progress. In our own times, scientific advance itself is seen to depend more and more on the government's allocating resources to the enterprise of science.

In the contemporary vision, the state is not itself considered as the sole immediate source of all potentialities for social advance, which, on the contrary, in a more and more complex society are presumed to be increasingly dispersed and differentiated. It is for this very reason that the state cannot stand as a transcendent power over against society, but in order to serve, it must thoroughly "innervate" it, interpenetrate itself with it. What supposedly distinguishes the state is the unique capacity for informed, effective decision making, for unitary vision, and for reliable execution of tasks built into it by the earlier achievements of the consolidation and the rationalization of rule.

It is by the standard set by this expectation that we may now seek to assess retrospectively the success of the story we have just reviewed. How much progress has *truly* been made over the last centuries in the development of the modern state? Of what attainments has the state been capable in the past and is capable today?

A TENTATIVE ASSESSMENT

"You will enter the Continent of Europe and, in conjunction with other United Nations, undertake operations aimed at the heart of Germany and the destruction of her armed forces."[15] These are the central words of the directive issued to General Eisenhower by the Combined Chiefs of Staff on February 25, 1944. It found execution in the sequence of military operations that began on D Day and lasted several months, involved vast and formidably equipped armies, and cost many thousands of lives.

This quotation reminds us of the persistent, ultimate involvement of the state with "blood and iron," of the irreducible element of contingency in the pursuit of its larger aims, and finally, of the inherent ambiguity of its connections with "progress" in any other than a purely technical sense. For although readers will probably agree with me that the successful outcome of those operations was "a Good Thing," we must recognize that one *might* think otherwise. It is also clear that in the nature of the case, the ultimate success of that directive was not a foregone conclusion and that its realization involved tremendous, lamentable human costs.

At the same time, the magnitude of the operations activated by that message does indicate the tremendous historical success constituted by the construction of the modern state. Only an extremely large, sophisticated, and efficient machine for generating power and bringing it to bear on collective purposes could have bridged the gap, as it were, between the terse command I have quoted, on the one hand, and, on the other, the gigantic amount of sustained, diverse, murderous effort it brought forth on the part of millions.

Yet it probably cannot be said that the development of the modern state has been unqualifiedly a success from the progressive standpoint in the sense of having securely fulfilled the expectations successively attached to that development by progressive opinion. On the face of it, what I have called the consolidation of rule appears to have registered a clear success, at any rate in its territorial aspect. "The Europe of 1500 included some 500 more or less independent political units, the Europe of 1900 about twenty-five,"[16] whose average size was of course dra-

15. Quoted in *Grand Strategy*, ed. John Ehrman (London: HMSO, 1956), V, 281.

16. Charles Tilly, "Reflections on the History of European State-Making," in *The Formation of National States in Western Europe*, ed. Charles Tilly (Princeton, N.J.: Princeton University Press, 1975), p. 15.

matically greater. Even on this account, however, some negative comments are in order.

First, it would be hard to claim that the larger political environment saw a corresponding reduction of its "turbulence potential." The frequency of armed conflicts may have decreased, but they became more massive, more intense, and much more bloody and destructive. Second, after asserting itself in the realization of many national states, the trend toward fewer and more inclusive political units seems to have lost its momentum. Originally, the progressive spokesmen for the national idea envisaged the national states themselves as the constituents of more embracing political entities, perhaps as members of a future world state. The latter remains today as implausible a prospect as it ever was; and even more modest attempts at constructing stable supranational political frameworks, at the regional, rather than world, level, are making little headway against the stubborn economic, political, and military interests that find their bases in the national state.

One major institutional theme associated with the national idea (and thus, in terms of the previous discussion, not just with the consolidation of rule but with its functionalization to the nation's interests)—the theme of citizenship as generalized bond attributing *some* political standing and significance to all individuals normally operating within a state's territory—may be said to have lost some credibility in that part of the world (the industrial West), in which one worker out of seven is not a citizen of the state in which he works. In various parts of the Third World, furthermore, statehood does not operate as a unifying force; on the contrary, claims to statehood have become the chief strategy of small elite groups, which use it to carve narrow, pseudo-independent constituencies out of larger ones. Finally, some states which in the past had imparted some political unity to more than one national component (for instance, the United Kingdom or Canada) currently see that unity threatened by separatist or autonomist movements.

As to that aspect of the consolidation of rule constituted by the monopolization by the state of the exercise of legitimate coercion, some of its progressive effects upon the nature of the internal political process seem to be jeopardized by recent developments. (This is one of the phenomena which convey to the historically informed student of contemporary politics the depressing sensation that ghosts apparently laid to rest by state building are coming back to haunt us.) I am thinking particularly of the apparent recent increase in the significance of both legitimate and illegitimate violence in internal politics.

During the nineteenth century the intrastate political process in Western countries seemed to have been largely "pacified." The enormous disproportion between the state's ability to *threaten* violence and the other social forces' ability to resist it, made the actual *exercise* of violence less frequent. The state's massive potential for coercion was organized in such a way as to segregate it from the normal political process; it was entrusted to specialized bodies of personnel, who in principle (and mostly in practice) left the ultimate decisions concerning its employment in the hands of civilian politicians.[17] A further differentiation took place between the personnel (and the resources) in charge of "external" and those in charge of "internal" uses of violence; and the operations of the latter—the police and other law enforcement personnel—were placed under juridical constraints inapplicable to the former. Various more or less effective arrangements for the organization and representation of political criticism and dissent allowed them to find legitimate expression and diverted them from their previous, largely violent means of expression. The modalities of law enforcement became milder, repression less frequent and savage.

Many current developments suggest that these progressive attainments are less secure in contemporary states (even Western ones) than the nineteenth-century experience promised them to become. Almost everywhere military establishments and the related security agencies operate under very little effective control by civilian governments and often threaten them with insubordination and takeover. Troops are being more frequently employed in internal repression operations. From what one gathers, the police forces of several so-called civilized countries routinely subject to torture those guilty or suspected of political opposition or dissent or for that matter of non-political crimes. For whatever reason, popular political demands often find expression through violent action, generally leading to indiscriminate repression.

If we now seek to assess the extent to which the rationalization and functionalization of rule have fulfilled their progressive promises, we must acknowledge in the first place a number of massive attainments. Compared with all other historical forms of permanent, large-scale rule, the modern state appears unequaled in its capacity to organize politico-administrative activities, to bring knowledge to bear upon rule, directing it to tasks of immediate, practical significance to vast populations. It has moderated the imbalances and inequities generated by accelerated economic development and sustained the latter when it has faltered. It has afforded most members of the population some measure of meaningful affiliation with the larger society. It has intervened to curb the most invidious forms of economic inequality and social discrimination and corrected the most punishing situations of insecurity and inferiority.

Yet today we are all acutely aware of the fragility and inadequacy of these attainments and of the magnitude of the price paid for them. We are sensitive to the fact that, currently, states are far from dis-

17. See Samuel P. Huntington, *The Soldier and the State: The Theory and Politics of Civil-Military Relations* (Cambridge, Mass.: Harvard University Press, 1957).

playing in the management of their affairs that spectacular ability to summon, organize, and deploy common effort so much in evidence in the follow-up to the directive of February 12, 1944.

One reason for this, of course, is that the directive envisaged a single, clearly defined objective, to which all relevant parties (on the Allied side, of course) subscribed and in view of which they could be counted on to make some sacrifices. On the other hand, most current symptoms of the state's inability to function well arise from its confrontation with a large and growing number of diverse, incompatible tasks, most of them of interest only to a section of the citizenry, which furthermore expects *other* sections to bear the relevant costs.

This plausible (though, of course, partial) account of the current political predicament suggests that some progressive aspects of the state's development may be at loggerheads with others; that, in particular, advances expressing the functionalization of rule (generating, in the above account, the state's openness to the claims of diverse social interests) may overload the state's capacity for rational decision making and efficient operation. I should like to comment on the above, disturbing (though hardly novel) suggestion, which can also be phrased by saying that some progressive attainments of the twentieth century jeopardize those of the nineteenth.

Let us reconsider, in particular, what I have indicated above as the institutional core of the rationalization of rule, the "right/duty shift." In feudal-patrimonial politics, interests (vested as rights) both motivated and cognitively oriented the exercise of rule; the latter took place, as it were, *under the propulsion* and *in the light* of interests. Accordingly, as rule became rationalized by enjoining those exercising it to suspend consideration of their interests, this opens up two problems: how that exercise is to be motivated and how it is to be cognitively oriented.

The solution of the first problem is, on the face of it, both simple and attractive from a progressive viewpoint: rule is to be carried out in a spirit of *service*. However, if it is to be morally creditable and emotionally compelling, such service must be *to* somebody or something; there must be a *Dienstherr*, a "lord of the service." Originally this emotional focus of the notion of service was provided by the person of the sovereign and his dynasty. When sovereigns, too, began to adopt *Ich dien'* as their motto, the state, or the law, or the public replaced them as such a focus. In the nineteenth century they were replaced in turn by a more concrete but also more diffuse entity, the nation. By the second half of the twentieth century, finally, one had begun to think of a somewhat nondescript entity, "the people" or, even worse, "people," as the beneficiary of the service.

Now, this succession of referents of the idea of service, while, on the one hand, it embodies the advance of the functionalization of rule, on the other, entails the following difficulty: the supposed *Dienstherr* becomes steadily less majestic, less easy to grasp intellectually and to cathect emotionally. By the same token, the idea of service becomes less potent as a motivational fuel for the exercise of rule. You can attach some moral resonance to the notion of being a servant of the king—because the king's service *exalts* you—but not to the notion of "serving" unmarried mothers, the producers seeking protection from imports, or file clerks threatened with unemployment by the goddamn microprocessor. Thus, as the state (with the progress of the functionalization of rule) becomes involved in regulating and assisting triter and humbler social interests, it becomes less and less psychologically feasible for its activities to be carried out in a spirit of service. Into the resulting motivational vacuum rush, once more, the individual and group interests of those exercising rule, under whatever disguise; and the motivational aspect of the "right/duty shift" is undermined.

Let us consider, now, its cognitive aspect: the expectation that rule be exercised in the light not of the particular interests of those charged with it, but of *knowledge*—objective, impersonal, discursively communicable knowledge. In the classical, nineteenth-century vision, the chief object of such knowledge was the legal system, particularly those parts of it establishing the governmental and administrative apparatus, controlling its activities, and regulating its relations to private individuals. Law was seen as the speech itself of the state, and legislation as the standard expression of sovereignty; the legal system was supposed to control and orient all other activities of the state, save exceptional ones of a specifically political nature.[18]

The progressive advances connected with the functionalization of rule—the undertaking by the state of a variety of responsibilities of societal management, from welfare activities to economic planning to the sponsorship of technological innovation—made untenable the above vision. It remained vital that the state's active posture should be sustained and oriented by knowledge; but the knowledge in question had to be much more diverse and "scientific" (in the Anglo-Saxon meaning of the term) than was compatible with the nineteenth-century emphasis on juridical knowledge as the distinctive cognitive resource orienting and controlling the exercise of rule.

From the progressive standpoint there is much to be said for the growing reliance of the state upon cognitive inputs from nonlegal disciplines.[19] But, ironically, there is also much to be said against it from the same standpoint, particularly with reference to some negative effects it has had upon previous progressive developments. Consider the following points.

First, in the classical conception, "the law" was a comprehensive,

18. See Poggi, *Development of the Modern State*, pp. 101-04.
19. The liabilities of juridical thinking in the context of advanced industrial societies are mostly related to the nature of its ultimate referents, normative (as against cognitive) expectations. See Niklas Luhmann, *Rechtssoziologie* (Reinbek: Rowohlt, 1972), I, 40ff; and N. Luhmann, "Die Weltgesellschaft," in his *Soziologische Aufklärung* 2 (Cologne: Westdeutscher, 1975), pp. 51-71.

gapless whole, a system where *tout se tient*. As such, it both reflected and sustained that basic acquisition of the process of consolidation of rule, the unity of the state. Again, as such, it was (as I indicated) the referent of a unitary, though ramified, body of knowledge. But there is no comparable unity among the cognitive resources supplied to the state by nonlegal disciplines. One might say that today's state runs no longer on knowledge but on knowledge*s* (compare the French *savoirs*) and that these are increasingly isolated from one another. The much lamented fragmentation of the state's administrative apparatus may be due in part to the intrinsic incommensurability of the several bodies of nonjuridical knowledge which supposedly orient the activities of its units and subunits.

Second, both the Continental doctrine of the *Rechtsstaat* and the English doctrine of the rule of law presuppose (among other things) that the activity of state organs can be programmed "conditionally," that is, by stating general circumstances under which those organs must carry out certain measures; for this makes it possible to monitor and correct a concrete course of administrative action (or inaction) by checking its correspondence with the general program in question. Instead, the increasing reliance on nonjuridical knowledge leads to administrative activity being programmed "by objective," that is, by assigning it a task and allowing it discretion in devising lines of action to that task. This may well be a (more) rational way of programming administrative activity; but it displaces the traditional (and perhaps the only?) way of binding and controlling its discretionality. In turn, this threatens the progressive requirements of objectivity and accountability in the operations of the state.[20]

Finally, a related, negative effect of the reliance upon nonjuridical knowledge is that it downgrades the significance of lay judgment and thus assigns the citizenry the role of passive, uncomprehending spectators (and perhaps beneficiaries) even of state activities which affect them quite closely. Basically, a view of the political process as activated largely by high-grade inputs of specialized, scientific knowledge discourages citizens from entertaining and expressing opinions on political matters based only on their natural competence for moral judgment. Such a delegitimation of critical, participant citizenship (and partisanship) is less likely when purely juridical knowledge is in question since law is man-made and ultimately embodies moral choice, amenable to persuasive argument and not to scientific demonstration. (Put otherwise, "There ought to be a law" is definitely *citizen talk*. "There must be a computer program" is not.)

The disruptive interferences between distinctive institutional embodiments of political progress do not all run one way, later embodiments interfering with previous ones, but also the other way around.

20. See Renate Mayntz and Fritz Scharpf, *Planungsorganisation* (Munich: Piper, 1973), Chap. 4.

In particular, during the process of functionalization of rule, the bureaucratic model, originally associated with its rationalization, has preserved its influence upon the state's organizational patterns, with particularly damaging effects in the twentieth century. The bureaucratic preference for hierarchy and vertical communication, the bureaucratic strategy of constructing for each line of activity a distinctive, permanent unit, with an establishment of its own enjoying secure employment and protected career expectations and viewing the size of its budget as its maximand, and a "passion for secrecy"—these legacies of eighteenth- and nineteenth-century organizational thinking, first embodied in the early ministerial apparatus, have played havoc in the context of a state seeking to perform more and more functions on behalf of a more and more complex, changing, and "demanding" society.

The persistence of bureaucratic organizational patterns is largely responsible for the most visible and lamentable trends in the structural configuration of the contemporary state apparatus: its sprawling gigantism, its fragmentation, and what could be called its introversion, that is, the tendency of each unit, subunit, and subsubunit to expend most of its energies in purely internal concerns rather than in attending to its original functional assignment. Gigantism, fragmentation, and introversion, in turn, largely account for two massive phenomena which impede the effective functionalization of rule to the society's welfare: the costliness of the state apparatus, and the tardiness and inefficiency of its mode of operation. In my view, consideration of both phenomena should counterbalance the tendency, in much contemporary literature, to account for current difficulties mainly by reference to the magnitude, urgency, and incompatibility of societal demands.

It may be noted that this last interpretation, though often advanced to "cool" some expectations placed on the state by progressive opinion, overlaps in fact with a particular line in progressive thinking, to the effect that the chief difficulty in the program of functionalizing rule lies in the essentially divided nature of society itself—for only a thoroughly unified society can be effectively and coherently *served* in its entirety.

A radical version of this line of thinking goes on to suggest that the notion itself of rule presupposes a divided society; that, therefore, the ultimate progressive target is the unification of society and, by the same token, the *suppression of rule*. A few concluding remarks are in order concerning this radical argument, which is of course best represented by Marxian thinking about the state.[21]

21. I am referring *exclusively* to Marx's own thinking on the state (as I read that thinking, of course). Whatever its justification, and its happy and unhappy outcomes, the orientation pragmatically pursued vis-à-vis the state by Marxist parties, both in the West and in the East, is a very different matter. For a recent commentary on the

The Marxian demand for the suppression of rule stands in a line of legitimate succession to the three phases of progressive thinking about rule we have discussed. Its legitimacy in this sense is suggested, if not proven, by the fact that the demand in question echoes the original aversion from politics of progressive thinking and, to that extent, represents a return to its roots. However, whether authentically progressive or not, one may wonder whether the position in question is correctly argued and whether the suppression of rule is feasible.

There probably is a logical connection between a divided society and the phenomenon of rule. It is also plausible that a divided society cannot be served (politically or otherwise) as a whole. However, Marx erred in seeing class interest as ultimately the sole significant cause of a divided society. His emphasis on economic antagonisms must be complemented by an insight best articulated by the so-called Machiavellian tradition, to the effect that whatever its relation to other social divisions, *rule itself divides society.* In and of itself, the possession of or exclusion from faculties and facilities of rule generates contrasting interest orientations between the respective groups. Indeed, any attempt at unifying society centered exclusively on its economic processes might well, paradoxically, reinforce the asymmetry and antagonism resulting from the *increased* significance of rule.

Machiavellian thinking disassociated itself from the progressive tradition by treating the phenomenon of rule as not only autonomously significant but also as utterly inevitable and as virtually unmodifiable.[22] To me, the succession (to use once more the terminology introduced above) of consolidation, rationalization, and functionalization of rule, in spite of all attendant limitations, difficulties, and setbacks, suggests that there can be (there has been) such a thing as "progress in politics." True, its achievements have so far been mixed, less permanent, and less radically innovative than one might have wished. But they have been substantial enough to establish that enlightened purpose can exercise some positive leverage even upon a phenomenon as dangerous as that of rule.

---

fateful mutual implication of socialism and the state, see Evan Luard, *Socialism Without the State* (London: Macmillan, 1979), Part 1.

22. See Vilfredo Pareto's sarcastic reference to the notion of "rule of law" (or, rather, *Rechtsstaat*, or "stato di diritto," in Italian): "I apologize to the reader for not defining this beautiful entity, but all my searches have failed to locate it, and I would as soon describe the Chimera"; *Trattato di sociologia generale* (Milan: Comunità, 1964), p. 632, par. 2182.

17

Progress and Public Policy

AARON WILDAVSKY

In the 1960s America fell in love with the Rachel of social reform and found itself instead married to the Leah of big government. She was bigger, but she wasn't better. It proved more inspiring to long after the unobtainable objectives of giant governmental programs than to wonder if they were worth having. Overinfatuated with the good they sought to do, Americans overemphasized the evil they had done. The idea of progress in public policy was, if not speedily seduced and abandoned, at least slowly suspended, if not discarded. Unrequited love easily turns on its object. Along the way, characteristic American optimism was subject to severe shock. Retrogression rather than progress became the expectation. Why?

Americans were better educated, more talented, and richer in human and material resources than ever before. Their sense of social justice, though far from perfect, was certainly sharper than in earlier times. Challenged to put up or shut up, they opened their coffers so wide as to shame a Croessus. Where, in the early sixties, defense took up some 45 percent of the federal budget and social welfare programs around 20 percent, a scant decade later these proportions and priorities were radically reversed. Relatively and absolutely, social welfare, from food stamps to Medicaid to Social Security, loomed larger on the government horizon. For those who doubt the relative decline in defense spending, see Figure 1, whose statistics are clear and convincing.

Why, then, weren't we-the-people happy? Why did we recoil from our fondest hopes, damning what we had so earnestly desired? Actually

This essay was written upon reflecting on the implications of doctrines of progress, as discussed by the other contributors to this volume, on my understanding of developments in public policy; see my *Speaking Truth to Power* (Boston: Little, Brown, 1979).

Fig. 1. Growth in Federal Government Spending

• • • • • • • Total defense spending
━ ━ ━ ━ ━ Total non-defense spending
━━━━━━━━━ Total federal spending as a percentage of GNP

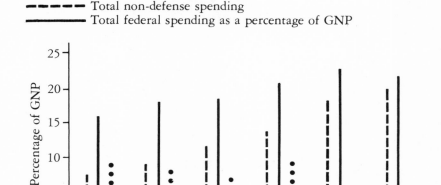

SOURCE: The Economic Report of the President, *Taxing and Spending*, February 1979, p. 15.

it wasn't all so bad or so consistent. Some social programs retain support. If not, they wouldn't be with us. Even so, the élan, the enthusiasm, the pure pleasure, the expectation of better things to come—all have gone. Wariness has replaced happiness. If the nation entered the seventies celebrating the change from warfare to welfare, it entered the eighties on a note of retrenchment. California's Proposition 13 became the lucky number for advocates of lower local real estate taxes; balance in public policy no longer signifies doing more to help the poor but now means restricting government spending. What happened?

Big government, which was supposed to institutionalize progress in public policy, has instead become identified as its main obstacle. There is little confidence that "doing more of the same" or "throwing money after problems," to use two of the current stock phrases, will make things better, and not a little that even bigger government will make them worse. At first blush, this reaction is surprising; the social welfare programs that have grown the fastest in the last two decades were introduced precisely as progress itself—sharing the wealth of the private sector in the form of redistribution by the public. Where the former was fueled by self-interest, the latter was said to be motivated by moral concern for the disadvantaged. Thus, a heightened awareness of duty to others less fortunate, a more exquisite moral sensibility, was to marry the wealth of society to the allocative efficiency of government to do good. Obviously, something happened on the way to public happiness.

On second thought, it is not surprising that something new, so much so soon, stumbled at the start. What would have been extraordinary, in view of our inexperience, would have been discovering that programs performed as intended, that each reinforced rather than crossed purposes with the other, so that social difficulties declined. Temporary dismay at the decline of high hopes is easy to understand; permanent disappointment leading to demands to dismantle the system of social welfare makes sense only if government is fatally flawed.

This essay is not a negation of the notion of public life. It is not a rejection of the sixties or a castigation of public policies to aid the poor. Not at all. I do not believe that the sixties were a dreadful decade. No people is wise to abandon its past, pretending it did not exist or preferring that it had taken a wholly different path (unless, of course, it was vile and mean-spirited, which ours was not).

For good or ill, our culture is self-conscious. We transport ourselves to the corners of our living rooms and observe our own behavior, subject and object together. If error recognition and error correction constitute the essense of right action, then we have had plenty of opportunity to learn in the school of public policy. Has there been progress, we ask ourselves, or only progression?

PROGRESSION VERSUS PROGRESS

The concept of progress (a radical innovation for its time) was originally coined by Condorcet as a reaction against the nostalgic notion of a beatific past from which time things were going downhill. The "golden age" was not so much a "has been" as a "never was." No need to worry, however, for education would sweep away the vestiges of the past. By overcoming prejudice and superstition, indeed by scientific understanding of the principles of society, mankind could continuously improve. Evidently, education and science were important prerequisites of progress. But from that day to this, the idea of progress has hidden ambiguities about process and purpose that we wish to explore.

It was certainly comforting, to be sure, that all kinds of progress went together—material, moral, mental. Earlier traditions, imbued with the doctrine of original sin, were likely to view the will as the servant of the passions and both as directing the weaker moral and material orders. Earlier also was a view of cycles that societies passed through but did not transcend. Change was permanent, but betterment was not. Rise and decline were related; as politicians climbing the "greasy pole" of success observe, the first step up is also the first step down. Man, who labored ceaselessly, was more like Sisyphus than Prometheus.

Without religion, without an afterlife to justify this one, the ultimate purpose of progression—life as history and history as dates—was unsettled. Whether there was to be evolution or revolution (or both) in this world, whether its saints were to be Darwin or Marx, the question of motivation remained. The need for an answer was particularly poignant under Marxism because it promised to liberate mankind not only from superstition but also from need. How would people arrange their lives? What would motivate them when they no longer had to work? (Some say not only fame but necessity is the mother of scientific invention.) If there were a secular side to motivation, it was tied to the conversion of history into meaning, that is, progression into progress.

Progress was bolstered by evolution, for here was not merely a prediction of glad tidings but a method assuring believers that the best had been chosen by natural selection, assuring survival of the fittest. What Protestant predestination did for the moral universe, evolution justified for the material world. The closed cycle of yore became an upward spiral. From the very beginning, however, there were doubters if not disbelievers, who thought it was all too neat.

Was there survival of the fittest, or did those who survive call themselves fit? Was there, in a word, progress or only power in disguise? That one thing succeeds another is undeniable; but is succession (the day-to-day effluvia of historical deposits) success? Religion left ultimate goodness to God, the last things appearing in all their perfection after history was over. For those who lived in history, however, the question remained: was it a random series of events, or was there a successful social mechanism for discarding the worst and selecting the best? The answer depends not only on whether enlightenment leads to progress but also on which of the rival principles of progress we choose as our inheritance.

THE TWO ENLIGHTENMENTS

Just as every constitution is written against the last usurper, it is important to understand what the philosophers of progress were arguing against as well as what they were for. In the political sphere, this is fairly obvious. The Anglo-Scottish Enlightenment found its government only moderately distasteful, but the French Enlightenment despised its nominal rulers. So the preference of the former for meliorative measures and the latter for wholesale housecleaning is understandable.

The economic sphere is more difficult to decipher. Leaders of the Enlightenment everywhere were opposed to mercantilism but not necessarily for the same reason. Though there is not entire agreement on the content of that doctrine, it apparently favored state control of commerce in order to export at the lowest possible price so as to accumulate gold with which to carry on grand projects of state. Unfortunately, a policy of export at all costs was interpreted to mean that wages had to be at the barest subsistence level. A gloomy doctrine, indeed, at least for most of the population.

Adam Smith and his teacher Adam Ferguson reacted against mercantilism by ridiculing and rejecting its vast array of intricate controls that got in each other's way. The French philosophers stressed the barrier of the state apparatus to its own restructuring. Between the conviction that the state should not act and the belief that it should act better lies an unbridgeable chasm.

What are the social sources of enlightenment? To the Scottish and English it is the interaction among individuals rather than the cogitation of any single one that produces wisdom.[1] Social interaction, bidding in economics and bargaining in politics, represents a search for the most advantageous relationships. How is it known that people have done the best for themselves? By results. When is it known? Afterwards. What is the criterion of good decision? Agreement.

By contrast, Condorcet or Diderot found truth in individual understanding. Knowledge is not about incessant error correction but about error prevention. Knowledge lies in the mind, which rationalizes all activity. When is it known? Beforehand. How is it known? By following the right design. The criterion of a good decision, therefore, was that it was correct, according to a previously ascertained body of principle.

Although each enlightenment did believe in progress and each was opposed to the practices of mercantilism, their diagnoses and remedies were different. Though both believed that society was a product of human action, the French saw it as potentially a product of human design. To the French philosophers, the design of the world could be formulated in the mind and imposed upon society. The Anglo-Scottish believed just the opposite: the world was created by interaction among people, interaction that was wiser than any single mind. The Anglo-Scottish fled from error; the French sped toward truth. Where the French Enlightenment justified itself prospectively by the belief it could make over the world in its own image, the Anglo-Scottish justified itself retrospectively, claiming that social interaction had been superior to intellectual cogitation in view of the results achieved.

Both formulations of enlightenment embraced evolution. Characteristically, interpretations differed drastically. The Anglo-Scottish strain saw individual adaptation to local conditions cumulating in a societal selection better than anyone could have foreseen. Human action might be purposeful, but it could not be predictable. The French variant saw society not as a cumulation of consequences of actions taken on other grounds and for other purposes but as a direct decision. The most knowledgeable forces in society shaped its evolution in a predetermined direction.

SPONTANEITY VERSUS CONTROL

The clash between spontaneity and control, interaction and cogitation, lies at the heart of the idea of progress. Of course, no control can be total, and no reaction can be entirely spontaneous. Interaction is always

1. For discussion of interaction versus cogitation, see Charles E. Lindblom, *Politics and Markets* (New York: Basic Books, 1978); and my *Speaking Truth to Power.*

bounded by constraints, and cogitation never quite gets it all. But what central controllers would call unfortunate unanticipated consequences, deviations from the blueprint of the future society, are the very staple of local social interaction. Only by knowing each situation as well as individuals do could all relationships be anticipated. The unexpected is the stuff of life that each person must communicate to the other precisely because no one else can possibly know. That is why it is so often observed that discoveries are made when the discoverer is not looking for them, at least not in the place they end up being found.

Serendipity is the rationale of spontaneity. Incessant search by many minds, it is claimed, produces more (and more valuable) knowledge than the attempt to program the paths to discovery by a single one. Why not go out after what is wanted? What is wrong with the common-sensical notion that the shortest path between two points is a straight line? For individuals to try and get what they want makes sense as long as it is understood that their objectives and the resources used to attain them are subject to modification with experience. What one wants depends on what one can get. The relevant others whose consent cannot be coerced sets limits to what would otherwise be an infinity of possible objectives. Formulating and reformulating objectives is sensible at the individual level. The question is whether it is similarly sensible at the collective level.

Not only markets rely on spontaneity; science and democracy do as well. In all three arenas, proof is retrospective rather than prospective. Looking back over past performance, adherents of free science, politics, and markets argue that on average their results are better than alternatives, but they cannot say what these will be. The foolishness and frustration of funding conferences (give us the money and we'll find something wonderful, especially if it is bound to be something we didn't expect) stems from the unpredictable character of social interaction.

The strength of spontaneity, its ability to seek out serendipity, is also its shortcoming—exactly what it will do as well as precisely how it will do it cannot be specified in advance (were it possible to specify what scientists would invent or who should get elected or how best to achieve economic growth, control could replace spontaneity).

The significance of serendipity lies in exploring why direct action may be counterproductive. Seeking social goals may undermine them. As soon as objectives get socialized, some people have to set them for others. It is not planning per se but who plans for whom that matters. Information is lost because objectives are necessarily attributed to all members that are in fact shared only by some. And other objectives that might emerge do not have an opportunity to manifest themselves. There can only be a small number of officially sanctioned goals on which social resources are employed. As these resources are used up, opportunities for other lines of endeavor, which might have emerged, lack open avenues of expression. Society literally does not know what it is missing because there is no way of measuring the alternatives there might have been had there been fewer socially supported objectives. Consequently, when new challenges emerge, the variety of practices and solutions that might have met them has been diminished.

Once there are collective objectives, it becomes difficult to switch support away from them. They develop clientele and consequences, which only can be dealt with in the existing entrenched context. Instead of objectives being treated as variables, changing according to the needs of the time, they become constants, around which other endeavors must move. Thus, present solutions limit future ones. Evolution only works one way—by addition but not by subtraction. Social objectives and their support staff grow bigger (the old that must be kept plus the new that must be tried) but not necessarily better.

To the extent that objectives are individualized and localized, their consequences are felt directly by their formulators. The more socialized and centralized the objectives, the more indirect and remote their consequences. Feedback becomes depersonalized. As the critical connection between causes and consequences is attenuated, the center becomes overloaded and out of touch. Evidently it can do evil as well as good. The manifest good it wishes to do becomes instead the very evil it wishes to avoid.

Since this basic argument is ordinarily buried beneath public discourse, it is worth glancing at a recent manifestation. In 1979 the *Wall Street Journal* carried this evocative headline: "Price of Progress? U.S. Inflation Blamed On Attempts to Avoid Slumps, Aid the Needy. Big Deficits, Flood of Money, Costly Regulation Ensue." This is not the place and I am not the person to argue about inflation. It is the form of the argument made by distinguished economists that is of interest:

> An extensive search for answers from private economists, businessmen and government officials leads to a more fundamental explanation that is gaining acceptance among experts of all political persuasions. It is that the U.S. inflation is the inevitable result of the kind of economy and society that we have been shaping for decades, a society in which both individuals and businesses are protected against the worst economic hazards of earlier eras and consumption is favored over savings and investment.

LIBERALS IN AGREEMENT

Sitting in his book-lined office at the Massachusetts Institute of Technology in Cambridge, Robert Solow, one of the nation's leading liberal economists, spells out a similar thesis. "The single most important reason for inflation is that we are a society that has tried to prevent deep recessions, to provide income security for people and to help those who suffer," he says. "We no longer let big businesses go bankrupt or people go unemployed for a long time."

Mr. Solow's MIT colleague, Nobel Prize-winner Paul Samuelson, sees inflation as the price paid for "our becoming a more humane society."

According to those who hold this view, a series of social policies, desirable in and of themselves, reduced the variety and flexibility of responses to price increases so that these went up and up instead of up and down. If security, humanity, and (less) suffering, to name a few of the policy objectives mentioned, lead to what the reporter quoted Arthur Okun, the eminent economist, as calling "a chronic disease," which, Amitai Etzioni, the sociologist, added, "is threatening the psychological safety of people," and which the reporter concluded is "endangering the nation's social fabric," evil may indeed come out of good.[2]

CRITERIA FOR CONSIDERING PROGRESS

What do these abstruse considerations have to do with progress and public policy? Everything. Is progress to be achieved by interaction or cogitation, a single mind or many, spontaneity or control? Is progress to be judged by process or by result, by whether it has followed the cogitators' initial design, or by whether conditions are better or worse than they once were? Even if progress has occurred according to some criterion, the causal connection is not necessarily self-evident. Has it occurred according to design or despite it?

Societies can interact but they cannot plan; only individuals can do that. What are called individualistic theories are in this sense misnomers. For it is only through social interaction that the preferences of individuals are known and valued. Collectivism, by contrast, contains an individualistic theory of decision—cogitation by a central supermind on behalf of others. Individualistic theories argue for the superiority of social interaction whereas collectivist theories are based on the superiority of a single supermind.

Summing up this tour of the horizon of ideas about progress, the men of the French Enlightenment believed that by stripping away the myths and superstitions of the past and by replacing them with an education based on science, mankind's essential morality would be set free. Enlightenment was then supplemented by evolution. To the learning of individuals was added the wisdom of the species. Each individual would benefit from the knowledge of others, about which he could not (and fortunately did not need to) know. There was coordination but without a coordinator. Some of the newly enlightened saw a benevolent social intelligence at work in the economy so that private interests willy-nilly produce public good whereas others placed this ultimate design in government, where professing public interests led to private good. The contradiction has never been resolved.

2. Richard J. Levine, in the *Wall Street Journal*, June 19, 1979, p. 1.

Education was the pathway to success. Accordingly, public officials with ever higher education should be more competent than people like them were before. Whose knowledge about whom—citizens about their own circumstances or experts about other people's—would matter most was unclear. Whether central controllers could be more competent than their societies was a question without an answer.

Even if they were not, the significance of evolution was that there existed a process for selecting good programs and discarding bad ones. Government was not only supposed to grow quantitatively but qualitatively as well. That sheer size might cripple quality was not considered, for with size went wealth. Growth of government was presumed to proceed apace with (not apart from) growth of society.

In the past, partisans of progress expected risk to be countered by resilience. Each generation would not only be richer than the one before; it would also be more resilient in the face of new challenges. It was not necessary, therefore, for each generation to pay all the costs of rapid technological change. These could be left to the future on the assumption that it would be more capable. Without faith in progress, without the belief that deficits would be made up by development, few would venture so far so fast. All of these conditions of progress as it has been understood—education, selection, growth, resilience—have been subject to severe challenge by experience with big government.

BIG GOVERNMENT AND LITTLE PROGRESS

By "big" I mean (1) large historically relative to the private sector; (2) large absolutely compared with past programs; and (3) large increase in number of programs, (4) in their diversity, and (5) in their impact on people's lives. Difficulties may arise along any of these dimensions.

Think of public programs as spheres existing in policy spaces. When these spaces are unoccupied, new programs have only their own consequences to consider. As these programs grow larger and are joined by others, they bounce off of one another. The larger the number of big programs, therefore, the more they bang into others, the more varied and indirect their consequences become. A new income maintenance program, for example, would have far-reaching effects on housing, consumption, transportation, and medical care, and far more than can be recounted here. The result is that complexity overcomes theory. Ability to control consequences by program design diminishes as unanticipated consequences increase. Even as available knowledge accumulates at a steady pace, the point is, the knowledge needed for large programs in big government grows by leaps and bounds. There is progress in understanding but retrogression in public policy.

Past progress, moreover, creates future problems. Just as yesterday's pneumonia victim is today's geriatric problem, overcoming easy difficulties may leave government stuck with intractable problems. The medical inflation we suffer from today is a direct result of subsidizing hospital construction, pouring money into Medicaid and Medicare, encouraging medical insurers to push comprehensive coverage, and otherwise flooding the medical market with money, thereby driving up prices. New programs—cost containment, second opinions on surgery, restriction of hospital beds, on and on—become necessary in order to cope with past consequences. When programs get big, involving millions of people and billions of dollars, they become such a large part of their sectors of policy that, by their very presence, they alter its outcomes.

The larger government grows, the more policies become their own causes. The more government does, the more it needs to fix what it does. The larger government gets, the less it responds to events in society, and the more it reacts to the consequences of its past policies. In an era of big government, policies increasingly become their own causes.

Just as any football coach knows that victories are in part a function of scheduling weak instead of strong opponents, capacity to control public policies depends on what one tries to do. The justification of big government must be that it does grand things. The upshot is that government undertakes tasks that no one knows how to accomplish—raising the cognitive abilities of deprived children, reducing crime and recidivism rates, and improving health. No matter how much money is spent, reading, health, and recidivism rates do not improve because there is no known way of doing these things. (By the way, Europeans are no more successful than Americans; they just don't advertise their failures as much.) A characteristic feature of all such programs is that change resides within the individual, not within government. Where governments seek to change their own behavior, the variable over which they have the most control, they sometimes succeed. The radical reorientation of priorities from defense to social welfare is evidence of that. But where government seeks to alter deep-seated human behavior, it often fails. Health, education, and welfare speak eloquently on this subject.

If it cannot do what it says, what does big government do? What it can. Government governs by input—the resources it controls. It pours money over problems as a sign of good intentions. It reorganizes itself endlessly. It tries everything at least once and some things, like tying welfare to work, many times. This is how the widespread impression of change for its own sake is created.

When programs do not work at all or as well as they might, the expectation is that efforts at error detection and error correction will take place. Efforts there are, but accomplishments are something else again. Actually, error correction goes on all the time; it is just that the solution is almost always larger than the problem.

If evolution were accompanied by devolution, the size of problems might be reduced to an intelligible scope. And if evolution took place in the midst of competition, the politically or economically fittest might survive, leading to public approval. Instead, what you see is what you get: the Dinosaur Syndrome operates so that every solution increases the size of programs without simultaneously increasing the intelligence of those who design and administer them.

This size syndrome operates according to well-known principles. Small errors are easy to correct but difficult to detect because it is hard to trace consequences to a multitude of possible causes among innumerable governmental programs. Large errors are easy to detect but difficult to correct because so many people and programs are connected to them that the effort appears disproportionate to the result.

How is opposition to large-scale change, requiring numerous adjustments in related programs, overcome? Decreasing size worsens internal competition by setting off a struggle for resources. The trouble with competition is that you can lose. Increasing size has happier internal consequences; everyone gets more as change is exchanged for growth. The inexorable collective consequence is giant government.

No better illustration of the dependence of change in public policy upon growing larger can be found than in social welfare. The principles are well known. No group once having received benefits may be denied; no level of benefits once raised may be lowered; with a choice between maximizing eligibles versus minimizing ineligibles, supporting the deserving is preferable to denying the undeserving. Notice that no change other than increasing income is compatible with these conditions, which do not permit decreasing either benefits or beneficiaries. Consequently, change in welfare policy can only be achieved by simultaneously raising benefits and broadening classes of beneficiaries. (When insiders talk about "upgrading" benefits, so that all receive the highest levels or "overlapping" categories, so that no one who might be entitled is left out, they are putting these principles into operation.) Since perfecting programs by cutting categories or benefits is not allowed, reordering program elements can only be accomplished within a larger matrix—more benefits and more beneficiaries. Progress appears to be guaranteed; no beneficiary is allowed to be worse off while some are bound to be better off.

A sad side of this situation is that size is incompatible with equality. Put differently, the original motive behind welfare policy—redistributing income to increase equality—is at odds with increasing size. Why this should be so is one of those entirely obvious observations that is perhaps too evident to be noticeable. When programs originate, they are designed to meet a need. A relatively small group is targeted to receive aid. Since the cash comes from the general population of taxpayers, people of plenty, so to speak, are paying for the poor. This is how programs begin but not how they end. Either the original beneficiaries want more money, or previously uncovered groups want to be included.

The way to do this, which adds to initial support, is to have larger benefits for a broader array of people. When this process has run its course, however, there are many more beneficiaries from more diverse social groups receiving higher levels of benefits. The people paying and the people receiving, though by no means identical, have come to resemble each other much more than they did before. Naturally, when proponents of redistribution check out these programs, they discover that their early egalitarian impulse has been much attenuated. The broader the social base and the higher the benefits, the less egalitarian the program. The end result is that though ever larger amounts are spent on ever larger numbers of recipients of welfare programs, there is less reduction of inequality.

"Learning" might be thought of as rules for retaining the best and discarding the worst of old solutions while trying on new ones. The process of learning prevents piling up of all solutions (old and new, good and bad) by establishing processes within which all have to compete because not all can survive at the same level. Just saying what we mean by "learning" is sufficient to make us uneasy, for we are aware, without quite saying so, that there is movement up but not out. Somehow the system does not discard but changes only by growing larger. Size substitutes for selection. Progression (one thing following another) prevails over progress (one thing improving another).

Why, in a period of enlightened social programs, in which huge sums are spent to right social wrongs, is there progression but not progress? Solutions create new problems faster than they solve old ones. Problem creation overtakes problem solution. Knowledge required to control public policy grows geometrically whereas understanding of them increases only arithmetically. The ability to measure failure ("evaluation," it is called) leaps ahead of capacity to cause success. Since people who give consent to public policies are often the same ones who are unwilling or unable to change their own behavior, they have every reason to know that particular programs are not working. Selection, citizens see, has given way to collection. This was not, needless to say, the way the system was supposed to work.

The radical reorientation of political philosophy by the framers of the American Constitution embodied a mixed idea of political progress. By the work of their own hands and minds, Americans would be able to create the political institutions under which they would govern themselves. This optimism about institutions was matched by pessimism about human nature. Motives were not to be made moral. In number 10 of *The Federalist Papers*, James Madison emphatically rejects this possibility. Individuals will always be tempted to act adversely to others; it is the task of government not to deny human nature but to mitigate its worst aspects. Interest is to be turned against interest. Institutions are to be arrayed so as to encourage cooperation on common grounds and obstruction on actions adverse to others. Put into the systems simile of John von Neumann,[3] the framer's belief was that institutions would interact so that the whole was more reliable (and, the framers would add, more just) than any of its parts.

Instead, big government has gone just the opposite way. By seeking to make each part superreliable, that is, by attempting to guarantee material progress to each and every part, it has reduced the reliability of the whole. The redundancy, the surplus resources, the resilience of the whole—all have been used to prevent any of the parts from suffering. Hence the only element in danger of failing is the whole.

MAKING PROGRESS POSSIBLE

Contemporary critiques of public policy are parodies of progress. Insisting that government move simultaneously in opposite directions is stultifying. Insisting that services be supplied and that people are becoming too dependent on government leaves no way out. Promoting safety and environmental measures while condemning decreased productivity is a paradox not a policy. Insisting that immense amounts be spent on income transfers while condemning the results as inegalitarian efforts to buy support increases anger without insight. These are not criticisms of public policy but condemnations of democratic government, which is programmed to fail no matter what it does.

There are two ways to do better—change the criteria and improve performance—and I propose we do both. The idea that problems are solved should give way to the notion that man-made solutions also create man-made problems. Policies do not succeed so much as they are superseded. It is not policy resolution but policy evolution that should be our concern. How well, we should be asking, have we detected and corrected our errors? More to the point, are we better able to learn from today's errors than we were from yesterday's?

Thinking that social ills are puzzles that can be solved instead of problems that may be alleviated or eventually superseded tends to make us despondent when these ills do not yield to our ministrations. A good comparison is to do something, as opposed to nothing, and then evaluate the result. The rub is that you do not know whether some other action might have been better or worse. A better comparison is to contrast the problems we have now with those we had before. Instead of thinking of permanent solutions, we should think of permanent problems in the sense that one problem replaces another. Then we might ask whether todays' problems are more moral or more effective than the solutions that they replaced. Are today's inflated medical costs preferable to yesterday's restricted access to medical care? I think they are. The capacity of policies to generate more

3. John von Neumann, "The General and Logical Theory of Automata," in *Modern Systems Research for the Behavioral Scientist*, ed. Walter Buckley (Chicago: Aldine, 1968), pp. 97-107.

interesting successors and our ability to learn from them what we ought to prefer may be their most important quality.

But how is quality to replace quantity as the measure of governmental success? By imposing limits on the size of government. The problem is to make existing knowledge more adequate for proposed public policy. The objectives sought and the intellectual resources available to achieve them should be brought into greater consonance. Whereas incentives inside government favor error protection, they should be altered to favor error correction. Selection should overtake size as the prevailing principle in government. And when crises occur, the new streamlined model should serve us better than the cumbersome creature we have come to know in recent times. Without going into detail, limiting the sheer size of government, for a time if not forever, would enforce selection. As soon as subtraction becomes part and parcel of decision making, government, if I am permitted a little rhetorical license, should look less like a dinosaur and more like a dolphin.

18

Social Progress
and Liberal Democracy

G. BINGHAM POWELL, JR.

Contemporary liberal democracy as a form of government is under assault from many quarters. Some of these attacks raise anew the familiar doubts about citizen capacity, which have been an element in Western political thought as long as the idea of democracy has existed. Other attacks are nourished by the failure of many liberal democracies to achieve social and economic equality for their citizens. The attacks with the most profound implications for the idea of progress, however, are those arguing that in the contemporary world, social progress and political, liberal democracy have become incompatible.

The idea that social progress and political democracy are mutually supportive was an important element in the original, bold American political experiment. It became an increasingly vital element in the "culture of progress" formed by nineteenth- and early twentieth-century thought and experience. If this idea is replaced by the assumption that social progress and political democracy are simply among the virtues that must be traded off against each other in a world of hard choices, we can, indeed, speak of a fundamental transformation of the idea of progress. In this essay I hope to sort out these attacks on democracy as an element in the culture of progress and suggest some implications.

I should particularly like to thank Lynda W. Powell, Gabriel A. Almond, William T. Bluhm, and William H. Riker for their comments on an earlier draft of this paper. Peter H. Lemieux and the various participants at the Conference on the Transformation of the Idea of Progress in Palo Alto, Ca., February 1979, contributed with their reactions to verbal presentations of some of these ideas.

HISTORICAL CONNECTION BETWEEN
PROGRESS AND DEMOCRACY

We can find many different images of democracy and many perspectives on its association with social progress.[1] Nonetheless, I see two primary strands of thought, each receiving vivid and articulate expression about the time of the formation of the American republic and then woven into the fabric of the idea of progress by the events and interpretations of the subsequent century.

The first strand of thought argues that social progress, and all that it implies in the scientific, economic, and moral spheres, will encourage development of a political process that involves meaningful participation of more and more of its citizens. Despite the frequently expressed cynicism of most of the eighteenth-century philosophes about the masses, the idea that proper education and conditions of greater prosperity and equality could develop citizens worthy of a role in government lurks at least at the fringes of Enlightenment thought.[2] For those who believed in the perfectability of man, the potential for a harmonious reconciliation of individual political man and the common, progressive good seemed limitless. In 1793, Condorcet's *Sketch for a Historical Picture of the Progress of the Human Mind* articulated an extreme form of the "progressive" view:

> What are we to expect from the perfection of laws and public institutions, consequent upon the progress of those sciences, but the reconciliation, the identification of the interests of each with the interests of all? . . . Will not a country's constitution and laws accord best with the rights of reason and nature when the path of virtue is no longer arduous and when the temptations that lead men from it are few and feeble?[3]

Condorcet is distressingly vague about the mechanisms through which individual and collective interests will become identified and reconciled, but there is no doubt that social progress is the condition that will make a democratic political process possible.

The second critical strand in the thought about democracy and progress is the idea that representative democracy can be a mechanism through which political leaders can be held accountable to the society

1. Louis Hartz argued that the most prominent nineteenth-century political theorists were primarily concerned with democracy as an antithesis to the repressive aristocracies against which they struggled, not with specific political visions of democracy in action. See his "Democracy: Image and Reality," in *Democracy in the Mid-Twentieth Century*, ed. William N. Chambers and Robert H. Salisbury (St. Louis, Mo.: Washington University Press, 1960), pp. 13-29.

2. See Peter Gay, *The Enlightenment: An Interpretation, Volume II: The Science of Freedom* (New York: Knopf, 1969), esp. Chap. 10, pp. 497-554; also see essay by Keohane, pp. 21ff.

3. Antoine-Nicolas de Condorcet, *Sketch for a Historical Picture of the Progress of the Human Mind*, trans. June Barraclough (New York: Noonday Press, 1955), p. 192.

for their actions. In this line of thought, interestingly, it is not the perfectability of man but the need to protect men against the inevitable imperfections of their rulers that is the driving force. The idea that new institutions can overcome fundamental social problems and individual flaws is also very much an Enlightenment idea.[4] The introduction of representative democracy as the institution through which the governors will be controlled, the solution to that ancient political problem, is a brilliant structural solution and a radical political experiment.[5] It is hard to improve upon the statement by Madison written as he and Hamilton sought support for the new American constitution in 1787-1788:

> The aim of every political constitution is, or ought to be, first to obtain for rulers men who possess most wisdom to discern, and most virtue to pursue, the common good of the society; and in the next place, to take the most effectual precautions for keeping them virtuous whilst they continue to hold their public trust.
>
> . . .
>
> All these securities, however, would be found very insufficient without the restraint of frequent elections. Hence, . . . the House of Representatives is so constituted as to support in the members an habitual recollection of their dependence on the people. Before the sentiments impressed on their minds by the mode of their elevation can be effaced by the exercise of power, they will be compelled to anticipate the moment when their power is to cease, when their exercise of it is to be reviewed, and when they must descend to the level from which they were raised; there forever to remain unless a faithful discharge of their trust shall have established their title to a renewal of it.[6]

Two points about the American experiment and Madison's analysis of it are worth special note. First, it was a remarkable and daring innovation. Despite the denial of suffrage to women, blacks, and some of the poor, it seems that a majority of adult males were eligible to cast an equal vote in judgment of their representatives.[7] Nearly a century

4. See the fine discussions of the American experiment as expression of Enlightenment thought in Gay, *The Enlightenment*, Chap. 11, esp. pp. 563-68.

5. Ibid., pp. 565-66.

6. *The Federalist Papers*, no. 57 (Cambridge, Mass.: Harvard University Press, 1961), p. 385.

7. There is substantial disagreement about the extent of the franchise restrictions on adult white males in the various American colonies and states in the late eighteenth and early nineteenth century. Robert E. Brown argued that eligibility approached 90 percent in Massachusetts and Virginia at the time of the Revolution; *Middle Class Democracy and the Revolution in Massachusetts 1691-1780* (Ithaca, N.Y.: Cornell University Press, 1955). A recent review of a variety of studies of different states concludes that eligibility of adult white males probably ranged from 50 to 60 percent in New York to 80 percent or more in Virginia. See Robert J. Dinkin, *Voting in Provincial America* (Westport, Conn: Greenwood Press, 1977), Chap. 3. The conclusion seems consistent

later, in the 1870s, only France and Switzerland could claim broad manhood suffrage among the European nations. Not until after the First World War could one point to some twenty nations, including most of the industrialized ones, having representative assemblies holding major political power and elected by most of the adult male population.[8] Second, it is obvious in the early discussions of American democracy that the founders believed that effective citizen control would require an informed and attentive citizenry, just the sort of citizenry that proponents of social progress like Condorcet were expecting to emerge everywhere.

Despite the many false starts and doomed hopes and despite the widespread condemnation by many progressive thinkers of just those new institutions of interest groups and political parties that were to prove essential in linking citizens and rulers in modern democratic societies, the nineteenth century found the pressures for increased popular involvement in political life inexorable. The processes of scientific, technological, economic, social, and cultural change carried with them an impetus for popular legitimation of government. The breakdown of traditional cultural and religious bases of authority, the increase in education and literacy, the growth of the belief that men can control their fate and act to improve their circumstances, the need of governments to expand their activities and extract greater resources from their citizens in order to cope with domestic changes and international threats—all these drove leaders in the countries achieving early modernization to increase the levels of citizen involvement.[9] Experimentation and international example, as well as ad hoc response to domestic pressure from the new groups whose cooperation was essential for national growth and stability, led to the creation of representative assemblies with growing powers and the spread of the suffrage.[10]

---

with the data and analysis of J.R. Pole, *Political Representation in England and the Origins of the American Republic* (New York: St. Martin's Press, 1966). The suffrage laws of each state were made the basis of eligibility for voting in Congressional elections in the constitution of 1787.

8. My own analysis suggests that even ignoring the question of women's suffrage, there were only about nine democracies among the forty-eight nations in 1902, twenty-two democracies among the sixty-four independent nations in 1920, twenty-one democracies among the sixty-five nations in 1929-1930, thirty democracies among the 121 nations in 1960. This analysis draws upon Arthur Banks, *Cross-Polity Time Series Data* (Cambridge, Mass.: MIT Press, 1971), for estimates of the selection bases and effectiveness of legislatures and upon a variety of sources for estimates of electoral suffrage, especially Stein Rokkan, "Mass Suffrage, Secret Voting, and Political Participation," *Archives Européen de Sociologie*, 2 (1961): 132-52; and Thomas T. Mackie and Richard Rose, *The International Almanac of Electoral History* (New York: Free Press, 1974).

9. See Rokkan, "Mass Suffrage"; and Stein Rokkan, *Citizens, Elections, and Parties* (New York: David McKay, 1970), for discussion of mass suffrage.

10. See Peter Gerlich, "The Institutionalization of European Parliaments," in Allan

These nineteenth- and early twentieth-century experiences seemed to offer powerful empirical support for each of the strands in the idea of an association of social progress and democracy. Those nations attempting democratic government without a basis of social progress, as in Latin America, seemed foredoomed to instability and failure.[11] Those nations achieving substantial progress seemed to be driven toward democratic government, whose workings in practice then seemed to help keep leaders in check and press government toward progressive reforms. Taken together, these experiences seemed to weave the two distinct strands of "progress and democracy" into a single, tight fabric of liberal thought.

Moreover, the practical experience with representative democracy in action also made visible, at least to the most clear-sighted observers, the essential role of political parties in organizing alternatives for the electorate and in aggregating enough of the diffuse political resources to make it possible to formulate, choose, and sustain public policies for citizens to evaluate. In his comparative study of six democracies, James Bryce observes quite matter of factly that parties are indispensable for democracy to work in practice and to link the inevitable "oligarchic" specialization of policy making and governing with the general choosing of policy orientation preferred by citizens:

> To begin with parties are inevitable. No free large country has been without them. No one has shown how representative government could be worked without them. They bring order out of the chaos of a multitude of voters. . . . So few people think seriously and steadily upon any subject outside the range of their own business interests that public opinion might be vague and ineffective if the party searchlight were not constantly turned on.[12]

Although more elegant formulations of the logic of competitive democracy have been developed since, most notably those of Schumpeter, Dahl, and Downs,[13] the basic consolidation of a modern image of democratic government, in theory and practice, seems to have been achieved in the 1920s and its place, implicitly and explicitly, in the vision of "progress" settled. Works by various social theorists in the subsequent decades have continued, despite some serious challenges to democracy (discussed below) to flesh out these images.

Kornberg, ed., *Legislatures in Comparative Perspective* (New York: David McKay, 1973), pp. 94-113.

11. See James Bryce, *Modern Democracies* (New York: Macmillan, 1921), II, 498-518; and James Bryce, *South America: Observations and Impressions* (New York: Macmillan, 1912).

12. Bryce, *Modern Democracies*, I, 119.

13. Joseph A. Schumpeter, *Capitalism, Socialism, and Democracy* (New York: Harper & Row, 1942), pp. 269-83; Robert A. Dahl, *A Preface to Democratic Theory* (Chicago: University of Chicago Press, 1956); and Anthony Downs, *An Economic Theory of Democracy* (New York: Harper & Row, 1957).

THEORETICAL CONNECTION BETWEEN
PROGRESS AND DEMOCRACY

It is useful at this point to consider more carefully the theoretical case for a mutually supportive relationship between social progress and liberal democracy. Progress and democracy have been seen as part of a common phenomenon for two different kinds of reasons. One reason is that they have been historically associated; the period of the emergence of liberal democracy was also the period of European industrialization. But compelling logical arguments can also be made for their interdependence, drawing upon the lines of thought I have here associated originally with Condorcet and Madison. Looking first at the theoretical case, then at some empirical evidence, will help put the various contemporary doubts and challenges into perspective.

Any model of the association of progress and democracy must, of course, rest on some assumptions about their meaning. In the arguments we are here exploring, "democracy" means the liberal, democratic form of government. Its presence is identified by open political competition between political parties, extension of the right to vote in the competitive elections to all citizens, transformation of the voting choices into the representation of parties in national assemblies that have authority to make public policies and control the executive that implements them, and the freedom of citizens to organize, persuade, and form new parties if dissatisfied with present alternatives.[14]

By "social progress" I mean to include the generally accepted elements of welfare and personal security.[15] The former include individual health and life expectancy, literacy and education, and living standards that enable the individual to choose among various ways of pursuing happiness. The latter include personal security and freedom from fear, as long as the individual acts within broad constraints of community opinion; absence of inequitable, as well as arbitrary, regulations of the behavior of groups and individuals; and control of violence and warfare. Involved in both welfare and security are the liberty to make individual choices about desired pursuit of personal goals and at least some equality of the opportunity to achieve these.

The argument that democracy and progress, seen in these terms, will be associated, has two major elements; some theorists would accept only one of them. One line of argument is that social progress will enhance the adoption of democracy or at least its maintenance once established. The other line of argument is that liberal democracy

14. For a brief summary of this vision of democracy and its requisites, see Dahl, *A Preface*; and Robert A. Dahl, *Polyarchy: Participation and Opposition* (New Haven, Conn.: Yale University Press, 1971), pp. 1-16. For a discussion of alternative twentieth-century visions of democracy, see Giovanni Sartori, "Democracy," in *International Encyclopedia of the Social Sciences*, ed. David Sills (New York: Macmillan and Free Press, 1960), IV, 112-21.

15. See also Gabriel A. Almond and G. Bingham Powell, Jr., *Comparative Politics: System, Process, and Policy* (Boston: Little, Brown, 1978), Chap. 14.

will encourage social progress or at least contribute to maintenance of important elements of it once they are established. We shall look briefly at each of these lines of thought.

We should note also that theorists have usually assumed that social progress and liberal democracy will be mutually supportive, perhaps interdependent, only after they pass some (usually unspecified) threshold. Appearance of some elements of liberal democracy, such as partial extension of the franchise or voting in noncompetitive elections, will not necessarily contribute to social progress. Partial improvement in some social circumstance, such as increased life expectancy, will not necessarily support democracy. Indeed, social theorists have long pointed out that early transition states in both conditions may be unsettling and disruptive.[16]

Progress Enhances Democracy

Although capable of great refinement, the arguments for the enhancement of democracy by means of social progress are relatively straightforward and have been very widely accepted. First, among individual citizens, education, information, health, and a wide range of personal skills and experiences facilitate all kinds of political involvement and make political participation and control through and over political parties meaningful. Without an informed and potentially involved citizenry, the mechanisms of controlling political representatives cannot work effectively. Second, greater economic resources facilitate political bargaining and lessen the intensity of political competition. It becomes possible to achieve a wide range of public policies, including the support of the disadvantaged, without great sacrifices on the part of others. Broad support for democratic regimes is enhanced.

A third argument avers that personal security and freedom from arbitrary and unequal regulation make it easier to accept changes in political control on the part of those in power and easier to wait and work through democratic channels on the part of those in opposition. Freedom from fear of violence makes political participation more meaningful. Another argument is that control of external violence and warfare makes internal democratic competition both more acceptable and more meaningful. Many liberal democracies severely limit competition and freedom of information during the "supreme emergency" of war; external dominance makes control by domestic leaders a sham. Finally, it is argued that the extension of scientific and technological progress in general enhances the abilities of governments to implement desired public policies. In the democracies, such policies are, presumably, those desired by the people. Their successful implementation will engender further support for democratic government. And

16. For example, Bryce, *Modern Democracies*, II, 498-518. More recently, see Mancur Olson, Jr., "Rapid Growth as a Destabilizing Force," *Journal of Economic History*, 23 (December 1963): 529-52.

the greater collective resources will make it easier to defend a democratic regime from both internal and external threat, enhancing its diplomatic, military, and policing capacity.

This line of argument, in various forms and with various nuances, can be found among the works of many social theorists in the last half-century. Bryce, for example, uses them in 1912 and 1921 to explain the poor chances for democracy in many South American nations;[17] Lipset similarly argues for economic development and modernization as requisites for democracy in 1960.[18] Merriam explains his confidence in the ability of democracies to resist "the new despotism" in 1939 by pointing in part to the enhanced strength of democracy under conditions of greater social progress.[19] In 1971 Dahl makes imaginative use of this line of thought to explain the historical exceptions of democracy being sustained under preindustrial conditions, as well as to reaffirm the general association of competitive democracy with social and economic development.[20]

Democracy Enhances Progress

That competitive democracy should encourage or sustain social and economic progress has also been part of progressive vision (despite some lingering doubts about the corrupting influence of political parties). This part of the broad argument is perhaps less in favor today,[21] but it is much too significant to ignore.

Above all, it is argued that competitive elections force leaders to anticipate citizens' needs and wants; where they fail to do so, they are replaced by other leaders. Since the majority of citizens would favor creating those conditions of welfare and personal security that are part of social progress, in the long run democratic policies tend toward sustaining economic growth, literacy, and communication and the control of violence. Second, competition creates incentives for leaders to appeal to marginal groups and bring them into new political coalitions and alignments; those out of power build new issue coalitions, create new issue dimensions. Hence, eventually all individuals and groups are brought into winning coalitions, at one time or another, and share in the benefits of policies implemented by their majority. Thus, in the long run democratic policies will contribute to the equalized distribution of the benefits of social progress.

In addition, competition gives incentives for political leaders and would-be leaders, as well as their active supporters, to watch and check those in power, preventing abuses that threaten citizen security, de-

17. Bryce, *Modern Democracies*, I and II.
18. Seymour Martin Lipset, *Political Man: The Social Bases of Politics* (Garden City, N.Y.: Doubleday, 1960), Chap. 2.
19. Charles Edward Merriam, *The New Democracy and the New Despotism* (New York: McGraw-Hill, 1939), pp. 252-62.
20. Dahl, *Polyarchy*, Chap. 5.
21. But see Carl Cohen, *Democracy* (New York: Free Press, 1971), Chap. 14.

fending those freedoms of information and choice that are essential both to citizens and leaders aspiring to office. Finally, democratic participation itself contributes to citizens' personal growth, enhancing their sense of self-worth and their knowledge and competence. (This idea was a part of the nineteenth-century democratic faith; it has become less pervasive as participatory democracy ideals have been replaced by party competition as the major control.)

It is important to note that the first three arguments do not depend on a mass participation vision of democracy but quite explicitly upon the model of party competition and its underpinnings. In considering all of these arguments, of course, we must keep in mind that it is not claimed that all democracies will always be superior to all nondemocracies. Many democratic theorists admit freely that they can imagine a philosopher-king who makes better decisions—decisions more closely reflecting the creation or sustaining of social progress—than the clumsy mechanisms of democratic competition. But democracy is here viewed as a type of government, and its policy consequences must be contrasted with achievements of other types of government, such as oligarchies, military dictatorships, one-party regimes, monarchies, and the like. Perhaps not surprisingly, the question of comparison of liberal democracy with other forms of government, rather than with some ideal of rulership, is most clearly kept in mind by those arguing against explicit alternatives, as in Bryce's comparison of democracies with aristocracies and monarchies,[22] or Laski's and Merriam's comparisons of democracies with the fascist challengers of the 1930s and 1940s.[23] As long as "progress" in general is believed to be unfolding, it is, of course, sufficient to see democracy as that form of regime that in the long run, and across the range of types of regimes, is most likely to enhance it. Under conditions under which progress in the social sphere is seen as extremely difficult or impossible to achieve, these arguments may not apply so clearly.

EMPIRICAL ARGUMENT FOR PROGRESS AND DEMOCRACY

The theoretical arguments for an association of social and economic progress with liberal democracy seem plausible. They are treated in greater detail in other studies. But there are also numerous counterarguments. The arguments for a positive association between democracy and progress have tended to hold the field among contemporary political scientists and broader publics as well because there is some plausible evidence to support them. Indeed, a good case can be made that the arguments follow the evidence as much as vice versa. Let us take a very brief look at the evidence pertaining to the association of

22. Bryce, *Modern Democracies*, II, 535-41.
23. Harold Laski, *Democracy in Crisis* (Chapel Hill: University of North Carolina Press, 1933); Merriam, *The New Democracy*.

democracy and progress over the last several decades. This brief review will help put present doubts in some perspective of recent experience, although we shall keep in mind that such doubts are generated in part by the feeling that a host of conditions are altering rapidly and that old patterns may no longer apply.

Social Progress and Democratic Performance

The argument that democratic performance will be enhanced, or sustained more successfully, in societies having achieved a substantial threshold of social progress is easily examined by looking at the working of liberal democratic regimes in more and less economically developed nations. Since education, health, life expectancy, mass media, social differentiation, and economic productivity are all highly associated with one another in the contemporary world, we cannot observe their independent impacts on the working of democracy. But we can see whether or not as a "package" they go together with the aspects of democratic performance suggested by our theoretical overview: enhanced citizen participation, broader support for democratic government, elite willingness to accept changes in governments, and the defense of democracy from internal and external threats.

In fact, a variety of studies have generally supported these expectations. My own recent investigation of performance in the thirty-odd democratic regimes between 1958 and 1976 also supports them, with a few minor caveats.[24] A variety of studies has demonstrated that citizens with greater social resources are more likely to participate in politics, particularly in the more time-consuming and complex forms of political activity.[25] My investigation of comparative voting turnout shows clearly that citizen participation is, on average, higher in the more economically developed nations, a relationship that is even sharper after taking account of registration laws and compulsory voting effects.[26] Among nations without compulsory voting, average turnout in national elections was about 66 percent of the eligible electorate in the poorer democracies and about 77 percent of the eligible electorate in the better-off ones. Serious political violence, as measured by average numbers of deaths by political violence per year, was much more prevalent in the poorer democracies than in the

24. G. Bingham Powell, Jr., *Contemporary Democracies: Participation, Stability, and Violence* (Cambridge, Mass.: Harvard University Press, 1982).

25. See, most recently, Sidney Verba, Norman H. Nie, and Jae-on Kim, *Participation and Political Equality: A Seven-Nation Comparison* (Cambridge, Mass.: Cambridge University Press, 1978); also see the review of various studies of individual participation by Lester W. Milbrath and M. L. Goel, *Political Participation: How and Why Do People Get Involved in Politics*, 2nd ed. (Chicago: Rand McNally, 1977).

26. G. Bingham Powell, Jr., "Voting Participation in Thirty Democracies," in *Electoral Participation: A Comparative Perspective*, ed. Richard Rose (London and Beverly Hills: Sage Publications, 1980).

economically developed ones, in both the 1960s and 1970s.[27] For the most part, such violence reflected armed attacks by political groups unwilling to accept the limitations and policies of the democratic regime. Despite the tragedy of Northern Ireland, and the urban riots and civil rights violence in the United States in the 1960s and early 1970s, the economically developed countries were far better able to prevent and contain such attacks, on average. (However, disorganized rioting was not particularly related to level of economic development, and peaceful protests were positively related to it.[28])

Most compellingly, the instances of democratic government being overthrown or suspended were almost exclusively confined to the less developed nations.[29] Among the more developed nations, only France in 1958 experienced a change of regime under (threat of) military force, although Italy was exposed to some severe crises. In the less developed democracies, it was often very difficult to sustain a working democracy: the armed forces overthrew democratic governments in Burma, Brazil, Greece, Chile, and Uruguay, and several times intervened directly in Turkey; incumbent executives toppled democracy in the Philippines and suspended democratic freedoms for substantial periods in India and Sri Lanka. Although we have no evidence in this period on the relative success of economically developed countries in the face of external threats, it seems quite clear that their advantages in enhancing citizen involvement, maintaining support, encouraging organized elites to keep within the democratic framework, and sustaining democratic regimes were substantial. To say this is not to denigrate the performance of democratic leadership or the seriousness of democratic commitment in the poorer nations. The institutionalization of political democracy in Venezuela, the remarkable stability of Costa Rica, the reestablishment of competition in Sri Lanka and India, with explicit rejection of leaders associated with authoritarian policies—all provide impressive evidence that economic development is not a necessary precondition for democracy. But the bulk of the evidence certainly supports the theoretical argument that social progress enhances the performance of democracies once they are established.

Liberal Democracy and Social Progress

The evidence that democratic regimes are more likely to enhance social progress is both more difficult to obtain and more mixed than the evidence for the other side of the coin. The one clear-cut area of superior performance is in sustaining civil rights and personal freedoms from elite abuse. The annual ratings of civil freedoms by Freedom House, a nonpartisan human rights organization based in New York, makes the superior performance of the liberal democracies quite

27. Powell, *Contemporary Democracies*, Chaps. 3, 4.
28. Ibid., Chaps. 3, 4, 6.
29. Ibid., Chap. 8.

clear.[30] Although some authoritarian governments permitted substantial civil freedoms (for example, Equador and Bolivia, in 1978), and some democratic governments did adopt some restrictions on press and personal rights (West Germany and Turkey, in 1978), the general intertwining of democracy and civil freedom is apparent. This relationship remains strong even after taking account of the level of economic development, although, as we would expect from the previous discussion, both democracy and civil rights were found more frequently among the most economically developed countries.

There is also some evidence that democracy contributes to containment of serious violence. The evidence is somewhat shaky because the nondemocracies, especially the communist regimes, control reporting of violence, and we no doubt underestimate the frequency of violence in some of them. This bias works, however, against the theory. Despite it, Hibbs's very careful and sophisticated analysis of mass political violence on a worldwide scale found that (1) regimes in which elites were electorally accountable to citizens were less likely to use repression and (2) elite restraints in the use of repression when confronted with citizen protest and turmoil helped prevent the escalation of serious violence. In his multivariate analyses of causal paths and dynamics, Hibbs summarizes the effects of democratic regimes as follows:

> In otherwise comparable situations, elites are less inclined to resort to repression in nations where political authorities are held accountable for their actions by free and competitive elections. Therefore, even though democratization does not have a significant direct impact on the level of violence, it clearly does have a causally important indirect influence by diminishing the extent of government repression.[31]

Thus, despite the breakdown of political order in some democracies, as in Lebanon, for example, there is evidence of at least indirect effects of democracy on the containment of violence. However, we do not want to exaggerate these findings because it is clear that where violence does get out of hand, democracy rather quickly disappears also; only a careful examination of evidence indeed can keep the causal sequence clear and see what independent effects democratic government may have.

The impact of democratic government on social welfare is even harder to ascertain. The reason is that the level of economic development and the nature of social needs, as well as international interdependence, have so much impact on social policies and their consequences. My study of policies and consequences within democracies

30. Raymond D. Gastil, ed., *Freedom in the World: Political Rights and Civil Liberties, 1978* (New York: Freedom House and G.R. Hall, 1978).

31. Douglas A. Hibbs, Jr., *Mass Political Violence: A Cross-National Causal Analysis* (New York: Wiley, 1973), pp. 186-87.

certainly found evidence, as have others, that outcomes of elections and party coalition formation in the developed countries had impact on public policies.[32] For example, the presence of a leftist government in power was associated with increases in the size of government revenue as a percentage of gross national product (GNP) between 1960 and 1970, with increased role of income taxes as a percentage of GNP in the same period, and with liberalism of national abortion policy in 1970. These relationships between democratic political outcomes and policies hold among the eighteen industrialized democracies even after taking account of relative wealth, the religious make-up of the population, and the nature of the party system.[33]

But it is very difficult to make acceptable comparisons between democracies and nondemocracies. The best studied area is that of economic growth. Bergson's careful analysis of investment and growth of the Soviet bloc nations and the almost entirely democratic nations of the Organization for Economic Cooperation and Development (OECD) in the 1950s and 1960s suggests some advantage to the latter, although there were wide variations within each type.[34] Among the nations at similar economic development levels, the OECD nations did somewhat better in growth, but not significantly. However, they were able to achieve their growth with lower levels of investment, suggesting more efficient production and less consumer sacrifice to yield the same outcomes. (These results hold if we exclude nondemocratic OECD nations.) The best performer in all respects was Japan.

Bergson's results do not necessarily demonstrate the superiority of democracy as a system, even under the limited condition of the 1950s and 1960s, as the primary contrast is between centrally controlled economies and market-oriented economies, not between regime types. But they are at least encouraging. Among poorer nations, C. H. Huang's recent analysis suggests only slight and not significant differences between democratic and nondemocratic countries in average economic growth rates in the 1960s and early 1970s, although democracy and higher degrees of competition were associated with greater use of inflationary policies.[35]

Examinations of income inequality patterns are also inconclusive.

32. Powell, *Contemporary Democracies*, Chap. 9; and see Edward R. Tufte, *Political Control of the Economy* (Princeton, N.J.: Princeton University Press, 1978), and the studies cited therein.

33. Powell, ibid., Chap. 9.

34. Abram Bergson, "Development Under Two Systems: Comparative Productivity Growth Since 1950," *World Politics*, 23 (July 1971): 579-617.

35. Chung-Hsiou Huang, "Democracy, Competition, and Development: The Political Economy of Inflation and Growth in Developing Countries," Ph.D. dissertation, University of Rochester, 1979, Chap. 4. My comparison of thirty-four nondemocracies and twelve democracies also shows identical median rates of growth in gross domestic product per capita 1968-1973 according to data in the World Bank, *World Tables 1976* (Washington, D.C: World Bank, 1976). (This comparison excludes major oil producers.)

Among the poorer nations there seems to be no significant relationship between the income share going to the lower 40 percent and whether or not the nation had a democratic regime, once one controls for level of economic development. Among the somewhat better-off countries, the communist nations for which data are available (as they are not for the U.S.S.R.) give a larger proportion to the lower 40 percent of citizens than the noncommunist countries, which are primarily democracies.[36] However, the large shares extracted by the government sector and the lack of citizen control over these expenditures, as well as the absence, at least until recently, of production response to consumer spending demand, limit the implications of such equality for utilization in pursuit of the individual's own desires. Moreover, the communist nations have patterns of political privilege and welfare inequality that do not show up in such statistics.[37] Within the developed democracies, the presence of political parties expressing clear-cut class groups seems a powerful factor in shaping redistributive policies.[38] Perhaps the absence of such parties in most of the poorer nations, along with fiscal constraints, helps explain the lack of democratic impact on redistributive policies there. One relevant set of studies does point out that military regimes are more likely to spend more of their income on "defense";[39] other studies indicate that defense spending is often at the cost of welfare expenditures.[40]

In summary, it seems that the democratic regimes have a clear advantage in the promotion and maintenance of citizens' liberty and security and, perhaps, in containing domestic violence. There are, however, few systematic differences between the performance of democratic and nondemocratic regimes in terms of welfare policies. Economic growth levels are similar, as best one can judge, and regime type is not the major factor shaping them, despite some inflationary tendencies among democracies. The communist systems probably do better in the income share going to the lower-income groups but sharply constrain the use of that income. Among poorer nations, regime type has apparently little impact on equality. Although exploration of differences between types of nondemocratic systems might reveal more suggestive patterns, the overall expectation that democratic regimes would promote greater citizen economic welfare is not

36. Calculated from data in Hollis Chenery et al., *Redistribution with Growth* (New York: Oxford University Press, 1974), pp. 8-9.

37. See the discussion in Almond and Powell, *Comparative Politics*, pp. 324ff.; and see John M. Echols, "Does Communism Mean Greater Equality?" paper delivered at the 1976 Annual Meeting of the American Political Science Association, September 2-5, 1976.

38. Harold Wilensky, *The Welfare State and Equality* (Berkeley: University of California Press, 1975); and Powell, *Contemporary Democratic Performance*, Chap. 7.

39. Eric A. Nordlinger, *Soldiers in Politics: Military Coups and Government* (Englewood Cliffs, N.J.: Prentice-Hall, 1977), pp. 66-68, 166-70.

40. Wilensky, *The Welfare State.*

supported. Yet, it is worth noting, given the contemporary doubts, that even in poorer countries the democratic regimes do not perform significantly worse, on average, than their authoritarian counterparts. The evidence for the association of progress and democracy in the past twenty years, then, finds that social progress seems to contribute to sustaining democracy; democracy contributes to sustaining liberty and security, but its impact on social welfare varies widely.

CONTEMPORARY DOUBTS ABOUT DEMOCRACY

The empirical record, although mixed, tends to be consistent with the broad theoretical argument for the association of democracy and progress. Yet we are beset with doubts about democracy. A number of writers, from many points of view, have predicted its forthcoming demise, in one form or another. Granted that democracy has always had its critics, even at the high point of its post-World War I triumph, it is notable that some of the present-day criticism and concern is coming from social critics and theorists who have long been defenders of the democratic faith. At least one line of thought seems to predict that another fundamental transformation of the idea that progress and democracy are associated is going to be forced upon us. To understand these doubts and their implications for the idea of progress, it is useful to classify the different doubts about democracy in terms of their relationship to expectations about progress.

Figure 1 presents an analytical classification of the doubts about democracy that have received some prominent recent expression. The

Fig. 1. A Typology of Contemporary Doubts About Progress and Democracy

Progress and Democracy Assumed to Be:

	Positively Related	Not Causally Related	Negatively Related
Predominant Independent Factor — Progress	A Progress Is Failing: So Will Democracy	C International, Cultural, and Historical Factors Predominate in Sustaining Both Progress and Democracy	D Progress Is Making Democracy Impossible
Predominant Independent Factor — Democracy	B Democracy Is Failing: So Will Progress		E Democratic Policy Making Undermines Progress

horizontal divisions distinguish doubts according to whether or not they assume that progress and democracy are, in fact, associated. On the left, we see arguments that they are positively related; in the center we see arguments that they are only accidentally associated, if at all; on the right we see arguments that they are, or are becoming, negatively related. The vertical division distinguishes arguments that assume democracy is somehow related to progress, in terms of whether the theorist thinks that it is progress or democracy that is the driving force in the presumed relationship. Our typology of doubts about democracy thus has five categories. Each of these, if they were realized, and accepted as true, would have somewhat different implications for the image of progress and democracy that has been broadly accepted for the past fifty years. It is, of course, possible that none of them will prove correct. It is also possible that more than one is or will shortly become true; some theorists have held, for example, both that social progress is at an end and that democracy contributes to its failure (*A* and *E*), a gloomy prospect, indeed, for the culture of progress as we have known it. We shall speculate briefly on such possibilities in conclusion.

Progress Is Failing: So Will Democracy

This line of argument accepts, by and large, the assumption that progress is necessary in order for democracy to be sustained. Its proponents would see the data presented above as consistent with their expectations. However, for a variety of reasons they see social and economic progress as we have known them as coming to an end. Democracy will be one of the many casualties of this fundamental reversal of the trends of the last several hundred years. The seriousness of the impending disaster is a matter of dispute among its forecasters, as is the possibility of prevention or alleviation. Serious dislocations are in store as, for example, the world shifts to new energy sources, although the collapse of industrial society is probably not at hand.

We might take note of two different variants of the position that "progress is failing; therefore, so will democracy." One of these emphasizes an *extended period of global resource scarcity*, in contrast to the growing abundance of the last two hundred years.[41] Such scarcity will intensify political conflict among different groups within democracies, as it is no longer possible to use a growing economy to satisfy different groups simultaneously. Politics becomes a totally redistributive process, and some democracies, especially those which have at present great inequalities between "haves" and "have-nots," such as Italy and France, will be unable to contain conflict within democratic boundaries. Rather, the situation will come to resemble that in Chile in 1973, or Weimar Germany, with intense conflicts spilling into violence, loss of support for democratic processes, and

41. For example, see Robert L. Heilbroner, *An Inquiry into the Human Prospect* (New York: Norton, 1974).

the eventual replacement of democracy by authoritarian rule. Moreover, the situation in the less industrialized nations will become even worse, and the already tenuous position of democracy in those societies will be further threatened as they are locked into levels of social progress far below those that can comfortably support democracy. Finally, the international conflicts between nations, especially between "haves" and "have-nots," will greatly intensify as well, with some democracies perhaps overrun by their neighbors, while others suppress internal democracy in the name of national necessity. (A worldwide nuclear holocaust will, of course, also dispose of democracy, along with mankind.)

In the other major version of "failing progress," the problem is one of governing. In this version an *age of ungovernability is at hand* in all the modern societies, not because of resource conflict but because of the impossible technological complexity of the modern world. Modern societies are or are becoming so technologically complex and interdependent, nationally and internationally, that rational and effective decision making is impossible under any system of government. Government decision makers simply cannot foresee the implications of actions they take; every effort in one direction to alleviate social problems exacerbates them elsewhere. Yet the system cannot function on its own. It drowns in its own waste of garbage, pollution, and maintenance failure. Interdependent communication and transportation systems collapse. Assigning responsibility for political decisions is impossible. Democratic control is meaningless. Frustration and anger pervade citizens of all the industrialized societies, leading to loss of governmental support and general political instability. Democracy is, again, one of the casualties, one of the first, in that the most advanced and complex societies are now democracies. The failure of progress, in the sense of man's ability to control his environment through rational decision, will bring with it the end of meaningful democracy. A particularly interesting presentation of this scenario, we might note, is LaPorte's and Abrams' review of "the California experience" as a preview of the loss of control in a technological society, and Lindberg presents a summary of the various approaches to the "failure of progress" literature and their political implications.[42]

Democracy Is Failing: So Will Progress

Throughout the nineteenth century it was easy to locate prophets of the internal contradictions of democracy. The problem of the age was how to deal with the pressures for democratization and yet retain the

42. Todd La Porte and C.J. Abrams, "Alternative Patterns of Postindustria: The California Experience," in *Politics and the Future of Industrial Society*, ed. Leon N. Lindberg (New York: David McKay, 1976), pp. 19-56; and Leon N. Lindberg, "Strategies and Priorities for Comparative Research," in the same volume, pp. 222-286. See also Michel Crozier, Samuel P. Huntington, and Joji Watanuki, *The Crisis of Democracy* (New York: New York University Press, 1975).

fruits of progress; how, in de Tocqueville's words, "to make liberty proceed out of that democratic state of society in which God has placed us."[43] Again in the 1930s, with democracies challenged by the new fascist states and the example of the consequences of the failure of the German Weimar Republic before their eyes, there were many who saw the contradictions and instabilities of democracy as likely to generate democratic collapse, with a subsequent loss of many of the most precious elements of social progress. But the experiences of the last two decades have made us far more optimistic about the resilience and the responsiveness of liberal democracy. Criticism has been directed at the failure of liberal democracy to attain the ideals of participatory democracy and at the continued entrenchment of corruption, the influence of the organized and better-off, immobilism under pressure, and so forth. But the adoption of welfare measures in much of Western Europe, the survival of all the industrialized democracies in the era since World War II, and the continued vigorous freedom of speech and press have answered many of the doubts about the survival of liberal democracy under progressive conditions and its achievement of its most basic claims.

Two questions are, however, worthy of brief note. One is the problem of the status of permanent minorities under democratic regimes. Where separate communities exist with clearly and permanently distinct values and goals, the assumption that democratic competition will eventually bring all elements of the society into a share of government may well not hold. Rabushka and Shepsle, for example, have argued that democratic competition is basically self-destructive under conditions of ethnic division, indeed, under any conditions of subcommunities with contradictory values.[44] It is indeed the case, as my own investigation of violence in the thirty contemporary democracies demonstrates, that democracies with ethnic divisions were more likely to experience deadly violence than their more homogeneous counterparts in the last twenty years and that such effects remain even after taking account of the level of economic development, growth rate, and so forth.[45] The American experience with racial conflict and British problems in Northern Ireland provide vivid examples even within the more prosperous nations. On the other hand, the experiences of Belgium and Switzerland show that ethnic divisions can be dealt with in a democratic context. Lijphart has explored some of the special mechanisms needed for obtaining consent and support under such conditions.[46] Hibbs's work demonstrates, moreover, that ethnic division

43. Alexis de Tocqueville, *Democracy in America* (New York: Knopf; Vintage edition, 1954), II, 340.

44. Alvin Rabushka and Kenneth Shepsle, *Politics in Plural Societies* (Columbia, S.C.: Merrill, 1972).

45. Powell, *Contemporary Democracies*, Chaps. 3, 4.

46. Arend Lijphart, *Democracy in Plural Societies* (New Haven, Conn: Yale University Press, 1978).

is not merely a problem for the competitive democracies.[47] Such divisions do have, however, serious implications for democratic performance.

A second question is raised by the possibilities of an interactive spiral of poorer "progress" conditions in the society and democratic poor performance. Our experience with more or less successful liberal democracy has been in recent years in quite favorable settings. It is possible that a decline in growth rates and the uncertainties of transition to new social, "postindustrial" conditions will set difficult problems to which democratic governments have a particularly difficult time responding because of the pressures of special interests and the incapacity firmly to enforce order. These failures may then, in their turn, undermine public confidence and government performance and contribute to a cycle in which serious problems become really intractable. Thus, Heilbroner, in his grim assessment of the impending disasters of the postindustrial age, sees liberal democracies as particularly vulnerable and contributing to the disaster and points to "the likelihood that there are obdurate limits to the reformist reach of democratic institutions within the class-bound body of capitalist society . . . ."[48] Such a prediction cannot, of course, be rejected by any information we have at present; although we can point to the ability of democracies to react well to some of the crises of the past, we cannot evaluate their response to new ones.

The doubts about democracy we have been considering view democracy and social progress as intimately connected. Over the past several generations they have operated to reinforce each other. However, it may be that "external" conditions—severe global scarcity, incomprehensible social and technological complexity, intractable value conflicts, and interactions of these—can break the positive cycle of progress and democracy and destroy them both. The "idea of progress" may retain its component elements, both political and social; democracy and social development remain part of the same package, so to speak, but the sense of optimism and inevitability in progressive thought is lost. We must also consider, however, a different version of the transformation of the idea of progress and democracy, one which decouples them and reformulates progress to stress the independence or even the antithetical nature of liberal democracy, on the one hand, and the welfare and security of citizens, on the other.

Progress and Democracy Independent of Each Other

Before considering those visions of the failure of democracy that would most fundamentally transform the idea of progress, those which see social progress and democracy as incompatible objectives, we must note those theorists who see progress and democracy as causally not

47. Hibbs, *Mass Political Violence.*
48. Heilbroner, *An Inquiry*, p. 24.

connected.[49] While there have, indeed, been strong patterns of association between social progress and liberal democracy, in the sense that a
country with the one is likely also to have the other, this association
can be seen as an accident of history or the consequence of other
factors.[50] With regard to the arguments, and empirical evidence, locating democracies in the more economically and socially "developed"
societies, the following criticisms are to be found in the current social
science literature.

First, the political economies of smaller and dependent nations are
strongly influenced by the political and economic structures of the
dominant powers. British and American international dominance in
the twentieth century coincides with the conjoining of liberal democracy and social progress in those two nations. They have imposed that
conjoining on much of the rest of the world. Second, regimes are
founded and sustained by the cultural values and preconceptions of the
elites. Liberal democracy and its appearance together with social progress elements simply reflects how Western culture, the culture of
progress itself, happened in the accident of its emergence in the eighteenth and nineteenth centuries to join those values. Few regimes
outside of Western Europe have liberal democratic institutions, and
most of these are British colonies or were subjected to British or
American tutelage. And third, as suggested by the example of the
Soviet Union with its record of economic growth but continued authoritarian repression, regimes have great internal continuity and are not
easily shaped by social and economic changes. Nor does major social
and economic change easily take place. Hence, the joining of progress
and democracy may be a contemporary reflection of an historical
coincidence.

With regard to the arguments and evidence about the performance
of the liberal democracies in promoting progress, the challenge might
be summarized as follows. First, the evidence on social and economic
performance suggests that factors other than regime type—elite decisions, internal bargains, international advantage, and internal resources—predominate in shaping economic growth and equality. Accountability of elites to citizens is a relatively trivial factor.[51] Second,
the evidence on security and the containment of violence is weak or
suspect and certainly only applies to broad averages at best. And,

49. We might also mention the argument that social and economic development
force a clearer choice between democracy and authoritarianism as national political
structures penetrate more deeply into the society. See Almond and Powell, *Comparative Politics*, pp. 68-76.

50. See, among others, the critical review of the empirical "democracy and social
conditions" literature in John D. May, *Of the Conditions and Measures of Democracy*
(Morristown, N.J.: General Learning Press, 1973).

51. See Bergson, "Development Under Two Systems"; Huang, "Democracy, Competition, and Development"; Chenery et al., *Redistribution with Growth*; and Wilensky,
The Welfare State.

finally, the association of democracy and the containment of government oppression may also be an accident of the cultural heritages and norms of internationally acceptable behavior that condition each of these.

These arguments, although likely to be of more interest to historians and social scientists than to popular thought about the underpinnings of progress and democracy, cannot be rejected out of hand. The evidence on the predominance of nonpolitical factors shaping economic performance seems largely consistent, although I think that one must push the institutional, international, and cultural arguments quite far to reject the impact of development on democratic stability or of democratic government on liberty. One must push them, in my opinion, well beyond what the evidence will bear. But it is worth noting the probable element of truth in this line of thought: simple correlations between aspects of "democracy" and "progress" can easily mislead the observer about the causal nature of the association. The implications are also interesting: the fate of democracy and the fate of social progress are *not* likely to be intertwined to any very great extent in the immediate future.

Progress Threatens Democracy

The most interesting of the visions of the decline of liberal democracy are those which foresee a continuation of "progress"—avoiding the economic disasters predicted by some—but the creation by that very progress of a set of conditions under which liberal democracy cannot survive. If this were to happen, either the idea of progress would have to be transformed to exclude its political component or the concept of "democracy" would again be modified to encompass a new set of arrangements. The different expectations about democracy and future progress have been generated largely from two sources: response to the upheavals within many of the industrialized liberal democracies appearing in the late 1960s and middle 1970s, and speculation about the meaning of the new "postindustrial" society that has begun to appear. Some of these doubts and expectations have to do with the new demands and pressures likely to emerge with increasing force in a postindustrial society—and the ability of liberal democracy to cope with these. Other doubts have to do with the capacity of democracy to cope with the nature of critical and possibly irreversible technological decisions.

The expectations about new demands and the doubts about the ability of democracy to cope with these without being destabilized were particularly stimulated by the numerous student protests and industrial strikes in the United States, Britain, Italy, and France, together with analyses of future trends. One expectation is that modernization has brought about fundamental value changes in contemporary society, as reflected in increased secularization, on the one hand, and increased emphasis on participation and self-fulfillment, on the other. These changes can be traced to changes in family structure, increased education and information, attainment of material security, and so forth. They imply intense pressures on governments to deal with social problems without a reserve of support for the regime; support becomes very oriented to short-term performance.[52] At the same time, demands for participatory involvement itself increase.[53] A related expectation is that traditional social groups are threatened by these events and demand government resistance to change and maintenance of order. In short, social transitions are likely to be destabilizing.[54] The great difficulty of democratic governments in dealing with these limitations on support and increased pressures for participation suggests more and more instability.

Moreover, education, mass communications and the growth of large numbers of organizations have made the mobilization of political pressure so easy and fluid that traditional mass linkage institutions, especially political parties, are obsolete and frequently by-passed. Hence, government has more and more to deal directly with pressure from citizen groups using a variety of direct protest and pressure tactics. Without effective political parties to set electoral choices and broadly mobilize and incorporate citizen support, governments will be too weak to keep citizen support.[55]

We might note at this point that although the theoretical bases of these arguments are unchanged, they do seem less threatening than at the high point of student unrest in the United States, Western Europe, and Japan in the late 1960s and early 1970s. Surveys continue to indicate some value and lifestyle changes among the young. But their containment within the more usual political bounds has been evident. Whether this is merely a short-term response to economic difficulties is not apparent. The continued low levels of political party support in the United States are, of course, a cause for concern, but it is difficult to separate the general impact of mobility, communications change, education, and other elements of "progress" from the especially American traumas of the Civil Rights movement, Vietnam, and Watergate.

A different type of concern is that technological specialization and the increased economic interdependence of modern societies give specialized groups increased power to disrupt society through strikes or

52. On legitimacy, see Lipset, *Political Man*, Chap. 3; and on secularization see Almond and Powell, *Comparative Politics*, pp. 46-51, 104-06.

53. See Ronald Inglehart, *The Silent Revolution: Changing Values and Political Styles Among Western Publics* (Princeton, N.J.: Princeton University Press, 1977); and the essay by Barnes, pp. 403ff.

54. See especially Samuel P. Huntington, "Postindustrial Politics: How Benign Will It Be?" *Comparative Politics*, 6 (January 1974): 163-92; Olson, "Rapid Growth."

55. See Huntington, "Postindustrial Politics"; and Crozier, Huntington, and Watanuki, *Crisis of Democracy*.

threatened withdrawal of support.[56] A strike by power plant workers, as Britain discovered, can cripple all economic activities. By giving such power to special minorities, "progress" actually undermines the possibility of citizen control over political decisions. The problem of pressure from specialized groups is, indeed, an interesting and important one, which does seem to follow at least in part from the very interdependence and specialization associated with economic development. Although a mass strike can always have a major impact on the economy and government, the new interdependence gives more weight to those in key bottleneck positions whereas the greater technical specialization makes it much harder to replace rebellious specialists. The National Guard can collect the garbage, but it is hard to see how it can run the nuclear power plants or computers. Democracies are presumably especially vulnerable to such specialist pressure because they facilitate the formation of pressure organizations. On the other hand, in the long run, the specialists, too, are dependent on other social groups and not invulnerable to various forms of government control and citizen pressure.

A final major concern is that in a highly technological society, critical and perhaps irreversible decisions must be made by political leaders: development of nuclear power plants, weapons planning, and social security structures. Citizens are often not involved in making these decisions and do not have the expertise to make rational choices. But once made, it is very difficult to alter the outcomes, as they involve huge amounts of planning and investment, and the implications may not be seen for very long periods of time. This problem is one of the most profound of the suggestions that the new social complexity will undermine democratic control. It is not, of course, the matter of elite specialization that is the problem. We saw that Madison long ago assumed that most citizens would not be involved in making the key decisions, that elites and specialized knowledge would be paramount. But the ability of citizens to tell leaders that they do not like what they are doing or do not like the consequences, even if they do not understand just what decisions were made, is the key to democratic control. The anticipation of citizen displeasure, the possibility of new aspiring challengers pointing to misdeeds of the incumbents and drawing upon citizen discontent, is the fundamental mechanism that propels elites to make decisions they think citizens will approve. And when they go wrong through misestimating citizen preference, through neglecting to bear it in mind, or through making real errors of policy, then the ability of the electorate to choose a different set of leaders can eventually rectify the situation. But if the implications of decisions can only be known long after the present leaders have left office or if the

56. See Samuel Brittan, "The Economic Contradictions of Democracy," *British Journal of Political Science*, 5 (April 1975): 129-159.

decisions, once made, are irreversible, then the mechanisms of democratic control are greatly weakened. Of course, this undermining does not necessarily imply that democracy will be replaced by a completely different regime form. Rather, it may mean increasingly that some very critical policy areas are simply removed from citizen control, and citizens will make their controlling decisions or exert their controlling anticipated pressure on grounds of other types of issues.[57]

Democratic Government
Incompatible with Social Progress

At least since the Greeks, opponents of democracy, and many of its defenders as well, have worried about the susceptibility of "the people" to "demogogues," their short-sighted concern with their personal interests, their unpredictable mob passions, their inability to grasp the broader issues of policy.[58] At least since the founding of the American republic, policy experts have groaned under the political pressures of the vote-seeking politician and resented the interference of popular sentiment into the serious business of administering "good" government. Such sentiments led the American Progressive movement to seek to eradicate political parties from local government and to emphasize professional city managers. These concerns appear again in a variety of doubts about the continued viability of the modern welfare state, the dangers of inflation, and the failure to sustain economic investment.[59]

One doubt is that political parties and politicians arouse citizen expectations to levels beyond what the society and the government can provide, generating, in effect, excess demand relative to capacity. To meet short-term political demands, especially when growth is slow, democratic politicians resort to various *inflationary policies*, directly or indirectly running the national printing press overtime. In

57. Since citizens are never offered in elections the total set of possible policy permutations from which to choose, the abandonment of citizen control over some policy areas may not in practice involve as radical an alteration in democratic performance as it would appear. Moreover, social choice theorists have demonstrated the existence of configurations of citizen preferences in which no single policy package is preferred by a voting majority to all other packages. The implications of social choice analyses, including the "Arrow Paradox" just alluded to, for democratic theory and practice are rigorously developed by William H. Riker, *Liberalism Against Populism: A Confrontation Between the Theory of Democracy and the Theory of Public Choice* San Francisco, Ca.: W.H. Freeman, 1981). Nonetheless, the appearance or recognition of large decision areas where policies are irreversible once they are made would seem profoundly to alter the potential for citizen control and elite accountability even where clear-cut majorities do appear.

58. See Hartz, "Democracy"; and Laski, *Democracy in Crisis.*

59. Brittan, "Economic Contradictions"; Huang, "Democracy, Competition, and Development," Chaps. 1-3; Richard Rose and Guy Peters, *Can Government Go Bankrupt?* (New York: Basic Books, 1978).

the long run, such inflationary policies undermine the economic prosperity of the country. To meet these short-term, competition-induced demands, politicians also encourage and compete to impose *taxation on profits and other sources of investment* in order to transfer the money to consumption-oriented sectors. This, too, undermines growth in the long run.

A second doubt is that competitive democracies encourage parties to offer elaborate welfare policies to the less well-off citizens. These and other *consumption-oriented projects limit needed economic investment*, encourage inflation, undermine the incentives for citizen work-productivity, and otherwise serve to destroy economic prosperity in the long run. A third is that the advantages enjoyed by organized groups in democracies enable them to *protect the economically inefficient and entrench them institutionally*. Such phenomena are seen in labor unions, firms in the military-industrial complex, farm organizations, welfare groups, and in many other areas. Once programs of support and relevant bureaucratic agencies are established, it is nearly impossible to eliminate them because of organizational leverage (see Wildavsky, pp. 360ff.). Hence, inefficiencies are increasingly built into the economy and society, undermining future progress.

These various charges that democracies make bad policies, especially short-sighted economic policies, depend in part on particular economic theories that are themselves far from securely established. But more profoundly, they depend also on the degree to which citizens, under the guidance of or responding to alternatives offered to them by political parties and leaders, will be capable of learning about relationships among inflation, consumption, and investment. Will citizens prove capable of taking into account long-term goals in choosing between alternative leaders? Will they prove forceful enough to demand that general interests be imposed over those of special organized interests, once it is shown that these seriously threaten generally desired goals?

These are not questions easily answered in the abstract. But the historical record of citizens on these issues is not as one-sided as many critics seem to believe. Citizens have certainly proven their willingness to accept serious sacrifices for the national interest in time of war. They have backed civil service legislation and programs over the temptations of corruption. Recent events in Britain, and elsewhere in Western Europe as well as in the United States, suggest that they have begun to appreciate the painful trade-offs that have to be made between investment in growth, taxation, and public expenditure and in income policies. Without either idealizing the educated citizen who is offered reasonable choices or minimizing the seriousness of the economic arguments about government interference, it seems, nonetheless, premature to conclude that citizens in democracies are incapable of learning.

TRANSFORMING THE VISION OF
PROGRESS AND DEMOCRACY

Ideas shape events, but they are also shaped by them. The specific form of the working democratic ideal and its inclusion in the culture of progress that had taken shape by the end of World War I was at least as much created by political events of the late nineteenth and early twentieth century as it altered them. The subsequent consolidation of that vision of progress and democracy has been buttressed by the success of their association. There have been some severe challenges, but "progress and democracy" have withstood them, and emerged stronger as a consequence.

Not long after liberal democracy was finally established as the dominating form of political regime by the victory of the democracies in World War I, it was shaken by the upheavals of the 1930s. It is easy to forget the impact upon social thought made by the collapse of Weimar Germany, a citadel of Western culture regardless of its lagged social and political progress, and the emergence of fascist authoritarianism as a challenge. The overthrow of democratic governments in Chile, Greece, Austria, Argentina, and Estonia and the intense conflict in other countries hit by the Depression were also significant. Doubts about both progress and democracy, as well as their association, were expressed that go far beyond those of our own time. But while the slow awakening of democracies to meet the challenge led to short-term despair, events after World War II again reestablished some confidence in the vision of progress and democracy.

The postwar period brought Soviet communism to the fore as a challenge. Here was a vision of progress and democracy, too, but with democracy, in particular, transformed into a claim of trusteeship by the Communist party—a claim to act in the interests of the people without engaging in divisive consultation of their wishes.[60] Participation becomes symbolic affirmation of leaders in elections without a choice. Liberty is "temporarily" sacrificed, but equality is more immediately introduced. The success of Soviet modernization, the impressive achievements of Soviet arms in the defeat of the German invasion, the spread of Soviet power in Eastern Europe and elsewhere, and the persuasiveness of an alternative vision of progress and democracy made this vision a real challenge to liberal democracy. Nonetheless, divisions in the Soviet camp, brutal use of Soviet forces in Eastern Europe, the ideological struggle between Russia and China, the failure of the communist vision to bring about rapid progress in the Third World, all served to weaken the force of the Soviet challenge. So, on the other side, did twenty-five years of growth and prosperity among the industrialized democracies.

The collapse of a number of the oldest democracies in less economically developed countries in the 1960s and early 1970s—Greece,

60. See Sartori, "Democracy"; and the essay by Meyer, pp. 67ff.

Chile, Uruguay, and the Philippines—has more recently shaken faith in democracy among those faced with the seemingly intractable problems of bringing about real progress in less modernized societies. Not only had democracy seemed shaky, as have all other regime forms in those societies, but the apparent success of some military governments, especially that in Brazil,[61] in turning democratic stagnation into rapid economic growth, presented a new challenge: technocratic or bureaucratic authoritarianism. As is pointed out by Crawford Young, the Third World retains its faith in material progress as a goal to be sought, but there is doubt that liberal democracy can bring it about (see pp. 100ff.). The economic success of Brazil has, of course, been counterposed by some dreadful failures of military, oligarchic, or single-party governments in the Third World. One need only think of Uganda, Nicaragua, or Guinea to observe economic stagnation without liberty; nor have the military governments in Uruguay and Chile been able to create economic miracles.[62] Still, Huang's work suggests that political competition in the Third World countries, whether or not associated with liberal democracy, has been associated with inflationary policies.[63] And it is easy to forget the democratic success stories (such as Costa Rica, for example). Many Third World citizens and elites may perceive that drastic measures are needed to create even a possibility of economic progress. Democracy may well seem unlikely to provide these drastic measures; too much bargaining and compromise is involved. Hence, such citizens, if offered a choice in the matter, might well choose the probability of elite irresponsibility and/or elite economic failure in order to create some possibility for economic success.[64] It is easy to understand, at least, the disintegration of the image of progress and liberal democracy under such conditions.

In the industrialized nations the impact of failure in the Third World has been rather slight.[65] There are, after all, strong elements in the history of progressive thought that foresaw the benign cycle of progress and democracy taking hold only after some basic level of "progress," at least education and literacy, had been achieved. The impact of the upheavals of the late 1960s and early 1970s in the

61. On Brazil's record, see Alfred Stepan, ed., *Authoritarian Brazil* (New Haven, Conn.: Yale University Press, 1973).

62. For quantitative evidence of the performance by such regimes, see the World Bank, *World Bank Atlas* (Washington, D.C.: World Bank, 1978).

63. Huang, "Democracy, Competition, and Development."

64. It is possible, and worth investigating, that the variance of economic success is greater under authoritarian regimes—that such regimes are prone both to greater elite abuse and economic disasters and greater economic investment and growth under elite control—than is true of democracies. If that were so and if the average democratic success is inadequate to sustain rapid growth, then the "rational" citizen in a poor country might not unreasonably choose authoritarianism as his best, if risky, hope of development.

65. An exception is the response of the Italian elite, especially the communists, to the overthrow of democracy in Chile.

industrial states themselves, however, was quite substantial. Racial violence in the United States and ethnic violence in Northern Ireland demonstrated that economic development does not necessarily bring social peace. Student riots and labor strikes, growth of extremist "protest" parties, a wave of political terrorism, economic recession and future economic dependence in the wake of the new oil cartel and oil price increases, all shook the confidence of democratic citizens, elites, and observers. Yet from broader historical and comparative perspective the record was quite impressive. Without an explicit challenging vision of a viable alternative political form, the concerned observers pointed vaguely to instability and technocratic authoritarianism or to democracy with diminished meaning as the prospects for the future either in a "regressive" or a "postindustrial" society. In the short run, the outburst of doubts about democracy seemed more evidence of a failure of nerve or simply a resurgence of those familiar antidemocratic sentiments that have their own tradition in "progressive" thought[66] than forerunners of a new transformation of the vision of progress and democracy.

In the longer run, of course, real transformations are quite possible. If economic progress comes to an end, then quite likely some democracies will collapse as well. The first three-quarters of the twentieth century may stand in history as that unique period in which the conditions for social progress and liberal democracy obtained. On the other hand, if a new, emergent set of conditions creates antipathies between progress and democracy—because of the irreversibility of policy decisions, the enhanced bargaining power of special groups, or the dynamics of short-term citizen preference—we might see a transformation of the idea of progress in which liberal democracy is dropped from the "package" of ideas that constitute progress, and democracy itself transformed, abandoned, or relegated to nostalgic memory and unsustainable ideal. I am inclined to believe, however, that the capacities of citizens to learn and the capacities of leaders to lead and to devise new, democratic arrangements for citizen involvement and organized control have been too little tried to justify such a pessimistic prediction. Faith in the resilience and inventiveness of the human spirit is, of course, an essential part of the progressive idea.

66. See the essay by Jeffrey D. Straussman, "Technocratic Counsel and Societal Guidance," in Lindberg, *Politics and the Future of Industrial Society*, pp. 126-66.

19

Changing Popular Attitudes
Toward Progress

SAMUEL H. BARNES

The idea of progress is a philosophical construct, elaborated and perpetuated by intellectuals. For the mass public, progress is a concrete
reality that is measured primarily by material well-being. A belief in
progress has been a dominant theme in Western culture for at least
two centuries, seemingly shared by elite and mass alike. Yet there is
little hard evidence for assuming similar elite-mass attitudes regarding progress. It is elites who create systems of ideas, and it is elites
who write and interpret history. Of the attitudes and beliefs of non-
elites we know very little.

Nevertheless, it is easy to believe that the mass public has shared in
the dominant belief in progress. In previous centuries, people lived
out their lives in environments quite similar to those into which they
were born. Historians, in retrospect, see change taking place in the
most stable of societies; but its pace must appear glacial to most
participants, for whom decline and progress seem due to forces beyond
their control, whether bad weather, invasion, overpopulation, or evil
or incompetent leaders. The idea of an ever-brighter future is modern,
and that idea seems to have been widely shared by elites and masses in
the United States and many other countries in the last two centuries,
during which Western publics—and especially North American publics
—have experienced expanding opportunities. The existence of a geographical frontier, of increasing scientific knowledge, and of rapid
economic growth combined to provide incentives for individual
achievement, rising material living standards, and egalitarian politics.
No systematic data exist to indicate what mass publics thought about

all this, but it is hard not to believe that every generation viewed its life as being better than the previous generation's. That is progress. How does it relate to the idea of progress?

The relationship between mass attitudes and philosophical systems is poorly understood. Few scholars would deny the existence of some form of linkage. But mass publics do not respond to events in terms of highly structured belief systems. Ideological sophistication is largely a monopoly of elites. And whatever else it is, the idea of progress is also an ideology, or ideological fragment, that is, a widely shared set of normative beliefs with implications for action. Without denying the impact of ideology on some mass publics at some times, we prefer to make no assumptions about the impact of ideology on mass publics. Instead, we will concentrate on mass needs and values and examine how they may or may not be linked with such elite concepts as the idea of progress.

Two caveats are in order before we proceed. One concerns the use of the term "mass." The distinction between "elite" and "mass" is in part a formal one. In contemporary societies, the expansion of education has raised the knowledge level of everyone and has vastly increased the percentage of the population that is able to respond to abstractions. What we treat as a dichotomy is in fact a series of subtle gradations. Moreover, populations are not an undifferentiated mass. They are composed of segments and groups with well-defined profiles. Some are in decline and some are ascending, with quite different perspectives on progress. Some subsets of the population are linked organizationally and culturally with philosophical positions—religious groups, for example—whereas other groups exist only in the tables of behavioral scientists. In short, speaking in general about mass attitudes grossly simplifies what is a complex and fascinating reality.

A second caveat concerns the nature of our data. For the distant past we are limited to the historical records left us—largely by elites. For the present, we have somewhat more information, at least for the last thirty years, in which systematic representative samples of mass publics have been interviewed on a reasonably regular basis. These studies permit us to generalize about mass populations. But interviews with representative samples must be restricted in length, complexity, and scope. They must be pitched at a level that can be understood by most of the respondents. Hence, questions often have a frustrating, even banal, simplicity. Studies that probe deeply into the conscious and subconscious structure of people's beliefs are of necessity limited to small populations. We trade off complexity for representivity in order to generalize about mass publics.

PERCEPTIONS OF PROGRESS

The study of mass opinions is still in its infancy. Investigations of popular evaluations of quality of life, of subjective indicators of aspirations, achievement, happiness, and satisfaction, are among the more recently mined terrain within this new field. Most of the evidence is from Western democratic systems, especially the United States. Although pioneering work by Hadley Cantril investigated people's hopes and fears around the world, and thus gives us some insights into a wider set of mass publics, this fruitful path has not been widely pursued so that our evidence is quite limited.[1] Even so, some results are so consistent in all the studies that they have the ring of universal applicability, though this is a dangerous claim to make in social science; of course, future findings may restrict their generalizability.

It is people's perceptions of progress that matter. Although these perceptions relate to reality in interesting ways, they are not closely correlated with objective indicators. At least *within* particular countries, income, educational level, quality of housing, job, and other "hard" indicators tell us very little about people's level of satisfaction, happiness, optimism for the future, or sense of achievement.[2] This runs counter to conventional wisdom. It seems sensible to expect that those who possess more, whether income, education, or material goods, would also be higher on subjective indicators of satisfaction or happiness or optimism concerning the future. Indeed, the relationship is consistently positive, both within countries and between countries. But what seems more important is the weakness of the relationship. Thus, in a study by Ronald Inglehart, a combined sample of nine European countries in 1973 showed that the percentage reporting that they were "very satisfied" with their lives as a whole rose from 28 percent of those with incomes of under $200 per month to 31 percent of those $800-$999 and 37 percent of those over $1000.[3] Richard A. Easterlin has reviewed studies on the relationship between income and happiness and reaches a quite different conclusion.[4] Easterlin is correct in his summary: "This positive relation between happiness and income appears in every single one of the thirty national surveys

1. Hadley Cantril, *The Pattern of Human Concerns* (New Brunswick, N.J.: Rutgers University Press, 1965).

2. These findings are documented in Ronald Inglehart, *The Silent Revolution* (Princeton, N.J.: Princeton University Press, 1977), p. 117; Angus Campbell, Philip Converse, and Willard L. Rodgers, *The Quality of American Life: Perceptions, Evaluations, and Satisfactions* (New York: Russel Sage Foundation, 1976), pp. 171-210; Stephen B. Withey and Frank M. Andrews, *Social Indicators of Well-Being* (New York: Plenum, 1976), pp. 283-334; and Ephraim Yuchtman (Yaar), "Effects of Psychosocial Psychological Factors on Subjective Economic Welfare," in *Economic Means for Human Needs: Social Indicators of Well-Being and Discontent*, ed. Brukhard Strumpel (Ann Arbor, Mich.: Institute for Social Research, 1976), p. 126.

3. Inglehart, *Silent Revolution*, Table 5.1, p. 126.

4. Richard A. Easterlin, "Does Economic Growth Improve the Human Lot?" in *Nations and Households in Economic Growth*, ed. P. A. David and M. W. Redes (New York: Academic Press, 1974), pp. 89-125; abbreviated in Easterlin's "Does Money Buy Happiness?" *Public Interest*, 3 (1973): 3-10. Note that Easterlin deals with "happiness" not "satisfaction." While the two measures are related, they are not the same. The differences need not concern us here but are suggested by the following: the old tend to be satisfied but unhappy, the young happy but unsatisfied. For a full explanation see Campbell, Converse, and Rodgers, *Quality of American Life.*

studied."[5] But very little of the variance in happiness is explained by income. For example, a correlation of 0.2 between two variables means that 4 percent of the variance in one is explained by the other. Moreover, it is not possible to demonstrate causality with correlations.

The weakness of the socioeconomic model in explaining satisfaction is suggested by Table 1. In it, Ronald Inglehart has utilized a set of standard social background variables as predictors of several attitudinal domains in 1973. It is clear that social background variables are much more powerful predictors of many other attitudes than they are of overall life satisfaction. And they are weakest in the United States.

TABLE 1
Attitudinal Variance Explained by Social Structure in Nine Nations (1973)[a]

Nation	Left-Right Self-Placement	Political Party Identification	Voting Intention	Value Priorities	Overall Life Satisfaction
France	51	37	28	35	12
The Netherlands	41	43	35	22	10
Belgium	16	49	43	23	12
Italy	58	25	25	24	10
Denmark	35	28	23	28	11
Britain	45	25	26	12	13
Germany	31	27	23	28	8
Ireland	10	2	4	15	12
United States	8	37	27	17	6
Mean (all nations)	33	30	26	23	10

[a]Percentage of total variance explained by multiple classification analysis model using standard social background predictor variables.

SOURCE: Ronald Inglehart, *The Silent Revolution* (Princeton, N.J.: Princeton University Press 1977), p. 130.

Data from both the Institute for Social Research (ISR) and the National Opinion Research Center (NORC) indicate that the correlations between income and perceived happiness have been declining since 1957 (see Table 2). The 1976 ISR survey shows a "blip" not present in the NORC data; presumably, it should be attributed to sampling problems.

This decline in the correlations through time adds support for the argument to be pursued here, which is that changing values are leading to changing conceptions of progress in the United States and that

5. Easterlin, "Does Money Buy Happiness?" p. 6.

TABLE 2
Correlations Between Income and Happiness
in the United States (1957-1978)

	Correlations (r)	
Year	Total Sample	College Graduates
ISR Surveys		
1957	0.24	0.08
1971	0.18	0.03
1972	0.15	0.13
1976	0.26	0.18
1978	0.12	0.04
NORC Surveys		
1963	0.25	
1972	0.12	
1973	0.20	
1974	0.15	
1975	0.14	
1976	0.16	
1977	0.19	
1978	0.14	

SOURCE: Unpublished research of Angus Campbell, Institute of Social Research, University of Michigan.

the educated are leading the way in this change. The weak relationship between family income and perceived happiness of college graduates, as indicated in Table 2, strengthens this argument. We conclude that income is not a strong predictor of satisfaction, that it is declining in importance, and that this decline will probably continue for reasons explored below.

The reason why the socioeconomic model explains little of the variance in evaluations of personal well-being is that popular attitudes are based on personal experience and are related not only to achievements but to expectations. Indeed, it is the gap between expectations and achievements that has the most significant societal consequences. This gap is as likely to be large among high achievers as lower achievers. This simple fact is quite relevant to understanding the current American malaise and the apparent disillusionment with progress within the intelligentsia. The dynamics of the process have been admirably summed up as follows: "Progress or success makes for rising levels of aspiration. Getting what one wants results in stepping up one's sights rather than in being satisfied and desiring nothing more than to keep and maintain what one already has. The achievement of a higher income and an improved standard of living results not in saturation but in new wants."[6] Robert Merton has written: "In the American Dream there is no final stopping point. . . . At each income level . . . Americans want about 25 percent more."[7]

Perhaps the process of aspiration formation can best be understood in Kurt Lewin's formulation of the concept of "person-environment fit." Lewin wrote that aspirations are not static; they "tend to grow with achievement and decline with failure." They are "reality-oriented." Consequently, aspirations fluctuate with the fortunes of individuals and the state of the economy. For example, the proportion of the American population listing unfilled wants *declines* in periods of recession, especialy among upper-income people.[8] The economic success of the United States undoubtedly contributes to the presumed current disillusionment with progress. "Rapidly growing expectations easily lead to disappointment—the greater the aspirations, the greater the danger of frustration. The more we feel we must have, the smaller the chance of gratifying all our wants and the greater the possibility of greater expectations making for stress, tension, and anxiety."[9] The malaise of intellectuals is undoubtedly related to frustrations growing out of the gap between aspirations and achievements. Two centuries of seeming progress in every field, the utopianism of many twentieth-century political movements, even the abandonment of the doctrines of original sin and the imperfectability of man have contributed to high aspirations for mankind on the part of intellectuals. The gap between these aspirations and the human condition looms large indeed. Among mass publics the gap is measured in a myriad of small defeats and victories with few perceived cosmic consequences. And among mass publics the gap is reduced by adjusting aspirations.[10]

There is no *necessary* relationship between general economic well-being, national decline, scientific discovery, improved welfare benefits or—seemingly—any other indicator of progress and individual perceptions of progress. Factors external to the individual's immediate experience must be translated into personal terms in order to have an

6. George Katona, Burkhard Strumpel, and Ernest Zahn, *Aspirations and Affluence* (New York: McGraw-Hill, 1971), p. 12.

7. Robert Merton, *Social Theory and Social Structure* (New York: McGraw-Hill, 1962), pp. 136-37.

8. Quoted in George Katona, *Psychological Economics* (New York: Elsevier, 1975), pp. 154, 157.

9. Katona, Strumpel, and Zahn, *Aspirations and Affluence*, p. 14.

10. Campbell, Converse, and Rodgers, *Quality of American Life*, p. 169.

impact. This translation process is not well understood. One point of view is that external factors simply have no impact. However, there are national differences in absolute levels of satisfaction, happiness, and optimism that suggest that something must be having a differential impact on people in different countries. We will return to this point later.

One likely explanation for the weak impact of many seemingly important factors is that they are taken for granted. For example, while there is no direct evidence that scientific discovery is discounted in advance, the ho-hum popular response to the moon landing suggests that science is now *expected* to produce spectaculars. There is considerable evidence that an increase in economic well-being leads only to temporary increases in satisfaction and happiness, after which the new higher level is taken for granted and aspirations resume their upward climb.[11]

SOME REASONS FOR A POPULAR BELIEF IN PROGRESS

We have emphasized the great variation in evaluations of personal well-being and the poor predictive power of such objective indicators as income and education. But there is one perception that, while subjective and individual, is so strongly held by Americans that it constitutes a cultural norm. That is the belief that individual progress reflects personal achievement. Americans believe in personal effort, that they are getting what they deserve.[12] Several studies document the tendency of Americans to blame themselves for their lack of achievement. Even low-status Americans are in general not prone to blame the system for their condition. Americans are more ego-involved in income increases than Europeans; the latter more often attribute increases to government and trade union activity.[13] This emphasis on the personal element in success and failure serves to isolate the individual from larger social explanations.[14]

Two other factors reinforce contemporary tendencies toward optimism concerning personal progress. One is the expansion of education, which has greatly increased both average levels of education and the percentage of the population with various forms of higher educa-

11. Inglehart, *Silent Revolution*, p. 119.
12. Katona, *Psychological Economics*, p. 400.
13. Katona, Strumpel, and Zahn, *Aspirations and Affluence*, p. 190.
14. Gerald Gurin and Patricia Gurin, "Personal Efficacy and the Ideology of Individual Responsibility," in *Economic Means for Human Needs*, pp. 150-51. An interesting comparative study of cultural differences noted that Americans "see personal progress as leading to the improvement of the collectivity" whereas Greeks see "personal progress as a consequent of the improvement of the collectivity"; Harry C. Triandis and Vasso Vassiliou, "A Comparative Analysis of Subjective Culture," in *The Analysis of Subjective Culture*, ed. Harry C. Triandis (New York: Wiley, 1972), p. 331.

tion. At least until very recently, individuals with higher education had every reason to be optimistic about their personal future. Furthermore, many were the first in their family to obtain higher education and could easily see their progress compared with their parents'.

A different but related factor emerges from the structure of occupations and careers.[15] In agricultural and other traditional societies, individual well-being was a result of status at birth and physical vigor. Most people were in the primary sector of the economy, and people reached their maximum levels of achievement and income while quite young; indeed, most died young. The structure of white-collar occupations is hierarchical, and they require education or experience, or both. Thus, individuals can expect their conditions to improve as they climb the career ladder. Peak earnings typically are deferred until age forty to fifty or after. Consequently, it is not unrealistic for people to be optimistic about their personal futures regardless of general trends. That is, individuals should progress even if the economy and society as a whole do not, assuming, of course, that the system continues to function.[16] The possibility of individual progress is scarcely questioned in the United States, though college students in the 1970s may be more anxious on that score than those of the past forty years.[17] The career patterns of advanced societies thus lead to expectations of individual progress and also encourage individuals to feel that they are themselves responsible for that progress, regardless of the despair of intellectuals, cosmic pessimism, or perhaps even national decline. This independence of individual from national evaluations is reflected in two sets of ratings from surveys conducted by Patrick Caddell. These indicate Americans' estimates of how well the country was doing and how well they were doing personally, for five years in the past, the present, and five years in the future. The methodology for these ratings is explained below. Table 3 shows the precipitous decline in the national ratings and the much more modest decline in the personal ratings.

NATIONAL DIFFERENCES IN OPTIMISM
ABOUT THE FUTURE

There are few studies that deal directly with mass attitudes toward progress, whether nationally or on a cross-national basis. However,

15. This point is emphasized in Katona, Strumpel, and Zahn, *Aspirations and Affluence*. The changing occupational structure is explored in Daniel Bell, *The Coming of Post-Industrial Society* (New York: Basic Books, 1973).

16. Preliminary reports from an Institute for Social Research study document a vast increase in the extent of repeated worrying among young people between 1957 and 1976, from about 30 percent to about 50 percent among those 21-29 and 30-39 (percentages estimated from graph on p. 5 of *ISR Newsletter*, winter 1979).

17. Two very useful studies of changing values of youth in the United States are by Daniel Yankelovich: *The Changing Values on Campus* (New York: Washington Square Press, 1973), and *The New Morality* (New York: McGraw-Hill, 1974).

TABLE 3
United States Satisfaction with Nation and with
Personal Life (Cantril Ladder Scores)

Year	Past (5 Years Ago)	Present	Future (5 Years from Now)
Nation			
1959	6.5	6.7	7.4
1964	6.1	6.5	7.1
1971	6.2	5.4	6.2
1975	6.4	4.3	5.4
1976	5.6	4.8	5.8
1977	4.8	5.0	6.3
1978	5.2	4.9	5.4
1979	5.7	4.7	4.6
Personal Life			
1959	5.9	6.6	7.8
1964	6.0	6.9	7.9
1971	5.8	6.6	7.5
1975	6.1	6.3	7.0
1976	5.8	6.4	7.4
1977	5.6	6.1	7.2
1978	5.5	6.2	6.9
1979	6.1	6.4	6.7

SOURCE: Patrick H. Caddell, "Trapped in a Downward Spiral," *Public Opinion*, 2 (October-November 1979): 2-8.

there are considerable data on personal satisfaction, data that permit comparisons between the past and present and the present and future. The earliest findings are from research by Hadley Cantril. Cantril utilized a self-anchoring ladder as a measure of satisfaction: respondents were asked to think of the top of the ladder as the "best possible" life and the bottom as the "worst possible," both as defined by the respondent. There are ten rungs on the ladder. The respondent places himself on the ladder where he thinks he is today, where he was five years ago, and where he will be five years in the future.[18] Everywhere, expectations for the future are higher than evaluations of the present.

18. Cantril, *Pattern of Human Concerns*, pp. 22-23.

But the national differences in the evaluation of the present and in the level of improvement anticipated in the future are striking (see Table 4).

TABLE 4

Evaluations of Past, Present, and Future Personal Ratings
(1-10 Cantril Ladder Scale)

Country	Past (5 Years Ago)	Present	Future (5 Years from Now)
United States	5.9	6.6	7.8
Germany	4.1	5.3	6.2
Yugoslavia	4.3	5.0	6.7
Poland	4.0	4.4	5.5
Brazil	4.1	4.6	7.3
Nigeria	2.8	4.8	7.4
India	3.4	3.7	5.1
Israel	4.7	5.3	6.9
Egypt	4.6	5.5	8.0
Cuba	4.1	6.4	8.4
Dominican Republic	1.6	1.6	5.8
Panama	4.5	4.8	7.0
Philippines	4.9	4.9	6.7
Japan	4.6	5.2	6.2

SOURCE: Hadley Cantril, *The Pattern of Human Concerns* (New Brunswick, N.J.: Rutgers University Press, 1965), passim.

The Cantril findings indicate a strong relationship between national economic development and mean national levels of satisfaction. Cantril constructed a composite measure of economic development based on eleven indicators of general welfare, communications, industrialization, urbanization, and education. The resulting socioeconomic index (converted to a 0.0-1.0 scale, with the United States equaling 1.0, India 0.0, and other countries in between) was then correlated with the personal ladder ratings for present, past, and future. The rank order correlations were 0.67 (significant at the 0.01 level) for the present, 0.56 for the past (significant at the 0.05 level), and 0.11 for the future.[19] As these data are aggregated to the national level, the relationships are moderate at best for present and past, and negligible

19. Ibid., pp. 193-94.

for the future. But the results do indicate that levels of economic development play a very important role in accounting for *national* differences in subjective evaluations of the present and past. Easterlin misinterpreted the Cantril findings concerning economic development and satisfaction, arguing that there was no relationship between the two.[20] A rank order correlation of 0.67 is rather strong; socioeconomic development does make a difference. Easterlin is correct in emphasizing that countries are often above or below where they should be if socioeconomic variables were the only important contributors to national levels of satisfaction. He also points out that increases in national levels of income do not lead directly to increases in satisfaction. He argues that people tend to compare their own level to the level of those around them, and if all are going up individuals are less aware of their own improvements.[21]

These results support the arguments we will make concerning changing values. Especially important is the very weak relationship between the socioeconomic index and future expectations. The gap between present and future is far greater in the less-developed than the developed countries. Part of this phenomenon is undoubtedly explained by a ceiling effect in the developed countries; they simply have less room for improvement. But there are vast national differences in expectations for the future. Five of the highest ladder ratings for the future are found in developing countries: Cuba (8.4), Egypt (8.0), Nigeria (7.4), Brazil (7.3), and Panama (7.0). The future is alive and well in the Third World!

In this same study, respondents were asked to rate national achievements and expectations as well as personal ones. The correlations of national rankings with the socioeconomic index are weaker than the personal ones: present (0.47—significant at the 0.05 level), past (0.39), and future (0.15).[22] Of the fifteen countries for which measures were obtained, in only three was the gap between past and present greater for the personal than for the national ladder. These three were the United States, Brazil, and the Philippines.[23] This suggests that individuals in those three countries feel that they have been doing better than their country and adds support for our contention that American mass publics view progress in highly personal terms. Personal and national ladder ratings for present and future show only two Israeli samples and India indicating a higher shift for the nation than for the individual; this too reinforces our point about the personal nature of belief in progress but suggests that Americans are not particularly distinctive in this assessment.[24]

The Cantril research provides evidence that ceiling effects and levels

20. Easterlin, "Does Money Buy Happiness?" pp. 7-8.   21. Ibid., pp. 8-9.
22. Cantril, *Pattern of Human Concerns*, p. 194.
23. Ibid., pp. 195-96.   24. Ibid., p. 188.

of socioeconomic development have a strong impact on national differences in optimism concerning the future. It is clear that much variance remains to be explained and that, in particular, there is great variation among countries that are quite close on socioeconomic indicators. Perhaps the low expectations for the future exhibited by respondents in the Dominican Republic, though deviating from the pattern of developing countries, does not merit an extensive search for explanations. But the considerable differences existing among countries that seem outwardly quite similar are a challenge to social scientists. The optimism of certain Third World countries such as Cuba, Egypt, and Nigeria seems related to the exhilaration of revolution or decolonization just prior to the field work. The low ladder ratings for the future in Japan and West Germany (both 6.2), two of the world's most prosperous countries, are striking; only Poland, the Dominican Republic, and India are lower.[25] A ready, ad hoc, explanation for the Japanese and German results might be that economic expansion was not yet well entrenched in 1959-1960 when the Cantril studies were carried out. However, replication of the ladder scales in Germany, the United States, and six other countries in 1974-1975 indicates that the pessimism of the Germans about the future was persisting.[26] Unfortunately, Japan was not included in the later study. In 1974, Germans ranked themselves 6.7 on the material satisfaction ladder and 7.1 on the life-as-a-whole satisfaction ladder. German expectations for five years in the future on the two ladders were 6.4 and 6.9. American ratings were 6.9 and 7.4 for the two present ladders and 7.7 and 8.2 for the future. Very pessimistic outlooks for the future were held by Germans (and Austrians) in the mid-1970s. In both countries, the percentage with decreasing expectations for the future (41 percent) is similar to those with increasing expectations (43 percent in Germany and 42 percent in Austria).[27] In the United States, the decreasing category was 22 percent and the increasing 63 percent. The figures for Britain were 29 percent and 53 percent, and for the Netherlands 30 percent and 45 percent. Thus, other European countries did not share the German and Austrian pessimism. These findings are even more surprising given the economic situation at the time of the 1974 field work, as the United States and Britain were still recovering from recession and other economic problems whereas the two Central European countries were prospering. Obviously, expectations for the future reflect far more than national economic well-being.

This optimism of Americans is well documented in other studies.

25. Ibid., p. 197.
26. Data reported here are from an eight-nation study. A first cross-national report is Samuel H. Barnes, Max Kaase, et. al., *Political Action: Mass Participation in Five Western Democracies* (Beverly Hills, Ca.: Sage Publications, 1979).
27. Ibid., p. 400.

Katona, Strumpel, and Zahn conclude that "Americans are more confident about further progress than West Europeans; the proportion of individuals who believe that they are making progress—not only that they are better off than a few years ago but that they will be better off a few years hence—is much larger in the United States than in Germany, Holland, or England."[28] The authors note that "in some thirty to forty surveys conducted between 1959 and 1968, the differences between the American and German data were found to be quite similar to those obtained in 1968."[29] German and American consumers react differently to improved expectations: the Americans respond expansively; Germans, defensively.[30] Whether the reasons derive from the exposed position and traumas of twentieth-century Central Europe, historical memories of runaway inflation, or deeply ingrained cultural pessimism, the American-European—and especially German —differences are very real. As Jean-Jacques Servan-Schreiber wrote, Europeans "continue to suffer progress rather than to pursue it."[31]

We are unable, in this paper, to probe any deeper into these national differences. We have established two points that are relevant for our larger concern with mass attitudes toward progress. The first is that levels of perceived achievement across countries are related to objective levels of socioeconomic development, but expectations for the future are affected by many other factors. The second point is that despite the overall relationship first mentioned, levels of perceived achievement and of future expectations vary greatly among countries at similar levels of socioeconomic development, with Americans much more optimistic than Europeans in general and Germans in particular.

CHANGING VALUES AND THE
IDEA OF PROGRESS

It is sometimes posited that human needs are insatiable. There seems to be no clear evidence on this point. Indeed, phrased in this manner it is doubtful that this is a scientific problem, that is, a question for which there is an empirical answer. But if we follow up on the thrust of the statement, we find that there are several aspects of needs about which we have a great deal of relevant theory and even some knowledge.

A basic point is that human needs are socially conditioned. They are not genetically programmed, except for the needs for food, water, and shelter, and—perhaps—some need for safety. Beyond these very basic needs—essentially those of the human animal—man's needs are formed by society, by the interaction of the personality with others.

28. Katona, Strumpel, and Zahn, *Aspirations and Affluence*, p. 42.
29. Ibid., p. 50.   30. Ibid., p. 84.
31. Jean-Jacques Servan-Schreiber, *The American Challenge* (New York: Atheneum, 1968), p. 185.

That this is true has been widely acknowledged at least since Marx.[32]

Needs are closely related to values. Many scholars use the terms interchangeably. Values may be viewed as deeply held attitudes concerning what one should get out of life. All values can be placed in a limited number of categories. Most life goals have some value; therefore, the most meaningful approach to the measurement of values is to rank them rather than simply to rate how much they are valued. Life forces choices on people; they must choose to maximize some values over others. The notion of choice is important. Many people are not presented with choices. Alternatives may be limited; many must choose basic necessities. Or they choose what others expect them to. Patterns of choice are thought to be established in childhood. Most of mankind has always lived amidst scarcity. Not only are material goods in short supply: love, esteem, belongingness are likewise elusive. Life is haunted by what is missing in childhood. We are driven by that of which we are deprived; we seek what we did not have. Even when we get it, we seek more of it. It follows that only those who are not deprived are spared this psychological determinism; only those few develop values free of the constraints of some kind of necessity.

Humanistic psychologists, and Abraham Maslow in particular, have erected a theoretical framework on these fragments of an economy of psychic scarcity. Maslow argues that human needs, and hence values, fit together in a hierarchical fashion, that some needs are more basic than others, and that higher-order needs are sought only after the lower-order ones are satisfied.[33] Needs are complex, and Maslow speaks of need areas encompassing syndromes of specific needs. The more fundamental needs are the physiological ones. Then come safety and security needs. Affection and a sense of belonging are next on the hierarchy, followed by the need for the esteem of others. The highest level is self-realization or self-actualization. Little is known about this level; it is the realm of creativity, self-fulfillment, "doing what he is fitted for."[34] The first four levels comprise deprivation needs. According to Maslow, people are driven not by what they do not currently have but by what they did not have in childhood. It is perhaps in this sense that needs are insatiable; the hungry child never gets enough food or wealth as an adult; the rejected child seeks love and belongingness as an adult; and so on. Maslow argues that needs higher up can be met only if the lower ones are met. Presumably, however, individuals can move up (and down?) the hierarchy. What this possibility seems to imply is that, in a probabilistic sense, the portion of the population "fixed" at a particular level should vary with changes in material well-being, security, national integration, and so on.

32. Carlo Tullio-Altan, *I valori difficili: Inchiesta sulle tendenze ideologiche e politiche dei giovani in italia* (Milan: Valentino Bompiani, 1974), p. 65.

33. Abraham Maslow, *Motivation and Personality* (New York: Harper, 1954).

34. Jean Knutson, *The Human Basis of the Polity* (Chicago: Aldine, 1972), p. 86.

It would seem that societies therefore should exhibit patterns of needs reflecting their levels of socioeconomic development and ability to meet the variety of psychic needs of their populations. We note that the latter may or may not be closely related to the former. We further note that it is not only national means that are important but also the pattern of distribution of needs throughout the population. An elite dominated by self-actualizers should behave quite differently from one containing large numbers of individuals with unmet lower-order needs, even if general population means are similar. It should also be pointed out that the fulfillment or satiation of a need does not mean its abandonment but only that it recedes from prominence and is replaced at the top of the ranking by other, more pressing concerns. The well-fed do not lose their interest in food, but they cease to be obsessed by it—unless driven by childhood deprivation—so that they rank other needs higher.

Let us admit that the empirical evidence for the existence of the need hierarchy, at least in the neat pattern laid out above and in the works cited above, is at best ambiguous. It "makes sense," but its existence has not been empirically demonstrated in an incontrovertible fashion. One major study found that all needs tended to be met together.[35] The thorough review in Jean Knutson's *Human Basis of the Polity* explicates the theory itself but does not attempt to disconfirm it. Perhaps, like other grand theories, the need hierarchy theory is useful to suggest middle-range theories but is not itself directly testable.

Maslow's need hierarchy has inspired a theory of value-change in advanced industrial society articulated by Inglehart in work first reported in 1971 and developed further in later works.[36] Inglehart argues that the affluence of the past generation has joined with the expansion of higher education to increase greatly the percentage of the population high on the need hierarchy. He does not label these people self-actualizers, and he did not originally set out to test Maslow's need hierarchy as such.[37] Rather, inspired by Maslow, Inglehart devised a method for separating those high from those low on the hierarchy through a battery of questions that tap respondents' ranking of the priorities attached to a series of national goals.[38] Those who choose

35. Erik Allardt, *About Dimensions of Welfare* (Helsinki: Research Group for Comparative Sociology, 1973).

36. For example, see the following by Ronald Inglehart: "The Silent Revolution in Europe: Intergenerational Change in Post-Industrial Societies," *American Political Science Review*, 65 (December 1971): 991-1017; *Silent Revolution*; "The Nature of Value Change in Postindustrial Societies," in *Politics and the Future of Industrial Society*, ed. Leon N. Lindberg (New York: David McKay, 1976), pp. 57-99; and "Value Priorities and Socioeconomic Change," pp. 305-42, and "Political Action: The Impact of Values, Cognitive Level, and Social Background," pp. 343-80, in Barnes, Kaase, et al., *Political Action*.

37. The research reported by Inglehart in "Value Priorities and Socioeconomic Change" (pp. 311-19) does deal with the value hierarchy but in an inconclusive fashion.

38. The original battery contained four items; Inglehart, *Silent Revolution*.

fighting inflation and maintaining law and order he labels materialists; those selecting giving people more say in decisions and protecting freedom of speech as the highest priorities he labels postmaterialists. A much larger battery of twelve questions developed later gives essentially similar results.[39]

This simple battery has impressive predictive power. Postmaterialists are well-educated, middle-class, leftist in politics, young, and ideologically sophisticated. More important from the point of view of the evolution of needs and values is the age distribution of postmaterialists: countries that achieved affluence and security early, such as Britain, have the highest proportion of postmaterialists among the older cohorts whereas countries such as Germany that have experienced recent expansion have the most among the young. This finding suggests the importance of childhood socialization, as national differences of two generations ago appear to be evident in the data. Additional support for the importance of childhood socialization is found by Inglehart in his examination of the relationship between affluence and percentage of postmaterialists. He finds a correlation of 0.67 between gross national product (GNP) per capita in 1950 (logarithmic transformation) and the ratio of materialists to postmaterialists in 1970-1976.[40] Sweden was the most postmaterialist country though it was second to the United States in 1950 in GNP per capita. Inglehart argues that Sweden was first because of its welfare policies and that it is "not sheer wealth per se but rather a sense of economic and physical *security*" that leads to a postmaterialist outlook. The ratio of materialists to postmaterialists is estimated best by the GNP per capita of 1950; the next best predictor is that for 1955; the 1960s are third; and 1975 is the weakest of the set. Clearly, there is a time lag of approximately one generation between economic changes and their maximum impact on the prevailing values of an adult national sample.[41]

If, as Inglehart argues, postmaterialists are harbingers of the values of the future, then the relationship between income and satisfaction could weaken even further. Among postmaterialists there is virtually no relationship between the two variables whereas for the materialists the relationship is moderate (see Table 5). Inglehart's thesis is holding up remarkably well in the face of the economic upheavals of recent years. Critics have argued that economic hard times would eliminate postmaterialism, that the present generation of college students is strongly materialist, and so on.[42] But the data continue to support the assumptions of the theory: that we are witnessing a massive shift in values among the affluent and the well-educated youth, that these

39. Inglehart, "Value Priorities and Socioeconomic Change," p. 312.

40. Ibid., p. 333.   41. Ibid., p. 332.

42. For an example of this line of criticism, see the review of *The Silent Revolution* by Mark Kesselman in the *American Political Science Review*, 73 (March 1979): 285-86.

TABLE 5
Satisfaction with Life as a Whole by Family Income, 1973:
Materialists vs. Postmaterialists[a]

Family Income per Month	Materialists		Postmaterialists	
Under $200	27	(933)	33	(55)
$200-399	26	(1,397)	16	(111)
$400-599	30	(1,297)	20	(102)
$600-799	31	(787)	23	(120)
$800-999	31	(728)	24	(98)
Over $1,000	40	(391)	23	(57)

[a]Percentage "very satisfied" among combined-nation European sample.

SOURCE: Ronald Inglehart, *The Silent Revolution* (Princeton, N.J.: Princeton University Press, 1977), p. 141.

changes are related to economic changes, and that they will not be reversed quickly. What seems to be happening is that the expansion of the proportion of the youngest cohorts that is postmaterialist has ceased, or at least peaked for a while; on the other hand, the cohorts that reached maturity in the 1960s and early 1970s, which were much more postmaterialist than their predecessors, are sustaining their postmaterialism on their long march through the life cycle. As older, more materialist, cohorts pass from the scene, the percentage of the total population that is postmaterialist can be expected to continue to grow for many years even with no increase in the percentage in the youngest age cohort.

Of course, a decline in postmaterialism is possible. The development of values is not well understood. Although there is a strong relationship between value change and socioeconomic development, many variables intervene. These can only be suggested here. For example, it is undoubtedly important that universities are in part subcultures, separate from the larger society, in which the young undergo an intense reexamination of their values in an environment that stresses postmaterialist themes and values. In other words, the educational system may to some extent have institutionalized the processes of value change, rendering them resistant to socioeconomic fluctuations. In the long run, of course, the relationship between value change and socioeconomic change should reassert itself—but how long is the long run? Family socialization is at least as important as the educational process in the inculcation of values. *Political Action* included interviews with parent-child pairs that permit direct examination of generation and lineage differences.[43] The results show that there are minimal differences of either type between parents and children. There is no support for generational conflict theories: "Similarity within the family is far more frequent than disagreement."[44] Thus, continuity between generations also reduces the likelihood of rapid alterations in the patterns of value change: postmaterialists simply exhibit in a purer or more extreme form tendencies present in their parents.

We must not neglect the importance of period effects on value change. We have examined generational change and found it to be incremental rather than revolutionary. We have noted, without much discussion, that life cycle effects are not likely to alter greatly the percentage of postmaterialists in each cohort, as the evidence suggests that the percentage is not declining as the cohorts age. The remaining source of change is the impact of events on the population as a whole, or what is known as "period effects." These are events of great impact that alter the perspectives of all who are exposed to them, such as war, depression, revolution, oil crises, and the like. Even these undoubtedly affect the young more than the old if only because the values of the former are more malleable than the latter. But everyone is changed by cataclysmic events. They intrude on the normal individual and societal learning processes and render theories about "normal" patterns of change irrelevant. For example, the extended loss of foreign oil would force a tremendous change in American expectations about the future. Indeed, the mere prospect of such a happening may be affecting American perspectives as we enter the 1980s. In other words, we must admit that there are factors that could drastically alter the processes of value change that we have described.

The relevance of value change for ideas about progress is clear. At lower levels of socioeconomic development, most people are at the lower reaches of the need hierarchy, and most view progress in material terms. With development, the concerns of the affluent and well-educated shift to nonmaterial matters; material well-being is still valued but is taken for granted. The primacy of youthful experiences leads to a lag of at least a generation in the impact of development on value change so that present levels of, for example, GNP per capita, are not the best indicators of values. Material indicators remain the criterion of progress for most of the population, but for those higher on the need hierarchy quality of life concerns assume primacy. High expectations lead to great frustrations, especially since so much of our

43. M. Kent Jennings, Klaus R. Allerbeck, and Leopold Rosenmayr, "Generations and Families: General Orientations," pp. 449-86, and Klaus R. Allerbeck, H. Kent Jennings, and Leopold Rosenmayr, "Generations and Families: Political Action," pp. 487-522, in Barnes, Kaase, et al., *Political Action*.

44. Allerbeck, Jennings, and Rosenmayr, "Generations and Families: Political Action," p. 515.

view of the good life stems from our perceptions of the lifestyles of elites of previous times, when they were few in number, were accorded deference, and were able to monopolize values. Material things can be expanded—greatly, if not infinitely. Some nonmaterial things can in principle also be greatly expanded, such as love, a sense of security, and self-esteem. But others are and will remain in short supply. And material growth itself eventually brings with it costs that cannot be ignored. Progress seems less assured. New conceptions of what constitutes progress alter the traditional equating of progress with growth in the material realm. It is not that economic prosperity and growth in scientific knowledge are no longer important; rather, they are taken for granted.

A NOTE ON THE DARK SIDE
OF THE FUTURE

Although self-actualization is not very well understood, it seems to be universally viewed as a "good thing," as a benign and socially constructive state. There may be good psychological reasons for the assumption that psychic growth and the achievement of the higher reaches of the need hierarchy are incompatible with socially destructive personalities. There may be political reasons for questioning such an optimistic view. Just below self-actualization on the hierarchy are the needs for belonging and esteem. Their relationship to out-group hostility, racism, and virulent nationalism has not been investigated, but the political consequences of there being substantial populations suffering from deprivations in these domains are frightening. Self-actualization may possess fewer implications for the collectivity, but why should we assume that self-actualizers will always pursue praiseworthy collective goals?

The key ingredient of self-actualization is control—control of self and control of environment. The self-actualizer is not driven by deprivation needs. He or she follows an inner voice. The subject of control is complex and the literature voluminous. One highly relevant work is *Personality and Democratic Politics* by Paul Sniderman.[45] Sniderman investigates the central role of self-esteem in mediating between personality and politics. Those with high self-esteem are likely to feel and actually to be more able to control themselves and manipulate their environment. And, of course, high self-esteem would place one high on the need hierarchy, as deprivation needs are destructive of self-esteem.[46] Persons with high self-esteem are likely to feel competent; they exhibit a great capacity for social learning so that they function

45. Paul Sniderman, *Personality and Democratic Politics* (Berkeley: University of California Press, 1975).
46. See Knutson, *Human Basis of the Polity*, p. 80.

well, understand and use the rules of the game, and have high levels of both expectations and achievement.[47] The irony is, as Sniderman points out, that self-esteem promotes the "learning of all socially approved values" so that those high on self esteem would probably prosper as well in a nondemocratic society.[48] The idealism of the civil rights movement and of opposition to the war in Southeast Asia seems to have contributed to the public-regarding values of the 1960s and 1970s. But there is no guarantee that the self-actualizers of the future will necessarily share these values. They could as easily be hedonistic, selfish, narcissistic, and self-aggrandizing.[49] These are, after all, values prominently displayed in the dominant culture of the United States. It is the advantage of self-actualizers that they—and only they—are truly free to choose; others are driven by deprivation needs. In contemporary American society, self-actualizers are faced with a cafeteria of values from which to choose, and with few guidelines for selection.

But the societal consequences may be enormous. The most significant may be an increasing difficulty in achieving consensus on national goals. The lower reaches of the need hierarchy are simple in their implications: economic prosperity, national and personal security, a sense of belonging to a family, group, and nation, the pursuit of dignity. To progress was to achieve more of these values. In the next stage, individuals must define for themselves what it means to progress, each in his or her own way. The agencies that traditionally developed and perpetuated common values all seem to be at best on the defensive and often discredited, including the family, religious and educational institutions, and those of the polity as well. In short, as populations move from the discipline of deprivation to the freedom of self-actualization, the potential exists for both public-regarding and socially disintegrative values.

The political consequences of the value preferences of self-actualizers are magnified by their social location and their tendency to act politically on the basis of their value choices. Their position within the elite stratum of society would by itself assure great societal impact for their choices. Their willingness to engage in both conventional and unconventional political action exaggerates the significance for society of their value preferences.

If we make the justifiable assumption that self-actualizers are well represented among Inglehart's postmaterialists, then it is evident that they tend to be highly participant in politics. They are also young, affluent, and well educated. A recent comparative study of five ad-

47. These results were also found by Gurin and Gurin, "Personal Efficacy," p. 141.
48. Sniderman, *Personality and Democratic Politics*, p. 323.
49. This is the thesis of Christopher Lasch, *The Culture of Narcissism* (New York: Norton, 1979).

vanced industrial democracies, including the United States, as reported in *Political Action*, documents the extensive political involvement of postmaterialists and their tendencies to engage in protest activities.[50] In the recent past, these propensities for demonstrations, confrontations, and the like have been on behalf of public issues that are widely viewed as deriving from idealistic motives even when tinged with self-interest, as in opposition to the draft and to war in general. But there is no reason to believe that self-actualizers will not utilize a wide range of political means to pursue their goals, no matter what these may come to be. Protest politics are available to everyone, and postmaterialists are among the groups that are most active in this form of participation. Whatever the substance of politics in the future, whether or not it is benign and socially constructive, postmaterialists will undoubtedly be among the leaders and will certainly be prepared to utilize protest as well as other forms of action to pursue their goals. And the high potential for protest activities merits concern as a component of the dark side of the future.

THE POLITICS OF PROGRESS

We have previously noted that whatever else it is, the idea of progress is an ideology with political consequences. A political ideology, at the minimum, is a set of widely shared beliefs prescribing certain collective actions. Ideologies are created by elites but gain historical significance when they gain mass followings. The process through which this occurs is a fascinating subject; it is not very well understood though it lies at the center of politics. Certainly elite ideas about progress have greatly influenced the public imagination for at least two centuries. We have emphasized the basic materialism of dominant mass views about progress, whatever subtleties elite ideologies might possess. Nevertheless, the idea of progress as an ideology has guided governmental policy making and has justified political decisions for a long time, during which there seems to have been great elite-mass congruence on what progress implied for public policy.

Progress as the justification for public policy has had its greatest impact in the United States; elsewhere, the idea of progress has been received more skeptically, though it has by now seeped into the core beliefs of most of mankind. Especially in the United States, most political debate has been about how best to achieve progress rather than over its definition: growth in material accomplishments has been viewed as progress. That view is probably still the dominant one among the American mass public. But contemporary intellectuals increasingly question the old assumptions, and our knowledge of opinion formation suggests that these elite divisions of opinion will diffuse to and through mass publics. What is now largely an intellectual's argu-

50. See Inglehart, "Political Action."

ment is becoming a public debate. With most people still concerned with lower-order needs, the potential for a period of rancorous political change is very great.

The redefinition of progress is a political issue, and it will take place in the political arena. It will be greatly affected by "expert" knowledge and opinion, as has always been the case in the past. That is, to some extent "objective" factors having to do with energy, pollution, scientific discovery, and military strength will establish the parameters of the possible and even serve to structure some of the alternatives. But the outcome will combine necessity and choice, as in all political decisions.

The current debate over the redefinition of progress illustrates two features of political ideology. One is that we tend to define as desirable that which is necessary and inevitable. Thus, the arguments concerning the limits to continued growth, and the genuine, if not completely understood, environmental factors underlying them, imply that we must redefine progress to render it compatible with the survival of our own species and others. The theory of the need hierarchy does just that: it justifies seeing self-actualization as superior to amassing material goods and hence provides a theoretical underpinning for the redefinition of progress in qualitative instead of material quantitative terms.

The second feature highlighted by the debate is the prescriptive nature of political ideology. Progress is good and not just a value-free description of human evolution. To climb the need hierarchy is desirable and not just a description of what populations do. We are in the process of converting the need hierarchy itself into a prescriptive ideology with vast political consequences: we must cease to consume at the present rate, we must not worry so much about security, we must redefine progress in terms of self-actualization. George Katona, who has emphasized the individual's desire to improve his position as the driving force of the American economy, articulates this prescriptive viewpoint quite well:

> At present . . . progress is identified by most Americans with growth of income and of the quantity of goods and services possessed. What is essential is to retain the prospect of improvement, regardless of what it is that may be considered improvement. A redefinition of progress is needed so that people identify an improvement in their situation less with an increase in the quality of material goods and more with other aspects of the quality of life. . . . What is required is the strengthening of wants and aspirations that use up fewer of our limited resources and contribute less to the deterioration of the environment than does the acquisition of increased quantities of consumer goods.[51]

51. Katona, *Psychological Economics*, p. 397.

Katona believes that the idea of progress makes people work hard, and that the alternative to growth is deterioration rather than a stable no-growth society.[52] As long as people believe in their own ability to advance, loss of faith in the government and economy in general will not lead to stagnation. But loss of the belief in personal progress would be disastrous. It would lead to economic stagnation and decline. Katona is optimistic. He concludes that "the proven adaptability of human motiviations to changing conditions offers the best hope for reconciling the need for belief in personal progress with measures required to improve the environment and to overcome the societal malaise."[53]

The capacity of a society to redefine progress is problematical. The general finding that aspirations seem over time to adjust to real-world conditions suggests that it is possible. The current emphasis of the intellectual debate on quality of life rather than on quantity of goods is a hopeful sign. The existence of substantial portions of the population, even in the United States, with unmet material aspirations and a deep sense of material deprivation suggests that the redefinition of progress will not be easy. The debate over progress is moving from the intellectual realm into the public arena. On that stage, superior arguments are only one form of currency, and not necessarily the one with the greatest purchase. The transformation of the idea of progress is now on the political agenda, where interest and passion mingle with reason as protagonists. The faith of the Enlightenment may be alive and well, but it must compete with other dreams in the political arena where aspiration and reality eternally confront one another.

52. Ibid.
53. George Katona, "Persistence of Belief in Personal Financial Progress," in *Economic Means for Human Needs*, p. 104.

PART V

Progress and Humanistic
Understanding

The essays in this final section view the idea of progress from a variety of humanistic perspectives. They explore but do not fully answer—as from their authors' abiding sense of the limitations of the specifically, generically human, they cannot—the question of humanity's potential for moral and intellectual growth commensurate with the deepest problems in its history. Although they are not exactly nay-saying, they are for the most part cautionary. The authors are fully aware of the ironic fact that humanistic research and speculation have derived a good deal of their power and import from their having been released long ago from the dictates of theology, a release central in the development of that very idea of progress which they in turn would question and qualify. Theirs is, however, only a modicum of this-worldly certitude. For the materials on which their research centers and their speculations focus—works of art, philosophical treatises, religious texts, and the like—are to be valued precisely as they are richly complicated, trying to see humanity whole, acknowledging and therefore celebrating affect as well as effect, confronting the unreasonable as well as the reasonable, the immoral as well as the moral. It is humanity conceived and expressed thus which does not appear necessarily to have been altogether amenable to progress. The humanist, as part of his very methodology, perhaps tends to understand the idea of progress in its extremest form, utopianism. And he is constitutionally suspicious of utopia even as, perhaps because, he is attracted to it. For in utopia, with all societal problems solved on a collective basis, there would still be the altogether existential, the individual, problems of life as against death, of the glory and the plenitude of human aspiration as against the agony and the tragedy of human limitation. It is just this existential problem that is at the heart of the documents which the humanist establishes, explicates, and interprets. Thus, his is a concern with the human project at its most individuated and particularized. His dialectic bids him believe that progress can be, in fact, progress only to the degree that it takes into account individuated human nature and its particular products in art, philosophy, religion, and the very forms of consciousness itself.

For the humanist, then, the matter of the self is of course absolutely central, since—from his perspective—belief, commitment, and behavior proceed on the basis of normative conceptions of self and the forms and thrusts of consciousness which those conceptions enable. In the first essay, Steven Marcus elucidates a principal conception of self in a portion of the nineteenth-century West—that is, a conception as it manifests itself in the great age of the idea of progress. He writes in the context of psychoanalysis—the mode of research whose aim is to comprehend that individuated "human nature" which is at the center, in turn, of all humanistic inquiry. He finds a paradox in the nineteenth-century English character type which, in its commitment to the idea of progress, felt itself to be not only regulated but empowered by the rational and orderly calculation which the idea entailed. On the one hand, as the result of such calculation, there were "the personal virtues of probity and integrity of character and of rectitude and moral uprightness in one's dealing with the world, other men, and one's self." On the other hand, also as a result of such calculation, there would result "aggressiveness," "materialism," "personal aggrandizement," and "a wide spectrum of hypocritical personal attitudes and institutional practices." Marcus then proceeds to show how these incompatible developments of the same character type, when it was no longer "possible to believe in the existence of some sort of transcendent value or moral authority that was, in certain senses, outside of one's self," resulted in a "drama of contradictions"—this in the writings of Thomas Carlyle, John Stuart Mill, Matthew Arnold, John Ruskin, William Morris, Walter Pater, and Oscar Wilde. Each of these "moralists," trying to resolve the contradictions, made manifest the essential instability and lack of integration in that nineteenth-century character type which derives from commitment to the idea of progress and foreshadowed the modern humanist's puzzled and puzzling discontents when he would consider, not to say understand, the modern self.

In the Western tradition at least, there has been since classical times a continuing need to defend the arts from the idea of progress since that idea, to the degree that it could comprehend the arts, would demand of us that we commit ourselves to the palpably absurd notion that an Eliot poem is necessarily better than a Milton poem, a Milton poem necessarily better than a Dante poem, and so on. Writing in this tradition, Murray Krieger, in the second essay, would "exempt" the arts from the idea of progress by defining them in terms of a collection of "single, complete, aesthetically satisfying" works—deriving from man's capacity to create glorious fictions which, because they are fictions, can be more inclusive in their scope of understanding than are other sociocultural products. Thus conceived, works of art are *given* once and for all, eternally present for those who would attend to them. And, so Krieger maintains, it may be said that there is, or can be, progress in the way the arts are "used" by society—the degree to which they are "available." This would allow progress in criticism, teaching, communication in general. And this of course would amount to progress in society—progress, as regards the arts, being such only to the degree that it centers on our knowledge that works of art themselves do not exhibit it. We must then strive to progress in our understanding of the arts in order all the more comprehensively to grant that they do not progress.

Complementary to Krieger's essay is Robert Elliott's, which follows it. Elliott treats of the literary form which directly derives from and is bound up in the idea of progress—the utopia. He inquires into the fate of literature in particular and the arts in general in a number of utopias. For the authors of utopias, the arts, precisely because they are fictive, generated by the creative imagination, play variously depreciated roles. That is to say, the proper utopian can concern himself only with the "real" as it exists in an about-to-be perfect, because potentially perfected, world. For those Marxists who are explicitly utopians, the dialectic of history would demonstrate either the ultimate withering away of the arts or, more likely, their absorption into "ordinary," nonfictive modes of expression and understanding—Everyman his own Shakespeare or Beethoven or Michelangelo, as it were. But since human nature would necessarily be perfected too, the substantive concerns of the arts would also be transformed. There would, for example, simply not be the stuff of tragedy in utopia. If utopia, then, is the necessary and extreme expression of the idea of progress, the literary humanist, constitutionally not a true believer, would point out that its costs are perhaps an index of at least some of the costs of progress itself.

Utopianism, in the form of millenialism and the eschatology relevant to it, would also appear to be necessarily implicated in religion, at least in that of the Western tradition. Martin Marty shows how, in modern theology, the idea of progress is brought to bear primarily as the theologian wants to relate his theology to specifically sociocultural issues. And this is a matter as much of the context of the various theologies of which he treats as of their intrinsic conceptualization. Like Daniel Bell, whose essay follows his, Marty points out the collapse of the Enlightenment assumption that true progress entailed the disappearance of religion. But whereas Marty sees no necessary connection between religion and the idea of progress, Bell is willing to envisage, following that "exhaustion of culture" which we are presently experiencing, a "return to the sacred"—"the sacred" being a necessary condition of those cultural universals which at the outset he carefully remarks and categorizes. His theology must at this stage remain indistinct, simply desiderated as that which will at once derive from and develop out of "the sacred." Set over against Elliott's account of the role of utopians in the Western tradition, the Marty and Bell essays suggest that from a humanistic perspective what is at issue as regards the idea of progress is precisely the tension between, the possible coexistence of, the secular and the sacred. We are all fated, in this understanding, to be failed utopians—aspiring, without hope of achieving it, to perfection—always perfectible, never perfected.

Concerned with "specifically ethical conceptions of the human good," Frederick Olafson in effect considers the matter of the secular and the sacred, so that his essay properly concludes this section and this volume; properly, too, because he asks more questions than he gives answers. He finds that the idea of progress has functioned in the Western tradition as an ideology (again, implicitly utopian) overdetermined by science and technology—an ideology being for him a belief passing for a criterion. Belief in progress, particularly when set by a commitment to science and technology, has for Olafson—and for the philosophical tradition which he represents—prevented the development of a genuine criterion for progress. What is called for, he writes, is "the kind of consciousness that is at once ethical in the sense of acknowledging a principle of obligation to one's fellow human beings; critical in the sense of being disposed to make appraisals of ethical validity an element in one's work in the world; and humane in the sense of an intelligent familiarity with, and enjoyment of, the variety of human goods and virtues." Surely, to say this is, without theologizing, to look to a return of the sacred, but the sacred locked inextricably in the context of the secular—the sacred, that is, somehow opposed to the holy. It is, as do all these essays written from an inclusively humanistic perspective, to look for the means whereby we may assess the costs as well as the rewards of progress. In the place of a theology, it assumes a philosophical anthropology—an inclusive *science humaine*—as a necessary condition of genuine progress. The humanist—meditating the idea of progress—thus turns out to be a progressivist not only in spite of himself but also in terms of himself.

20

Conceptions of the Self in an Age of Progress

STEVEN MARCUS

Why is it that we customarily look to art, to literature, to cultural developments and scientific theory as the indicators in advance of large changes in fundamental attitudes, as the first notices of alterations in collective sensibility? I assume that today there is general agreement on the theoretical principles of determination and over-determination in human affairs and in particular on that part of those affairs which may be described as mental; and I am in agreement with this settled group of assumptions. At the same time, the activities that constitute art, literature, and cultural and scientific theorizing appear, when compared with such realms of activity as economics, politics, or family life, to be relatively free and less directly dependent upon specific social circumstances. What I am suggesting is that in shifting the direction of the arrow of determinate analysis, we are by no means abandoning the principle of determination or overdetermination. Whether we think of these activities in an interior sense as comparatively conflict-free functions of the ego or, less doubtfully perhaps, in an exterior sense as the quasi-autonomous domain of the superstructure vis-à-vis the base is not, at this juncture, of compelling importance. What is at issue is our recognition of the differential quality of determinateness in these realms and the uses to which those differences and that recognition may be put.

In the dim light cast by these scandalously foreshortened theoretical remarks, I should like to turn to my subject or to the way into it. I should like to direct us to what I take to be an often overlooked contradiction or set of contradictions in the dominant character type in nineteenth-century middle-class or bourgeois society and culture. This character type has been habitually, and properly, associated with the historical life of industrial capitalism in its early expansive and even heroic phase; and the contradictions within it may be seen to fall within the ambiguities inscribed by the activities associated with acquisitive behavior and the social and economic institutions that légitimized and promoted such behavior. On the one hand, this character type was thought to be highly governed by certain normative rules and values that derived directly from economic rationality. Hence, this character type regulated much of its life by rational calculation and, in particular, by the kind of calculation that relied upon the supposed consequences of what the unremitting practice of the virtues of thrift, frugality, and industry might have upon one's individual life. These virtues were to be realized largely in the quality of devotion to work or vocation that was internalized within this character type, but they extended to more general deferrals of gratification in other regions as well. They entailed sobriety of thought, dress, and demeanor; moderation of impulse and speech; and temperation of behavior that often transformed itself into demands for temperance that were nothing short of intemperate. This character type also believed in, and believed it practiced, self-discipline; and the purpose of such self-discipline was not merely the socially desirable subordination of unruly and disorderly impulses but the still higher purpose of self-improvement, which, it was believed, should be carried on throughout life and literally unto death.

At the center of this type stood the personal virtues of probity and integrity of character and of rectitude and moral uprightness in one's dealings with the world, other men, and one's self. It was from these austere virtues that the behaviors of rational economic calculation were understood to issue; and it was to these same severities that the successful results of such behaviors returned, to confirm them and to reinforce one's conviction of their lawfulness. On one side, thus, this character type represented itself in the world through ordinances (issued to itself and to that world) that were ascetic and self-denying; and these ordinances, indeed, constituted the heart of its claim to a high spirituality. This spirituality, of course, is the mainspring of Max Weber's unsurpassed account of the Protestant Ethic.

On the other hand, this same character type, when regarded from another perspective, seemed to be constituted out of very different elements. This other perspective might be supplied by a different social location, or it might be supplied by a shifting of internal focus within the dominant character type itself. The same acquisitive behaviors were now construed as bearing a negative valence. Rational calculation was in fact an institution for the methodical expression of aggressiveness. The thrifty, frugal, and industrious middle-class merchant or bourgeois manufacturer or financier was at the same time greedy and rapacious. Deferral of gratification was by no means incompatible with a wide variety of appetitive practices, and the middle classes of the period were represented as often in pleasure-seeking and pleasure-taking activities as they were in their dedication to work. The claims to high spirituality were a permutated and incompletely sublimated form of materialism; self-discipline was regularly put into the service of personal aggrandizement; sobriety did not extinguish the love of comfort and luxury and the desire for consumption; self-improvement coexisted comfortably with a wide spectrum of hypocritical personal attitudes and institutional practices; and appeals made on behalf of probity and integrity of character did not simply cancel out the existence of a moral double standard. The member of the bourgeoisie was not simply ascetic; he was equally sensual and was referred to conventionally as *l'homme moyen sensuel*. And his ordinances of self-denial, however often they were issued, were regularly accompanied in the mass by an extravagant and vulgar display of objects and acquisitions both inanimate and animate.

I do not raise these opposing accounts to impute singular truth to either of them. I raise them as what they were—covert and unacknowledged contradictions of character and of the structure of individual selfhood that are connected in very deep and complex ways with the historical character of the society in which they were played out and with its large contradictions. They refract those conditions, they express them, and they react back on them, although they are not, it seems to me, finally reducible to them. It was, in my view, possible to live with these contradictions, to adjust to or deal with them, to overlook or avoid them, or to go on with the business of living as though they did not exist, so long as it was still possible to believe in the existence of some sort of transcendent value or moral authority that was, in certain senses, outside of one's self. Whenever this belief seemed imperiled, the contradictions rose toward the surface; when the belief became impossible, they erupted.

In the writings of the great Victorian moralists, literary and social critics, and cultural sages, this drama of contradictions was played out in extraordinary detail, complexity, and consequentialness, as it was in other idioms in the works of the great nineteenth-century bourgeois novelists and their successors, the central creative figures of twentieth-century modernism (I will not have time here to deal with or even touch upon this corresponding line of development). The writings of the chief Victorian critics form a coherent, complex, and yet sequential set of discourses. In them we can see prefigured, for what well may have been the first time, much of what has come today, a century later, to be enacted on a much larger cultural scale.

The first and most exemplary figure in this cultural drama was Thomas Carlyle. Born in 1795 and raised in the tradition of Scottish Calvinism, Carlyle attended Edinburgh University where he was exposed to the chilly winds of eighteenth-century rationalism and skepticism. Recalling these experiences in his spiritual autobiography, *Sartor Resartus*, he writes: "The hungry young . . . looked up to their spiritual Nurses; and, for food, were bidden eat the east-wind. . . . Often we would condole over the hard destiny of the Young in this era: how, after all our toil, we were to be turned-out into the world, with beards on our chins indeed, but with few other attributes of manhood; no existing thing that we were trained to Act on, nothing that we could so much as Believe."[1] The young Carlyle's deconversion took the form of a personal crisis that became emblematic for the era. Thrown back upon his isolated self, the universe, he writes, in a memorable passage, "was all void of Life, of Purpose, of Volition, even of Hostility: it was one huge, dead, immeasurable Steam-engine, rolling on, in its dead indifference, to grind me limb from limb."[2] With the loss of belief in a celestial salvation, of an afterlife to be paid for by suffering here on earth, he asked himself the fatal question, "Why am I not happy?" The question was fatal because, of course, in this context it has no answer. As he recovered from his crisis (which I cannot discuss in any detail), Carlyle formulated a number of central insights. First, in a world deserted by a traditional transcendent authority, the question of individual happiness and self-realization becomes a central problematic:

> Man's Unhappiness, as I construe, comes of his Greatness; it is because there is an Infinite in him, which with all his cunning he cannot quite bury under the Finite. Will the whole Finance Ministers and Upholsterers and Confectioners of modern Europe undertake, in joint-stock company, to make one Shoeblack HAPPY? They cannot accomplish it, above an hour or two: for the Shoeblack also has a Soul quite other than his Stomach; and would require, if you consider it, for his permanent satisfaction and saturation, simply this allotment, no more, and no less: *God's infinite Universe altogether to himself*, therein to enjoy infinitely, and fill every wish as fast as it rose. Oceans of Hochheimer, a Throat like that of Ophiuchus: speak not of them; to the infinite Shoeblack they are as nothing. No sooner is your ocean filled, than he grumbles that it might have been of better vintage. Try him with half of a Universe, of an Omnipotence, he sets to quarrelling with the proprietor of the other half, and declares himself the most maltreated of men. Always there is a black spot in our sunshine: it is even, as I said, the *Shadow of Ourselves*.[3]

It is this direct claim upon life, Carlyle argued, that had to be renounced, before life, properly speaking, could begin again. And hand

1. Thomas Carlyle, *Sartor Resartus*, ed. Charles F. Harrold (New York: Odyssey Press, 1937), pp. 113, 116.
2. Ibid., p. 164.   3. Ibid., p. 190.

in hand with this self-renunciation, Carlyle discovered a new transcendent value. He discovered it in conduct, in action. "Doubt of any sort," he wrote, quoting Goethe, "cannot be removed except by Action." And the form of action that he invested with special moral authority was work—indeed he called it the "Gospel of Work."

> I too could now say to myself: Be no longer a Chaos, but a World. . . .
> Produce! Produce! Were it but the pitifullest infinitesimal fraction
> of a Product, produce it, in God's name! 'Tis the utmost thou hast in
> thee: out with it, then. Up, up! Whatsoever thy hand findeth to do,
> do it with thy whole might. Work while it is called Today; for the
> Night cometh, wherein no man can work.[4]

Even in a world given over to Mammon, there is hope, so long as one is earnest about something. "Idleness," Carlyle continues, "is worst, Idleness alone is without hope: work earnestly at anything, you will by degrees learn to work at almost all things. There is endless hope in work, were it even work at making money." These insights and formulations were immensely influential, insofar as one can say that the written utterances of one man influence others. They were syntonic with a number of the central impelling forces of society at that time and were, indeed, in part articulate expressions of those forces. Yet they did not hold permanently for Carlyle. The capitalism of the period did not bring forth the heroic figures that he thought it would; nor did it produce the new "religious mythus" that he believed, in larger measure correctly as I think, human beings required. It did not, in other words, transcend itself; it did not produce the "natural supernaturalism" that Carlyle believed the modern world had to invent for itself. It produced economic and social crises; it produced wealth and continued to distribute that wealth with sinful inequity. And as it did so, Carlyle's critical asperity went sour; the anti-intellectual tendencies that were always powerfully latent in him rose to expression, and the high spirituality of the middle-class values that he put in idiosyncratic and powerful form gave way to an illiberal authoritarianism that was as hostile to bourgeois individuality as it was to almost anything else. He had reached a dead end.

The second great figure in this discourse is John Stuart Mill, who, starting out at a point remote from Carlyle, went through a similar situation and crisis and arrived at similar conclusions. Mill had been deliberately raised by his father to have no religious beliefs and to have no experience of religious sentiments. Yet at the age of fifteen, John Stuart Mill underwent an experience of conversion. He read the works of Jeremy Bentham, his father's philosophical master, and found religion in, among other things, the "greatest happiness principle." From that moment, he writes, "I had what truly might be called an object in life; to be a reformer of the world. My conception of my own

4. Ibid., p. 197.

happiness was entirely identified with this object." For five years he lived with this faith, but in 1826 at the age of twenty, he found himself out of sorts and in a state of incipient depression:

> In this frame of mind it occurred to me to put the question directly to myself, "Suppose that all your objects in life were realized; that all the changes in institutions and opinions which you are looking forward to, could be completely effected at this very instant: would this be a great joy and happiness to you?" And an irrepressible self-consciousness distinctly answered, "No!" At this my heart sank within me: the whole foundation on which my life was constructed fell down. All my happiness was to have been found in the continual pursuit of this end. The end had ceased to charm, and how could there ever again be any interest in the means? I seemed to have nothing left to live for.[5]

Mill's crisis was prolonged, profound, and quasi-suicidal. His passage out of it is described in his *Autobiography* in considerable and illuminating detail. When he emerged on the other side, he felt that his experiences of this period had left two very marked effects on his opinions and character:

> In the first place, they led me to adopt a theory of life, very unlike that on which I had before acted, and having much in common with what at that time I certainly had never heard of, the anti-self-consciousness theory of Carlyle. I never, indeed, wavered in the conviction that happiness is the test of all rules of conduct, and the end of life. But I now thought that this end was only to be attained by not making it the direct end. Those only are happy (I thought) who have their minds fixed on some object other than their own happiness; on the happiness of others, on the improvement of mankind, even on some art or pursuit, followed not as a means, but as itself an ideal end. Aiming thus at something else, they find happiness by the way. The enjoyments of life (such was now my theory) are sufficient to make it a pleasant thing, when they are taken *en passant*, without being made a principal object. Once make them so, and they are immediately felt to be insufficient. They will not bear a scrutinizing examination. Ask yourself whether you are happy, and you cease to be so. The only chance is to treat, not happiness, but some end external to it, as the purpose of life. Let your self-consciousness, your scrutiny, your self-interrogation, exhaust themselves on that; and if otherwise fortunately circumstanced you will inhale happiness with the air you breathe, without dwelling on it or thinking about it, without either forestalling it in imagina-

5. John Stuart Mill, *Autobiography*, ed. Jack Stillinger (Boston: Houghton Mifflin, 1969), p. 81.

tion, or putting it to flight by fatal questioning. This theory now became the basis of my philosophy of life.[6]

The second important result of these experiences, Mill said in his *Autobiography*, was that they led him for the first time to give "its proper place among the prime necessities of human well-being, to the internal culture of the individual." What he meant by this first became clear to him when he read the poetry of Wordsworth at this time and found there what he called "the very culture of the feelings." Yet what one feels in Mill, and what makes the reading of his autobiography so poignant an experience, is the sense that it communicates of transcendence lost never to be regained. This may not be the worst thing in the world, and to have gone on to become John Stuart Mill, the saint of rationalism and much else, is nothing to sneeze at. Nevertheless, his book, and indeed his life (apart from his work, which he pursued with Carlylean dedication), is characterized by pervasive emotions of loss, of absence, of the unrecoverable.

To mention Wordsworth, culture, and loss brings us inevitably to the third figure in this extended cultural discourse. Matthew Arnold begins with the conviction that traditional moral and religious authority are moribund. He begins as well with the insight that Carlyle's central project had failed and that this central project had been, in fact, to import the ideals of the French Revolution into England. For Carlyle those ideals were largely captured in the phrase, "the career open to talents," or as a subdoctrine in the Gospel of Work, "the tools to those that can use them." The overriding moral authority behind the middle-class claims to social and political hegemony were to be found in the ideal of society reorganized as a meritocracy—an open hierarchy in which individual talents could freely express themselves and find their appropriate place and rewards.

For Arnold, as for Carlyle, and I am quoting Arnold, the French Revolution remained "the greatest, the most animating event in history," and it remained so precisely by virtue of the "force, truth and universality of the ideas which it took for its law, and from the passion with which it could inspire a multitude for these ideas, a unique and still living power." It had changed the world, and yet it had failed as well. For the exacerbating circumstance that all these exceptionally creative figures had to face was that even in the wake of the French Revolution and of reform in England, mind and power remained radically alienated from one another. Confronted by a society in which, as he described it, "our upper class is materialized, our middle class [is] vulgarized, and our lower class is brutalized," Arnold chose a less direct route than that pursued by Carlyle or Mill. He put together a remarkable discourse that was controlled by a number of connected

6. Ibid., pp. 85-86.

and sometimes interchangeable terms: these were criticism, culture, literature or poetry, and humane letters or education. And it was in the arena composed by these activities that he tried to reinscribe transcendent value. In criticism he saw a disinterested and free play of the mind upon all things, an activity whose purpose was to see the object as in itself it really is, in which the mind as a rule takes up an adversary position toward the social and cultural situation in which it finds itself, while yet remaining at the same time in the ultimate service of that society and culture. The culture that he proposed was not the culture in which he lived. It too was an ideal practice whose final aim was that "of all great spiritual disciplines ... man's perfection or salvation." Through getting to know the best that has been thought and said, in cultivating our inwardness and responsiveness to great and high thoughts and books, we would be doing our best to, in the end, make "reason and the will of God prevail." Literature was, he repeatedly remarked, "a criticism of life," and poetry was the highest form of that utterance.

> The future of poetry is immense, because in poetry, where it is worthy of its high destinies, our race, as time goes on, will find an ever surer and surer stay. There is not a creed which is not shaken, not an accredited dogma which is not shown to be questionable, not a received tradition which does not threaten to dissolve. Our religion has materialised itself in the fact, in the supposed fact; it has attached its emotion to the fact, and now the fact is failing it. But for poetry the idea is everything; the rest is a world of illusion, of divine illusion. Poetry attaches its emotion to the idea; the idea *is* the fact. The strongest part of our religion to-day is its unconscious poetry.[7]

Nothing could be clearer, more appealing, or, as we now can see, more questionable. The redemptive powers of religion were to be displaced into literature and art. Arnold, of course, had no way of knowing to what future uses these notions were to be put, but several things may be at this point noted about them. In this unprogrammatic program, still greater stress was put upon the cultivation of individuality in the form of inner selfhood.

Moreover, Arnold himself saw the disparities and contradictions we have been discussing in terms of an opposition that he ascribed to fundamental impulses in human nature. Those impulses he denominated as Hebraism and Hellenism. Victorian society and culture were, he observed, dominated by the Hebraic; they needed an infusion of the Hellenic that they tended to be frightened of and deny. Here is one of Arnold's descriptions of the Hellenic:

7. Matthew Arnold, "The Study of Poetry," in *English Literature and Irish Politics*, vol. 9 of *The Complete Prose Works of Matthew Arnold*, ed. R.H. Super (Ann Arbor: University of Michigan Press, 1973), p. 161.

To get rid of one's ignorance, to see things as they are, and by seeing them as they are to see them in their beauty, is the simple and attractive ideal which Hellenism holds out before human nature; and from the simplicity and charm of this ideal, Hellenism, and human life in the hands of Hellenism, is invested with a kind of aërial ease, clearness, and radiancy; they are full of what we call sweetness and light. Difficulties are kept out of view, and the beauty and rationalness of the ideal have all our thoughts.[8]

In such a passage, as we move ahead in the dialectic of discourse we have been reconstructing, we can make out the first contradictory part of the hypothetical character type giving way to a refined, attenuated, and hypertrophied version (in part) of the second, although it does not quite recognize itself as such.

Arnold himself was intermittently aware of such contradictions, both in terms of the dominant character type and of the larger social and cultural contradictions of which they were in some measure refractions. And he proposed to deal with them by a deliberate process of distancing:

It will be said that it is a very subtle and indirect action which I am thus prescribing for criticism, and that, by embracing in this manner the Indian virtue of detachment and abandoning the sphere of practical life, it condemns itself to a slow and obscure work. Slow and obscure it may be, but it is the only proper work of criticism. The mass of mankind will never have any ardent zeal for seeing things as they are; very inadequate ideas will always satisfy them. On these inadequate ideas reposes, and must repose, the general practice of the world. That is as much as saying that whoever sets himself to see things as they are will find himself one of a very small circle; but it is only by this small circle resolutely doing its own work that adequate ideas will ever get current at all. The rush and roar of practical life will always have a dizzying and attracting effect upon the most collected spectator, and tend to draw him into its vortex; most of all will this be the case where that life is so powerful as it is in England. But it is only by remaining collected, and refusing to lend himself to the point of view of the practical man, that the critic can do the practical man any service.[9]

Arnold's contribution to the classical humanist tradition in its modern phase was decisive; there are few of us who have not in one way or another been touched by it. But it is no discredit to him to say that

8. Matthew Arnold, *Culture and Anarchy*, vol. 5 of *The Complete Prose Works of Matthew Arnold*, ed. R.H. Super (Ann Arbor: University of Michigan Press, 1965), p. 167.

9. Matthew Arnold, "The Function of Criticism at the Present Time," in *Lectures and Essays in Criticism*, vol. 3 of *The Complete Prose Works of Matthew Arnold*, ed. R.H. Super (Ann Arbor: University of Michigan Press, 1962), pp. 274-75.

we can now see that it was a holding action, that it brought time and space within the prevailing social order for certain protected and privileged kinds of thought and behavior, and that it has not prevailed.

The next major figure in the tradition, I shall have to address with shameful brevity. John Ruskin began as a disciple of Carlyle, a conventionally religious evangelical Christian, and a critic of painting and architecture, who believed in the redemptive power of art as well. He believed that an appropriate response to and appreciation of art and architecture were in a society inseparable from sound public behavior, morality and justice, and he strove in his writings to amend and correct public taste in the hope of establishing social and moral deliverance in his own time. Despite his great success with a large public, he was dissatisfied, since his prophetic utterances seemed to be going unheeded. By the mid-1850s he had lost his faith in dogmatic religion, turned away from writing about art, and began to write a series of brilliant critical denunciations of political economy, the industrial capitalist system as it was functioning at the time, and the styles of life and of self of the dominant middle class. Redemption and transcendence could now only be achieved by direct interventions into the social and economic order itself although Ruskin was never altogether consistent about what those interventions should be or how they might take place.

I can think of no more dramatic demonstration of the contradictions that I have been referring to than this eruption and about-face. These writings of Ruskin were greeted, not surprisingly, with a storm of outrage and abuse. But Ruskin went even further. He tried to put these two different tendencies together in a series of writings and social experiments that he sponsored and paid for, in which the transcendent powers of art were to be combined with efforts at social restoration. These noble projects were not merely contradictory; they soon revealed that they were incoherent, and Ruskin himself, a member of the bourgeoisie in England (his father was a wealthy wine merchant), whose Protestant ethical side was overdeveloped to the point of deformation and who was tormented by personal as well as cultural demons, lapsed into general incoherence and then into the silence of deranged mental powers.

An astute foreign observer had been taking note of these developments. "I have been reading the life of Thomas Carlyle," he writes:

> this unconscious and involuntary farce . . . Carlyle: a man of strong words and attitudes . . . constantly lured by the craving for a strong faith and the feeling of his incapacity for it. . . . The craving for a strong faith is no proof of a strong faith, but quite the contrary. If one has such a faith, then one can afford the beautiful luxury of skepticism. . . . [In Carlyle there is] a constant passionate dishonesty against himself—that is his *proprium*; in this respect he is and remains interesting. Of course, in England he is admired precisely

for his honesty.... At bottom, Carlyle is an English atheist who makes it a point of honor not to be one.

The foreign observer continues his observations about his Victorian contemporaries:

> They are rid of the Christian God and now believe all the more firmly that they must cling to Christian morality. That is an English consistency.... In England one must rehabilitate oneself after every little emancipation from theology by showing in a veritably awe-inspiring manner what a moral fanatic one is. That is the penance they pay there.
>
> We others hold otherwise. When one gives up the Christian faith, one pulls the right to Christian morality out from under one's feet. This morality is by no means self-evident.... Christianity is a system.... By breaking one main concept out of it, the faith in God, one breaks the whole: nothing necessary remains in one's hands....
>
> When the English actually believe that they know "intuitively" what is good and evil, when they therefore suppose that they no longer require Christianity as the guarantee of morality, we merely witness the *effects* of dominion of the Christian value judgment and an expression of the strength and depth of this dominion.... For the English, morality is not yet a problem.[10]

The inimitable ferocity, superiority and hyperbole of tone and statement belong, of course, to Nietzsche, and the passages I have just cited come from *The Twilight of the Idols*, whose subtitle is *How One Philosophizes with a Hammer*. It was written in 1888, the last year of Nietzsche's sane life. In it, Nietzsche is saying that the entire development that I have synoptically and inadequately recounted was misconceived, misbegotten, and corrupted from the very beginning; that the entire Victorian effort to find other and alternate centers of authority and value when the one supreme transcendent value had absconded was cowardly and farcical. What he, even in his genius, fails to see is that this very effort constitutes part of the abiding interest and value (as well as the limitations) of the central Victorian figures.

What he fails to see as well is the sociocultural element, the element of class, in these intellectual goings-on. For all of these creative-critical figures were individual members of the middle class or bourgeoisie, who addressed that class from *within* its social and cultural order. If their careers and writings embodied the cross-purposes of that order and the strains of what it was like to be an individual within it, those writings were also directed toward their fellow members of the middle class. Such works were as often as not fiercely critical of the audience they were written for, and one of the singular circumstances

10. Friedrich Nietzsche, *The Twilight of the Idols*, in *The Portable Nietzsche*, ed. and trans. Walter Kaufmann (New York: Viking Press, 1954), pp. 521, 515-16.

in all of this is that these writings were actually read; they were attended to, responded to, they even may be said to have exerted an influence on the middle-class readers who were the object of their critical intentions.

What Nietzsche also fails to see is that other developments were going on. These developments represent two distinct and coherent branchings out from the mainstream of critical discourse that we have been tracing. The first of these is to be found in the life and work of William Morris. Morris begins as a disciple of Carlyle, Ruskin, and Arnold. He starts out as a Pre-Raphaelite, moves on to restore ancient buildings, founds the Kelmscott Press, designs books, cloth, and furniture of preindustrial integrity, and becomes a leader in the effort to design a new style of civilized individual life within a vulgarized, ugly, and industrialized capitalist world. But he also does something else; he becomes a socialist, reads Marx, and goes on to become a revolutionary communist. This succession, integral and consequent as it is, represents the first structural break in the discussion, the first stepping outside the boundaries in which the discourse had been contained. It represented a new conception of the relation of classes, offered a new group of notions of what an individual person within society might be or become, and, above all, held out the hope, to be realized in the revolutionary future, of a recaptured transcendence, a redeemed humanity, and an impeccable moral authority external to ourselves here on earth.

The second development had occurred some years before and was incidentally connected with the first. In 1868 there appeared in the *Westminister Review* a review essay of three volumes of William Morris's early poetry. It divided itself into two parts—the first was an intelligent appraisal of the works under discussion; the second was a kind of tacked-on conclusion, which does not really derive from what has come before. Here are some extended passages from that concluding section of the review:

> To regard all things and principles of things as inconstant modes or fashions has more and more become the tendency of modern thought. Let us begin with that which is without—our physical life. Fix upon it in one of its more exquisite intervals—the moment, for instance, of delicious recoil from the flood of water in summer heat. What is the whole physical life in that moment but a combination of natural elements to which science gives their names? ... Our physical life is a perpetual motion of them—the passage of the blood, the wasting and repairing of the lenses of the eye, the modification of the tissues of the brain by every ray of light and sound— processes which science reduces to simpler and more elementary forces. Like the elements of which we are composed, the action of these forces extends beyond us; it rusts iron and ripens corn. Far out on every side of us these elements are broadcast, driven by

many forces; and birth and gesture and death and the springing of violets from the grave are but a few out of ten thousand resulting combinations. That clear, perpetual outline of face and limb is but an image of ours under which we group them—a design in a web the actual threads of which pass out beyond it. This at least of flame-like our life has, that it is but the concurrence renewed from moment to moment of forces parting sooner or later on their ways.

Or if we begin with the inward world of thought and feeling, the whirlpool is still more rapid, the flame more eager and devouring. ... At first sight experience seems to bury us under a flood of external objects, pressing upon us with a sharp, importunate reality, calling us out of ourselves in a thousand forms of action. But when reflection begins to act upon those objects they are dissipated under its influence, the cohesive force is suspended like a trick of magic, each object is loosed into a group of impressions, colour, odour, texture, in the mind of the observer. And if we continue to dwell on this world, not of objects in the solidity with which language invests them, but of impressions unstable, flickering, inconsistent, which burn, and are extinguished with our consciousness of them, it contracts still further, the whole scope of observation is dwarfed to the narrow chamber of the individual mind. Experience, already reduced to a swarm of impressions, is ringed round for each one of us by that thick wall of personality through which no real voice has ever pierced on its way to us, or from us to that, which we can only conjecture to be without. Every one of those impressions is the impression of an individual in his isolation, each mind keeping as a solitary prisoner its own dream of a world.

Analysis goes a step further still, and tells us that those impressions of the individual to which, for each one of us, experience dwindles down, are in perpetual flight; that each of them is limited by time, and that as time is infinitely divisible, each of them is infinitely divisible also, all that is actual in it being a single moment, gone while we try to apprehend it, of which it may ever be more truly said that it has ceased to be than that it is. To such a tremulous wisp constantly reforming itself on the stream, to a single sharp impression, with a sense in it, a relic more or less fleeting, of such moments gone by, what is real in our life fines itself down. It is with the movement, the passage and dissolution of impressions, images, sensations, that analysis leaves off, that continual vanishing away, that strange perpetual weaving and unweaving of ourselves.

Such thoughts seem desolate at first; at times all the bitterness of life seems concentrated in them. They bring the image of one washed out beyond the bar in a sea at ebb, losing even his personality, as the elements of which he is composed pass into new combinations. Struggling, as he must, to save himself, it is himself that he loses at every moment....

The service of philosophy, and of religion and culture as well, to the human spirit, is to startle it into a sharp and eager observation. Every moment some form grows perfect in hand or face; some tone on the hills or sea is choicer than the rest; some mood of passion or insight or intellectual excitement is irresistibly real and attractive for us for that moment only. Not the fruit of experience but experience itself is the end. A counted number of pulses only is given to us of a variegated, dramatic life. How may we see in them all that is to be seen in them by the finest senses? How can we pass most swiftly from point to point, and be present always at the focus where the greatest number of vital forces unite in their purest energy?

To burn always with this hard gem-like flame, to maintain this ecstasy, is success in life. Failure is to form habits; for habit is relative to a stereotyped world; meantime it is only the roughness of the eye that makes any two things, persons, situations—seem alike. While all melts under our feet, we may well catch at any exquisite passion, or any contribution to knowledge that seems by a lifted horizon to set the spirit free for a moment, or any stirring of the senses, strange dyes, strange flowers and curious odours, or work of the artist's hands, or the face of one's friend. Not to discriminate every moment some passionate attitude in those about us and in the brilliance of their gifts some tragic dividing of forces on their ways, is on this short day of frost and sun to sleep before evening. With this sense of the splendour of our experience and of its awful brevity, gathering all we are into one desperate effort to see and touch, we shall hardly have time to make theories about the things we see and touch. What we have to do is to be for ever curiously testing opinion and courting new impressions, never acquiescing in a facile orthodoxy of Comte or of Hegel or of our own.... The theory or idea or system which requires of us the sacrifice of any part of this experience, in consideration of some interest into which we cannot enter, or some abstract morality we have not identified with ourselves, or what is only conventional, has no real claim upon us....

Well, we are all *condamnés*, as Victor Hugo somewhere says: we have an interval and then we cease to be. Some spend this interval in listlessness, some in high passions, the wisest in art and song. For our one chance is in expanding that interval, in getting as many pulsations as possible into the given time. High passions give one this quickened sense of life, ecstasy and sorrow of love, political or religious enthusiasm, or the "enthusiasm of humanity." Only, be sure it is passion, that it does yield you this fruit of a quickened, multiplied consciousness. Of this wisdom, the poetic passion, the desire of beauty, the love of art for art's sake, has most; for art comes to you professing frankly to give nothing but the highest quality to your moments as they pass, and simply for those moments' sake.[11]

These passages, with omissions, were reprinted in 1873 as the conclusion to Pater's *The Renaissance: Studies in Art and Poetry.* Pater was, I should hasten to add, a disciple of Arnold and Ruskin. He also, it seems, did not quite realize what he had written, and as a result of the clamor these pages aroused, he dropped the section from the second (1877) edition of the work because, as he said, "it might possibly mislead some of those young men into whose hands it might fall." And when he did restore the conclusion in later editions, he progressively modified its wording so that its force was diluted and weakened. In any event, and nevertheless, the cat had been let out of the bag, and we can appropriately regard these pages as the specimen text of modernism. The physical universe, modern science has revealed, is nothing but forces and elements in a state of flux, of combination and decomposition. Our mental existence fines down to no more than a succession of discrete, evanescent impressions. Individual identity is unstable; communication with others is an impossible illusion. And all effort and activity are without point or meaning except as they lead to sensations that are intensely pleasurable. There is no transcendence; there is nothing above or beyond us; the above or beyond have become identical with the indubitable nothing that is beneath us and upon whose edge we stand. Conventional morality, with its demands for constancy, habit, and stability, are failure and death, as is any other idea or system that requires us to sacrifice or renounce some new intensity of experience. Experience itself is the end, and there is nothing beyond it. Self-realization consists in "getting as many pulsations as possible" into the time allotted to us. If Morris's career eventuates in a break with the tradition of discourse we have been describing, Pater's statement represents its collapse upon itself and its inner evacuation.

Pater's chief inevitable disciple took this program and dramatized it in his exemplary life, which culminated in exemplary disaster. In the aesthetic and decadent movements of the late 1880s and 1890s, nonconformity to middle-class expectations became fashionable, and repudiation from within of the dominant character type became a public project. These movements were overtly antibourgeois, antiphilistine, and antimaterialistic. They were explicitly based on snobbery and on the aping of aristocratic exclusiveness. They cultivated refinement of sensibility, floridity of individual expressiveness, and autonomy of self that chiefly appeared as insolence toward others and a worship of youth in both its beauty and its ignorance. They were explicitly narcis-

11. Walter Pater, Unsigned review of *The Earthly Paradise, Westminster Review,* 34 n.s. (October 1868): 309-12.

sistic and almost explicitly homosexual. In their dandyism they were treating their physical selves as if they were works of art. In the prophetic and transitional figure of Oscar Wilde these tendencies, these early forays into the outskirts and badlands of modernity, come to a focus. As for Wilde, it may be said that almost nothing about him is memorable except himself. What one recalls is the effect of wit and paradox, the effort through ridicule to explode firecrackers along the lines of contradiction in middle-class character and social life. Yet whenever one returns to his writing, one finds there matters that one had overlooked or forgotten. Here are two passages from "The Critic as Artist":

> What is termed Sin is an essential element of progress. Without it the world would stagnate, or grow old, or become colourless. By its curiosity Sin increases the experience of the race. Through its intensified assertion of individualism, it saves us from monotony of type. In its rejection of the current notions about morality, it is one with the higher ethics. . . .

And again:

> The mere existence of conscience, that faculty of which people prate so much nowadays, and are so ignorantly proud, is a sign of our imperfect development. It must be merged in instinct before we become fine. Self-denial is simply a method by which man arrests his progress, and self-sacrifice a survival of the mutilation of the savage, part of that old worship of pain which is so terrible a factor in the history of the world.[12]

Pater and Nietzsche, we see, have here joined forces—as they do in Wilde's repeated assertion that "the sphere of art and the sphere of ethics are absolutely distinct and separate." His flawed but important work *The Picture of Dorian Gray* is, of course, central to any discussion of the development we have been outlining. Dorian Gray undertakes to treat himself as a work of art—to make his life into a work of art. In the preceding historical period of Western culture, Faust made a pact with the devil: he would sell his soul for transcendent knowledge and power. Dorian Gray's implicit pact is that he will sell his soul for eternal youth. What we see here in the domain of cultural discourse is, it seems to me, a process of devolution: from a powerful fantasy in which the autonomous ego is invested with demonic powers, to a fantasy in which autonomy is imagined beneath the sign of a narcissistic investment. But there is more to it than this. Wilde wrote of Dorian that he is "haunted all through his life by an exaggerated sense of conscience which mars his pleasures for him and warns him that youth and enjoyment are not everything in the world. It is finally

12. Oscar Wilde, "The Critic as Artist," in *The Works of Oscar Wilde*, ed. G. F. Maine (New York: E. P. Dutton, 1954), pp. 962-63.

to get rid of the conscience that dogged his steps from year to year that he destroys the picture; and thus in his attempt to kill conscience Dorian Gray kills himself."[13] Wilde seems to imply that this outcome was an unfortunate accident and that in someone more happily endowed the killing of conscience might not not have entailed the larger fatality. In the light of both cultural and clinical evidence, that implied assertion by Wilde seems very doubtful indeed.

It certainly was not true for Wilde, for as we now understand, he undertook unconsciously to destroy himself, largely out of feelings of guilt—and in this sense too, we can perceive him as a transitional figure. At his first trial Wilde was questioned by his old schoolmate, Edward Carson, who was counsel for the Marquess of Queensbury:

> *Carson*: Is it good for the young?
> *Wilde*: Anything is good that stimulates thought in whatever age.
> *Carson*: Whether moral or immoral?
> *Wilde*: There is no such thing as morality or immorality in thought. There is immoral emotion.
> *Carson*: "Pleasure is the only thing one should live for"?
> *Wilde*: I think that the realization of oneself is the prime aim of life, and to realize oneself through pleasure is finer than to do so through pain. I am, on that point, entirely on the side of the ancients—the Greeks. It is a pagan idea.
> *Carson*: "A truth ceases to be true when more than one person believes in it"?
> *Wilde*: Perfectly. That would be my metaphysical definition of truth; something so personal that the same truth could never be appreciated by two minds.[14]

And after his release from prison, Wilde remarked in answer to a question put to him by André Gide: "Would you like to know the great drama of my life? It is that I have put my genius into my life—I have only put my talent into my work."[15] We have arrived at the point at which Carlyle has been stood on his head; and indeed Wilde's forward-looking statements amount to an inversion of the values through which bourgeois society and culture, in the historical period under discussion, represented itself to itself, in its notions of what makes up an individual.

What I have been trying to demonstrate here is that there occurs across a seventy-year period in English literature and culture a coherent discourse at the very highest pitch of consciousness among the

13. Letter to the editor of the *Daily Chronicle*, June 30, 1890, in *The Letters of Oscar Wilde*, ed. Rupert Hart-Davis (New York: Harcourt, Brace & World, 1962), pp. 263-64.
14. H. Montgomery Hyde, ed. *The Trials of Oscar Wilde* (London: William Hodge, 1948), p. 123.
15. André Gide, "Oscar Wilde: In Memoriam," in *Oscar Wilde: Interviews and Recollections*, ed. E.H. Mikhail (London: Macmillan Press, 1979), p 297n.

most acute minds of the dominant culture. This discourse in all its ramifications amounts in uncanny ways to a prefiguration in thought and culture of what in the last thirty years we have begun to see being acted out in the lives of large numbers of individuals in advanced or late capitalist society and certain institutions peculiar to it. I do not know whether there are lessons to be learned here; and I do not believe that what we know historically enables us to predict what will happen next. I do think, however, that this consultation of part of the history of our culture helps clarify for us how we have come to be where we are, where we came from, and to what, indeed, we are not returning.

21

The Arts and the
Idea of Progress

MURRAY KRIEGER

In my undertaking here, I feel something of a lonely outsider, or at least I feel that way on behalf of my subject. In treating the various humanistic, scientific, or near-scientific disciplines so that we may explore the idea of progress reflected in them, we realize that the arts must be singled out from the rest as an exceptional case, indeed must be singled out for exemption. Historians and theorists have customarily treated the arts, in their relation to progress, in a radically different way from that of other disciplines. So much is this the case that in response to the question, "Can we apply the idea of progress to the arts?" most of our colleagues, thinking the question naïve, would at once reply in the negative. And at the level at which they make this answer, it is difficult to disagree. So long as by "the arts" one means only the individually created artifacts and so long as by the history of the arts one means only the sequence throughout history in which such artifacts are produced, critics and historians have properly resisted applying the idea of progress to them.

Art, at least in the Western tradition, is a special subject for us because, as a collection of artifacts ordered chronologically but held as a single group in our minds, it constitutes a canon (however shifting its members and whatever the disagreements among us about them in individual cases) of fixed works that are, in a simple sense, always and identically present for us. These works, individually valued and judged as we seek to make a selection of the best among them, are taken by us to be fictions, illusionary "realities," which themselves do not change, though our perceptions of them surely do as we move through time with them as our companions. But in this limited conception of the arts with which I have begun, my concern is with progress in *them*, as individually ordered works of art viewed as an historical collective, and not with progress in our commentary or conception of them. The latter may well have to be taken up later in these remarks since, before

I finish, I want to suggest all the problems attendant upon putting the two terms—progress and the arts—together and even to suggest how the idea of progress might be transformed so that it and the arts might coexist, indeed how their special place in relation to progress might make them uniquely helpful to our considerations of progress in other areas.

THE NEOCLASSICAL PROBLEM: THE ANCIENTS VERSUS THE MODERNS

But in this first, common-sense notion of the arts as a collection of completed, illusionary works in a variety of media, we can understand why the consideration of progress in the arts has always stood apart from our considerations of progress in other fields of human endeavor. I am accepting a nonproblematic definition of progress—any of those with which Nannerl Keohane began (see pp. 22f.), all of them characterized by Charles Van Doren's notion of "irreversible meliorative change."[1] The question, then, presents itself quite simply: can it be maintained that later works are (in some as yet unspecified sense) better than earlier ones and that, therefore, works being produced today are the best of all? To argue for progress from this perspective, we must argue that works of more recent periods represent an improvement over those of earlier periods since obviously the individual work does not itself improve. The text of *King Lear* does not get better, or alter at all, with the years, however we may improve our capacity to appreciate it.

Even in the early and least self-critical enunciations of the idea of progress during the eighteenth century, there was usually some reluctance, in the field of the arts, to deflate the ancients in order to inflate the moderns. The authority of the classics was too central to the self-definition of neoclassicism to suggest so one-sided a victory in the competition moderns may have felt with them. For the competition was held on the ancients' ground, with the modern gesture of imitation sufficient to guarantee the authority of the original, however improved in refinements the current version may have appeared. Even those on the progressive side in the battle between ancients and moderns rarely hid altogether their sometimes grudging acknowledgment of the excellence and priority of original authority in the arts.

Thus, we have the propagation of two myths, the myth of origins, which leads to the idolatry of the ancients by attributing "original genius" uniquely to them, as if they were the absolute beginning; and the myth of the "advancement of learning," which was to account for the superiority of the moderns in those areas in which—since they came along too late in history to be "original"—learning would have to be enough. In the arts, the division of labor sponsored by the two

1. Professor Keohane is referring to Charles van Doren, *The Idea of Progress* (New York: Praeger, 1967), p. 3.

myths allowed the moderns to excel in technical refinements ever more impressive without threatening the profundity of the genius that was there, however primitively, at the start. So it was the lasting power of the extant art object of the distant past thrusting itself, always anew, upon the present which set the arts apart from those disciplines of science and philosophic thought which could more single-mindedly turn against the past since these latter were, without qualification, to be responsive to the advancement of learning. The work of art was thus divided in two: the greatness of vision which was there in the earliest works and is always with us in them, beyond competition, and the elegance of refinement which is increasingly ours since, thanks to the advancement of learning, we know so much more than our unhappily ignorant precursors.

In pointing to this distinction between progress in science and progress in art, I cannot do better than quote from David Hume, clearly a liberal who sides with the moderns in their battle with the ancients because he is committed to the belief in intellectual progress. In his "Of the Standard of Taste" (1757), he rescues art unambiguously from the framework imposed by the idea of progress, even though he grants that "modern authors" have "an advantage" over the ancients because of "the want of humanity and of decency" in the "rough heroes" of the ancients, which the moderns, no longer barbarous, have in their civilized manner refined:

> Theories of abstract philosophy, systems of profound theology, have prevailed during one age: in a successive period, these have been universally exploded: their absurdity has been detected: other theories and systems have supplied their place, which again gave place to their successors: and nothing has been experienced more liable to the revolutions of chance and fashion than these pretended decisions of science. The case is not the same with beauties of eloquence and poetry. Just expressions of passion and nature are sure, after a little time, to gain public applause, which they maintain forever. Aristotle, and Plato, and Epicurus, and Descartes, may successively yield to each other: but Terence and Virgil maintain a universal, undisputed empire over the minds of men. The abstract philosophy of Cicero has lost its credit: the vehemence of his oratory is still the object of our admiration.[2]

In Hume we see the advantage to fiction in its evasion of any criterion of falsifiability. There is no empirical truth or falsity in art and, hence, no obsolescence: we need not pull down Virgil to set up Shakespeare. A great work remains always present, commandingly there, undiminished, however much we may learn or read. Unlike the history of other disciplines, the history of an art throws up a series of discrete,

2. "Of the Standard of Taste," in *The Philosophy of David Hume*, ed. V. C. Chappell (New York: Random House, 1963), p. 495.

value-laden objects as its "facts," and, as repositories of value responsible finally to themselves, they do not lend themselves to being treated
in comparison to other similar, though utterly different, entities which
constitute the historical sequence of which they may be seen to be a
part.

Recent semiology has alerted us anew to the "intertextual" character of literary works and their meanings so that what may seem to be a
discrete work, with its own closure, actually has all sorts of prior
works flowing into it as it in turn flows into others. Thus, all are to be
seen as elements in a single historically developing semiotic code, all
of whose members are mutually cooperative—and hence comparable.
Nevertheless, I would claim, in the aesthetic experience bounded by
one work, what we are caught by is the development of a system of
internal manipulations which argues for a momentary integrity that
transcends history and disdains comparison, shunning any terms more
general than itself. And even if, in spite of such experiences, we
should try to treat our masterworks comparatively, the history of their
succession hardly suggests a consistently upward movement among
them as we move forward through time.

Now it is certainly true that Hume has left room for the refinements
of more civilized modern authors, and, as I have suggested, it has
become commonplace to provide for progress in all those aspects of
the arts in which learning and sophistication can pave the way for
advancement—for example, in styles and techniques. Here we can find
problems to be solved and the elements of a given medium, within an
accepted genre, to be manipulated more and more successfully. The
solutions and manipulations can be compared and placed within a
progressive pattern. But, as Hume suggests, these descriptive judgments, as they relate to sensible and teachable matters, probably do
not determine our ultimate aesthetic judgments of candidates for the
canon.

Indeed, on this question Hume sounds all too much like his conservative antagonist, Samuel Johnson, who also wanted to free his
contemporaries to go beyond their classical forebears where they could,
although they still would not match that originality of perception
which is the special attribute of antique crudeness. In his dissertation
upon poetry in *Rasselas* (1759), Imlac sets forth this limited doctrine
of progress, which allows the moderns to be superior in everything
that is of secondary importance in aesthetic creativity:

> And yet it fills me with wonder, that, in almost all countries, the
> most ancient poets are considered as the best: whether it be that
> every other kind of knowledge is an acquisition gradually attained,
> and poetry is a gift conferred at once; or that the first poetry of
> every nation surprised them as a novelty, and retained the credit by
> consent which it received by accident at first: or whether, as the
> province of poetry is to describe nature and passion, which are

always the same, the first writers took possession of the most striking objects for description, and the most probable occurrences for fiction, and left nothing to those that followed them, but transcription of the same events, and new combinations of the same images. Whatever be the reason, it is commonly observed that the early writers are in possession of nature, and their followers of art: that the first excel in strength and invention, and the latter in elegance and refinement.[3]

When Johnson comments on Pope's translation of the *Iliad* of Homer in his "Life of Pope" (1779-1781), he seems, like a proper neoclassicist, to be leaning more heavily toward the advantages of the progress which has led to the civilized moderns:

There is a time when nations emerging from barbarity, and falling into regular subordination, gain leisure to grow wise, and feel the shame of ignorance and the craving pain of unsatisfied curiosity. To this hunger of the mind plain sense is grateful; that which fills the void removes uneasiness, and to be free from pain for a while is pleasure; but repletion generates fastidiousness, a saturated intellect soon becomes luxurious, and knowledge finds no willing reception till it is recommended by artificial diction. Thus it will be found in the progress of learning that in all nations the first writers are simple, and that every age improves in elegance. One refinement always makes way for another, and what was expedient to Virgil was necessary to Pope.[4]

From Homer to Virgil to Pope, Johnson is apologizing for the loss of Homeric qualities by praising those which Pope has substituted from his later vantage point. In what may seem to be an enormous concession to the progressive advantages enjoyed by Pope, Johnson has subtly displayed his remarkable balance in judgment. Terms like "elegance" and "refinement" carry their negative underside along with the praise they intend. And however splendid Pope's accomplishment, however unequaled anywhere before (as Johnson announces), its greatness is tied to the fact that it is an imitative achievement, an achievement in translation, the carrying over into these times and this language of the original vision of another.

In Johnson's distinction between original, barbaric ancients and imitative, elegant moderns, as in Hume's distinction between the history of the arts and the history of thought, we can find the implicit opposition between the intuitive and the rational, the instinctual and the learned. From the earliest days of aesthetics in the West, theorists

3. Samuel Johnson, *The History of Rasselas, Prince of Abyssinia,* in *Rasselas, Poems, and Selected Prose,* ed. Bertrand H. Bronson (New York: Holt, Rinehart, and Winston, 1958), p. 627.
4. Samuel Johnson, "Pope," *Lives of the English Poets* (London: Oxford University Press, 1952), II, 320.

had distinguished between the endowments of nature and the enhancements of art. Always it was the first that was the source of genius and absolute artistic vision, beyond all rules and instruction, and it was the second which—though only a subsidiary advantage to be pursued in conjunction with the first—frequently had to be substituted by derivative poets in derivative periods for what history or the genes had denied them. And, in a Hume or in a Johnson, it was only the second sort which was susceptible to rules and hence could be taught and learned; the first remained, in its untouchable mystery, a *je-ne-sais-quoi*. Hence, progress could be predicated only in the limited area of the arts (style, devices, general questions of craft) to which reason and learning had access. Progress was denied to the artist's original genius, which was built into his nature. Paradoxically, then, the original creative center of art was proclaimed to be *nature* whereas what was termed the *art* in art was really the science of art. It was only this technical element in the arts, only this scientific element, which turned natural art into artifice with its refinements; it was only this element which, like all science, could be seen as subject to the law of progress—whereas the essence of art, and its greatness, its very nature, presumably escaped this as it escaped all laws.

We can now review the standard arguments that we have seen urging the nonprogressive character of the arts. First, there is the most obvious argument: "there were giants in those days" and, by contrast, almost exclusively pygmies in our own time. This is an appeal to the greater number of masterpieces in all the arts of older periods. It is a claim that is widely unchallenged. If it is a just claim, these masterpieces would seem to represent prima facie empirical evidence against progress in the arts. The second argument rests on the opposition between instinct or intuition on one side and reason on the other; and since art is seen as the product of the first and science as the product of the second, it leads to the claim that art is independent of rational knowledge and its advancement. As another way of putting the first argument, it asks, in effect, how it is that we can be so much more knowledgeable than, say, Homer, and yet cannot boast of nearly so great a poet. The conclusion must be that knowledge is not sufficient to the achievement of greatness in art. A corollary would be that craft or technique—know-how that is of course subject to knowledge—is not the same as art and can progress without art itself progressing: *poeta nascitur*, and no amount of technical education can produce him. A third argument also follows: the great art work never becomes obsolete, as scientific formulae can. The art work cannot be falsified since our appreciation of it should not be dependent on our agreement with the set of beliefs on which it rests. Therefore, the work is not exposed to the aging process, which wears out all doctrines, and it cannot be superseded by its successors.

Based on these arguments, the exemption of the arts from the idea of progress was common among progressives and conservatives alike in those early ideological debates about progress in the eighteenth century. The progress in refinement in the arts would then seem to come only at the cost of original genius, to which it moves in an inverse relation. From this perspective, the arts—insofar as they are characterized by the masterworks of genius—have achieved their highest moment at the beginning. And, ever since, they have—despite the compensatory progress in elegance—been in an apparent decline, which can produce only the refinements of imitation. This "primitivistic" notion (to borrow a term used by Roy Harvey Pearce to characterize this line of thought)[5] conceives of an artless art, which had its fullest realization in an antique moment before developments in learning and in scientific and material progress led it on its downward path. (How strange it is that such primitivistic idolatry should accompany the celebration of refinement which constituted the neoclassical aesthetic, a guide for artists to do the best with what history left to them—namely, an imitative task.)

Here indeed is what I earlier referred to as the myth of origins, a narrative structure plotted on the analogy to the Fall of man. Artistic genius is born in innocence and, as a simple tragic hero, falls victim to rational progress and sophistication in other realms. The "noble savage" of late eighteenth-century thought is created for us by the retrogressive myth of origins and then is destroyed as that myth is forced to coexist with, and give way before, the progressive myth of the advancement of learning. As in the original myth of the Fall, it is reason—together with reason's knowledge—that is the enemy to genial instinct and brings it down. Whatever takes the place of genius is a talent of another sort, one more akin to the scientist's and more at home in the scientist's world of progress.

So to the progressive's belief that "later is better" was opposed the equally reductive belief that so far as art was concerned, "later is worse" (though with compensations that neoclassical artifice could provide). Except for matters of technique, the doctrine of decline often replaced the doctrine of progress in discussions of artistic genius. Obviously, later critics had less unbalanced or unqualified views: they would no longer be simply content with an upward or downward movement. Instead, some might argue that the individual great work was somehow outside the historical continuum, an unpredictable sport that occurs when it will, early or late. Or some might argue for an historical relativism, which saw only a sequence of sealed historical periods, answerable only to themselves, so that they cannot be com-

5. Pearce adapts the notion of the "primitivistic" to his own purposes in an unpublished essay, "Poetry and Progress," which he wrote for a meeting of the academy devoted to "The Transformation of the Idea of Progress." A summary of this essay appears in the *Bulletin of the American Academy of Arts and Sciences*, 31 (October 1977): 26-27.

pared with one another. Consequently, one cannot judge across periods
to establish a general movement upward or downward. In both these
variations of the arguments about progress in the arts, however, the
case against applying a progressive model to the arts is consistently
supported.

There have, of course, been exceptions, especially among poets interested in keeping up their own hopes for a greatness to surpass that
of the past. For example, to return to the late eighteenth and early
nineteenth centuries, we observe, in early preromantic or romantic
writers like Schiller or Wordsworth, a desperate attempt to find progress after all in the substitution of the new "sentimental" poet (Schiller's term for the modern poet of a dissociated culture) for the old
"naïve" poet (Schiller's term for the original, un-self-conscious, instinctual poet). Of course, Schiller finds a high place for the contemporary poet in the name of his contemporary, Goethe, as Wordsworth
does on behalf of himself and his fellows. These poets, fighting what
Walter Jackson Bate has called "the burden of the past,"[6] would re-
invent the hope of progress for the sake of their own role in creating
out of themselves a new poetry that could more than compensate for
what had been lost, converting poetry's Fall into a fortunate one.[7] But
the nonpoets who look beyond them may be less convinced. Thus,
Schiller tries to find a uniquely different kind of genius in the "sentimental" poet, which in its own way might match or even surpass the
accepted genius of the "naïve" poet, although Schiller seems to concede
that an objective greatness seems to have vanished, not to be replaced.
His humanism thus creates a consoling alternative, if not a wholly
competitive one. But for those who had less of a personal commitment
to authorize their contemporary arts, there may have been a more
willing acceptance of what was acknowledged to be the unprogressive
character of these arts, especially in contrast to the rational disciplines.
A belated neoclassicist like Thomas Love Peacock was just such a
skeptic about the powers of poetry in the modern world.

It is useful for us to watch as Peacock extends the arguments against
progress in the arts to their logical extreme, though with a positivistic
antagonism to the role of poetry, in contrast to the protective sympathy we have observed in Hume and Johnson. Peacock turns against
poetry precisely because of its resistance to the idea of progress, which
blesses all other disciplines, bringing them out of primeval darkness
with the light of reason that is denied to poetry. With an attitude to
science that is uncritically progressive, he exemplifies the positivist's
exclusive valorization of that which is capable of progress. Here is a

6. W. Jackson Bate, *The Burden of the Past and the English Poet* (Cambridge, Mass.:
Harvard University Press, 1970).

7. See "William Wordsworth and the *Felix Culpa*," in my *The Classic Vision: The
Retreat from Extremity in Modern Literature* (Baltimore, Md.: Johns Hopkins University Press, 1971), pp. 149-95. In this chapter, I relate Wordsworth to Schiller and others.

composite of condescending quotations from Peacock's *The Four Ages of Poetry* (1820):

> While the historian and the philosopher are advancing in, and accelerating, the progress of knowledge, the poet is wallowing in the rubbish of departed ignorance, and raking up the ashes of dead savages to find gewgaws and rattles for the grown babies of the age. . . .
>
> A poet in our times is a semibarbarian in a civilized community. He lives in days that are past. His ideas, thoughts, feelings, associations, are all with barbarous manners, obsolete customs, and exploded superstitions. The march of his intellect is like that of a crab, backward. The brighter the light diffused around him by the progress of reason, the thicker is the darkness of antiquated barbarism, in which he buries himself like a mole, to throw up the barren hillocks of his Cimmerian labors. . . .
>
> Poetry [originally] was the mental rattle that awakened the attention of intellect in the infancy of civil society: but for the maturity of mind to make a serious business of the playthings of its childhood, is as absurd as for a full-grown man to rub his gums with coral, and cry to be charmed to sleep by the jingle of silver bells.[8]

So poets, useful "while society was savage, grow rabid, and out of their element, as [society] becomes polished and enlightened." I thought it worth quoting these excesses at some length so that we could savor the full rhetorical impatience with which the unbridled idolatry of scientific progress has to view the one area of human activity which is apparently excluded from it and even prides itself on its exclusion. In other words, Peacock accepts the division between instinct and reason, but only to celebrate the expulsion of instinct from a mature and civilized culture. He is forecasting that this is the destiny of the one previously valued area of human creation (the arts) which—by both admirers and detractors of the idea of progress—has been singled out as being unaffected by that idea, if not operating historically as an inversion of it.

Actually, of course, there were many in the nineteenth century who —unlike Peacock—insisted that the arts, no less than anything else, moved only in an upward direction until reaching the summit of the present day. But I shall here skip over these apostles of universal progress who uncritically used the evolutionary metaphor to construct their models of history. Because their too easily optimistic doctrines were so obviously out of accord with what was revealed by a less doctrinaire look at the shape of history's narrative of the arts, they were not long credited. So these doctrines need not distract us now

8. Thomas Love Peacock, "The Four Ages of Poetry," in *The Works of Thomas Love Peacock*, ed. Henry Cole (London: Richard Bentley & Sons, 1875), III, 334-36.

from our concern with more skeptical observations about progress in the arts. Peacock's faith in scientific progress—indeed his faith in progress in everything except the arts—was no less naïve, but the immunity from general progress, which it inflicts upon the arts—even when put in so extreme a form as Peacock's—is part of an intellectual tradition which, because of its later positivistic affiliations, is not without influence even today.

Peacock's quasi-positivistic optimism on behalf of progress and reason points toward a scientific utopianism, though one which protects its progressive character by leaving the retrograde, even childish, arts far behind. The hope apparently is that they will wither away, like the vestigial state in the communist dream. Strangely, both protectors and disparagers of the place of art in the modern world can share this utopianism in behalf of rational progress. The question that divides them asks whether the arts are to be taken along with science or left behind. And if, unlike Peacock, they want art taken along into the modern, rational utopia, they must decide what sort of art they are speaking for: is it the old masterworks—the unchallenged elite of earlier and less advanced cultural moments—which are seen as our permanent companions? Or is it the more progressive, up-to-date companions, which an advancing culture produces to symbolize its own moment of greatest enlightenment? Is a utopia a cultural condition in which everybody will be able to enjoy Bach or Rembrandt or Shakespeare, or is it one in which Bach will be rejected for current inventions which reflect, as they are a match for, the state of our advancement? What is at stake is whether we wish theoretically to justify our feelings concerning the absolute superiority of a Bach or a Rembrandt or a Shakespeare over the moderns who have pretensions to being their successors, or whether the arts themselves progress as reflections of the progress in the other disciplines (for example, music that reflects recent experiments in electronic sound, or paintings that reflect what we now know about optics, or narrative structures that reflect what psychology tells us about the motives behind actions).

THE MODERN PROBLEM:
SOCIAL VERSUS AESTHETIC PROGRESS

To move to our own times, many modern theorists of the avant-garde argue that recent artists should not try to do better than older masters in performing the same function but should recognize instead that a different function is now called for. There is in such theorists an outright rejection of elitism in the arts, an insistence on the egalitarian alternative which welcomes all symbolic expressions without discrimination. They would tear down the walls of our museums and turn the world itself into a "museum without walls." Their democratic receptivity claims to represent an advance over the outmoded class consciousness which finds its aesthetic analogue in our setting apart a few select masterworks into a canon (a term whose unfortunate theological implications are now exploited). The avant-garde critics see political (and theological) metaphors as implicit everywhere in older and traditional criticism, and they press such metaphors to their literal consequences since they wish to condemn the aesthetic convention, out of which older cultural moments produced their masterworks, for its aristocratic exclusiveness. And those works most admired in the past are treated as though they were as obsolete as the discarded social and political institutions that are now seen reflected in their elitist pretension to be high art.

This rejection of the entire concept of an elite corps of art works, now treated as if we were dealing with class distinctions among citizens within a social structure, is really a rejection of the political institutions at work in the cultures which produced these works. It is as if, by turning against an aesthetic monument, which history has carefully segregated—and lifted above—its fellows, we somehow can wish out of existence the reactionary political context which was thriving when the work was created. Better yet, we are implicitly acknowledging that the special endowments of the elite work somehow require, and grow out of, the undemocratic characteristics of its social-political context. Hardly a sample of "people's art," the great work seems to demand the metaphors of an aristocratic body politic even to find the audacity to ask for the privileged treatment, the idolatry, the claim of special "value," which has been accorded it.

For some antielitist moderns, the most objectionable character of the great work of art is its assumption of the absolute value of man-created *order*, its order. Instead of authorizing the human creator to seek a triumph with his order over ordinary life, the antielitist asks for the embrace of the ordinary and the condemnation of any order that would disdain it. As antielitist, he distrusts as politically suspect our every impulse to refine the ordinary into a transcendent order that would improve aesthetically upon it. As he relates art to society, he relates aesthetic order to social-political order, believing that a high degree of the first usually has been found only where there is a high degree of the second. And he is aware that a highly ordered society has hardly been the most progressive; indeed, the unprogressive nature of societies in which our greatest art has been produced is hardly an encouragement to his hopes. He fears that, to the extent that art reflects its culture, the art most conducive to order (our high art) is reflective of a most regressive social order since it emerged out of such an order. Conversely, the progress of society, with its breakdown of accepted orders in the name of freedom and equality, may well carry with it the subversion of the potential greatness of elite objects of art. And the continuing insistence on producing such objects poses a threat to the progress of the culture it is to reflect because, if it does indeed reflect its culture, it would still have to work toward a society within which its own penchant for order felt comfortable.

If, then, society dedicates itself to preserve cultural conditions under which such elite objects can still be produced, must it not put a priority on a social order which may well play against the egalitarian impulse usually associated with social progress? So either we try to restrict progress in the arts to progress in their capacity to serve—at whatever cost to themselves—progress in a society moving forward toward liberation, or we accept retrograde notions of social order so that we may encourage a still revered aristocratic art. To insist on such an either/or may seem to represent a strangely unfortunate surrender of art to society, a surrender based on a simplistic and fearful equation made between aesthetic and social orders, as if "order" was the same thing in both realms. Nevertheless, inimical to order as necessarily hierarchical and idolatrous, and in love with indiscriminate, pedestrian experience at large, the antielitist rejects elite art along with the obsolete society that cherished its elites. He has come to accept a newer and literally revolutionary notion of (what, for lack of another term, I shall still call) art, and he sees it as more progressive (and hence, in his special sense, better) than the rejected notion of art. He can even claim to find progress in art through the ages, although he is speaking of its function, the immediacy of its relations with an entire society, rather than of its rarefied value as a thing in itself, which he gladly has given up.

So in the avant-garde (and we must note the progressive implications of this metaphorical epithet itself) there must be an implied assertion of progress in the arts quite apart from any claim to an increasing value for the individual work that has been more recently produced. I started this essay by explicitly defining progress in the arts only as the improvement in quality in individual works as we move from earlier to later ones. But the antielitist attitude I have been considering deliberately disdains such discriminating individual judgments of aesthetic quality, seeing them as irrelevant, if not reactionary; that attitude must disdain them because, as antielitist, it wishes to affirm progress in the arts as a whole as reflections of the progress in institutionalized relations among persons in society. The interest is in historical continuity among equals and not in the ahistorical discontinuity of a transcendent single work. Progress in the arts can be affirmed, then, only because it is now related to their role in fostering an open, egalitarian society.

But does this attitude not shortchange the aesthetic qualities which have undermined the argument for progress by their assuring us our permanent experience of the unsurpassable greatness of early masterpieces? And do we not take such aesthetic judgments and such masterworks for granted even as we try to be receptive to the social and antielitist arguments which justify an often antiaesthetic avant-garde? In our self-prompted, postmodernist enthusiasm, we may reluctantly accept many of the most antiaesthetic experiments as peculiarly representative of our culture. But we can afford to do so, perhaps, because we feel secretly assured that our antique gems of art have already been made and are still with us to be valued in their rarefied separateness. I wonder whether, when we try to respond to electronic music, for example, we do so knowing we can count on Mozart to be there to go back to. In other words, for all our attempts to cooperate with the revolutionary art (or antiart) that may reflect our moment at this end of the progressive continuum, we quietly rely upon our antiprogressive commitment to works of art with which the modern world does not seek to compete, and very likely could not if it tried.

But now we have moved beyond the single definition of artistic progress with which I began, as we have moved from individual elite works to the historical continuum made up of all our symbolic expressions. And we have seen how some kind of progress could be predicated of the second, but not of the first, provided we were speaking of progress in society (rather than in the arts themselves as isolated entities), or rather—to be more precise—provided we were speaking only of progress in the conception of how the arts were to function in a progressive society as they moved toward the sacrificial end of self-obliteration in the service of the equality of all things. So, besides the obvious notion which would have progress in the arts depend on a simple comparison between the aesthetic qualities of earlier and later works (in which notion progress in the arts is usually denied), we have this second notion, in which the argument for progress depends on a comparison between earlier and later assumptions about how art functions in society. And this turns out to depend on how we judge the respective societies since we see that progress in society leads it to reshape its role for art in a progressive direction (irrespective of our judgment, on "merely" aesthetic criteria, of the individual works).

PROBLEMS OF TECHNIQUE AND
CRITICAL RESPONSE

There is a third notion of what progress in the arts might mean, one that I have referred to earlier: it is the matter of craft, the changing and teachable methods of manipulating the expressive medium of the particular art. As readily discernible techniques, these *can* be put into the context of historical progress. Now it is not that we can claim a long-term upward movement so much as we can claim refinements in the solutions being offered within defined areas of problems concerned with craft. Thus, we find a limited degree of what might be called technical progress within various genres in the arts as these develop their traditions. (We must understand the claim that Milton knew more than Virgil to mean, among other things, that this "more" which Milton knew was Virgil himself.) We find such progress also within and between artistic movements, usually within genres: initial breakthroughs in craft, in response to a given problem, give way to the consolidation of gains, perhaps only then revealing dead ends—

end-of-the-line problems which suggest nowhere left to go with this peculiar manipulation of the medium—until someone breaks through to a new lode to be explored and exploited, so that the process begins again. This sequence—the exhaustion of once vital movements, then experimentation and successful invention that get it all going again—accounts for the cry, heard in experimental moments in the history of the arts, to "make it new." In this repeated process there may be some significant gains, some technical problems which are taken care of so successfully that they will not present themselves again as problems—at least not in the same form.

Yet it may be too optimistic to claim a single line of improvement, even in small matters of craft, since one can demonstrate progressive development more easily within movements than between them. It may be misleading to apply the organic metaphor too literally to artistic movements or genres, projecting a birth, development, maturity, decay, and death to each movement as if it was a separate life, with each successive one having to start all over again. But it is equally misleading to expect that each movement necessarily stands on the shoulders of its predecessor, each an improvement over what has come before. Further, it must be repeated, critics in our history have generally avoided confounding technical judgments with aesthetic judgments. An aesthetician like R.G. Collingwood, in the post-Crocean tradition, distinguished the technical and external aspects of art as mere matters of "craft" from the internal intuition which for him is the essence of the work of art.[9] It is only the first of these, technique or craft, which is subject to the sequence of learning experiences, to the successive improvements, which constitute progress. But rather than defining art, this discernible element of craftsmanship functions largely to keep us critics in business by giving us something firm to talk about. So observations about craft may indicate more about changes in criticism than about changes in the arts themselves.

Thus, as a fourth way to make a connection between progress and the arts (and the last I shall consider here), we can shift the attempt to find progress from comparing works of several periods to comparing the responses of audiences (and their most specialized representatives, the critics) of several periods. In other words, in speaking about progress in the arts, we may really mean to speak only about progress in criticism, that is, about the increasing self-consciousness with which a culture can account for the power of its arts, past or present. The concern with progress in the arts becomes the concern with progress in the criticism of the arts, and this in turn becomes the concern with progress in criticism as an art, perhaps in the end *the* art. For criticism is seen as a rational (and, for some hermeneuticians among us, as a quasi-scientific) discipline capable of continuous development and

9. R.G. Collingwood, *The Principles of Art* (Oxford: Clarendon Press, 1938), pp. 15-41.

thus able to think of itself as progressing. Indeed, it is common, in recent days, for some literary critics, in their arrogance, to argue that what they create is a form of art that has the same status as poetry and is a rival art to it. Thus, the usual distinction between the art work as primary and the criticism of it as subsidiary is put in question.

Though one may well wish to qualify this aggrandizement of criticism, the history of criticism does indeed suggest that there has been progress in the rational manipulations of this discipline. To the extent, then, that criticism is a form of literary art, does not critical progress lead to some degree of progress in the arts? It is at least progress in what we expect or want of art and in how we interpret and respond to what we get in art. And might not this in turn lead to a hoped-for progress in art itself insofar as it follows criticism (even if such is rarely the case, since—modern self-inflating critics to the contrary notwithstanding—history rather suggests that it is criticism which follows art)? In view of what I have said so far, I would remind the reader that whatever progress art might make in the wake of its criticism is likely to occur only in the conscious manipulation of the medium, that is, in the areas supervised by craft. Further, whatever the artist learns from advances in the critical art over the centuries would not be likely to confer advantages on him which would lead to the creation of works of greater aesthetic power than what was generated by earlier artists unblessed by such articulate companions.

Yet here is another way in which we can speak of progress in the arts of succeeding cultural moments while we evade the obvious fact that the history of our artifacts suggests otherwise. Indeed, each of these ways of construing progress in the arts as something other than the upward march of a culture's monuments is similarly evasive. Whether we find progress in a culture's conception of how arts should function in society (which ends by finding progress in society's own functions), or find progress in the development of the technical aspects of the arts, or find progress in the art of criticizing the arts, we have managed to affirm something progressive about our traffic with the arts—but only by turning away from the works themselves, which prove so resistant to the idea of progress. And however persuasive our arguments for these other sorts of progress may be, they should not distract us from this resistance; they should rather remind us of the evasive nature of our efforts to find a way of bringing the arts into the alien realm of discourse about progress.

THE ENTIRE QUESTION QUESTIONED

My earlier discussion about relating progress to the changing social function of art leads to a larger questioning of the entire enterprise engaged by this essay. The fact that societies and audiences have through history defined in such different ways the art which reflects and serves them may lead us to ask whether we have been deceived into using the single term "art" to characterize very different entities. Should we, perhaps, turn this essay on itself by asking whether it has not cut its subject out from under itself?

The question to which this essay is devoted, "Can the idea of progress be applied to art?" is itself put in question by the essay, especially if we examine the question from the perspective of recent poststructuralist semiology. The original question assumes a constant entity, "art," that gets better, or gets worse, or stays much the same, as it moves through history. It thus reifies the word "art." But do we fool ourselves by using the one word as one thing, making "art" a single protagonist, whether in a lengthy history of upward growth, or in an equally lengthy history of decline, or in a sporadic sequence of ups and downs, or—as historical relativists would have it—in an indeterminate succession of enclosed and autonomous periods which cannot withstand mutual comparisons that would produce any larger tendency toward movement one way or the other? In speaking of progress, however we may relate the entity "art" before change to the entity "art" after change, it is risky to treat the two as one entity. And if they are different things (by which, in a poststructuralist mood, we would have to mean different functions), then they cannot be entered as one item into a simple model of progress. On the contrary, art, as the "thing" that does or does not become better, is not a constant thing or a thing at all, so much as it is a changing function.

The problem is that our linguistic habit of reifying our words leads us to speak of all these functions (which we summarize with the one word "art") as if they were the same entity first in a more primitive and then in an improved state. It is our anthropomorphism of language which leads us to speak (and to think) this way as we try to shape the moving world into the stasis of our substantives. This is, in short, a problem in semiology: dare we tie down the "floating signifier," "art," as one "thing" undergoing progress, instead of recognizing its dynamic, unsubstantial character? Each cultural moment, we have observed, seems to require its own "art," which—given its change of function with each successive moment—may hardly deserve to be denominated by a single word. As a changing function (and no longer a thing) within the disposition of the functional forces that constitute culture from moment to moment, we may well question—as poststructuralists —whether art, any more than culture itself, has earned its generic operational name, and whether it would bear it except for the ontologizing habit of our language. If we are dealing with functions so radically different from moment to moment in our cultural history, can our original question—depending as it does on a transhistorical (and transcultural) definition—any longer have any meaning? Or do nominalistic questions about what we call "art" at any given moment swallow it up?

Thus can the poststructuralists—with their "moves" replacing any ontological claims—deconstruct the language in which the myth of progress comes wrapped, thereby undoing that myth, if only—it turns out—to enhance their own. They thus seek to free us from a mystification by language which has caught the rest of us but which they abjure. Earlier, we must remember, the structuralism of Claude Lévi-Strauss sought to undo the notion of historical sequence required for the idea of progress by urging a purely synchronic analysis which revealed similar structures in primitive and in advanced cultures.[10] But of course, in spite of himself, Lévi-Strauss's own perspective on these structures became a privileged position and hence one which—with whatever inconsistency—represented significant progress over perspectives which had been held before. He was claiming to advance our capacity to understand the fact that there could be no advancement in our capacity to understand.

Now, however, the poststructuralist presses such matters with deconstructive instruments more keenly applied. Through efforts of thinkers like Jacques Derrida and Michel Foucault (though these two proceed in profoundly different ways), the final triumph of discourse, representing the high point in the progress of our reasoning about its capacity to mean, seems to lead to the emptying out of its meaning. An ironic triumph indeed. I have been indulging in a nominalistic deconstruction of the carefully built claims that filled the rational language of progress for two centuries. The ultimate consequence of such semiological self-knowledge is a confidence in methodological linguistic progress that would bring our confidence in substantive progress to naught. But this war on the metaphysical is self-defeating. In spite of the intentions of the poststructuralist critique, language can bring us to the zero point only by itself becoming a negative meaning, an apocalypse of nonbeing; and this unprogressive claim has an implicit ontology in it that contradicts the vision of language as a field of forces always in motion. So this would-be deconstruction is not a final move, but is—or would be—a final claim (or rather a final anticlaim). As what comes to be a negative metaphysic, it has all the metaphysical force of the positive metaphysic it would undo. It is not the end of arguments about progress, then, so much as it is a counterargument that reminds us of our logocentric illusions. Nevertheless, after we have paid these illusions due regard, we find the same problems about

10. The final lines of Claude Lévi-Strauss's "The Structural Study of Myth," *Structural Anthropology*, trans. Claire Jacobson and Brooke Grundfest Schoepf (New York: Basic Books, 1963), gives us a pithy summary of the strongly antiprogressive nature of his synchronic appeal:

> What makes a steel axe superior to a stone axe is not that the first one is better made than the second. They are equally well made, but steel is quite different from stone. In the same way we may be able to show that the same logical processes operate in myth as in science, and that man has always been thinking equally well; the improvement lies, not in an alleged progress of man's mind, but in the discovery of new areas to which it may apply its unchanged and unchanging powers. (p. 230)

progress in the arts still there confronting us: the failures in the language we have been using to resolve them have not dissolved them after all.

If semiology cannot deconstruct our problem out of existence, it is because the art work itself is continually reconstructing itself. The poststructuralist critique permits us to recognize that progress in the arts is, as a notion, self-contradictory: to the extent that there is progress—any of the sorts of progress that have been proposed—the term "arts" becomes increasingly unstable, even to the point of utter decomposition. The more progress, the less confident we should be that there is *an* "art" which undergoes it. But if there is no such constancy of term, then clearly there is no progress in what becomes of it but only a constantly shifting field of differences. The (so-called) arts produced by the several cultural moments necessarily represent such different functions and thus take such momentarily different forms that it would seem self-mystifying for them to claim the same generic term. But there is "art" as a deceiving collective term, and there is the individual work of art. The first may shift about without substantive meaning, but the second is constant. After all our semiological involutions, the single, utterly complete work of art, as it reappears in each cultural moment, is the same work, no matter how differently each culture perceives and conceives it, and the persistence of its presence lifts it beyond the destructive power of our demystifying instruments.

PROGRESS AND THE WORK OF ART

No matter how I have turned our question around in this essay, no matter how I have tried to alter our subject, I always come back to that individual work of art. At first we observed the resistance to applying the idea of progress to the arts and found the work itself at the base of every argument used to press that resistance. Then, as I sought definitions which might permit more affirmative answers to our question, none of the alternative definitions could finally displace our original concern about the comparative relationship among works of art produced through the centuries. And when I finally made the reflexive move of turning against the question by showing it was linguistically misleading and at odds with itself, still the substantive issue—and the individual work—remained. And it remains with us now.

But this is just what the work of art has been advertised to do from the beginning: to establish for itself a permanent presence with us. It recurs and recurs and will not go away. It may be that we can use this unique function of the art work, its continuous presence—so at odds with all our other ways of thinking and writing—to make a last effort to rescue our subject, though in an unexpected and perhaps distorted way. If we have not been able to look from the work outward—to society, to critics, to genres and artistic movements, to our deceiving language—perhaps we can look inward within the work. If we do, we may well find there—no matter how early or how late in history it was produced—a microcosmic model for the idea of human progress.

Let us think of the single, complete, aesthetically satisfying work of art as an ultimate "commodity," different from other desirable "goods" in that it is a permanent "good." Each art work is perceived to be a single, finite, framed, and self-enclosed entity, an absolute and perfected version of all those fleeting "goods" in the human economy (including scientific advances). The attainment of these goods in increasing numbers is supposed to constitute progress—except that with these other goods our satisfaction palls with our gratification. But the art work is an emblem of a lasting power in things which we do not otherwise find because there is, we seem to feel, something terminal about it as its own fictional reality. If we feel dissatisfied with each experience of the work, we are often dissatisfied with ourselves more than we are with it.

Think of the expression on the face of a colleague, filled with an ecstasy of anticipation, who reports that he is shortly to witness a new performance of *King Lear* (or *Giselle* or a late quartet of Beethoven), which is supposed to be an extraordinary and fully satisfying appearance of the work, as if in this appearance the work has achieved its once-and-for-all finality. (I use the word "appearance" in the Platonic sense because our colleague has in effect become a Platonist who takes this word with metaphysical seriousness, hoping this once with it to leap to the work's ultimate reality.) He is looking forward to the reenactment of a ritual in which yet newer and more highly qualified pretenders will seek again to unmask the god, the work-in-itself. And though his previous experiences suggest that in the end he will sense a failure, he wants to witness again and again the experience—however frustrating—of coming close. In the nonperformance arts (another silent reading of a poem to ourselves, another viewing of a painting), we would find—*mutatis mutandis*—the same kind of promise, frustration, and hope for another occasion. The phrase "work-in-itself" suggests an absolute ontological status which belies the role of the audience in constructing the reality of the work. Epistemological honesty should lead us to admit that the aesthetic form which holds this promise for us is, after all, a system of signs which depends on *our* interpretive energy if it is to become the work we worship. Paradoxically, we have in effect created the completeness of the ideal object, which is the standard of judgment for the less complete experience we have also created.

There is, I grant, something fetishistic about what we feel about those highest members of the canon of the elite art in our culture. Matthew Arnold was in part right about art's functioning as a substitute for a defunct religion precisely because (as we saw Hume suggest) it can—with a merely fictional commitment—outlast the obsolescence of the doctrines in the world that produced it. So these idolatrous expectations do suggest a fetishism, with each work seen as sacred even if our experience of it is not: each work is seen as containing its own Platonic archetype which any appearance (that is, any experience) of it permits us only to approach inadequately. As I have repeatedly observed in this essay, from this point of view, even technique (and progress in it), like criticism (and progress in it), is only an illusion since the beckoning absolute of the work itself continues to retreat and remains teasingly beyond its reach. Yet each time we approach the work, through another performance or another private experience, we open ourselves to it as the source of an always elusive ultimate satisfaction toward which it promises to lead us if we can but get beyond our imperfect experiences of it.

I have already observed that this is hardly a function our contemporary art would care about and that many of us who respond to this art do so while reserving to ourselves the right to seek in older masterworks the idolatrous satisfactions I have been describing. We sanction the new antielitist alternatives, the egalitarian translation of everything into art (or art into everything), presumably as a reflection of our culture's freedom; but we do so in large part because we have the assurance of another sort of art that persists, though that art is now torn away from the cultural values that produced it and is serving our culture which, with another revolutionary "art" of its own, probably needs such works more than ever to fall back on.

The value of each of these works to us and our culture rests upon the dream of its perfection which I have spoken of. Its completeness, sufficiency of self, and the special satisfactions these promise, all these derive from our sense of its internal teleology, that special, disinterested purposiveness of which Kant spoke. This leads, in Kant, to a "finality of form," which suggests the "final things" of eschatology. And I want to suggest that there is something eschatological in what the work's finality (as we project it out of our experience) promises us: an end to history's incompleteness by a final breakthrough which transcends historical contingency, replacing it with its own system of absolute relations. Of course, the work can do so because it *is* free of history. Its finality is possible only because—as our aesthetic habit constitutes it out of the signs before us—it is a fictional finality; and the claim that the work of art is freed as well as limited by its fictional character has been central to criticism since Matthew Arnold. Its eschatological promise allows the work to become the emblem of the conquest of alien elements by the imposition of form, the emblem, in other words, of the breakthrough to utopia, a microcosm of satisfied ends, difficulties overcome, and problems resolved, so that all that threatens as the random is now overwhelmed into an ultimate teleology. It thus becomes an emblem also of the idea of progress, the fiction of progress in the real world, which gains mythic authority, thanks to the internal completeness of the individual work of art, in which progress does occur and does lead to a utopia of ultimate satisfactions. We find progress in the joint relations among the elements within the work as we continually seek to put them together to satisfy its promise of utopia; or at least this is another fiction we entertain as we see ourselves moving from one imperfect experience of the work to the next, coming closer and closer to its own Platonic archetype. And yet again it gives us the progressive dream of a world that is an aesthetic improvement over our own in the completeness of its system of satisfied ends.

So the work of art comes out of history, seems to violate our present by managing to make itself into *its* present—an always-now—and thus leads us into itself as a continuously circular history. Yet it points to a future beyond our grasp—another experience of it in which its Platonic archetype can at last be realized—thus beckoning us toward indefinite progress, toward utopia, a totally humanized utopia which demands our total indulgence and receives our partial failings—though we like to think each time less partial—every time we experience it. The work's capacity to achieve its own fullness of power—irrespective of its "progressive" place in history or its "progressive" role in the history of its art or its genre—by itself can transform the idea of progress. The "free play" of total breakthrough achieved in the work (free with respect to history and to the empirical world) yet leads—as it caters to our perceptual habit of seeking completion—to the realization of the teleologies latent in the human power to impose form, the power to create an order we cannot find. Art contributes to the idea of progress, then, not as a result of its own historical sequence of artifacts but through the very process of fabrication within each object. This may seem to be mere aestheticism, though I think not. It is more profoundly anthropological than that in its giving to the arts a major role in maintaining—and perhaps transforming—our capacity to imagine an idea—a narrative—of progress. As the emblem of its own quest, art represents the dream which, as a model, it presents. Its very being thus keeps alive the human habit to narrate progress and imagine utopia. And it is this habit that keeps alive the humanity in the rest of us.

22

The Costs of Utopia

ROBERT C. ELLIOTT

In his book *Inventing the Future*, Dennis Gabor, the distinguished physicist, winner of the Nobel Prize, accuses literary intellectuals of a new *trahison des clercs*. Scientists continue to shape the world by their discoveries, says Gabor, and technology advances with giant strides toward a new golden age "with all the wonders that would be," quoting Tennyson; but the poets and writers of our time have lost faith in the future. They no longer, he says, provide a faith for living. But of course many scientists as well as poets have long been aware of the paradoxes associated with progress: the blessings of anaesthesia and antibiotics born of the same Faustian powers that produced the atomic bomb and the population explosion. Konrad Lorentz's comment about progress in the medical sciences is representative of many chilling ironies: "all those gifts that have sprung from man's deep insight into the nature of his surroundings . . . work in a horrible paradoxical way toward the destruction of mankind." Not that earlier periods were unaware that what we call progress might have negative connotations. Lucretius's tone has almost the cynical ring of the twentieth century as he describes man's primitive state before he had fire or any of the arts: "At that time it was famine that brought their fainting limbs to death; now, on the contrary, it is abundance that destroys us. In those days men often took poison in ignorance; now, better instructed, they give it to others."

The eighteenth century, that age of Enlightenment which saw the

This essay was originally published in *Studies on Voltaire and the Eighteenth Century*, vol. 152 (1976), ed. Theodore Besterman (Transactions of the Fourth International Congress on the Enlightenment, 11), and is reprinted here in an expanded form by permission of the Voltaire Foundation at the Taylor Institution, Oxford.

burgeoning of the idea of progress, had of course its own notable disbelievers: Swift, to whom the whole idea of progress was a squalid joke; Rousseau, whose position is equivocal but who in the *Second Discourse* links the development of language and the discovery of the arts—traditionally the origin of human progress—with the ruination of humanity; Hume, Gibbon, Voltaire, whose awareness of the strength of human folly armored their skepticism. But by the late years of the century the pessimists and the skeptics were in the minority. Most of those who concerned themselves about such matters were comfortable with the belief that man normally progresses from savagery through barbarism to civilization; that by the exercise of his reason man will continue to advance in desirable ways to desirable ends. Just over the horizon of the future they saw a society organized according to principles of justice and devoted to increasing the happiness of its members —the fortunate heirs of the dark ages. Utopia lay not far ahead.

As everyone knows, there were varying degrees of commitment to this notion. The most extreme devotees of progress like Turgot and Condorcet, believing in the infinite perfectibility of man and society, foresaw a dynamic utopia, one forever changing for the better. So heady was this vision that neither man, despite occasional private qualms, allowed consideration of a possible price to be paid for progress to qualify his speculations.

Other believers in progress, less doctrinaire, had a strong sense of the tragic dynamics of history. Kant, for example, associates what happiness is possible on earth with man's advance from barbarism; but that advance, in his view, is a direct function of the very characteristics of man that have made for his tragic fate: his aggressiveness, his avarice, his lust for power. Just as today Claude Lévi-Strauss maintains that the enslavement of some men by others was a necessary condition of progress, so Kant claims that social conflict, and all its attendant misery, is necessary to awaken men's powers for social good. Without conflict, says Kant, "all talents would remain hidden, unborn in an Arcadian shepherd's life, with all its concord, contentment, and mutual affection." An idyllic scene, one that men have dreamed of always, but not acceptable to Kant. In his view men in this situation would be little better than the sheep they herd. Kant recognizes the pathos in this cruel law of history: we must thank nature, he says, for our heartless vanity, our ambition, our greed. "Man wishes concord; but Nature knows better what is good for the race; she wills discord."[1] In another essay Kant speaks of human inequality, "that rich source of so many evils but also of everything good." Even war, that terrible scourge of man, is, he says, indispensable to the further development of human culture.[2] Thus though progress may be necessary and in the final analysis desirable, it entails a frightful cost.

1. Immanuel Kant, "Idea for a Universal History," in *On History*, ed. Lewis W. Beck (Indianapolis: Bobbs-Merrill, 1963), pp. 14-21.
2. Immanuel Kant, "Conjectural Beginning of Human History," in ibid., pp. 64-67.

Looking far into the future, Kant does foresee a time when, after humanity has suffered the cruelest hardships, a perfect culture will flourish in perpetual peace. Despite his generally positive perspective, Kant is not always sure that the long struggle is worth it. "Rousseau was not far wrong," he says, "in preferring the state of savages, so long, that is, as the last stage to which the human race must climb is not attained."[3] Except for the positive intimations, dimly foreseen, in the last clause of that sentence, the tone is nearly as sombre as that of Freud at the end of *Civilization and Its Discontents*, where he suggests that the whole agonizing effort to establish civilization has not been worth the pains. It is a tone similar to that we hear from Lévi-Strauss today.

Other writers of the Enlightenment saw the price of progress in quite different ways. Adam Ferguson, for example, that luminary of enlightened Edinburgh, carefully balanced the gains and losses entailed by man's advance from a savage to a civilized condition. No primitivist, Ferguson still found things to admire in the savage state as he and his contemporaries conceived it. The move toward civilization, Ferguson recognized, meant a loosening of the simple and strong bonds of community found in savage society, meant an increase in domestic disorders, meant the institutionalization of social inequality.[4] These sacrifices to progress Ferguson regretted, just as he regretted the loss of great poetry which civilization necessarily entailed. Ferguson was among those like Thomas Blackwell, Bishop Hurd, and the brothers Warton, about whom René Wellek has written so magisterially, and like Herbert Read in our own time, who believed that the greatest poetry could be written only in an age of imagination—a heroic age. Civilization and the heroic were incompatible. Great poetry was a necessary victim. We may regret the loss of pleasure from "the sublimer kinds of Writing," says Blackwell, in a famous phrase, but we pray that "*we may never be a proper Subject of an Heroic Poem.*" The nostalgia for the world of fine fabling was doubtless genuine enough, and many recognized how literature and the life of the imagination were being depreciated as civilization advanced toward regularity and order; but when it came to choosing between poetry and social progress, for Ferguson and Blackwell and the rest only one choice was possible.

I have an interest in utopian literature, and it occurred to me to inquire whether the negative correlation between poetry and progress continues in the depictions of utopia made by Enlightenment writers and their successors. Most of those who write about utopia, after all, are merely trying to envisage the state of affairs toward which progress is presumably conducting society. If by the eighteenth century poetry in its higher reaches is thought to be an acceptable sacrifice to

3. "Idea for a Universal History," in ibid., p. 21.
4. Adam Ferguson, *An Essay on the History of Civil Society* (1767), ed. Duncan Forbes (Edinburgh: Edinburgh University Press, 1966), pp. 181ff.

progress, which will be the attitude toward literature and the arts in the society to which progress is to give birth? As progress intensifies, so to speak, will the costs of progress intensify too? Will literature itself suffer the fate of heroic poetry? The questions seemed worth following up.

As one might expect, answers are by no means uniform or consistent with one another. But before looking at some of them, we should recognize that for good reason chroniclers of utopia rarely speak except in the most general and abstract terms about the literature of their imagined societies. Whereas vivid descriptions of scientific and technological advances, sometimes startlingly prophetic, have come readily to the utopian imagination, specific accounts of literature and art have not. Paul Valéry points out that Jules Verne's Captain Nemo, cruising the oceans in a submarine of the future, plays Bach and Handel on his organ, not the electronic music truly contemporary with his mode of travel. George Orwell said that not even the genius of Jonathan Swift was equal to producing a specimen by which we could judge the poetry of Swift's rational horses, the Houyhnhnms. Gulliver exclaims ecstatically over their poetry, which abounds in expressions of friendship and benevolence and is devoted in good measure to celebrating the prowess of victors in athletic contests— especially, of course, the victors in horse races. This is a poetry appropriate to a people of the heroic age; and, indeed, Houyhnhnm society has many characteristics of the heroic period as the eighteenth century conceived it. The utopia of Houyhnhnmland is a pastoral society of great simplicity and asceticism, founded on an economic base, as A. L. Morton says, roughly that of the Neolithic age. The Houyhnhnms have no clothing, do not know the use of metals; they have no word for law or government; they have no history. Their poetry, in the loftiness of its sentiments and the justness of its similes, reflects superbly the character of the society. That poetry would surely have been of the greatest interest to Blackwell and Hugh Blair. But, as Orwell says, Swift did not give us a sample of their verse.

Orwell perhaps did not know, however, that a Houyhnhnm poem actually exists—at least it is signed "Houyhnhnm"—and if it is not by Jonathan Swift, it is by his good friend Alexander Pope. Pope's poem is said to have been written by one of the horses in Gulliver's stable in England; it is entitled "To mr. Lemuel Gulliver the grateful address of the unhappy Houyhnhnms, now in slavery and bondage in England." The first stanza reads:

> To thee, we wretches of the Houhynhnm band,
> Condemn'd to labour in a barbarous land,
> Return our thanks. Accept our humble lays,
> And let each grateful Houyhnhnm neigh thy praise.

If this hardly comes up to Gulliver's enraptured account of Houyhnhnm verse, we must recognize that the horses in his stable are sadly degenerated from the noble breed of the island far away. Furthermore, this Houyhnhnm poet has been exposed to civilization (which, confusingly, he calls barbaric); the costs of progress have been exacted. No wonder his—or perhaps her—verse is banal.

Well, all this is playing games a bit: clearly Houyhnhnmland is a special case. Our interest is in how literature is said to fare under the utopian conditions projected by writers of the Enlightenment and those who succeed them. In many cases literature is said to fare very well indeed. For example, even as he hid from the Terror in France, the Marquis de Condorcet, writing of the infinite perfectibility of man, sees the arts of the future burgeoning in pace with the sciences to ever-mounting heights of perfection. Each of the coming generations will experience exquisite joy from the flow of ever more perfect works of art, but even here there will be a price to pay—at least to us it must seem a price. In Condorcet's utopia the great artistic monuments of the past will cease to have significance as they are submerged in the flood of progress. What is lost, says Condorcet, will be the "more reflective pleasure of comparing products of different ages and countries. . . . As works of art genuinely worthy of preservation increase in number, and become more perfect, each successive generation will devote its attention and admiration to those which really deserve preference, and the rest will unobtrusively fall into oblivion."[5] This casual observation makes me think of a passage in Aldous Huxley's *Brave New World* in which the controller, Mustapha Mond, dismisses the importance of history: "He waved his hand; and it was as though, with an invisible feather whisk, he had brushed away a little dust, and the dust . . . was Ur of the Chaldees; some spider webs, and they were Thebes and Babylon and Cnossos and Mycenae. . . . Whisk, Whisk, King Lear and the Thoughts of Pascal." The whisk of Condorcet, as he consigns the art of the past to oblivion, is equally relentless and equally thorough. Men of the future, Condorcert writes, will experience the same pleasures to be derived from the simpler, more striking, more accessible aspects of beauty that their predecessors enjoyed; but these pleasures will be found only in the latest works.

A somewhat more complex situation is heralded in Louis Sebastian Mercier's utopian fiction called *Memoirs of the Year 2500* (published in France in 1771; translated into English in 1772). The narrator, an eighteenth-century Frenchman, visits a utopia of the far future in a dream—a remarkably bad dream, I would call it. While exploring the state of the arts in the twenty-sixth century, he visits the mammoth king's library in Paris only to find it practically denuded of books. Puzzled, he makes inquiries and is told that millions of books judged frivolous, useless, or dangerous have, by unanimous consent of the

5. Antoine-Nicolas de Condorcet, *Sketch for a Historical Picture of the Progress of the Human Mind*, trans. June Barraclough (New York: Noonday Press, 1955), pp. 195-96.

people, been burned. "We have done from an enlightened zeal," says his utopian informant, "what the barbarians once did from a zeal that was blind." Ours was an "expiatory sacrifice to veracity, to good sense, and true taste." Some relics of the past have been preserved. The substance of thousands of volumes has been extracted and condensed into a "small duodecimo," and the literature considered worth saving has been carefully abridged and then reprinted. Homer, Plato, and Sophocles have been saved entire, but Herodotus, Sappho, Anacreon, and "the vile Aristophanes" have been burned and only their names survive. Cicero, Ovid, and Horace have been heavily purged. Among authors more contemporary with the narrator, Molière's works survive, but he is no longer understood—social improvements have made nearly incomprehensible the manners of the seventeenth century— Corneille is revered, a large part of Voltaire has been expunged, Rousseau exists complete.[6] The narrator is discreetly silent about authors between Rousseau and the twenty-sixth century; all we know is that they are immensely superior to their predecessors: more useful and interesting, says the informant, more closely related to progress in philosophy, politics, and morality. Why should we read Plato or Sophocles? he asks, when progress has left them so far behind. The situation is the same with paintings which so far surpass those of the past that the only persons interested in Raphael and Rubens are a few obstinate and opinionated antiquaries.

Thus for Mercier (as for Condorcet) the price to be paid for progress is history, which in any case is something of an embarrassment in utopia. The only records of political history preserved in the year 2500 are those that do honor to humanity. All the rest—the whole appalling story of man's follies and his crimes—has deservedly been expunged. Mercier's attitude is neatly encapsulated in his account of his narrator's visit to the theater, where he witnesses a tragedy on a subject familiar to him: the affair of the unfortunate Calas, whom Voltaire made famous. The play was superlative, says the narrator, the language exquisitely that of nature. At the end of the performance the narrator is introduced to the audience as a contemporary of Calas. "I hid my face," he says, "while I blushed for the age in which I was born."[7]

If the past is relentlessly devalued in Mercier's utopia, literature is not: poetry, opera, the theater ride the same tide of progress as do the sciences, and are swept to the same unimaginable—and certainly indescribable—heights. Only Fourier three-quarters of a century later surpasses Mercier in his manic enthusiasm for the future of literature. Fourier looks forward to the time when the three billion inhabitants of earth are organized into phalansteries. In that glorious era, Fourier

6. Louis S. Mercier, *Memoirs of the Year 2500,* trans. W. Hooper (Dublin: W. Wilson, 1772), II, 1-27.

7. Ibid., I, 198.

calculates, there will be thirty-seven million mathematicians living equal to Newton, thirty-seven million poets living equal to Homer, thirty-seven million writers of comedy as good as Molière. These are, Fourier admits, estimates only.

Other explorers of utopian existence foresee an entirely different status for literature and the arts—a distinctly inferior status. Some writers hold that the arts could not flourish in a society devoid of conflict; even if literature continues to be written it will be a tepid affair compared with the glories of the violent past. The Abbé Turgot believed that although the knowledge of nature and of truth is infinitely cumulative, the arts, which exist primarily to give us pleasure, have fixed limits that were reached ages ago by the Greeks and Romans. (Condorcet, Turgot's follower, specifically rejected this notion in the tenth epoch of the *Esquisse*.) If science, technology, morality, and other areas of human activity are linearly progressive, while the fine arts are not, clearly the arts will play a diminishing role in the new world to be born. Turgot, like a number of his contemporaries, accepts the future impoverishment of the life of the imagination with marked complacency.

Another theorist who depreciates the role of literature in the good society is Morelly. As he sets down the laws for his utopia in *Nature's Code* (1755), Morelly allows the fine arts a place, but a carefully circumscribed place only. Poetry, painting, and oratory are confined to celebrating the beauties of nature and science and the achievements of culture heroes. Other products of the imagination like tales, fables, or absurd fictions, or speculative arts or sciences not immediately useful to society—these are frowned upon, sacrifices to a mode of life in which, as Morelly says, all things have been brought to perfection.[8]

The arts fare even worse in Megapatagonia, a country described by Restif de la Bretonne in a utopian fiction known in English as *The French Daedalus* (1781). Here in this primitivistic society, whose language is French written backwards, the arts are generally despised. When asked if they have theaters and plays in their country, a Megapatagonian informant replies that such entertainments are for children or a nation of children only. We want true pleasures, not artificial ones, he says. "We want only the real." The Megapatagonians have outlawed myth and allegory—modes of saying that which is not—as obstacles to truth; and they look on most poetry, other than the celebratory mode, as absurd and dangerous. Painting is equally despised as child's play and useless: "Our portraits," they say, "are our handsome men and our beautiful women whom we see every day."[9] The key statement in this utopian denigration of the arts is "We want

8. Morelly, *Code de la nature*, ed. Gilbert Chinard (Paris: R. Clavreuil, 1950), pp. 22, 318, 321.

9. Nicolas-Edmé Restif de la Bretonne, *La Découverte australe par un homme-volant; ou le dédale français* (Leipzig, 1781), III, 503, 505, 514.

only the real." Restif touches here on a persistent theme in utopian literature. The Megapatagonians echo Socrates's question in the *Republic*: "If a man were able actually to do the things he represents as well as to produce images of them, do you believe he would seriously give himself up to making these images and take that as a completely satisfying object in life?" In utopia, where life is good, the mimetic arts are often said to be superseded by life itself—they become superfluous. Literature, painting, and the rest become sacrifices to that happiness which it is the function of progress to bestow on man.

Successors to Enlightenment writers pick up this problematic theme in interesting ways. A good example is William Morris's *News from Nowhere*, one of the most attractive of all utopian fictions. In the green and pleasant England of the future that Morris envisages, only Ellen's grandfather regrets the progressive enfeeblement of literature that he has noticed in the years since the new order was established. Why is it, the old grouch complains, writers no longer produce novels like *Vanity Fair*? Ellen, a clear-eyed, forthright representative of a good many utopian women, puts the old-fashioned novel-reader in his place. Books once had a positive function, Ellen says, when they helped palliate the miseries of people's lives; but they have no place today. "When will you understand that after all it is the world we live in which interests us; the world of which we are a part, and which we can never love too much? Look!" she says, laying her hands on the shoulders of the two lovers, "look! these are our books in these days!"[10] Ellen echoes the Megapatagonians' sentiments: "We want only the real."

It is disheartening to realize that there is no more place for great literature in the good society imagined by Morris than there is in the bad society of Huxley's *Brave New World*, where art is replaced by obstacle golf and the feelies. Everyone knows of Huxley's own personal devotion to literature and painting and music. I find it peculiarly poignant that at the end of his life, when he tried to negate the negation of *Brave New World* by writing the positive utopia *Island*, Huxley found it necessary to devalue the arts and to denigrate literature savagely. Literature, concludes his spokesman in *Island*, is incompatible with human integrity, with philosophical truth, with a decent social system—incompatible with everything, he says, "except dualism, criminal lunacy, impossible aspiration, and unnecessary guilt." Huxley was convinced like so many others that the negative correlation between literature and the good life was absolute. One had to choose between them; and for him, as for his eighteenth-century predecessors, only one choice was possible.

Among the twentieth-century heirs of the Enlightenment who have pondered most carefully the fate of the arts in a putative good society

10. William Morris, *News from Nowhere* (Boston: Roberts Brothers, 1890), Chap. 22.

of the future are the Marxists. It is well known that Marxist eschatology contains no clear picture of man's estate on the other side of
history. However, when progress has brought man from the kingdom
of necessity to the kingdom of freedom, when there is no basis for
class conflict and the state has withered away, when man's labor is no
longer alienated and he has immensely increased leisure, then art—if
art there be—will doubtless take forms far different from those we
know today. Marxists differ inevitably on how they foresee these
developments. One of the central points of difference is on the question of whether art and literature will develop in the new society in
forms recognizable to us, or whether the need for art, as such, will
disappear, supplanted by the satisfactions of the good life.

Trotsky is characteristically vigorous on these issues:

> In a society which will have thrown off the pinching and stultifying
> worry about one's daily bread, in which community restaurants will
> prepare good, wholesome and tasteful food, for all to choose, in
> which communal laundries will wash clean everyone's good linen,
> in which children, all the children, will be well fed and strong and
> gay, and in which they will absorb the fundamental elements of
> science and art as they absorb albumen and air and the warmth of
> the sun, in a society in which electricity and the radio ... will come
> from inexhaustible sources of super-power at the call of a central
> button, in which there will be no "useless mouths," in which the
> liberated egotism of man—a mighty force!—will be directed wholly
> toward the understanding, the transformation and the betterment
> of the universe—in such a society the dynamic development of
> culture will be incomparable with anything that went on in the
> past.[11]

Even in this society of the future, founded on friendship and sympathy and love for one's neighbor, there will still be competition, says
Trotsky, but competition sublimated to a higher and more fertile
form. Energies which once went into political struggles will be chan-
nelized into technique, into construction, which also includes art. Parties will form over social issues: the location of a new canal, the
distribution of oases in the Sahara, the regulation of climate, a new
theater, two competing tendencies in music. In the tense debates over
aesthetic schools and tastes the human personality will grow and
become polished. The explosions of collective nervous energy and the
collective psychic impulses which make for the creation of new artistic
tendencies will continue.

Certain literary modes will, of course, be ruled out: mysticism, for
example, and the kind of romanticism that is really mysticism in
disguise. "Our age cannot have a shy and portable mysticism," Trotsky

11. Leon Trotsky, *Literature and Revolution* (Ann Arbor: University of Michigan
Press, 1960), pp. 188-89.

writes, "something like a pet dog that is carried along 'with the rest.' Our age wields an axe." Similarly, "we shall no longer accept a tragedy in which God gives orders and man submits." Moreover, he adds, "there will be no one to write such a tragedy." In general, however, Trotsky thinks that the new art will revive all the old forms: comedy, because "the man of the future will want to laugh," the lyric, because "the new man will love in a better and stronger way" than did his predecessors. "All that is necessary," says Trotsky, "is for the poet of the new epoch to re-think in a new way the thoughts of mankind, to re-feel its feelings." As in the new society man relocates mountains and rivers, rebuilding the world to his own taste, Trotsky has not the slightest fear that the taste will be bad, so thoroughly will the wall between nature and art have been demolished. Man will reform nature in art's image. In a final peroration, rivaling the utopian vision of Fourier, Trotsky foresees the forms of life that progress is to bring: "The average human type will rise to the heights of an Aristotle, a Goethe, or a Marx. And above this ridge new peaks will rise."[12]

Some of the speculations of Herbert Marcuse are almost equally exuberant, although they take a different form. Marcuse, one of the most utopian of contemporary Marxist theoreticians, envisages a society in which the abolition of poverty and toil makes possible the domination of the sensuous, the playful, the calm, the beautiful, to the point where these qualities *become* the forms of existence and thereby the form of society itself. Once consciousness is liberated and science and technology are brought into the service of life rather than of repression, then, says Marcuse, "Technique would tend to become art and art would tend to form reality: the opposition between imagination and reason, higher and lower faculties, poetic and scientific thought would be invalidated." We would see, in short, the emergence of a new reality principle. Marcuse speaks several times of the aesthetic as the "possible form of a free society." Art, he says, would become a "productive force in the material as well as the cultural transformation." This would mean the end of the segregation of the aesthetic from the real. Thus Marcuse foresees as a distinct historical possibility the breaking up or dissolution of art as we know it—the "end" of art through its realization.[13]

As later publications show, however, Marcuse is not entirely comfortable with this position, and he dislikes particularly some of the misapprehensions easily associated with it. The end of art is notoriously a truism for the radicals of the New Left: the Living Theater, for example, tries programmatically to dissolve the gap between art and life. According to Julian Beck, one of the founders of the Living Theater, a major purpose behind the play *Paradise Now* was to "make a

12. Ibid., pp. 231ff.

13. Herbert Marcuse, "The New Sensibility," in *An Essay on Liberation* (Boston: Beacon Press, 1969), pp. 24-45.

play which would no longer be an enactment but would be the act itself."

Beck is stating in another form that central doctrine of the Mega-patagonians: "We want only the real." Clearly Marcuse's ideas tend here too, although his emphases are very different. In a lecture at the Guggenheim Museum, Marcuse carefully dissociated himself from Beck's position and from "anti-art" movements in general, the "fre-netic efforts," as he put it, "to produce the absence of form, to substi-tute the real for the aesthetic object. . . . The gap which separates art from reality," says Marcuse, "the essential otherness of art, its 'illusory' character, can be reduced only to the degree to which *reality itself* tends toward art as reality's own form." This can only be in a qualita-tively different society, one in which might be experienced what Marx called "the sensuous appropriation of the world." Traditional arts would not be invalidated in this society, Marcuse believes, shifting his ground somewhat, nor the capacity to understand and enjoy them. "Perhaps," he comments, "for the first time men would *see* with the eyes of Corot, of Cézanne, of Monet because the perception of these artists has helped to form this reality."[14] Whether there would be new Monets, however, or new novels or tragedies, Marcuse does not say.

One further example: in the 1930s Joseph Wood Krutch recorded a conversation he had had with Eisenstein, the great Soviet film director. Eisenstein calmly informed Krutch that his aim was to de-stroy the motion picture. Pressed for an explanation, Eisenstein re-plied somewhat as follows:

> There are two kinds of art, bourgeois art and proletarian art. The first is an attempt to compensate for unsatisfied desire. The second is a preparation for social change. In the Perfect State there will be no bourgeois art because there will be no unsatisfied desires. There will also be no proletarian art because there will be no necessity for further social change. Therefore, since I am working for the perfect state, I am also attempting to destroy the motion picture.[15]

I do not know with what seriousness we should take this account. Perhaps Eisenstein was trying to shock Krutch, and if he was, he succeeded. In any event, his statement, I take it, is another version of the "We want only the real" theme.

The golden age of the future about which Eisenstein and Marcuse—and their Enlightenment forebears—speculate has its counterpart, of course, in the other golden age—the one before history began. Among the defining characteristics of that mythical time as Hesiod and Ovid describe it are these: its people were happy and they had no art. The

14. Herbert Marcuse, "Art as a Form of Reality," in *On the Future of Art*, intro. E. F. Fry (New York: Viking Press, 1970), pp. 122-34.

15. Quoted in Joseph Wood Krutch, *Was Europe a Success?* (New York: Farrar and Rinehart, 1934), p. 62.

myth tells us that the arts and the sciences were the gift of Prometheus, that magnificently ambiguous culture hero; and with the gift came the curse of the gods which brought conflict, exploitation, misery —the whole complex of evils that Kant asserts is necessary for progress. Rousseau in both the *First* and *Second Discourses* subscribes to a form of this myth; and so does his twentieth-century successor, Lévi-Strauss, who considers the acquisition of writing by primitive man a precondition of progress, but also a kind of secular fall. Even the earliest writing, says Lévi-Strauss, is invariably associated with power over things and over people—with the exploitation of human beings by each other. Thus, in our conjectural histories of the prehistoric past conflict and misery are often taken as necessary energizing forces of the arts—and particularly of literature, necessary preconditions of its very existence.

No wonder that in projecting the golden age of the future some theorists come full circle, reinstating the artless conditions of the mythical past. Instead of regression, however, their new state represents transcendence. The new dispensation, it is claimed, would produce men quite unlike Kant's happy sheep; they would be men like gods, but it is well known that gods do not require books or paintings or motion pictures to fulfill their lofty destinies. It comes down to Socrates's question in the *Republic*, which put into Freud's terms amounts to this: if real gratifications were available, would we be content with the substitute gratifications of art? From the Enlightenment to today the answer of a number of utopian writers has been to say No; we would not be satisfied. We want only the real. The new reality principle supposes that society itself will *be* a work of art, and artists will find their occupations gone: "These are our portraits," say Restif's Megapatagonians, pointing to their handsome men and women—the end of art, as Marcuse puts it, through its realization. Those who respond in this way have a dazzling, almost hallucinatory sense of what progress will have wrought in the golden age they contemplate. To all but the true believer, however, the costs exacted by that progress must seem high indeed.

23

The Idea of Progress in Twentieth-Century Theology

MARTIN E. MARTY

Although the idea of progress has biblical roots, according to the vision of most modern and secular prophets of progress, biblical faith was expected to fade away with the rest of religion. Commitment to the idea of progress entailed commitment to the idea that, as humans increasingly came to master nature and rational processes, the priests, who were custodians of unmastered mystery, would have increasingly less work to do. Theologians, who were interpreters of the language of believing communities, must certainly become obsolete.[1]

After two centuries of these prophecies, religion seems to be as large a factor in the human story as ever. People in most societies persist in regarding themselves as being impinged upon by unseen powers to which they owe response. Sociologists like S.S. Acquaviva and Bryan Wilson speak of the decline of the sacred and of massive secularization,[2] but even they have to account for abundant vestiges of religion, and many of their colleagues encounter an ever more bewildering diffusion of religious impulses in most cultures. In international affairs religion has played its part in the revolution in Iran, in conflicts in the Middle East and Ireland, in resistance to communism in Poland, and in a flowering of revivals in North America and Africa.

---

1. For this definition of religion, see James M. Gustafson, *The Contributions of Theology of Medical Ethics* (Milwaukee, Wisc.: Marquette University Press, 1975), pp. 97, 5; Gustafson also cites Julian Hartt as a contributor to this definition.
2. S.S. Acquaviva, *The Decline of the Sacred in Industrial Society*, trans. Patricia Lipscomb (New York: Harper & Row, 1979); and Bryan Wilson, *Religion in Secular Society* (London: Penguin Books, 1969).

Theologians have done more than merely survive along with vital religion. From time to time they have prospered, and they have done so in part because of the stands they have taken in relation to secular notions of progress. Thus, in some periods they won favor for resisting the encroachments of science and technology in the name of progress when people thought these were working against human freedom. At other times they co-opted the motif of progress and themselves claimed credit for having helped advance the human impulse to master the world in its name. Modernity did pose a problem for theologians, however, because it made for that sort of division of labor that led to the sequestering of their profession. Although their natural habitat was the university, the language on which they drew was that of the sanctuary, a domain with which the academy dealt only marginally and sporadically. Despite all they had at stake in the language of progress and regress, members of the theological community were often left out of interdisciplinary discourse about progress.

From time to time their apologists have felt the need to protest. Speaking to the academy for the Jewish community in a period when both were especially ambivalent about the theological enterprise, Arthur Cohen all but pleaded:

Theology need not be a pretentious discipline; it need not usurp the sciences, dismiss natural philosophy, nor overturn logic. It is a modest discipline founded, to be sure, upon an immodest history. Once theologians ruled the sciences and held court in universities, whereas presently they are hidden away in drafty seminaries and muster disciples from the thin readership of lugubrious journals. The unhappy condition of theology has undoubtedly made theologians snappish and defensive, but we can ill afford to forget that whereas theologians are human their object of concern remains God.[3]

Once the word "God" is introduced, both believers and unbelievers have reason to take notice. For it was God, the *theos* of theology, who was at the heart of the earlier controversies over progress. Believers divided over the question whether their God was disdainful of human achievement or the initiator of all human improvement. Unbelievers divided over whether the belief in God was the retardant to progress when progress was desired or the main impeller of progress when it was under suspicion. So long as such debates have raged, the theologians had much at stake.

What made the problem of isolating the relation of belief and theology to progress so perplexing was the irregularity of correlations between progress, as conventionally conceived, and religious faith. Acquaviva could point to the desacralization of industrialized Scandi-

3. Arthur A. Cohen, *The Natural and the Supernatural Jew* (New York: Pantheon, 1962), p. 301.

navia, where literacy, technology, and politics were highly developed; and George Gallup found high levels of sacrality in India, where they were not.[4] What could they make of Japan and Southern California, which are proverbial for their mixtures of ancient and new religions in the very heart of industrialized economies, hedonistic cultures, and, by definition, desacralized societies?

Some critics, therefore, dismissed religion as being epiphenomenal. Religion attached itself to movements of progress or regress, which can get along just as well without its symbols. If religion was thus merely epiphenomenal, then theologians could be seen as opportunists who reached for the pro- or antiprogress resources in their traditions, depending upon which version their secular peers currently favored. In Alfred Schutz's term, they would rely on a system of "imposed" as opposed to "intrinsic" relevance:

> Imposed upon us as relevant are situations and events which are not connected with interests chosen by us, . . . which we have to take just as they are. . . . The intrinsic relevances are the outcome of our chosen interests, . . . to bring forth a projected state of affairs.[5]

Schutz points out that these realms of relevances are intermingled; such blending is most likely the case in the instance of Western theology and modern views of progress. Hannah Arendt once noted it was often claimed that all modern revolutions are essentially Christian in origin. Yet, she added, secularization had to occur before any Christian revolutionary seed could ever sprout "so that the best one can say in favor of this theory is that it needed modernity to liberate the revolutionary germs of the Christian faith. . . ."[6]

So with the germs of progress, biblical faith witnesses to a God who is active in history, who controls its beginning and end, and who determines the good that happens in it. Good was to come from the divine command to humans on page two of Genesis to "fill the earth and subdue it; and have dominion. . . ." They were to be faithful stewards of what God would work. But it would never have occurred to anyone to identify this with progress—until secular notions of progress "liberated" biblical theologians.

ITS DUBIOUS CLAIM

In the period of the Enlightenment and the nineteenth century, thinkers of Jewish, Catholic, and Protestant traditions alike were liberated with a vengeance. The laity may have made their own adjustments,

4. Acquaviva, *Decline of the Sacred*, pp. 77-78; George Gallup, *Religion in America 1976*, Gallup Opinion Index Report no. 130 (Princeton, N.J.: American Institute of Public Opinion 1976), esp. pp. 6-21, which offer comparative international data.

5. Alfred Schutz, *On Phenomenology and Social Relations*, ed. Helmut R. Wagner (Chicago: University of Chicago Press, 1970), p. 114.

6. Hannah Arendt, *On Revolution* (New York: Viking Press, 1963), pp. 18-19.

and defenders of orthodoxy resisted modernity. It was essential to liberal theology of the sort that dominated in the universities of Western Europe and Anglo-America to give impetus to progress as though this school of theology had invented the idea. One detects almost nothing of a grudging character in the liberal religious embrace of progress or the invention of metaphysical schemes to legitimate it. These theologians were so confident that they were bringing to fruition what had lain latent as a seed in their tradition that they saw their outlook to be grounded in a system of intrinsic relevance. Their conservative critics for a century and a half have scorned them for capitulating to modernity in order to look respectable and current—not because faith in progress squared with historic religion as the liberals claimed it did.[7]

The liberal era was sufficiently long, and its effort for a period was so successful that the idea of progress came to be bonded with faith and theology in modernist schools of thought. No matter what setbacks the belief in progress has suffered in the twentieth century, many Christian thinkers have been ready to reassert fresh versions of it whenever cultural circumstances made it possible for them to gain a hearing. Belief in progress and, better, theological interpretations of progress turn out to be episodic. They go into eclipse or fall out of fashion but then remain in the stream as a latent virus, ready to reactivate themselves.

To say a theological word in favor of progress or even to express the view that such words will again be spoken would have been unremarkable in 1913 or 1965, but they seem fantastic in 1919 or 1980. Writers on the theme now take for granted the stigma associated with any concept of a metaphysics of progress. They are even more disdainful about any empirically verifiable evidence for progress. One of the more persistent and audacious reflectors on the theme, Langdon Gilkey, posed it this way:

> One of the most important questions for contemporary theology . . . has been, *granted that the theory of progress is barely credible to us*, how [are] eschatology and future history to be related so that creative political and social praxis may have sound theological bases[?][8]

Gilkey has shown how modern theology was genetically programmed to include progressive thinking. This school of thought reflected the guiding ideas of the nineteenth century, which to Gilkey meant that it was scientific, immanentist, optimistic, and progressivist. Old notions of human depravity and impotence "seemed barbaric in the extreme, a

---

7. See James Hitchcock, *Catholicism and Modernity: Confrontation or Capitulation?* (New York: Seabury Press, 1976).

8. Langdon B. Gilkey, *Reaping the Whirlwind: A Christian Interpretation of History* (New York: Seabury Press, 1976), p. 203; emphasis mine.

function of the priestly gloom of earlier times." Gilkey boldly summarized a century:

> The divine force, said liberal theology, whose immanent work in the process has brought about such progress toward higher, more coherent, more adaptive, and more moral goals, is what men have called God....[9]

He could call to witness an array of thinkers as varied as those Warren Wagar linked in support of "the theology of progress": Friedrich Schleiermacher, Albrecht Ritschl, the philosopher Hermann Cohen, Adolf von Harnack, Alfred Loisy, Maurice Blondel, George Tyrell, and, in a more modest mode, John Cardinal Newman, the Catholic prophet of the idea of "development."[10] In words Harnack wrote in 1898, the Christian Gospel intended to form the widest human community, based on love, as

> a high and glorious ideal, and we have received it from the very foundation of our religion. It ought to float before our eyes as the goal and guiding star of our historical development. Whether mankind will ever attain to it, who can say? But we can and ought to approximate to it, and in these days—otherwise than two or three hundred years ago—we feel a moral obligation in this direction. Those of us who possess more delicate and therefore more prophetic perceptions no longer regard the kingdom of love and peace as a mere Utopia.[11]

ITS PESSIMISTIC PHASE

A symbolic date for the total eclipse of liberal optimism was 1919, when Swiss theologian Karl Barth looked up from the trenches of World War I and back to the writings of St. Paul. Barth's *Epistle to the Romans* set the tone for almost a half-century of Protestant theology, a tone echoed in interwar Catholic thought and deepened and amplified in Jewish reflection. After reaching back to nineteenth-century doom-sayers like Franz Overbeck and Søren Kierkegaard, Barth found nothing in the Bible but the language of distance between the divine and the human. There was to him "nothing in the whole range of human possibilities ... which is capable of realizing the moral objective, the goal of history. Our range of possibilities is certainly capable of being increased and broadened, but its relation to the ... final goal must ... continue to be as 1:00."[12] Barth was later to temper this

9. Langdon B. Gilkey, *Naming the Whirlwind: The Renewal of God-Language* (Indianapolis, Ind.: Bobbs-Merrill, 1969), p. 75.

10. W. Warren Wagar, *Good Tidings: The Belief in Progress from Darwin to Marcuse* (Bloomington: Indiana University Press, 1972). Wagar's is a good summary of interwar thought, and I draw on it at several places.

11. Cited by ibid., p. 85.

12. Karl Barth, *The Word of God and the Word of Man*, trans. Douglas Horton (London: Hadden & Stoughton, 1928), p. 166.

gloom slightly, but no true idea of progress ever reappeared. Between 1932 and 1967 this dominating thinker published his thirteen volumes of *Church Dogmatics*. In 112 columns of a fine-print "Subjects" index, the category appears as meagerly as this: "Progress?, III, 4:670; IV, 1:607; ecclesiastical IV, 1:705."[13]

To Gilkey, this Barthian-era theology of crisis looked like part of a system of imposed relevance, thanks to World War I's "prolonged and senseless bath of blood" and the economic depression, which were followed by fascist and communist totalitarianisms and World War II: "History seemed to manifest demonic regress not progress in the social, political, and moral realms." But the neoorthodox theology also grew out of an intrinsic biblical theme:

> If God works in history at all, he cannot, therefore, work providentially through the developing social structures that have become self-destructive and so have produced *this* chaos. The dominant cause of the dialectical or Krisis theology was, therefore, the breakdown in the theory of progress, the loss of confidence in the development of civilization and the conviction that if there be meaning at all in historical life, it must be transcendent to history's developments in a God beyond immanence, and inward in existential appropriation where alone meaning could be found.[14]

In the period between the world wars, other major theologians offered alternative philosophies of history without again coming into congruence with secular theories of progress. In Eastern Orthodoxy the Russian Nicolai Berdyaev kept alive some faith in the freedom that engenders hope of progress. But his was a muted faith; it also issued in a view of progress that looked chiefly beyond temporal life to the eternal.[15] Rudolf Bultmann, the period's preeminent biblical theologian, considered old belief in progress to be a "kind of secularizing of the Christian teleology of history." He concluded: "This belief in progress is not in accord with the Christian faith; indeed, it is opposed to it. It originated in the polemics against the Christian belief in providence." Bultmann propagated a Heideggerian existentialism that stressed "the eternal now" and a call to authenticity through present decision for faith.[16]

In the United States, the brothers, Richard and Reinhold Niebuhr, the most important mid-century native-born Protestant theologians, did not allow their criticism of the idea of progress to paralyze them politically. They developed an ethics of responsibility that did not depend upon meliorism to sustain itself. But Reinhold Niebuhr, be-

---

13. Karl Barth, *Church Dogmatics: Index Volume with Aids for the Preacher*, ed. G.W. Bromiley and T.F. Torrance (Edinburgh: T. and T. Clark, 1977), p. 249.

14. Gilkey, *Reaping the Whirlwind*, pp. 223-24.

15. See Wagar, *Good Tidings*, p. 214.

16. Rudolf Bultmann, *The Presence of Eternity: History and Eschatology* (New York: Harper & Brothers, 1957), p. 70.

cause of his influence in the political order and his journalistic visibility, remained especially nettling to those secular thinkers who wanted to revive faith in progress. Sidney Pollard singled him out:

> More powerful [than the Austrian conservative economic school] has been the Christian opposition to the idea of progress. Shattered by the achievements of science and rationalism, the Church has had little new to contribute to European thought until now, suddenly, the belief in original sin, and the need of an ethical anchor outside the historical framework of this world, appear to have become necessary. . . .
>
> Niebuhr, a product of the modern dilemma, is . . . destructive. Since original sin, the evil in man's nature, is permanent, the belief in progress is not only misguided, but also harmful. It is responsible for the follies, self-deceptions, and arrogant hopes on which the modern era has misspent its energies. . . . The belief that when man progresses in knowledge he also progresses in virtue explains why science has been erected into a false Messiah.[17]

Paul Tillich, the refugee from Nazi Germany, also helped import to America some of the continental distrust in progress. A religious socialist in Germany and not politically passive in America, Tillich reached to his Lutheran roots in order to decry any faith in "a metaphysics of progress." Nothing ontological, in the structure of being, brought the promise of progress—though its absence did not mean for Tillich that humans were free to be irresponsible. They would not be likely to break off the quest for meaning in life. But times changed "for the better," and shortly before he died in 1965, Tillich had trouble recalling how and why he could ever have joined in the radical celebration of the "breakdown of progressivism" after 1914. In his *Systematic Theology* he agreed that there could be progress in technology ("better and better") and methodology.[18] He also found some progress in education and the overcoming of spatial divisions and separations within and beyond mankind. Still, in creativity and morals Tillich found no progress.

Jews had even more dramatic reasons than these Orthodox and Protestant thinkers to undergo a crisis of faith in progress. Some Jewish thinkers feel that their loss of faith may be permanent because of the Holocaust. In the nineteenth century, Jewish religious thought in Western Europe had undergone an emancipation and an enlightenment. In various modern or Reform versions, Jews embraced progress as enthusiastically as did Protestant liberals and Catholic modernists.

---

17. Sidney Pollard, *The Idea of Progress: History and Society* (Baltimore, Md.: Penguin Books, 1971), pp. 197-98.

18. Cited by Wagar, *Good Tidings*, p. 216; see Paul Tillich, *Systematic Theology* (Chicago: University of Chicago Press, 1963), III, 338-39.

Thus, the French Orientalist James Darmesteter in 1892 fused humanist and biblical thought:

> Two great dogmas ... ever since the prophets, constitute the whole of Judaism: the divine unity and Messianism, unity of law throughout the world and the terrestrial triumph of justice in humanity. These are the two dogmas which at the present time illuminate humanity in its progress both in the scientific and the social order of things, and which are termed in modern parlance, unity of forces and belief in progress.
>
> For this reason, Judaism is the only religion that has never entered into conflict, and never can, with either science or social progress, and that has witnessed, and still witnesses, all their conquests without a sense of fear. These are not hostile forces that it accepts or submits to merely from a spirit of toleration or policy in order to save the remains of its power by a compromise. They are old friendly voices which it recognizes and salutes with joy, for it has heard them resound for centuries already, in the axioms of free thought and in the cry of the suffering heart.[19]

Few Jewish theologians could find such a faith at all credible after Hitler. Typical of North Americans who have completely revised their views of historical progress after the attempts to extinguish European Jewry is the theist philosopher Emil Fackenheim, a Canadian who survived Auschwitz. His thought has grown ever more radical, as has that of many Jewish theologians since the Israeli wars of 1967 and 1973, after which Jewish survival became a vivid issue. But as early as 1955 Fackenheim was reflecting autobiographically on "Judaism and the idea of progress." In pre-Hitler Germany, in the climate of enlightenment and romanticism, he had developed the firmest belief that history had a purpose, that it "had followed a path of necessary progress in the past, and the guarantee for its infinite perpetuation was implicit in history itself." Only in one respect did the liberal Jew ever have to do any tailoring: "History no longer required irrational incursions of a supernatural God; its purposes were realized by men inspired by the Ideal."[20] In that context the Jew had to discover his place. Judaism must contribute to progress.

Fackenheim and his generation later rebelled against this firm belief on three grounds. The first was religious; being "neoorthodox" themselves in many ways, they had a religious objection. "If history is necessary progress, brought about by men, then there is, so to speak, nothing left for God to do." Second was the concept of a Jewish mission. Jews were losing their necessary sense of superiority needed

19. Quoted in Nahum N. Glatzer, ed., *The Dynamics of Emancipation: The Jew in the Modern Age* (Boston: Beacon Press, 1965), p. 32.

20. Emil L. Fackenheim, *Quest for Past and Future: Essays in Jewish Theology* (Boston: Beacon, 1968), p. 84.

to pursue a mission as teachers of mankind, and this was morally and intellectually intolerable. But most important was the brutal fact of Nazism:

> A view still popular in America holds that history progresses necessarily but intermittently; relapses may occur, but these become ever less serious. But to me Nazism was, and still is, not a relapse less serious than previous relapses, but a total blackout.... History is regarded as necessary progress only by those who are relatively remote from the evils of history.... The real conclusion I derived ... is that if even a single brave and honest deed is in vain, if a single soul's unjust suffering goes unredeemed, that then history as a whole is meaningless. With this conclusion, the progress view of history, so far as I was concerned, had suffered total shipwreck.

Yet God did not die and history was not meaningless for Fackenheim and others in the mainstream of Jewish theology. Nor would the Jewish thinker use his loss of faith in progress as an occasion for moral inactivity: He must work harder than ever before for the survival of Judaism and for justice—all in the name of God.[21]

A POSITIVE STEP

Roman Catholics generally shared the mistrust in progress from World War I until the 1950s, though we shall note two or three important exceptions. Then in the 1960s they could point to a kind of official stamp on a faith in progress thanks to *Gaudium et Spes*, a forward-looking document of Vatican II. Its linkage of human progressivism with the Gospel of the Kingdom was rather cautious and unsatisfying to restless Catholic liberals. But this document showed a move far from the old antimodernism of the Church. In one frequently quoted text, it could play both ends in terms of the middle it so assuredly occupied: "Earthly progress must be carefully distinguished from the growth of Christ's kingdom. Nevertheless, to the extent that the former can contribute to the better ordering of human society, it is of vital concern to the kingdom of God."[22] A papal encyclical, *Populorum progressio*, was a far more emphatic stamp of approval on this impulse to create human progress under divine authority.

A gathering of well over two thousand bishops from all over the world may well have been influenced by the spirit of the early 1960s, but it was also in the strand of a long-developing more positive Catholic view of human endeavor. The towering figure in Catholic philosophy on both sides of the Atlantic in the period when neo-

21. Ibid., pp. 85-87.
22. Austin P. Flannery, ed., *Documents of Vatican II* (Grand Rapids, Mich.: Eerdmans, 1975), p. 938; see a critical discussion in Gustavo Gutierrez, *A Theology of Liberation: History, Politics, and Salvation*, trans. Sister Cardida Inda and John Eggleson (Maryknoll, N.Y.: Orbis Books, 1973), pp. 168ff.

orthodoxy reigned in Protestantism was Jacques Maritain. Through the decades he developed a moderate view of progress, which he called "integral humanism." Maritain was more positive than Tillich, who had been the Protestant figure bridging the eras. Maritain discerned moral progress developing as "the explicit knowledge of the various norms of natural law grows with time." This progress produced the prohibition of slavery and a more humane mode of waging war and governing. But even as Maritain mentioned these signs, he had to point to a comparable growth in evil, a fact that made Christian grace necessary. Yet the fact that Christians had higher extratemporal goals never left them free to let up on their effort "better and better" to serve society. Maritain's "New Christendom" was to be a semisecular and truly free civilization.[23]

France was the source of much preconciliar progressivist thought. Wagar has singled out as a leader Emmanuel Mounier, editor of *Esprit* and a leader in the French Resistance. This personalist thinker, influential far beyond French Catholic theological circles, attacked the Christian pessimism of the decades. He advocated a "tragic optimism" that saw in the midst of evil some human progress. Thus, technology had led "from a condition of immanent servitude to an inhuman nature, to a considered mastery over a humanized nature." Mounier was explicitly Christian in his progressive claims, a fact that made his thought congenial to otherwise more timid Church leaders: "Christianity gives man his full stature and more than his full stature. It summons him to be a God, and it summons him in freedom. This, for the Christian, is the final and supreme significance of progress in history." God wished human liberation: "Humanity, *farà da sè*, slowly, progressively."[24]

The voice of a new episode and the most unguardedly progressive thinker in recent Catholicism was the Jesuit Pierre Teilhard de Chardin. No one could accuse him of shaping his outlook to match the spirit of the times in the church or the world. As far as the Church was concerned, Telhard was so out of step that the Jesuit order permitted almost no publication of his writings until after his death in 1955. As far as the mood of the world was concerned, he was committed to a metaphysic of progress that was consistent through both world wars; indeed, he could in some writings reduce those wars to a footnote. He even incorporated the invention of nuclear armaments into his ideology of progress. Today the Teilhardian star has declined, but in the mid-sixties, "when wise men hoped," it shone. The lure of his having been silenced may have helped Teilhard find a following in the freer post-conciliar climate. Catholics were also hungry to find a synthesis between faith and science or evolution and Providence, and Teilhard provided many with that.

23. Quoted by Wagar, *Good Tidings*, pp. 246-48.
24. Ibid., pp. 249-50.

"Barely credible," Gilkey would have to call his "Note on Progress" written after the World War I experience in 1920. Even then Teilhard already defied the "immobilists" who lacked passion. "The truth can now be seen: Progress is not what the popular mind looks for, finding with exasperation that it never comes." Progress is not immediate ease, but a *force.* "It is the Consciousness of all that is and all that can be," wrote the enthusiastic evolutionist:

"Nothing moves," a first sage will say. "The eye of commonsense sees it and science confirms it."

"Philosophy shows that nothing can move," says a second.

"Religion forbids it—nothing must move," says a third.

Disregarding this triple verdict the Seer leaves the public place and returns to the firm, deep bosom of Nature. . . . Gazing upward, towards the space held in readiness for new creation, he dedicates himself body and soul, with faith reaffirmed, to a Progress which will bear with it or else seep away all those who will not hear.

In 1941, in another work that remained unpublished until 1959, the priest sustained this absolute faith in progress, an outlook that so many Catholics and humanists found inspiring in the mid-sixties. "Some Reflections on Progress" were the reflections of a man who proudly identified himself as a palaeontologist but who was more mystical than scientific. "There are stronger scientific reasons than ever before for believing that we do really progress," he wrote in spite of bitter disillusionment with human goodness in recent years. "We are dealing with a question of facts and we must look at the facts." First looking back on three hundred million years, Teilhard then looked ahead and showed that humans still possessed "a *reserve,* a formidable potential of concentration, i.e., of progress." And the "blind" forces of the universe, he thought, were in inexorable complicity with the human. But "we can progress only by uniting," as a law of life; for this, a common human vision would develop. Such language is rare in the eighties, but a century from now it is likely that historians will be quoting people like Teilhard to recreate the theological and secular mood of the early 1960s: "I am convinced that finally it is upon the idea of progress, and faith in progress, that Mankind, today so divided, must rely and can reshape itself."[25]

The work in which those essays appeared, *The Future of Man,* appeared in the United States in 1964. A few years later Teilhardian faith was being seriously challenged, and disillusionment again set in. But had he lived, nothing in Teilhard's outlook would have prepared him to let short-term setbacks deny his vision of human complexity and unity on the way to "the Omega point" of consummation in Christ.

25. Pierre Teilhard de Chardin, *The Future of Man,* trans. Norman Denny (New York: Harper & Row, 1964), pp. 19, 24, 61, 63, 64, 69-75.

A FURTHER POSITIVE STEP

Protestantism had no towering figure to match Teilhard, but its own progressive episode did rely on the thoughts of a more restrained believer in human development, the martyr to Hitler, Dietrich Bonhoeffer. He was a Lutheran theologian schooled in the qualified vision of that tradition. But in the very heart of darkness, a Nazi prison, he went against the *Zeitgeist* and began to reach for resources in the biblical and Protestant tradition to explain his vision of "a world come of age."

If one had explicitly posed the notion of progress to Bonhoeffer, it is not likely that he would have simply subscribed to it. Yet he did picture a developmental view of reality in which God progressively withdrew from the role as nurturer of human processes while humanity was coming past adolescence to "religionlessness" yet still faithful adulthood. "Religion" to Bonhoeffer connoted routine and repressive pieties, obsolete patterns of metaphysics, and a view of God as the filler of gaps in human knowledge:

> Man has learnt to deal with himself in all questions of importance without recourse to the "working hypothesis" called "God." In questions of science, art, and ethics this has become an understood thing at which one now hardly dares to tilt. But for the last hundred years or so it has also become increasingly true of religious questions; it is becoming evident that everything gets along without "God"—and, in fact, just as well as before. As in the scientific field, so in human affairs generally, "God" is being pushed more and more out of life, losing more and more ground.[26]

One would have thought that to a theologian who remained Christocentric this development would cause dismay, but Bonhoeffer and those of his outlook came to cheer it. His biographer Eberhard Bethge said that Bonhoeffer did not turn optimistic about humans "becoming better and better"—how could he in a Nazi prison? But he did believe in "responsibility," "the unreversible capability and duty of adults individually to answer the questions of life in their own particular fields and within their own autonomous structures."[27]

The secular theologians like Harvey Cox and the Anglican Bishop John A. T. Robinson, author of *Honest to God*, drew upon Bonhoefferian concepts of technological and political "adulthood" to develop theologies that sounded very progressivistic. Cox in *The Secular City* took the image and the reality of the modern city as exemplars of postsacral progress. "Massive residues of magical and superstitious world-views" survived, but Cox saw these being exorcised. The city, he

26. Dietrich Bonhoeffer, *Letters and Papers from Prison*, ed. Eberhard Bethge (New York: Macmillan), pp. 325-26.

27. Quoted in James W. Woelfel, *Bonhoeffer's Theology: Classical and Revolutionary* (Nashville, Tenn.: Abingdon, 1970), p. 306, n. 49.

thought, was the sphere of liberation and renewal. The very anonymity of the city contributed "to the maturation of persons" as the world moved toward its own adulthood. Cox asked his readers to celebrate the unfolding of this city.[28] Several years later he was back with *The Feast of Fools, The Seduction of the Spirit,* and *Turning East,* works which seemed to represent a complete about-face because they returned to the celebration of what had to Cox earlier looked residual: myth and symbol. Yet in his best-selling prime, Cox gave great impetus to both the Protestant and Catholic belief in progress. Jewish reviews, written out of the spirit of post-Holocaust musing, were almost unanimously critical of his optimism and belief in "better and better" human situations.

My contention that some sort of belief in progress remains latent in liberal theological thought finds confirmation in this eruption of progressive theology that began in the fifties and came to a climax around 1965. The public situation briefly encouraged its vision. Western intellectuals momentarily took cheer from the progressive example of Pope John XXIII and took hope from the Second Vatican Council which ended that year. Martin Luther King embodied the hope of many that a racially and economically divided society would progress toward integration and social justice. The New Frontier and Great Society of John F. Kennedy and Lyndon B. Johnson looked like the unfolding kingdom of God to many Americans and some sympathizers elsewhere.

Alongside the new views of progress in religion and politics there also developed a faith in technology among humanists and theologians. Christian thinkers called an end to their disgraceful retreat in the face of scientific discovery and an unwillingness to defend a "god of the gaps" who was located wherever human knowledge gave out and mysterious ignorance began. They then reached for the language of progress and even utopian optimism. Less than a generation later, to borrow Gilkey's phrase, people would not only find such a theory of progress "barely credible" but would dismiss it as simply *in*credible. To recover something of the movement's mood, it is worthwhile to listen to an exuberant statement by a member of the "secular theology school," William Hamilton. The Baptist professor published his essay "The New Optimism" in the quarterly *Theology Today* in January 1966. Given what we know of the time that the editing processes take and the internal evidence of the text, we may deduce that Hamilton must have written it in the spring of the Selma to Montgomery civil rights march or in the early summer of 1965 when Congress was passing progressive legislation. It must have been just before the cities began to burn in a time of racial unrest or immediately before the administration heated up American involvement in the Vietnamese War.

28. Harvey Cox, *The Secular City* (New York: Macmillan, 1965), pp. 150, 83-84.

The faith in progress came back with a vengeance to the theologians of Hamilton's breed. Theologies change for many reasons, wrote Hamilton. "Everybody knows, or at least feels, that the time of troubles for the neoorthodox ecumenical-biblical-kerygmatic theology has arrived." It was on the defensive because its doctrine of man, as voiced by Reinhold Niebuhr, was now no longer plausible simply because it was "in part a pessimistic theology." Hamilton suspected that "one of the reasons neoorthodoxy now doesn't work is that this pessimism doesn't persuade any more." Belief in progress or optimism, "an increased sense of the possibilities of human action, human happiness, human decency, in this life," was regnant.[29] The death of the gloomy Christian poet T. S. Eliot and President Johnson's State of the Union message, both on January 4, 1965, symbolically signalled the move from pessimism to optimism, from alienation to politics, from blues to the freedom song.

Hamilton noted an instance of the new belief in progress in the writings of Marshall McLuhan, the technological optimist; his thought would "remind some of the venerable doctrine of progress over which we have preached so many funeral orations." Also, the "gaiety, ... absence of alienation, [and] vigorous and contagious hope at the center" of the civil rights movement were Hamilton's "most decisive piece of evidence." He prophesied that "the sixties may well be the time for play, celebration, delight, and for hope." This was the language of imposed systems of relevance because Hamilton now urged "hunting up of biblical or theological foundations for something... that has already taken place...." Now, "we trust the world, we trust the future, we deem even many of our intractable problems just soluble enough to reject the tragic mode of facing them." This was to be not an optimism of grace, said Hamilton, but an optimism of worldliness.[30]

What sounds now like puffery for the passing *Zeitgeist* of 1965 was an effervescent expression of a spirit shared by many more sober thinkers, whether secular or theological. The period from the mid-1950s to the mid-1960s in some respects bore resemblances to the "national period" in America, which Alfred North Whitehead characterized as a period when "wise men hoped, and... as yet no circumstance had arisen to throw doubt upon the grounds of such hope."[31] It was as if two world wars, economic depression, the Cold War, and a nonaffluent world beyond American borders were nonexistent, or out of memory and sight. One could argue that theology should stay with what is intrinsic to its tradition and philosophical development and

29. William Hamilton, "The New Optimism," in Thomas J. J. Altizer and William Hamilton, *Radical Theology and the Death of God* (Indianapolis, Ind.: Bobbs-Merrill, 1966), pp. 157, 158, 159.

30. Ibid., pp. 164, 165, 168, 169.

31. Alfred North Whitehead, *Essays in Science and Philosophy* (New York: Philosophical Library, 1948), p. 114.

that profound thinkers would do well to be aloof from or in opposition to the spirit of the times. Thus, during the period between the wars they might well have reasserted a compensatory faith in progress born of their heritage when people were dispirited, and they might just as well have questioned the heady optimism of 1965. But being as steadfast as that would demand a vision and heroism that few thinkers can sustain.

An exception and a bridge to the next period was Jacques Ellul, a French Protestant lawyer and lay theologian, who has through a variety of changes in cultural mood been persistently denunciatory in his view of progress. Ellul makes a sharp distinction between a supernatural hope that looks for divine intervention in history and a faith in progress that derives from a "shallow" view of the empirical situation. Christian hope to the theologian, says Ellul, should exist "in spite of."

> Thus hope is . . . a "giving the lie to the realm of death." All hope is always in that category. At whatever level it is encountered, it is always *this* giving the lie to something *obvious* which man considers unimpeachable, to a *fatality* to which man bows. It arouses man to go beyond that. This is indeed why it has no place except in a situation without hope.

Ellul was utterly pessimistic about technology, modern politics, mass media of communication, and the other spheres of life from which the new progressives of the mid-sixties took hope.

Ellul saved his most acid tone for the theologian whose book better than any other captured the progress-minded "secular theology," Cox's *The Secular City.* Wrote Ellul, this work

> offers the public a justification for what is going on in the world, for what man is in process of doing. It is true that modern man in his most fallen aspect wants exactly above everything else that someone should come along to tell him that he is right in doing what he is doing. That was the springboard for all the propaganda.
>
> It supplies precisely the "solemn complement" (that Marx rightly accuses religion of supplying). . . . Since man's technological power is constantly increasing, the Church's message consists in giving assurance that it is up to man to create his own destiny. . . .
>
> *The Secular City* is the prime example, for our modern society, of the opiate of the people.[32]

Cox, of course, did not see himself as someone who used religion as an opiate but as someone who reached into the tradition for latencies that went back to the biblical creation and exodus accounts. He and Hamilton were the more public and effervescent exemplars of a school of thought that had been developing in spite of Jewish thought about

32. Jacques Ellul, *Hope in Time of Abandonment* (New York: Seabury Press, 1973), pp. 204, 152-53.

the Holocaust, in the face of Catholic traditionalism, and during the growth of antiliberal Protestant fundamentalism. In the period of neoorthodoxy's and neoscholasticism's decline, this new progressivism revealed how durable is the latent faith in progress, how ready it is to seize its moments.

ANOTHER DECLINE

Ten years after the crest of secular theology, a cultural malaise set religious thought into opposite directions. The sense of progress again, as after 1919, seemed "barely credible." Now came prophecies that never again would progress gain a hearing. It would be foolish to try to refute such claims by reference to a future that has not yet unfolded, but a historian who has surveyed past recurrences can be fairly confident that the virus of progress is only latent. Barring a cultural upheaval of unimaginable proportions, it is likely to reappear.

If any theologians do believe in progress, they certainly do not speak of inevitability or uniformity of progress in their own discipline. Almost unanimously they speak of their craft as itself being in a bad state. Thor Hall, who in the 1970s made studies of the current practitioners of the discipline, agreed with most of his respondents that after a half-century of giants, most of his contemporaries were nothing more than "pretenders." Nor did one school of thought predominate in the 1970s:

> There are theologies of biography, black liberation, change, culture, death of God, ecumenics, fantasy, freedom, history, holocaust, hope, humor, imagination, joy, liberation, love, mystery, myth, narrative, oppression, paradox, peace, personality, play, politics, process, psychotherapy, revolution, sensibility, story, symbol, tradition, transcendence, women's liberation, et cetera—each representing a different point of view, and each laying claim to priority on the agenda of the theologians of the day.[33]

In Hall's list, two families especially pointed to the most recent theological transformations of progress. One of those is "process," an extremely durable school that derives from Whitehead's metaphysics. An academic mode of discourse that has had little impact in the Christian congregations, "process" recognizes scientific progress. Its key terms include "potentiality" and "becoming"—even in the godhead. God has a "consequent" nature through involvement with the world of entities. God also has a "superject" nature, which is the repository of all that has been accomplished. Evil there can be, but the consequent nature of God sees to it that the world does not fall into chaos "as it passes into the immediacy of his own life." This is a motif that process theologians have picked up as they may speak of divine

33. Thor Hall, *Systematic Theology Today: The State of the Art in North America, Part I* (Washington, D.C.: University Press, 1978), pp. 3-4.

grace and human hope. Theologians often listed in the process camp
are John B. Cobb, Schubert M. Ogden, and Daniel Day Williams.[34]

The other family of thought in Hall's sequence connects his terms
"freedom," "hope," "liberation," "politics," and "revolution" in a
school that passes most frequently under the code name "liberation
theology." Influenced by the maverick Marxist Ernst Bloch, author of
Das Prinzip Hoffnung,[35] this began as a "theology of hope" in the
writings of two German Protestants, Wolfhart Pannenberg and Jürgen
Moltmann, and the Roman Catholic Johannes-Baptist Metz. "Hope"
and "progress" are by no means the same thing, but by positing God
as the power of the future, these theists saw an opening toward the
greater and the better in the future.

Less ambiguous in its progressivism is the form of the theology
which, especially in the Third World, has come to be called "liberation
theology." Now that the world's Christian majority is soon to pass to
the southern hemisphere, voices from that sphere are being heard in
Europe and America. In *Theology in a New Key* Robert McAfee
Brown has summarized responses to "liberation themes." He shows
how the secular mentor for this school is not finally Bloch but Marx.
For some liberationists, Marx represents a world view, a framework
for decision about thought and action. In this all-encompassing sense,
Brown thinks that Marxism is incompatible with Christianity. For
others, Marxism, he says, is a plan for political action, as it has turned
out to be for many Christian activists in Latin America. And for most
it is an instrument of social analysis, just as Catholic Christianity once
used Aristotelianism as an instrument of philosophical analysis.[36]

Brown may hold a too circumscribed view of the Marxist dimensions
of much liberation theology; it often has come to be encompassing.
Thus, the Spanish Marxist Alfredo Fierro in *The Militant Gospel*
described his own as a "historico-materialistic theology."[37] How one
regards progress in this theology that looks for liberation depends
largely on how one relates progress to Marxism. Certainly there is
nothing simply developmental or progressive about it; "no antagonism, no progress"—the Marxian dictum, applies well. All the liberationists picture class struggle and violent revolution as a step in which
God is working toward the next stage, but that stage is "better," and
thus progress somehow rules, if in almost utopian forms.

34. See especially Alfred North Whitehead, *Process and Reality* (New York: Macmillan, 1979). Daniel Day Williams discussed progress in one of his earlier books, *God's
Grace and Man's Hope* (New York: Harper & Brothers, 1949), pp. 107ff., 186ff. This
approach has prevailed during the years of process theology's revival through the
1970s.

35. Ernst Bloch, *Das Prinzip Hoffnung*, 3 vols. (Frankfurt am Main: Suhrkamp,
1969).

36. Robert McAfee Brown, *Theology in a New Key* (Philadelphia, Pa.: Westminister, 1978), p. 66; Brown includes a helpful annotated bibliography.

37. Alfredo Fierro, *The Militant Gospel*, trans. John Drury (Maryknoll, N.Y.: Orbis,
1977).

The liberationist who has posed the issues of progress best is Rubem A. Alves, author of *A Theology of Human Hope*. He includes a Christian critique of conventional human optimism. Progress, he notes, is not natural or simply evident. "Nothing indicates that the horizons are becoming more open." On the contrary, conservatism makes repressive powers seem more dominant than ever. "Humanistic messianism" looks for human deliverance by the powers of man alone and thus turns romantic or faithless to history.

> The problem with the messianism of technology and the idea of progress, from the perspective of the historical experience of humanistic messianism and messianic humanism, is that the rationality operative in technology is not derived from the experience with the liberating movement of freedom in history but rather from the rationality of nature. It makes room for the quantitatively different but not for the qualitatively new. It is a rationality that depends on quantitative changes to survive but dies if qualitative changes occur. Progress or economic development, as the creation of technology, would thus become a different sort of opiate that would prevent qualitative changes, changes created by freedom by making freedom tamed through the marvels and power of the quantitative factor. It would make freedom domesticated, thereby destroying it as freedom.

The hope of human liberation in "humanistic messianism and messianic humanism," on the other hand, has a kind of transcendent character, but to the theologian humanistic messianism relies too much on human powers. Messianic humanism, however, "offers a different assessment of what is possible to history, thereby providing a different ground for the hope of human liberation."[38] This prospect appears in drastic social change on Marxist models, but it finds symbolization among Christian populations also in the divine activity of a God who sides with the poor against the oppressor, promising them a better day.

Theologians of the liberationist schools strenuously differentiate between progress and hope, but from the viewpoint of secular observers, the two will look similar. At the very least, liberation theology seeks to counter the pessimism and apathy of the oppressed or the malaise of people who are frustrated over the way history is not malleable to their purposes. In the present context, it reveals again how the virus of faith in progress—though this time progress beyond conflict and after antagonism—has reappeared.

THE FUTURE

This essay has concentrated on the theologies that regularly erupt on the soil of liberal or radical biblical faith, where thinkers have stressed the ties between nature and supernature, the immanent and the tran-

38. Excerpted in Alistair Kee, ed., *A Reader in Political Theology* (Philadelphia, Pa.: Westminster, 1974), pp. 36-41.

scendent. They represent only the yang of a Jewish and Christian yin and yang. For the rest of this century it is possible that the negative motif about the future will prevail. The growing communities of Christianity are presently evangelical, pentecostal, and fundamentalist. These are devoted more to private morale in bad days than to a belief in "better and better" social morale toward good days. Much of their thought is "premillennial," which implies a theological commitment to the belief that everything must get worse and worse until the second coming of Jesus. That coming will be followed by a millennium of good days, but in no way can the idea of progress be associated with its transformation.[39] Given the experience of millennial apocalypticisms around the year 1000 and following other signs, we can expect a reappearance of these toward the year 2000, especially if the empirical world gives little reason for belief in progress.

Yet the alternative strain of Christian thought, open as it is at times to utopianism, will continue to use the language of human hope. It will still embody the ethos of progress, which never disappears entirely from the believing communities of the Western world in good times and despite recurrent bad times.

39. See Robert G. Clouse, ed., *The Meaning of the Millennium: Four Views* (Downers Grove, Ill.: Inter-Varsity Press, 1977).

24

The Return of the Sacred: The Argument About the Future of Religion

DANIEL BELL

RELIGION AND THE ENLIGHTENMENT

At the end of the eighteenth and to the middle of the nineteenth century, almost every enlightened thinker expected religion to disappear in the twentieth century. The belief was based on the power of Reason. Religion was associated with superstition, fetishism, unprovable beliefs, a form of fear which was used as protection against other fears—a form of security one might associate with the behavior of children—and which they believed, in fact, had arisen in the "childhood" of the human race.

Religion, in this view, arose out of the fears of nature, both the physical terrors of the environment and the dangers lurking in the inner psyche, which were released at night or conjured up by special diviners. The more rational answer—we owe the start, of course, to the Greeks—was philosophy, whose task was to uncover *physis* or the hidden order of nature. The leitmotif was the phrase which occurs first in Aristotle and is resurrected later by Hegel and Marx, "the realization of philosophy." For Aristotle, nature had a *telos*, and within it man would realize his perfected form. For Hegel, this *telos* lay in History, in the *marche générale* of human consciousness, which was

"The Return of the Sacred? The Argument on the Future of Religion" was given as the Hobhouse Memorial Lecture at the London School of Economics in the spring of 1977 and published under the terms of the lecture in the *British Journal of Sociology*, December 1977.

wiping away the fogs of illusion and allowing men to see the world more clearly. "The criticism of religion," Marx said, "ends with the precept that the supreme being for man is man...."[1]

The end of History would come in the "leap" from "the kingdom of necessity to the kingdom of freedom." The end of History would be the unbinding of Prometheus and Man stepping onto the mountain top to take his place with him among the Titans. As Shelley proclaimed:

> The painted veil ... is torn aside;
> The loathsome mask has fallen, the man remains
> Sceptreless, free, uncircumscribed, but man
> Equal, unclassed, tribeless, and nationless,
> Exempt from awe, worship, degree, the king
> Over himself. ...[2]

From the end of the nineteenth century to the middle of the twentieth century, almost every sociological thinker—I exempt Max Scheler and a few others—expected religion to disappear by the onset of the twenty-first century. If the belief no longer lay in Reason (though in Emile Durkheim there remained a lingering hope, and in a book he expected to write after the *Elementary Forms of the Religious Life* [1912], but never did, he planned to sketch the forms of a new universalism that he thought might arise by the end of the century), it now lay in the idea of Rationalization. Reason is the uncovering—the underlying structure—of the natural order. Rationalization is the substitution of a technical order for a natural order—in the rhythms of work, in the functional adaptation of means to ends, in the criteria for use of objects, the principal criterion being efficiency. And since, as most sociologists believe, men are largely shaped by the institutions in which they live, the world has become, in Max Weber's terrifying phrase, "an iron cage." As Julien Freund sums up Weber:

> With the progress of science and technology, man has stopped believing in magic powers, in spirits and demons; he has lost his sense of prophecy and, above all, his sense of the sacred. Reality has become dreary, flat and utilitarian, leaving a great void in the souls of men which they seek to fill by furious activity and through various devices and substitutes.[3]

This is the view, I dare say, of most sociologists today, though much of the poignancy has been drained away and replaced if not by jargon, then by bare utilitarian prose—as if the language itself has become proof of the proposition.

1. Karl Marx, "A Criticism of Hegel's Philosophy of Right," in *Selected Essays*, trans. M.J. Stenning (London: Leonard Parsons, 1926), pp. 26-27.
2. "Prometheus Unbound," in *The Complete Poetical Works of Percy Bysshe Shelley*, ed. Thomas Hutchinson (Oxford: Oxford University Press, 1935), p. 249.
3. Julien Freund, *The Sociology of Max Weber* (New York: Pantheon, 1969), p. 24.

The sociological term for this process is "secularization." Yet I find the term to be a muddle, for it mixes together two very different kinds of phenomena, the social and the cultural, and two very different processes of change that are not congruent with each other. Changes in social structure are determinate, and there is a clear principle of change. There is a historicity in man's growing consciousness, particularly in the awareness of his powers. For this reason, there is often a linear direction in the realm of sociotechniques. If something is cheaper, better, more efficient, we use it as a substitute for the previous process. If an institution becomes too large, it differentiates and sets up specialized parts. But changes in culture follow no such trajectories. Boulez does not replace Bach or Jackson Pollock "succeed" Raphael. Changes in culture are syncretistic and, at best, enlarge the moral and aesthetic repertoire of mankind; at worst, as in the meditative mingling of consciousness, East and West, syncretism trivializes culture.

Since I sort out the different processes of institutional change from cultural change, I would break apart the concept of secularization and divide the meanings. The word "secularization" has an original meaning that I would like to restore. It was originally employed, in the wake of the Wars of Religion, to denote the removal of territory or property from the control of ecclesiastical authorities. In this sense, secularization means the disengagement of religion from political life—the classic instance is the separation of church and state—and the sundering of religion from the aesthetic so that art need no longer bend to moral norms but can follow its own impulses, wherever they lead. In short, it is the shrinkage of institutional authority over the spheres of public life, the retreat to a private world where religions have authority only over their followers, and not over any other section of the polity or society.

But when such secularization has taken place, as has clearly been the case in the last two hundred years, there is no necessary, determinate shrinkage in the character and extent of beliefs. In fact, all through this "progressive" secularization of religious institutions, we find extraordinary revivals in religious enthusiasm among masses of people, as in the burned-over districts and camp-fire evangelicism in the United States, and the Methodist revivals in England, and, in the culture, the powerful replies of a Schleiermacher to the cultured despisers, the conversion of a John Henry Newman, the existential faith of a Kierkegaard, the powerful religiosity of a Soloviev, the personalism of a Mounier, the neoorthodoxy of a Barth or Tillich, the agony of a Simone Weil, and other renewed well-springs of faith that have not ceased to come forth again and again in that period.

There has been, of course, in the culture of the last two hundred years, the more dominant trend of disbelief. This is the idea that the world has lost its mystery, that men not gods can rule the world, or that beyond there is nothing, just the void; the underlying thread of modernism is nihilism. This is what Weber has called *Entzauberung*, the disenchantment—or, more cumbersomely, the demagicification—of the world. Yet this tendency, which indeed has been very powerful, has very different roots from the process of rationalization (whose sources are technological and economic—I *do* leave aside science, not only because of its early affiliations with Puritanism but because it has been only one strand of science that has supported rationalization, the Baconian influence) or the process of secularization (whose roots were primarily political, in the diminution of ecclesiastical power). The sources of disenchantment lie, I believe, in somewhat autonomous tendencies in Western culture, and it is those tendencies that have to be the starting point, I believe, for an understanding of the future of religion in the contemporary world.

There is, thus, a double process at work. One is secularization, the differentiation of institutional authority in the world, which is reinforced by the processes of rationalization. The second, in the realm of beliefs and culture, is disenchantment, or what I would prefer to call, for the parallelism of the term, profanation. Thus, the sacred and the secular become my pair terms for the processes at work within institutions and social systems, the sacred and the profane for the processes within culture.

The thread I wish to pursue is the changes within culture. Here, too, there is a double level, for changes in culture arise in reaction to changes in institutional life (to justify or to attack), and changes in culture relate to the changes in moral temper and sensibility, to expressive styles and modes of symbolization, to the destruction of old symbols and the creation of new ones. Since changes in the character of religion, not institutional authority, begin primarily at this second level, it is there that I want to develop my story.

I come now to the fulcrum of my argument, the definition of culture. By culture, I mean less than the anthropological notion of the artifacts and patterned ways of life of a bounded group, and more than the "genteel" notions of a Matthew Arnold as the cultivation of taste and judgment. I would define culture as the modalities of response by sentient men to the core questions that confront all humans in the consciousness of existence: how one meets death, the meaning of tragedy, the nature of obligation, the character of love—these *recurrent* questions which are, I believe, cultural universals that are asked in all societies where men have become conscious of the finiteness of existence.

It would make little sense to seek an exhaustive list of cultural universals. But in all cases they go back to the fundamental questions of epistemology, morality, *techne*, and consciousness of the self, which all human groups begin to ponder. These universals would include:

The idea of order, some notion of regularities in the universe and of regularities in social life.

A sense of the past, some notions of origin and of creation.

An idea of group identity, a distinction between oneself and others.

A conception of courage. The exact definition may vary, yet all human groups have some notion of the idea in positive form.

A concept of fate and chance, often related to the idea of order.

The necessity for instruction, the idea that growing up always involves a learning process.

An aesthetic sense, an idea of decoration, of imagery.

A conception of the sacred—if only through that which is taboo.

The idea of ritual, an act that unites the sacred with awe and regularity.

The burial of one's dead, and the sense of grief.

Culture, thus, is always a *ricorso*. Men may expand their technical powers. Nature may be mastered by scientific knowledge. There may be progress in the instrumental realms. But the existential questions remain. The answers may vary—and do. This is the *history* of human culture, the variations in myth, philosophy, symbols and styles. But the questions always recur. The starting point in understanding culture is not human nature (as in Greek thought), or human history (as in Hegel and Marx), but the human predicament: the fact that man is "thrown" into the world (who asked to be born?) and in the growing knowledge of that situation becomes aware of some answers—the received residues of culture—and gropes his way back to the questions to test the meanings for himself.

All cultures, thus, "understand" one another because they arise in response to the common predicaments. Cultures are expressed in different languages, each of which, having its own sounds and references, thus assumes idiosyncratic and historical character. Yet as Walter Benjamin observed in an essay on translation: "Languages are not strangers to one another, but are, a priori and apart from all historical relationships, interrelated in what they want to express."[4] If I follow the sense of Benjamin's remarks, translation reproduces meaning not by literalness or even context, but by the relatedness of the response to the existential questions to which the original meaning was addressed. Translation cannot reproduce the "color" of culture—the exact syntax, the resourcefulness of its phonology, the particular metaphors or the structure of associations and juxtapositions that the original tongue provides. What it can render is its significant meanings. In that sense, the color is the *parole*, and meanings the *langue* of culture.

Within this purview, religion is a set of coherent answers to the

4. Walter Benjamin, "The Task of the Translator," in *Illuminations*, ed. Hannah Arendt (New York: Harcourt, Brace and World, 1968), p. 72.

core existential questions that confront every human group, the codi-
fication of these answers into a credal form that has significance for
its adherents, the celebration of rites which provide an emotional
bond for those who participate, and the establishment of an institutional body to bring into congregation those who share the creed and
celebration and provide for the continuity of these rites from generation to generation.

The attenuation or the breakdown of a religion can be along any of
these dimensions—institutions, rites, creed, or answers. The most
crucial of all are the answers, for these go back most piercingly to the
human predicaments that gave rise to the responses in the first
instances.

THE ADVENT OF THE SELF

From the seventeenth through the nineteenth century there occurred
a change in moral temper, in the relation of the individual to the
existential questions of culture, which undermined the cultural foundations of the Western religions, answers that had given men a coherent
view of their world.

Identifying modal changes in culture is a very difficult undertaking.
Political changes, like revolutions, announce themselves with the sound
of a thunderclap. Socioeconomic changes, such as industrialization, are
visible in the material structures that are created. But changes in
culture and moral temper—until the twentieth century at least—came
in more subtle and diffuse ways, and it is difficult to locate them in
specific time and place. At best, one can single out some representative
figures to symbolize such changes.

In his essays *Sincerity and Authenticity*, Lionel Trilling remarks:

> Historians of European culture are in substantial agreement that, in
> the late sixteenth and early seventeenth century, something like a
> mutation in human nature took place. Frances Yates speaks of the
> inner deep-seated changes in the psyche during the seventeenth
> century: "One way of giving a synopsis of the whole complex psycho-
> historical occurrence is to say that the idea of society, much as we
> now conceive it, had come into being."[5]

In the context of his essay, Professor Trilling was concerned to
show that in this period, "If one spoke publicly on great matters as an
individual, one's only authority was the truth of one's experience,"[6]
and it is for this reason that the idea of sincerity began to matter. One
can broaden the argument to say that, at this time, experience, not
revelation, or tradition, or authority, or even reason, became the touch-

5. Lionel Trilling, *Sincerity and Authenticity* (Cambridge, Mass.: Harvard University Press, 1972), p. 19.
6. Ibid., p. 23.

stone of judgment, and the emphasis on experience became the emerging cultural norm.

In the story that I am pursuing, there were three changes that, woven together, made up this change in moral temper. These were (1) the growth of the idea of a radical individualism in the economy and the polity and of an unrestrained self in culture; (2) the crossover from religion to the expressive arts (literature, poetry, music, and painting) in the problem of dealing with restraints on impulse, particularly the demonic; and (3) the decline of the belief in heaven and hell and the rise in the fear of nothingness, or the void, in the realm beyond life; the coming to consciousness, in short, of nihilism.

The interrelatedness (but not integration) of these three we call "modernity"—the turning away from the authority of the past, the shrinking of the realm of the sacred, and the Faustian quest for total knowledge, which sets man spinning into the vortex of the *Wissendrang* from which there is no surcease. To take these up seriatim:

1. "The impulse to write autobiography may be taken as virtually definitive of the psychological changes to which the historians point," writes Professor Trilling.[7] The clearest case in point is Rousseau's *Confessions*. What scandalized his contemporaries was not his scatological remarks but the very first word in the book and the very tone of that first paragraph. Rousseau begins:

> I am commencing an undertaking, hitherto without precedent, and which will never find an imitator. I desire to set before my fellows the likeness of a man in all the truth of nature, and that man myself.
>
> Myself alone! I know the feelings of my heart, and I know men. I am not made like any of those I have seen; I venture to believe that I am not made like any of those who are in existence. If I am not better, at least I am different. Whether Nature has acted rightly or wrongly in destroying the mould in which she cast me, can only be decided after I have been read.[8]

(Nature may have destroyed the mold, but the culture recreated it, and the imitators, unfortunately, have written endless advertisements for themselves.)

It is not just Rousseau's claim to uniqueness that is central; that is merely a matter of psychology. It is a deeper change in the nature of culture and character structure. In the polity, the claim of individualism was for liberty, to be free of all ascriptive ties. But in the culture, the claim was for *liberation*: to be free of all constraints, moral and psy-

7. Ibid., p. 24.
8. *The Confessions of Jean-Jacques Rousseau* (New York: Modern Library, n.d.), p. 3.

chological, to reach out for any experience that would enhance the self.

2. Religion has always lived, dealing as it does with the most basic human impulses, in the dialectical tension of release and restraint. The great historic religions—Buddhism, Confucianism, Judaism, and Christianity—have all been religions of restraint. Underneath have been the subterranean impulses—the Dionysian frenzies, the Manichean dualities, the gnostic assaults on the exoteric doctrines, the idea of the Holiness of Sin—that have beat against the great walls of religious taboos.

The crossover from religion to the expressive arts has not only meant that restraint has gone slack; it has also meant that the demonic impulses in men (once channeled into religion, once used by particular religions against others) have now become polymorph perverse and pervade all dimensions of modernist culture. If experience is the touchstone of the self, then there can be no boundaries; nothing is unattainable, or at least unutterable; there are no sacred groves that cannot be trespassed upon and even trampled down.

That movement, which we call Modernism, was of course a great source of energy and vitality, and the century from 1850 to 1950 (and its peaks, from 1890 to 1920) can probably be seen—in painting, literature, poetry, and music—as one of the great surges of creativity in human culture.

But there was a price: the fact that the aesthetic was no longer subject to moral norms. Men's true metaphysical destiny, Nietzsche declared, lay not in morality (a paltry, dispirited ethic of slaves) but in art. In the modernist imagination, all is permitted—murder, lust, sodomy, incest, degradation—in order to nourish the rich fantasies of the unconscious and to express the diffuse primary process, which is polymorph perverse. Passion is no longer the identification with religious suffering and sacrifice, but carnal sensuality, which carries one beyond the self. Murder is no longer the mark of Cain but man's uncontrollable excitement with his secret impulses. In the great works of imagination—a Karamazov or Gide's *Vatican Caves*—these transmutations are contained by the constraining forms of art.

But when the distinctions between art and life begin to break down, when some proclaim that their life itself is a work of art, when there is the democratization of Dionysius in the acting out of one's impulses, then the demonic spills over all bounds and suffers a double fate. At one extreme, violence becomes the aesthetic of politics (no longer of art), as in the calls to a cleansing of the polluted selves by a Sorel, a Marinetti, a Sartre, or a Fanon; at the other, the demonic becomes trivialized in the masochistic exorcisms of the cultural mass.

3. The fear of nothingness—the nihilism that now suffuses the culture—has given rise to new forms of aggression and domination. The great divide is the understanding of death. The source of con-

science, said Hobbes, is the fear of death; the source of law, the fear of violent death. Yet within a religious culture, death could still be viewed —though feared—as the prelude to *something* beyond. But what if there was *nothing* beyond?

The implication of this new view of consciousness is spelled out powerfully by Hegel in his Kafka-like parable, that of *Herr und Knecht*, Lord and Bondsman in the *Phenomenology*. In that parable, the *ur*-encounter between two men is a duel, in which one risks his life for freedom or submits to the will of the more powerful one. If this is the fundamental paradigm of human relations, one can ask: why should the two engage in a duel? Or why, as the emerging rationality of a Locke or Adam Smith suggests, should they not cooperate and thus increase their yields?

But each man knows—and this is the secret of Hegel's parable— that whatever his striving, no matter how much he can master nature, or even expand his own powers, there is, *au fond*, the nagging sense of mortality, the realization of negation, the annihilation of what is his greatest achievement as man, his self-consciousness, his *self*. Some few men can and do live in that stoic realization, but fewer modern men because their very character is their striving, their claim to free-dom or liberation, the impulse to burst all bonds, strike off all con-straints. The sense of death is too heavy a burden, and what we—all of us—do is to blot it out of consciousness, beginning as children with solipsistic fantasies: it will never happen to me; when I turn around the world does not exist; *I* can imagine myself dead, but it is *I* that stands outside all that. In short, the fundamental defense against death is a fantasy of omnipotence. But what happens when two omnip-otences meet? They cannot occupy the same psychic space at the same time. And so, there is a duel—to the death or submission.

Is it an accident that the modern world, having delimited the au-thority of religion in the public sphere, has been the first to create "total power" in the political realm—the fusion of beliefs and institu-tions into a monolithic entity that claims the power of a new faith? With the "Oriental despot," to use Hegel's language, "one was free." Today, in the regimes of total faith, "all are bound." And the mode of rule is Absolute Terror—the mode that Hegel discerned in the first of the political religions, the French Revolution.[9]

THE ALTERNATIVES TO RELIGION

These are broad brush strokes. They lack shade and nuance, detail and qualification. I would hope that in a larger work, of which this essay is a précis, these elements will be filled in. But within this limited space, I can only continue the argument as a sketch.

9. G. F. W. Hegel, *The Phenomenology of Mind*, ed. Sir James Baill (London: Allen & Unwin, 1955), pp. 599-610.

In the nineteenth and twentieth centuries, the culture, freer now from traditional restraints, no longer tied in intellectual and expressive areas to the modalities of the religious beliefs, began to take the lead, so to speak, in exploring the alternatives to the religious answers. There have been, in that time, in the West, five alternative responses to the disenchantment with traditional religions. These have been—and to some extent still are—rationalism, aestheticism, existentialism, civil religions, and political religions. In this essay I would like to deal, very briefly, with two of them, aestheticism and political religions, as illustrations of the power of these alternatives. It is also, I would argue, the failure of these particular two which has opened up the beginnings of various searches for new, religious answers. I cannot do justice here to the very complex histories of each theme, but I shall call attention, in each instance, to a single motif.

Aristotle said that if a man were not a citizen of the *polis*, he would seek to be either a beast or God. This is the secret of nineteenth-century aestheticism: it rejects society, and man, and seeks to be *both* beast and God.

Aestheticism began to emerge at the end of the eighteenth century, when men of letters sensed the opening of a void: if the secure meanings of religion could no longer provide either certitude or a road to the divine, where was the way? If God is no longer "there," how does man satisfy the desire for "the unattainable" and his dream of the infinite?

In his essay *Le Triangle Noir*, André Malraux locates this first awareness in the work of the French novelist Choderlos de Laclos, the Spanish painter Francisco de Goya, and the French revolutionary Louis de Saint-Just. For Laclos, who is our thread, if God no longer bars the way, men can pursue the infinite along the paths of eroticism, cruelty and terror. The freeing of the erotic from the religious—one of the earliest and most intertwined of the orgiastic couplings of religion and sexuality or, making a religion of the erotic, free of all other norms of morality and rational conduct—was the foundation of aestheticism, and its later bastard offspring, the decadent movements of the end of the nineteenth century.

It is in Baudelaire that the poet as the man accursed by this vision of *le curiosité du mal* receives his fullest expression. Baudelaire stands as *homo duplex*, or in his own words *l'homme dieu*, seeking to invoke God and embracing the devil. Divided between the desire for "thrones and dominations" and the compulsion to taste the vices of sin, he puts forth the motto at the end of his *Voyages*, "To the depths of the unknown to find the new."

As Pierre Emmanuel has written in his book *Baudelaire: The Paradox of Redemptive Satanism*, Baudelaire recognizes in Laclos "the rigorous logic of an eroticism which, out of hatred for nature, pushes the natural to an excess; a movement which, in him, reaches the extremes of bestiality only to bring him toward another extreme, an angelic one."[10]

For Baudelaire, sexuality is separated from love and must be explored for the sensations it can provide. He experiments with opium (*cette drogue enivrante et maudite*) and seeks release through drink (*cette autre vie que l'on trouve au fond des breuvages*). And, as he writes in his *Aesthetic Curiosities*, "the beautiful is what is bizarre." In *Les Fleurs du Mal*, the poem which brought him to trial in 1857 for outraging the morals of the public, he seeks to distill flowers from evil. The poem is lascivious and blasphemous, and extraordinarily beautiful.

Yet beauty and the bizarre are evanescent. One can only tarry with these. Earth—boredom—is *hell*, and one must go below it. In the morning life, one wears a cold mask. At night one explores the subterranean rivers and unconscious beliefs, the dreams and unsatisfied aspirations that feed the wellsprings of appetite. But Baudelaire finds that man is only *in tenebris*. The world stands in the last days of Holy Week, and the candles are progressively being extinguished. Yet it is not Christ who is coming but Satan. And in this extremity of spirit, there is left only the "furious and desperate appetite for death," the final darkness.

In the aesthetic movement, poetry, not religion, is sacred. The poet is a seer, or *voyant*, replacing the priest, or rather, becoming the new prophet in the historic tension of prophet and priest. In the beginning was the word; but the word now belonged to the poet. The "prophetic tribe" of poets, in Baudelaire's phrase, had extralucid powers, a belief that led, in Rimbaud's incantations, to the idea that the poet possesses the "alchemy of the word."

But the word is neither *logos* nor law. The way becomes the wayward, Halakha becomes apocrypha. The impulse replaces the idea, the sense—the sensations that tantalize—overpower the mind. In the aesthetic mode, will and passion are the primary coordinates of the paths of action.

The foundation of a political religion is a messianism which makes the eschatological promise of the leap to the kingdom of freedom— the release from all necessity—on earth. The vision of Marxism is such a speaking of tongues. In his earliest essays, such as the *Critique of Hegel's Philosophy of Right*, one finds this prophetic language. The idea of the "leap" itself—a term that was central to Kierkegaard—is a metaphor with religious connotations.

Yet the development of Marxism itself—the effort of the "mature" Marx to be scientistic (for example, the Newtonian language such as "the laws of motion" in *Capital*) and the rise of mass social democratic

---

10. Pierre Emmanuel, *Baudelaire: The Paradox of Redemptive Satanism* (University, Ala.: University of Alabama Press, 1967), p. 48.

parties that became integrated, even negatively, into the life of their societies—gradually smothered the messianic tone in favor of the language of progress and inevitability. Sorel might say that it is to violence that Socialism owes those high ethical values by means of which it brings salvation to the modern world.[11] But few listened to this syndicalist appeal.

The political religion which transformed Marxism came out of the crucible of World War I and the Russian Revolution. After so long a period of progress and economic growth, the war suddenly seemed to be an apocalyptic shock, the more so because of the senseless mass slaughter which led a generation of poets and writers to proclaim that the nihilism only a few had discerned was now covering the world like thick mud. The October Revolution brought with it an orgiastic chiliasm, the heady feeling that the eschatological opening of History was at hand. And, added to these, was a third necessary element, a charismatic agency that would bring purification through terror, the Party.

Two men became the formulators, at the deepest gnostic level, of this creed. One was Georg Lukács, the other Bertolt Brecht.[12] For the "New Left," Lukács was the man who brought back to Marxism the ideas of alienation and historical consciousness. But for the smaller, initial group of apostles, Lukács provided the "theory of two truths," the "noble lie," the inner formula which is the binding cement of faith for the initiated.

The starting point in understanding Lukács is the final page of his most interesting book, *The Theory of the Novel*, written in 1914-1915. We live, he said, following the phrase of Fichte, in the epoch of absolute sinfulness. It is in the words of Dostoevsky that one can glimpse what may lie beyond. "It will be the task of historico-philosophical interpretation to decide whether we are really about to leave the age of absolute sinfulness or whether the new has no herald but our hopes."[13]

In 1915 a small group of Hungarian intellectuals began to meet with Lukács and his closest friend, Bela Balazs, every Sunday afternoon for discussion, meetings patterned after the group that used to

---

11. Georges Sorel, *Reflections on Violence* (London: Allen & Unwin, 1950), Chap. 6.

12. In this essay I discuss only Lukács. My reference to Brecht is to the *Lehrstücken*, particularly *The Measures Taken*, in which Brecht justifies murder of a comrade for the sake of the Party. In the play, Brecht has a song entitled "Praise of the Party." It says, in part:

> A single man has two eyes
> The party has a thousand eyes....
> A single man can be annihilated
> But the Party cannot be annihilated.

In *The Modern Theatre*, ed. Eric Bentley (New York: Anchor Books, 1960), VI, 277-78.

13. George Lukács, *The Theory of the Novel* (Cambridge, Mass.: MIT Press, 1971), p. 152.

meet at the home of Max Weber, which Lukács had regularly attended. Among those who came were Karl Mannheim, Arnold Hauser, Frederick Antal, and Michael Polanyi. As Lee Congdon, the young historian to whom I am indebted for the reconstruction of this period of Lukács' life, remarks: "The subject for discussion was always chosen by Lukács and it invariably centered on some ethical problem or question suggested by the writings of Dostoevski and Kierkegaard. Politics and social problems were never discussed."[14]

The Hungarian Communist party was organized on November 24, 1918. Lukács joined the party in December, along with Yelena Grabenko and Bela Balazs, and became one of the editors of *Vöros Ujsag* (Red Gazette). Most of the members of the Sunday discussion circle were stunned. They had heard Lukács speak of Dostoevsky and Kierkegaard but had never heard him speak of Marx. One member, Anna Leszani, remembered that "Lukács' emergence as a communist occurred in the interval between two Sundays: Saul became Paul." A proletarian writer, Lajos Kassak, in his autobiography, recalled:

> I was a little surprised [at Lukács' presence], he who a few days earlier had published an article in *Szabadgondolat* (Free Thought) in which he wrote with philosophical emphasis that the communist movement had no ethical base and was therefore inadequate for the creation of a new world. The day before yesterday he wrote this, but today he sits at the table of *Vöros Ujsag* editorial staff.

In the *Szabadgondolat* article, "Bolshevism as a Moral Problem," Lukács had asked why the victory of the proletariat, the reversal of oppressors and oppressed, would bring all class oppression to an end rather than simply bring in a different kind of oppression. Any answer, said Lukács, would have to rest on faith. People would have to believe that good (the classless society) could issue from evil (dictatorship and terror). And this was an instance of *credo quia absurdum est*, which he could not accept.

Yet within that fateful week, he had taken the leap of faith. In an essay he wrote in 1919, "Tactics and Ethics," he sought to resolve the moral dilemma. It had become his conviction that there was no escape for men who wished to preserve their moral purity in the "age of absolute sinfulness." "All men," he believed, "were caught in the tragic dilemma of having to choose between the purposeful and ephemeral violence of the revolution and the meaningless and never-ceasing violence of the old corrupt world," as Congdon puts it. One had to sign the devil's pact.

14. Lee Congdon, "The Unexpected Revolutionary: Lukács' Road to Marx," *Survey*, 20(2/3) (spring-summer 1974): 194; all quotations in my text concerning Lukács' conversion to communism may be found in this article. See also Lee Congdon, "The Making of a Hungarian Revolutionary: Béla Balázs," *Journal of Contemporary History*, 8(3) (July 1973): 57-74.

In this remarkable essay, Lukács cited the novels of Boris Savinkov, the Russian socialist revolutionary who was one of the assassins of Minister of Interior von Plehve.

Murder is not permitted; murder is an unconditional and unforgivable sin. Yet it is inescapably necessary; it is not permitted, but it must be done. And in a different place in his fiction, Savinkov sees not the justification of his act (that is impossible), but its deepest moral root in that he sacrifices not only his life, but also his purity, morality, even his soul for his brothers.

The corruption of political religions is not just the ebbing away of revolutionary fervor and the establishment of a new bureaucratic class in office. It is, to use theological language, the victory of the devil in seducing anguished men to sign that pact which makes them surrender their souls. And if the thought of Savinkov could induce Lukács to make that leap of faith over the *credo absurdum*, what is one to say of Lukács' silence when, in 1924, the Bolsheviks murdered Savinkov, by throwing him out of a window, for his continued opposition to the Bolshevik regime? But Lukács had already sold his soul. As Theodor Adorno said of Lukács, he "is desperately tugging at his chains, imagining all the while that their clanking heralds the onward march of the world-spirit [*Weltgeist*]."[15]

I believe that the "ground impulses" behind aestheticism and political religions are exhausted. These were the impulses to abolish God and assume that Man could take over the powers he had ascribed to God and now sought to claim for himself. This is the common bond between Marx and Nietzsche and the link between the aesthetic and political movements of modernity.

The phrase "God is dead" clearly has no denotative meaning. Nor do I think Nietzsche meant it so. It is a form of religious pornography, and I have to explain my restricted meaning of the term.[16] The *Fröhliche Wissenschaft* (translated variously as *The Gay Science* or *The Joyful Wisdom*) is a form of pornography in the sense that Machiavelli's *The Prince* is a kind of political pornography and de Sade's *Justine* sexual pornography—not so much for the content as for the intention to shock people in a highly specific way. We cannot believe that when Machiavelli wrote *The Prince*, people did not know of the actual practices of the Borgias, but one simply did not talk about them. Similarly, if one looks at the libertinism of eighteenth-century France, only a child might not know of the perverse games played in the Deer Park. But again, one did not talk of such things in polite society. What Nietzsche was seeking to do was to utter the unutterable. In every religion there is a sacred circle that engirdles the name that cannot be

15. For Theodor Adorno's assessment of Lukács, see the essay "Reconciliation under Duress," in *Aesthetics and Politics* (London: NLB, 1977), p. 175.
16. I owe this formulation to my friend Irving Kristol.

named. What Nietzsche was saying was that people knew the religious facts of life, but they persisted in the polite hypocrisy of refusing to utter what should not be mentioned. What Nietzsche was saying—and to that extent he was repeating Kierkegaard—is that without God, there is only the void of nihilism. Kierkegaard made the leap over that void, which he called the absurd, to religious faith. Nietzsche felt that such a leap was no longer possible.

Man was a rope dancer over the abyss, with the beast or *Knecht* at one end and the superman or *Herr* at the other. In his growing obsession with this dilemma, Nietzsche believed one could no longer accept the submission which every religion requires. Having challenged God on the mountain, Nietzsche believed that his *Zarathustra* was the Fifth Gospel, the gospel to obliterate the preceding four.

Nietzsche, hating modernity, carried out its logic to its end, or trans-end, which is to explode all limits, to dare all and to be all. In the end, his brain itself exploded, and he passed into the austistic realm of a oneness turned back on itself, the oneness of silence.

It is in the contrast between Goethe's *Faust* and Mann's *Doktor Faustus* that we see the trajectory of this *Wissendrang*. Goethe's Part 2 ends with Faust, now blind, but still striving, still believing, as his life ebbs away, that the digging he hears—the digging of his grave—is the digging of the great works of progress he has commanded. Mann's Faustus, Adrian Leverkühn, who embodies the Nietzschean temper, makes his pact with the devil as well. But instead of the affair with the pure and innocent Gretchen, he is passionately attracted to a prostitute he calls the "Hetaera Esmeralda" and contracts syphilis. The poison in his blood is the source of the "towering flights of . . . upliftings and unfetterings, of ecstasy in the music he writes that unites him with eternity." But the price he pays is the inability to establish a human relationship, the exhaustion of the art which is drawn from the subconscious, which the Germans call *das Musiche*, sterility and derangement. Leverkühn's final work, the work of negation, is intended to destroy Beethoven's Ninth Symphony. The Cantata *D. Fausti Weheklag* is, in its wail, agony, and pain, the negation of Faust. And instead of *Licht, Licht, mehr Licht*, we have *nichts, nichts, mehr nichts*.

The exhaustion of political religions follows a double trajectory. One was laid out quite directly by Weber in his "Politics as a Vocation":

> The materialist interpretation of history is no cab to be taken at will; it does not stop short of the promoters of revolution. Emotional revolutionism is followed by the traditionalist routine of everyday life; the crusading leader and the faith itself fade away, or, what is even more effective, the faith becomes part of the conventional phraseology of political Philistines and *banusic* technicians.[17]

17. H.H. Gerth and C. Wright Mills, *From Max Weber* (New York: Oxford University Press, 1946), p. 125.

Once a revolution has taken place, the major problem for any chiliastic regime is how to maintain enthusiasm. Revolutionary regimes must therefore try to sustain zeal by maintaining an atmosphere of war, by mobilizing emotions against an outside or internal enemy, or by some kind of "revitalized" faith.

I need not rehearse here all the difficulties and travails that have occurred in the Soviet Union and in the People's Republic of China. But there is a crucial logic that has bearing on my argument. In revolutionary Marxism, that is, the canon according to Lenin, the "Party" had a sacred character. The Party was the vanguard of the masses, and it was the "collective wisdom" of the Party that interpreted the will of History. Stalin, even when he made extreme claims of omniscience, did so because he claimed to embody the Party. And when his name was blackened, when the seals were opened, his successors could do so on the ground that he had violated Party norms and that the new collegial leadership was restoring the legitimacy of the Party.

What Mao succeeded in doing—and this is the historical change in the "religious" nature of the creed—was to substitute himself for the Party. That ever-present, ever-quoted breviary, the little Red Book, made it clear that whatever charisma the Party may possess derives solely from the person and thought of Mao Tse-tung.

Men can carry on a revolution (that is, live by moral rather than material incentives) if they become "new men," if there is a transvaluation of values. The dilemma for all revolutionary theorists from Saint-Just and Babeuf to the present is how to carry through a revolution that is "tainted" or corrupted by the bourgeois past. The existence of that taint has always been the justification put forth by the revolutionary elite in setting up a dictatorship to protect the people from themselves (to censor what they read, to forbid sad or pessimistic tales, to create "positive heroes"). In China, Mao took the final step, which was to set up his own person and his own thought as the first and final arbiter and, in the Cultural Revolution, to change the character of men and thus change society. This has been the quest of all great religions. The irony is that it has been attempted on the most spectacular scale in human history by a political religion. The obvious paradox is the Marxism that begins as a movement of Reason and ends as a cult. It begins with an attack on all Gods and ends as Idolatry.

Each Great Profanation, in its own dialectic, has its small negation. The profanation of Modernism is that the great works which were created by wrestling with the demonic (as Jacob wrestled with the angel and became Israel) become trivialized by the *culturati*; what has been art becomes trendy lifestyle, and what has been incorporation (as in transubstantiation) becomes consumption. And the profanation of Marxism is the debasement of socialism not just in the great political religions but in the grotesque totemic forms of African socialism,

Arab socialism, Baath socialism, and the hundred different socialisms that have erupted like weeds in the wastelands of Marxism.

THE *RICORSO* OF RELIGION

On the double level of social structure and culture, the world has been secularized and profaned. The secularization derives from the rationalization of life, the profanation from the imperious self of modernity. Religion is no longer the "collective conscience" of society, as Durkheim believed was its elementary form, because society is radically disjointed, its different realms of the technoeconomic sphere with its principle of functional rationality, the polity and its surge for equality, and the culture with its demands for self-fulfillment creating increasingly intolerable strains. And if religion was once the opium of the people, that place has been taken by *pornotopia*, where the straight and narrow have become the kinky and the twisted.

Hobbes once said that Hell is truth seen too late. Hell is the Faustian bargain, the pact which compels man to strive endlessly, for if he acknowledges any point as final, he loses his soul. But if there are no limits or boundaries, life become intolerable. The ceaseless search for experience is like being on a merry-go-round, which at first is exhilarating but then becomes frightening when one realizes that it will not stop. As Don Giovanni discovered, endless pleasure is endless torment precisely because it is endless. And today we have the democratization of the erotic.

Will there be a return of the sacred, the rise of new religious modes? Of that I have no doubt. Religion is not an ideology or a regulative or integrative feature of society—though in its institutional forms it has, at different times, functioned in those ways. It is a constitutive aspect of human experience because it is a response to the existential predicaments which are the *ricorsi* of human culture. That complex German writer Walter Benjamin maintained that "the concrete totality of experience is religion," and he gave to this form of authentic experience the word "aura."[18]

Religions, however, unlike technologies or social policies, cannot be manufactured or designed. The multiplicity of exotic consciousness-raising movements—the Zen, yoga, tantra, I Ching, and Swami movements—which have spread so quickly among the *culturati*, is itself an illustration of that fad. These are not religions. They are an illustration of the confusions of authenticity, the search in this multiple, discordant world for the authentic "I." America in the mid-seventies, writes the counterculture historian Theodore Roszak, is launched on "the biggest introspective binge any society in history has undergone." He may well be right. The "authentic I," having become a bore to others, has now become even more of a bore to itself.

18. Benjamin, "The Task of the Translator."

When religions fail, cults appear. When the institutional framework of religions begins to break up, the search for direct experience which people can feel to be "religious" facilitates the rise of cults. A cult differs from a formal religion in many significant ways. It is in the nature of a cult to claim some esoteric knowledge which had been submerged (or repressed by orthodoxy) but which is now suddenly illuminated. There is often some heterodox or esoteric figure who functions as a guru to present these new teachings. The rites that are practiced permit, or more often prompt, an individual to act out impulses that hitherto had been restrained or repressed so that there is a sense of *ex-stasis* or some transfiguring moment.

But the deception—and the undoing—of such experience—however "sincere" and anguished like so much of "enthusiastic" quest—occurs because the search rests basically on some idea of a *magical* moment and on the power of magic. Like some headache remedy, it gives you fast, fast, fast belief, if not relief. And it is no accident that the half-life of these movements is so short and that the heteroclites move on ceaselessly, to a new nostrum.

When we think of the possibility of new religions, we turn, naturally, to Max Weber, who, more than anyone else, has given us the comprehensive picture of the way religions arise. But if we are looking in the direction Weber pointed, we may be looking in the wrong direction. For Weber, new religions arose with prophecy and with the charismatic figure who had the power within him to shatter the bonds of tradition and to tear down the walls of the old institutions. But what is there to shatter or to tear down today? Who, in the culture, defends tradition? And where are the institutional walls? We live in a culture which is almost entirely antiinstitutional and antinomian. How could it be otherwise when the radical self is taken as the touchstone of judgment?

If there are to be new religions—and I think they will arise—they will, contrary to previous experience, return to the past, to seek for tradition and to search for those threads which can give a person a set of ties that place him in the continuity of the dead and the living and those still to be born. Unlike romanticism, it will not be a turn to nature, and unlike modernity it will not be the involuted self; it will be the resurrection of memory.

I do not know how these will arise, but I have some dim perception of the forms they may take. I would be bold enough to say that in the West they would be of three kinds. The first I would call "moralizing" religion. Its roots and strength are in a fundamentalist faith, evangelical and scourging, emphasizing sin and the turning away from the Whore of Babylon. In the United States, in recent years, the largest-growing voluntary associations have been the Fundamentalist churches. To some extent this is an aggressive reaction on the part of the "silent majority," so to speak, against the carryover of modernist impulses into politics—especially the claims of complete personal freedom in sexual areas (for example, Gay rights), morals, abortion, and the like. But that is too simple an explanation. I think, given the history of Western culture, that a large substratum of society has always felt the need for simple pieties, direct homilies, reassurances against their own secret impulses (such as in Nathaniel Hawthorne's powerful story "Young Goodman Brown") but that until recently these people have been derided by the predominantly liberal "culture" (not society) and, more importantly, abandoned by the clergy, who, coming from the educated classes and subject to the conformist pressures of the liberal culture, had lost their own nerve and often, as well, their belief in God. The exhaustion of Modernism and the emptiness of contemporary culture mitigate that social pressure, and Fundamentalist ministers can step forward, with less fear of derision from their cultured despisers. These groups, traditionally, have been farmers, lower-middle class, small-town artisans, and the like. In the long-run occupational sense, they are in the decline. Yet in the more immediate future they may be the strongest element in a religious revival.

The second—which I think will find its adherents in the intellectual and professional classes—I would call "redemptive" and derives, I think, from two sources. One is the retreat from the excesses of modernity. One can face death, perhaps, not by seeking to be self-infinitizing but by looking back. Human culture is a construction by men to maintain *continuity*, to maintain the "un-animal life." Animals seeing each other die do not imagine it of themselves; men alone know their fate and create rituals not just to ward off mortality (the pretty stories of heaven and hell) but to maintain a "consciousness of kind," which is a mediation of fate. In this sense, religion is the awareness of a space of transcendence, the passage out of the past from which one has come, and to which one is bound, to a new conception of the self as a moral agent, freely accepting one's past (rather than just being shaped by it) and stepping back into tradition in order to maintain the continuity of moral meanings. It is a "redemptive process" (in Kenelm Burridge's term), whereby individuals seek to discharge their obligations—and if one claims *rights*, at some point there has to be recognition of *obligations* as well—to the moral imperatives of the community: the debts in being nurtured, the debts to the institutions that maintain moral awareness. Religion, then, begins, as it must, in the mutual redemption of fathers and sons. It involves, in Yeats's phrase, becoming "the blessed who can bless," the laying on of hands.[19]

There is a second, more direct sociological source of the redemp-

19. Kenelm Burridge, *New Heaven, New Earth* (Oxford: Basil Blackwell, 1969).

tive. This is in the growth, as I believe it will come, of what Peter Berger has called "mediating institutions."[20] In the reaction against central government, against large-scale bureaucracy and the mega-structures of organization, there is a desire to reinstate a private sphere—of family, church, neighborhood and voluntary association—to take back the function which it has lost of *caring*: of caring for the afflicted and the ill, of caring for welfare, of caring for one another.

The mediating institutions, centered as they will be on the idea of caring, resurrect the idea of *caritas*, one of the oldest sources of human attachments, a form of love that has been crushed between rational-ized *eros* and profaned *agape* and superseded by the welfare state. Whether the mediating institutions that I think will arise become the cenacles of a new religion remains to be seen.

The third religion, more diffuse, will be a return to some mythic and mystical modes of thought. The world has become too scientistic and drab. Men want a sense of wonder and mystery. There is a persis-tent need to overcome the dualisms that prize apart the tendrils of self which yearn for unification of being. There is also the temptation to walk along the knife-edge of the abyss. As Rilke began his *Duino Elegies*: "For Beauty's nothing but the beginning of Terror." Yet myth tames the terror and allows us to look at the Medusa's head without turning to stone. Myth returns us to what Goethe called the *Urphä-nomene*, the *ricorsi* of the existential predicaments.

Such mythic modes cannot take the form of primitive animism or shamanistic magic; for such invocation is simply the substitution of meaningless Castanedas for abstract cause-and-effect relationships. A mythic mode, since it will come from our past, will derive from the prescientific and preconceptual roots and transform them.

A mythic mode, if it comes, will probably be closer to what Marcel Granet calls *emblème*, the sign which evokes the totality of things.[21] One such emblem, classic to Chinese thought, is the Tao, a mode which emphasizes the singular rather than the general, the sign rather than the concept, the resemblance rather than the identity, the precur-sive image rather than the efficacious cause. It is a world of symbolism, in which contrasts are not contradictions but intimate interdependen-cies. Its purpose is not to discover sequences but to uncover solidarities, not cause and effect but the common root of phenomena in which pictorial images can be substituted for one another as symbolic images that unite the event and the world.

Is any of this possible—in the West? The West, as Weber pointed out, had created a unique civilizational pattern of institutionalized

20. Peter Berger and Richard Neuhaus, "To Empower People: Mediating Struc-tures and Public Policy" (Washington, D.C.: American Enterprise Institute, 1977).

21. Marcel Granet, *La Pensée Chinoise* (Paris: Editions Albin Michel, 1950), pp. 334f.

rationality, one that, through the power of technology, has permeated all parts of the world. Yet if East has to come West, would Weber have trouble in admitting that at some future time beginning in the present, the West could, in some new fashion, find itself looking to the East? What is striking—in the serious realm of philosophers, poets, physicists, and artists—is that the journey is now being undertaken.

I began with the Enlightenment, but I find that its conception of religion was misleading. It regarded religion as primitive and fetishist in origin, to disappear by the cold light of reason or, a century later, through the antisepsis of science. In the last quarter of the nineteenth century, Andrew D. White, the president of Cornell, could publish a book with the title *A History of the Warfare of Science with Theology*, and John W. Draper, a chemist turned historian, could write a bestseller entitled *A History of the Conflict Between Religion and Science*. Draper, whose animus was largely against the Catholic Church, believed in a severely planned society under the tutelage of a scientific elite. It is a view that has had a long history, from the French social philosopher Henri de Saint-Simon down, perhaps, to the later Leo Szilard.[22]

Few scientists today would make this hubristic claim. More important, we have come to realize a necessary distinction between science and religion as relating to two totally different realms. Science, if I follow C. F. von Weizsäcker, is the search for the unity of nature. In physics, this takes two forms: one is the effort to state a "closed system" in mathematical terms—through transformation groups such as, in relativistic quantum theory, the Lorentz group defining the structure of space and time, and the unitary groups defining the metric of Hilbert space. The second is an effort of unity through reductionism, in which chemistry is united with physics, biology united with chemistry, while evolution links the molecule and man.[23]

If science is the search for the unity of nature, religion is the search for unity of culture. Culture is a different realm from nature. If one is reductionist, the other is emergent, through consciousness. And, it is the concern with the knower and less with the known. Culture seeks meaning on the basis of purpose. It cannot be indifferent to the imperatives of nature (for example, the death of the individual for the necessary continuation of the strength of the species), for it is the *conscious response* of men to the existential predicaments that arise out of the interaction of men with nature, and with one another.

22. Andrew D. White, *A History of the Warfare of Science with Theology in Christendom* (London: Macmillan, 1896); John W. Draper, *A History of the Conflict Between Religion and Science* (New York: Appleton, 1875).

23. C. F. von Weiszäcker, *The Unity of Nature* (New York: Farrar, Straus & Giroux, 1980).

The thread of culture—and religion—is memory. As Louis Mac-Neice once wrote: "I cannot deny my past to which my self is wed / The woven figure cannot undo its thread."

TO REGAIN THE SACRED

There is an old Midrashic parable that asks, Who first discovered water? We do not know. But one thing we do know: the fish did not. We may be in the position of the fish, for the world of religion is the world of the nonrational, and we can only go so far in our understanding, for the realization of the nonrational (a category that sociology has rarely tried to define) is the recognition that the existential predicaments we confront derive from a mystery, one that we may never be able to penetrate. For Aristotle, man's highest capacity was not *logos* (that is, speech or reason) but *nous*, the capacity for contemplation whose constitutive character is that its content cannot be rendered in speech. The eternal, for Aristotle, was *aneu logou*—without words. That is also the source of the *kairos* which breaks into time, or the "holy sparks" of the *Shekinah*, which becomes the sacred.

The sacred is the space of wonder and awe, of the noumenal which remains a mystery and the numinous which is its aura. With the sacred is the principle of *Havdolah*, the principle of distinction, of the realm which is reserved for the days of awe and lament, and the realm of the mundane and profane. It is a dualism whose content has been redefined by various cultures and different generations. But until contemporary times, this principle has been observed by almost every human group we know. Ours is the first to annul the boundaries which maintained the preciousness of the principle of life itself. The viciousness of that annulment emerges when a society is wholly dissolved into the political maw of the "sacred" (as in the Soviet Union) and when all spheres of life become subordinated to it, or where a society is wholly absorbed into the economic engorgement of the profane, as in a capitalism that treats nothing as sacred but converts all objects into commodities to be bought and sold to the highest bidders. When there are few rituals to mark the turns in the wheel of life, if all events become the same with no ceremony to mark the distinctions—when one marries in ordinary dress, or receives a degree without a robe, or buries one's dead without the tearing of cloth—then life becomes gray on gray, and none of the splashiness of phosphorescent pop art can hide that grayness when the morning breaks.

The exhaustion of Modernism, the aridity of communist life, the tedium of the unrestrained self, and the meaninglessness of the monolithic political chants, all indicate that a long era is coming to a close. The theme of Modernism was the word beyond: beyond nature, beyond culture, beyond tragedy—that was where the self-infinitizing spirit was driving the radical self. We are now groping for a new vocabulary whose keyword seems to be limits: a limit to growth, a limit to spoliation of the environment, a limit to arms, a limit to torture, and a limit to *hubris*—can we extend the list? If we can, it is also one of the relevant portents of our time.

What will come out of that clearing, I do not wholly know, but since I believe that the existential questions of culture are inescapable, I feel that some new efforts to regain a sense of the sacred point to the direction in which our culture—or its most sentient representatives—will move. Whether that new vision will be genuine, that is, fully responsive to the deepest feelings of people, I do not know; and, even more, whether such new threads can be woven into meanings that will extend over generational time and become embodied in new institutions is something even further beyond my purview.

All these are conjectures, and we shall have to wait, in the fullness of time, for their refutations. But I am bound, in the faith of my fathers, to one obligation. In the *Pirke Avoth*, there is the "tablet" of Rabbi Tarfon. He used to say: it is not your part to finish the task; yet neither are you free to desist from it.

25

The Idea of Progress:
An Ethical Appraisal

FREDERICK A. OLAFSON

I

The most obvious ethical question that can be raised in connection with the idea of progress is a question of fact: have human beings in the course of their history shown substantial improvement in the way they treat one another? Even if we succeeded in answering this question to our satisfaction, we would surely also want to know what accounts for such ethical improvement as may or may not have occurred. In this essay, I do not directly deal with either of these questions but with one that is probably closer to the second than it is to the first. I am interested in determining whether or not one of the influences that can facilitate or block a specifically ethical form of human betterment may not be the idea of progress itself, and, if so, what the character of that influence may be. My guiding intuition here is a feeling that from the ethical standpoint the idea of progress probably has more drawbacks than it has advantages although it clearly has some advantages to which I will try to do justice. It should also be made clear that the idea of progress I am going to be concerned with here is not just a conception of a widespread improvement in the conditions of human life but one that also connects such improvement, however it may be understood in detail, with the advance and dissemination of knowledge. Such knowledge need not be scientific knowledge in any special or highly restrictive sense of the term; but I think it is fair to say that in recent times at least the achievements and the methods of the natural sciences have been the principal paradigm of the kind of knowledge from which widespread social benefits have

been expected to follow. In this connection it should also be understood that the idea of progress I have in mind is not so much a set of
explicit theses that can be attributed to some thinker or school of
thought but rather one of those background assumptions by which the
thought and practice of a civilization are so often shaped, at both the
popular and the learned levels, without their ever being subjected to
real critical scrutiny.

Since my intuitions about the ethical role of the idea of progress are
negative in character, let me begin by drawing attention to a positive
aspect of this same conception. Whatever else it may say, the idea of
progress at the very least says that even the most general arrangements
of human life are not immutably fixed; and it thus implies that some
alternatives to a given prevailing state of affairs may be possible. As a
result, we are invited to entertain ideas as to what these other possible
orderings of human life may be instead of being told that we must
reconcile ourselves to things as they are. When we are authorized to
think about the future in terms of possible alternatives to our present
set of arrangements, beliefs that we may have about what would
constitute a more desirable ordering of life will obviously have a
chance to find expression; and among these may be specifically ethical
conceptions of the human good. Of course, a theory of progress may
be deterministic and thus discourage people from believing that their
ideas of what is right and good can have any influence in determining
which possible alternative to the status quo actually takes its place. But
if this is not the case, it seems reasonable to assume that the idea of
progress will tend to loosen the grip of the actual on people's minds
and thus make it more likely that it will make sense to them to take
seriously and perhaps even act on their notions of what is morally
right if they are otherwise disposed to do so. This last proviso is an
important one; and if in other ways the idea of progress were to have
the effect of weakening our disposition to take our ethical intuitions
seriously, the advantage I have just attributed to it might well be
canceled out.

There is another point to be made in this same general connection.
It seems clear that the ideas of what constitutes an improvement in
the conditions of human life on which most exponents of the idea of
progress rely are drawn from common-sense views on the subject and
have nothing especially original about them. As I will have occasion to
point out later, this reliance upon received views may contribute to a
certain dangerous ambiguity that is inherent in the idea of progress;
but that is another matter. What I want to emphasize at this juncture
in my argument is rather the fact that these shared intuitions of
common sense as to what is desirable in human life are for the most
part entirely sound. It is better to be able to prevent or to cure small-
pox than it is to have to suffer its ravages; and it is better to have
machines that can relieve human beings of back-breaking, life-long
labor than it is not to have them. I would in fact want to argue that

judgments like these, which are typical of the assumptions on which the idea of progress builds, are so well established that if some new principle of evaluation were to be invoked that called them into question, its incompatibility with them would have to count heavily against it. These observations lead me to the conclusion that even if it should turn out to be the case that in certain important respects the idea of progress is defective when appraised from an ethical standpoint, we would nevertheless be able to accept a great deal of the "progress" postulated by that idea as a net improvement in the human condition. There is, therefore, no intention on my part of offering a critique of the idea of progress as a kind of comprehensive repudiation of the assumptions as to what is good and worth having that have been associated with that idea. To say this is not, of course, to endorse the ways in which human beings have acted on these assumptions or the actual scale of priorities they have observed; and it may be that one implication of such a critique will be to make a revision of some of those priorities seem appropriate. However that may be, I am not proposing any wholesale substitution of a new set of judgments as to what is to count as good and what as bad.

By way of introducing the negative aspects of the idea of progress into the argument, it may be useful to point out that the idea of progress we inherited from the nineteenth century was at least as much an ideology as it was an idea. An idea of progress in its most general form would be simply a criterion by reference to which one can determine whether a large-scale change in the condition of human life is good or bad or indifferent; and it seems beyond dispute that all of us make use of some such criterion and can hardly avoid doing so. We do so, moreover, both when we judge that an improvement has taken place and when, in our view, there has been deterioration of some kind; and in respect of these contrasting possibilities our criterion of judgment would normally be expected to remain neutral and uncommitted. An ideology, by contrast, is not so much a criterion as it is a belief and a belief to which a special status is implicitly assigned that protects it against refutation by the ordinary experiential methods. In the case of the idea of progress, that belief is one that asserts a connection between various kinds of scientific and technological advance and a general improvement in the condition of mankind; and its ideological character consists in the ambiguity it maintains with respect to the more precise character of this connection.

In one aspect, it is an empirical connection since it is certainly possible to show persuasively that the achievements of science and technology have made possible changes in our mode of life which by any reasonable *criterion* of progress would have to count as improvements. But the peculiarity of the idea of progress which marks it as an ideology is the fact that it does not seem at all readily to permit this inference to run the other way so as to establish that some change attributable to science or technology is bad and ought not to have occurred. It is as though the source of such changes in scientific knowledge itself carried such validating force that the common-sense criteria cited by way of confirmation in the positive case cannot avail against it in the prima facie negative case. When this happens, as it typically does in the case of ideological beliefs, our normal criteria of evaluative judgment fail to maintain the requisite degree of independence from the very changes which they are used to judge; and one sign of this lack of independence is that one can reason from the fact that a given change is the result of an advance in technology to the conclusion that it must represent an improvement and thus progress. There is, in other words, a quasi-definitional connection between scientific and technological advance and general improvement or progress. Since it is also assumed on independent grounds that scientific and technological advance is inevitable and will continue indefinitely, it follows on the strength of this implicit definition that human improvement is equally inevitable and will continue indefinitely. It is hardly surprising that when tied to a self-certifying set of assumptions and definitions of this kind, the idea of progress in its criterial aspect suffers from the peculiar disability of being allowed to count only in favor of the hypothesis of progress and never, at least in any decisive way, against it.

It may be thought that this criticism of the idea of progress is a purely conceptual one and that accordingly, although it may correctly diagnose an unfortunate vice in the internal logic of that idea, it does not demonstrate or even suggest that any untoward consequences are to be expected as a result of the presumably remediable defect to which it points. Plausible as this sounds, I will contend that the vice in question is in fact much more serious and that so far from being the result of mere carelessness in the details of logical formulation, it is, in fact, functional just as it stands and manifests certain strategic elisions on which a whole ordering of life depends and about which serious ethical doubts need to be raised. More specifically I propose to argue that if the principal ethical advantage associated with the idea of progress is to open up whole sectors of human life to revisionary choice, its principal disadvantage is that it also tends to "close down" for ethical purposes the very situations it has opened up by declaring that change in the general conditions of life is possible. It closes them down by offering assurances based on the scientific/technological character of the source of change to dissuade us from insisting upon a genuinely independent, ethical evaluation of what is, in fact, coming to pass. Such assurances can be very persuasive and understandably so in light of the manifestly beneficial character of many of the changes so produced and the equally obvious hazards and uncertainties connected with the idea of an independent appraisal that could claim some sort of collective authority. In any case, the vital function of the idea of progress seems to me to lie in its appearing to validate certain kinds of changes that take place in people's lives and to do so with a minimum of institutional controls and without the requirement of close ethical scrutiny that could hardly be resisted if the acceptability of those changes were a genuinely open issue. Such a mode of validation or pseudo-validation has of course quite definite presuppositions as regards both economic realities and ethico-religious authority within society; and I will attempt to characterize some of these as well as the complexion a society tends to assume in the various departments of its activity when the ideology of progress has established itself.

First, however, it is essential that something be said about the notion of ethics that is to play such a central role throughout this essay. Especially when the featureless terminology of "values" dominates all discussions of this type as it tends to do at present, that notion can easily lose all distinctiveness of contour and become simply a general term of reference to the things people in one way or another care about. When that happens, an ethical approach to the idea of progress can be no more than a comparison of the items that appear on our preference lists with those that have in fact been made more widely available as a result of changes attributable to science and technology; and the conclusion in which that comparison issues is almost certain to be that there is indeed a positive correlation between progress and ethics. When ethics is more narrowly construed in terms of a particular subset of the items on that comprehensive preference list—those, namely, that have to do with the varying and often inconsistent expectations as to other-regarding conduct that human beings address to one another—more caution is usually shown in the matter of a positive correlation between progress and ethics; but this lower likelihood is treated as though it were simply another contingent fact about the probable rate of satisfaction of desires cherished by individual human beings. The sense, if there is one, in which ethical considerations must take precedence over all others in an assessment of progress—the sense in which, as Santayana put it, the only true progress is moral progress—clearly cannot emerge from such ways as these of approaching the ethical dimension of progress. It cannot do so because human beings are being considered solely in their capacity as individual consumers of goods of various kinds—ethical goods among them—and this means in abstraction from any underlying ethical relationship to one another which does not depend for its authority upon its being an item included in their individual preference lists. Viewed in such a light, even so central a social virtue as justice becomes a contingent desideratum and as such hardly suited to any stronger role as a central axis of evaluation along which the movement of a society—its progress and its regressions—could be plotted. It is obviously not possible within the compass of this essay even to begin to suggest what the character of such a stronger conception would be; but it should be possible at least to raise some doubts about the conception of ethics on which the idea of progress I have been discussing rests; and in the next section I will turn to that task.

First, however, I would like to note in passing that there are a good many signs that we may now be moving beyond the kind of historical situation in which an idea of progress functioning in the way I have described can find the strong acceptance it has enjoyed in the past. Indeed, if a transformation is taking place in our way of conceiving progress, I think that is in large part because we have become aware of the ideological function of that concept and because we feel a new need to formulate an idea—a criterion—of progress that is genuinely independent and will accordingly not lend itself to the uses to which the old one has been put. Perhaps because there is such a widespread perception that we are nearing the end of a period in which resources of all kinds have been prodigally available, there is much less willingness to license all sorts of private undertakings whose eventual costs to society as a whole are unknown and a much greater insistence that the implications of such initiatives for the set of relationships—ethical and political and social—in which, willy-nilly, we stand to one another be clarified and justified in appropriate terms. Perhaps this new mood has found its aptest expression in the subtitle of E. F. Schumacher's well-known book *Small Is Beautiful: Economics as Though People Mattered.*[1] Of course, such a reaction can take some unintelligent forms. Among these is the inference that, since science and technology are not automatically good, they must be automatically bad. Another is the belief that since one criterion of progress has proved to have serious defects, the notion of progress itself is meaningless and that it is no use looking for another, more satisfactory criterion to replace the old one. Even if we do not jump to conclusions like these, it is still not going to be easy for us to give effect to this new aspiration to free our criterion of progress from question-begging assumptions, but the opportunity to do so is, nevertheless, an extraordinarily valuable one of which we should make every effort to take proper advantage.

II

It may seem quite implausible to suggest that developments within moral philosophy itself may have had a significant influence on the emergence of an idea of progress such as the one I have been describing, especially when the latter is, as I believe it to be, a phenomenon of broad social import and by no means confined to some arcane domain of speculation. That nevertheless is the claim I want to venture. It is not a claim about the origination of this idea of progress nor about the vested interests and motives that have supplied the power for its

---

1. E. F. Schumacher, *Small Is Beautiful: Economies as Though People Mattered* (New York: Harper & Row, 1973).

subsequent development. The role of moral philosophy has rather been that of a parallel development which may be said to have reinforced the main movement of the idea of progress in the society at large precisely because it did not oppose it where otherwise it might have been expected to do so and in fact increasingly appeared to ratify at least implicitly the new design of moral concepts that was the product of the ideology of progress. Once again, I have to disclaim any intention of attempting to substantiate this view in any serious way in this paper; and in particular I propose to avoid entering the controversy about the special role of the eighteenth-century *philosophes* in this evolution I will be sketching. Instead, I would like to put forward an interpretation of the movement of modern philosophical thought as it bears on morality and issues relating to the explanation of human action—an interpretation that has been developed principally by members of the Frankfurt school like T. W. Adorno and Jürgen Habermas and that has not as yet received the kind of attention in this country that I think it deserves.[2]

In its broadest sense, the movement of "enlightenment" that has been in process in the Western world over the past two or three centuries has the character of a comprehensive conceptual reform through which the domains of, first, nature and, then, human society and human nature are reinterpreted in such a manner as to guarantee the applicability to them of the forms of order upon which scientific understanding and technological control depend. Negatively, this means that whatever is in principle resistant to, or unincorporable into, those forms of order must be denied a place within the system of the natural and the human world; and this sentence of banishment is obviously imposed in the first instance on all those magical forces and presences that have been the source of so much of the terror—and, it must be added, of so much of the interest as well—with which the scene of nature has been filled for its human occupants. The word *Entzauberung* ("disenchantment") has been very appropriately used to characterize this lifting of the magical spell under which nature had lain for so long and the resultant emergence of a neutralized domain of objects and processes to which human intelligence can be confidently applied without any inhibiting fear of an irrational residue in nature or of extranatural forces. From such a standpoint, religious belief in all but its most innocuously deistic forms must be regarded as the great embodiment of the antirational principle that first found expression in magic. Accordingly, the continuing alliance between

2. I have in mind especially Theodor Adorno and Max Horkheimer, *Dialektik der Aufklärung*, English trans. John Cumming, *Dialectic of Enlightenment* (New York: Seabury Press, 1972); and Jürgen Habermas, *Erkenntnis und Interesse*, English trans. J. Shapiro, *Knowledge and Human Interests* (Boston: Beacon Press, 1971), and his "Science and Technology as Ideology," in *Toward a Rational Society* (Boston: Beacon Press, 1970).

certain sectors of human life—most notably those that have to do with standards of conduct and morality—with religion or with views of the world that are teleological and dramatic in the way systems of religious belief typically are, must be greatly deplored. Not surprisingly, it is just this relationship of human experience, especially in its evaluative and moral dimensions, to the forms of natural order revealed by scientific inquiry that puts this "enlightened" world view to its severest test.

It is unquestionably in the philosophy of Immanuel Kant that one can discern the first phase of this "dialectic of enlightenment." It may be for just this reason that in the English-speaking world at least Kant is not so often thought of as a commanding philosophical figure in the same intellectual world as Gibbon and Voltaire and is perceived instead as the pioneer of an alternative world view whose antienlightenment and antiscientific character was to emerge fully in the work of his successors. If Kant's first philosophical objective was to provide sound foundations for the Newtonian world view in a theory of experience of a radically novel kind, he was equally convinced that the questions "What should I do?" and "What can I hope for?" were as much in need of answers as the question "What can I know?" What made him an atypical philosopher of the Enlightenment was his insistence that practical reason cannot be interpreted as an at bottom prudential adjustment of competing desires to one another on the analogy with empirical knowledge that utilitarianism was to develop into its own theory of morals and that it must instead be grounded in a theory of free moral personality for which no place can be found within the natural world of Newtonian science. It is true that in Kant's view the central demand of practical reason as of theoretical reason was for universality and necessity; and he has been very severely criticized for holding that the formal test of universalizability can generate substantive moral directives to which a unique validity attaches. I am not at all sure that these criticisms are sound or that even now we have succeeded in getting to the bottom of Kant's profound, although not always clearly articulated, intuitions as to the kind of reciprocity that rational beings cannot help recognizing as in some sense governing their relationships with one another. There can be no doubt, however, that, revolutionary as Kant's ideas on these matters were, they were too closely associated with the language and the hopes of traditional theism not to appear to many as a lapse on the part of an otherwise radical mind into an outmoded and indefensible posture of belief and into the kind of absolute dualism of scientific knowledge and morality, which the main movement of enlightened thought was attempting to overcome.

It is fascinating to see how in the course of the nineteenth century successive attempts were made to interpret the character of the rationality of which human conduct is capable in its relationship to the rationality illustrated by the natural sciences. As Habermas has shown, these efforts were marked by a gradual but steady assimilation of the former to the latter and thus by a failure to disengage the features of a distinctively human form of reciprocity that might have provided a clue to an understanding of ethical principles and their proper form of validation. In the ever subtler forms of utilitarianism that were being worked out, a calculative and predictive form of rationality was elaborated, which, as John Rawls has shown, in certain important respects abstracted from the essential plurality characterizing ethical situations and in so doing inevitably missed just those substructures of the communicative relationships among a plurality of selves that are of such vital significance in the understanding of justificatory activities, whether ethical or otherwise.[3] In these circumstances ethical problems came to be understood as being technical problems of maximizing happiness or well-being over a population of potential recipients and in the light of the advantages and disadvantages that the situations of these persons present to the overall maximizer. The net result of this approach is that little, if any, attention is paid to the position of the moral agent who has to define his course of conduct in a constant relation to the other human beings whose goals impinge so variously upon his own. Once rationality in the sphere of conduct has been defined in terms of such comprehensive maximization of well-being, it becomes well-nigh impossible to raise questions about the motives that could possibly induce anyone to accept an equivalence between his position and that of all the other like beings who are competing for the same good things that he seeks. That equivalence has in effect been presupposed as a defining condition of rationality in the setting up of the ethical problem in the form of a maximization of the general well-being; and as a result of the conception of moral personality that yields that equivalence, it does not appear *within* a moral philosophy reared on that foundation but instead as a kind of background condition of a peculiarly anonymous character whose status within the lives of the actual human beings who have to make ethical decisions has never been more determinately specified.

Now it is just this peculiar anonymity attaching to the most fundamental assumption on which the ethical life is to rest and its detachment from the real-life context of moral choice that have led some of the thinkers who have elaborated the line of analysis I am presenting here to argue that its deployment within our lives will inescapably have what can only be called an unmediated character. It is suggested, in other words, that the likely result of this failure to associate the highest principle of rational choice with an adequate concept of moral personality will be that in its application to human beings the effort to

3. John Rawls, *A Theory of Justice* (Cambridge, Mass.: Harvard University Press, 1971), Chap. 1.

maximize the general well-being will take on a managerial and manipulative character that derives from the techniques found useful in establishing scientific/technological control over natural processes. Typically, it will make its appearance as the policy of an institution rather than of individual human beings acting in their own right; and as is so often the case with institutional policies, it will exist in a peculiarly indefinite kind of relation to the purposes that are realistically imputable to the human beings who enact them as well as to those for whose benefit they are applied. The effect is, therefore, very likely to be a kind of forced assimilation of the human realities that are approached in this way to the natural processes in relation to which these techniques of analysis and control have been developed. If that happens, the last stage in the dialectic of enlightenment will have been reached and the great effort to liberate man from the terrors and sufferings of his condition within nature will have resulted in subjecting him to a new form of control through a managerial, technological form of rationality that is essentially empty of any sense of moral personality, either in its bearers or in its clients.

If this analysis of the hazards to which a certain kind of utilitarian ethic is exposed is at all persuasive, then its implications for the idea of progress outlines above should be readily apparent. The idea of progress is in fact simply a more primitive version of the same general conception of the maximization of well-being as the organizing principle of human life, both individual and social. It is more primitive in that it no longer troubles itself about the kind of difficulty that the utilitarians still recognized and attempted to deal with, most notably the problem of justice. For such concerns as these, it simply substitutes a massive assurance to the effect that the effective deployment of an ever expanding capability to control and redirect the processes of both nature and society will inevitably generate such a plenitude of the conditions of well-being that everyone can expect to find satisfaction in a world so enriched. The imperatives governing the production of such expanding wealth and of the knowledge that makes it possible will accordingly take precedence over all other social concerns; and the assumption that all other important social virtues will accrue, in whatever measure it is reasonable to expect their realization at all, to a society so organized will take on the status of an ideological postulate. In these circumstances it can be expected that the distinction between the procedures that are appropriate to the sphere of production and those that have traditionally been thought appropriate to the sphere of human relationships will undergo a steady process of erosion. The idea of progress thus would operate as a kind of charter for the institutions that are primarily responsible for the production of useful knowledge and of wealth and as an advance justification for not subjecting them to any form of responsibility that would involve the application to their activities of any ethical standard or any conception of collective interest more demanding than the general principle of the maximization of well-being. As a recent statement by a distinguished social scientist makes clear, what is required of the general population by the idea of progress is "belief"—"belief in the value of economic growth and prosperity; confidence in the powers of reason, particularly as manifested in the practical arts and sciences; acceptance of material advancement as one of the signs of intellectual and moral advancement."[4] Clearly, in this "belief" the criteria that would be characteristic of a critical and moral consciousness do not seem to find any natural place.

What I have been describing is a model of society in which a great many useful objects are produced and widely distributed and in which as the result of the steady accumulation of knowledge it becomes possible to eliminate many of the most obvious sources of human suffering. It is also a society in which there is at best a weak sense of the distinctive features of moral personality. It needs to be pointed out once again that such a society is not necessarily worse in an ethical sense than a society that reverses this order of priority. Such a society may in fact seem to its members to have a decidedly benign aspect partly because it may still incorporate forms of social order informed by a stronger conception of the social bond and partly because it may be so prosperous as to soften the edges of the various forms of competition and conflict that arise within it. Certainly this has been true in the United States, and even in a period like the present in which critical doubts about these assumptions suggest themselves ever more insistently, there is still a widespread feeling that dissent from them is attributable for the most part either to adherence to some rival and probably "undemocratic" ideology or simply to a chronic incapacity for satisfaction in any achievable set of real-world conditions. In light of these predispositions it is all the more important to see the negative possibilities associated with this peculiar combination of a strong commitment to the production of "goods" (in both senses of that term) with a weak sense of the person. In that connection one of the few analyses of which one can avail oneself is that proposed by Michael Polanyi in his 1960 Eddington lecture, "Beyond Nihilism." The central concept he is concerned to develop there is that of the "moral inversion" which he believes to have been a dominant tendency within the Western world during the last century. Moral inversion is a kind of excess of moral zeal generated by the secularization of the Christian aspiration for a better world; but the more interesting aspect of this phenomenon is its association with "skeptical rationalism" and a naturalistic world view. Polanyi's argument is that as a result of these rationalistic and naturalistic prepossessions, it became impossible for the extraordinarily strong moral impulse that was undertaking to

4. Robert Nisbet, "Nuclear Power: Victim of an Intellectual Lynching," *Los Angeles Times*, July 7, 1979, Section 6, p. 1.

reconstruct the whole human and social world to recognize itself *as* the moral impulse it really was, with all the implications that fact carries for the way in which such ends would have to be pursued. Because such a mode of self-identification was ruled out by the naturalistic world view to which these reformers and revolutionaries of personal and political life subscribed, the constraints that are inherent in a moral approach to social questions dropped away, and the only real alternative proved to be a theory that sanctioned unrestricted violence as the only realistic means of achieving power and holding it and that offered a deterministic or a voluntaristic but in any case a completely nonethical account of the motives inspiring this effort to change the world. The result, according to Polanyi, was moral inversion in the sense of "a condition in which high moral purposes operate only as the hidden force of an openly declared inhumanity."[5]

I am not as interested in the judgment Polanyi offers of the tendency toward violence and totalitarian rule that he believes to be inherent in moral inversion as I am in the more general proposition that underlies it. That is the claim that it is possible to pursue goals that are in some valid sense "good" and therefore worthy of being pursued and yet to do so without being able to represent to oneself the distinctively moral character of this effort. If I understand his argument correctly, Polanyi is also arguing that when this unusual combination of mental states prevails—as he claims it has in the past hundred years as a result of the superseding of Christianity (the source of this moral impetus) by rationalistic naturalism (the source of the incapacity to form a concept of moral personality and distinctively moral motivation)—it will prove unstable because the second of these will have a denaturing effect upon the first. The specific character of that effect will presumably vary a good deal, but in one way or another it can be assumed that it will tend to make the human beings that are involved in such processes of change the *objects* rather than the *subjects* of the effort to reach the goals in question. This is so because as a result of the occlusion of moral personality as such, they will have been conceptualized in a way that does not assign primary importance to their capacity for participation in, and fidelity to, reciprocal understandings that define the goals and the limits of permissible social action. To the degree that these capacities are disregarded or treated as being relatively insignificant by comparison with other, more potent determinants of behavior, other more "behavioristic" methods of social control will have to be utilized. But once one of these fundamentally nonethical ways of envisaging one's fellow human beings has established itself, the latter cannot in any very meaningful sense be partners in the effort to bring into being a better world, and this fact in turn entails a serious danger that the substitutes for partnership based on true reciprocity will be of such a

5. Reprinted in M. Grene, ed., *Knowing and Being: Essays by Michael Polanyi* (Chicago: University of Chicago Press, 1969), p. 16.

character as to push us in the direction of the terrible perversions of high moral purpose by which our century has been disfigured. Whether the horrors of totalitarianism are as directly chargeable to "moral inversion" as Polanyi claims is a matter on which I hesitate to offer a judgment. It does seem clear, however, that any society in which this peculiar combination of aggressive moral idealism and an incapacity to think in distinctively moral terms has established itself will not be in a good position to protect itself against these evils, whatever their origin may be.

In this connection it seems appropriate to take note of a recent book—*On Human Nature* by Edward O. Wilson—in which both the component elements of moral inversion as I have characterized them above are clearly present but in an apparently benign form that may well make any suggestion of dangerous moral tendencies inherent in them seem quite implausible.[6] This book also has an added interest stemming from the fact that its perspective is that of evolutionary theory—the ultimate theory of progress—which he believes to be just as valid for the study of human societies as it is for the insect societies, to which he devoted much of his earlier work. Scientific naturalism is thus the *only* valid way of looking at human behavior and the life of human societies; and Professor Wilson's most biting contempt is reserved for those moral philosophers who appear to think that there is some independent set of moral concepts by means of which valid conclusions can be reached about such matters as the requirements of justice. These presumptuous persons are described as having derived their intuitions of the right and the good from their hypothalamus which they apparently consult in a covert manner while representing whatever that organ intimates to them as the expression of a universal reason. Moral reasoning as such is clearly viewed by Wilson as being hopelessly vitiated by its failure to bring its claims into the mandatory scientific form in which they would become testable propositions about, for example, the place of justice in the evolutionary economy of human societies. The study of moral phenomena is thus quite emphatically to be cast in the same third-personal mode as obtains in the study of other natural phenomena; and this means more specifically that the one admissible sense that can be given to the evolutionary notion of progress is one that turns on having one's genes represented in succeeding generations. Moreover, since human culture, including its ethical component, is much more extensively controlled by genetic factors than social scientists are willing to concede and since morality is taken to be mainly a matter of dispositions to altruistic behavior toward other members of one's social group, the scientific study of ethics takes on the character of an inquiry into the evolutionary role of

6. E.O. Wilson, *On Human Nature* (Cambridge, Mass.: Harvard University Press, 1978). A review of this book by Stuart Hampshire (*New York Review of Books*, 25 [1978]: 64) makes many of the same criticisms that I do.

altruistic behavior and it postulates the existence of an altruistic gene that controls such behavior. Wilson further lays it down that "the species lacks any goal external to its own biological nature" and that "human behavior . . . is the circuitous technique by which human genetic material has been and will be kept intact"; and from these propositions he infers that "morality has no . . . demonstrable function" other than just this pursuit of genetic advantage.[7]

What strikes one as most disconcertingly simplistic in Wilson's naturalistic treatment of moral phenomena is his complete lack of attention to the way in which the dispositions said to be implanted by the altruistic gene actually work. One may well agree with him that the fact that human beings are in some measure capable of regulating their conduct by reference to moral considerations has neurophysiological and thus genetic preconditions; but what these preconditions make possible is not simply some instinctual willingness to sacrifice oneself or one's interest, if need arises, in someone else's behalf. (Nor, for that matter, is it, as Wilson's account of "soft-core altruism" has it, simply selfishness modified by strategic considerations that motivate concessions to others.) Instead, it centrally involves a discursive and rational component, in which the principle of intersubjective equivalence and reciprocity are centrally important elements; and if it is fair to call attention, as Wilson does, to the way human beings constantly violate the obligations imposed by this kind of reciprocity, it is no less in order to show how constantly we appeal to the very principles we may at other times violate. The network of duties and rights generated within specific sets of circumstances by this principle of equivalence is not simply the expression of some instinct that is unable to interrogate itself as to its own guiding tendency. However rigid it may be in its first manifestations and however bound to the scope that self-interest is willing to allow it, the moral point of view is not a blind, implanted inclination but an instrument of justification and of criticism; and as such it may fairly be said to enjoy a significant measure of independence from whatever biological basis is assigned to it although not in the sense—apparently the only one recognized by Wilson—that would make it the spokesman for some transcendent and absolute domain of moral truth. What it in fact does is to construe the world in which human beings encounter one another as a practical field governed by rules of equivalence and reciprocity that apply to the positions we occupy in relation to one another; and progress toward a civilized state is precisely the growing identification of the interests and the feelings of the self with the requirements of that nascent intersubjective order of volition among human beings. Altruism as a blind willingness to sacrifice oneself is, no doubt, a reality in human life just as the calculating selfishness that Wilson calls "soft altruism" is, but any analysis of the moral life that treats it as a mixture of these

7. Wilson, *On Human Nature*, p. 167.

two components misses altogether the way the moral life transmutes the interests of the self by constituting at the level of reflective understanding a domain of compatibility and of cooperation in terms of which those interests can redefine themselves.

The vital question that arises for any evolutionary approach to ethics and thus for Wilson's theory as well is whether once such a capability for moral understanding, on however limited a scale, has been brought into being (thanks perhaps to the "altruistic gene") the prospects for the kind of continuing advance that would satisfy a moral criterion have to be regarded as being dependent upon our degree of success in governing our relations with one another in accord with the requirements of this new moral level we have reached or whether such progress must be viewed as being still dependent upon genetic changes that proceed in full independence of cultural processes. This is an especially vital question in the context of a discussion of moral inversion. It seems clear that if the kind of scientific naturalism that presides over evolutionary theory up to the point at which the process of evolutionary change issues in the emergence of the kind of incipient moral understanding I have been describing were to treat the latter as "epiphenomenal" and thus extraneous to the executive order of evolutionary change, it would be almost irresistibly tempting to try to use our growing knowledge of genetic processes to intervene in those processes so as to bring about the kinds of change that it does not expect to be achieved through what it calls cultural processes. In that case, human beings might well find themselves the objects of forms of intervention and control that would altogether bypass their status as codeterminers of what may legitimately be done to them; and it is quite possible that the denial of freedom such measures would entail would make the relatively primitive political terrorism of the early twentieth century pale by comparison. Nor does it seem at all likely that in such circumstances the scientific elite responsible for such forms of intervention would feel at all constrained by any "cultural" principles for the epistemic standing of which they have such contempt. On all of these matters and particularly with respect to genetic engineering, Wilson remains quite vague and appears to want to have things both ways by arguing that through an acceptance of a true scientific view—presumably that of morality as the preservation of genetic material—we will be put in a position to choose a new set of cultural, that is, moral, values that will replace the old ones.

But to the degree that these new cultural values—some of which by the way seem to have been quite directly borrowed from the old condemned codes—involve real constraints on what can permissibly be done by one human being to another and do not function simply as a charter justifying in advance everything that a scientific elite undertakes in the way of genetic engineering, how can we be sure that a cast of mind defined by its rejection of any distinctive status for the normative that does not translate into some sort of biological fact will understand or respect those constraints? Accustomed as it is to operating outside such antiquated frameworks of pseudo-knowledge, will the scientific mind really understand that "universal human rights," if seriously acknowledged, set multiple obstacles in the way of what it may attempt in reconstructing the human species, and, if it does, will it be prepared to work within constraints of a type so different from those that its sense of reality is prepared to recognize? There is nothing in Wilson's book that offers any ground for reassurance on these matters, and it therefore seems fair to conclude that the dangers of moral inversion are indeed present in the program of objective cultural values which it so enthusiastically proposes.

III

Earlier, I suggested that the idea of progress is in fact an ideology that serves as a justificatory charter for the institutions that are the principal bearers of the scientific/technological revolution. Now I would like to examine the impact of the priorities implicit in that ideology upon certain institutions and interests within our society. The institutions I have in mind are in the first instance the cultural and educational institutions that have traditionally been thought to require for purposes of defining their own function a substantially stronger conception of the ethical basis of society than the one typically associated with the idea of progress.

The great hope entertained by the philosophers and moralists who expected a general improvement of the human condition from the advance and dissemination of knowledge was that a movement toward a mode of understanding of natural phenomena by reference to universal laws and principles would quite naturally be associated with a similar movement transcending the particularism of human loyalties and the blindness and indifference to the fate of other human beings that is the fruit of such particularism. The light of reason would, in other words, dispel the ignorance and prejudice that have for so long stood in the way of an acknowledgment of the solidarity of the human community. In light of the considerations that have been reviewed in this essay, it seems very doubtful whether these expectations were ever well founded.

If it is assumed that in the moral sphere the work of reason is primarily negative in the sense that its function there is to undermine the claims of dogmatic religion and metaphysics that covertly serve the interest of an established and unjust social order, there is a real danger that the magnitude of the task of reconceptualizing moral reason in positive terms, once the forces of obscurantism have been put to flight, will be seriously underestimated. More specifically, since the idea of progress did not acknowledge on any equal basis the possibility of a negative as well as a positive value attaching to changes brought about through the agency of science, there was clearly a danger that the new "enlightened" institutions that were to be the vehicles of these changes would be in their own way just as particularistic and just as problematically related to the general interest as were the institutions of the old prescientific world whose selfishness and stupidity were so severely censured by the party of progress. One of the characteristic features of most institutions, both old and new, is their capacity for sealing up their members within a justificatory rationale, which serves both as their medium of communication with one another and as a shield against such rude inquiries about what they are doing as may reach them from the outside world.

That in itself is nothing new in human history, although now we are much less likely to claim supernatural forms of legitimation for the missions of such institutions as a defense against challenges from without. But this change has not noticeably diminished the capacity of such institutions to exclude from their own internal domains of discourse anything that does not fit their presiding rationales or to make untenable the position of any member who fails to adjust his actions to that code or who appeals to considerations that lie outside it. Specifically, the fact that the functions of such institutions are "rational" in the sense of being based on scientific understanding of the relevant contexts of action does not appear to immunize them against the tendency I am describing. Indeed, it may have the effect of intensifying the conviction of being in the right on the part of those who work within such institutions and thus of lessening the chances of their being able to respond otherwise than in a *pro domo* manner to external criticism. It is not too much to say that such institutions may in fact come to regard themselves as the sole repositories of rationality and the world, insofar as it has not been brought under their control, as a state of nature in which the only maxim by which their actions can be guided is that of self-preservation. In this way they may come to reproduce the predatory characteristics of the institutions of unenlightened ages and fail, in spite of all the massive and often beneficial changes they bring about on the human scene, to modify significantly the ethical relationships in which they stand to one another and to the people they are said to serve.

Perhaps the most concise way of expressing the import of the idea of progress as it bears upon the activities of the kinds of institutions I have in mind is to say that it authorizes them to abstract from, or as one might put it, to "bracket" ethical considerations as such in the course of their operations and to do so on the strength of a guarantee of the long-run beneficence of the work that they perform and in fact feel they can perform only in this special kind of abstraction from the ethical. A great deal of attention has been devoted to the way in which this ideologically authorized "bracketing" of the ethical worked itself out in the case of the private enterprises in the economic field upon which so many of the hopes for a new enlightened conduct of the business of society were originally founded. On the whole it seems fair to say that these hopes have been disappointed and that there is now little willingness to believe that it is tolerable to allow the economic life of a society to be governed by corporate entities that are required to pay only minimal attention to any social interest more inclusive than that of their stockholders. But these are by no means the only institutional vehicles for the kinds of changes that come under the rubric of "progress." Especially in a time when industrial and economic development depends ever more directly upon the production of new, technologically exploitable scientific knowledge, it is the institutions that are responsible for that production of knowledge that have become the bastions of the idea of progress in the contemporary world. These are, of course, in the first instances the universities, but in an even more direct way the scientific disciplines themselves within which the work of original scientific inquiry is carried on. It will accordingly be useful to devote some attention to the espousal of the idea of progress on the part of these disciplines and especially to its wider implications for the interpretation of progress in society as a whole.

It seems clear that it is precisely in the domain of knowledge and its several component areas that the idea of progress has its most unchallengeable application. Whatever complexities may be introduced into our understanding of the history of science by a more sophisticated awareness of conceptual discontinuities that render problematic straightforward comparisons of, say, Greek with modern physics, they do not seem sufficient to shake the almost universally shared conviction that it is possible to discern a linear growth of scientific knowledge and thus a movement from a less advanced to a more advanced state about which no skeptical doubts can arise. It is therefore not surprising that when representatives of these disciplines are invited to assess the present status of the idea of progress from the standpoint of their disciplines, their response is overwhelmingly positive. They are generally confident that their disciplines will continue to achieve notable successes in their understanding of the phenomena with which they concern themselves; and they view doubts about progress as the expression of an antiscientific and obscurantist mentality. It is extremely difficult on such occasions to get a hearing for the view that the idea of progress is precisely an *idea* and that as such it may have logical features that are not only objectionable in themselves but also susceptible of being challenged without questioning the reality and magnitude of the scientific achievement. And yet the view that the idea of progress is a kind of ideological carapace for science is by no means antiscientific in inspiration. It could in fact serve to clarify in a helpful way many of the vexing issues that grow out of the assumed implication of science itself in a configuration of our intellectual world that serves quite different purposes from those of disinterested inquiry.

When those who identify themselves with the perspective upon the world of a special discipline of inquiry turn outward and attempt to assess the prospects for progress in some wider sense that would embrace the life of society as a whole, one senses that they have some difficulty in moving beyond that disciplinary perspective. They tend in fact, more often than not, to project the apparatus of their discipline rather indiscriminately upon the social world as a whole and even to talk in ways that incongruously assimilate the substantive life and concerns of human society to the scientist's own distinctively epistemic preoccupations. When this happens, we hear of the "poor experiments" that history is systematically conducting and of how poorly ordered social phenomena are—as though these were not matters that are entirely relative to our epistemic expectations which may well be based on other and perhaps quite irrelevant paradigms. At other times, the momentum of disciplinary achievement is so strong that it overcomes any sense of such deficiencies in the real world; and a bright prospect of progress under the guiding auspices of the discipline in question is opened up to the denizens of that world, provided only they do not succumb to doubts about the idea of progress.

In one way or another, however, the point seems to be elided that a society is not a discipline or even in any primary sense a field of deployment for a discipline, and that the standards that are used to assess progress in a discipline are not the appropriate ones when it is progress in a society as a whole that is in question. When the latter sort of question does have to be confronted in its own right, and the inadequacy of disciplinary frameworks to that task has to be conceded, the most common reaction on the part of those who are accustomed to work within such a framework is skepticism. Since it is clear that the only mode of thought that would be adequate to this new task must be ethical in nature, this is ethical skepticism—skepticism with respect to any possibility that ethics as an independent province of thought can exhibit a principle of conceptual integrity that is strong enough to compel assent to its conclusions. I would not want to claim that ethical skepticism does not deserve to be taken seriously. In fact it seems undeniable to me that any form of philosophical thought that does not bear in one way or another the mark of its encounter with such radical doubt is likely to be irrelevant to our intellectual situation. Too often, however, there is something facile and even complacent about current skepticism as though it were felt to be, after all, not such a very uncomfortable resting-place for thought, or at any rate not for those whose priorities of inquiry are such as to make them rather uninterested in the effort that a serious alternative to skepticism would entail. It may also be worth pointing out that the nihilistic implications of such skepticism are typically evaded by an incongruous association of ethical skepticism with the principle of liberalism. From the fact that all ethical postulations are equally gratuitous, it is thought to follow that all of them are to be treated, to the degree possible, with toleration. By means of this glaringly invalid inference, a completely nonethical point of view is made to appear as though it generated a set of ethical implications which in a liberal society we all find congenial.

In the aftermath of the unhappy events in our recent national life, there has been a reaction in some quarters against such attitudes as the ones I have been describing and a corresponding interest in examining and strengthening the ethical codes of various institutions and professions and in changing the character of professional education in such a way as to include within it a study of the ethical issues that practitioners confront. These efforts are welcome, and one can only hope that they will at the very least be successful in changing the predominantly negative attitude toward ethical issues that has for so long been the rule in most professional schools. At the same time, it would not do to underestimate the indifference and opposition such a movement of ethical "consciousness-raising" is likely to encounter. The ways of thought I have been describing here are very deeply entrenched in our professions as elsewhere, and their collective investment in the assumptions that are now being questioned is too great to permit any easy process of accommodation to a new set of requirements.

There is, in addition, another source of potential difficulty in the fact that the very institutions that would have to assume the principal responsibility for the new kind of preparation for professional work—institutions of higher education—are by no means free from the influence of the very attitudes which have helped to bring about the situation which ethical education is now supposed to correct. Indeed, one is tempted to claim that, among the institutions in our society, none has been more intimately associated with the belief in progress than have educational institutions. In fulfillment of the role assigned to them within a broad social conception of progress, they have vastly expanded their activities and their clienteles in the course of the last century; and it has been in these schools and universities that young people have acquired both the general literacy and the specialized forms of competence that are necessary in a progressive modern society. One would expect, therefore, that in institutions dedicated to this purpose, a society would have a unique opportunity to address the issues of social morality and to impart to new generations some shared conception of the human character and aspirations of the society they are to serve. There is no doubt that many schools and colleges have in fact interpreted their broader responsibilities in some such manner as this; and in certain of their more exalted statements of educational philosophy the claim has even been advanced that in their own ways of conducting their internal affairs educational institutions should prefigure the form of the good society that is gradually to be realized in the world at large. But such declarations as these will remain quite meaningless unless the institutions that make them give as much attention to general education as to specialized vocational or professional education and unless they conceive their educational priorities in humanistic terms that set as high a value on the preparation of the citizen and the human being as on that of the doctor or the mechanic. Unfortunately, the priorities of our institutions of higher education have *not* been so construed, and one suspects that the high-sounding principles to which they subscribe have themselves taken on an ideological quality and may in fact be functioning as a justificatory interpretation of the way these institutions actually operate in the society they serve rather than as a critical instrument for assessing their performance.

It is a matter of great importance, if we are to move toward an explicitly and independently ethical alternative to the idea of progress as we have known it, to assess the degree of success of our educational institutions in forming the kind of consciousness that is at once ethical in the sense of acknowledging a principle of obligation to one's fellow human beings; critical in the sense of being disposed to make appraisals of ethical validity an element in one's work in the world; and humane in the sense of an intelligent familiarity with, and enjoyment of, the variety of human goods and virtues. If we were to attempt such an assessment now after two centuries or so of national life under the auspices approximating to those of the idea of progress as I have described it, I do not think we would find much cause for self-congratulation. The notion of a school or university as a place in which a critical understanding of the human and social context of professional scientific and economic activity is formed either tends to assume a narrowly political form or it is treated with contempt by reason of the alleged "softness" of the kind of knowledge it represents. These polar attitudes tend, moreover, to beget and to reinforce one another; and between them they effectively squeeze out efforts to think in terms of a wider conception of reason—practical, ethical, and social—than either one is typically prepared to countenance. Although it seemed possible two or three decades ago that we might, here in the United States, develop a form of general or humanistic education suited to the circumstances of a democratic society, it now seems all too clear that that effort which was made principally in the colleges and universities has failed and that by reason of the even more serious failures of the schools we are now confronted by a major crisis of sheer literacy in which the fundamental human skills of expression in and comprehension of a common language are not being successfully transmitted. If we fail to perceive this crisis (and there is no evidence that it is being perceived for what it is and for what it implies for the higher forms of humane literacy, not to speak of the ideal of shared participation in a genuinely democratic society), I suspect that the idea of progress, in the form in which we have typically embraced it, must bear at least part of the blame. Supervening as it does on the old human predispositions to blindness and indifference to any larger life than one's own, it recognizes these only as a residue of ignorance that will disappear with the spread of knowledge and it thus gives us another reason which we really do not need for not being interested in ourselves as moral beings or in those modes of experience and understanding that do not readily accommodate themselves to the paradigms of knowledge from which we have become accustomed to expect the benefits with which progress is identified. For that reason, I suggest, the *idea* of progress has been an obstacle in the way of a more deeply conceived and adequate view of human betterment. If that idea is, indeed, now in the process of being transformed, one can only hope that its successor will understand its inadequacies and will build intelligently upon that understanding.

CONTRIBUTORS

MOSES ABRAMOVITZ, Professor of Economics, emeritus, Stanford University, received his Ph.D. at Columbia University in 1939. He served as president of the American Economic Association in 1979-80 and has been an advisor to the secretary-general of the Organization for Economic Development and Cooperation and a visiting fellow at All Souls College. He is managing editor of the *Journal of Economic Literature* and the author of *Price Theory for a Changing Economy, Inventories and Business Cycles*, and (with Vera Eliasberg) *The Growth of Public Employment in Great Britain*.

GABRIEL A. ALMOND, Professor of Political Science, emeritus, Stanford University, received his Ph.D. at the University of Chicago in 1938. A former president of the American Political Science Association, he has taught at Princeton and Yale and is co-author or author of *The Politics of the Developing Areas, The Civic Culture, Comparative Politics, Political Development*, and *Crisis, Choice and Change*.

FRANCISCO J. AYALA, Professor of Genetics and Director of the Institute of Ecology, University of California, Davis, was born and educated in Madrid. He came to the United States in 1961 to study evolution and genetics with Theodosius Dobzhansky at Columbia, obtaining his Ph.D. in 1964. His scientific career has centered on the study of evolution. He is the editor of *Molecular Evolution* and co-author of *Evolution*, a statement of the current status of evolutionary theory, and *Modern Genetics*.

SAMUEL H. BARNES, Professor and Chairman of Political Science, University of Michigan, received his Ph.D. at Duke University in 1957. In that year he came to Michigan and has been a program director of the Institute for Social Research since 1969. He served as coordinator of the Project on Expectations and Political Action in Eight Advanced Industrialized Democracies. He is the author of *Party Democracy* and *Representation in Italy*, and co-author of *Political Action: Mass Participation in Five Western Democracies*.

DANIEL BELL received his Ph.D. at Columbia University. He has taught at the University of Chicago and Columbia, and currently is Henry Ford II Professor of Social Sciences at Harvard University. He is the author of, among other works, *The End of Ideology, The Radical Right, The Coming of Post-Industrial Society*, and *The Cultural Contradictions of Capitalism*.

HARVEY BROOKS, Benjamin Peirce Professor of Technology and Public Policy at Harvard, received his Ph.D. in physics at Harvard in 1940. He served as dean of the Harvard Division of Engineering and Applied Physics from 1957 to 1975, as president of the American Academy of Arts and Sciences from 1971 to 1976, and as a member of the president's Science Advisory Committee and the National Science Board. He is the author of *The Government of Science*.

HOLLIS B. CHENERY, Vice-President of the World Bank, received his Ph.D.

in economics at Harvard in 1950. He was a professor of economics at Stanford and Harvard and is the author of *Structural Change and Development Policy* and the co-author of *Redistribution with Growth*.

MARVIN CHODOROW, Professor of Applied Physics, emeritus, at Stanford, received his Ph.D. in physics at M.I.T. in 1939. He served as chairman of the Department of Applied Physics at Stanford from 1962 to 1969, and from 1959 to 1978 as director of the Edward L. Ginzton Laboratory. He is the co-author of *Fundamentals of Microwave Electronics* and many articles in the field of microwave theory and electronic and acoustic devices.

JOEL COLTON, Professor of History, Duke University, received his Ph.D. in history at Columbia in 1950. Formerly Director for Humanities at the Rockefeller Foundation, he is the author of *Compulsory Labor Arbitration in France, Léon Blum: Humanist in Politics*, and *Twentieth Century*, and co-author with R.R. Palmer of *A History of the Modern World*.

BERNARD D. DAVIS, Adele Lehman Professor of Bacterial Physiology at the Harvard Medical School, received his M.D. at Harvard in 1940. He is a member of the National Academy of Sciences and a former vice-president of the American Academy of Arts and Sciences, the editor of *Human Diversity: Its Causes and Social Significance*, co-author of *Microbiology*, and author of more than two hundred scientific papers.

JOHN T. EDSALL, Professor of Biochemistry, emeritus, at Harvard University, received his M.D. at Harvard in 1928. He has served as president of the American Society of Biological Chemists, and as chairman of the Committee on the History of Biochemistry and Molecular Biology, American Academy of Arts and Sciences. He is co-author of *Proteins, Amino-Acids, and Peptides*.

ROBERT C. ELLIOTT was until his death Professor of English Literature at the University of California, San Diego. He is the author of *The Power of Satire: Magic, Ritual, Art*; *The Shape of Utopia*; and the forthcoming *The Literary Persona*.

GERALD FEINBERG, Professor of Physics at Columbia University, received his Ph.D. there in 1957. He is the author of *The Prometheus Project, What Is the World Made Of?*, and *Life Beyond Earth*.

GERALD HOLTON, Mallinckrodt Professor of Physics and Professor of the History of Science at Harvard, received his Ph.D. at Harvard in 1948. He is author of *Introduction to Concepts and Theories in Physical Science, The Thematic Origins of Scientific Thought: Kepler to Einstein, The Scientific Imagination: Case Studies*, and other works. He was the Jefferson Lecturer for 1981 and is president-elect of the History of Science Society.

H. STUART HUGHES received his Ph.D. in history at Harvard. He has taught at Stanford and Harvard and is currently Professor of History at the University of California, San Diego. He is the author of *Consciousness and Society, The Obstructed Path*, and *The Sea Change*.

GEORG IGGERS, Distinguished Professor of History, State University of New York at Buffalo, received his Ph.D. at the University of Chicago in 1951. He is the author of *The Cult of Authority: The Political Philosophy of the Saint Simonians, The German Conception of History*, and *New Directions in European Historiography*.

NANNERL O. KEOHANE, President of Wellesley College, received her Ph.D. from Yale in 1967. A former member of the Stanford faculty and fellow of the Center for Advanced Study in the Behavioral Sciences, she is the author of *Philosophy and the State in France: The Renaissance to the Enlightenment*.

MURRAY KRIEGER, University Professor, University of California, and Director of the School of Criticism and Theory, received his Ph.D. in English at Ohio State University in 1952. He is the author of *The New Apologists for Poetry, The Tragic Vision, A Window to Criticism: Shakespeare's Sonnets and Modern Poetics, The Play and Place of Criticism, The Classic Vision, Theory of Criticism, Poetic Presence and Illusion,* and *Arts on the Level.*

STEVEN MARCUS, George Delacorte Professor in the Humanities at Columbia University, received his Ph.D. at Columbia in 1961. He is the author of *Dickens: From Pickwick to Dombey, The Other Victorians,* and *Engles, Manchester and the Working Class.*

MARTIN E. MARTY is the Fairfax M. Cone Distinguished Service Professor at the University of Chicago, where he earned his Ph.D. in 1956 and has taught the history of modern Christianity in the Divinity School since 1963. He is a member of the university's Committee on the History of Culture and an associate in the Department of History.

ALFRED G. MEYER, Professor of Political Science at the University of Michigan, received his Ph.D. at Harvard in 1950. He has taught at Harvard, the University of Washington, and Michigan State University and has written *Marxism: The Unity of Theory and Practice, Leninism,* and *The Soviet Political System.*

FREDERICK A. OLAFSON, Professor of Philosophy at the University of California, San Diego, received his Ph.D. at Harvard in 1951. He also served as Professor of Education and Philosophy at Harvard. He is the author of *Principles and Persons, Ethics and Twentieth-Century Thought,* and *The Dialectic of Action.*

ROY HARVEY PEARCE, Professor of American Literature at the University of California, San Diego, received his Ph.D. at the Johns Hopkins University in 1945. He served as a professor of English at Ohio State University and as a dean of Graduate Studies at the University of California, San Diego. He is the author of *The Continuity of American Poetry, The Savages of America: A Study of the Indian and the Idea of Civilization,* and *Historicism Once More: Problems and Occasions for the American Scholar,* and is a general editor of the Centenary Edition of the *Works* of Nathaniel Hawthorne.

GIANFRANCO POGGI, Professor of Sociology at the University of Edinburgh, received his Ph.D. at the University of California, Berkeley, in 1963. He is the author of *Catholic Action in Italy, Images of Society: Essays on the Sociological Theories of Tocqueville, Marx, and Durkheim,* and *The Development of the Modern State: A Sociological Introduction.*

G. BINGHAM POWELL, JR., Professor of Political Science at the University of Rochester, received his Ph.D. at Stanford University in 1968. He is the author of *Social Fragmentation and Political Hostility* and *Political Performance in Contemporary Democracies: Participation, Stability and Violence,* and the co-author of *Comparative Politics: System, Process, Policy.*

MARC J. ROBERTS, Professor of Political Economy, School of Public Health, Harvard University, received his Ph.D. at Harvard in 1969. He has served as consultant to the National Water Commission and the Environmental Protection Agency and as member of the Committee on Energy and the Environment of the National Academy of Sciences. He is editor and co-author of *Regulating the Product* and principal author of *The Choices of Power: Utilities Face the Environmental Challenge.*

NATHAN ROSENBERG, Professor of Economics and Director of the Public

Policy Program at Stanford University, received his Ph.D. from the University of Wisconsin in 1955. He has been editor of the *Journal of Economic History* and is the author of *Perspectives on Technology* and (with Walter Vincenti) *The Generation and Diffusion of Technological Knowledge: The Case of Britannia Bridge.*

AARON WILDAVSKY received his Ph.D. at Yale University in 1959, is Professor of Political Science at the University of California, Berkeley, and a former dean of the Graduate School of Public Policy. He is author or co-author of *The Politics of the Budgetary Process, Planning and Budgeting in Poor Countries, Budgeting: A Comparative Theory of Budgetary Processes,* and *Speaking Truth to Power.*

CRAWFORD YOUNG, Professor of Political Science, University of Wisconsin, received his Ph.D. at Harvard University in 1964. He has been an associate dean of the graduate school at Wisconsin and a dean of the faculty of social sciences, National University of Zaire. He is the author or co-author of *Politics in the Congo, Issues of Political Development,* and *The Politics of Cultural Pluralism.*

INDEX

adaptiveness, 34, 146, 336
aestheticism, 510, 511, 514
Afghanistan, 87, 89, 101, 104
Africa
  and colonialism, 88-89, 91-92
  and nationalism, 93
  need for acceleration of economic growth
    in, 330
  pessimism in, 100-101
  progress in, 87, 104
  role of, in history of world, 55
al-Qadafi, Wanie Muammar, 95-96
American Progressive Movement, 398
Amin, Idi, 99
Andes, 87
Angola, 101
Arendt, Hannah, 484
Aristotle
  and aestheticism, 510
  and evolution, 106
  and idea of progress, 70
  and man's capacity for contemplation, 522
  and "the realization of philosophy," 501
Arnold, Matthew
  and art as substitute for religion, 467-68
  and cultivation of individuality, 437
  and drama of contradiction, 428
Aron, Raymond, 61, 65, 84, 99
art
  fixed limits of, 476
  function of, 458-60
  future of, and Marxism, 477-78
  as highest wisdom, 444
  idea of progress in, 12, 449-69
  and instability of the term, 464, 466
  and nature, 34
  nonprogressive character of, 454-56
  and prefiguration of change in society,
    447-48
  progress in, 24, 428-29
    and ancients versus moderns, 450-58
    and craft, 461-62
    defined, 460
    Enlightenment idea of, 11
    and problems of technique and critical
      response, 461

  and progress in criticism, 462-63
  and the work of art, 466-69
  redemptive power of, 440
  as religion, 438, 467-68
  and utopia, 468-69, 474-81
Asia, 87, 88-89, 93
  East, 320
  South, 330
atoms, 164, 165-66
Augustine, Saint, 2, 42

Bacon, Francis
  and "civil" knowledge, 32
  and idea of progress, 29, 30, 84, 253
  and rationalism, 47
Baudelaire, 510-11
Benin, 101
biochemistry
  and genetics, 130, 140
  progress in, 138-44
  and unity of life, 139
biology
  acceleration of discoveries in, 137-38
  cost of progress in, 155-56
  decline of important advances in, 138
  ecological threats to future of, 157-59
  evolutionary, 130
    and eugenics movement, 151-53
    and formation of new species, 147-48
    key concepts in, 145-48
    mechanistic concepts in, 149-51
    progress in, 144-48
    teleological concepts in, 149-51
    teleonomic theory of, 150-51
  future of, 136
  great discoveries in, 137-38
  molecular, 130, 138-44
  progress in, 11, 135-60
    cost of, 138
    defined, 135
    fear of, 156, 182-201
    measurement of, 112-15
    as model for progress in other
      domains, 106
  and study of human behavior, 191
Bohr, Niels, 164, 178

Bolivia, 386
bourgeoisie, 43, 431-33
Brazil
    capital-intensive development strategy of,
        324
    economic growth and equity in, 323, 327
    and high-speed industrialization, 320
    income distribution in, 325 graph, 326,
        328-29 table
    optimism toward progress in, 412 table, 413
    overthrow of democratic government in, 385
    problem of debt in, 103
    and Western model of progress, 101
Brecht, Bertolt, 512
Bretonne, Restif de la, 476
Britain, optimism toward progress in, 414
Buddhism, 19, 85, 86, 508
Burke, Edmund, 50
Burkhardt, Jakob, 18, 56, 59
Burma, 103, 385
Bury, J. B.
    and definition of progress, 22
        in Third World, 85
    and idea of progress, 26, 84
    and idea of Providence, 25
    and history of idea of progress, 45
    and progress as ultimate stage of history, 6

capitalism, and the Protestant Ethic, 277
Caribbean, 87-88
Carlyle, Thomas
    as critic of rationalism, 433-35
    and drama of contradictions, 428
    and gospel of work, 435, 437
    and Nietzsche, 440-41
    and problems of economic growth, 275-76
Castro, Fidel, 75, 99
Catholicism, and idea of progress, 490-92
Chad, 105
change
    and amelioration, 97, 109
    causes of, 25, 26
    cultural, 504, 506
    defined, 107
    determination of, 202
    and "four stages" theory, 34
    historical, 2, 3
    interconnectedness of areas of, 5 diagram
    in moral temper, 506-507
    and progress, 3, 22
    in society, prefiguration of, in art and
        literature, 447-48
    technological effect of, 305-306
Chile, 385
China
    economic growth and equity in, 321, 323, 327
    and high-speed industrialization, 320
    and idea of socialist transformation, 102
    and imperialism, 87
    revolution in, 99
    role of, in world history, 55

Christianity
    and colonialism, 91
    and control of nature, 27, 182
    and doctrine of salvation as political
        theory, 81
    and idea of progress, 32, 70
    and Marxism, 498
    opposition of, to progress, 488
    and restraint, 508
    and revolution, 484
    classical beliefs, and progress, 26
Colombia, income distribution in, 328-29
    table
colonialism, 73, 85-92
communism
    and British and American model of progress,
        61
    and doubts about progress, 81
    and inequality, 67
    Lenin's definition of, 76
    and Marx, 78
    and progress, 13, 19
    and scientific management, 78
    in Third World, and failure to bring about
        rapid progress, 400
    and war, 67
    and welfare inequality, 388
Comte, Auguste
    and application of natural-science methods
        to social sciences, 133
    and elimination of conflict, 45
    and elite of scientists, 52
    as expositor of progress, 2, 3, 38
    and idea of progress, 44, 65
    and progressive approach to history, 18
    and science and industry, 53
Condillac, Étienne, 33
Condorcet, Marquis de
    and application of natural-science methods
        to social sciences, 133
    and arts of utopia, 474, 475
    and coining of idea of progress, 363
    and elimination of conflict, 45
    and equality of women, 36-37
    as expositor of progress, 2, 84, 471
    and history as march of reason, 59
    and idea of golden age, 23
    and idea of progress, 35-38, 43
    and individual understanding, 365
    and limits of the arts, 476
    and linkage among various spheres of
        progress, 11
    and optimism toward progress, 17, 45
    and perfectability of man, 376
    and progressive approach to history, 17
    and Sketch for a Historical Picture of the
        Progress of the Human Mind, 49
    and vision of betterment, 39
    and vision of the future, 53
conflict, 57, 59
Confucianism, 19, 85, 508

Congo-Brazzaville, 101
Copernicus, 204-205, 217
cosmology, 8
Costa Rica, 328-29 table, 385, 401
Crick, Francis, 141, 142
criminal rehabilitation, 5
Cuba
  economic growth and equity in, 321, 323, 327
  optimism toward progress in, 412 table,
    413, 414
  and socialist transformation, 102
culture
  changes in, identification of, 506
  defined, 504
  history of, 505
  modern, crisis of, 1
  universals of, 504-505
Curie, Marie and Pierre, 168

Darwin
  and adaptive variation, 146
  and conflict, 57
  disbelief in natural selection theory of, 144
  and evidence of fossil record, 148
  and evolutionary progress, 38
  and Marx, 73
  as philosopher of progress, 38
  and religious traditionalists, 191
defense
  and progress, 13
  proportion of federal budget for, 361, 388
democracy
  and civil freedom, 386
  contemporary doubts about, 389-99
  and economic development, 385, 387
  effect of the Depression on, 400
  effect of war on, 381
  impact of, on social welfare, 386-87, 389
  and income inequality patterns, 387-88
  incompatibility of, with social progress,
    398-99
  and inflation, 387-88, 398-99
  liberal
    attacks on, 375
    challenge of postwar Soviet communism
      to, 400
    and civil rights, 385-86
    doubts of Third World concerning, 401
    role of political parties in, 379
    and social progress, 375-402
    and suffrage, 377-78
  and Madison, 397
  and progress, 13, 381-83, 391-93
    empirical argument for, 383-89
    historical connection between, 376-80
    independence of, 393-95
    theoretical connection between, 380-83
    in Third World, 13
  and social complexity, 397
  and socioeconomic progress, 335
  status of minorities under, 392

threat of progress to, 395-98
threat of strikes to, 395, 396
and violence, 386, 392, 394-95
Descartes, René, 29, 31, 32, 47, 84
deserts, spread of, 157-58
de Tocqueville, Alexis
  and advance of equality, 58-59
  and characterization of American society,
    318
  and liberty and democracy, 392
  as skeptic of progress, 18
Diderot, Denis, 2, 11, 17, 33, 365
Dirac, Paul, 127, 174-75, 205
divine plan
  and historical change, 3
  and progress, 27, 32, 35, 40, 337
  see also Providence
DNA
  early research on, 140-41
  formation of structure of, 141
  as genetic material, 140-41
  measurement of, 115-16
  non-coding, 157
  recombinant
    concern over research in, 132-33, 156,
      184-86, 199
    consequences of, 125, 316
    public reaction to, 187-88
  replication experiments with, 149
  research on, 140-44
  role of
    in evolution, 146
    in transformation of pneumococcal types,
      155
Dobzhansky, Theodosius, 123, 145, 147
Dominican Republic, 412 table, 414
Dostoevsky, Fëdor, 512
Durkheim, Emile, 18, 57-58, 243-44, 517

Easterlin, Richard, 266-67, 405-406
ecology, 8, 154, 157-59
economic growth
  benefits of, 262-66
  Club of Rome model of, 312
  compulsions of, 274
  constraints on, 285-99
  costs of, 262-66
  and democracy, 385, 387
  and energy needs, 307-308
  and environmental concerns, 313-15
  and equality, 251
  and equity of income distribution, 289-90,
    321-32, 328-29 table
  and exhaustion of resources, 283-91
  and goods-intensive consumption, 271
  and habituation, 268-69
  opposition to, 261
  and pessimism, 310-13
  postwar, 282-83
  reappraisal of, 262-71

and redistribution, 322
  relation of, to social welfare, 327
  and rising price of space and time, 269-71
  role of government in, 289
  and satisfaction, 266-71, 412-13
  in Third World, 251, 331
  Western model of, 331
economic progress, 249-332
  concerns affecting, 313-18
  contemporary disillusionment with, 249
  costs of, 13
  and environmental concerns, 313-15
  and equity of distribution, 12, 321-32
  and limits of resources, 301-18
  mistrust of, 12
  and national product estimates, 257-58
  postwar emphasis and achievement in,
    259-62
  retreat from, 253-80
  and work, 272-73
economics
  laws of, 238
  methodological precepts of, 232
  and national product, 264-65
  and progress, 47
education
  ability to alter human behavior of, 234
  benefits of, 264
  and ethics, 541-44
  and inculcation of values, 419
  and pathway to success, 369
  and personal progress, 409-10
  and progress, 33, 40, 363
  as theme of international expositions, 5
  in Third World, 97, 103
educational institutions, and belief in
    progress, 543
Egypt, 95-96, 102, 412
Einstein, Albert, 129-30
  the Age of, 165-66
  and development of comprehensive
    Weltanschauung, 220
  and geometry of space, 177
  and kinetic-atomic research program, 207
  and nuclear phenomena, 222
  and opposition to quantum physics, 222
  and parsimony, 213
  and presuppositions, 211-14, 215
  and progress in physics, 178
  and suspension of disbelief, 210-11, 222
  and theory of relativity, 165, 166
  and theory of scientific development,
    207-209
  and totality of experience, 221-23
  and unification, 213, 217, 218
Eisenstein, Sergei, 480
elitism, and progress, 24
energy
  and evolutionary progress, 118
  need for, and economic growth, 307-308
  problem of, 297-99, 305
  saving of, 309-10

Engels, Friedrich
  and ambivalence toward historic
    phenomena, 68
  and criticism of Rousseau, 69-70
  and disappearance of government, 52
  as exponent of progress, 3, 67-74
  and history, 52
  and human cost of progress, 70
  and results of economic liberation, 57
Enlightenment
  Anglo-Scotch, and government, 364, 365
  and disenchantment, 530
  first stage of, 32-35
  French, and government, 364
  and idea of progress, 6, 21-40, 43-57
  idea of religion in, 521
  and interpretation of evolution, 365
  and man as progressive organism, 20
  and religion, 501-506
  zenith of idea of progress in, 35-38
environment
  concerns over, 313-15
  control over, 119, 421
  damage, to, 12, 263-64
  destructive burden of economic progress on,
    242
  pollution of, 250
    and changes in global climate, 291, 294-95
    and deterioration of natural ecosystems,
      291, 293-94
    and material progress, 291-95
    threat to health from, 291-93
  sacredness of, 13
enzymes, 140, 142, 143
Equador, 386
ethics
  and assessment of progress, 528-29
  defined, 528
  and education, 543
  evolutionary approach to, 538
  and rationality, 531-32
  scientific study of, 536-37
Ethiopia, 87, 89, 101
eugenic movement, 151-53
Europe
  as bearer of progress, 49, 53
  civilizing mission of, 44
  and history of the world, 55
  opposition to economic growth in, 262
  postwar economic growth in, 261
evolution
  Enlightenment interpretation of, 365
  and formation of new species, 147-48
  and fossil record, 147-48
  key concepts in, 145-48
  measurement of, 115-18
  as progress, 38, 73, 106-24, 364
  and religion, 130-31
  retrogressive, 112
  tempo of, 147-48
  theory of, 148-51
  unpredictability of, 149

555

Febvre, Lucien, 244
Ferguson, Adam
  and conjectural history, 47, 48
  and costs of progress, 472
  and *Essay on the History of Civil Society*, 34
  and idea of Providence in history, 26
  and progressive approach to history of, 17
  and reaction against mercantilism, 364-65
Fermi, Enrico, 170-71
food, and economic growth, 295-96
Foucault, Michel, 63, 465
Fourth World, 84-85
Franklin, Benjamin, 2
French Revolution, 51
Freud, Sigmund, 220, 472
Freudianism, as historical paradigm, 242-43

genes
  "altruistic," 537
  and heterozygosity, 147
  and natural selection, 146
  regulatory systems controlling, 143
  role of, in evolution, 144-45
  synthesis of, in vitro, 144
gene therapy, 188-90
genetic research, 156
genetics
  and biochemistry, 130, 140
  and cloning, 189-90
  human behavioral, 191, 199
  Mendelian, and eugenics movement, 151
  molecular, 157
  progress in, 182, 184-93
  and racial discrimination, 191-93
Germany, and philosophies of progress, 38
Germany, West
  and civil freedom, 386
  optimism in, 412 table, 414
Ghana, 104
Gibbon, Edward, 44, 46, 471
God
  abolishment of, 514-15
  and progress, 25-26, 30, 31, 35, 40, 483
Goethe, Johann, 71, 515
golden age
  concept of, 363
  destruction of, 31
  and the future, 470
  happiness of, 480-81
  lack of art in, 480-81
  movement of progress toward, 23
  regression from, 2
Goldsmith, Oliver, 275
government
  and alteration of behavior, 370
  and Anglo-Saxon Enlightenment, 364
  and complexity of society, 391
  disappearance of, 52
  and French Enlightenment, 364
  and knowledge, 341
  measurement of success of, 374
  as obstacle to progress in public policy, 362

and progress, 13, 369-73
  and public welfare, 334
  role of, in economic growth, 289
  and social welfare programs, 362
governmental bureaucracies, 9-10
Goya, Francisco de, 510
Greece, 385, 400-401
Greeks, ancient, 26, 28
Guatemala, 87
Guinea, 401

Haiti, 104
happiness
  correlation of, with income, 405-407
  and level of aspiration, 408
  and the millennium, 39
  national differences in, 409
  and progress, 32, 98
  and rationalism, 434
health
  mental, and religion, 14
  public, government involvement in, 315-16
  as theme of international expositions, 5
  threats to, from technological progress, 8
Hegel, Georg
  and destructive aspects of man, 58
  as expositor of progress, 2, 38
  and history as march of reason, 59
  and idea of progress, 3, 44
  and idea of Providence in history, 26
  and leadership of Europe, 53
  progressive approach to history of, 18
  and "the realization of philosophy," 501-502
  and role of India and China in history, 55
  on rule, 348
  and theory of history, 51-52
  and war, 53
Helmholtz, Hermann, 164
Helvétius, 33
Herder, Johann Gottfried von, 50-51, 63-64
Hinduism, 19, 85
historiography
  basic paradigms of, 241-44
  contemporary, 240-48
  cumulative approach of, 44
  developmental approach of, 44
  and idea of progress, 41-66
  and psychohistory, 246
  and quantification, 246
  research approaches to, 246
  scientific, 54, 133
  twentieth-century, 57-66
historism, 49-51, 54-55
history
  approaches to, 17-18
  as cause of change, 25, 26
  Christian concept of, 67
  and conflict, 57
  as development of human powers, 68
  divine plan of, 31
  earlier view of, 3
  end of, 501-502

and four stages of development, 42
as history of scientification, 59
as march of reason, 59
Marxian concept of, 68
model of progress in, 11
as obstacle, 76
philosophies of
  and *Annales* circle, 63, 64
  anthropocentric, 63
  and Augustine, 2
  Christian, 2
  conjectural, 47-48
  Copernican, 63
  cyclical, 6, 18, 28, 31
  and decline, 31
  and diversities of cultures, 63-64
  German, 38
  and historical necessity, 52
  and historism, 49-51, 54-55
  and ideology of progress, 6-7
  Marxist, 71
  narrative developmental, 47
  and Nietzsche, 6
  and one history, 44
  and patternlessness of history, 31
  and Plato, 2
  and Providence, 6
  questions concerned with, 2
  retrogressive, 28
  and Spengler, 6
  spiral, 71
  synchronic, 64
  and Toynbee, 6
  and unity of man, 47
and progress, 26, 41, 136-37
progressive approach to, 17-18
as retrospective anthropology, 65, 244
stages of, 26, 33-34
and theme of cumulative development, 44
unity of, 63-64
Whig interpretation of, 136
as the work of men, 44
world, 55, 65
Ho Chi Minh, 75, 99
Hume, David, 44, 48, 451-52, 471
Huxley, Aldous, 477
Huxley, Julian, 62, 114-15, 122, 145, 147
Huxley, Sir Andrew, 155
Huxley, Thomas, 117

imperialism, 74, 87, 98
India
  income distribution in, 321-22, 328-29 table
  optimism toward progress in, 412, 414
  progress and religion in, 484
  role of, in world history, 55
  suspension of democratic freedoms in, 385
individualism, 506-509
industrialization, 272-74
inequality
  and communism, 67

and economic progress, 12
and progress, 25, 36-37
of women, and progress, 36-37
inflation, 367-68
Iran
  and crisis of the state, 104
  and imperialism, 87
  integralist Islam in, 96-97
  religion and revolution in, 482
  and Western model of progress, 101
Ireland, 402, 482
Islam
  idea of progress in, 85
  integralist, 95-96
  and progress, 19, 87
Israel, 101, 321, 327, 412
Ivory Coast, 101

Japan
  and adaptive technology, 306
  and "catching up" model of economic
    growth, 261, 320, 321, 387
  and defensive modernization, 90
  and imperialism, 87
  opposition to economic growth in, 262
  optimism toward progress in, 412 table, 414
  religion and progress in, 484
John XXIII, Pope, 494
Johnson, Samuel, 452-54
Judaism
  and control of nature, 27, 182
  and idea of progress, 488-90
  and restraint, 508

Kant, Immanuel
  as believer in progress, 471-72
  and destructive aspects of man, 58
  and dialectic of enlightenment, 531
  as expositor of progress, 2, 342
  and "finality of form," 468
  and necessity of evil for progress, 481
  as skeptic of progress, 17, 33
Kelvin, Lord, 164, 174-75
Khomeini, Ayatollah, 95-96
Kierkegaard, Sören, 503, 511, 515
King, Martin Luther, 494
knowledge
  as agent of progress, 3
  concern over consequences of, 199
  and control, 73
  control of nature through, 2, 17
  danger of, to social justice, 191-93
  and government, 341
  and historical change, 3
  and improvement of institutions, 2
  and increase of material welfare, 2
  increase in, and progress, 26
  and justice, 192
  and loss of paradise, 27
  and material welfare, 6

and moral progress, 10, 11, 14, 17, 26, 28, 35, 39, 191, 539
objective, possibility of, 196-99
and organizations, 6, 9
political consequences of, 11, 17
problematics of, 25
and progress, 2, 20, 36-37
and reform of legislation, 2
and religion, 40
restriction of scientific, 190-91
and rule, 345-46
spread of, and correlation with other changes, 5 diagram
Korea
and high-speed industrialization, 320
income distribution in, 325 graph, 327, 328-29 table
labor-intensive development strategy of, 324
rapid economic growth of, 320-21

Latin America, 87, 88, 102, 330
Lebanon, 386
Lenin, Nikolai, 76, 170
Leninism, 19, 101
Lévi-Strauss, Claude
and enslavement of men as condition of progress, 471
and equal validity of cultures, 18
and Marxism and psychoanalysis, 248
and notion of historical sequence, 465
and role of scientific reason, 62-63
and writing as downfall of man, 481
Libya, 95-96
literature, 438, 447-48
Lorentz, Konrad, 207, 470
Lucretius, 28, 42, 43, 470
Lukács, Georg, 512-14

Macaulay, Thomas Babington, 55-56, 86
Mach, Ernst, 164, 179, 219, 220
Madison, James, 373, 377, 397
magic, 7-8
Malaysia, 101
Malraux, André, 510
Mao Tse-Tung, 75, 84, 95, 516
Marcuse, Herbert, 62, 242, 276, 479-80
Maritain, Jacques, 491
Marx, Karl
and abolishment of God, 514
ambivalence of, toward historic phenomena, 68
and application of natural-science methods to social sciences, 133
and communism, 78
and criticism of Rousseau, 69-70
and Darwin, 73
and disappearance of government, 52
and elimination of conflict, 45
and the end of prehistory of human society, 43
and history, 18, 44-45, 52

and human cost of progress, 70
and idea of progress, 2, 3, 8, 19, 44, 65, 67-74, 498
and laws of social development, 60
and problems of economic growth, 275
and the realization of philosophy, 501-502
and relationship of man to nature, 62
and results of economic liberation, 57
and role of science and industry, 53
Marxism
and Christianity, 498
contemporary Western, 79-82
as cult, 516
and future of arts, 477-78
as historical paradigm, 242-43
and history as spiral, 71
as movement of Reason, 516
as political religion, 511-12
and sacredness of the Party, 516
suppression of, 359-60
in Third World, 74-76, 76-77, 101
transformation of, by Russian Revolution, 512
Maslow, Abraham, 416-17
mass media, 9, 10
Mauritania, 105
Mayr, Ernst, 145, 147, 148, 149
medical care, cost of, 369-70
meritocracy, 58
Mexico
capital-intensive development strategy of, 324
economic growth and equity in, 323
and imperialism, 87
income distribution in, 325 graph, 326, 327, 328-29 table
Middle East, 482
Mill, John Stuart
and drama of contradictions, 428
and elimination of conflict, 45
as expositor of progress, 2, 3, 53, 54, 65
and happiness principle, 435-37
and problems of economic growth, 275
and science and industry, 63
as skeptic of progress, 254
millennium, 3, 27, 39, 42-43
Monod, Jacques, 141, 143, 149
Montaigne, Michel de, 31
Montesquieu, Baron de
and control of nature through knowledge, 2
and historism, 50
interest in intercultural comparison of, 44
and technology and human needs, 71
moral consequences of science and technology, 7
moral improvement
connectedness of, to other changes, 5 diagram
and development of organizations, 6
moral phenomena, scientific study of, 536-37
moral philosophy, and scientific progress, 206

moral progress
  and knowledge, 10, 11, 14, 24, 26, 28, 32-33,
    35, 191, 529-30, 539
  and material progress, 10, 534-35
  and scientific method, 33
  and scientific progress, 11, 48, 195
  and technology, 14, 182
Morris, William, 275, 428, 442, 477
Mounier, Emmanuel, 491, 503
Mozambique, 101
mystery, 7

Nasser, Gamal Abdel, 84, 98, 99
nature
  and art, 34
  balance between man and, 63
  control of, 68
    and Judeo-Christian beliefs, 27, 182
    through knowledge, 2, 17
    and maximizing of well-being, 533
    and progress, 3, 26, 30, 97, 119, 253
    by rationalism, 57
    and science, 7
    and technology, 7
  and disenchantment, 530
  fear of, and religion, 501
  and limits to growth, 304-305
  plot of, 31
  and progress, 30, 73
  relationship of man to, 62, 64, 293-94
  return to, 46-47
  Taoist approach to, 182
Nehru, Jawaharlal, 83, 94, 99, 101
Netherlands, 414
Newman, John Cardinal, 486, 503
Newton, Sir Isaac, 176, 205, 218
Newtonian cosmology, 8
Nicaragua, 401
Nietzsche, Friedrich
  and abolishment of God, 514-15
  and cyclical view of history, 6
  and loss of religion and English morality,
    440-41
  and sacrifice for progress, 72
  and struggle, 59
  and underestimation of violence, 57
Nigeria, optimism toward progress in,
    412 table, 413, 414
nihilism, 507, 515
Nkrumah, Kwame, 84, 94, 95, 99
Novalis, 57
nuclear destruction, 12, 126
nuclear fission, 126
nuclear power plants, 316
nuclear technology, 15
nucleic acids, 140, 141-42
nutrition, 139

optimism
  of Descartes, 31
  of eighteenth century toward progress,
    17, 20, 45, 46

and French Revolution, 51
  of historism, 50
  and idea of progress, 27
  modern, 60
  national differences in, 409, 410-15,
    412 table
  of nineteenth century European historical
    writing, 55-56
  and progress, 13, 26
  of seventeenth century, 29-32
  in Third World, 413
  in United States, 414-15
organizations, 6, 9
Orwell, George, 62, 473

Pascal, Blaise, 32, 35, 38
Pater, Walter, 428, 442-45
Peru, 102, 328-29 table
pessimism, 46, 58, 310-13
Peter the Great, 89-90
Philippines
  collapse of democracy in, 385, 400-401
  income distribution in, 328-29 table
  optimism toward progress in, 412 table
physics
  and chemistry, 180
  development of, 163-68
  and mathematics, 175-76
  and molecular biology, 180
  predictive nature of concepts of, 149
  progress in, 161-81
    and atomic research, 163-64
    and black holes, 180
    defined, 161, 163
    and discovery of new phenomena, 168-71
    and electromagnetic field, 164
    and "empty" space-time, 179
    forms of, 168-78
    future of, 178-81
    and geometry of space, 177
    and laws of thermodynamics, 165
    and new modes of explanation, 173-76
    and new theory of gravity, 166
    from 1929 to the present, 165-66
    and quantum mechanics, 165-67, 174
    and quark theory, 176
    and radiation, 164
    and radioactivity, 168-69
    and relativity theory, 165, 166, 167
    and statistical thermodynamics, 174
    and subatomic particles, 169
    and theoretical understanding, 171-73
    and theory of matter, 167, 169-70
    and what needs to be understood, 176
  relationship of, to other sciences, 180-81
  theoretical, 161
Planck, Max, 207, 210, 217, 220-21
Plato, 2, 28
poetry
  and the heroic age, 472
  as religion, 438
  resistance of, to idea of progress, 456

sacredness of, in aestheticism, 511
Poland, 412 table, 482
political parties, 9
political progress
    and economic transformation, 98
    and knowledge, 11
    and material productivity, 11
    and scientific progress, 11
political religion, 511-17
politics
    and progress, 333, 338-43, 360
    and religion, 482
    and scientific method, 33
    and violence, 384-85
pollution. *See* environment, pollution of
Pope, Alexander, 473
population, 38, 295-98
population growth, 285-99
poverty
    alleviation of, 321-22, 328-31, 362
    and progress, 319-32
progress
    as accumulation, 24
    and adaptiveness, 34, 146, 336
    in Africa, 87
    and alienation, 19, 71
    ambiguity of, 18
    in the arts. *See* art, progress in
    in Asia, 87
    as aspiration, 15
    assessment of, and ethics, 528-29
    belief in, and educational institutions, 543
    in biochemistry, 138-44
    biological. *See* biology, progress in
    and Buddhism, 19, 86
    and bureaucracy, 77
    as change, 22, 106-109
    Christian idea of, 70
    and classical beliefs, 26, 58
    and colonialism, 73, 85-92
    and communism, 13, 19
    and conceptions of self, 431-48
    Condorcet's vision of, 36, 100
    and conflict, 53-54, 59
    and Confucianism, 19
    consciousness as driving force of, 75
    and consolidation of rule, 343-45
    and control over nature, 26, 30, 97, 253
    and corporations, 9
    costs of, 18, 24
    criteria of, 118, 368-73
    and cultural heritage, 94
    and cultural self-affirmation, 92-97
    and cumulative truth, 27
    decline of, and dissolution of bourgeois
        civilization, 46
    and defense, 13
    and defensive modernization, 87, 89-90
    defined, 1, 22-26, 109, 112-13, 227-30, 450
        in Third World, 85
    and democracy. *See* democracy, and progress
    and destructive trends, 72

as development, 97-100
and direction, 106-109
direction of, and thematic pluralism,
    223-25
disillusionment with, 7
and diversity, 23
and divine plan, 32, 35, 40, 337
and DNA, 114
and ecology, 8, 157-59
economic. *See* economic progress
and economics, 47
and education, 33, 40, 363, 369, 409-10
and elitism, 25
emerging culture of, 3-5
and enslavement, 471
European attitude toward, 415
Europe as bearer of, 49
evaluation of, 122-24
and evolution, 38, 73, 364
evolutionary
    and ability to process information about
        environment, 118-22
    concept of, 106-24
    criteria of, 122-24
    and energy flow, 118
    measurement of, 115-18
in evolutionary biology, 144-48
"four stages" theory of, 35
in Fourth World countries, 103
four types of, 24
in genetics. *See* genetics, progress in
and goals, 22-23
and God, 25-26, 30, 31, 35, 40, 483
and government, 13
and happiness, 32, 98
and health, 8
and Hinduism, 19
historical model of, 11
and historism, 49-51
and history, 26, 41, 136-37
hope of, 159-60, 499, 500
and human control, 40
human cost of, 70
and human reason, 33
idea of, 109-10
    and John Adams, 2
    ambiguities of, 59
    and anthropocentric perspective, 38, 39
    and the arts, 12, 449-69
    and Bacon, 29
    and bourgeoisie, 43
    and Buddhism, 19, 85, 86
    and Catholicism, 490-92
    and changing values, 415-21
    and Chinese historical literature, 42
    and Christian Platonists, 32
    and civilizing mission of Europe, 44
    as coined by Condorcet, 363
    collectivist, 2
    and communist ideology, 67-82
    and Comte, 2, 44
    and Condorcet, 2, 35-38, 43, 45, 363

and Confucianism, 85
constituents of, 26-29
as criterion of reference, 526
cyclical, 44
and D'Alembert, 2
dangers of, for study of history, 136-37
decline of, 46
and de Floris, 28
and Descartes, 29
deterministic, 73
and Diderot, 2
as distortion of past, 41
and divine plan, 27
drawbacks to, 524
effects of First World War on, 58
in eighteenth century, 2, 3, 24, 26, 33,
    45, 46
in Enlightenment, 6, 12, 21-40, 43-57, 342
ethical alternatives to, 544
ethical appraisal of, 524-45
ethical role of, 525
evolutionary, 2
in France, 38, 47-49
and Benjamin Franklin, 2
in Germany, 38, 47
in Great Britain, 47-48
and Greeks, 26, 28, 42
and Hegel, 2, 3, 44
and hierarchy of needs, 420-21
and Hinduism, 85
and historiography, 41-66
history of, 45
and idea of historical sequence, 465
and idea of Providence, 338, 487
incompatibility of a sense of history with,
    41
indictment of, by Rousseau, 69
individualist, 2
and institutions, 539-41
and Islam, 85
and Judaism, 488-90
and Kant, 2
and knowledge, 541
and Leninism, 19
logical features of, 541
and Lucretius, 28, 43
and Marx, 2, 3, 8, 19, 44
and maximizing of well-being, 533-34
and John Stuart Mill, 2
and the millennium, 3, 27
and the modern state, 337-60
and Montaigne, 31
and Montesquieu, 2
negative aspects of, 525
in nineteenth century, 2, 3, 26, 44
as opposed to ideology of, 526
optimism toward, 27, 45, 46
origins of, in Third World, 85-92
and Pascal, 35
pessimism toward, 46
as philosophy of history, 1-3

and Plato, 28
poetry's resistance to, 456
as political issue, 424
positive aspects of, 525
post-Enlightenment, 41-66
and postmaterialist outlook, 418-19
principal ethical advantage of, 527
and regression, 3, 46
and relationship between mass attitude
    and philosophical systems, 404
and religion, 7
in Renaissance, 28-29
revolutionary, 2
Roman contributions to, 28, 42
and Saint-Simon, 2
shortcomings of, 65
and Adam Smith, 2, 39
in social thought, 41-66
and Socrates, 28
and Herbert Spencer, 2, 44
and spontaneity versus control, 365-67
in Third World, 19, 83-105, 319-32
and Turgot, 2, 35
in twentieth-century theology, 482-500
and unity of man's history, 43-44, 47
and upward development, 51
and Voltaire, 2
in Western thought, 84, 85
and Xenophanes, 28
zenith of, 35-38
ideology of
    and change, 3, 5 diagram
    and Comte, 3
    effect of, on institutions, 539-44
    in eighteenth century, 3
    and Engels, 3
    and Marx, 3
    and John Stuart Mill, 3
    in nineteenth century, 3
    as opposed to idea of progress, 526
    and philosophy of history, 6-7
    and Herbert Spencer, 3
and imperialism, 87
as improvement, 22
inequality of, 25, 36-37
interconnection of elements of, 37, 39
and Islam, 19, 87
and Judeo-Christian beliefs, 26
kinds of, 110-12
and knowledge, 3, 20, 26, 36-37
in Latin America, 87
and legislation, 33, 40
and level of aspiration, 408
and the liberal state, 88
and liberation, 94
limitlessness of, 37
limits of, in material welfare, 8
linkage of various spheres of, 11
man as agent of, 3
and Marxism, 498
and mass media, 9

material
  and "catching up," 320-21
  criticisms of, 281
  and cultural heritage, 90
  dimensions of, 320-23
  and environmental pollution, 291-95
  and equity, 321-22
  and moral progress, 534-35
  obstacles to, 299-300
  prospects for continuing, 281
  and science, 282
  and technology, 281-300
meaning of, 227-30
measurement of, 38, 340, 403
medical, 14, 470
and meritocracy, 58
and method, 29
and the millennium, 42-43
modern idea of, 3
in the modern state, 353-60
in molecular biology, 138-44
moral. See moral progress
and motive, 29, 30
as movement, 22-23, 38
and nature, 30, 73
negative connotation of, 470
"net," 25, 110-12, 116, 118, 123
non-Western idea of, 100
as obligation, 15
obstacles to, 84
opposition of Christianity to, 488
optimism toward, 13, 17, 21, 26, 29-32
as ordering theme for modern history, 18
particular, 111-12
perceptions of, 404-409
perpetual, 111
personal, 409-10
in physics. See physics, progress in
political. See political progress
politics of, 423-25
and politics, 333, 338-42, 360
and pollution. See environment, pollution of
popular attitudes toward, 335-36, 403-25
and population, 38, 285-89, 295-98
and poverty, 319-32
predicted failure of, 390-91
price of, 9
and progression, 34, 363-64
as protest, 81
and Providence, 31, 42, 45
and public policy, 361-74
questioning of, 6
and reason, 57
as refinement, 24
rejection of, 6
and religion, 19, 25-26, 40, 45, 67, 86, 363, 364, 429-30
in religion, 95-96, 494
as religion of Western society, 67
and retrogression, 19, 71, 112, 154-55, 361, 369

and revolution, 74
and rise of disillusion, 100-105
role of nature in, 30
scientific. See science, progress in
skepticism toward, 12, 17, 18
social. See social progress
through socialist transformation, 101-102
and social welfare programs, 362
socioeconomic, and democracy, 335
and Soviet ideology, 76
spiral development of, 19, 71
and the state, 333-35
technological. See technological progress
and technology, 76-77
theological. See theological progress
in Third World, 13, 74-76
threat of, to democracy, 395-98
uniform, 23, 110-11, 112, 115, 123
and universities, 9
and values, 112-15
and violence, 59
and war, 45, 53, 65, 471
Protestant Ethic, 277, 432-33
Providence
  as cause of change, 25
  as philosophy of history, 6
  and progress, 25-26, 31, 42, 45, 487

racial discrimination, and genetics, 191-93
rain forests, disappearance of, 158
rationalism
  character type associated with, 431-33
  and ethics, 531-32
  and man's unhappiness, 434
  and science, 7-8
  and secularization, 517
  as substitute for religion, 502
  as a value-free abstraction, 57
reason, 33, 57, 59
regression
  and idea of progress, 3
  and positivism, 244, 248
  and progress, 54
religion
  and advent of self, 506-509
  and aestheticism as alternative to, 510-11
  alternatives to answers of, 510-17
  and approach to knowledge, 40
  changes in, and changes in culture, 504
  as collective conscience of society, 517
  complaint of, 517-22
  and consciousness-raising movement, 517
  defined, 505-506
  disappearance of, 501, 502
  and Enlightenment, 501-506, 521
  and evolution, 130-31
  failure of, and cults, 518
  and fear of nature, 501
  and Fundamentalist churches, 518-19
  future of, 501-23
  and idea of progress, 7, 45, 482-500

and ideology of progress, 67
literature as, 438
and mental health, 14
and modernity, 507
new forms of, 518-20
and Newtonian cosmology, 8
and nihilism, 507
and politics, 482
and progress, 19, 25-26, 40, 86, 95-96, 363,
    364, 429-30
as response to existential predicament, 517
and restraint, 508
return of, 507, 517
the ricorso of, 517-22
and science, 128, 196, 223
and scientific progress, 13, 206
and secularization, 504
and trend of disbelief, 503-504
and unity of culture, 521
and utopia, 486
resources
    enlarging bases of, 307-309
    exhaustion of, 283-84, 285-91, 390
    extension of, 286-87
    limits of, and economic progress, 301-18
    output of, as proportion of gross national
        product, 303
    and population growth, 290-91
retrogression
    expectation of, 361
    as idea of progress in Marxism and
        Leninism, 19
    in muscle research, 154-55
    and progress, 71, 369
revolution
    in China, 99
    and Christianity, 484
    and Marxist idea of progress, 3
    Romanticism of, 99
    tainting of, by bourgeois past, 516
Rilke, Rainer Maria, 520
Rimbaud, Arthur, 511
Rousseau, Jean-Jacques
    and indictment of idea of progress, 69
    and individualism, 507-508
    and necessity of evil for progress, 481
    as prophet of idea of progress, 84
    and return to nature, 46-47
    as skeptic of progress, 33, 471
rule
    consolidation of, 343-45, 353-54
    and divided nature of society, 360
    duty base of, 346-47
    functionalization of, 348-53
    Marxist concept of, 359-60
    rationalization of, 345-48
    right of, 346-47
Ruskin, John, 275, 428, 440
Russian Revolution, 512

sacred, return of, 501-23
Saint-Pierre, Abbé

and application of natural-science methods
    to social sciences, 133
and idea of golden age, 23
optimism of, toward progress, 17
as philosopher of progress, 38
and progressive approach to history, 17
and progress in morality and politics, 32-33
Saint-Simon, Henri de
    and disappearance of government, 52
    as expositor of progress, 2, 38
    and planned society under scientific elite, 521
    and progressive approach to history, 18
Saint-Simonians, 45, 48
satisfaction
    connectedness to other changes of, 5 diagram
    correlation of
        with income, 405-407
        with objective indicators, 405-407
    and development of organizations, 6
    and economic development, 412-13
    and growth in consumption, 266-71
    and knowledge, 7
    and level of aspiration, 408
    national differences in, 409
    and progress, 6
    and science, 7
    and technology, 7
    in the United States, 411, 412 tables
Saudi Arabia, 96
savages, 34
Schelling, Friedrich, 38, 219
Schiller, Johann, 456
Schleiermacher, Friedrich, 486, 503
science
    and adaptiveness, 34
    benefits of, 131-32
    contract of, with society, 182-84
    and control over nature, 7
    and decline of human condition, 58
    development of, and correlation with other
        changes, 5 diagram
    disaffection with, 182-83
    domination of, 12, 58
    as instrument of political system, 183
    and magic, 7
    and material progress, 6, 8, 282
    method of growth of, 11
    moral ambiguity of, 7, 195, 206
    and moral progress, 8, 11, 13-14, 48
    and mystery, 7
    objectivity of, 198-99
    paradigms in, 153-55
    philosophies of, 128-30
    and political progress, 11, 132
    as prerequisite of progress, 363
    problems of, 124-34
    and progress, 47, 128
    progress in
        ambivalence toward, 126
        analytic method of, 204
        exhaustion of, 182
        methods of, 11

and moral philosophy, 206
and morality, 13-14
problems of, 125-34
and reference systems, 203
and religion, 13, 206
resistance to, 12
and restriction of knowledge, 190-91
and the state, 352
synthesis method of, 204, 205-206
theory of, 202-25
two-dimensional model of, 208-11
and unification of fields, 144
and scientifically planned society, 52
and self-actualization, 416-25
pure, 30
rationalist-empirical view of, 7-8
and religion, 13, 128, 196, 223
resistance to progress in, 12
and satisfaction, 7
and scientifically planned society, 52
as search for unity of nature, 521
and social problems, 194
and social progress, 7, 48, 65
and spontaneity, 366
and the state, 341
threat of, 12
and unified field theory, 217-23
scientism
dangers of, 193-95
defined, 193
and objectivity, 193-99
and the role of objective knowledge, 195-96
secularization, 503, 504, 517
Seneca, 28
Senghor, Leopold, 94-95
Sierra Leone, 103
Singapore, 320-21, 327
Smith, Adam
and conjectural history, 47, 48
as expositor of progress, 2, 84
and idea of progress, 39
and problems of economic growth, 275
and reaction against mercantilism, 364-65
socialism
Third World, 101-102
and violence, 512
social progress
versus aesthetic progress, 458-71
and democratic performance, 384-85
incompatibility of democratic government
with, 398-99
and liberal democracy, 375-402
and science, 48
and social complexity, 39-40
in social sciences, 11, 226-39
and the state, 352
and welfare policies, 399
social sciences
and criteria of progress of hard sciences, 133
difficulties of, 230-34
model of progress in, 11
progress in, 226-39

and statistical methods, 232-33
social welfare
policies of, 371-72
proportion of federal budget for, 361
relation of, to economic growth in
developing countries, 327
and state, 351
society, divided nature of, 359-60
sociobiology
concepts of, 156-57
and relation of science to social
problems, 194
Socrates, 28
Soviet ideology, and progress, 77-79
species
increase in number of, 117-18
loss of, 158
Spencer, Herbert
and disappearance of government, 52
as expositor of progress, 3, 38, 44
and pessimism, 59
and progressive approach to history, 18
and role of conflict in progress, 54
and science and industry, 53
and theory of progress, 2
Spengler, Oswald
and cyclical model of history, 6, 18
and diversity of cultures, 64
and polemic against scientific world view
of West, 220
and value of conflict, 59
Sri Lanka
economic growth and equity in, 321, 323, 327
income distribution in, 325 graph, 326, 328-
29 table
suspension of democratic freedoms in, 385
Stalin, 516
state
bureaucratic model of, 359
changes in, 351-53
and consolidation of rule, 343-45, 353-54
and divided nature of society, 359-60
inability to function of, 356
and knowledge as basis of rule, 345-46
and Machiavellian tradition, 360
and political repression, 354-55
and processes of rule, 343-53
and progress, 333-35
progress in the modern, assessment of,
337-60
and promotion of social welfare, 351
and rationalization of rule, 345-48
and science, 341
and scientific progress, 352
social function of, 348-49, 352
Stent, Gunther, 157, 182, 195-96
sterilization laws, 152
Sudan, 103

Taiwan
income distribution in, 325 graph, 326,
328-29 table

labor-intensive development strategy of, 324
pattern of economic growth and distribution
    in, 327
rapid economic growth of, 320-21
and Western model of progress, 101
Tanzania, 102, 321, 323
Taoism, 182, 520
technological change, 5 diagram, 305-306
technological progress
    ambivalence toward, 126
    problematics of, 25
    resistance to, 12
technology
    adaptiveness of, 305-306
    and antiscience movement, 201
    and control over nature, 7
    and decline of human condition, 58
    domination of, 12, 58
    effects of, 25, 65, 126
    fear of, 12, 265
    and human improvement, 7
    lack of, in savages, 34
    and material progress, 6, 8, 281-300
    moral ambiguity of, 7
    and moral progress, 14, 182
    and organizations, 6, 9
    and political capacity for utilizing optimally,
        132
    and progress, 76-77
    resistance to progress in, 12
Teilhard de Chardin, Pierre, 94, 491-92
Thailand, 87, 89, 320, 323
theological progress, 486-90, 497-98
Third World
    democracy and progress in, 13
    doubts of, concerning liberal democracy, 401
    and economic growth, 251, 331
    educational investment in, 97
    failure of communism to bring about
        rapid progress in, 400
    geographical definition of, 84
    idea of progress in, 19, 83-105, 319-32
    Marxism in, 74-76, 76-77
    material welfare of, 8
    modernization of, 60, 102-103
    nationalism in, 354
    optimism in, 413
    and progress, 13
    spokesmen of progress in, 84
    and triumph over imperialism, 98
Thucydides, 42
Tillich, Paul, 488, 503
totalitarianism, 535, 536
Toynbee, Arnold, 6, 18, 64
Trotsky, Leon, 478-79
Turgot, Anne Robert Jacques
    and elimination of conflict, 45
    as expositor of progress, 2, 471
    and fixed limits of arts, 476
    and idea of golden age, 23
    and idea of progress, 35, 48-49

and linkage among various spheres of
    progress, 1
and optimism toward progress, 17
and progressive approach to history, 17,
    33-34
Turkey
    and civil freedom, 386
    economic growth and equity in, 323
    and high-speed industrialization, 320
    income distribution in, 328-29 table
    problem of debt in, 103
    threat to democracy in, 385

Uganda, 104-105, 401
universities, 9, 10
Uruguay, 385, 400-401
utopia
    arts in, 468-69, 474-81
    and Bacon, 30-31
    cost of, 470-81
    literature in, 474-81
    and Marxism, 43
    and Megapatagonia, 476-77
    and the millennium, 43
    and progress, 427, 429-30
    and religion, 486
    theme of literature in, 477
    withering away of, 80

Valéry, Paul, 473
values, and progress, 112-15
van Doren, Charles, 22, 43, 85, 450
Veblen, Thorstein, 275
Venezuela, 385
Vietnam, 102
violence
    and democracy, 386, 392, 394-95
    and equality, 59
    and minorities, 392
    and moral inversion, 535
    and progress, 59
    reservoir of, 57
    and socialism, 512
Voltaire
    and control of nature through knowledge, 2
    and idea of regression, 46
    and linkage among various spheres of
        progress, 11
    and progressive development of intellect,
        culture, and society, 44
    as skeptic of progress, 17, 33, 471
von Neumann, John, 373

war
    as agent of progress, 53
    and communism, 67
    effect of, on democracy, 381
    as heroic value, 59
    and progress, 45, 65, 471
    self-elimination of, 53
Watson, J.D., 141

Weber, Max
  and ambiguities of the idea of progress, 59
  and comparison of Chinese and Western
    civilizations, 73
  and *Entzauberung*, 504
  and exhaustion of political religions, 515
  and historical paradigm, 243
  on institutionalized rationality of the
    West, 521
  and loss of sense of the sacred, 502
  and Lukács, 513
  and progress of science, 7-8
  and Protestant Ethic, 432-33
  as skeptic of progress, 18
  on technology, 25
  and the way religions arise, 518
welfare
  material
    and knowledge, 2, 6
    limits of progress in, 8
    problematics of, 8
    and science, 6, 8

  and technology, 6, 8
  of Third World, 8
  "net" progress in, 25
  and organizations, 6, 9
  public, and government, 334
  social, and democracy, 386-87, 389
Whitehead, Alfred North, 495
Whitman, Walt, 4
Wilde, Oscar, 428, 446-47
Wilson, Edward O., 156-57, 194, 536-39
work, gospel of, 435, 437

Xenophanes, 28

Yeats, William Butler, 519
Yugoslavia
  income distribution in, 321, 325 graph, 326,
    327, 328-29 table
  optimism in, 412 table

Zaire, 103, 104
Zambia, 103

Designer: William Snyder
Compositor: Sallie Wells/Sue Somit
Text: Compset 500 Garamond
Display: Compset 500 Garamond
Printer: Vail-Ballou Press
Binder: Vail-Ballou Press